Recognition of Family Judgments in the Commonwealth

Commonwealth Law Series

General Editor: Sir William Dale, KCMG, Hon LLD

This volume is one of a series of books published, or to be published, by Butterworths devoted to Commonwealth Law. The titles in the series are intended to serve the needs of law officers and legal practitioners, as well as academic lawyers throughout the Commonwealth. The volumes so far commissioned are as follows:

The Modern Commonwealth by Sir William Dale, KCMG, Hon LLD Barrister formerly Legal Adviser to the Commonwealth Office

Recognition of Family Judgments in the Commonwealth by J D McClean, BCL, MA, Barrister, Professor of Law, University of Sheffield

Recognition of Commercial Judgments and Awards in the Commonwealth by Keith W Patchett, LLM, Professor of Law, University of Wales Institute of Science and Technology

Recognition of Family Judgments in the Commonwealth

J. D. McClean BCL, MA
Barrister, Professor of Law, University of Sheffield

London
Butterworths
1983

England	Butterworth & Co (Publishers) Ltd, 88 Kingsway, **London** WC2B 6AB
Australia	Butterworths Pty Ltd, **Sydney, Melbourne, Brisbane, Adelaide** and **Perth**
Canada	Butterworth & Co (Canada) Ltd, **Toronto** Butterworth & Co (Western Canada) Ltd, **Vancouver**
New Zealand	Butterworths of New Zealand Ltd, **Wellington**
Singapore	Butterworth & Co (Asia) Pte Ltd, **Singapore**
South Africa	Butterworth & Co (Pty) Ltd, **Durban**
USA	Mason Publishing Co, **St Paul,** Minnesota Butterworth Legal Publishing, **Seattle,** Washington **Boston,** Massachusetts, **Austin,** Texas D & S Publishers, **Clearwater,** Florida

© Butterworth & Co (Publishers) Ltd 1983

British Library Cataloguing in Publication Data

McClean, J. D.
    Recognition of family judgments in the Commonwealth.—(Commonwealth law series, ISSN 0264–8288)
    1. Domestic relations—Commonwealth of Nations
    I. Title   II. Series
    341′.04
    ISBN 0 406 40321 x

Made and printed in Great Britain
by Butler & Tanner Ltd, Frome and London

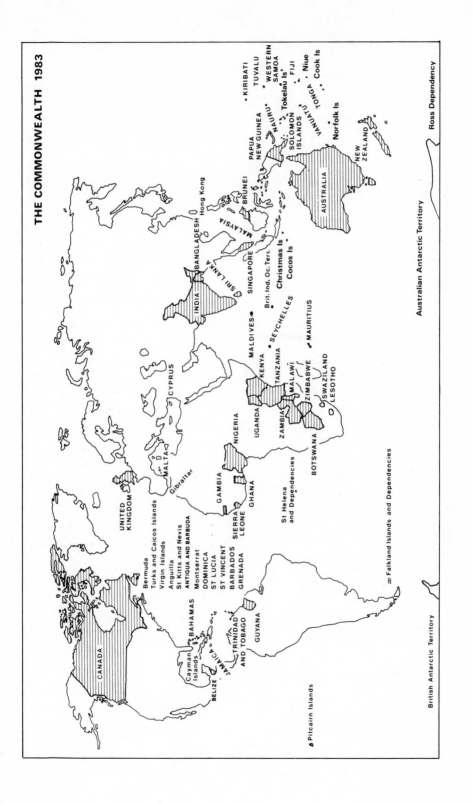

THE COMMONWEALTH 1983

Preface

Whatever its constitutional or political significance, the Commonwealth is about people. Its people, despite the current strictness of immigration policies, display a great and growing mobility, for settlement, business, education or recreation. That mobility can enrich family life; but it can also lead to marital breakdown, breach of maintenance obligations, and painful disputes as to the custody of children. The law of Commonwealth countries has to deal with the recognition of divorce decrees, and of maintenance and custody rights, in cases which cross national boundaries, and that legal provision forms the subject-matter of this book.

In academic terms, this is a study in the comparative conflict of laws of Commonwealth countries; but its shape has been determined by very practical considerations. In terms of content, I have dealt only incidentally with the recognition of nullity decrees or of judicial separations; in practical experience, divorce maintenance and custody are the pressing issues. The law of domicile is a necessary introduction to the whole, and gives an interesting example of the way in which a concept, supposedly common currency throughout the Commonwealth, can acquire not inconsiderable diversity of meaning; the process may pass almost unnoticed, so presenting unexpected pitfalls for the practitioner.

Practical considerations were to the fore in the actual preparation of the book. To survey even a small part of the law of some 85 jurisdictions presents formidable problems. I have tried hard to avoid writing from a narrowly English perspective; but the book was written in England using sources available in that country. I have received an enormous amount of assistance from government legal officers in many jurisdictions, both in correspondence and in meetings, from successive Directors of the Legal Division of the Commonwealth Secretariat, Kutlu Fuad (now a Judge of Appeal, Hong Kong) and Jeremy Pope, and from the heroic staff of that treasure-store of admirably-ordered material, the Commonwealth legal library in the Foreign and Commonwealth Office. For all that, there are inevitable limitations on what is available in England (particularly in case law) and delays in the transmission of published material. Despite the use of the grapevine to supplement more orthodox research methodologies, there is a period of time stretching back from the completion of the text early in 1983 in which some developments will have occurred which are not included; where I encountered particular difficulty in obtaining up-to-date information, that fact is noted in the text.

There are, I believe, some practical conclusions to be drawn from this study. Fifty years ago uniformity in legal principles throughout the British Empire would seem a reasonable aim; common law principles were often exported from the Strand and model legislation from the Colonial Office. Today it is axiomatic that each Commonwealth country should have a legal system which reflects its own distinctive qualities; nobody would advocate, or expect to find, for example, uniform grounds for divorce. But where, as with the topics examined here, political issues are a stage removed, there is a very strong case for countries with a shared and valued legal heritage to avoid unnecessary diversity; uncoordinated law reform, of which there are too many examples in this book, does a disservice to legal practitioners and their clients. Commonwealth law reform agencies already co-operate in many ways but there seems to be room for a greater willingness to seek common solutions to shared difficulties.

Of the topics examined, financial provision has attracted most attention from Commonwealth legislators. The Commonwealth schemes are highly developed and their principles have become well accepted. Here the need for law reform is at a more technical level; adherence to an outmoded requirement of reciprocity, coupled with failure to take account of constitutional changes, has led to confusion and disarray in the law of a number of jurisdictions and greatly reduces the overall effectiveness of the schemes. Remedial action is urgently needed.

Throughout the book, much attention is given to the work of The Hague Conference on Private International Law. In the past the work of that Conference was little known in common law countries, and so had little influence. One important practical conclusion I draw from the present study is that the greater involvement of common law countries, and more recently of the Commonwealth Secretariat on behalf of Commonwealth countries not in individual membership of the Conference, is making the Hague Conventions, not merely more acceptable, but a vital ingredient in the development of Commonwealth law, either in dealings with non-Commonwealth states or as a model for the further development of Commonwealth co-operation.

Finally my thanks are due to many who have helped in this exercise. To Keith Patchett, with whom I first explored this subject, for his generous friendship; to Jean Hopewell for her secretarial expertise and tolerance; to the British Academy and the University of Sheffield Research Fund for contributions towards research expenses; to Butterworths and to Sir William Dale for their encouragement; and, above all, to Pamela, Michael and Lydia McClean in the hope that they will continue to find nothing in this book of the slightest possible use to themselves.

David McClean

St Mark's Day 1983

Contents

Table of Legislation

This Table also includes Uniform Acts recommended by the Uniform Law Conference of Canada.

References in this Table to *Statutes* are to Halsbury's Statutes of England (Third Edition) showing the volume and page at which the annotated text of the Act will be found.

Table of Cases

Abbreviations

A	Atlantic Reporter (United States)
AC	Appeal Cases
ACT	Australian Capital Territory
AD	Appellate Division
AIR	All India Reporter
All	Allahabad Series (of the All India Reporter)
All ER	All England Reports
ALR	African Law Reports *or* American Law Reports
ALR Mal	African Law Reports, Malawi Series
Alta	Alberta
Alta LR	Alberta Law Reports
Am Jo Comp L	American Journal of Comparative Law
Am Univ LR	American University Law Review
BC	British Columbia
BCR	British Columbia Reports
Bing	Bingham's Common Pleas Reports
Blatch	Blatchford's United States Circuit Courts Reports
Bom	Bombay Series (of the All India Reporter)
CA	Court of Appeal
Cal	California
Can	Canada
CBR	Canadian Bar Review
CCC	Canadian Criminal Cases
Cd	Command Paper
Cl & Finn	Clark and Finnelly's House of Lords Reports
CLR	Commonwealth Law Reports (Australia) *or* Cyprus Law Reports
Cmd, Cmnd	Command Paper
Col Jo L Soc Prob	Columbia Journal of Law and Social Problems
Colo	Colorado
CPD	Cape Provincial Division (South Africa)
DC	District of Columbia *or* Divisional Court
DLR	Dominion Law Reports (Canada)
Dow	Dow's House of Lords Cases
EA	East Africa Law Reports
Fam	Family Division
Fam RZ	Zeitschrift für das gesamte Familienrecht
FC	Full Court
Fed Ct	Federal Court
FLC	Family Law Cases (Australia (CCH))
FLR	Family Law Reports (UK) *or* Fiji Law Reports
Gaz	Gazette
GLR	Ghana Law Reports *or* Gazette Law Reports (New Zealand)

GN	Gazette Notice *or* Government Notice
H Ct	High Court
HKLR	Hong Kong Law Reports
HLC	House of Lords Cases
ICLQ	International and Comparative Law Quarterly
ILQ	International Law Quarterly
ILR	Indian Law Reports
IR	Irish Reports
Ir Eq Rep	Irish Equity Chancery Reports
KB	King's Bench Division
KLR	Kenya Law Reports
LI	Leeward Islands
LLR	Lagos Law Reports
LN	Legal Notice
LQR	Law Quarterly Review
Mad LJ	Madras Law Journal
Mal	Malawi
Man	Manitoba
Man R	Manitoba Law Reports
MLJ	Malayan Law Journal
MLR	Modern Law Review
N	Natal Division (South Africa) *or* Notice
NB	New Brunswick
NC	North Carolina
Newf	Newfoundland
NILR	Northern Ireland Law Reports
NMLR	Nigerian Monthly Law Reports
NS	Nova Scotia
NSW	New South Wales
NSWLR	New South Wales Law Reports
NW Jo Int Bus L	Northwestern Journal of International Business Law
NWT	Northwest Territories of Canada
NY	New York Reporter
NZ	New Zealand
NZLR	New Zealand Law Reports
NZULR	New Zealand Universities Law Review
OB & F	Ollivier Bell and Fitzgerald's Reports (New Zealand)
OLR	Ontario Law Reports
Ont	Ontario
OR	Ontario Reports
OWN	Ontario Weekly Notes
P	Probate Divorce and Admiralty Division *or* Pacific Reporter (United States)
PC	Privy Council
PD	Probate Divorce and Admiralty Division
PEI	Prince Edward Island
PNG	Papua New Guinea
Proc	Proclamation
Pun & Har	Punjab and Haryana Series (of All India Reporter)
QB	Queen's Bench Division
QSCR	Queensland Supreme Court Reports
QWN	Queensland Weekly Notes

Rev crit de dip	Revue critique de droit international privé
RFL	Reports of Family Law (Canada)
RL	Revised edition of the Laws
RSC	Revised Statutes of Canada *or* Rules of the Supreme Court
Russ & Ry	Russell and Ryan's Crown Cases Reserved
SA	South Africa
SALJ	South African Law Journal
Sask	Saskatchewan
Sask BR	Saskatchewan Bar Review
SASR	South Australian State Reports
SC	Session Cases (Scotland) *or* Supreme Court
SCR	Supreme Court Reports (India)
SCR (NSW)	Supreme Court Reports, New South Wales
SE	South Eastern Reporter (United States)
SI	Statutory Instrument
SLT	Scots Law Times
SQ	Statutes of Quebec
SR	Southern Rhodesia Law Reports
SR (NSW)	State Reports, New South Wales
SRO	Statutory Rules and Orders
Sub Leg	Subordinate Legislation
Sup Ct	Supreme Court
SW	Southwestern Reporter (United States)
Sw & Tr	Swabey and Tristram's Ecclesiastical Reports
Terr LR	Territorial Law Reports (Northwest Territories, Canada)
TLR	Times Law Reports (England)
TPD	Transvaal Provincial Division (South Africa)
UK	United Kingdom
Ves	Vesey's Chancery Reports
Vic	Victoria
VLR	Victoria Law Reports
VR	Victorian Reports
W	Witswatersrand Division (South Africa)
WIR	West Indian Reports
WLR	Weekly Law Reports
WN	Weekly Notes
WN (NSW)	Weekly Notes, New South Wales
WWR	Western Weekly Reports (Canada)

CHAPTER 1

Domicile

A. THE COMMON LAW RULES

Introduction

1.01 For more than a century, the notion of domicile has been a central feature in the conflict of laws rules of Commonwealth jurisdictions in the field of family law. Words originally spoken by Lord Penzance in 1872[1] were endorsed 'without reservation' by the Judicial Committee of the Privy Council in *Le Mesurier v Le Mesurier*:[2]

'... [T]he only fair and satisfactory rule to adopt on this matter of jurisdiction is to insist upon the parties in all cases referring their matrimonial differences to the courts of the country in which they are domiciled. Different communities have different views and laws respecting matrimonial obligations, and have a different estimate of the causes which should justify divorce. It is both just and reasonable, therefore, that the differences of married people should be adjusted in accordance with the laws of the community to which they belong, and dealt with by the tribunals which alone can administer those laws. An honest adherence to this principle, moreover, will preclude the scandal which arises when a man and woman are held to be man and wife in one country and strangers in another.'

The sophisticated modern observer will detect some confusion in that passage of notions as to jurisdiction, choice of law, and the recognition of foreign decrees; but there is no doubt that the primacy of the court of the domicile, and of the law of the domicile, of the parties was fundamental to judicial policy.

That remains substantially true in a very large number of Commonwealth jurisdictions; hence the attention given in this chapter to the nature of domicile and the uncertainties which surround it, in terms both of its precise definition and of its future. But it has also to be said that there has been a considerable retreat from domicile. Lord Scarman has referred with evident exasperation to 'the long and notorious existence of this difficult concept in our law, dependent on a refined, subtle and frequently very expensive judicial investigation of the devious twists and turns of the mind of man'.[3] In the areas of divorce and judicial separation domicile was early established and survives tenaciously, but even there it is supplemented (and in some jurisdictions virtually supplanted) by other connecting factors. In the areas of financial provision and child custody domicile is mentioned much less often; yet these are the areas of growing importance.

It is not, therefore, surprising that the proposal has been aired in several jurisdictions—and acted upon in one—that domicile should be replaced in toto by the concept of 'habitual residence'. This is examined in more detail below;[4] but it is important first to examine the nature of domicile and the way in which the traditional certainties established in the middle years of the 19th century have come to be threatened.

1 Wilson v Wilson (1872) LR 2 P & D 435.
2 [1895] AC 517, PC.
3 *Shah v Barnet London Borough Council* [1983] 1 All ER 226, [1983] 2 WLR 16, HL.

4   Paras 1.38–1.43 below.

A shared heritage?

1.02   The great majority of Commonwealth jurisdictions share a common corpus of law as to domicile. Inevitably there are some differences in emphasis, conditioned in part by the diverse personal circumstances encountered in different jurisdictions. In a few places, aspects of the law of domicile have been codified, and in another group of Commonwealth jurisdictions the legislature has acted to reform the law of domicile, either generally or in its application in particular contexts, to remedy what are widely seen as unsatisfactory features of the traditional concept.

There is of course no reason why the rules as to domicile should be entirely uniform in all jurisdictions and in all contexts, but it can lead to difficulties and confusion if what is generally thought of as a uniform concept comes to be governed by different rules (not perhaps *very* different, so that the differences which do exist are not immediately obvious) in neighbouring jurisdictions as a result of unco-ordinated law reform.

The first part of this chapter examines the traditional concept of domicile as developed by case law; the emphasis is not on the traditional 'leading cases', which tend to be English decisions, but on the practical working-out of domicile in cases from different regions of the Commonwealth. Those statutes which appear to codify the common law rules are examined in the course of this treatment, but overtly reforming statutes, together with the related work of law reform agencies, are examined in a second part. Thereafter the possible replacement of domicile is considered.

The function of domicile

1.03   'Domicile' is a legal concept which links a person, including in some contexts a corporation or other legal person, to a particular country. It identifies 'his' country, the law of which is in some sense proper to him.

Individuals are increasingly mobile. They often spend periods of time travelling to different countries. They may own property in several countries, and have family or business links with many more. It is, however, a rare individual who does not have a country which he regards as his 'home' country. Of course there will be individuals who have divided loyalties, whose current way of life points to one country as home, but whose upbringing, family tradition and sentimental attachments are focussed on another; the Commonwealth, better than any other group of countries, knows well the expatriate and his love/hate relationship with his host country. For most people, however, the notion of 'a home country' is a real one, and the law recognises this; the law of domicile provides a framework of rules to guide the courts in the identification of an individual's 'home country'.

It is not possible to read off from these general statements of the function of domicile any absolute requirements as to its content. Like nationality, a concept serving similar legal purposes, domicile may be differently understood in different countries, though in practice Commonwealth countries do draw upon a common body of domicile law.[1]

Within one particular country, domicile may be given different meanings in different contexts. It is common to find it used, with a special definition, in immigration legislation[2] and domicile for fiscal purposes may well differ from that applying to the same person for the purposes of matrimonial jurisdiction.

For most purposes, a person has only one domicile, but some uses of the term domicile do not require it to be exclusive, not precluding double or even multiple domiciles.[3]

The traditional use of domicile is to identify an individual's 'personal law'.[4] It is so used in most common law countries, although religious persuasion is used for the same purpose in the Indian subcontinent[5] and nationality has traditionally been the corresponding connecting factor in civil-law jurisdictions. Roman–Dutch law makes great use of domicile, though on some points the content of the concept may differ from that traditionally adopted in common law countries.[6] Despite the effects of legislation in many Commonwealth jurisdictions, it remains central to the conflict of laws rules relating to the family.

1 See generally Dicey and Morris *The Conflict of Laws* (10th edn, 1980) ch 7.
2 Eg the Immigration (Restriction) Law 1941 (Cayman Islands), s 2 discussed in *Re McDonald (No 2)* (1975) 23 WIR 332; Immigration Act (Canada), s 4(1). Cf Admissions of Persons to the Union Regulation Act 1972 (South Africa), s 5(1).
3 Eg Civil Jurisdiction and Judgments Act 1982 (UK) giving effect to the EEC Convention on Jurisdiction and the Execution of Judgments in Civil and Commercial Matters 1968.
4 See a modern statement to this effect: *Henderson v Henderson* [1967] P 77 at 79.
5 See D. Pearl *Interpersonal Conflict of Laws in India, Pakistan and Bangladesh* (1981).
6 See E. Kahn *The South African Law of Domicile of Natural Persons* (1972); C. F. Forsyth *Private International Law* (1981) ch 5; B. Ranchod 'The Concept of Domicile in South African Law' 1970 *Acta Juridica* 53.

A basic definition

1.04 The facts of a Malawi case, *Gray v Gray*,[1] illustrate the factual complexities with which a definition of domicile must cope.

Mr Gray was born in South Africa in 1906. His father was Scottish. His mother was English and at the time of his birth was actually en route for Malawi (then Nyasaland). After attending schools in both Nyasaland and Rhodesia, Mr Gray spent the years 1924–1930 in Scotland where he qualified as a veterinary surgeon. In 1930 he took a post in the Sudan, moving to New Zealand in 1934. During his stay in New Zealand he was visited by his mother and decided that he ought to live in Nyasaland to be near her. He applied to join the Colonial Service and after a short spell in Tanganyika was posted to Nyasaland in 1940. At the time of the case he had been in that country for some eight years and hoped to remain there, so far as he was able to refuse transfers within the Colonial Service.

It is by no means obvious what was his 'home country',[2] and the facts certainly demonstrate that an individual's *current* home can change from country to country quite frequently, too frequently for that notion to be very suitable for the purposes for which domicile is used. For this reason the courts have adopted as the basic content of domicile the idea of a *permanent* home.[3]

This notion of the permanent home involves looking beyond the established facts of a person's residence to his intentions for the future pattern of his life. That in turn requires special rules to govern cases in which the propositus through infancy or mental disorder[4] is unable, or, not being sui iuris, is regarded as not entitled, to have views on the matter. These operate to make it impossible to equate domicile with 'permanent home' in every case, and that equation is further hindered by the special rules as to the domicile of origin, the domicile acquired at birth, which is given special importance.

1 1923–60 ALR Mal 160 (Nyasaland H Ct, 1948).
2 He was in fact held to have acquired a domicile of choice in Nyasaland.

3   Although the present discussion is concerned for the most part with the common law tradition, it is important to recall that the origins of the concept lie in Roman and Canon law. See B. Wortley 'Proposed Changes in the Law of Domicile' (1954) 40 Grotius Society Transactions 121, 124 citing Canon 92 (*Domicilium acquiritur commoratione in ... dioecesi ...; quae commoratio vel coninuncia sit cum animo ibi perpetuo manendi, si nihil inde avocet, vel sit protracta ad decennium completum*) and drawing attention to the use of the notion of 'permanent home' in Spanish, Portuguese and Mexican Civil Codes.

4   The rules as to the domicile of the mentally disordered are unclear. For an examination of the position see Dicey and Morris *The Conflict of Laws* (10th edn, 1980) pp 139-141. As the problem seldom arises in the contexts with which this book is concerned, it is not further examined here; but see para 1.37 below.

The country identified by domicile

1.05   Domicile is used to identify a country possessing a distinct legal system. One implication of this is that it is usually unnecessary to identify a particular place (town, country, province) within the country as the place where the propositus is domiciled. There can be exceptions in particular statutory contexts,[1] and in the special cases presented by boundary changes.

An example of the latter is *Evans v Evans*,[2] concerning the reconstitution of the Colony of the Leeward Islands in 1940 when one of its five presidencies, Dominica, became a separate colony. Mr Evans was born in Dominica before 1940 and claimed to have a domicile of origin in the Colony of the Leeward Islands. The court rejected this argument, holding in effect that his domicile of origin was in Dominica despite its being at the relevant date merely one area of a country; but Mr Evans' residence in Antigua, a continuing presidency, was the basis of the decision that he had acquired a domicile of choice in the post-1940 Colony of the Leeward Islands.[3]

1   The Civil Jurisdiction and Judgments Act 1982 (UK) provides a number of illustrations, but the concept of domicile used in that Act is distinct in all but name from common law domicile.

2   (1960) 2 WIR 246 (Sup Ct of Windward Is and Leeward Is).

3   Cf *A-G for NSW v McLean* (1876) 14 NSW SCR 72 (separation of Queensland from NSW); *Egan v Egan* [1928] NI 159 (a much criticised case) and *Re M* [1937] NI 151 (partition of Ireland).

Federal states

1.06   Where a federal state is concerned, each component unit having a separate body of law, the unit is the 'country' for the purposes of the conflict of laws. To an immigrant in particular, the boundaries between the various units may be of little significance; he plans to live in Britain, Australia, Malaysia or Nigeria, and may have no attachment to any one unit, and no awareness of whether the legal structure of the federation gives significant legislative power to its component units. He must nonetheless be domiciled in such a unit; to acquire such a domicile as a domicile of choice requires more than the establishment of the necessary links with the federation as a whole.[1] This feature of the law of domicile has been much criticised and has been the subject of legislation in some jurisdictions; the reforming statutes are considered below.[2]

This statement of the position in federal states needs to be qualified to take account of the exercise (in the family law area the apparently increasing exercise) of legislative power by federal legislatures, whose Acts supersede the previous legislation of the various units on the same topic.[3] Until 1967, the relevant rule in Dicey's treatise read that 'no person can at the same time have more than one domicile'.[4] Fatayi-Williams J of the Western Nigeria High Court observed in *Odiase v Odiase*,[5] 'I doubt whether Dicey's proposition ...

can fit into the modern concept of the exercise of legislative power in a federation.' His view, now widely accepted, was that where the subject-matter is governed by federal legislation, it is proper to speak of domicile in the federation as a whole; where the relevant law is that of the federal unit, we must still speak only of domicile in the unit. It is a difficult question whether this approach is possible in Kenya, where statutory force has been given to the rule that 'no person may have more than one domicil at any time'.[6]

The position that a 'federal domicile'[6] can exist has been reached, not without some controversy, in Nigeria,[7] Australia[8] and Canada.[9] Although the determination of domicile is a matter for the lex fori,[10] it is believed that in appropriate contexts a court sitting outside one of these federal states would accept the reality of the 'federal domicile' so introduced, despite a dictum to the contrary in the Zimbabwe case of *Smith v Smith*.[11]

1 *Bell v Kennedy* (1868) LR 1 Sc and Div 307 (component parts of Great Britain; the composite structure of the United Kingdom, with distinct legal systems but a single sovereign legislature is akin to that of a federation for this purpose); *A-G for Alberta v Cook* [1926] AC 444, PC (Provinces of Canada); *Trottier v Rajotte* [1940] 1 DLR 433 and *Gatty v A-G* [1951] P 444 (States of the USA); *Bates v Bates* (1951) 17 MLJ 95 (States of Malaya); *Re Benko* [1968] SASR 243 (States of Australia) (criticised as 'bizarre' in P. E. Nygh *Conflict of Laws in Australia* (3rd edn, 1976) p 131, citing dicta advocating a different approach).
2 See para 1.36, below.
3 Eg, the Family Law Act 1975 of the Commonwealth of Australia, superseding the legislation of the Australian states, mainland territories and Norfolk Island on the same subject-matter.
4 It is now qualified by the insertion of the words 'for the same purpose': Dicey and Morris *The Conflict of Laws* (10th edn, 1980) p 104. Compare the hesitations expressed by C. F. Forsyth *Law of Domicile* pp 98–99 in the South African context.
5 [1965] NMLR 196 at 198.
6 Law of Domicil Act 1970, No 6 (Kenya), s 10(1).
7 As a result of the Matrimonial Causes Decree 1970. For the controversy which raged before the enactment of that decree, see E. I. Nwagugu *Family Law in Nigeria* pp 98–99, and the cases there cited.
8 By the Matrimonial Causes Act 1959 and the Family Law Act 1975 (both of the Commonwealth Parliament). See *Lloyd v Lloyd* [1962] VR 70.
9 Divorce Act 1968 (now RSC 1970, cap D-8). See *Jablonowski v Jablonowski* [1972] 3 OR 410 at 415 (Ontario H Ct); *Khalifa v Khalifa* (1971) 19 DLR (3d) 460 (NS).
10 Subject to certain statutory exceptions giving binding force to the decisions of foreign courts on the matter, eg Recognition of Divorces and Legal Separations Act 1971 (UK), s 3(2); Indian and Colonial Divorce Jurisdiction Act 1926 (UK), s 1(5).
11 1970 (1) SA 146 (Rhodesia H Ct). Cf the criticism of P. B. Carter in [1970] *Annual Survey of Commonwealth Law* at p 612.

Domicile of origin

1.07 The common law traditionally ascribes to every person a domicile of origin from the moment of his birth. In the standard case of the legitimate child born during his father's lifetime, his domicile of origin will be the country in which the father was then domiciled. Although much else about the domicile of origin is controversial, that much is well established in case law[1] and is reproduced in statutory codes of domicile in Cyprus,[2] India[3] and Kenya.[4] In Barbados and New Zealand, the statutory reform of the law of domicile has effectively abolished the domicile of origin; the reforming legislation is examined below.[5]

Outside the standard case, the position is less clear cut. A legitimate but posthumous child is usually declared by the text-writers to take the domicile of his mother,[6] but no authority is given for there appears to be none.[7] To the same effect is legislation in Cyprus,[8] but both the Indian Succession Act 1925[9] and the Kenyan Law of Domicil Act 1970[10] prefer the law which the father had at the time of his death.

The rule that the domicile of origin of an illegitimate child is that of his mother at the date of his birth is universally accepted.[11] In some jurisdictions the status of illegitimacy has been abolished, all children enjoying equal status.[12] The effect on the law of domicile is not always clear. The English Law Commission in their examination of a proposal for similar action considered that there was an open choice between (a) applying to all children the principles which now operate in relation to legitimate children and (b) introducing in relation to all children a new rule, namely that a child's domicile should be governed by that of the mother; the Commission preferred the second alternative.[13]

The position as to the domicile of origin of a child conceived in wedlock but born after the dissolution of his parents' marriage is unclear. A foundling is regarded as having a domicile of origin in the country in which he is found[14] but where this rule is expressed in legislation the domicile attributed to a foundling is not expressly declared to be one of origin.[15]

At common law it would seem that no subsequent event can alter the domicile of origin ascribed to a child at his birth. The child's adoption will only have this effect if statutory provision is made, either in the legislation as to adoption[16] or in that on domicile.[17]

1   Since 1801: *Somerville v Lord Somerville* (1801) 5 Ves 750 at 787.
2   Wills and Succession Act, RL cap 195 (Cyprus), ss 6(a), 7.
3   Indian Succession Act 1925, Act 39 of 1925, s 7.
4   Law of Domicil Act 1970, No 6 of 1970 (Kenya), s 3(a).
5   See paras 1.23, 1.30 below.
6   So Dicey and Morris *The Conflict of Laws* (10th edn, 1980) Rule 9(1)(b); J.-G. Castel *Canadian Conflict of Laws* (1975) p 107; P. E. Nygh *Conflict of Laws in Australia* (3rd edn, 1976) p 132.
7   Cf *Re Callaghan* [1948] NZLR 846 (Compensation Court) where it was necessary to attribute a domicile to an *unborn* child and it was held that this followed the domicile of the father until the father's death; but this was not a domicile of *origin*.
8   Wills and Succession Act, RL cap 195 (Cyprus), s 8.
9   Indian Succession Act 1925, s 7.
10 Law of Domicil Act 1970 (Kenya), s 3(a).
11 For legislative expressions of this rule, see Wills and Succession Act (Cyprus), RL cap 195, s 8; Indian Succession Act 1925, No 39, s 8; Law of Domicil Act 1970 (Kenya), No 6, s 3(b).
12 Eg Status of Children Act 1969 (New Zealand) No 18; comparable provisions exist in most Australian jurisdictions. For details see H. Finlay *Family Law in Australia* (2nd edn, 1978) paras 961–965.
13 Working Paper No 74 (1979), paras 8.3–8.5. The Commission's final Report on Illegitimacy (Law Com No 118) (1982) made no recommendation: para 13.3.
14 See *Re McKenzie* (1951) 51 SRNSW 293 (NSW Sup Ct).
15 This is the case in Kenya (Law of Domicil Act 1970, No 6, s 4) and also in Barbados and New Zealand where the domicile of origin is effectively abolished; see para 1.30 below.
16 As in the United Kingdom: Children Act 1975, s 8 and Sch 1, para 3(1) and in most of the Australian jurisdictions (but see now next note).
17 See the uniform Domicile Act of the Australian states, s 8(3) and, for the effect of rescission of an adoption, s 8(6).

Domicile of choice

1.08 The acquisition of a domicile of choice is in issue in the overwhelming majority of reported cases, which are very numerous. There is general agreement that two elements must be proved; the factum of residence and the animus manendi, an intention to remain. Perhaps the use of Latin is significant, suggesting a precision which is lacking. Certainly the courts have experienced much difficulty in applying the criteria to the astonishingly varied facts of the cases before them.

The factum of residence

1.09 It is clear that the propositus must become 'resident' in the country,[1] but this appears to mean nothing more than physical presence other than casually or as an itinerant traveller. Ramaswami J of the Supreme Court of India stated the position in these terms: 'For this purpose, residence is a mere physical fact, and means no more than personal presence in a locality, regarded apart from any of the circumstances attending it. If this physical fact is accompanied by the required state of mind, neither its character nor its duration is in any way material.'[2] Residence even for a few hours may be sufficient,[3] but must be proved: an intending immigrant deterred from disembarking from his ship by reports of an epidemic will not acquire a domicile of choice.[4] If the period of physical presence in a country was intended as a short visit, eg a holiday, it may be disregarded even if the visitor intends ultimately to return to settle in that country.[5]

It appears that a rather different rule as to the acquisition of a domicile of choice applies in Cyprus. Although the relevant provisions of the Wills and Succession Act[6] appear to be designed to codify the common law, section 9 provides:

'A person acquires a domicile of choice *by establishing his home at any place* in [Cyprus] with the intention of permanent or indefinite residence therein, but not otherwise . . .'[7]

Although 'home' is often used as a convenient and readily understood synonym for domicile,[8] it is not, in normal usage, the same as 'residence'. Arguably a man setting foot on Cyprus intending to remain there permanently, and clearly acquiring a domicile of choice there under the traditional rules, would not do so immediately for the purposes of the Wills and Succession Act; it would have to be proved that he had done something which constituted 'establishing his home'. No authority on the point has been found.

There is Canadian authority for the proposition that a domicile of choice can be acquired even by an illegal immigrant.[9] The weight of Commonwealth authority is to the contrary, with reported decisions from two Australian states,[10] England[11] and Zimbabwe.[12]

1   *Gordon v Gordon* [1929] NZLR 75 is a striking illustration.
2   *Kedar Pandey v Narain Bikram Sah* AIR 1966 SC 160 at 163.
3   *Miller v Teale* (1954) 92 CLR 406; *White v Tennant* 8 SE 596 (West Virginia, 1888) (a case which, despite its US provenance, has become the stock illustration in Commonwealth discussions).
4   The facts are those of *Clayton v Clayton* 1922 CPD 125 (influenza in Cape Town).
5   *IRC v Duchess of Portland* [1982] Ch 314, [1982] 1 All ER 784.
6   RL cap 195, ss 6–13, applying to regulate succession only (s 5).
7   Italics added; for a Proviso to this section, see para 1.14 below.
8   As in the much cited passage from *Whicker v Hume* (1858) 7 HLCas 124 at 160.
9   *Jablonowski v Jablonowski* [1972] 3 OR 410.
10   New South Wales: *Solomon v Solomon* (1912) 29 WN (NSW) 68; Victoria: *Lim v Lim* [1973] VR 370.
11   *Puttick v A-G* [1980] Fam 1, [1979] 3 All ER 463.
12   *Smith v Smith* 1962 (3) SA 930 (Rhodesia and Nyasaland Fed Ct). There is some South African authority to the same effect (*Ex p McLeod* 1946 CPD 312 at 315) but United States courts share the Canadian view (*Seren v Douglas* 489 P 2d 601 (Colo, 1971); *Rzeszotarski v Rzeszotarski* 296 A 2d 431 (DC, 1972)).

The animus manendi

1.10　The element of intention is very much more difficult both to state with precision and to establish in a disputed case. Dicey and Morris's treatise speaks of 'an intention of permanent or indefinite residence' (words reproduced in the Cypriot Act cited above). A South African writer has commented that at least four types of intention can be distinguished:

(1)　An intention to reside in the country for a definite period, eg for the next six months, and then to leave;

(2)　An intention to reside in the country until a definite purpose is achieved, eg until a particular piece of work is completed, and then to leave;

(3)　An intention to reside in the country for an indefinite period, ie until and unless something, the happening of which is uncertain, occurs to induce the person to leave;

(4)　An intention to reside forever.[1]

An intention falling into classes (1) or (2) will *not* suffice; that in class (4) is sufficient for the acquisition of a domicile of choice; the problem cases are in class (3).

This can be illustrated by presenting a selection of the formulae used by judges, in many different parts of the Commonwealth, to describe the necessary intention. This is not, of course, other than highly selective, and in some cases nothing will have turned on the words used; but it serves to reveal some of the shades of meaning behind a supposedly common concept:

'the intention of residing there for a period not limited as to time';[2]

'an intention of continuing to reside there for an unlimited time';[3]

'an intention to remain so firm and positive as to exclude any intention to make an ultimate home in another jurisdiction';[4]

'a deliberate intention to settle there';[5]

'a present intention to reside for ever';[6]

'an intention of remaining [there] permanently';[7]

'an intention never to leave';[8]

'the intention of permanently settling there: of remaining there, that is to say, as Lord Cairns says, "for the rest of his natural life", in the sense of making that place his principal residence indefinitely';[9]

'the establishment of a home in a place where a man intends to reside for an indefinite time is, of itself, of no great importance [for] residence and domicil are two perfectly distinct things';[10]

'make up his mind to live and die [there]';[11]

'an intention of living and dying in this country'.[12]

1　W. Pollak 'Domicile' (1933) 50 SALJ 449 at p 465. For a full discussion of South African law using this typology see C. F. Forsyth *Private International Law* (1981) pp 103-107.

2　*King v Foxwell* (1876) 3 Ch D 518 at 520 per Jessel MR.

3　*Udny v Udny* (1869) LR 1 Sc & Div 441 at 458 per Lord Westbury.

4　*Marshall v Marshall* (1956) 22 MLJ 122 (Singapore) per Taylor J.

5　*Kedar Pandey v Narain Bikram Sah* AIR 1966 SC 160 at 163 per Ramaswami J.

6　*Central Bank of India v Ram Narain* AIR 1955 SC 36 at 39; *Malkiat Singh v State of Punjab* AIR 1966 Pun & Har 250 at 254 per Sandhwalla J.

7　*Sanders v Sanders* (1953) 4 Fiji LR 73.

8　*Re Mrs Aga Begum* 1971 1 Mad LJ 18; *Gordon v Gordon* [1965] EA 87 at 89 per Reide J (Tanzania H Ct).

9　*Trottier v Rajotte* [1940] 1 DLR 433 at 436 per Duff CJC. The reference to Lord Cairns is semble to his judgment in *Bell v Kennedy* (1868) LR 1 Sc & Div 307 but the precise phrase is not used there. Its 'interpretation' by Duff CJC highlights the contrast between 'permanently' and 'indefinitely'.

10   *Donald v Donald* [1922] NZLR 237 at 240 per Stringer J.
11   *Linton v Guderian* AIR 1929 Cal 599 at 602 per Rankin CJ.
12   *Coombe v Coombe* 1923–60 Mal 115 at 119 per Mathew Ag CJ (Nyasaland H Ct, 1945).

The grey area

1.11   There are a number of factors which contribute to the creation of a 'grey area', identified in part by this range of dicta. The first is the simple observation that a person's attitude and plans can change slowly and imperceptibly. The testimony of a Singapore judge could have been given, mutatis mutandis, in very many jurisdictions: 'The vast majority of both officials and businessmen of non-Malayan origin still contemplate ultimate retirement to some other country and therefore do not become domiciled here, however long their residence, but there is a noticeable tendency to remain longer, to return after provisional retirement for further periods of residence and, in a few instances, to settle finally.'[1]

The second is the phenomenon of the uncertain future event.[2] A robust Scottish statement is that of Lord Fullerton in *IRC v Gordon's Executors*:[3]

'If in order to constitute a domicile there were required an *animus remanendi* so permanent and so absolute, as to be independent of any possible change of circumstances, I do not understand how, in the constant uncertainty and transition of all sublunary events, a domicile ever could be established.'[4]

On the other hand a much harder line was taken in the South African case of *Eilon v Eilon*.[5]

The third is a semantic, but nonetheless important, point, the uncertainty inherent in the use of the word 'permanently' in this context. This was fully analysed by Asprey JA in the New South Wales Court of Appeal in *Hyland v Hyland*,[6] in a passage which also touches upon the other factors mentioned above and which deserves to be set out in full.[7]

'The contrast in this context between the words "permanent" and "indefinite" was discussed by Langton J in *Gulbenkian v Gulbenkian* where Dicey's use of "indefinite" was held to be justified.[8] There are many shades of "permanence" which are too obvious and well-understood to need detailed discussion here. The *Shorter Oxford Dictionary* defines "permanent" as "lasting or designed to last indefinitely without change; enduring; persistent; opposite to temporary". It is not synonymous with "everlasting".[9] A very usual sense is that of indefinitely continuing.[10] ... In the context of the principles applicable to a domicile of choice I am of the opinion that the use of the word "permanent" means nothing more than Lord Westbury's phrase "general and indefinite" which, as I understand it, produces the result that the person's intention is one which, when formed, is to remain as a resident of the country of choice for a period then regarded by him as unlimited in point of time and without having addressed himself to the question of giving up such residence and leaving the country of his choice upon the happening of some particular and definite event in the foreseeable future notwithstanding that he may entertain in the phraseology which appears to have been coined by Story[11] a floating intention to return at some future period to his native country.[12] Firstly, it appears to me to be quite unreal to ask the average person who has arrived to settle in a particular place to determine whether his intention is to reside there forever for his answer well might be that he proposes to remain so long as the political climate continues as it is or the economy remains stable or his own financial position or health permits him to do so—and there might be a dozen or more other remote contingencies which, if suggested to him, would place a qualification on the word "permanent" if it were otherwise to mean the duration of that person's life.[13] Secondly, the intention which is necessary to the acquisition of a domicile of choice may be formed without the individual being conscious of having taken any deliberate decision at any particular point of time.[14] Whilst undoubtedly there are many learned judges who have expressed themselves on this subject in terms of a "permanent home", there are others who have preferred a phraseology connoting a term of indefinite residence.'

1   Taylor J in *Marshall v Marshall* (1956) 22 MLJ 122 at 123.
2   As in class (3) in para 1.10 above.
3   (1850) 12 D 657 at 662, cited by Anton in his *Private International Law* at p 178 as deserving to be better known.
4   See to the same effect the Appellate Division of the Supreme Court of South Africa in *Ley v Ley's Executors* 1951 (3) SA 186 (AD) at 195.
5   1965 (1) SA 703 (AD) at 721. Criticised by C. F. Forsyth *Private International Law* (1981) at pp 106–7.
6   (1971) 18 FLR 461 at 464–465.
7   See also *Re Furse, Furse v IRC* [1980] 3 All ER 838 (residence for 39 years; intended to leave if health prevented enjoyment of present way of life; domicile established as this intention too vague and uncertain).
8   See also 7 Halsbury's Laws (3rd edn) para 31; *Re Fuld's Estate, Hartley v Fuld (No 3)* [1968] P 675 at 682–686, per Scarman J.
9   *Henriksen v Grafton Hotel Ltd* [1942] 2 KB 184 at 196, per du Parcq LJ.
10   *Federal Commissioner of Taxation v Austin* (1932) 48 CLR 590 at 601–602.
11   *Conflict of Laws* (8th edn) p 50.
12   See *Henderson v Henderson* [1967] P 77 at 80–81, and the authorities there referred to.
13   *Re Fuld's Estate, Hartley v Fuld (No 3)* [1968] P 675 at 684–685.
14   *D'Etchegoyen v D'Etchegoyen* (1888) 13 PD 132 at 134; *Gulbenkian v Gulbenkian* [1937] 4 All ER 618 at 627; *Qureshi v Qureshi* [1971] 1 All ER 325 at 338, [1971] 2 WLR 518 at 531.

Codifying statutes

1.12   No analysis of the case law, however exhaustive, can resolve these difficulties. There is clearly a case for a statutory definition of the required intention, to produce at least a common starting point, and some of the reforming statutes considered below include such a provision. It remains to note the provisions of those Commonwealth statutes which aimed to restate rather than reform the common law rules. That in force in Cyprus has already been cited;[1] India and Kenya have more elaborate provisions.

The Indian Succession Act contains two relevant sections. One introduces a concept of domicile quite different from that existing under the usual common law rules, acquired by the deposit of a written notice to that effect in a government office, subject only to residence for the past 12 months.[2] A provision much more in line with the common law principles is also included. Section 10 provides that 'a man acquires a new domicile by taking up a fixed habitation in a country which is not that of his domicile of origin'. This seems to lack the requirement of permanence, certainly if that is equated with an intention of life-long residence.[3]

The Kenyan Law of Domicil Act 1970 appears to reflect the common law position but with an unusual extra provision. The basic test for acquiring a domicile of choice is 'Where a person ... takes up residence in a country ... with the intention of making that country his permanent home ... '.[4] It is then further provided: 'A person may intend or decide to make a country his permanent home even though he contemplates leaving it should circumstances change.' It seems likely that this provision was prompted by the decision of the East African Court of Appeal in *Thornhill v Thornhill*[6] where an immigrant from Sri Lanka who had set up in Uganda as a manufacturer of instant tea was held in all the circumstances to have acquired a domicile of choice in Uganda despite 'the hypothetical opinion that if things do not go the way he hopes they will, he might have to leave the country in which he has decided to establish himself and make his home'.[7] This seems to accord with the generally accepted position at common law.

1   Para 1.09 above.
2   Indian Succession Act 1925, Act 39, s 11.
3   For the exception and illustrations to s 10, see para 1.14, below.
4   Law of Domicil Act 1970, No 6, s 8(1).
5   Ibid, s 8(2).
6   [1965] EA 268.
7   Per de-Lestang VP at 277.

Particular cases

1.13   Even if Commonwealth jurisdictions were more clearly of one mind in identifying the required animus manendi, their courts would still have to apply those criteria. This involves the courts in an examination of an individual's life-story, and often of his family history; the material is utterly fascinating in its endless variety, but, equally, cannot be made the subject of easy formulae. A very large number of cases from the major Commonwealth jurisdictions are analysed to demonstrate relevant considerations in standard treatises such as Dicey and Morris[1] and there would be little value in a repetition of that exercise, but it may be observed that similar factors have been relied upon in cases reported in other Commonwealth jurisdictions. So the purchase of land,[2] especially the purchase of a retirement home and grave-plot,[3] marriage to a local girl[4] or other local family connections,[5] and a change of religion[6] are factors which have been regarded as evidence of the acquisition of a new domicile. The question of naturalisation has been treated as of less importance,[7] though where such cases concern residence in pre-independence times they must be interpreted with caution. Prolonged residence is evidence of domicile[8] and is given more weight than a man's statements as to his own domicile.[9]

1   *The Conflict of Laws* (10th edn, 1980) pp 115–120.
2   *Santhumayor v Santhumayor* [1959] EA 204 (Uganda H Ct); *Saminathan v Saminathan* (1941) 10 MLJ 79 (Straits Settlements).
3   *Re De Veaux* (1967) 11 WIR 365 (Guyana H Ct).
4   *Gordon v Gordon* [1965] EA 87 (Tanzania H Ct). Cf *Bates v Bates* (1951) 17 MLJ 95 (Selangor) (marriage to a girl from a different state of Malaya weighed against acquisition of domicile); *Unwin v Unwin* (1966) 11 WIR 10 (Trinidad and Tobago H Ct) (cohabitation with local woman after desertion by foreign wife semble of no weight; the decision is, with respect, surprising on the reported facts).
5   *Ferris v Ferris* (1951) 35 HKLR 17 (favourite brother).
6   *Saminathan v Saminathan* (1941) 10 MLJ 79 (Straits Settlements) (Hindu converted to Christianity and estranged as a result from his family).
7   *Abu-Jaudeh v Abu-Jaudeh* [1972] GLR 444 (Ghana H Ct) (Lebanese in Ghana); *Thornhill v Thornhill* [1965] EA 268 (CA) (Sri Lankan in Uganda).
8   *Santos v Pinto* (1916) ILR 41 Bom 687 (58 years); *Rodriguez v State of Bombay* AIR 1956 Bom 729 (20 years). Cf *Kanmani v Sundarampillai* (1957) 23 MLJ 172 (Jaffna Tamil from Sri Lanka working in Malaysia; 34 years residence discounted because pattern of migration by Tamils indicates that they frequently return later in life); *Re Ah Chong* (1913) 33 NZLR 384 ('British colonists' a different class from 'Chinese residents' in New Zealand).
9   *Saminathan v Saminathan* (1941) 10 MLJ 79; but 'if the court sees no reason to doubt a man's words, why should it not believe him?': ibid, per McElwaine CJ. Cf *Re Mohamed Siad Nabi* [1965] 1 MLJ 121 (declarations in will inconsistent with facts); *Biggar v Biggar* [1930] 2 DLR 940 (BC).

Special statutory rules

1.14   Statutory provisions in a few jurisdictions draw attention to certain special cases. In Cyprus it is provided that 'no person shall be held to have acquired a domicile of choice in [Cyprus] by reason only of his residing there in Her Majesty's naval, military, air or civil service',[1] a provision remaining on the republican statute book but arguably of little or no current effect. The Indian Succession Act 1925 contains a similar but more extensive provision:

'A man is not to be deemed to have taken up his fixed habitation in India merely by reason of his residing there in the civil, military or air force service of the Government, or in the exercise of any profession or calling.'[2]

It will be seen that this applies only to domicile *in India*, and not to cases in the Indian courts in which it is argued that a person has lost an Indian domicile of origin and acquired a domicile in, say, Bangladesh. Nor would it apply were it a relevant issue whether the propositus was domiciled in a particular part of India. Despite this limitation the reference to 'profession or calling' is of some general importance.

Both provisions use the phrase 'merely by reason . . .'; they do not preclude soldiers, businessmen and others from acquiring a domicile of choice in appropriate circumstances, but do require a positive decision to settle in the country, a decision not governed by the exigencies of service or profession.[3] So understood, these legislative provisions are wholly in accord with the position in Commonwealth jurisdictions generally, where what were once seen as 'special cases' are now treated merely as special illustrations of the general rules in operation. This is true in respect of diplomats,[4] other government officials (in the older cases typically colonial officers),[5] members of the armed forces,[6] and members of religious orders.[7] A modern legislative code would accordingly make no special provision for cases of this sort.

1   Wills and Succession Act, RL cap 195 (Cyprus), s 9 Proviso.
2   Indian Succession Act 1925 s 10, Exception.
3   See the Illustrations to s 10 of the Indian Act: Illustrations (iv) and (v) concern a man travelling to India solely to attend to the affairs of a dissolved partnership and planning to leave having dealt with that business (no domicile acquired), then changing his intention and deciding to take up a 'fixed habitation' in India (domicile acquired). Cf the position in Quebec (a civil law jurisdiction): art 82 of the Civil Code of Lower Canada provides, 'A person appointed to fill a temporary or revocable public office retains his former domicile unless he manifests a contrary intention.'
4   Eg, *Naville v Naville* 1957 (1) SA 280 (C) (Swiss consul in Cape Town acquired domicile there); *Re De Veaux* (1967) 11 WIR 365 (Guyana H Ct) (Panamanian consul in Georgetown acquired domicile there).
5   Eg, *Gray v Gray* 1923-60 ALR Mal 160 (Nyasaland H Ct, 1948), stated at para 1.04 above; cf *Gordon v Gordon* [1965] EA 87 (Tanzania H Ct) (18 years residence by colonial office servant, but domicile not acquired as he planned to end his days in England).
6   The case law is enormous. See eg *Donaldson v Donaldson* [1949] P 363; *Willar v Willar* 1954 SC 144; *Schache v Schache* (1931) 31 SRNSW 633; *Armstead v Armstead* [1954] VLR 733; *Patterson v Patterson* (1955) 3 DLR (2d) 266 (NS); *McBeth v McBeth* [1954] 1 DLR 590 (BC); *Stephen v Stephen* (1965) 51 MPR 65 (NB); *Ex p Readings* 1958 (4) SA 432 (C) (but cf *McMillan v McMillan* 1943 TPD 345); *Ferris v Ferris* (1951) 35 HKLR 17.
7   *Re Laprade* [1974] FC 196. Cf *Thorne v Board of Education* (1891) Leeward Is App Cases 148 (itinerant Wesleyan Methodist minister).

Loss of domicile of choice and its results

1.15   It is well established that a domicile of choice is only lost when the propositus both ceases to reside in the country and ceases to have the animus manendi. Both are required: the fact that the propositus may intend to leave the country, and may even have made travel arrangements and obtained accommodation and employment in another country, is not in itself sufficient to deprive him of his domicile of choice.[1] Equally a change of residence is insufficient without proof of an unequivocal intention to abandon the domicile of choice, although the evidence required has been said to be less strong than that required to establish the acquisition of such a domicile;[2] but it has also been held that where it is clearly proved that the propositus has lost the intention to return that suffices, without proof of a positive intention *not* to return.[3]

If one domicile of choice is lost without at the same time another being acquired, the domicile of origin 'revives' and becomes the effective domicile so as to prevent there being a 'gap'. This rule, known from its source as the Rule in *Udny v Udny*,[4] applies however remote the links between the propositus and his domicile of origin.[5] It is accepted in many Commonwealth jurisdictions[6] but, as will be seen below, has attracted much attention from law reform agencies.

1 The facts are those of *Foo v Foo* (1956) 40 HKLR 112 (refugee placement in the United States accepted just prior to case). See also *Santos v Pinto* (1916) ILR 41 Bom 687 (Bombay resident resolved on falling mortally ill to return to Goa) and the old case of *Re Raffenel's Goods* (1863) 3 Sw and Tr 49.
2 *Re Eu Keng Chee* (1961) 27 MLJ 210 (Singapore).
3 *Re Flynn, Flynn v Flynn* [1968] 1 WLR 103 at 113–115 per Megarry J.
4 (1869) LR 1 Sc and Div 441.
5 Eg that of Mr Gray (semble Scottish) in the case stated in para 1.04 above.
6 See eg, *Re Rattenbury Estate* (1936) 51 BCR 321; *Barton v Barton* [1940] 3 DLR 211 (Sask) (but cf *Nelson v Nelson* [1930] 3 DLR 522); *Ex p Donnelly* 1915 WLD 29 (a case of deportation from the country of domicile of choice); *Santos v Pinto* (1916) ILR 41 Bom 687 at 693; *Strike v Gleich* (1879) OB & F 50 (NZ CA); *Holden v Holden* (1914) 33 NZLR 1032.

Domicile of dependence

1.16 Certain categories of persons are for the purposes of the law of domicile *alieni iuris*. That is, they are not capable of acquiring an independent domicile of their own and are instead deemed to share the domicile of some other person, their domicile changing as his changes. There is general (though not always wholly unqualified) acceptance of this proposition in Commonwealth jurisdictions, but legislatures and law reform agencies have been active in considering two aspects of the matter, the scope of the rule in terms of the categories of persons properly regarded as dependent, and the selection of the person on whom the domicile is to depend; these points are considered in the context of reforming statutes below.[1]

At common law, the categories of dependent persons comprise:

(a) children below the age of majority;
(b) married women; and
(c) the mentally disordered.

A minor child's domicile follows that of his father, if the child is legitimate,[2] of his mother if he is illegitimate or fatherless. A married woman (even if she is below the age of majority[3]), takes the domicile of her husband[4] or if he is a minor that of her father-in-law; a woman widowed while still under age becomes again dependent upon her father.[5]

1 See paras 1.32–1.35 below.

2   Eg *Henderson v Henderson* [1967] P 77; *Kilpatrick v Kilpatrick* [1930] 1 DLR 288 (BC).
3   See Law of Domicil Act 1970 (Kenya), No 6, s 9(2) for a statutory statement of this rule.
4   *A-G for Alberta v Cook* [1926] AC 444, PC; *Lord v Lord* (1902) 28 VLR 566; *Neelakantan v Neelakantan* AIR 1959 Raj 133.
5   *Shekleton v Shekleton* [1972] 2 NSWLR 675.

Qualifications and exceptions

1.17   Although these rules are almost always stated as absolute, there is a trickle of authority from a number of Commonwealth jurisdictions which suggests the existence of exceptions to or a discretionary element within the rules, and (quite apart from the major reforms reviewed below) some adjustments have been made by statute.[1] One possible exception arises in the case of children whose parents have been divorced, custody of the children being awarded to one parent or the other (and, arguably, this could be extended to any other situation in which one parent is given exclusive custody). This view was advanced in Manitoba[2] and adopted in Northern Ireland,[3] but rejected in Scotland.[4] It has been expressly adopted by statute in Kenya.[5] It has been held in India that a child may retain its domicile of origin in India despite the emigration of its father if the father is in desertion, even if there is no decree of divorce or custody award.[6]

The Indian Succession Act 1925 contains a more extensive exception. Section 14 reads:

'The domicile of a minor follows the domicile of the parent from whom he derived his domicile of origin.
Exception. The domicile of a minor does not change with that of his parent, if the minor is married or holds any office or employment in the service of the Government, or has set up, with the consent of the parent, in a distinct business.'

There is virtually no support for an exception in these terms in other Commonwealth common law jurisdictions, although there is occasional discussion of the proposition that a minor may acquire the capacity to select his own domicile on marriage or on 'engaging in trade'.[7] There is however a similar approach in the United States, where the influential *Restatement of the Conflict of Laws*[8] states

'An emancipated child may acquire a domicile of choice. . . . Some states require actual court proceedings [for emancipation], but the majority insist upon no more than that the minor, having attained years of discretion, maintain a separate way of life, either with his parents' consent or because they are dead or have abandoned him. It is frequently held that the contraction of a valid marriage emancipates a minor.'

In Scotland, a minor (ie in Scots law a boy over 14 or a girl over 12) may have legal capacity to choose his own domicile in circumstances very similar to those described in the *Restatement* as emancipation.[9] The civil law in force in Quebec[10] and Roman–Dutch law as developed in South Africa appear also to regard an emancipated minor as having this capacity.[11]

A related question which has arisen in the jurisdictions following the common law is whether the parent has a discretion, whether he can determine the child's domicile independently of any change in his own domicile. It has been held that a widow changing her domicile on remarriage, or as a result of a change in the domicile of her new husband subsequent to the date of the remarriage, can decide whether or not the domicile of her children should also change;[12] Scots law is to the same effect.[13] In New Zealand it has been held that the mother has this power even in cases where her own domicile is unchanged, Wilson J advancing a general proposition that:

'a dependent person's domicile changes when his parent intends it to change and the change is for his benefit, irrespective of whether the domicile of the parent also changes'.[14]

In terms that proposition applies to all parents, whatever the family circumstances, but there appear to be no Commonwealth cases in which such a generous rule has been put into effect.[15]

1 In Cyprus, the Wills and Succession Act RL, cap 195, which contains provisions generally restating the law of domicile is wholly silent on the domicile of dependence; semble the common law rules are left wholly intact.
2 *Hannon v Eisler* (1954) 62 Man R 440 at 448 (CA). It is the prevalent rule in the United States: eg, *White v Bickford* 244 SW 49 (Tenn, 1922), 26 ALR 129.
3 *Hope v Hope* [1968] NI 1. *Duncan v Duncan* [1963] NZLR 510 has been cited as authority for the same proposition, but the most that can be said is that the judge appeared to contemplate the possibility of the child's domicile not remaining that of its father.
4 *Shanks v Shanks* 1965 SLT 330. Cf *Re B(S)* (*an infant*) [1968] Ch 204 (issue raised but not resolved).
5 Law of Domicil Act 1970, No 6 (Kenya), s 9(1) Proviso. See also the same rule in a civil law context in Quebec: Civil Code of Lower Canada, art 83, para 2 (as replaced in 1980).
6 *Rashid Hasan v Union of India* AIR 1967 All 154.
7 See *Costie v Costie* [1947] 3 DLR 541 at 542 (Ont) (revsd on the merits [1947] 4 DLR 472).
8 2nd edn, 1971, s 22, comment (f).
9 See E. M. Clive 'The Domicile of Minors' 1966 Judicial Review 1; Anton *Private International Law* pp 171-2.
10 Civil Code of Lower Canada, art 83 (as replaced in 1980).
11 *Ochberg v Ochberg's Estate* 1941 CPD 15; Forsyth *Private International Law* p 123.
12 *Re Beaumont* [1893] 3 Ch 490.
13 *Crumpton's Judicial Factor v Finch-Noyes* 1918 SC 378 at 386.
14 *Re G* [1966] NZLR 1028.
15 An early Irish case *Stephens v M'Farland* (1845) 8 I Eq R 444 contains material supporting a wide rule, though in that case a widowed mother was the relevant parent; *Spurway v Spurway* [1894] 1 IR 385 is inconsistent with a discretion vested in a father. See W. R. Duncan 'The Domicile of Infants' (1969) 4 Irish Jurist 36 at 41-43.

Domicile of married women

1.18 There is a clear trend in the law of Commonwealth jurisdictions to abolish or limit the scope of the rule that a married woman takes the domicile of her husband as a domicile of dependence throughout the existence of the marriage. Reforming statutes to this effect are considered below.[1] Here it is necessary to notice two variants on the common law position in the Indian and Kenyan legislation.

The Indian Succession Act 1925 provides as follows:

'15. By marriage, a woman acquires the domicile of her husband, if she had not the same domicile before.
16. A wife's domicile during her marriage follows the domicile of her husband.
    Exception. The wife's domicile no longer follows that of her husband if they are separated by the sentence of a competent court, or if the husband is undergoing a sentence of transportation.'

The Exception to s 16 is clearly inconsistent with the common law position expounded by the Judicial Committee of the Privy Council in *A-G for Alberta v Cook*.[2]

The Kenyan Law of Domicil Act 1970 contains provisions of some subtlety:

'7. A woman shall, on marriage, acquire the domicil of her husband.
8. (3) An adult married woman shall not, by reason only of being married, be incapable
of acquiring an independent domicil of choice.
(4) The acquisition of a domicil of choice by a married man shall not, of itself,
change the domicil of his adult wife or wives, but the fact that a wife is present with
her husband in the country of his domicil of choice at the time when he acquires
that domicil or subsequently joins him in that country shall raise a rebuttable
presumption that the wife has also acquired that domicil.
9. (2) The domicil of an infant female who is married shall change with that of her
husband.'

The apparent simplicity and elegance of these provisions conceals some
points of real difficulty.

(a)   An adult woman domiciled in Kenya marries a man domiciled in England. They live together in Nairobi. It is clear that she becomes domiciled
in England, even if she would herself regard Kenya as her permanent
home notwithstanding the marriage. It is not clear how, or even whether,
she can resume a Kenyan domicile.

(b)   The facts are as in (a), except that the man has a domicile of choice in
Kenya. He later returns to England and resumes his domicile *of origin*
there. What is the effect of section 8(4) which is in terms of a domicile *of
choice*? Semble it is intended to apply to any deliberate change of domicile
by the husband, but the point is unclear.

(c)   An infant wife's domicile changes with that of her husband. It is not clear
precisely what is the position on her reaching the age of majority. Would
her de facto domicile of choice in another country take effect immediately?[3]

1   See para 1.32.
2   [1926] AC 444, PC.
3   Cf *Re Scullard, Smith v Brock* [1957] Ch 107.

B. REFORM: PROPOSALS AND ACTION

Reform of the law of domicile

1.19   A considerable number of Commonwealth jurisdictions have taken
action in the last 20 years to reform their law of domicile.[1] In some cases the
reforms have been limited in scope, often focussing on a single issue (the
domicile of married women) and sometimes on that issue as it arises in a
particular context (jurisdiction in matrimonial causes). A number of
initiatives by law reform agencies have contributed to this process.

1   The Domicile Ordinance 1948, No 18 (Seychelles) (now RL cap 92) repealed arts 13 and
102–111 of the Seychelles Civil Code and provided (s 2) that the law of domicile should be
the law of England for the time being; a new Civil Code including fresh provisions as to
domicile and residence was, however, enacted in 1975: see para 1.26 below. Similarly, s 2(1)
of the Matrimonial Causes Law 1976, No 9 (Cayman Islands) gives 'domicil' for the purposes
of that Law the meaning ascribed to it from time to time in English law.

Britain 1954–63

1.20   One of the earliest, and in the event one of the least fruitful, initiatives
took place in England. The First Report of the Private International Law
Committee[1] was concerned with the Draft Convention to Regulate Conflicts

between the Law of the Nationality and the Law of the Domicile negotiated at The Hague Conference. It advised that the law both of England and Scotland should be reformed, and produced a Code of the Law of Domicile as the basis for legislation. The Code largely restated the existing law but would have effected a number of reforms:

(a) it would have abolished the rule in *Udny v Udny* as to the revival in certain circumstances of the domicile of origin;

(b) it would have defined a domicile of choice and provided rules for its ascertainment in article 2 of the Code:

'(1) Subject to the provisions of this Code, the domicile of a person shall be in the country in which he has his home and intends to live permanently.

(2) Unless a different intention appears, the following are rules for ascertaining a person's intention to live permanently in a country:

Rule 1: Where a person has his home in a country, he shall be presumed to intend to live there permanently.

Rule 2: Where a person has more than one home, he shall be presumed to intend to live permanently in the country in which he has his principal home.

Rule 3: Where a person is stationed in a country for the principal purpose of carrying on a business, profession or occupation and his wife and children (if any) have their home in another country, he shall be presumed to intend to live permanently in the latter country.

(3) Paragraph (2) shall not apply to persons entitled to diplomatic immunity or in the military, naval, air force or civil service of any country, or in the service of an international organisation.'

(c) it would, while preserving the general rule as to the domicile of a married woman have entitled a woman separated from her husband by a competent court to acquire an independent domicile; and

(d) it would have enabled a court to vary in certain cases the domicile of an infant or of a lunatic.[2]

A Bill to implement the Report's recommendations on domicile failed in 1958, principally as a result of fears expressed on behalf of the expatriate business community in England as to the possible consequences upon their liability to tax of the shift in the burden of proof brought about by art 2 of the Code. A less ambitious Bill in the following session also failed, and the Private International Law Committee was invited to reconsider the matter.[3] Its Seventh Report[4] contained a 'businessman's formula' designed to meet the earlier fears but concluded that such a formula would make reform of the law hardly worthwhile. The Committee also reviewed the whole question of the domicile of married women, reaching the pessimistic conclusion that action on that score would involve legal complications outweighing any advantages that might accrue. Not surprisingly, no legislative action followed.

1 Cmd 9068 (1954).

2 For discussion see B. Wortley 'Proposed Changes in the Law of Domicile' (1954) 40 Grotius Society Transactions 121; R. H. Graveson 'Reform of the Law of Domicile' (1954) 70 LQR 492.

3 For the background, in which the correspondence columns of *The Times* played an important part, see M. Mann 'The Domicile Bills' (1959) 8 ICLQ 457.

4 Cmd 1955 (1963).

Canada 1961

1.21 The British Committee did not refer to the work of the Canadian

Uniform Law Commissioners undertaken between the dates of the two British reports. If the British initiative erred on the side of caution, the Canadian Commissioners were ahead of their time. They produced a draft model Act, the Domicile Code, which in effect abolished the domicile of origin and the domicile of dependence, and introduced a new definition of domicile with presumptions to aid its ascertainment. Children and married women were to be treated in the same way as adults generally; so were mental incompetents, except for a power vested in the courts to approve a change in their domicile made by their guardian.[1] The principal provisions of the proposed Act were as follows:

4. (1) Every person has a domicile.
   (2) No person has more than one domicile at the same time.
   (3) The domicile of a person shall be determined under the law of the province.
   (4) The domicile of a person continues until he acquires another domicile.
5. (1) Subject to section 6, a person acquires and has a domicile in the state and in the subdivision thereof in which he has his principal home and in which he intends to reside indefinitely.
   (2) Unless a contrary intention appears,
       (a) a person shall be presumed to intend to reside indefinitely in the state and subdivision where his principal home is situate, and
       (b) a person shall be presumed to have his principal home in the state and subdivision where the principal home of his spouse and children (if any) is situate.
   (3) Subsection (2) does not apply to a person entitled to diplomatic immunity or in the military, naval or air force of any country or in the service of an international organization.
6. The person or authority in charge of a mentally incompetent person may change the domicile of the mentally incompetent person with the approval of a court of competent jurisdiction in the state and subdivision thereof in which the mentally incompetent person is resident.

No province has adopted the model Act.

1   See the Commissioners' Proceedings for 1957 (p 153), 1959 (pp 24, 91), 1960 (pp 29, 104), 1961 (pp 23, 139) and 1964 (p 92) and, for commentary, W. S. Tarnopolsky 'The Draft Domicile Act—Reform or Confusion' (1964) 29 Sask BR 161.

Australia and New Zealand 1970–82

1.22   Almost ten years later another initiative got under way, this time in Australia. The Standing Committee of Federal and State Attorneys-General (a body which has close links with officers in neighbouring jurisdictions such as Papua New Guinea and, especially relevant in this context, New Zealand) considered the reform of the law of domicile at its 1970 meeting. The matter was considered within the several jurisdictions,[1] and by a further meeting of Ministers and Law Officers in 1974, which approved a draft Bill prepared in New Zealand. A revised version of this Bill was enacted in New Zealand as the Domicile Act 1976, though its coming into effect was postponed in the expectation of parallel action in the Australian jurisdictions; it eventually came into force on 1 January 1981. In Australia there was a very limited reform in the context of the Family Law Act 1975 but it was only in 1982 that uniform legislation was brought into force for a general reform, and that legislation is not identical with the New Zealand model.

1   See, eg, the published report of the (Victorian) Chief Justice's Law Reform Committee on the Reform of the Law of Domicil (dated 25 October 1972).

New Zealand (and Barbados and Trinidad and Tobago)

1.23 The New Zealand Domicile Act 1976,[1] which has been adopted, save for two provisions,[2] in Barbados and in Trinidad and Tobago,[3] effects a comprehensive reform of the law. It is reproduced in Appendix A. The Act

(a) abolishes, in effect, the concept of a domicile of origin and, expressly, the rule in *Udny v Udny* as to the revival of that domicile;[4]

(b) abolishes the dependent domicile of married women;[5]

(c) enables a child to acquire an independent domicile on attaining the age of 16 or on marrying below that age;[6]

(d) makes provision as to the domicile of children below that age, including provision for cases in which the child's parents are living apart;[7]

(e) restates the rules for the acquisition of a new domicile (ie, in traditional terminology, a domicile of choice), so that, in essence, the propositus must be 'in' the country and intend 'to live indefinitely in that country';[8]

(f) applies to cases concerning the acquisition of a new domicile the standard of proof formerly appropriate for the abandonment of a domicile *of choice* and the acquisition of another domicile of choice (ie, a lower standard than is required where the domicile being lost is one *of origin*);[9] and

(g) deals with the special problems of domiciles in federal or composite states (called 'unions' in the Act) by ensuring that a person domiciled in the union as a whole is always domiciled in a country forming part of the union (and providing rules to identify which is that country),[10] and that a person domiciled in such a country is also domiciled in the union as a whole.[11]

No provision is made concerning the domicile of insane persons, the law on that topic being expressly saved in s 7.[12]

1 No 17 of 1976.
2 Those concerning the age at which a child can acquire an independent domicile and domicile in 'unions'.
3 Domicile Reform Act 1979, No 31 (Barbados); Family Law (Guardianship of Minors, Domicile and Maintenance) Act 1981, No 15 (Trinidad and Tobago).
4 Domicile Act 1976 (New Zealand), s 11.
5 Ibid, s 5.
6 Ibid, s 7.
7 For the case of children whose parents are living apart, see further para 1.34 below.
8 Domicile Act 1976 (New Zealand), s 9(c), (d).
9 Ibid, s 12.
10 Ibid, s 10.
11 Ibid, s 13. Ss 10 and 13 are not reproduced in the Domicile Reform Act 1979, No 31 (Barbados) nor in the Trinidad Family Law (Guardianship etc) Act 1981 although cases involving domiciles in the United Kingdom or the United States must present themselves in those countries. For these 'federal' provisions, see further para 1.36 below.
12 For commentaries on the Act see P. R. H. Webb 'The New Zealand Domicile Act 1976' (1977) 26 ICLQ 194; W. R. Atkin 'The Domicile Act 1976' (1977) NZULR 286.

Australia

1.24 The Australian uniform Domicile Act[1] is now in force in all Australian jurisdictions.[2] It is slightly less radical than its New Zealand counterpart. It is reproduced in Appendix A. The Act

(a) abolishes the rule in *Udny v Udny* as to the revival of the domicile of origin,[3] without however abolishing the domicile of origin itself;

(b) abolishes the dependent domicile of married women;[4]

(c)   enables a child to acquire an independent domicile on attaining the age of 18 or on marrying below that age;[5]

(d)   makes provision as to the domicile of children below that age, including provision for cases in which the child's parents are living apart and for children the subject of adoption orders or whose adoption has been rescinded;[6]

(e)   redefines the intention needed to acquire a domicile of choice,[7] but without establishing any presumptions to guide the ascertainment of such a domicile;

(f)   contains a rule as to the evidence required to establish a domicile of choice similar in its effect to that in the New Zealand Act;[8]

(g)   contains a provision affecting domicile in a federal 'union', so that a person domiciled in the union is domiciled in one country forming part of the union,[9] but with no provision dealing expressly with the reverse case.[10]

No provision is made concerning those lacking mental capacity; the law on this topic is expressly saved in s 7(2).

1   Or almost uniform: s 8 of the Victorian Act as originally enacted used a different drafting technique from the other Acts (but amending legislation to adopt the uniform text was introduced in 1982), and the Commonwealth Act, because of some additional material (mainly concerning application to territories) and further differences in drafting has a variant numbering of the principal sections.

2   Domicile Act 1982, No 1 (Commonwealth), Domicile Act 1978, No 9231 (Victoria), Domicile Act 1979, No 118 (New South Wales), Domicile Act 1979, No 78 (Northern Territory), Domicile Act 1980, No 81 (South Australia), Domicile Act 1980, No 38 (Tasmania), Domicile Act 1981, No 51 (Queensland), Domicile Act 1981, No 91 (Western Australia). For commentary see M. Pryles 'Reform of the Law of Domicile in Victoria' (1979) 5 Monash LR 236.

3   Uniform Domicile Acts, s 6.

4   Ibid, s 5.

5   Ibid, s 7(1).

6   Ibid, s 8. For the cases of children whose parents live apart, see further para 1.34 below.

7   Ibid, s 9.

8   Ibid, s 11.

9   Ibid, s 10. See further para 1.36 below.

10   A provision which was included in the New Zealand Act because that Act replaces and does not merely amend the common law rules.

Britain 1973

1.25   As part of its work on family law, the English Law Commission examined questions of jurisdiction in matrimonial causes, reporting on the matter in 1972.[1] It recommended the abolition of the dependent domicile of married women, but for the purposes of jurisdiction in matrimonial causes only. Just before the publication of this Report, a Private Member's Bill had been introduced to abolish that domicile for all purposes, but it was not given a second reading, the issue being considered by a special Working Party set up by the Lord Chancellor. The outcome was the Domicile and Matrimonial Proceedings Act 1973,[2] Part 1 of which introduced reforms in the law of domicile, effective for all purposes. The relevant provisions are reproduced in Appendix A; ss 1 and 4 are in force throughout the United Kingdom, but s 3 is not applicable in Scotland. The Act deals with three matters only; it

(a)   abolishes the dependent domicile of married women;[3]

(b)   enables a child to acquire an independent domicile on obtaining the age of 16 or on marrying under that age;[4]

(c) makes provision as to the domicile of children under that age whose parents are living apart.[5]

1 Law Com No 48. Parallel work was undertaken by the Scottish Law Commission.
2 Cap 45. For commentary, see T. C. Hartley and I. G. F. Karsten (1974) 37 MLR 179.
3 Domicile and Matrimonial Proceedings Act 1973, s 1.
4 Ibid, s 3.
5 Ibid, s 4. See further para 1.34 below.

Seychelles

1.26 After a period in which domicile was given the meaning it had in the law of England for the time being,[1] a new set of provisions was incorporated in the Civil Code of Seychelles Ordinance 1975. Under the influence of Professor A. G. Chloros, the principal adviser on the drafting of the new Code, definitions based on those recommended by the Council of Europe were adopted both for domicile and for habitual residence.[2] This was considered appropriate in view of the French influence on Seychelles law.

Article 3 of the new Civil Code declares that domicile (the spelling 'domicil' is used in the text) is to be inferred from the fact that a person retains or voluntarily establishes his sole or principal residence in a country with the intention of retaining or making that country the centre of his personal, social and economic interests.[3] Married women are given their own domicile for all purposes,[4] and any person can acquire a domicile of his own at age 18 or on marrying below that age.[5]

The law of England for the time being continues to govern domicile but subject to these new provisions.[6] The effect of this is not at all clear: the new definition clearly supplants English rules as to the acquisition of a domicile of choice, and unmarried children under 18 will continue to have a domicile of dependence determined by reference to English principles; but the status of the rules as to the domicile of origin, and especially its revival in the case of certain adults under the Rule in *Udny v Udny* is obscure.

1 Domicile Ordinance, cap 92 RL (Seychelles), s 2, first enacted in 1948.
2 See para 1.39 below.
3 Civil Code (Seychelles), art 3(3).
4 Ibid, art 3(5).
5 Ibid, art 3(4).
6 Domicile Ordinance, cap 92 RL (Seychelles), s 2, as amended by the Civil Code of Seychelles Ordinance 1975, Sch 3.

Ontario and Prince Edward Island

1.27 The Family Law Reform Act 1978[1] of Ontario made a large number of amendments to the relevant common law, including that of domicile. It provides that 'the same rules shall be applied to determine the domicile of a married woman as for a married man',[2] and makes fresh provision for the domicile of minors in s 68, which is in these terms:

'(1) Subject to subsection (2), a child who is a minor,
    (a) takes the domicile of his or her parents, where both parents have a common domicile;
    (b) takes the domicile of the parent with whom the child habitually resides, where the child resides with one parent only;
    (c) takes the domicile of the father, where the domicile of the child cannot be determined under clause (a) or (b); or

(d) takes the domicile of the mother, where the domicile of the child cannot be determined under clause (c).

(2) The domicile of a minor who is or has been a spouse shall be determined in the same manner as if the minor were of full age.'

The Family Law Reform Act 1978[3] of Prince Edward Island contains identical provisions.[4]

1   Cap 2.
2   S 65(3)(c).
3   Cap 6.
4   Ss 60(3)(c) (married women), 61 (minors).

Irish proposals 1981

1.28   The Law Reform Commission of Ireland published in 1981 a Working Paper on 'Domicile and Habitual Residence as Connecting Factors in the Conflict of Laws'. It takes serious account of the possible replacement of domicile by habitual residence,[1] but also makes detailed proposals for the reform of domicile on the assumption that it will be retained. The proposals are comprehensive, and would

(a) abolish the rule in *Udny v Udny* as to the revival of the domicile of origin, without abolishing the concept of a domicile of origin;
(b) abolish the dependent domicile of married women;
(c) enable a child to acquire an independent domicile at the age of 16 (or possibly 18) or on marrying below that age;
(d) make detailed provision as to the domicile of children below that age, both in terms of domicile of origin and of dependence, including provision for cases in which the parents are living apart,[2] adopted children and foundlings, and would give a court power to change the domicile of a child on the application of any interested person in certain prescribed circumstances;[3]
(e) restate the rules for the acquisition of a new domicile in precisely the same terms as are used in the New Zealand Act;
(f) deal with the problems of domicile in federal states, in terms closely following the New Zealand model;[4]
(g) codify the law as to the domicile of the mentally ill.

The Commission's Paper[5] proposes that legislation should abolish the rule that a domicile of origin is more difficult to abandon than a domicile of choice; but no provision to this effect is included in their scheme for a Bill.

1   See below, para 1.40.
2   See further for these cases, para 1.34 below.
3   Cf W. Binchy (a counsellor of the Commission) 'Reform of the Law Relating to the Domicile of Children: a Proposed Statute' (1979) 11 Ottawa LR 279.
4   See further para 1.36 below.
5   Para 122.

C. REFORM: THE COMMONWEALTH POSITION

Introduction

1.29   The great majority of Commonwealth jurisdictions have made no legislative reforms in the field of domicile, and the common law (or civil law or Roman-Dutch law) principles remain fully operative.[1] A few jurisdictions have received the effect of United Kingdom legislation by virtue of applying for this purpose 'the law of England for the time being'.[2] In the paragraphs which follow an account is given of the changes which have been made, or officially proposed, on particular issues.

1 In Quebec amendments were made to the Civil Code in respect of the domicile of minors in 1980 (Act to establish a new Civil Code and to reform Family Law, SQ 1980, cap 39); further reforms were proposed in ss 60–65 of Book 1 of the Report of the Civil Code Revision Office.
2 See para 1.19 above.

(a) Domicile of origin

1.30   Note has already been taken of the minor variations in the rules as to the domicile of origin of particular groups, principally posthumous children.[1] The numbers affected are tiny. The principal objection taken to the common law rules concerns the rule in *Udny v Udny* as to the revival of the domicile of origin should any 'gap' be threatened in a person's effective domicile. This rule has been abolished in Australia, Barbados, New Zealand and in Trinidad and Tobago;[2] the Kenyan Law of Domicil Act 1970 appears to achieve the same result by providing[3] that 'notwithstanding that he may have left the country of his domicil with the intention of never returning, a person shall retain such domicil until he acquires a new domicil in accordance with the provisions of [the] Act'. It would also appear to be excluded by the Seychelles Civil Code provisions, which do not make any express reference to the domicile of origin but which define domicile in a way which seems to leave no room for the operation of the rule.[4]

Although the *Udny v Udny* rule was to be abolished under the proposal of the English Private International Law Committee in 1954, reiterated in 1963, no action has been taken in the United Kingdom. Similarly the Canadian Uniform Law Commissioners proposed its abolition in 1961 but no province has responded. The Irish Law Reform Commission has provisionally made the same proposal, though it also refers to a possible new approach. The Commission sees the disadvantages both in the *Udny* rule and in the usual alternative which continues the domicile of choice recently de facto abandoned, and considers a new possibility, that during any threatened 'gap' in domicile as a result of the application of the usual rules, a person should be held to be domiciled in the country with which he is most closely connected.[5]

Once the rule in *Udny v Udny* is abolished, the significance of the domicile of origin is considerably reduced. The traditional rules make the domicile of origin harder to lose than one of choice, but this position is abandoned in Australia, Barbados, New Zealand and in Trinidad and Tobago.[6] The Barbados, New Zealand and Trinidad and Tobago Acts go further and cease to make any use of the concept of a domicile of origin, a child's first domicile being one of dependence. There appears to be no disadvantage in this approach which was also taken by the Canadian Commissioners and semble in the Seychelles Civil Code of 1975,[7] but it is not adopted in Australia, nor was it proposed by the Irish Law Reform Commission.

1 See para 1.07 above.
2 Uniform Australian Domicile Acts, s 6; Domicile Act 1976 (NZ), s 11; Domicile Reform Act 1979 (Barbados), s 10; Family Law (Guardianship of Minors, Domicile and Maintenance) Act 1981 (Trinidad & Tobago), s 42.
3 S 10(2).
4 Civil Code of Seychelles Ordinance 1975, Sch 1, art 3(3); see para 1.26 above.
5 Working Paper No 10 (1981), para 122.

6   Uniform Australian Domicile Acts, s 11; Domicile Act 1976 (NZ), s 12; Domicile Reform Act 1979 (Barbados), s 11; Family Law (Guardianship etc) Act 1981 (Trinidad & Tobago), s 43.
7   See para 1.26 above.

(b) Domicile of choice

1.31   The traditional definition in terms of the factum of residence and the animus manendi is wholly or partially replaced in a number of jurisdictions. In Barbados, New Zealand and in Trinidad and Tobago, the requirements for the acquisition of a new domicile are restated (inter alia) as being that the propositus 'is in that country' and 'intends to live indefinitely in that country'.[1] The Irish Law Reform Commission propose the same text, merely substituting 'State' for 'country'. The uniform Australian legislation addresses itself only to the element of intention: the propositus must have 'the intention to make his home indefinitely in that country'.[2] It remains to be seen whether 'to make his home' acquires shades of meaning different from 'to live'; it is unfortunate that the two models differ at this point where no principle is involved.

1   Domicile Act 1976 (NZ), s 9; Domicile Reform Act 1979 (Barbados), s 9; Family Law (Guardianship of Minors, Domicile and Maintenance) Act 1981 (Trinidad & Tobago), s 41. For Seychelles, see para 1.26 above.
2   Uniform Australian Domicile Acts, s 9.

(c) Domicile of dependence—married women

1.32   Although many commentators object, on general grounds of sexual equality, to the rule that a married woman cannot have an independent domicile, it has been recognised for many years that there are particular difficulties in respect of jurisdiction in matrimonial causes. Where domicile is the sole basis of jurisdiction, a wife whose husband has always been domiciled abroad, or who acquires such a domicile after deserting her, may be unable to petition. Various techniques have been used to deal with that problem:

(a)   In some jurisdictions, the bases for divorce jurisdiction have been extended to cover at least the second of these cases, without altering the rules as to domicile. This was done, for example, in England in s 13 of the Matrimonial Causes Act 1937, which was adopted in many other jurisdictions.

(b)   In other jurisdictions, the rules as to domicile have been altered to provide for the wife to be deemed to be domiciled in the jurisdiction in such cases. An early example was s 3 of the Divorce Act 1898 of New Zealand.[1] This technique is used in Nigeria,[2] both in respect of deserted wives and other wives who have been resident in Nigeria for three years, and (in almost identical words) in Papua New Guinea.[3]

(c)   A third technique is to allow a married woman a separate domicile, as if she were an adult single person, for all purposes of the law of matrimonial causes. This was formerly the position in the Australian jurisdictions[4] and New Zealand,[5] and is the current technique in Bermuda,[6] Canada[7] and Ghana.[8]

The final step is of course to abolish the married woman's domicile of dependence for all purposes. This has been done in all the Australian jurisdictions,[9] Barbados,[10] Gibraltar,[11] New Zealand,[12] Ontario,[13] Prince Edward Island,[14] Seychelles,[15] Singapore,[16] Trinidad and Tobago[17] and in the United Kingdom.[18] Legislation on the Australian and New Zealand models provides that the domicile of a married woman at any time after the commencement of the legislation is to be determined as if the legislation had always been in force;[19] the United Kingdom model provides however that the wife's domicile immediately before the commencement of the Act is retained as a domicile of choice 'unless and until it is changed by acquisition or revival of another domicile either on or after' the commencement date.[20] It has been pointed out that the effect is to treat women who were married before the commencement date somewhat less favourably than those who marry after that date,[21] a result which was probably not intended.

1 For the history of that provision, see P. R. H. Webb (1977), 26 ICLQ 194-5.
2 Matrimonial Causes Decree 1970, No 18 (Nigeria), s 7.
3 Matrimonial Causes Ordinance 1963, No 18 of 1964 (sic) (PNG).
4 Family Law Act 1975 (Commonwealth), s 4(3)(b).
5 Matrimonial Proceedings Act 1963 (NZ), s 3.
6 Matrimonial Causes Act 1974, No 74 (Bermuda), s 3.
7 Divorce Act 1968 (now RSC 1970, c D-8), s 6(1), in force throughout the dominion.
8 Matrimonial Causes Act 1971, Act 367 (Ghana), s 32.
9 Uniform Australian Domicile Acts, s 5.
10 Domicile Reform Act 1979, No 31 (Barbados), s 5.
11 Domicile, Matrimonial Proceedings and Recognition of Divorces and Legal Separations Ordinance 1974, No 23 (Gibraltar), s 3 (in the same terms as the UK Act, below).
12 Domicile Act 1976, No 17 (NZ), s 5.
13 Family Law Reform Act 1978, c 2 (Ontario), s 65(3)(c).
14 Family Law Reform Act 1978, c 6 (PEI), s 60(3)(c).
15 Civil Code of Seychelles Ordinance 1975, Sch 1, art 3(5).
16 Women's Charter, RL cap 47 (Singapore), s 45A inserted by the Women's Charter (Amendment) Act 1980, No 26 (in similar terms to the UK Act, below).
17 Family Law (Guardianship of Minors, Domicile and Maintenance) Act 1981, No 15 (Trinidad and Tobago), s 37.
18 Domicile and Matrimonial Proceedings Act 1973, c 45 (UK), s 1. Reference has already been made to the modification but not total abolition of the special rules for married women in the Law of Domicil Act 1970, No 6 (Kenya): see para 1.18 above.
19 This appears to be the intention of the Irish proposals of 1981, but they are not clear on the point.
20 Domicile and Matrimonial Proceedings Act 1973, c 45 (UK), s 1(2).
21 *IRC v Duchess of Portland* [1982] 1 All ER 784 at 789.

(d) Domicile of dependence—children

1.33 Rather less attention has been paid to the rules as to the domicile of dependence of children. The age at which a person first becomes capable of acquiring a domicile of choice (21 at common law) is expressly lowered to 18 in the Australian jurisdictions[1] and to 16 in Gibraltar,[2] New Zealand[3] and the United Kingdom.[4] In some other jurisdictions, the age may have been affected by more general legislation as to the age of majority (though domicile is commonly expressly excluded from such legislation); in Barbados the Domicile Reform Act 1979, while following the New Zealand model in other relevant respects, omits the definition of 'child' which fixes the age at 16. All the statutes referred to also provide that a child who is (or has been) married while under the prescribed age can acquire an independent domicile.

1 Uniform Australian Domicile Acts, s 7.
2 Domicile, Matrimonial Proceedings and Recognition of Divorces and Legal Separations Ordinance 1974 (Gibraltar), s 4.
3 Domicile Act 1976 (NZ), s 6(2).
4 Domicile and Matrimonial Proceedings Act 1973 (UK), s 3.

Children whose parents live apart

1.34   A common criticism of the traditional common law rules was that they produced unsatisfactory results where a child's parents were living apart; this is particularly important where married women are able to acquire an independent domicile. Special rules have been introduced by statute in several jurisdictions to deal with this type of case, but unfortunately the approaches adopted are not identical.

Most jurisdictions can be considered together, Ontario, Prince Edward Island and Trinidad and Tobago being the exceptions. Within the major group three different forms of words are used, though in most cases the effect is the same.[1] If the parents are alive but living apart, a child whose home is with his father (or who had a home with his father and has not since had a home with his mother) takes his father's domicile; a child whose home is with his mother (or who had a home with his mother and has not since had a home with his father) takes his mother's domicile (and on her death retains her last domicile). In Australia, Barbados and New Zealand a child who formerly had a home with his father, who is now dead, and has not since had a home with his mother keeps the last domicile of his father; in Gibraltar and the United Kingdom the common law rules will apply in this situation, and the mother's domicile will be taken. In Barbados and New Zealand, the position of the child whose parents are living apart but who may be held to have a home with *both* of them is obscure; it is dealt with in the Australian Acts (which use the phrase 'principal home') and in Gibraltar and the United Kingdom (where the father's domicile prevails in such a case).

The Ontario and Prince Edward Island statutes, already quoted,[2] adopt a rather different approach, not using 'home' and providing directly only for the cases where the parents have a common domicile or where the child habitually resides with only one parent. In other cases the father's domicile prevails, the mother's domicile being applied only if the father's cannot be determined (eg, because he had died).

The Trinidad and Tobago legislation[3] is generally based on that of Barbados, but on this point variant, and seemingly defective provisions are included. They are declared to replace all rules of law relating to the domicile of minor children[4] but make no provision for cases in which one parent is dead. The relevant factor is 'residence' or actual custody, rather than 'home'[5] or habitual residence. The relevant provisions in s 38 of the Family Law (Guardianship of Minors, Domicile and Maintenance) Act 1981 are as follows:

(2)   A minor whose parents are living together has the domicile for the time being of his father;

(3)   A minor whose parents are living apart shall have the domicile of the parent with whom he resides and if he resides with neither parent then of the person who for the time being has actual custody of him; and a minor who is in the care of an institution established in Trinidad and Tobago shall be deemed to be domiciled in Trinidad and Tobago;

(4)   Until a minor who is a foundling has its home with one of its parents both of his[6] parents shall for the purpose of this section, be deemed to be alive and domiciled in the country in which the minor who is a foundling was found.

1   One is the New Zealand model (Domicile Act 1976 s 6(4)(5)) also used in Barbados (Divorce Reform Act 1979, s 6(2)(3)); the second the Australian (uniform Domicile Acts, s 8, originally with a variant form in Victoria); the third is the British (Domicile and Matrimonial Proceedings Act 1973, s 4) also used in Gibraltar (Domicile, Matrimonial Proceedings and Recognition of Divorces and Legal Separations Ordinance 1974, s 5).

2   Ie, Family Law Reform Act 1968 (Ontario), c 2, s 68, and the Family Law Reform Act 1978
    (PEI), c 6, s 61; see para 1.27 above.
3   Family Law (Guardianship of Minors, Domicile and Maintenance) Act 1981, No 15 (Trinidad
    & Tobago).
4   Ibid, s 38(5).
5   But see ibid, s 38(4), reproduced below, re foundlings.
6   The use of 'its' and 'his' in the same subsection is strange, suggesting that these provisions were
    amended at some stage in the course of enactment.

Other points

1.35   Legislation which is designed wholly to replace the common law rules as
to the domicile of children must deal with the special cases of posthumous
children and foundlings, as does that in Barbados and New Zealand. The
Australian uniform Act does not cover the whole field, though it caters for
posthumous children; it does, however, include full provision in respect of the
domicile of adopted children which in other jurisdictions is commonly covered
by general provisions in the adoption legislation. The Gibraltar and United
Kingdom provisions are limited to children whose parents are alive but living
apart; but within that area apply to adoptive as well as natural parents.

(e) Domicile in federal or composite states ('unions')

1.36   The legislation in Australia and New Zealand deals with this problem,
but in different ways. The Australian approach uses the notion of the 'closest
connexion', New Zealand that of 'ordinary residence'.[1] So, s 10 of the uniform
Australian Acts provides:

'A person who is, in accordance with the rules of the common law as modified by this
Act, domiciled in a union but is not, apart from this section, domiciled in any particular
one of the countries that together form the union is domiciled in that one of those
countries with which he has for the time being the closest connexion.'

The New Zealand provision, s 10 of the Domicile Act 1976, provides:

'A person who ordinarily resides and intends to live indefinitely in a union[2] but has not
formed an intention to live indefinitely in any one country forming part of the union
shall be deemed to intend to live indefinitely—
(a)   In that country forming part of the union in which he ordinarily resides; or
(b)   If he does not ordinarily reside in any such country, in whichever such country he
    is in; or
(c)   If he neither ordinarily resides nor is in any such country, in whichever such
    country he was last in.'

The disadvantage of the latter approach is that in certain cases, where the
propositus is for example outside the union for a period of months, his domicile
may turn on the identity of the port or airport by which he found it convenient
to leave.

1   The Irish proposals of 1981 are based on the New Zealand text, but use both 'habitual
    residence' and 'ordinary residence'.
2   Note that this is a stricter test than would be required for domicile in the union, for domicile is
    acquired when a person is 'in' a country, ordinary residence not being essential: see Domicile
    Act 1976 (NZ), s 9(c).

(f) Domicile of the mentally disordered

1.37   There appears to be no legislation on this topic. The common law position is not well established, and cases can arise in which considerable amounts of property are at stake, so the inclusion of provisions on the point in a code of domicile seems very desirable. The Irish Law Commission has proposed[1] statutory provisions modifying what is generally supposed to be the common law position in one respect, to provide that where a mentally disordered minor reaches the age of majority his then domicile remains fixed. The Commission would also give the courts power to alter the domicile of a mentally disordered person, a similar proposal having been made in 1954 by the English Private International Law Committee.[2]

1   Working Paper No 10 (1981), paras 123-4 and pp 92-3.
2   First Report (Cmd 9068).

D. THE REPLACEMENT OF DOMICILE BY HABITUAL RESIDENCE

The emergence of 'habitual residence'

1.38   Sir Otto Kahn-Freund, the distinguished comparative and conflicts lawyer, described domicile in 1964 as being 'a superannuated concept',[1] but it must be said that domicile is enjoying a very active retirement. Arguably the reforms undertaken since 1964 in several leading common law jurisdictions will have established the concept on a firmer footing. Even a reformed domicile faces determined criticism. Some comes from within the common law tradition[2] but the most persistent critics are those concerned with the negotiation of international conventions, to whom 'domicile' is unsatisfactory on account both of its technical nature and of the variation in its meaning as between the legal systems which make use of it.[3] Recent international legal instruments, especially the conventions produced by the Hague Conference on Private International Law[4] have made use of a different concept, 'habitual residence', and one commentator has claimed that domicile has been 'practically ousted ... in modern Private International Law' as a result.[5]

The first use of habitual residence, in its French version 'résidence habituelle', appears to have been as a translation of a technical concept of German law, 'gewöhnliche Aufenthalt', in a Franco-Prussian treaty of 1880. It was first used in a Hague Convention, that on Civil Procedure, in 1895, and has since been used frequently both in Hague Conventions and in draft texts produced by the International Law Association, and in those contexts has repeatedly been presented as a notion of fact rather than law, as something to which no technical legal definition is attached so that judges from any legal system can address themselves directly to the facts.[6] This has not prevented judges and commentators from attempting to analyse and define the scope of the new concept.

1   (1964) 27 MLR 55, 57.
2   A recent example is C. T. Corson 'Reform of Domicile Law for Application to Transients, Temporary Residents and Multi-Based Persons' (1981) 16 Col Jo L Soc Prob 327, criticising the mechanical nature of existing rules, even in their flexible American form, and arguing that some individuals should be recognised as having no domicile and others multiple domiciles.
3   See in particular L. I. de Winter 'Nationality or Domicile? The Present State of Affairs' (1969) Hague *Recueil des Cours* III, 349 at 419 ff.
4   For the work of this body see G. A. L. Droz and A. Dyer 'The Hague Conference and the Main

Issues of Private International Law for the Eighties' (1981) 3 NW Jo Int L Bus 155. Cf a more critical view: P. M. North 'Hague Conventions and the Reform of English Conflict of Laws' (1981) 6 Dalhousie LJ 417.
5   De Winter, op cit, at 423. See, for a US view, D. F. Cavers ' "Habitual Residence": a useful concept?' (1972) 21 Am Univ LR 475.
6   See for the detailed history, M. H. van Hoogstraten 'La codification par traités en droit international privé dans le cadre de la Conférence de la Haye' (1967) *Recueil des Cours* III, 337 at 359 ff; L. I. de Winter, op cit, at 423 ff.

Towards a definition

1.39   It has sometimes been suggested that habitual residence is in essence the same as domicile;[1] it has been interpreted as meaning the 'life-centre'[2] or the 'social domicile'[3] of an individual. German courts, considering the Hague Convention on the Protection of Minors 1961, have interpreted a child's habitual residence as the 'centre of gravity of its life'[4] and a Dutch decision is to the same effect.[5] The English Law Commission, considering the phrase 'habitual residence' in the context of the Hague Convention on Recognition of Divorces and Legal Separations, commented as follows:

'[Habitual residence] is clearly distinguishable from domicile, a necessary element of which is a particular intention as to the future. Such an intention is not needed to establish habitual residence; it can be proved by evidence of a course of conduct which tends to show substantial links between a person and his country of residence. . . . To be habitual, a residence must be more than transient or casual; once established, however, it is not necessarily broken by a temporary absence.'[6]

Other official bodies have proposed partial definitions of 'habitual residence', while seeking to preserve its status as a 'notion of fact'. The Council of Europe's Committee of Ministers, responding to proposals of CCJ (the European Committee on Legal Cooperation), adopted a Resolution on the Standardisation of the Legal Concepts of 'Domicile' and of 'Residence' on 18 January 1972.[7] The Resolution recommended certain rules, including the following:

'7. The residence of a person is determined solely by factual criteria; it does not depend upon the legal entitlement to reside.
9. In determining whether a residence is habitual, account is to be taken of the duration and the continuity of the residence as well as of other facts of a personal or professional nature which point to durable ties between a person and his residence.
10. The voluntary establishment of a residence and a person's intention to maintain it are not conditions of the existence of a residence or an habitual residence, but a person's intentions may be taken into account in determining whether he possesses a residence or the character of that residence.
11. A person's residence or habitual residence does not depend upon that of another person.'

Paragraphs 7 and 9 of these rules are reproduced, with only minor drafting changes, in art 102 of the Civil Code of Seychelles as enacted in 1975.[8]

1   F. A. Mann 'Der Gewöhnliche Aufenthalt im internationalen Privatrecht' Deutsche Juristen Zeitung, 1956, p 466; R. de Nova 'Current Developments of Private International Law' (1964) 13 Am Jo Comp L 542 at 562: 'domicile in modern garb for international consumption'.
2   van Hoogstraten, op cit, using a French neologism 'centre-vie'.
3   L. I. de Winter *De maatschappelijke woonplats als aanknopingsfaktor in het internationaal privaatrecht* (1962); and see (1963) 17 Diritto Internazionale 233.
4   Landgericht Zweibrücken, 26 July 1973, Fam RZ 1974, 140; Kammergericht, 4 December 1973, Fam RZ 1974, 144; Oberlandesgericht Hamm, 12 December 1973, Fam RZ 1974, 155; Amtsgericht Iserlohn, 17 December 1973, Fam RZ 1974, 141; Oberlandesgericht Stuttgart, 23

June 1975, Fam RZ 1975, 644 (requiring a certain integration into the social environment); Kammergericht, 17 February 1976, 1 W 1273, 1274/75; Oberlandesgericht Saarbrücken, 6 December 1976, 5 W 170/76; Landgericht Berlin, 7 July 1978, 83 T 256/78.

5 Arrondissementsrechtbank Maastricht, 13 July 1976, NILR 1979, 66.
6 *Report on Jurisdiction in Matrimonial Causes*, Law Com No 48, para 16. A footnote adds, 'This does not mean that evidence of intention is irrelevant; it may throw light on particular facts and emphasise a person's degree of connection with a country.'
7 Resolution (72) 1, reproduced in the Council of Europe publication *European Committee on Legal Cooperation 1963-1973* p 72.
8 See para 1.26 above, and *Govindan v Govindan* (1978) Case No 18.

Irish proposals

1.40 The Irish Law Reform Commission has gone further, and proposed a set of guidelines and presumptions which would be given statutory effect were domicile to be replaced by habitual residence in Irish law. These included a provision that the habitual residence of a person should be determined 'having regard to the centre of his personal, social and economic interests', including the duration of those interests and the intentions of the propositus. In the case of a married person, the habitual residence of the other spouse might be taken into account, and if the spouses were living together there would be a rebuttable presumption that they shared a common habitual residence. There would similarly be a rebuttable presumption that an unmarried child has the habitual residence of his parents, or of the parent with whom he has his home.[1] 'Habitual residence' is already used in Irish law without definition,[2] but the Commission felt that its more widespread use would create a need for a general indication of its meaning; the risk is that a statutory formulation, even in the form of commonsense presumptions, could lead to the development of technical rules.

1 Working Paper No 10 (1981) on Domicile and Habitual Residence as Connecting Factors in the Conflict of Laws, chapter 12 and pp 102-3.
2 Succession Act 1965, No 27 (Ireland), Part VIII.

English judicial views

1.41 Reference may be made to two English cases in which the meaning of 'habitual residence' has been considered. In *Cruse v Chittum*[1] Lane J accepted a number of propositions advanced by counsel in an undefended case:

(a) Habitual residence requires an element of intention, an intention to reside in that country;
(b) 'Habitual' indicates a quality of residence rather than a period of residence;
(c) Habitual residence denotes a regular physical presence, not temporary or secondary in nature, which must endure for some time;
(d) Habitual residence is something more than 'ordinary residence';[2]
(e) Habitual residence is similar to the residence normally required as part of domicile, without the element of animus necessary in domicile.

The relationship between propositions (a) and (e) is far from clear, and proposition (e) seems mistaken given that residence as an element of domicile is little more than presence, and in some cases presence for a very brief period indeed.[3] In *Oundjian v Oundjian*,[4] French J rejected an argument that continual physical presence, subject to de minimis absences, was required, noting the Oxford English Dictionary's definition of 'habitual' as 'in the way of habit or settled practice, constantly, usually, customarily'.

1 [1974] 2 All ER 940. See C. Hall '*Cruse v Chittum*, Habitual Residence Judicially Explored', (1975) 24 ICLQ.
2 See *R v Barnet London Borough Council, ex p Shah* [1982] QB 688, [1980] 3 All ER 679, speaking of a scale from presence, via residence, ordinary residence and habitual residence, to domicile.
3 Cf para 1.09 above.
4 (1979) 1 FLR 198.

Domicile and habitual residence: the relative merits

1.42 The merits of habitual residence as a connecting factor have sometimes been overstated. It is not a self-defining concept, and the literature already contains ominous references to 'subjective' and 'objective' tests.[1] On the other hand it has several major advantages over the traditional, or even the reformed, concept of domicile. The main advantage is that there is nothing equivalent to either a domicile of origin or a domicile of dependence, so that the technical rules which surround those concepts, and which have troubled law reform agencies, are swept away. Because the element of intention is of much less importance to habitual residence than to domicile,[2] the uncertainties as to the best formulation of the animus manendi and the practical difficulties in applying any test are both removed.

It may be argued that the thorough reform of the law of domicile already achieved in Barbados, New Zealand, and in Trinidad and Tobago, and proposed in Ireland secures these same advantages while retaining the traditional connecting factor of domicile. The result of such reforms is, however, to produce considerable variety, even as between Commonwealth jurisdictions, in the meaning of domicile. 'Domicile' is not a term readily understood by laymen; lawyers are familiar with the word, but may well be troubled by the variant meanings attached to it. The case for 'starting again' with the concept of habitual residence is a strong one. The Irish Law Reform Commission has indicated its view that, on balance, habitual residence constitutes a more satisfactory connecting factor than domicile; and experience with the new concept in the jurisdictions which use it, notably in connection with the recognition of foreign divorces,[3] suggests that it presents few difficulties.

1 L. Palsson *Marriage and Divorce in Comparative Conflict of Laws* vol 1 (1974), pp 76–80 with full citation of the European literature; but note Palsson's optimistic conclusions (at p 80).
2 However, in Quebec the Civil Code Revision Office is considering the use of 'principal residence' which would be differentiated from 'habitual residence' by the inclusion of an element of intention.
3 See para 3.32 below.

Legislative action

1.43 It is to Nauru, one of the smallest Commonwealth jurisdictions, that one must look for a pioneering reform in this field. The Conflict of Laws Act 1974[1] applies the rules of private international law in force in England on 31 January 1968 to cases coming before the courts of Nauru.[2] However this is subject to section 3:

'Where the proper law to which effect would have to be given under the provisions of section 2 [which states the general rule] for the purpose of deciding any question would be the law of the country of any person's domicile, the proper law to which effect is to be given for the purpose of deciding that question is the law of the country in which that person habitually resides.'[3]

It remains to be seen whether other jurisdictions will follow the lead set by Nauru.

1   No 14 of 1974.
2   S 2.
3   Sadly, no explanatory report as to the origins of this Act is available.

CHAPTER 2

Divorce: The Common Law Rules

Introductory

2.01　This chapter is concerned with the common law principles governing the recognition of a decree of divorce granted in some other country. Much more attention has been given in recent years to the recognition of foreign divorces than to the recognition of foreign marriages. Given that many more people marry than are divorced, this may seem surprising. In reality it is readily explained.

Marriages take place between persons who are either in love with one another or, if the conventions of the society are not based on romantic love, are at least consenting to the change in status which is taking place. In all but the rarest of circumstances, in which proxy marriages are allowed, they will be present in one country; normally they will be planning to set up a matrimonial home, and looking to the establishment of a family, and to mutually beneficial rearrangement of their financial affairs. Divorce takes place in much less happy circumstances, often of bitterness and mutual hostility. The parties may be living in different countries; one may be opposed to the divorce; their financial interests may now be conflicting; and the fate of any children may be hotly fought over.

Attitudes to divorce have changed in many societies. Chief Justice Seaton of the Supreme Court of Seychelles could write, in a paper prepared for the 1983 Commonwealth Law Conference, that many of his audience would be surprised to learn that countries still existed which retained a fault-based system of divorce; and he could go on to question the extent to which judicial intervention was still a desirable feature of no-fault divorce procedures. These changes may have made divorce a more 'civilised' operation, but in themselves they create pressure for review of the conflict of law rules as to the recognition of decrees. As Lord Pearce argued in *Indyka v Indyka*:[1]

'The world had become more shifting and mobile than it was in the last century. Moreover, divorce had become much more common and easier to obtain. . . . In the last century if a wife was deserted by her husband . . . she was tied to him until he died. Now society in this and other countries was no longer content with that situation. She must be freed to live a normal life; and it was felt that on the grounds of morals, humanity and convenience she should be able to obtain divorce in the country where she genuinely lived.'

The result has been rapid change first in the rules as to divorce jurisdiction —where statutory intervention was required—and second in the rules as to the recognition of foreign divorces—where case-law development proved possible, though statutory reform has also taken place.

This chapter is concerned with the common law position. Much of the available material is drawn, inevitably, from the major Commonwealth jurisdictions; these are also the jurisdictions most likely to have enacted statutory provisions covering much of the ground. If a reader in one of these jurisdictions finds the following paragraphs of largely historical interest, he should recall that the common law principles still apply in many Commonwealth jurisdictions whose judges must do their best to build upon work begun, especially in England, but never fully completed because of parliamentary intervention.

1   [1969] 1 AC 33, [1967] 2 All ER 689, HL.

Decrees granted in the common domicile of the parties

2.02   The primary basis for the recognition of foreign decrees of divorce at common law is that they are granted by a court in the common domicile of the parties. This principle was firmly established a century ago by the House of Lords in *Harvey v Farnie*[1] and endorsed by the Privy Council in 1895 in *Le Mesurier v Le Mesurier*.[2]

Until these cases, the legal position was confused. Much of the confusion can be traced to the criminal case of *R v Lolley*[3] argued before all the judges in Serjeants' Inn in December 1812. Lolley was convicted of bigamy despite the fact that his first wife had obtained a divorce in Scotland (where she had resided for some five months only) on the ground of Lolley's adultery. The judges were unanimously of the opinion 'that no sentence or Act of any foreign country or state could dissolve an English marriage a vinculo matrimonii, for ground on which it was not liable to be dissolved a vinculo matrimonii in England'.[4]

Lolley's case was briefly reported and can be interpreted in a number of different ways. It could mean that a marriage in England could only be dissolved in England, which at that time would involve an Act of Parliament. This was certainly the interpretation offered a few months later by Lord Eldon LC in *Tovey v Lindsay*,[5] although there was no final decision in that case. Such a restrictive rule, even if intended by the judges, clearly could not survive for long; it would be wholly unacceptable in a more mobile society.

Another possible interpretation of the judges' opinion would leave open the possibility that a foreign court might dissolve a marriage celebrated in England, but would deny recognition if the dissolution were on a ground unknown to English law. This seems too sophisticated a proposition for its formulation in 1812 to be at all probable. Sir James Hannen P at first instance in *Harvey v Farnie*[6] treated it as axiomatic that 'we have nothing to do with the grounds upon which the tribunals of [a foreign] country may proceed in declaring what shall entitle the man or woman to have his or her marriage dissolved'.

The interpretation of *Lolley's case* which ultimately prevailed was that it was limited to 'English marriages' in the special sense of marriages the parties to which were domiciled in England at the time of the divorce proceedings, but the 19th-century cases show the judges in a number of minds as to the meaning of 'English marriage' and also perplexed by a distinction, later abandoned, between 'matrimonial' and 'actual' domicile.

Developments in Scottish and Irish law paved the way for clarification. The Scottish courts, alone of United Kingdom courts before 1857, had the power to dissolve marriages. In *Warrender v Warrender*[7] in 1835, the House of Lords on appeal from Scotland upheld the proposition that the domicile of the parties in Scotland was a good basis of jurisdiction, even if the marriage had been celebrated in England. Although the recognition of the divorce elsewhere was not strictly in issue, Lord Brougham went out of his way to demonstrate the difficulties which would be produced by a strict interpretation of *Lolley's case*, essentially those of the 'limping marriage' syndrome: a divorce, which must be regarded as valid in the forum state even if nowhere else, affects the property and social interests of the parties outside as well as inside that state.[8]

It was the Lord Chancellor of Ireland, Blackburne LC, who applied these considerations in a recognition context. In *Maghee v M'Allister*[9] he recognised a Scottish divorce of 1846 as having validly dissolved a marriage celebrated 18 years earlier in England. The crucial point was that it was a 'Scottish marriage' in the sense that the parties were domiciled in Scotland by virtue of the Scottish domicile of the husband at all relevant times. *Lolley's case* was expressly distinguished on the ground that there the parties were not domiciled in Scotland, and had gone there merely for the purpose of getting rid of the marriage.[10]

Maghee v M'Allister was followed in England in *Harvey v Farnie*[11] where the facts were substantially identical. The House of Lords accepted as the general opinion of 'almost every writer and speaker upon the subject',[12] that personal status was a matter for the domicile of the parties. In the divorce context they would apply that principle so as to recognise a decree of the courts of the domicile, and declared that the fact that the marriage was celebrated in England was irrelevant.

Some residual doubts remained because of a decision in a jurisdictional context. In *Niboyet v Niboyet*,[13] the Court of Appeal, over the strong dissent of Brett LJ, had held that the English courts had jurisdiction in divorce where the respondent was resident in England and was alleged to have committed adultery there. James LJ found it 'a violation of every principle to make the dissolubility of a marriage depend on the mere will and pleasure of the husband, and domicil is entirely a matter of his will and pleasure'.[14] Such statements were plainly inconsistent with those to be accepted in *Harvey v Farnie*; the majority of the *Niboyet* court (James and Cotton LJJ) sat in the Court of Appeal in *Harvey v Farnie* and Cotton LJ argued that *Niboyet* turned not on any point of general principle but on the construction of a specific statutory provision.[15]

The matter was finally settled in *Le Mesurier v Le Mesurier*,[16] a Privy Council decision on appeal from what was then Ceylon. The narrow point in issue concerned the jurisdiction of the courts in Ceylon to dissolve marriages where the parties' true domicile was in England. The Board rejected any notion of a special matrimonial domicile, and cited Bar as holding that only the judge of the parties' domicile or nationality was competent and entitled to recognition elsewhere; and in the common law tradition the key reference was to domicile, that to nationality not being pursued.

1   (1882) 8 App Cas 43, HL. The official Law Reports are in error in indicating in the margin that this was a Scottish appeal; the case concerned a Scottish divorce, but the litigation was English.
2   [1895] AC 517, PC.
3   (1812) Russ & Ry 237.
4   At 239.
5   (1813) 1 Dow 117 at 124–125. Cf Lord Selborne LC in *Harvey v Farnie* (1882) 8 App Cas 43 at 54–55.
6   (1880) 5 PD 153 at 156.
7   (1835) 2 Cl & Finn 488.
8   See (1835) 2 Cl & Finn 488 at 541–547.
9   (1853) 3 Ir Ch Rep 604.
10   At 609.
11   (1882) 8 App Cas 43.
12   Per Lord Blackburne at 58.
13   (1878) 4 PD 1, CA.
14   At 8.

15   (1880) 6 PD 35 at 50–51, CA.
16   [1895] AC 517, PC.

Application of the domicile basis

2.03   The rule established in *Harvey v Farnie*[1] and *Le Mesurier v Le Mesurier*[2] that the common domicile of the parties is the primary basis for divorce jurisdiction and so for the recognition of divorce decrees is accepted at common law throughout the Commonwealth.[3]

Domicile is to be tested at the time proceedings are commenced, by the presentation of the petition or equivalent procedural step. If the domicile test is satisfied at that time, the resulting decree will be entitled to recognition even if the test would not have been satisfied had it been applied at the date of the decree.[4] In this respect, the recognition rule mirrors that applying in the context of jurisdiction.[5]

At common law, the domicile of a married woman is of course that of her husband, so that in the context of divorce 'the common domicile of the parties' means the domicile of the husband; reference has already been made to James LJ's protest that it is 'a violation of every principle to make the dissolubility of a marriage depend upon the mere will and pleasure of the husband',[6] and there were suggestions in a number of cases that a married woman might be entitled to a separate domicile in certain circumstances for the purposes of jurisdiction in matrimonial causes.[7] The door was firmly shut on any such developments by the decisions of the House of Lords in *Lord Advocate v Jaffrey*[8] (where it was held that the Scottish courts had no jurisdiction to entertain a divorce petition by a wife whose 'drunken and dissipated' husband had acquired a domicile in Queensland, despite the alleged desertion and adultery he had committed) and of the Privy Council in *A-G for Alberta v Cook*[9] (where the wife had obtained a decree of judicial separation in Alberta, but was held not to be thereby entitled to a domicile separate from that of her husband who was domiciled throughout in Ontario). These decisions prompted legislative action in a number of jurisdictions, including Canada,[10] Victoria,[11] New Zealand[12] and England[13] to remedy the situation, but only for the purposes of giving divorce jurisdiction to the courts of the enacting country; the legislation did not by itself affect the recognition of overseas divorces. A review of the current legislation on this point has already been given;[14] the more radical domicile reform statutes which allow a married woman a separate domicile for all purposes do not necessarily affect the recognition of foreign divorces insofar as the basis of recognition is the grant by a court of the *common* domicile of the parties.

1   (1882) 8 App Cas 43, HL.
2   [1895] AC 517, PC.
3   See, for example, *Magurn v Magurn* (1884) 11 AR 178 (Ont); *R v Woods* (1903) 7 CCC 226 (Ont CA); *Adams v Adams* (1909) 14 BCR 301; *Casavallo v Casavallo* (1911) 1 WWR 212 (Alta); *Cutler v Cutler* (1914) 6 WWR 1231 (BC); *Potratz v Potratz* [1926] 1 DLR 147 (Sask); *MacDonald v Nash* [1929] 4 DLR 1051 (Man); *Yates (Davis) v Davis* [1960] OWN 201 (Ont); *Schwebel v Ungar* (1965) 48 DLR (2d) 644 (Can SC); *Kretzschmar v Kretzschmar* (1873) 4 AJR 131 (Vic FC); *Wood v Wood* (1875) 4 QSCR 136 (FC); *Jackson v Jackson* (1892) 18 VLR 766; *Forster v Forster* [1907] VLR 159 (FC); *Armstrong v Armstrong* (1892) 11 NZLR 201; *Gardner v Gardner* (1897) 15 NZLR 739; *McCartie v McCartie* (1903) 23 NZLR 161; *Owen v Robinson (Otherwise Owen)* [1925] NZLR 591; *Murray v Murray* (1950) 34 HKLR 28. The earlier the case, the more likely it is to raise the jurisdictional aspect of the rule rather than the question of recognition, but dicta repeatedly link the two issues in a single principle.
4   *Mansell v Mansell* [1967] P 306, [1966] 2 All ER 391. But cf *Harris v Harris* [1947] VLR 44.
5   *Slater v Slater* [1928] SASR 161; *Russell v Russell* [1935] SASR 85 (FC); *Pearson v Pearson* [1951]

2 DLR 851 (Ont); *Howard v Howard* 1966 (2) SA 718 (SR); *Leon v Leon* [1967] P 275, [1966] 3 All ER 820. Cf *Kerrison v Kerrison* (1952) 69 WN (NSW) 305.

6   *Niboyet v Niboyet* (1878) 4 PD 1 at 8, CA; see para 2.02 above.

7   *Le Sueur v Le Sueur* (1876) 1 PD 139; *Armytage v Armytage* [1898] P 178; *Stathatos v Stathatos* [1913] P 46; *De Montaigu v De Montaigu* [1913] P 154. See also *Jewell v Jewell* (1913) 30 WN (NSW) 130 (distinguishing *Stathatos v Stathatos*).

8   [1921] 1 AC 146, HL.

9   [1926] AC 444, PC. See also the earlier New Zealand case of *Hastings v Hastings* [1922] NZLR 273.

10   Divorce Jurisdiction Act 1930 (of the Dominion Parliament).

11   Marriage Act 1928 (Vic), s 95. For a very much earlier Australian provision see Matrimonial Causes Act 1899 (NSW), s 16(a) (three years' residence).

12   Divorce and Matrimonial Causes Act 1928 (NZ), s 12.

13   Matrimonial Causes Act 1937 (UK), s 13. Earlier legislation in several of the Australasian jurisdictions had gone some way in this direction: see *Indyka v Indyka* [1969] 1 AC 33 at 102, HL.

14   See para 1.32 above.

The grounds relied upon in the foreign forum

2.04   It is now clearly established that the foreign decree will be recognised if the jurisdictional test is satisfied, ie in the present context if it is established that both parties were domiciled in the forum state. It is quite immaterial, subject to the possible invocation of the doctrine of public policy in exceptional cases,[1] what factual grounds were relied upon by the foreign court in granting the divorce. Despite the suggestion to the contrary in *Lolley's Case*,[2] it is irrelevant that the ground for divorce would not be sufficient in the law of the country in which recognition is sought. Given the great variation in divorce law as between different states this is a very necessary rule; any other rule would produce great uncertainties and many 'limping' marriages.

So it is immaterial that no matrimonial offence was alleged against the respondent in the foreign proceedings even if the recognising country requires such an offence;[3] or that the petitioner relied upon his *own* misconduct.[4] Divorces founded on a husband's adultery (at a time when such conduct was not a ground for divorce in most jurisdictions),[5] or on bad temper falling short of the usual 'cruelty' ground,[6] or 'mental' cruelty similarly falling short,[7] or on a 'violation of matrimonial duty' consisting of insulting behaviour and incompatibility of temper,[8] or on the existence for a stated period of a legal separation[9] will be recognised.[10] This proposition applies equally to the other bases for recognition now to be considered.

1   See para 2.13 below.

2   (1812) Russ & Ry 237.

3   *Gardner v Gardner* (1897) 15 NZLR 739.

4   *Burpee v Burpee* [1929] 3 DLR 18 (BC).

5   *Harvey v Farnie* (1882) 8 App Cas 43, HL; *Bater v Bater* [1906] P 209, CA.

6   *Pemberton v Hughes* [1899] 1 Ch 781.

7   *Perin v Perin* 1950 SLT 51.

8   *Mezger v Mezger* [1937] P 19, [1936] 3 All ER 130.

9   *Pastre v Pastre* [1930] P 80; *Manning v Manning* [1958] P 112, [1958] 1 All ER 291.

10   See also *Henderson v Muncey* [1943] 3 DLR 515; affd [1943] 4 DLR 758 (BC CA) and *Walker v Walker* [1950] 4 DLR 253 (BC). For a reaffirmation of the principle that the grounds relied on are irrelevant see *Indyka v Indyka* [1969] 1 AC 33 at 73, HL, per Lord Morris.

Decrees granted in third states and recognised in the common domicile

2.05   The question was raised in England in 1906 'are we to recognize in this country the binding effect of a decree obtained in a State in which the husband is [and therefore both parties are] not domiciled if the Courts of the State in which he is [and therefore they are] domiciled recognize the validity of that decree?'[1] The parties to a marriage celebrated in England were domiciled in New York. After a deed of separation had been entered into in England, the wife went to South Dakota where she obtained a divorce on the ground of cruelty and desertion. There was evidence that the decree would be recognised in New York, despite the differences between the laws of New York and South Dakota.[2] Sir Gorrell Barnes P held that the English courts must recognise the decree: 'It seems to me impossible to come to any other conclusion, because the status is affected and determined by the decree that is recognized in the State of New York—the State of the domicil—as having affected and determined it.'[3] The result was that the subsequent marriages of each party could be upheld and the four children of the wife's second marriage held legitimate.

This rule in *Armitage v A-G* seems a natural and desirable extension of the basic domicile rule. It rests on principle, but also on the practical point that had recognition of the South Dakota decree been refused and the parties required to obtain a New York divorce, the courts of that state (on the evidence as to the law of New York presented in *Armitage v A-G*) would dismiss a petition, on the ground that there was no subsisting marriage to dissolve. A mere declaratory judgment to that effect would be little more than was already available to the parties in the *Armitage* case.

This principle has won general acceptance in Commonwealth common law jurisdictions.[4]

1   *Armitage v A-G* [1906] P 135 at 141.
2   See the controversy between Morris (1946) 24 CBR 73 and Tuck (1947) 25 CBR 226.
3   *Armitage v A-G* [1906] P 135 at 141. Cf the restrictive restatement of the ratio of *Armitage v A-G* advanced, but not pressed, by Davies J in *Mountbatten v Mountbatten* [1959] P 43 at 78.
4   *Owen v Robinson* [1925] NZLR 591 (following *Cass v Cass* (1910) 26 TLR 305); *Wyllie v Martin* [1931] 3 WWR 465 (BC); *Walker v Walker* [1950] 4 DLR 253 (BC) (cf earlier Canadian references in *Burnfiel v Burnfiel* [1926] 2 DLR 129 (Sask CA) and *Holmes v Holmes* [1927] 2 DLR 979 (Alta); *Guggenheim v Rosenbaum* (2) 1961 (4) SA 21 at 31-2 (W); *Yuan v Yuan* [1964] 34 HKLR 895; *Perin v Perin* 1950 SLT 51.

Reciprocity: Travers v Holley

2.06   Much more controversial, perhaps because it involved a more radical departure from established principles, was the English decision in *Travers v Holley*.[1] From the date of *Le Mesurier v Le Mesurier*,[2] it was clear law that the common domicile of the parties was the primary basis for both jurisdiction in divorce and the recognition of decrees granted elsewhere. Domicile was seen as central to the issue of personal status and, that being established, jurisdiction and recognition were different faces of the same coin; in the reported cases, authorities on jurisdiction and recognition are cited as almost interchangeable. The rule in *Armitage v A-G* could only apply in a recognition context, and could have no jurisdictional counterpart; but it was seen as an extension of the domicile basis rather than resting on any new principle. Once *A-G for Alberta v Cook* had been decided, and more legislatures sought to remedy the injustice felt by married women, a new situation was created: jurisdiction was now claimed in circumstances in which the domicile principle could not be relied upon. Did the common law tradition, in which recognition rules had mirrored jurisdictional principles, suggest that the new, statutory, jurisdictional principles should be matched by corresponding, judge-made, recognition rules? This question was answered in the affirmative in *Travers v Holley*.

It had earlier been expressly rejected in Scotland. In *Warden v Warden*,[3] the parties were domiciled in Scotland and a divorce decree was granted in Nevada on the jurisdictional basis of six weeks' residence. The pursuer sought to argue that the decree could be recognised in Scotland where the Law Reform (Miscellaneous Provisions) Act 1949[4] had given the Scottish courts jurisdiction on the basis of residence by the petitioning wife. Lord Strachan said that he could not accept a general proposition that Scottish courts must concede to foreign courts any ground of jurisdiction which they claim for themselves. In the 1949 Act, Parliament could well have dealt with recognition, but had chosen to limit the provisions to jurisdiction. In any event, there was no evidence that the Nevada basis for claiming jurisdiction (six weeks' residence) corresponded to the Scottish residence test, which required three years' ordinary residence. No point was taken on the date of the decree, January 1947, which was before the Scottish Act.

The English Court of Appeal, without considering *Warden v Warden*, reached the opposite conclusion two years later. In *Travers v Holley*[5] the decree was granted in New South Wales on the basis of the three years' residence of the wife petitioner.[6] The Court of Appeal could have decided the case solely on the domicile basis, for it held (Jenkins LJ dissenting) that the parties were domiciled in New South Wales at the relevant time. However it also held (Jenkins LJ apparently agreeing, though he still indicated that he would dismiss the appeal) that the decree was entitled to recognition because the New South Wales court was asserting a jurisdiction substantially similar to that conferred on the English courts by s 13 of the Matrimonial Causes Act 1937. Somervell LJ thought the matter plain: 'On principle it seems plain to me that our courts should recognize a jurisdiction which they themselves claim. I do not myself readily understand on what grounds it was submitted that the result should be otherwise.'[7]

The precise limits of the rule in *Travers v Holley* are explored below. It should be noted here that the case has been widely accepted in Commonwealth jurisdictions including Alberta,[8] Manitoba,[9] Ontario,[10] Cyprus,[11] India,[12] New South Wales,[13] Victoria (by legislation following a judicial refusal to follow *Travers v Holley*,[14]) and (not following *Warden v Warden*) in Scotland.[15] In England itself, the rule was applied in a series of cases but doubts lingered. In 1958, counsel for the Queen's Proctor in *Mountbatten v Mountbatten*[16] submitted that it was not easy to reconcile the new principle with those laid down by the Privy Council in *Le Mesurier v Le Mesurier* (the ground upon which O'Bryan J of the Supreme Court of Victoria rested his refusal to follow *Travers v Holley*) and expressly reserved for future argument the question whether *Travers v Holley* was rightly decided. In the end the new principle was endorsed by the House of Lords in *Indyka v Indyka*;[17] as that case developed a wholly new basis of recognition it is considered separately below.

1   [1953] P 246, [1953] 2 All ER 794, CA.
2   [1895] AC 517, PC.
3   1951 SC 508.
4   S 2.
5   [1953] P 246, [1953] 2 All ER 794, CA.
6   Under Matrimonial Causes Act 1899 (NSW), s 16(a).
7   [1953] P 246 at 251, CA.
8   *Bednar v Deputy Registrar General of Vital Statistics* (1960) 24 DLR (2d) 238; *Re Allarie and Director of Vital Statistics* (1963) 41 DLR (2d) 553; cf *La Pierre v Walter* (1960) 24 DLR (2d) 483 (and see *Pledge v Walter* (1961) 36 WWR 95).
9   *Januszkiewicz v Januszkiewicz* (1965) 55 DLR (2d) 727.

10   *Re Capon* (1965) 49 DLR (2d) 675 (Ont CA; applied in a nullity context). See *Bevington v Hewiston* (1975) 16 RFL 44 (Ont) for the limiting effect of the Divorce Act 1968 (Canada) on the scope of the doctrine in practice.
11   *Serghi v Serghi* (1958) 24 CLR 20 (where *Travers v Holley* distinguished as divorce granted in Oregon after only 20 months' residence).
12   *Satya v Teja Singh* [1975] 2 SCR 197.
13   *Sheldon v Douglas (No 1)* [1963] NSWR 129 (FC).
14   Marriage (Amendment) Act 1957 (Vic), s 4, reversing *Fenton v Fenton* [1957] VR 17.
15   *Galbraith v Galbraith* 1971 SC 65; *Bain v Bain* 1971 SC 146.
16   [1959] P 43. See at 59.
17   [1969] 1 AC 33, [1967] 2 All ER 689, HL; see para 2.09 below.

Limitations on the rule in Travers v Holley

2.07   The precise scope of the rule in *Travers v Holley*[1] took some time to work out; the decisions are English ones, and it is possible—though unlikely—that courts in other Commonwealth jurisdictions would limit the principle in rather different ways.

A major obscurity in the rule as originally propounded was the degree of equivalence required between the law of the country in which the decree was granted and that in which it was to be recognised. In *Travers v Holley* itself, the New South Wales legislation required that the wife should have been domiciled there for three years before the institution of the suit and provided that desertion by the husband during a period of domicile would not deprive her of that domicile. The corresponding English Act merely required the wife to have been domiciled in England immediately before desertion by her husband. The courts eventually adopted a test which did *not* depend on any equivalence between the legal principles relied on, or forming part of the law of, each country: the test concerned the factual links between the parties and the foreign forum as compared with the jurisdictional rules in the country of recognition.

So, if the English courts have jurisdiction in divorce where the wife petitioner was ordinarily resident in England for three years before the presentation of the petition, those English courts will recognise any decree granted to a wife petitioner who had been ordinarily resident in the foreign forum for the three-year period. The ground upon which the foreign court relied in claiming jurisdiction is immaterial, whether it is the separate domicile of the wife in the eyes of the foreign country's conflict of laws rules,[2] or the nationality[3] or the last common residence of the parties,[4] or residence for a relatively short period.[5] But it is essential for the English jurisdictional rules to be met mutatis mutandis: despite suggestions to the contrary,[6] a shorter period of residence than the English court would require is insufficient.[7]

Just as the legal basis upon which the foreign court claimed jurisdiction is immaterial, so also is the state of that country's conflict of laws rules. 'Reciprocity', a word often used in connection with the rule in *Travers v Holley*, does not strictly apply; it is not necessary to establish that the foreign country has a rule corresponding to that in *Travers v Holley*.[8]

The question of a possible limitation on the rule in *Travers v Holley* in terms of time was raised by the facts of *Indyka v Indyka*.[9] A Czechoslovak decree was pronounced a few months before English jurisdictional rules were changed (by the Law Reform (Miscellaneous Provisions) Act 1949) so as to allow divorce petitions where a wife had been ordinarily resident there for three years; as the wife had been ordinarily resident in Czechoslovakia for more than three years, it was argued that the decree should be recognised in England, even though it could not have been recognised at the date it was pronounced. The House of Lords held that the decree should be recognised. On this particular point, Lord Morris argued that the issue was the husband's freedom to remarry, an issue which became relevant only after the coming into force of the new legislation as to English jurisdictional rules.[10] Lord Pearce based his decision on a more general proposition.[11]

'The facts which made it right for our courts to have wider jurisdiction and give wider recognition existed at the date of the Czech decree even though those facts did not until a few months later result in the statute by which this country took wider jurisdiction. When once the appreciation of these facts has been brought home to our courts by parliamentary extension of their jurisdiction, their recognition should be retrospective. ... In my opinion the question whether a foreign decree should be recognised should be answered by the court in the light of its present policy, regardless (within reason) of when the decree was granted.'

The parenthetical 'within reason' is not explained; but there could easily be cases in which reliance upon the previous legal position had led the parties to act in certain ways so that retrospective application of the new rules would be unjust.[12]

The point arose in the Ontario case of *Bevington v Hewitson*,[13] although that case was ultimately decided on a different ground. The divorce decree was pronounced in the State of Maine in 1954. The husband was domiciled, and so at common law both parties were domiciled, at all relevant times in Ontario. The wife was, however, born in Maine and remained at all times resident in the township of her birth; de facto she was 'domiciled' in Maine. In 1968, the Canadian jurisdictional rules in divorce were altered; by s 6(1) of the Divorce Act 1968 the domicile of a married woman was to be determined for jurisdictional purposes as if she were unmarried. Lacourciere J of the Ontario High Court expressed the view that the fact that the divorce antedated s 6(1) did not, of itself, render that section inapplicable 'as a matching domestic jurisdictional base' for the purposes of the rule in *Travers v Holley*. On the facts, however, he would not apply the argument.[14] The husband had remarried in 1958, and the proceedings concerned the validity of that marriage; in 1958 Ontario would not have been able to recognise the decree. This was not a case in which Ontario was relevant merely as a country in which recognition was now sought; as the lex domicilii of the husband, Ontario law governed his capacity to remarry in 1958.[15]

Two other 'time-factor' points arose in *Bevington v Hewitson*. Between 1930 and 1968, the Canadian courts had jurisdiction where a married woman had been deserted for more than two years. The relevant legislation[16] was repealed in 1968. Did this mean that a Canadian court, asked, at some date after 1968, to recognise a foreign decree granted during the earlier period, should ignore the repealed legislation? *Indyka v Indyka*[17] might suggest this, insofar as it applied the *Travers v Holley* principle by reference to jurisdictional rules current at the date of recognition not of the original decree, but Lacourciere J was not prepared to deny recognition on that basis. In effect, he was prepared to let those seeking recognition 'have it both ways'; the decree would be recognised if the domestic jurisdictional rules at *either* the date of the decree *or* the date of recognition were in appropriate terms.[18] Finally, s 6(2) of the Divorce Act 1968, establishing a new recognition rule, contained an express provision as to its temporal scope, which would of course be respected.[19]

For the rule in *Travers v Holley* to be applicable, there must be real correspondence between the facts and the appropriate jurisdictional rule of the
recognising country. If, for example, the jurisdictional rule based upon three
years' residence applies only in the case of petitions presented *by a wife*, the
recognition rule developed in *Travers v Holley* will be similarly limited, and will
not even apply to decrees pronounced on a husband's cross-petition filed in
response to a petition by a wife.[20] Where joint petitions are permitted, it is
thought that recognition would be accorded to the resulting decree, but no
authority has been found on the point.

1   [1953] P 246, [1953] 2 All ER 794, CA.
2   As in *Robinson-Scott v Robinson-Scott* [1958] P 71, [1957] 3 All ER 473 (wife in fact resident in
    Zurich forum for at least 10 years).
3   *Indyka v Indyka* [1969] 1 AC 33, [1967] 2 All ER 689, HL.
4   As in *Arnold v Arnold* [1957] P 237, [1957] 1 All ER 570 (wife, a Finnish national, in fact
    resident in Finnish forum for 17 years, and also domiciled in Finland at time of desertion by
    the husband); *Manning v Manning* [1958] P 112, [1958] 1 All ER 291 (wife, of Norwegian
    origin, had been resident in Norwegian forum for 6 years); *Gerrard v Gerrard* (1958) Times, 18
    November.
5   See *Mountbatten v Mountbatten* [1959] P 43 at 83.
6   *Arnold v Arnold* [1957] P 237 at 253, per Mr Commissioner Latey: 'two years' residence or
    more, or even less, and the residence is genuine and bona fide and not merely for the purpose
    of getting a divorce in a convenient court'.
7   *Robinson-Scott v Robinson-Scott* [1958] P 71 at 87; *Manning v Manning* [1958] P 112 at 120. See
    Dunne v Saban [1955] P 178, [1954] 3 All ER 586 where, however, no reliance was placed on
    the two-year residence by the wife.
8   See the hypothetical question raised in *Manning v Manning* [1958] P 112 at 118, and the
    comments by P. R. H. Webb at (1958) 7 ICLQ 376–7. See also Lord Reid's comments on
    'reciprocity' and 'comity' in this context in *Indyka v Indyka* [1969] 1 AC 33 at 58, HL.
9   [1969] 1 AC 33, HL.
10 At 75–6.
11 At 91.
12 Cf the issues raised in *Starkowski v A-G* [1954] AC 155, [1953] 2 All ER 1272, HL.
13 (1974) 47 DLR (3d) 510 (Ont).
14 At 515.
15 Cf *R v Brentwood Superintendant Registrar of Marriages, ex p Arias* [1969] 2 QB 956, [1968] 3 All
    ER 279, DC.
16 Divorce Jurisdiction Act 1930 (Canada).
17 [1969] 1 AC 33, [1967] 2 All ER 689, HL.
18 Cf P. M. North *The Private International Law of Matrimonial Causes in the British Isles and the
    Republic of Ireland* p 161.
19 See para 3.03 below.
20 *Levett v Levett* [1957] P 156, [1957] 1 All ER 720, CA.

Relationship between the bases of recognition

2.08   In an important article published in 1957, P. R. H. Webb asked the
question, 'Are the rules in *Le Mesurier v Le Mesurier*, *Armitage v A-G* and *Travers
v Holley* each separate rules, so that a foreign divorce, valid under any one of
them, must be recognised?'[1] The particular point in practice is the relationship
between the two latter rules, and it arises in two different contexts.

The first is one of possible conflict. A decree is presented for recognition in a
Commonwealth country which has accepted both *Armitage v A-G* and *Travers
v Holley*. The petition leading to the decree was presented by the wife who had
been resident in the forum country for at least three years; three years' residence
by a wife is a basis for jurisdiction in the recognising country, so the decree is
prima facie entitled to recognition under the rule in *Travers v Holley*. But the
parties are domiciled in a third country which will not recognise the decree, so

that prima facie it must be denied recognition under the rule in *Armitage v A-G*. This situation does not seem to have arisen in a reported case, where requests for recognition have been made in the country of domicile not in a third country. In *Mountbatten v Mountbatten*,[2] Davies J, obiter, seemed to be of opinion that were it to arise the decree would not be recognised, but this view rests (as does the formulation of the issue in this paragraph) on the assumption that *Armitage v A-G* has a negative aspect, that a decree not recognised in the common domicile must be denied recognition elsewhere. Most writers and judges treat *Armitage v A-G* as a facultative extension of the domicile basis, to which *Travers v Holley* is an exception. On this argument, which it is submitted is much to be preferred, not least for its practical convenience, a decree can be recognised under either principle; the rules are independent of one another.[3]

The second is one of possible combination. Can *Travers v Holley* and *Armitage v A-G* be combined to create a more extensive recognition principle? This possibility was explored in *Mountbatten v Mountbatten*,[4] which concerned a Mexican decree. The parties were domiciled in England, and their only link with Mexico was a period of two days' residence. The argument was summarised by Davies J as follows.[5]

'(1) The New York court is the court of the residence of the wife.

(2) The New York court would recognize the Mexican decree.

(3) While formerly our courts took the view that the court of the domicile of the parties was the only court which had jurisdiction to dissolve their marriage, nevertheless we would recognize the validity of a decree pronounced alibi if such a decree was recognized as valid by the court of the domicile (*Armitage v A-G*).

(4) As a result of the decisions in *Travers v Holley* [and following cases], the English courts now recognize foreign decrees pronounced at the suit of the wife if the wife at the time of the presentation of her petition had been for three years resident within the jurisdiction of the court which pronounced the decree, even though the jurisdictional test of the foreign court is other than that of three years residence and the ground of the decree was not a ground upon which this court could act.

(5) Therefore, this court by an extension of the principle of *Armitage v A-G*, should in the present case recognize the Mexican decree, since it is recognized by the court in whose jurisdiction the wife has resided for three years and whose competence to dissolve the marriage we would now recognize.'

However, the argument was firmly, and it is submitted rightly, rejected. *Armitage v A-G* is a development of the domicile principle; the whole rationale of the case was the primacy of domicile in matters of personal status, and it is simply not possible to treat the same principles as transferable to a mere residence context.

1 (1957) 6 ICLQ 608 at 615.
2 [1959] P 43 at 83-4.
3 See, eg, *Bevington v Hewitson* (1974) 47 DLR (3d) 510 at 514, 'a further test'.
4 [1959] P 43.
5 At 70.

Real and substantial connection: Indyka v Indyka

2.09 Although the principle developed in England in *Travers v Holley*[1] was expressly adopted in a good number of Commonwealth jurisdictions[2] and may fairly be said to have become part of Commonwealth common law, there has been little elaboration of the principle in reported cases outside England. The principal reason for this is that the *Travers v Holley* principle has been overtaken, or at least over-shadowed, by a more radical and more inclusive principle expounded in the opinions in a House of Lords case, *Indyka v Indyka*[3] in 1967. This concerned a Czechoslovak divorce pronounced in 1949 on the wife's petition. The parties were Czech, had married in Czechoslovakia in 1938, and had established their matrimonial home there. The wife had never ceased to reside in Czechoslovakia, but the husband, caught up in the 1939–45 War, spent a number of years in Poland and Russia before coming to England in 1946 and acquiring a domicile of choice there.

In the lower courts, the case turned on the application of the rule in *Travers v Holley*[4] but in the House of Lords the whole question of the recognition of foreign divorces was explored.

Lord Reid offered a powerful critique of the rule in *Travers v Holley*. He argued that to use domestic jurisdictional rules, enacted by Parliament with only 'the particular circumstances' in that country in mind, as the determinant of recognition rules would not lead to a rational development of the law. In particular, he thought that it was unsatisfactory that courts which themselves exercised jurisdiction on the basis of the wife's residence for three years should be required to recognise foreign decrees granted in corresponding circumstances;[5] though it must be said that Lord Reid's view seems to be based primarily on his dislike of the English jurisdictional rule itself, as creating 'limping' marriages. Lord Reid's speech does not ignore Parliamentary action in reforming jurisdictional rules; what Parliament had done, by creating a residential basis of jurisdiction, was to destroy the primacy of domicile asserted, for recognition and jurisdictional purposes alike, in the opinion in *Le Mesurier v Le Mesurier*.[6] This freed the judges to develop new bases of recognition, but in no way dictated the shape of those new bases. The basis Lord Reid proposed was that of the matrimonial home. He would recognise decrees pronounced in the country of the matrimonial home, expressly including cases where the husband had left that country leaving the wife behind. He would also allow cases where the wife had become *habitually* resident in a new country. But he would exclude cases where the spouses went to live in a country for only a few years (even it seems if they set up their matrimonial home there) and in which one spouse tried to take advantage of their short stay to obtain a divorce on trivial grounds.[7]

Lord Reid's approach was in some respects notably conservative; but it did lead him to advocate what was, despite some references to the concept of matrimonial home or domicile in the 19th-century cases, a wholly new basis of recognition. The other members of the House were equally innovative. Lord Morris traced the development of the law leading up to *Travers v Holley* which he expressly approved.[8] But he wondered whether development should stop there:

'... [O]nce the rigidity of insistence upon domicile has been displaced the question must be asked whether it is reasonable only to recognise decrees where the foreign jurisdiction is founded upon rules which mutatis mutandis are like ours.[9] There is peril in assuming that only our rules are rational and justifiable.'[10]

Lord Morris said that he would recognise the decree on a 'wider basis', which he explained by reference to the circumstances of the case: the parties were Czech citizens, and the wife was in Czechoslovakia and she undoubtedly had a real and substantial connection with that country.[11]

Lord Pearce followed a similar line of reason. It would be 'insular and unreasonable'[12] to go back on *Travers v Holley*; but its effect could properly be broadened. Jurisdictional rules should only be an approximate test of recognition, and the courts should go further 'when this is justified by special circumstances in the petitioner's connection with the country granting the decree'.[13] He would recognise decrees of the court of the nationality of the parties, at least when jurisdiction was taken by the foreign court on that ground, but also noted that in the instant case the matrimonial home factor could also be relied upon.[14]

Lord Wilberforce addressed himself in more detail to the content of an expanded recognition rule. He considered the adoption of a nationality or a residence basis, but concluded in each case that it would be going too far to adopt the new basis as generally applicable without qualification. He indicated that in some cases nationality *combined with other factors* could be taken into account; and he would recognise divorces given to wives by the courts of their residence wherever a real and substantial connection was shown between the petitioning wife and the country whose courts granted the decree. The length and quality of the wife's residence, and other factors such as nationality, could all be weighed.[15]

Finally Lord Pearson would recognise 'subject to appropriate limitations' a divorce granted on the basis of nationality or domicile (including cases in which the forum's idea of domicile was less exacting than that applied in England), and would extend this to cases where the court granting the decree had relied upon a separate nationality or domicile allowed to married women for the purpose of matrimonial proceedings.[16] One of the 'appropriate limitations' was a requirement of a real and substantial connection between the petitioner and the forum; this qualified the other factors so that, for example, nationality might not be a good basis for recognition in the absence of such a connection.[17] Lord Pearson would express no decided opinion on the residential basis for recognition.

1   [1953] P 246, [1953] 2 All ER 794, CA.
2   See para 2.06 above.
3   [1969] 1 AC 33, [1967] 2 All ER 689, HL (decided in May 1967).
4   On this aspect, see para 2.07 above.
5   [1969] 1 AC 33 at 59–60, HL.
6   [1895] AC 517. See the passage cited in para 2.01 above.
7   [1969] 1 AC 33 at 68, HL.
8   At 75.
9   This is of course a less than accurate reflection of the principle underlying *Travers v Holley*, which rests on the factual situation vis-à-vis the foreign jurisdiction and not on that country's rules.
10 [1969] 1 AC 33 at 76, HL.
11 At 76–77. Lord Reid had mentioned but declined to express an opinion on nationality as a basis for recognition: at 68–69.
12 At 84.
13 At 87.
14 At 90–91.
15 At 104–105.
16 At 111.
17 At 112.

Reception of Indyka v Indyka in England

2.10   It seems a fair assessment of the position immediately after the decision in *Indyka v Indyka*[1] that the law as to the recognition of foreign divorces was 'in an unstable state'.[2] Ormrod J, speaking four years after the House of Lords' decision, commented sorrowfully that their Lordships had refrained from formulating in precise terms the correct test or tests to be applied, leaving it, rather, to the judges to work out the rules in the light of the general observations contained in their Lordship's speeches.[3] He went on to subject the speeches to close analysis, and developed a number of cautiously worded propositions;[4] but meanwhile other judges had taken a simpler, if somewhat cavalier, approach.

Three cases decided within a year of *Indyka v Indyka* established a pattern. In *Angelo v Angelo*,[5] which Ormrod J himself decided, counsel submitted that the true ratio of *Indyka v Indyka* was to be found in Lord Morris's reference to a party having a real and substantial connection with the foreign forum state. In *Peters v Peters*,[6] Wrangham J, without actually deciding whether *Indyka v Indyka* went that far, declared that the 'high-water mark' was the proposition that an English court would recognise the validity of a foreign decree wherever such a real and substantial connection existed. Finally, in *Brown v Brown*[7] Cumming-Bruce J stated the test as being the existence of a real and substantial connection between the wife petitioner and the foreign jurisdiction.

Although individual judges have expressed doubts, hinting that violence was being done to the speeches in *Indyka v Indyka*,[8] it has come to be accepted that a 'real and substantial connection' is a basis for recognition, despite the fact that the original use of the phrase was as a factor to be used in weighing the circumstances, or even as an 'appropriate limitation' on other rules.

In its original context, and in a number of later formulations, the new rule enabled the English courts to recognise a decree obtained as a result of a petition by the wife.[9] It soon became accepted that no distinction should be drawn between wives and husbands for this purpose; the status of each was changed and it could be quite incidental who initiated the proceedings.[10]

Having identified the new test, the judges proceeded to give it a generous interpretation. The mere fact of the celebration of the marriage in a country did not create the necessary real and substantial connection,[11] but other facts were readily treated as satisfying the test. The combination of nationality and residence (even residence of recent origin) suffices;[12] residence since birth of one party is a clear case,[13] but shorter periods of residence coupled with other elements have also been accepted. So residence for some two years before the decree, with evidence that it had continued thereafter was accepted in *Welsby v Welsby*;[14] even residence for 12 months between marriage and decree was sufficient where there had been previous residence for much of a two-year period[15] or where it was accompanied by a determination to remain indefinitely.[16]

1   [1969] 1 AC 33, [1967] 2 All ER 689, HL.
2   *Messina v Smith* [1971] P 322 at 331 per Ormrod J.
3   Ibid.
4   At 335–6.
5   [1967] 3 All ER 314, [1968] 1 WLR 401.
6   [1968] P 275 at 279.
7   [1968] P 518 at 521.
8   Eg Ormrod J in *Messina v Smith* [1971] P 322 at 336; Bagnall J in *Law v Gustin* [1976] Fam 155 at 159.
9   See eg *Brown v Brown* [1968] P 518, [1968] 2 All ER 11; *Messina v Smith* [1971] P 322, [1971] 2 All ER 1046.
10 *Blair v Blair* [1968] 3 All ER 639, [1969] 1 WLR 221; *Mayfield v Mayfield* [1969] P 119, [1969] 2 All ER 219; *Munt v Munt* [1970] 2 All ER 516. See also *Turczak v Turczak* [1970] P 198, [1969] 3 All ER 317.
11 *Peters v Peters* [1968] P 275, [1967] 3 All ER 318.
12 *Angelo v Angelo* [1967] 3 All ER 314, [1968] 1 WLR 401; *Brown v Brown* [1968] P 518, [1968] 2 All ER 11.
13 *Turczak v Turczak* [1970] P 198, [1969] 3 All ER 317.

14   [1970] 2 All ER 467, [1970] 1 WLR 877. See also *Perrini v Perrini* [1979] Fam 85, [1979] 2 All
     ER 323 (nullity).
15   *Munt v Munt* [1970] 2 All ER 516.
16   *Law v Gustin* [1976] Fam 155, [1976] 1 All ER 113 (nullity).

Reception of Indyka v Indyka outside England

2.11   *Indyka v Indyka*[1] was a decision as to the law of England, and could have
been disregarded elsewhere. This was the case even in Scotland, despite the
fact that appeals lie from Scottish courts to the House of Lords. The new
principle expounded in *Indyka v Indyka* was, however, accepted by the Court of
Session. As Lord Wheatley put it in *Galbraith v Galbraith*,[2] 'That a more liberal
view should be taken than the more restricted traditional view seems to find
encouragement if not authority (at least for a Scottish court) from the speeches
of their Lordships.'

Outside the British Isles, the position was much less predictable. The leading
cases for Commonwealth jurisdictions were the Privy Council decisions in *Le
Mesurier v Le Mesurier*[3] and *A-G for Alberta v Cook*,[4] and there is no doubt that
the principle developed, or, perhaps more accurately, initiated, in *Indyka v
Indyka* is inconsistent with those cases. These facts led O'Sullivan JA of the
Manitoba Court of Appeal to the conclusion that *Indyka v Indyka* could not be
followed. His reasoning deserves to be quoted at some length:[5]

'Where the House of Lords to this day expounds a principle of common law as being
one of ancient standing, albeit adapted to modern circumstances, it may still be safe for
Canadian lower courts to accept the exposition of the House of Lords as a sound
statement of the common law, the basic principles of which are, and it is desirable
should be, the same here as in England.

But where the House of Lords expressly departs from the received common law or
exercises its power to make new law, then in my opinion it is quite wrong for Canadian
courts of first instance or of intermediate appeal to follow the latest House of Lords
decision in preference to cases binding on us. A decision to follow the House of Lords in
effecting a change in our law is one that, in my opinion, should be left to the Supreme
Court of Canada....

To follow *Indyka v Indyka* in preference to *Le Mesurier v Le Mesurier* and *A-G for Alberta
v Cook* [gives] an unwarranted authority to an extra-territorial tribunal.'

This might well have been said, mutatis mutandis, in many other Commonwealth jurisdictions. But O'Sullivan JA was in a minority even in his own
court, and despite the refusal of the Supreme Court of Canada to decide the
point in the one case where opportunity presented itself,[6] *Indyka v Indyka* has
been applied, or treated as applicable, in Alberta,[7] British Columbia,[8] Manitoba[9] and Ontario.[10] Nor is the willingness to accept *Indyka v Indyka* a purely
Canadian phenomenon. It is equally accepted in Australia,[11] India,[12] New
Zealand[13] and Singapore,[14] and can now be regarded as an established part of
the common law as generally applied in Commonwealth jurisdictions.

In England, *Indyka v Indyka* has been treated as laying down a test of 'real
and substantial connection'. This same approach has been gratefully adopted
in other jurisdictions and, with a few exceptions, judges have given the same
liberal interpretation to the test as has been found in England. It must be
stressed that all the circumstances of each case have to be considered, including
'many diverse factors from residence, employment, nationality, citizenship and
holding property',[15] and there are therefore great dangers in any attempt to
state briefly the effect of the various decisions; it will be attempted, for all that.

It is clear that the life-long residence of one party in the relevant country will suffice[16] especially if it is coupled with citizenship.[17] A rather odd variant is a combination of domicile and nationality used in *Haut v Haut*,[18] odd because domicile alone was of course itself a sufficient basis for recognition.

Residence alone has been relied on in a large number of cases. The quality of the residence is important, and depends on all the surrounding circumstances, but the starting-point in practice is its length. Strictly what must be relevant, it seems, is the existence of a real and substantial connection at the time proceedings are commenced, but in some cases the date of the decree is cited (perhaps because it is more readily available) and residence even after that date may be relevant as establishing the quality of the earlier residence. Decrees have been recognised where a party has been resident in the granting country for periods of twelve years,[19] ten years,[20] seven years,[21] six years,[22] five years,[23] three years (with an intention to remain permanently),[24] and two years (coupled with citizenship and a long period of residence as a child).[25]

The outcome is a good deal less predictable where the period of residence is even shorter. A generous approach was taken in three Canadian cases. Twelve months' residence was sufficient in *Clarkson v Clarkson*[26] and in *La Carte v La Carte*;[27] in the latter case the wife was living with her mother, so some intention to remain may have been inferred. In *Wood v Wood*[28] the petitioning wife had been resident in Utah for only eight months, though she remained for about a year after the decree; her husband had been in the United States for about four years, but not in the relevant state; but the decree was recognised. These may be contrasted with three cases in which residence for ten to twelve months was regarded as insufficient. Two are New Zealand cases, *Re Darling*,[29] in which there was a period of some two years further residence after the decree, and *Godfrey v Godfrey*[30] where a period of ten months in Arizona was part of a total of four years in the United States. The third is from Ontario: in *El-Sohemy v El-Sohemy*[31] the petitioning wife was a native-born citizen of Egypt, as was her husband. After four years' residence in Canada, she returned to Egypt where she obtained a divorce after about one year of what became a three-year period of residence. Osler J held that this could not be a real and substantial connection 'even under the allegedly relaxed rule of *Indyka v Indyka*'.[32]

There seems in the three cases just cited to be a significantly different approach to the test. Most judges simply ask whether there is a real and substantial connection with the country in which the decree was granted. It is immaterial that another connection, perhaps even stronger, exists with some other country; indeed in most cases the domicile will be elsewhere. In the New Zealand case of *Re Darling*, however, the parties were held to be 'mere sojourners' in Liberia during their three-year working trip;[33] the implication being that their real links were with New Zealand. Similarly in *El-Sohemy v El-Sohemy* property and other links with Canada were emphasised and set against what must be regarded as substantial links with Egypt. It is submitted that the approach is incorrect: *a* real and substantial connection must be found, not *the most* real and substantial connection.

Citizenship alone has not been treated as sufficient. An example is *Keresztessy v Keresztessy*;[34] the parties were Hungarian citizens (though they had also acquired Canadian citizenship) and had lived in Hungary until their emigration in 1956. But it was held that to describe their connection with Hungary as 'real and substantial' was 'wishful thinking'.

To complete the record, it is not surprising that residence for six weeks (in the house of a 'professional divorce witness')[35] and residence for four days[36] have been regarded as insufficient for the present purpose. But residence for a single day was sufficient in *Nicholson v Nicholson*[37] where the petitioning wife was resuming residence in California, where she was born and had lived for all but the last four of her 26 years.

1 [1969] 1 AC 33, [1967] 2 All ER 689, HL.

2 1971 SC 65 at 70. *Galbraith v Galbraith* was followed in *Bain v Bain* 1971 SC 146.

3 [1895] AC 517, PC.

4 [1926] AC 444, PC.

5 *Holub v Holub* (1976) 71 DLR (3d) 698 at 703-4 (in a dissenting judgment).

6 *Powell v Cockburn* (1976) 68 DLR (3d) 700. The headnote in the Dominion Law Reports errs in suggesting that *Indyka v Indyka* was followed.

7 *Re Kish and Director of Vital Statistics* (1973) 35 DLR (3d) 530; *Wood v Wood* [1974] 5 WWR 18.

8 *La Carte v La Carte* (1975) 60 DLR (3d) 507; *Siebert v Siebert* (1978) 3 RFL (2d) 338 (where the decree not recognised on the facts); *Gwynn v Mellen* (1979) 101 DLR (3d) 608 (BC CA) (where the principle was applied to the recognition of a foreign nullity decree).

9 *Holub v Holub* (1976) 71 DLR (3d) 698 (Man CA); *Clarkson v Clarkson* (1978) 86 DLR (3d) 694.

10 *Abbruscato v Abbruscato* (1973) 12 RFL 257; *Rowland v Rowland* (1973) 42 DLR (3d) 205 (expressly obiter: see at 212); *Bevington v Hewitson* (1974) 47 DLR (3d) 510; *MacNeill v MacNeill* (1974) 53 DLR (3d) 486; *Haut v Haut* (1978) 86 DLR (3d) 757; *Re Karnenas* (1978) 3 RFL (2d) 213; *Re Casterton* (1978) 94 DLR (3d) 290; *Goldin v Goldin* (1979) 104 DLR (3d) 76; *Szabo v Szabo* (1980) 15 RFL (2d) 13. In the following cases the principle was treated as applicable, but the decree was refused recognition on the facts: *Keresztessy v Keresztessy* (1976) 73 DLR (3d) 347; *Bate v Bate* (1978) 1 RFL (2d) 298; *El-Sohemy v El-Sohemy* (1978) 3 RFL (2d) 184.

11 *Nicholson v Nicholson* (1971) 17 FLR 47 (NSW). Cf *Alexsandrov v Alexsandrov* (1967) 12 FLR 360 (S Australia).

12 *Satya v Teja Singh* AIR 1975 SC 105 (semble: no final decision as decree not recognised on the facts).

13 *Re Darling* [1975] 1 NZLR 382; *Godfrey v Godfrey* [1976] 1 NZLR 711 (though in neither case was the decree recognised on the facts).

14 *Sivajaran v Sivajaran* [1972] 2 MLJ 231 (where decree not recognised on the facts).

15 *Bate v Bate* (1978) 1 RFL (2d) 298 at 311 (Ont) per Boland J.

16 *Bevington v Hewitson* (1974) 47 DLR (3d) 510 (Ont); *Re Casterton* (1978) 94 DLR (3d) 290 (Ont); *Szabo v Szabo* (1980) 15 RFL (2d) 13 (Ont).

17 *Bain v Bain* 1971 SC 146 (Scotland); *Re Kish and Director of Vital Statistics* (1973) 35 DLR (3d) 530.

18 (1978) 86 DLR (3d) 757 (Ont).

19 *Abbruscato v Abbruscato* (1973) 12 RFL 257 (Ont).

20 *Re Karnenas* (1978) 3 RFL (2d) 213 (Ont).

21 *Gwynn v Mellen* (1979) 101 DLR (3d) 608 (BC) (nullity).

22 *Rowland v Rowland* (1973) 42 DLR (3d) 205 (Ont).

23 *Holub v Holub* (1976) 71 DLR (3d) 698 (Man).

24 *MacNeill v MacNeill* (1974) 53 DLR (3d) 486 (Ont).

25 *Galbraith v Galbraith* 1971 SC 65 (Scotland).

26 (1978) 86 DLR (3d) 694 (Man).

27 (1975) 60 DLR (3d) 507 (BC).

28 [1974] 5 WWR 18 (Alta).

29 [1975] 1 NZLR 382.

30 [1976] 1 NZLR 711.

31 (1978) 3 RFL (2d) 184 (Ont).

32 At 188.

33 [1975] 1 NZLR 382 at 383-4.

34 (1976) 73 DLR (3d) 347 (Ont).

35 *Bate v Bate* (1978) 1 RFL (2d) 298 (Ont) (decree in Nevada).

36 *Siebert v Siebert* (1978) 3 RFL (2d) 338 (BC) (despite some evidence of an intention to remain).

37 (1971) 17 FLR 47 (NSW) (where the petition was in fact originally for maintenance, but was substantially the initial step to a divorce).

Relationship of Indyka v Indyka to the other bases for recognition

2.12 In the English case of *Mather v Mahoney*,[1] the parties were domiciled in England. The wife obtained a divorce in the State of Nevada. Payne J in an extempore judgment held that as the decree would be recognised in the State of Pennsylvania, with which the wife had a real and substantial connection (having been resident there for most of her life, apart from a few years in Italy), it must be recognised in England.

Without apparently realising it, His Lordship was combining the rule in *Armitage v A-G* with that in *Indyka v Indyka*, and in so doing did considerable violence to both. The decision in *Armitage v A-G* rests upon the primacy of the domicile in matters of status; if a decree is recognised in the country of the domicile other countries must take note. That thinking cannot be appropriately transferred to the country of a real and substantial connection. Similarly *Indyka v Indyka*, which Payne J purported to follow, required a connection with the country granting the decree, not with a third country.

In many cases, this issue cannot arise. If the country in which the divorce decree is granted has realistic jurisdictional requirements, it is unlikely that the party satisfying these requirements will have a real and substantial connection with another country. But the point may arise by reference to the other party's circumstances, or in relation to decrees granted, as are those of the State of Nevada, on the basis of requirements as flimsy as six weeks' residence.

Mather v Mahoney was expressly doubted in *Davidson v Davidson*[2] decided in the following year, but the point was not resolved as on the facts no real and substantial connection with the recognising state was established. The *Mather v Mahoney* principle was however again applied, in another undefended case in 1970[3] and approved after full argument in *Messina v Smith*[4] in 1971. This last-named case is a strong one: it again involved a Nevada decree pronounced after six weeks' residence. The wife had been resident in the United States for six years, and there was evidence that the decree would be recognised in all those states; but there was no evidence at all as to her connection with any specific state. Ormrod J declared that to refuse recognition to the decree would be 'to produce an entirely artificial result which would in no way advance the cause of justice'.[5]

It is noteworthy that these cases all concern federal countries. Ormrod J's argument is most persuasive in that context, and involves interpreting *Indyka v Indyka* as requiring a real and substantial connection with *either* the jurisdiction actually granting the decree *or* the federation which includes that jurisdiction and within which the 'full faith and credit' principle makes wide recognition of decrees certain or very likely. It is submitted that such a principle could be accepted, but that a wider interpretation of *Mather v Mahoney* is unjustified. Although the point was not pressed to decision, even the narrower rule was treated with disapproval in the New Zealand case of *Godfrey v Godfrey*.[6] A period of some nine months in Arizona was not sufficient as a basis of an alleged real and substantial connection; the parties had lived in the United States for four years, but this was treated as unhelpful. The point seems not to have been taken in other Commonwealth jurisdictions.

---

1   [1968] 3 All ER 223, [1968] 1 WLR 1773.
2   (1969) 113 Sol Jo 813.
3   *Spencer-Churchill v Spencer-Churchill* (1970) 114 Sol Jo 806.
4   [1971] P 322, [1971] 2 All ER 1046.
5   At 338.
6   [1976] 1 NZLR 711.

Grounds for refusing recognition

2.13 The common law approach to the recognition of foreign divorce decrees is essentially one of examining the jurisdiction of the court which granted the decree. The factual grounds on which the divorce is granted are not examined, and even if those facts have been established by false evidence the decree will be recognised.[1] There are, however, some grounds upon which recognition may be refused, though their precise limits are ill-defined.

One proposition supported by authority is that a decree obtained in some fashion which is contrary to natural justice will be treated as invalid.[2] In many contexts, a failure to give a defendant or respondent notice of proceedings will render the proceedings contrary to natural justice, and in a number of cases it has been asserted that a divorce decree obtained in such circumstances will be refused recognition;[3] in all these cases, however, the statement was strictly obiter, as the foreign court did not have jurisdiction. There are a large number of cases in which a decree has been recognised despite want of notice on the part of the respondent,[4] and it is clearly desirable to recognise some such decrees. The New South Wales case of *Brown v Brown*[5] provides an example. The parties displayed a startling mobility. The husband was Australian by birth, the wife a French citizen born in Manchuria. They married in Switzerland and later lived in Canada and Australia. After their separation, the husband settled in Canada and became a Canadian citizen. He obtained a divorce in Mexico, giving no notice to the wife and merely placing advertisements in newspapers in the Mexican State of Chihuahua. Despite his initial suspicions, Selby J held that the husband was domiciled in Chihuahua, and that at the time of the divorce proceedings he was genuinely unsure of the wife's whereabouts, her recent addresses having included places in Sarawak, Hong Kong, Switzerland and the Netherlands. There was no reason to refuse recognition to the decree, especially as the husband had remarried in Mexico (to a lady whose name suggests German origins) in reliance upon it.

It was this sort of consideration which led Sachs J in *Macalpine v Macalpine* to declare that where it is proved to be the case or where it can be assumed to be the case that upon information bona fide given to it the foreign court has held that its own rules as to service or substituted service have been duly complied with, the decree will be recognised despite the fact that no notice of the proceedings was received by the respondent.[6]

It is important that the information should be given bona fide. If deliberately false information is given to the foreign court on matters going to its jurisdiction the decree will be refused recognition. False evidence going to the merits will not be material, but false evidence as to jurisdiction will be; this principle has been applied in many cases in different Commonwealth countries,[7] and, although it has been criticised, was reasserted after full consideration by the Supreme Court of Canada in *Powell v Cockburn*.[8]

Fraud of a rather different type is mentioned in some of the cases. This is where the action of the petitioner in selecting a particular forum is characterised as being for any 'fraudulent or improper reasons'.[9] Lord Pearce in *Indyka v Indyka*[10] argued as follows:

'I think, however, that our courts should reserve to themselves the right to refuse a recognition of those decrees which offend our notions of genuine divorce. They have done so when decrees offend against substantial justice, and this, of course, includes a decree obtained by fraud. But I think it also includes or should include decrees where a wife has gone abroad in order to obtain a divorce and where a divorce can be said not to be genuine according to our notions of divorce . . . Where jurisdiction is taken on one day's residence and divorce is granted on incompatibility of temperament . . . it is clear that a court is simply purveying divorce to foreigners who wish to buy it; and that does not accord with our notions of a genuine divorce. . . . I feel sure that our judges could distinguish reasonably in practice between those jurisdictions which purvey divorces to the foreign market and those who are genuinely trying to make laws for the divorce of its citizens (including its genuine residents) to whom its duty lies.'

That argument is attractive but goes well beyond the position established in the common law tradition, which reflects a marked reluctance to look behind compliance with jurisdictional criteria and at the factual grounds. But it is believed that two elements of Lord Pearce's proposition can be supported.

The first arises only in the context of the principle in *Indyka v Indyka*. The considerations Lord Pearce refers to must surely be relevant to the reality of the parties' connection with the forum state. A 'real and substantial connection' must be a genuine connection, not a spurious one designed for the purposes of easy divorce.

The second is the reference to 'substantial justice', a phrase used also by judges in earlier[11] and later[12] cases. The courts have claimed a residual discretion, based on public policy, to refuse to recognise foreign decrees which offend their notions of substantial justice. Just as, according to the Supreme Court of Canada, 'even within the limited area of what might be termed jurisdictional fraud there should be a great reluctance to make a finding of fraud',[13] so there is a marked reluctance to exercise this discretion. It has been exercised so as to refuse recognition to *nullity* decrees granted in circumstances suggesting discrimination on religious grounds.[14] In the divorce context it was relied on, as an alternative basis for the decision, in *Middleton v Middleton*[15] which was however a case of jurisdictional fraud, and in *Re Meyer*.[16]

The latter case was one of racial persecution. The wife petitioner was in effect compelled to obtain a divorce in the German courts in 1939 from her Jewish husband who had escaped from Nazi persecution and was living in England. The decree was in form based upon failure to maintain and desertion, and was not contested in the immediate post-war years under an Ordinance concerning 'judicial decisions based solely or predominantly on racial, political or religious grounds'. In a not dissimilar case, *Igra v Igra*,[17] where the divorced husband had accepted the decree and remarried, the validity of the decree was recognised despite elements of racism. In *Re Meyer*, Bagnall J based himself on duress, not alleged in *Igra v Igra*. He held that a court would declare a foreign decree of divorce invalid if the will of the party seeking the decree was overborne by a genuine and reasonably held fear caused by present and continuing danger to life, limb or liberty arising from external circumstances for which that party was not responsible; 'danger to limb' included serious danger to physical or mental health, and 'danger' included, at least, danger to a parent or child of the party.[18]

The important point about the judgment in *Re Meyer* is its careful refusal to go beyond procedural issues. Bagnall J took the view that the original reference to 'substantial justice' in Sir Nathaniel Lindley MR's judgment in *Pemberton v Hughes*[19] was limited to questions of the propriety of the proceedings.[20] Bagnall J was of course aware of the nullity cases of *Gray v Formosa* and *Lepre v Lepre*, but denied that those cases established a general discretion to substitute his own view of the merits of a foreign decree for the view of the court of competent jurisdiction.[21]

Accordingly, it has to be said that the residual discretion is an elusive creature. Footprints are regularly found in the snow—Sir Jocelyn Simon P discussed the residual discretion, but declined to exercise it a few months after *Re Meyer* had been decided (but not reported)[22]—but reliable sightings of the beast are very few.

1　See para 2.04 above; *Bater v Bater* [1906] P 209, CA; *Middleton v Middleton* [1967] P 62 at 69.
2　*Macalpine v Macalpine* [1958] P 35 at 45; *Norman v Norman (No 3)* (1969) 16 FLR 231 (ACT).
3　*Rudd v Rudd* [1924] P 72; *Crabtree v Crabtree* 1929 SLT 675; *Scott v Scott* 1937 SLT 632.
4　*Boettcher v Boettcher* [1949] WN 83; *Maher v Maher* [1951] P 342, [1951] 2 All ER 37; *Igra v Igra* [1951] P 404; *Arnold v Arnold* [1957] P 237, [1957] 1 All ER 570; *Wood v Wood* [1957] P 254, CA; *Brown v Brown* (1962) 4 FLR 94 (NSW); *Hornett v Hornett* [1971] P 255, [1971] 1 All ER 98.
5　(1962) 4 FLR 94 (NSW).
6　[1958] P 35 at 45. Sachs J reserved the question of foreign rules as to service which were themselves contrary to natural justice.
7　*Bonaparte v Bonaparte* [1892] P 402 (false evidence as to domicile led to grant of Scottish divorce enabling wife to marry in the Isle of Man the legitimated son of Prince Lucien Bonaparte); *Bavin v Bavin* [1939] 2 DLR 278 (Ont) (revsd on other grounds [1939] 3 DLR 328); *Rothwell v Rothwell* [1942] 4 DLR 767 (Man); *Grissom v Grissom* [1949] QWN 52; *Macalpine v Macalpine* [1958] P 35, [1957] 3 All ER 134; *Terrell v Terrell* [1971] VR 155. Cf *Norman v Norman (No 3)* (1969) 16 FLR 231 (ACT) (shameful and shoddy deception by solicitors, but decree recognised).
8　(1976) 68 DLR (3d) 700 at 703-714.
9　*Re Kish and Director of Vital Statistics* (1973) 35 DLR (3d) 530 (Alta) at 543. See also *Wood v Wood* [1974] 5 WWR 18 (Alta).
10　[1969] 1 AC 33 at 88, HL.
11　Most notably in *Pemberton v Hughes* [1899] 1 Ch 781 at 790, per Lindley MR. See below.
12　See eg *Norman v Norman (No 3)* (1969) 16 FLR 231 (ACT).
13　*Powell v Cockburn* (1976) 68 DLR (3d) 700 at 713-714, per Dickson J.
14　*Gray v Formosa* [1963] P 259, [1962] 3 All ER 419, CA; *Lepre v Lepre* [1965] P 52, [1963] 2 All ER 49. See the criticism in Dicey and Morris *The Conflict of Laws* (10th edn, 1980) p 385; but contrary to what is there suggested it was not the absence of a religious ceremony which was decisive in the foreign court but the absence of a religious ceremony according to the rites of a particular Church.
15　[1967] P 62 at 76-7.
16　[1971] P 298, [1971] 1 All ER 378.
17　[1951] P 404.
18　[1971] P 298 at 307. See also *Burke v Burke* (1955) Times, 17 March.
19　[1899] 1 Ch 781 at 790.
20　[1971] P 298 at 308.
21　Ibid, at 309.
22　*Qureshi v Qureshi* [1972] Fam 173 at 201.

Extra-judicial divorces

2.14　The common law rules as to the recognition of foreign divorces were formulated in the context of the 'typical' judicial decree. That is, they assumed that what was presented for recognition was a decree of a court forming part of the judicial system established under the constitution of a particular state, either a specialised Family Court or a court exercising general jurisdiction. But the 'typical' divorce is not the only form of divorce. Should a divorce obtained in the country of the parties' domicile, for example, be refused recognition if it did not conform to the standard model?

A number of variant forms of divorce can be identified.[1] One involves a judicial process, satisfying the ordinary rules of natural justice, but taking place in a court deriving its authority not from the law of the state in which it sits but from some system of canon or religious law. Although Christian canon law in the West does not provide for a divorce jurisdiction (the Roman Catholic Church's tribunals exercising a liberal nullity jurisdiction), Orthodox churches take a different view. Their courts function wherever Orthodox Christians are to be found, and accordingly they are active not only in countries where Orthodoxy is established or the courts legally recognised (as in Greece or Cyprus) but in London, Melbourne, and other centres.

Another group of variants allow for divorce by act of the parties. Some understandings of marriage present it as an act of the parties, authenticated by church or state; an analogous view of divorce is not inappropriate. In some forms, registration by a court is required, notably in the case of a Jewish bill of divorcement or gett which has to be inscribed in a Rabbinical court. In other cases a written instrument must be registered in a state administrative office or registry, as in Iran, Japan, and the Soviet Union in certain cases. In Pakistan official involvement is extended, since the Muslim Family Laws Ordinance 1961,[2] to the provision of compulsory reconciliation proceedings during a period before the divorce can be effective. But in other cases again no official procedures are required, except perhaps for purposes of proof; and in some the divorce may be achieved by the unilateral act of one party without the other being present or even in the same country. Some forms of Islamic divorce, the talak (or talaq), and the khula, are in this category, as are Thai divorces and divorces under many systems of customary law of Chinese or African origin.

At the other extreme are divorces by private Act of Parliament or state decree, that is divorces by legislative rather than judicial process. England had this system until 1857, and Quebec and Newfoundland as recently as 1968.

If the parties are married and divorced in the country of their domicile, and the divorce though extrajudicial, is recognised by the general law of that state, there seems never to have been any doubt that the divorce would be entitled to recognition. Although the circumstances were rather special, because of the existence of a British court with extra-territorial jurisdiction in the country of origin, the Privy Council decision in *Sasson v Sasson*[3] lends support to this proposition. A clear illustration is *Lee v Lau*[4] where the parties married in Hong Kong in accordance with Chinese customary law and dissolved their marriage there in accordance with the same law by means of a written instrument authenticated by the seal ('chop') of the Sai Kung Northern Rural Committees' Association; the divorce was recognised in England. A similar result was arrived at in *Khan (otherwise Worresck) v Khan*[5] where a marriage and subsequent divorce by talak in Pakistan were recognised in British Columbia; but the decision proceeded on the fiction, regarded by the judge as of doubtful validity and repudiated in later cases,[6] that the Pakistan Embassy in Washington was to be treated as subject to Pakistan law.

On the other hand, where a divorce is obtained in the country of the parties' domicile by some means not recognised by the general law of that state, there seems to be no case for giving the divorce any recognition notwithstanding the ecclesiastical or other authority which the decree may possess.[7]

These propositions leave a large area to be resolved. The range of possibilities is indicated in Sir Jocelyn Simon's formulation of the issue in *Qureshi v Qureshi*:[8]

'The issue which I have to determine is whether there is a rule of English law which compels refusal of recognition to a divorce valid by the law of the domicile, if it is not the creature of judicial activity or performed in judicial presence, either generally, or if the marriage is celebrated in England, or the purported divorce takes place in England, or both.'

It seems to be clear that there is no such rule; a divorce recognised in the domicile of the parties will be recognised elsewhere despite the existence of the other factors listed. This has been declared to be the case in England,[9] Hong Kong,[10] New Zealand[11] and Scotland;[12] but the position was not reached without some controversy and difficulty.

The difficulties were caused principally by a decision of the English Court of Appeal, *R v Hammersmith Superintendent Registrar of Marriages, ex p Mir-Anwaruddin*.[13] The parties were domiciled in India, but had married in England and had supposedly been divorced by a talak pronounced by the husband in England. There was no doubt that the talak would be regarded as effective in the country of the parties' common domicile, and that no court (either in England or India) had jurisdiction to dissolve the marriage. The divorce was refused recognition in both the Divisional Court and the Court of Appeal, for a remarkable variety of reasons.[14]

In the Divisional Court, Viscount Reading CJ and Bray J sought to avoid the application of the rule in *Armitage v A-G*[15] by limiting it to judicial decrees.[16] Swinfen Eady and Bankes LJJ based their judgments on the nature of the marriage, an English monogamous marriage: it was not 'a marriage in the Mahomedan sense which can be dissolved in the Mahomedan manner'.[17] Lawrence J took the point of natural justice; it was contrary to natural justice that a man should be judge in his own cause and determine his marriage at his own will and pleasure.[18]

Although sometimes followed,[19] the *Hammersmith Registrar* case was more often ignored. A large number of first instance decisions, including one decided before the *Hammersmith Registrar* case and not cited in it,[20] recognised extra-judicial divorces granted in the common domicile of the parties (a fact which did of course distinguish the facts from those in the *Hammersmith* case itself) as validly dissolving English marriages.[21] Eventually a case of this type was taken to the Court of Appeal in *Russ v Russ*.[22] The Court of Appeal, taking a number of points of difference on the facts, distinguished—effectively, refused to follow—the *Hammersmith* case. The ratio of *Russ v Russ* appears to be that attributed to it in the later Scottish case of *Makouipour v Makouipour*,[23] that an extra-judicial divorce, at least if judicially recognised and registered in the books of the courts of the domicile, will be recognised as dissolving any marriage; but even the emphasis on proceedings involving court registration was soon to disappear.

It had already been established that a *foreign* marriage could be dissolved by an extra-judicial divorce, even one pronounced in England, if the divorce was recognised by the law of the domicile of the parties; this represented a logical application of *Armitage v A-G*. It was established in England in *Har-Shefi v Har-Shefi (No 2)*,[24] which was followed in Victoria[25] and New Zealand.[26]

A final and possibly most difficult set of cases reflects the *Hammersmith* facts in that both marriage and extra-judicial divorce are in the state in which recognition is sought, but the divorce is valid by the law of the foreign domicile of the parties. *Mahbub v Mahbub*[27] is an interesting example, in that the talak involved was posted in Pakistan but was effective where it was received, in England. A second case, also unreported in official series, is *Varanand v Varanand*[28] where a marriage in England, involving a Thai prince, was dissolved by consent in London. The divorce was valid in Thai law; it took place in the Thai Embassy in London, but nothing can turn on that point.[29] Finally in an elaborately argued judgment, Sir Jocelyn Simon P in *Qureshi v Qureshi*[30] recognised a talak, delivered in London where the reconciliation procedures prescribed by Pakistan law were also arranged so that the law of the Pakistan domicile of the parties was fully complied with, as effective to dissolve a marriage celebrated in an English registry office. The *Hammersmith Registrar* case was declared inconsistent with later Court of Appeal authority[31] and was effectively buried.

There would seem now to be no reason for treating extra-judicial divorces as a distinct class. Negatively, that implies that the nature of the proceedings, even if a unilateral talak is involved, will not be a reason for withholding recognition. Positively, it suggests that all the bases for recognition, including *Indyka v Indyka*, might be available in appropriate circumstances. This has not been explored judicially, although in *Hassan v Hassan*[32] Somers J of the Supreme Court of New Zealand, recognising a talak pronounced in New Zealand, noted that only the husband was domiciled in Egypt, the wife (so far as she was capable of having an independent domicile) being domiciled in New Zealand.

1   For detailed survey, see P. M. North *The Private International Law of Matrimonial Causes in the British Isles and the Republic of Ireland* pp 218–222.
2   Ordinance VIII of 1961.
3   [1924] AC 1007, PC (Jewish divorce in Egypt). See also *Sarabai v Rabiabai* (1905) ILR 30 Bom 577 (talak in India) cited by the Board in *Sasson v Sasson* but again not involving a *foreign* divorce in the strict sense.
4   [1967] P 14, [1964] 2 All ER 248.
5   (1959) 21 DLR (2d) 171 (B Col).
6   *Radwan v Radwan* [1973] Fam 24, [1972] 3 All ER 967.
7   See, eg, *Preger v Preger* (1926) 42 TLR 281; *Spivack v Spivack* (1930) 46 TLR 243, DC; *Joseph v Joseph* [1953] 2 All ER 710, [1953] 1 WLR 1182; *Corbett v Corbett* [1957] 1 All ER 621, [1957] 1 WLR 486.
8   [1972] Fam 173.
9   *Russ v Russ* [1964] P 315, [1962] 3 All ER 193, CA; *Qureshi v Qureshi* [1972] Fam 173, [1971] 1 All ER 325.
10 *Ives v Ives* [1967] HKLR 423 (FC).
11 *Hassan v Hassan* [1978] 1 NZLR 385.
12 *Makouipour v Makouipour* 1967 SC 116.
13 [1917] 1 KB 634, CA.
14 Cf the analysis essayed by Donovan LJ in *Russ v Russ* [1964] P 315 at 330–331, CA.
15 [1906] P 135; see para 2.05 above.
16 [1917] 1 KB 634 at 643, 652–3.
17 Ibid, per Swinfen Eady LJ at 659; cf Bankes LJ at 661.
18 Ibid, at 662.
19 *Maher v Maher* [1951] P 342, [1951] 2 All ER 37 (English marriage, Muslim divorce in Cairo not recognised; a 'Christian marriage, which cannot be dissolved by a method of divorce appropriate to a polygamous union').
20 *Seni-Bhidak v Seni-Bhidak* (1912) Times, 3 December (divorce in Thailand).
21 *Yousef v Yousef* (1957) Times, 1 August (talak in Zanzibar); *El-Riyami v El-Riyami* (1958) Times, 1 April (same facts); *Ratanachai v Ratanachai* (1960) Times, 4 June (divorce by agreement in Thailand); *Gillon v Gillon* (1961) Times, 4 July (gett in Israel).
22 [1964] P 315, [1962] 3 All ER 193, CA.
23 1967 SC 116 (Scottish marriage dissolved by consent decree filed in Iranian registry).
24 [1953] P 220, [1953] 2 All ER 373 (Jewish divorce in Beth Din, London).
25 *Mandel v Mandel* [1955] VLR 51 (Jewish divorce in Beth Din, Melbourne).
26 *Hassan v Hassan* [1978] 1 NZLR 385 (talak in New Zealand dissolving marriage celebrated in Egyptian consulate in Athens).
27 (1964) 108 Sol Jo 337.
28 (1964) 108 Sol Jo 693.
29 See the report in (1964) Times, 25 July, commented upon in *Qureshi v Qureshi* [1972] Fam 173 at 199–200.
30 [1972] Fam 173.
31 Ie, *Russ v Russ* [1964] P 315, [1962] 3 All ER 193, CA.
32 [1978] 1 NZLR 385.

Remarriage

2.15 It should be borne in mind that the recognition of a foreign divorce does not necessarily mean that the parties are free to remarry. There may be obstacles by reference either to the law of the country granting the divorce or to the law of the domicile of the party wishing to remarry.

The former case arises where a decree of divorce, though a decree absolute, does not immediately permit the parties to remarry. There may be a delay, designed either to ensure that no remarriage takes place before any time for appealing against the decree has expired or to minimise the possibility of disputes as to the paternity or legitimacy of children conceived close to the relevant time.[1] Certainly where both parties are subjected to a restraint on immediate remarriage, the restraint will be recognised. 'As the foreign law effecting the dissolution which alone sets the party free to remarry treats the dissolution as incomplete and not yet productive of that consequence, the law by which the validity of the subsequent marriage is determined cannot disregard it.'[2] Accordingly, a remarriage within the prescribed period will be void. There are a large number of decisions to this effect, in England,[3] Australia[4] and Canada.[5]

On the other hand, to quote again from the High Court of Australia's decision in *Miller v Teale*,[6] 'Once the status of the marriage is completely destroyed as by a final decree absolute any attempt by the law under which the decree of dissolution is granted to impose upon a party to the marriage a prohibition on remarriage is treated as territorial only if it is by way of punishment, discipline or example.' So a prohibition on remarriage by the spouse found guilty of adultery will not be recognised,[7] nor will any other discriminatory restraint applying only to one party.[8]

The second case arises because of the choice of law rule that capacity to marry is a matter for the law of the domicile of each party to the marriage. If a divorce is not recognised by the domiciliary law, or is not effective under that law to free the parties to remarry,[9] its recognition in other jurisdictions will not avail the parties on this particular point in the absence of a special statutory provision.[10]

1   For an example of the latter see the Belgian ten-month delay considered in *Lundgren v O'Brien* (*No 2*) [1921] VLR 361. African customary laws commonly have similar delays for the same reason.
2   *Miller v Teale* (1954) 92 CLR 406 at 415 (H Ct of Australia).
3   *Warter v Warter* (1890) 15 PD 152 (remarriage in England after Indian divorce); *Le Mesurier v Le Mesurier* (1930) 46 TLR 203 (remarriage in Sri Lanka after Indian divorce; parties semble domiciled in England); *Boettcher v Boettcher* [1949] WN 83 (remarriage in England after divorce in State of Indiana).
4   *Miller v Teale* (1954) 92 CLR 406 (H Ct of Australia) (remarriage in NSW by wife domiciled there after divorce in South Australia).
5   *Gill v Gill* [1947] 2 WWR 761 (BC) (remarriage in Washington after BC divorce); *Dahl v Dahl* [1951] 2 WWR 392 (BC) (same facts); *Turner v Turner* (1953) 9 WWR (NS) 684 (Alta) (remarriage in Idaho after BC divorce); *Bevand v Bevand* [1955] 1 DLR 854 (NS) (remarriage in NS after BC divorce); *Hellens v Densmore* (1957) 10 DLR (2d) 561 (Sup Ct Can) (remarriage in Alberta after BC divorce); *Sakellaropoulo v Davis* (1960) 24 DLR (2d) 524 (Ont) (remarriage in Ontario after BC divorce).
6   (1954) 92 CLR 406 at 415.
7   *Scott v A-G* (1886) 11 PD 128.
8   *Lundgren v O'Brien* (*No 2*) [1921] VLR 361.
9   *R v Brentwood Superintendent Registrar of Marriages, ex p Arias* [1968] 2 QB 956, [1968] 3 All ER 279 (where the decree was actually granted in the country of the domicile, but by the conflict of laws rules of that country capacity to remarry was referred to the law of the nationality which did not recognise the decree).
10 Cf *Schwebel v Ungar* (1964) 48 DLR (2d) 644 (Sup Ct Canada) (a converse situation).

Costs and damages

2.16   Recognition of a foreign divorce does not entail enforcement of any order for costs or damages made in the divorce proceedings.

So in *Redhead v Redhead*,[1] costs had been awarded in an English divorce case against a co-respondent resident in New Zealand. The New Zealand court held that in the circumstances (of an appearance having been entered on the co-respondent's behalf without his having given any instructions to that effect) the 'judgment' could not be registered for enforcement as a money-judgment under the Administration of Justice Act 1922 of New Zealand. Explaining dicta in *Rayment v Rayment*,[2] MacGregor J held that the mere fact that the English Divorce Court had jurisdiction (the parties to the marriage being domiciled in England) did not mean that orders against co-respondents could be enforced elsewhere.

To the same effect is an Ontario case, *Patterson v D'Agostino*.[3] Damages and costs were awarded in divorce proceedings in Wales on the basis of adultery. The co-respondent was not domiciled or resident in Wales and did not appear in the Welsh proceedings. After examining the law of Ontario as to the enforcement of money-judgments, the judge refused to allow the order as to costs and damages to be enforced in that province.

In England, the position at common law remains unclear. In *Phillips v Batho*,[4] Scrutton J enforced an award of damages, against a co-respondent resident in England, made in divorce proceedings in British India. He recognised that none of the usual rules as to jurisdiction in personam[5] were applicable, but nonetheless applied a special rule in the instant case relying upon the fact that both the English court and the court of origin were 'Courts of the same Sovereign' and upon the judgment being ancillary to a judgment in rem. Neither argument is persuasive; the former being plainly inappropriate in modern Commonwealth law and the latter inconsistent with later authority.[6]

1   [1926] NZLR 131.
2   [1910] P 271.
3   (1975) 58 DLR (3d) 63.
4   [1913] 3 KB 25.
5   As set out in *Emanuel v Symon* [1908] 1 KB 302.
6   See *Jacobs v Jacobs* [1950] P 146, [1950] 1 All ER 96 and Dicey and Morris *The Conflict of Laws* (10th edn, 1980) p 356. See further para 4.10 below.

Unrecognised foreign divorces: estoppel or preclusion

2.17   If a divorce obtained abroad cannot be recognised, the marital status of the parties must be regarded as unchanged. It has, however, been argued in a number of Commonwealth jurisdictions that the divorce, or the act of the petitioner in seeking it, may give rise to an estoppel, or may preclude him from relying upon his married status in order to claim some financial or property advantage. In England and Australia there are dicta hostile to any such argument,[1] but in Canada, partly as a result of the influence of United States' principles, the 'preclusion' doctrine is well developed and was approved in the Supreme Court of Canada in *Downton v Royal Trust Co*.[2]

In that case Laskin J, reviewing earlier authorities, upheld the applicability of the doctrine against a spouse who, having obtained a decree from a foreign court incompetent to give it, seeks thereafter to assert that incompetence in order to gain a pecuniary advantage against his or her spouse or the estate of the spouse. The doctrine can be applied, for example, to applications for provision out of a deceased's estate,[3] to claims to take on intestacy[4] or to fall within a class of beneficiaries under a will[5] or an insurance policy,[6] but its precise limits are still unclear. This lack of clarity is most acute where the spouse who was respondent in the foreign proceedings submitted to the jurisdiction, or where third parties are concerned. Laskin J, having spoken of the ethical basis of the doctrine, continued:

'The ethical basis is lost, however, where there has been both invocation and submission to the foreign jurisdiction by the respective spouses; and if there is to be a modification or rejection of the preclusion doctrine in respect of one or both of the spouses, other considerations may be brought into account; there may, for example, be an alleviating explanation for the submission to the jurisdiction of an incompetent foreign court. So too, where third parties are involved in a case where a spouse who has obtained an invalid foreign divorce or decree of nullity seeks to rely on its invalidity.'[7]

In *Downton v Royal Trust Co* the wife respondent had submitted to the foreign jurisdiction, apparently to protect her financial interests, and the Supreme Court found this an 'alleviating explanation' so that the doctrine was not applied so as to bar her application for provision out of her deceased husband's estate under the Newfoundland Family Relief Act 1962. The range of possible such explanations remains obscure.

It is however clear, and was reasserted in *Downton v Royal Trust Co*, that the preclusion doctrine cannot be relied upon in 'a strictly matrimonial cause in which divorce or nullity is sought'.[8] It is only pecuniary advantage which may be denied. Even in that limited area, it is far from clear that the doctrine is soundly based despite the asserted ethical foundation, and there is certainly no sign of its adoption in Commonwealth jurisdictions outside Canada.

1   *Bonaparte v Bonaparte* [1892] P 402 (subsequent nullity petition); *Travers v Holley* [1953] P 246 at 254, CA (subsequent divorce proceedings); *Hornett v Hornett* [1971] P 255 at 261 (resumed cohabitation no bar to reliance on divorce); *Alexsandrov v Alexsandrov* (1967) 12 FLR 360 at 363 (S Australia) (subsequent divorce proceedings). See also *Gaffney v Gaffney* [1975] IR 133 (Sup Ct of Ireland).
2   (1972) 34 DLR (3d) 403. See G. Battersby 'The Doctrine of Preclusion in Canada' (1977) 16 Uni W Ont LR 163.
3   As in *Downton v Royal Trust Co*, though the doctrine was excluded on the facts.
4   Eg *Re Capon* (1965) 49 DLR (2d) 675 (Ont), approved in *Downton*.
5   *Re Jones* (1960) 25 DLR (2d) 595 (BC).
6   *Re Williams and Ancient Order of United Workmen* (1907) 14 OLR 482; *Re Banks* (1918) 42 OLR 64.
7   (1972) 34 DLR (3d) 403 at 412–413.
8   *Stephens v Falchi* [1938] 3 DLR 590 (Sup Ct Can) (relied on in the Australian case of *Alexsandrov v Alexsandrov* (1967) 12 FLR 360); *Foggo v Foggo* (1952) 5 WWR (NS) 40 (BC CA); *Fife v Fife* (1964) 49 DLR (2d) 648 (Sask); *Schwebel v Schwebel* (1970) 10 DLR (3d) 742 (Ont); *Seagull v Seagull* (1974) 53 DLR (3d) 230 (Ont CA); *Holub v Holub* [1976] 3 WWR 437 (Man) (revsd on other grounds [1976] 5 WWR 527 (Man CA)); *Fromovitz v Fromovitz* (1977) 79 DLR (3d) 148 (Ont).

CHAPTER 3

Divorce: Statutory Bases

Introduction

3.01 The common law rules as to the recognition of foreign divorces examined in the last chapter remain in force in many Commonwealth jurisdictions, but there are some two dozen jurisdictions which have enacted statutory provisions supplementing or replacing the common law rules. Those provisions are examined in this chapter.

The arrangement of this chapter hinges upon important events in the late 1960s. The common law rules reached their point of furthest development with the leading decision of the House of Lords in *Indyka v Indyka*[1] decided in 1967. That decision opened up so many possibilities that a systematic review of the principles of recognition was clearly indicated. This coincided with work being done at The Hague Conference on Private International Law towards a convention on the subject, eventually opened for signature in 1970. It was to prove very influential within the Commonwealth, and its provisions are examined in some detail below.[2] The United Kingdom ratified the Convention, but the legislation passed in the United Kingdom, while satisfying the Convention's requirements, adopted significantly wider recognition rules, based upon but more generous than those acceptable to the authors of the Convention. This Act, the Recognition of Divorces and Legal Separations Act 1971 (UK), is also examined in some detail below.[3]

The Convention and the United Kingdom legislation inspired by it form the central part of this chapter. Before they are examined, an account is given of various pieces of legislation, of earlier origin, modifying the common law rules and still in force in some 11 jurisdictions. In the last part of the chapter, an account is given of legislation derived from either The Hague Convention or from the United Kingdom Act. This latter section seems to indicate the general direction of Commonwealth legal development in this area; Australia and Trinidad and Tobago each had pre-1970 legislative provisions but have decided to replace them by fresh legislation on The Hague or Hague/UK model.

To assist the reader, the following Table lists the jurisdictions whose legislation is referred to in this chapter with an indication of the paragraph(s) in which some account of the relevant provisions may be found.

Jurisdiction	*Paragraph(s)*
Ascension	3.41
Australia[4]	3.42
Barbados	3.42
Bermuda	3.43
British Antarctic Territory	3.41
Canada	3.03
Cayman Islands	3.44
Falkland Islands	3.41

Falkland Islands' Dependencies	3.41
Fiji	3.04–3.06
Ghana	3.07
Gibraltar	3.41
Guernsey	3.41
Hong Kong	3.41
Jersey	3.41
Isle of Man	3.41
Nauru	3.45
New Zealand	3.08–3.12
Nigeria	3.04–3.06
Papua New Guinea	3.04–3.06
Saint Helena	3.41
Saint Lucia	3.08–3.12
Tanzania	3.13
Trinidad and Tobago	3.41
Tristan da Cunha	3.41
United Kingdom	3.29–3.40
Western Samoa	3.08–3.12
Zimbabwe	3.14

1   [1969] 1 AC 33, [1967] 2 All ER 689, HL.
2   Paras 3.15–3.28. The text of the Convention is printed in Appendix B.
3   Paras 3.29–3.40. The text of the Act is printed in Appendix B.
4   The text of the relevant Australian provisions is printed in Appendix B.

A. COMMONWEALTH LEGISLATION OF PRE-1970 ORIGIN

The Indian and Colonial Divorce Jurisdiction Act 1926 (UK)

3.02   Although now of very limited effect, this Act is of very considerable historical interest.

As is well known, a large British community was to be found in India during the century prior to independence. Many members of this community were intent on an eventual return to Britain, even though most of their lives may have been spent in India. It followed that they never acquired a domicile in India (and, indeed, the courts flirted with the idea of an 'Anglo-Indian domicile' in an attempt to overcome some of the difficulties which resulted[1]).

So far as divorce jurisdiction was concerned, it was for many years assumed that the Indian Divorce Act 1869[2] conferred jurisdiction over persons resident, though not domiciled, in India. This view seemed to derive from the emphasis on residence in *Niboyet v Niboyet*[3] and survived the virtual repudiation of that case in *Le Mesurier v Le Mesurier*.[4] It was emphatically rejected in *Keyes v Keyes and Gray*[5] in 1921 by Sir Henry Duke P. He refused to recognise a divorce granted in India, purporting to dissolve a marriage itself celebrated in India; the parties were resident in India, though not domiciled there, and the adultery relied upon by the husband took place in India.

The result of *Keyes v Keyes and Gray* was that the recognition in England of a large number of divorces granted in India and in various colonial territories was placed in doubt. The Indian and Colonial Divorce Jurisdiction Act 1926[6] was passed to remedy the problem.

As its name suggests the primary purpose of the Act was to confer jurisdiction upon the courts to which it applied. The jurisdiction only existed when the parties were British subjects domiciled in England or in Scotland (and so not in Northern Ireland),[7] where the petitioner was resident in the country taking jurisdiction and the parties last resided together there;[8] the court was to apply the English grounds for divorce;[9] and 'act and give relief on principles and rules as nearly as may be conformable' to those applying in England.[10] No decree on the ground of adultery, cruelty or any crime could be granted except where either the marriage was celebrated in the country concerned or the adultery, cruelty or crime was committed there.[11] By the Indian and Colonial Divorce Jurisdiction Act 1940,[12] the effect of the 1926 Act was extended to cover cases where a husband had been domiciled in England or Scotland but had changed his domicile on deserting his wife;[13] and by the Colonial and Other Territories (Divorce Jurisdiction) Act 1950[14] the earlier Acts were extended to cover persons domiciled in Northern Ireland[15] and were made capable of application to protectorates, trust territories and certain protected states.[16]

The importance of this legislation so far as recognition is concerned lies in the provision that a decree made under it was to be transmitted to the court of the domicile and was to be registered in that court on receipt.[17] This constitutes an exception to the common law recognition rules, although in fact since *Travers v Holley*[18] and *Indyka v Indyka*[19] the decrees, insofar as they operate to dissolve the marriage, would almost certainly be entitled to recognition at common law.

The legislation was applied at various times to decrees of courts in Burma, India, Jamaica, Kenya, Malawi, Malaysia, Pakistan, Singapore, Sri Lanka, Tanganyika, Uganda and Zambia, but none of the Orders in Council so extending the legislation remain in force. It now applies only in respect of Hong Kong, by virtue of the Hong Kong Divorce Jurisdiction Order in Council 1935.[20] Its effect therefore is merely that certain divorces granted in Hong Kong which might possibly be denied recognition at common law will be recognised on registration in any part of the United Kingdom.

---

1   See *Re Mitchell, ex p Cunningham* (1884) 13 QBD 418 at 425, CA.
2   Act 4 of 1869.
3   (1878) 4 PD 1, CA.
4   [1895] AC 517, PC. See *Re Norton's Settlement, Norton v Norton* [1908] 1 Ch 471 and for pre-1895 cases, *Warter v Warter* (1890) 15 PD 152 at 154.
5   [1921] P 204.
6   16 and 17 Geo 5, c 40.
7   Indian and Colonial Divorce Jurisdiction Act 1926, s 1(1).
8   Ibid s 1(1)(c) as substituted by Indian and Colonial Divorce Jurisdiction Act 1940, s 2(1).
9   Indian and Colonial Divorce Jurisdiction Act 1926, s 1(1)(a).
10   Ibid, s 1(1)(b). See *Buckle v Buckle* [1956] P 181 for the effect of those words in enabling parties to an Indian divorce to remarry immediately.
11   Indian and Colonial Divorce Jurisdiction Act 1926, s 1(1)(c) as substituted by the Act of 1940, s 2(1).
12   3 & 4 Geo 6, c 35.
13   S 3.
14   14 Geo 6, c 35.
15   S 1.
16   Ss 2, 3.
17   1926 Act, s 1(2); 1940 Act, s 4(1); 1950 Act, s 1(c).
18   [1953] P 246, [1953] 2 All ER 794.
19   [1969] 1 AC 33, [1967] 2 All ER 689, HL.
20   SR & O 1935/836, as amended by SI 1969/1060.

Canada

3.03 The recognition of foreign divorces in Canada remains a matter for the common law rules, subject only to s 6(2) of the Divorce Act[1] originally enacted in 1968.[2] This provides as follows:

'For all purposes of determining the marital status in Canada of any person and without limiting or restricting any existing rule of law applicable to the recognition of decrees of divorce granted otherwise than under this Act, recognition shall be given to a decree of divorce, granted after the 1st day of July 1968, under a law of a country or subdivision of a country other than Canada by a tribunal or other competent authority that had jurisdiction under that law to grant the decree, on the basis of the domicile of the wife in that country or subdivision determined as if she were unmarried and, if she was a minor, as if she had attained her majority.'

The effect is that a decree pronounced in a country in which the wife alone is, by virtue of s 6(2), deemed to be domiciled will be recognised in Canada. If the husband is domiciled where a decree is granted, s 6(2) does not prevent the recognition of the divorce; it does not abrogate the rule that a married woman takes the domicile of her husband for many purposes,[3] but rather enables her also to rely on a separate domicile if she asserts it for the purpose of obtaining the recognition of a divorce.

In *Bevington v Hewitson*[4] (where the foreign divorce was in fact granted before 1968 so that s 6(2) was inapplicable) Lacourciere J expressed the opinion that, in relation to divorces granted to a wife after 1 July 1968 resort should first be had to this provision.[5] However, the existing rules of law saved by s 6(2) included the recently developed rule in *Indyka v Indyka*.[6]

1 Chap D-8, RSC.
2 Divorce Act 1967–68, c 24, s 6(2).
3 But not for the purposes of the Canadian courts' divorce jurisdiction: Divorce Act, cap D-8, s 6(1).
4 (1974) 47 DLR (3d) 510 (Ont HC).
5 At 517.
6 [1969] 1 AC 33, [1967] 2 All ER 689, HL.

Fiji, Nigeria and Papua New Guinea

3.04 The Commonwealth of Australia legislated for the recognition of foreign divorces in s 95 of the Matrimonial Causes Act 1959. That Act was repealed in 1975 and different provisions now apply in Australia.[1] It was, however, used as a model by draftsmen in other jurisdictions, and legislation on that model remains in force in Fiji,[2] Nigeria[3] and Papua New Guinea.[4] The text as currently in force in Fiji is reproduced here; there are insignificant differences of drafting in the other countries' legislation and one difference of substance: in Nigeria the equivalent of Fiji's s 92(6) continues 'or that the dissolution or annulment had been obtained by fraud'.[5] Commentary on the provisions is to be found in the following paragraphs.

'92.—(1) A dissolution or annulment of a marriage effected in accordance with the law of a foreign country shall be recognised as valid in Fiji where, at the date of the institution of the proceedings that resulted in the dissolution or annulment, the party at whose instance the dissolution or annulment was effected (or if it was effected at the instance of both parties, either of those parties) was—

(a) in the case of the dissolution of a marriage or the annulment of a voidable marriage, domiciled in that foreign country; or

(b)   in the case of the annulment of a void marriage, domiciled or resident in that foreign country.

(2)   For the purposes of subsection (1) —

(a)   where a dissolution of a marriage was effected in accordance with the law of a foreign country at the instance of a deserted wife who was domiciled in that foreign country either immediately before her marriage or immediately before the desertion, she shall be deemed to have been domiciled in that foreign country at the date of the institution of the proceedings that resulted in the dissolution; and

(b)   a wife who, at the date of the institution of the proceedings that resulted in a dissolution or annulment of her marriage in accordance with the law of a foreign country, was resident in that foreign country, and had been so resident for a period of three years immediately preceding that date shall be deemed to have been domiciled in that foreign country at that date.

(3)   A dissolution or annulment of a marriage effected in accordance with the law of a foreign country, not being a dissolution or annulment to which subsection (2)[6] applies, shall be recognised as valid in Fiji if its validity would have been recognised under the law of the foreign country in which, in the case of a dissolution, the parties were domiciled at the date of the dissolution or in which, in the case of an annulment, either party was domiciled at the date of annulment.

(4)   Any dissolution or annulment of a marriage that would be recognised as valid under the common law rules of private international law but to which none of the preceding provisions of this section applies shall be recognised as valid in Fiji and the operation of this subsection shall not be limited by any implication from those provisions.

(5)   For the purposes of this section, the Court, in considering the validity of a dissolution or annulment effected under the law of a foreign country, may treat as proved any facts found by a court of the foreign country or otherwise established for the purposes of the law of the foreign country.

(6)   A dissolution or annulment of a marriage shall not be recognised as valid by virtue of subsection (1) or (3) where, under the common law rules of private international law, recognition of its validity would be refused on the ground that a party to the marriage had been denied natural justice.

(7)   Subsections (1) to (6) apply in relation to dissolution and annulment effected, whether by decree, legislation or otherwise, before or after the commencement of this Act.

(8)   In this section "foreign country" means a country, or part of a country, outside Fiji.'

1   See Family Law Act 1975 (Cmwth of Australia), ss 3(1) (repeals) and 104 (new provisions as to the recognition of foreign divorces).
2   Matrimonial Causes Act, cap 51, RL 1978 (Fiji), s 92.
3   Matrimonial Causes Decree 1970, No 18 (Nigeria), s 81.
4   Matrimonial Causes Act 1963, No 18 of 1964 (sic).
5   Matrimonial Causes Decree 1970 (Nigeria), s 81(7). The subsection numbers are different in Nigeria as s 81(1) contains provisions as to the recognition of decrees made in one region of Nigeria in the other parts of the federation.
6   This must be an error; the reference must be to subsection (1). The error is not reproduced in Nigeria or Papua New Guinea.

A codification of common law principles

3.05   The general purpose of this legislative model has been described as 'to facilitate recognition and to clarify and in some respects widen common law principles of recognition, while preserving those principles'.[1] The model is very largely a codification of the common law principles as they were understood in England before *Indyka v Indyka*.[2]

So s 92(1) (using the Fijian numbering) restates the domicile basis.[3] It uses, as do subsections (2) and (3), the phrase 'effected in accordance with the law of a foreign country'. This has been interpreted as requiring that the foreign court should have competence to pronounce divorces under the law of the system of which it was a part, or that (in the case of extra-judicial divorces) the divorce should be regarded as valid by that law.[4]

Section 92(2) states the effect in the context of the Act as a whole of the Rule in *Travers v Holley*,[5] mirroring the jurisdictional rules set out elsewhere in the Act. It has been observed that the provision 'still clings desperately to domicile'[6] because it uses the device of deeming the wife to be domiciled in a country, rather than providing for new bases of recognition in favour of wives who had been deserted or who had a three-year residence qualification. The relevant date, in both limbs of subsection (2) is that of the institution of proceedings.

Section 92(3) codifies the rule in *Armitage v A-G*[7] as to decrees recognised in the country in which both parties were domiciled at the date of the decree.

Section 92(4) expressly saves any common law recognition rules not reflected in the preceding provisions. After a good deal of hesitation,[8] it is now clear that this enables courts to apply the principles in *Indyka v Indyka*,[9] for the reference to the 'common law rules of private international law' is to 'those rules, modified and developed from time to time, as they exist when a relevant matter arises for consideration';[10] the common law is not 'frozen' at the date of enactment of the legislation.

It is clear from s 92(7) that the provisions apply to legislative and other extra-judicial divorces.[11] The effect is to go some way beyond the current development of common law principles. For example, a gett entered into at the wish of both parties in a country in which the wife alone had been resident for three years would appear to be entitled to recognition under s 92(1)(a) and (2)(b), regardless of the domicile (in the common law sense) of the parties; though the parties to that divorce might still lack capacity to remarry.

Section 92(8) defines foreign country as meaning a country or part of a country. This simplicity conceals some uncertainties. If a wife had been resident in a foreign country with a federal system, such as Canada, can she rely on s 92(2)(b) and the interpretation in s 92(8) to secure the recognition of a divorce from any Canadian province or territory whether or not she had resided for three years in that particular jurisdiction? At common law the decree would not be recognised under *Travers v Holley*[12] principles without such a specific link, and arguably s 92 will be interpreted to keep the provisions as far as possible in line with the common law, but a more radical interpretation seems also to be possible.

So far as grounds for the refusal of recognition are concerned, s 92(6) expressly incorporates the common law principles so far as they are based on a denial of natural justice.[13] It is not clear whether this operates to exclude any ground existing at common law. Fox J of the Australian Capital Territory Supreme Court observed in *Norman v Norman* (*No 3*) that fraud was not mentioned. He continued:

'It would be odd if fraud were not a ground because most divorces given recognition by [the legislative provision] would now be given recognition at common law. Perhaps the answer lies in giving a specially wide meaning to the phrase "denial of natural justice" ... Another, and independent ground, for non-recognition at common law is that the decree offends against our concepts of substantial justice ... This ground could perhaps be encompassed by [in Fijian numbering, section 92(6)] more readily.'[14]

In Nigeria, some of this uncertainty is removed by the addition to the equivalent of s 92(6) of an express reference to fraud.[15]

The legislation applies retrospectively, that is to divorces obtained before as well as after the date of enactment.[16] It has been judicially recognised that this can create extremely difficult situations, where parties may have arranged their affairs on assumptions as to the validity of a divorce which though correct at the time are falsified by the Act; the example was given in *Alexsandrov v Alexsandrov*[17] of a party entering upon a marriage believing that his prior marriage was void because the other party to that marriage was not validly divorced from her earlier marriage. There seem no discretionary powers enabling such hardship to be alleviated.

1   *Norman v Norman (No 3)* (1969) 16 FLR 231 (ACT) at 233 per Fox J.
2   [1969] 1 AC 33, [1967] 2 All ER 689, HL. See *Nicholson v Nicholson* (1971) 17 FLR 47 at 57 (NSW) per Selby J.
3   See *Norman v Norman (No 2)* (1968) 12 FLR 39 at 44 (ACT) emphasising that the concept of domicile used is, of course, the common law concept.
4   *Norman v Norman (No 3)* (1969) 16 FLR 231 at 232-233, (ACT).
5   [1953] P 246, [1953] 2 All ER 794. Its adoption in the original Australian legislation was the more striking because of the refusal two years earlier of the Supreme Court of Victoria to follow *Travers v Holley: Fenton v Fenton* [1957] VR 17 (FC).
6   Per Selby J in *Nicholson v Nicholson* (1971) 17 FLR 47 at 56 (NSW).
7   [1906] P 135. See *Bishop v Bishop* (1970) 18 FLR 35 (NSW).
8   See especially *Alexsandrov v Alexsandrov* (1967) 12 FLR 360 (S Australia).
9   [1969] 1 AC 33, [1967] 2 All ER 689, HL.
10 *Nicholson v Nicholson* (1971) 17 FLR 47 at 59 (NSW) per Selby J.
11 *Brown v Brown* (1962) 4 FLR 94 at 99 (NSW); *Norman v Norman (No 3)* (1969) 16 FLR 231 at 233 (ACT).
12 [1953] P 246, [1953] 2 All ER 794.
13 See *Brown v Brown* (1962) 4 FLR 94 at 98 (NSW); *Terrell v Terrell* (1970) 16 FLR 323 at 326-327 (Vic).
14 (1969) 16 FLR 231 at 245-246.
15 Matrimonial Causes Decree 1970 (Nigeria), s 81(7).
16 S 92(7) in the Fijian numbering. Cf Lucke and Kelly, 'Recognition of Foreign Divorces: the Time Factor' (1968) 3 Adelaide LR 179.
17 (1967) 12 FLR 360 at 367 (S Australia).

Proof of facts

3.06   Section 92(5) contains a novel provision. A court considering 'the validity' of a divorce 'may treat as proved' any facts found by a court of the foreign country or otherwise established for the purposes of the law of the foreign country. This provision has received a good deal of judicial attention.

'Validity', it has been held, does not refer to validity in accordance with the municipal law of the foreign country, but to validity for the purposes of the recognising jurisdiction.[1] In other words the provision applies whenever a recognition issue is being determined.

The 'facts' referred to 'are, or include' facts relevant to jurisdiction in the international sense, such as domicile, and residence for the three-year period.[2] It may be that the facts are expressly found by the foreign court, but such a finding may be inferred from the actions of that court (for example, because it could only have exercised jurisdiction had it taken a certain view of the facts).[3]

However, 92(5) is merely permissive. The court invited to recognise a divorce *may* rely on the finding of facts in the foreign court but is not obliged to do so;[4] where the foreign proceedings were undefended and the facts strongly disputed in the recognising court 'the only satisfactory course' was for that court to examine for itself the relevant jurisdictional facts.[5] Accordingly, the effect of the subsection may in practice turn out to be very limited.

1   *Norman v Norman (No 3)* (1969) 16 FLR 231 at 233 (ACT).
2   *Norman v Norman (No 2)* (1968) 12 FLR 39 at 45 (ACT).

3 See *Norman v Norman (No 3)* (1969) 16 FLR 231 at 233-4 (ACT).
4 *Norman v Norman (No 2)* (1968) 12 FLR 39 (ACT); *Suko v Suko* [1971] VR 28; *Terrell v Terrell* (1970) 16 FLR 323 at 327 (Vic).
5 *Norman v Norman (No 3)* (1969) 16 FLR 231 at 234 (ACT).

Ghana

3.07 The Matrimonial Causes Act 1971 of Ghana[1] provides as follows:

'The court shall recognize as valid a decree of divorce, nullity, or presumption of death and dissolution of marriage, obtained by judicial process or otherwise, which is not contrary to natural justice, and which—
(a) has been granted by any tribunal which had[2] a significant and substantial connection with the parties to the marriage; or
(b) is in accordance with the law in the place where both parties to the marriage were ordinarily resident at the time of the action dissolving or annulling the marriage.'

This provision gives rise to a number of difficulties of interpretation.

It is not clear from the Act whether s 36 is intended to be exhaustive or to provide additional bases for the recognition in Ghana of foreign divorces. In other words, it is not clear whether common law recognition rules survive; they are not expressly saved. The point arises most acutely in connection with the Rule in *Armitage v A-G*[3] as to divorces recognised in the common domicile of the parties, and in connection with extra-judicial divorces similarly recognised. Section 36(b) refers to the common ordinary residence of the parties which need not coincide with the common domicile.

Most decrees which could be recognised at common law will be capable of recognition by virtue of s 36(a) which is clearly related to the 'real and substantial connection' test of *Indyka v Indyka*. As the common law doctrine has developed, however, it has become clear that it is sufficient if either party has the appropriate connection with the country in which the decree was granted; but s 36(a) speaks of a connection with the parties, in the plural. This appears to exclude cases in which one party has a close connection with the relevant country, including citizenship and virtually life-long residence, if the other party has no link except the marriage itself. It might however be argued that, given the existence of the marriage in the time prior to its dissolution, the connection of one party with a particular country must be effective to link both parties.

A divorce which does not qualify under s 36(a), either because of the lack of any significant and substantial connection or because it was extra-judicial (and so not granted 'by any tribunal'), may qualify under s 36(b). The drafting of the latter provision is most unhappy, in particular the use of the phrase 'in accordance with the law in the place ...'. The reader familiar with the common law principles expects to find 'recognised under the law in the place ...' but this language is not used. The statutory text suggests that the grounds relied upon when the divorce was obtained (eg adultery) must be found in the law of the country of ordinary residence; or perhaps that the choice-of-law rule relied upon is not at variance with the conflict of laws rules in that country; but it is unlikely that either was intended. There are similar difficulties in the case of extra-judicial divorces. If a talak is pronounced in, say, Kuwait, the parties being ordinarily resident in Pakistan, must it be shown that the reconciliation procedures prescribed in the law of Pakistan had been complied with (regardless of the parties' domicile or nationality)? It is greatly to be hoped that the section will be interpreted as requiring simply that the law of the common ordinary residence would recognise the validity of the decree.

No divorce can be recognised under s 36 if it is contrary to natural justice. This arguably excludes any divorce obtained without due notice to the respondent (except where substantial service is resorted to in good faith),[4] and must raise some difficult questions where extra-judicial divorces, involving no judicial proceedings and perhaps mere unilateral declarations (as in the case of the talak in some systems of law), are under consideration.

1   Act 367, s 37.
2   Semble, at the date of the decree.
3   [1906] P 135.
4   Cf *Macalpine v Macalpine* [1958] P 35, [1957] 2 AUER 134, and para 2.13 above.

New Zealand, St Lucia and Western Samoa

3.08   The present form of the New Zealand legislation on the recognition of foreign decrees dates from 1958 when it was introduced by s 2 of the Divorce and Matrimonial Causes Amendment Act.[1] It has since been re-enacted a number of times, and was amended on its re-enactment in 1963 in connection with decrees obtained in the courts of the domicile[2] and again in 1968 by the insertion of a reference to decrees granted by 'public authorities'.[3] The present text is s 44 of the Family Proceedings Act 1980[4] which reads as follows:

'44. *Recognition of overseas orders*—(1) The validity of a decree or order or legislative enactment for divorce or dissolution or nullity of marriage made (whether before or after the commencement of this Act) by a Court or legislature or public authority of any country outside New Zealand shall, by virtue of this section, be recognised in all the Courts of New Zealand, where—

(a)   One or both of the parties were domiciled in that country at the time of the decree, order, or enactment; or

(b)   That overseas Court or legislature or public authority has exercised jurisdiction—
(i)   In any case, on the basis of the residence of one or both of the parties to the marriage in that country, if, at the commencement of the proceedings, any such party had in fact been resident in that country for a continuous period of not less than 2 years; or
(ii)   In any case, on the basis that one or both of the parties to the marriage are nationals or citizens of that country or of any sovereign State of which that country forms part; or
(iii)   In any case, on the basis that the wife has been deserted by her husband, or the husband has been deported, and that the husband was immediately before the desertion or deportation domiciled in that country; or
(iv)   In any case, on the basis that the wife was legally separated from her husband, whether by an order of a competent Court or by agreement, and that the husband was at the date of the order or agreement domiciled in that country; or

(c)   The decree or order or enactment is recognised as valid in the Courts of a country in which at least one of the parties to the marriage is domiciled.

(2) Nothing in this section shall affect the validity of a decree or order or legislative enactment for divorce or dissolution ... or of a dissolution of marriage otherwise than by judicial process, that would be recognised in the Courts of New Zealand otherwise than by virtue of this section.'

In Western Samoa, the Divorce and Matrimonial Causes Ordinance 1961 contains provisions[5] following the 1958 New Zealand text; that is without the amendments made in New Zealand in 1963 and 1968 noted above.

In St Lucia, the Divorce Act 1973 contains provisions[6] following the 1963 text of the New Zealand legislation, that is substantially the text as reproduced above minus the references to 'public authorities' added in New Zealand in 1968.

These provisions are examined in the paragraphs which follow. Provisions corresponding to those in force in St Lucia were in force in Trinidad and Tobago prior to the Matrimonial Proceedings and Property (Amendment) Act 1982.[7]

1 No 30 of 1958, substituting a new s 12A of the Divorce and Matrimonial Causes Act 1928.
2 Matrimonial Proceedings Act 1963, No 71, s 82. See below.
3 Matrimonial Proceedings Amendment Act 1968, No 60, s 12.
4 No 94 of 1980. S 44(1)(b)(v) dealing with nullity decrees is not reproduced.
5 Divorce and Matrimonial Causes Ordinance 1961, No 20 (W Samoa), s 37.
6 Divorce Act 1973, No 2 (St Lucia), s 51.
7 Matrimonial Proceedings and Property Act, cap 45: 51, RL, s 62.

Types of divorce covered

3.09 Although it has long been clear that certain types of extra-judicial divorce were capable of recognition at common law, the New Zealand legislation is unusual in making express references to 'a decree or order or legislative enactment . . . made by a Court or legislature or public authority'.[1] The precise meaning of 'public authority' awaits judicial examination, but it seems apt to cover cases in which a marriage is dissolved by some instrument executed by the parties and lodged in a state registry. If the reference to a court is given a restricted interpretation, some ecclesiastical tribunals might be regarded as 'public authorities'. Common law rules as to the recognition of extra-judicial divorces are preserved by s 44(2).

1 Family Proceedings Act 1980 (NZ), s 44(1). The St Lucia and Western Samoan legislation does not include the reference to 'public authorities': Divorce Act 1973 (St Lucia), s 51(1); Divorce and Matrimonial Proceedings Ordinance 1961 (WS), s 37(1).

The domicile basis

3.10 In New Zealand and St Lucia, a foreign divorce will be recognised if one or both of the parties was recognised in the foreign country at the time of the divorce.[1] This departs from the common law rule in that it relates to the date of the decree, order or enactment, and not to the commencement of proceedings. Accordingly, loss of domicile after the presentation of the petition, or initiation of administrative proceedings, or introduction of a Bill in the legislature, might prove fatal to the recognition of the divorce.

The provision also departs from the common law rule in contemplating separate domiciles for the parties. In New Zealand the separate domicile for a married woman is established by the Domicile Act 1976 applicable in all contexts, not just that of matrimonial proceedings.[2]

In Western Samoa, the fact that one or both parties are domiciled in the foreign country is not in itself a sufficient basis for recognition. In addition it must be shown that the foreign court or legislature exercised jurisdiction on the basis of the domicile of one or both parties.[3] This additional requirement is of no significance in practice where *both* parties are domiciled in the foreign country, for then the decree would be entitled to recognition under the common law rules which remain in force;[4] but it is relevant where a foreign court is prepared to exercise jurisdiction on the basis of the domicile of the petitioner or respondent alone.

1   Family proceedings Act 1980 (NZ), s 44(1)(a); Divorce Act 1973 (St Lucia), s 51(1)(a).
2   See para 1.32 above.
3   Divorce and Matrimonial Causes Ordinance 1961 (WS), s 37(1)(a)(i). For the phrase 'has exercised jurisdiction' see the next para.
4   Ibid, s 37(2).

Other bases for recognition

3.11   Five other bases for recognition are established. The first corresponds closely to the rule in *Armitage v A-G*[1] as to a decree recognised in the domicile of the parties. In all three countries with this legislative model the rule is adopted and extended to cases in which one only of the parties is domiciled in a country which recognises the decree.[2] In Western Samoa it is further extended to cases in which at least one of the parties is deemed to be domiciled in the relevant country by the law of *that* country.[3] This means that, for example, a decree obtained in Nevada on the basis of six weeks' residence, and denied recognition in Quebec, where both parties were domiciled in accordance with the understanding of domicile in the law of Quebec and of Western Samoa, would be recognised as valid in Western Samoa if it was recognised by, say, the law of France in which, under French notions, the wife was still domiciled.

All the other bases depend upon the fact that the overseas court or legislature (or, in New Zealand, public authority) 'has exercised jurisdiction' on certain bases. It is not sufficient to establish that, for example, both parties had been resident in the foreign country for more than two years; it must be shown that the foreign court took jurisdiction because that test was satisfied. So, had the parties in *Godfrey v Godfrey*[4] lived in Arizona for two years, the decree would still have been denied recognition as Arizona courts are given divorce jurisdiction under the law of that state after 90 days' residence. Presumably the basis upon which the foreign court assumed jurisdiction can be established by evidence of the law of the foreign state, and need not be recited in the decree presented for recognition.

What is much more difficult is to see how the requirement as to the basis of jurisdiction could operate in relation to the Act of a foreign legislature; the Act is unlikely to recite any reason for the legislative competence of the state in question, and no other legislative provision, save possibly a constitutional one, will give any guidance. Legislative divorces are extremely rare in practice, so the problem may be merely academic; but similar difficulties might arise in New Zealand in respect of 'public authority' divorces.

The other bases for recognition are set out in the legislative text reproduced in paragraph 3.08 above, and do not call for detailed exposition. It is, however, noteworthy, that the bases set out in s 44(1)(b)(iii) and (iv) of the New Zealand Act (desertion, deportation and legal separation) depend solely on the domicile of the husband at the relevant time. The wife's connection with the foreign country, or the absence of such a connection, is for these purposes quite immaterial. It would appear that in this context, which is that of the basis upon which the foreign court assumed jurisdiction, 'domicile' must be according to the understanding of that concept in the foreign country.[5] In earlier versions of the current New Zealand legislation it was provided that for the purposes of the legislation, 'the domicile of any person shall be determined in accordance with the law of New Zealand',[6] but this general provision would not necessarily prevail over the specific provision dealing with foreign decrees.

In the text of the legislation, there are repeated references to the 'country' concerned. In *Godfrey v Godfrey*,[7] Mahon J held that 'country' means not only a sovereign state with a unified system of law but also any province or state forming part of a federation in which such province or state exercises its own independent system of divorce law. The correctness of this view is borne out by the language of s 44(1)(b)(ii) dealing with nationality.

1   [1906] P 135. See above, para 2.05.
2   Family Proceedings Act 1980 (NZ), s 44(1)(c); Divorce Act 1973 (St Lucia), s 51(1)(c); Divorce and Matrimonial Causes Ordinance 1961 (WS), s 37(1)(b).
3   Ibid.
4   [1976] 1 NZLR 711. Mahon J's statement, at 714, that the husband 'had to show that he or both parties had been resident in Arizona for not less than two years' is, with respect, not a complete statement of the position.
5   Semble, the point could have been taken in *Godfrey v Godfrey* [1976] 1 NZLR 711 where the 90 days' residence test of Arizona law was a 'domiciliary provision'.
6   See Matrimonial Proceedings Act 1963 (NZ), s 3(2).
7   [1976] 1 NZLR 711

Common law bases retained

3.12   In all three countries with this legislative model, it is expressly provided that the legislation does not affect the validity of a divorce (including an extra-judicial divorce) which would be entitled to recognition otherwise than under the Act, that is in accordance with the common law principles.[1] There is no reference to any date by reference to which the state of the common law is to be determined, and it has been held that *Indyka v Indyka*,[2] which introduced a new common law principle well after the New Zealand legislation took its present form, is applicable in New Zealand by virtue of the saving provision of the Act.[3]

1   Family Proceedings Act 1980 (NZ), s 44(2); Divorce Act 1973 (St Lucia), s 51(2); Divorce and Matrimonial Causes Ordinance 1961 (WS), s 37(2).
2   [1969] 1 AC 33, [1967] 2 All ER 689, HL.
3   *Re Darling* [1975] 1 NZLR 382; *Godfrey v Godfrey* [1976] 1 NZLR 711.

Tanzania

3.13   The Law of Marriage Act 1971 of Tanzania[1] contains provisions dealing respectively with judicial and extra-judicial divorces. So far as judicial decrees are concerned the Act provides:[2]

'Where a court of competent jurisdiction[3] in any foreign country has passed a decree in any matrimonial proceedings, whether arising out of a marriage contracted in Tanganyika[4] or elsewhere, such decree shall be recognized as effective for all purposes of the law of Tanganyika—

(a)   if the petitioning party was domiciled in that country or had been resident there for at least two years prior to the filing of the petition; or

(b)   being a decree of annulment or divorce, it has been recognized as effective in a declaratory decree of a court of competent jurisdiction in the country of the domicile of the parties or either of them.'

This provision appears to be in substitution for the common law jurisdiction rules which are not saved by any provision of the Act.

Section 91(a) preserves the domicile principle but also adds a residential basis. Only the petitioner's residence is relevant, and the 'residence' is not qualified by any adjective such as 'habitual' or 'ordinary'. Presumably occasional absences from a country, for business or holiday reasons, would nonetheless not be taken as breaking what overall amounted to a two-year period.

Section 91(b) is related to the rule in *Armitage v A-G*,[5] but is more restrictive in requiring, not merely evidence that the decree would be entitled to recognition in the country of the domicile of the parties,[6] but an actual declaratory decree to that effect granted by a court in that country. If no such decree has been obtained, and even if the courts in the relevant country have no power to make declaratory judgments (or no jurisdiction to do so in the particular circumstances, perhaps because of a residential test), s 91(b) will not be satisfied.

Extra-judicial divorces are dealt with in s 92. Such a divorce will be entitled to recognition if 'it was effective under the law of the country of domicile of each of the parties at the time of the divorce'[7] or in circumstances corresponding to those in s 91(b).[8] When is a divorce 'effective under the law of' a country? If the reference is to cases in which an extra-judicial divorce is obtained in country X but will be recognised as valid in country Y, where the parties are domiciled, there is little sense in the inclusion, as an alternative basis for recognition, of the existence of a declaratory decree to that effect granted in country X. Accordingly, it is believed that s 92(a) is limited to extra-judicial divorces obtained *in* the country in which both parties are domiciled, and regarded as effective by the law of that country. This interpretation would accord with the usage in s 2(b) of the Recognition of Divorces and Legal Separations Act 1971 of the United Kingdom.[9]

1   No 5 of 1971.
2   S 91.
3   The reference is presumably to 'internal' competence, ie under the rules of the legal system of which the court formed part.
4   Sic. The provisions do not apply in Zanzibar, the other component part of the United Republic of Tanzania.
5   [1906] P 135.
6   The words 'or one of them' are apt for the nullity cases also covered by s 91(b).
7   Law of Marriage Act 1971 (Tanzania), s 92(a).
8   Ibid, s 92(b).
9   '... effective under the law of that country', ie the country in which the decree was obtained.

Zimbabwe

3.14   Section 13 of the Matrimonial Causes Act of Zimbabwe[1] provides as follows:

'13. (1) The General Division [ie of the High Court] may recognize the validity of any decree or order made in any country in any case in which the husband is not domiciled in that country if—
(a)   it is satisfied that the laws of that country contain provisions which correspond substantially to the relevant provisions of section *twelve*; or
(b)   the President has, by proclamation in the *Gazette*, declared that the laws of that country contain provisions which correspond substantially to the relevant provisions of section *twelve*.
(2) No proclamation shall be issued under paragraph (b) of subsection (1) unless the President is satisfied that adequate provision is made under the law of the country concerned for the recognition by the courts of that country of the decrees and orders

made under the provisions of section *twelve* in any case in which the husband is not domiciled in Rhodesia.

(3) The President may at any time revoke any proclamation issued in terms of paragraph (b) of subsection (1).'

The reference to 'section twelve' is to a provision extending the jurisdiction of the Zimbabwe courts in three sets of circumstances: (a) where the wife was deserted and her husband was immediately before the desertion domiciled in Zimbabwe; (b) where the wife had resided in Zimbabwe for at least four years immediately preceding the commencement of the action, and was still so resident, and the marriage was celebrated in Zimbabwe; and (c) where the wife satisfied the same residential tests and was a citizen of Zimbabwe.

Those provisions in s 12 are in fact rather unusual in points of detail, so that the usefulness of s 13 depends very much upon the generosity with which the phrase 'correspond substantially' is interpreted. If however another country does have such provisions, its divorces are entitled to recognition in all circumstances; nothing is said about the foreign court having taken jurisdiction in reliance on any such provision. On the other hand, s 13 provides that the Zimbabwe court *may* recognise decrees; it will retain the power to refuse to recognise, for example, decrees obtained by fraud or in defiance of natural justice.

As far as is known, no proclamation has been issued under s 13(1)(b). It seems unlikely that the section as a whole (based on a South African model) is useful in practice; this is certainly so if, as appears to be the case, the common law bases of recognition (including *Travers v Holley*[2] and *Indyka v Indyka*[3]) can also be relied upon in Zimbabwe.

1 Cap 39, RL.
2 [1953] P 246; [1953] 2 All ER 794.
3 [1969] 1 AC 33, [1967] 2 All ER 689, HL.

B. THE HAGUE CONVENTION OF 1970

The Hague Convention

3.15 Although only one Commonwealth member country[1] has ratified it, the Hague Convention on the Recognition of Divorces and Legal Separations has had a marked effect on Commonwealth law, and seems likely to have a continuing and growing effect. Accordingly, it is desirable to examine its provisions in some detail.

The Convention was drawn up at a series of meetings between 1964 and 1968, culminating in the Eleventh Session of the Hague Conference on Private International Law in October 1968. In accordance with the then practice of the Conference, the draft convention was not formally opened for signature until a later date, 1 June 1970. It has been ratified by Czechoslovakia, Denmark, Egypt, Finland, the Netherlands, Norway, Sweden, Switzerland and the United Kingdom. Luxembourg has signed but not yet ratified the Convention. It is however open to accession not only by other member states of the Hague Conference, but by any state which is a member of the United Nations or of any specialised agency of the United Nations or which is a party to the Statute of the International Court of Justice.[2]

The negotiation of the Convention, which was presided over by the United Kingdom delegate,[3] was a considerable achievement; but the price paid was in the complexity both of the basic rules of the Convention and of the qualifications and reservations which surround them. The details are set out in the paragraphs which follow.[4] The text of the substantive articles of the Convention is reproduced in Appendix B.

1   The United Kingdom. Canada was also represented at the Session at which the Convention was drawn up.
2   Convention, art 28.
3   Professor R. H. Graveson.
4   Apart from the official Explanatory Report (in French only) by P. Bellet and B. Goldman in *Actes et Documents de la Onzième Session* Tome II, p 209, see A. E. Anton 'The Recognition of Divorces and Legal Separations' (1969) 18 ICLQ 620; H. H. Foster and D. J. Freed 'The Hague Draft Convention on Recognition of Foreign Divorces and Separations' (1967) 1 Family Law Q 83; F. Juenger 'Recognition of Foreign Divorces: British and American Perspectives' (1972) 20 Am Jo Comp L 1.

Subject-matter and approach

3.16   The Convention is concerned with the recognition of divorces and legal separations obtained in other contracting states.[1] For the sake of clarity the word 'divorce' in the following paragraphs includes 'legal separations', except where a different usage is clear from the context.

The Convention is limited to *recognition*. Although this necessarily involves paying a great deal of attention to the jurisdictional competence, in the international sense, of the state of origin (the state in which the divorce was obtained), the authors of the Convention did not attempt the much more difficult task of agreeing common jurisdictional rules.

It is also a closed Convention, in the sense that it is limited to divorces obtained in other contracting states. Although the rapporteurs observed that 'it is not destined to form, in those states, the general law as to the recognition of divorces',[2] there is nothing to prevent a contracting state, or indeed a non-signatory state, taking the Convention's rules and applying them generally to the recognition of divorces obtained anywhere in the world; and this has already occurred in a number of Commonwealth jurisdictions.

The recognition of a divorce involves an acceptance that the marital relationship is at an end with all the necessary consequences in accordance with the private international law rules of the recognising state. To cite examples given by the French delegate in the course of discussions at The Hague, divorce will have effects on succession rights, on the matrimonial property regime, and in some countries at least, on the wife's right to use her husband's surname.[3] In particular, divorce implies the right to remarry, and the Convention underlines this by providing[4] that a state which is required to recognise a divorce under the Convention may not preclude either spouse from remarrying on the ground that the law of some other state does not recognise the divorce; though of course there may be other obstacles to a particular further marriage which could be relied upon, eg the nonage of the proposed second partner.

It is expressly provided that the recognition of a divorce does not apply to findings of fault—which could be relevant, for example, in jurisdictions which award damages for adultery—or to ancillary orders, in particular orders relating to pecuniary obligations or to the custody of children, both being topics covered by other Hague Conventions and raising other types of issue.[5]

In accordance with all conventions on recognition of foreign judgments and orders, the Hague Convention on Divorces prohibits review of the merits of the decision presented for recognition.[6]

1   See Convention, preamble and art 1, first paragraph.
2   Explanatory Report, para 11 (translated from French original).

3   *Actes et Documents de la Onzième Session* Tome II, at p 105.
4   Convention, art 11.
5   Ibid, art 1, second paragraph.
6   Ibid, art 6, third paragraph; without prejudice to such review as is required to establish that the Convention provisions do in fact apply.

'Divorces'

3.17   The authors of the Convention spent much time on issues relating to the definition of divorces entitled to recognition, taking a firm decision not to attempt any formal definition.[1] They were clear that nullity decrees, even those in voidable marriage cases, were excluded; divorces pronounced in connection with presumption of death are, semble, included, but no vote was recorded on the point as the meeting decided not to refer to the point even in the Explanatory Report!

Extra-judicial divorces were, however, discussed at some length. The Convention speaks of divorces 'which follow judicial or other proceedings officially recognised in that State [ie, the state in which they are obtained] and which are legally effective there.'[2] This includes administrative and legislative divorces, as well as those obtained in religious as well as secular tribunals, provided the requirements of the Convention are satisfied in other respects. The text needs careful interpretation, as the official Explanatory Report indicates:

'In principle, this requirement [of "proceedings officially recognised"] comprises two distinct elements: on one hand, there must be *proceedings*, that is a minimum of acts, steps or formalities lawfully prescribed and carried out by some authority, or at least with its approval or in its presence; on the other, there must be proceedings *officially recognised*, that is prescribed or authorised by the State as a means of divorce ... This second element of the requirement allows, for example, the exclusion from the benefit of the Convention of religious divorces pronounced in a State which does not recognise proceedings before confessional courts. But notice the significance too of the first element: "proceedings" according to the definition just given is a matter of objective fact; recognition can be refused to the dissolution of a marriage, *even one legally effective in the State of origin*, which does not result from such "proceedings".'[3]

The best-known forms of extra-judicial divorce, the Jewish gett and the Islamic talak were discussed not only in connection with this provision but again in relation to art 8, which allows recognition to be refused if, in the light of all the circumstances, adequate steps were not taken to give notice of the proceedings for a divorce to the respondent, or if he was not afforded a sufficient opportunity to present his case. The delegates of Israel and of Egypt both explained the operation of religious laws in their legal systems, which require either the presence of the respondent or formal steps before a court officer or both; the 'bare' talak, a simple unilateral divorce by the husband was not fully considered. It seems clear from the debates however that this type of talak, like consensual divorces not requiring formal procedures, would fall outside the scope of the Convention.

1   See generally Procès-verbal No 2 (8 October 1968) in *Actes et Documents de la Onzième Session* Tome II, pp 95-101.
2   Convention, art 1, first paragraph.
3   Explanatory Report, para 13. (Author's translation from French original.)

Basic rules of recognition

3.18   Articles 2 to 4 of the Convention contain the basic rules, which are subject to certain possible qualifications under other provisions, indicating the circumstances in which the links between the parties and the state of origin are sufficiently strong to entitle the divorce to recognition. In every case, the time at which the circumstances are to be judged is the date of the institution of proceedings in the state of origin,[1] and this will be referred to as 'the relevant date'. Where there has been a cross-petition, a divorce will be recognised if either the petition or the cross-petition falls within the rules, ie the relevant date may be taken to be either that of the petition or that of the cross-petition whichever favours recognition.[2]

1   Convention, art 2.
2   Ibid, art 4.

Basic rules: habitual residence

3.19   A divorce is entitled to recognition in the following cases:

(1)   the *respondent* had his habitual residence in the state of origin at the relevant date;[1]

(2)   the *petitioner* had his habitual residence there at that date and the habitual residence had continued for not less than one year immediately prior to that date;[2]

(3)   the *petitioner* had his habitual residence there at that date and the spouses last habitually resided together there.[3]

The content of the notion of habitual residence, a concept much used in Hague conventions, has already been discussed.[4]

1   Convention, art 2, 1.
2   Ibid, art 2, 2, a.
3   Ibid, art 2, 2, b.
4   Paras 1.38–1.41 above.

Basic rules: domicile

3.20   The Convention text concentrates upon habitual residence and nationality. References to domicile were included in the earliest draft, but at that stage it was possible that domicile would be interpreted as meaning habitual residence, so that the two types of case would be merged in practice.[1] In the final text, however, domicile becomes a connecting factor which can be relied upon in its own right, but it is given a special interpretation. The 'domicile' in question is domicile as the term is used *in the state of origin*;[2] whatever the views of that state, however, it does not include the domicile of dependence of a wife,[3] that notion being unacceptable to the delegates at The Hague as seeming to be based upon sexual discrimination.

The domicile bases of recognition under the Convention are available only 'where the State of origin uses the concept of domicile as a test of jurisdiction in matters of divorce or legal separation'.[4] The Convention does not, however, specify that the domicile test of jurisdiction should have been relied on in the instant case in the state of origin. It seems possible, also, that the domicile bases of recognition could be available in the case of a decree of divorce (in this context, as opposed to one of legal separation) whenever the state of origin made use of a domicile jurisdictional test in matters *either* of divorce *or* of judicial separation; ie if State A were to base jurisdiction in judicial separation alone on domicile, its divorces would also be within the Convention's rules.

Where the domicile bases are available under the rules just considered, a divorce will be recognised in the following cases:

(4)   the *respondent* had his domicile (in the above sense) in the state of origin at the relevant date;[5]

(5)   the *petitioner* had his domicile (in that sense) there at that date and the domicile had continued for not less than one year immediately prior to that date;[6]

(6)   the *petitioner* had his domicile (in that sense) there at that date and the spouses' last common domicile (again, in that sense) was there.[7]

Although the exclusion of the wife's dependent domicile was designed to avoid discrimination against women, the effect will of course be to exclude certain divorces from recognition. These are those in which her domicile of dependence in the state of origin is the only link with that state.[8]

1   See the Draft of 15 October 1965 (*Actes et Documents de la Onziéme Session* Tome II, p 13) and the Secretary-General's provisional report, para 14 (ibid, p 20).
2   Convention, art 3, first paragraph.
3   Ibid, art 3, second paragraph.
4   Ibid, art 3, first paragraph.
5   Ibid, arts 2, 1 and 3.
6   Ibid, arts 2, 2, a and 3. (See Explanatory Report, para 32, for the second reference to 'domicile'.)
7   Ibid, arts 2, 2, b and 3.
8   Cf the English Law Commission in Law Com No 34 (1970), para 21, to the same effect.

Basic rules: nationality

3.21   A divorce is also entitled to recognition in the following cases:

(7)   *both* spouses were nationals of the state of origin at the relevant date;[1]

(8)   the *petitioner* at the relevant date was a national of that state and also had his habitual residence there;[2]

(9)   in the cases in which the domicile bases are available and in accordance with the interpretations examined in the last paragraph, the *petitioner* at the relevant date was a national of that state and also had his domicile (in the sense previously identified) there;[3]

(10)   the *petitioner* was a national of that state at the relevant date and had habitually resided there for a continuous period of one year falling, at least in part, within the two years preceding the relevant date;[4]

(11)   in the cases in which the domicile bases are available, the *petitioner* was a national of that state at the relevant date and had his domicile (in that sense) there for a continuous period of one year falling, at least in part, within the two years preceding the relevant date;[5]

(12)   in cases of divorce (but *not* judicial separation), the *petitioner* was, at the relevant date, a national of that state and present there, and the spouses last habitually resided[6] together in a state whose law, at that date, did not provide for divorce.[7]

In an attempt to deal with the complexities of nationality law (of which the United Kingdom provides a notorious example), the Convention provides that contracting states may from time to time declare that only certain categories of their nationals are to be considered their nationals for the particular purposes of the Convention.[8]

The special position arising where the state of origin has in matters of divorce two or more legal systems applying in different territorial units is dealt with by providing in effect that the nationality rules apply where the spouses, or the petitioner, as the case requires, have the nationality of the state of which the territorial unit where the divorce was obtained forms a part.[9]

1   Convention, art 2, 3.
2   Ibid, art 2, 4, a.
3   Ibid, arts 2, 4, a and 3.
4   Ibid, art 2, 4, b.
5   Ibid, arts 2, 4, b and 3.
6   'Domicile' is not available as an alternative as art 3 relates in effect only to domicile in the state of origin and not in a third state.
7   Convention, art 2, 5.
8   Ibid, art 22.
9   Ibid, art 14.

An additional case: divorces by conversion

3.22   In some countries judicial separation is the usual, or invariable, first phase of divorce proceedings. Under the principle of perpetuatio fori, once the requirements of the Convention are satisfied so that a separation obtained in a particular state is entitled to recognition, a divorce granted in the same state as the second phase of the process will equally be entitled to recognition. This is so even if at the time of the institution of divorce proceedings none of the bases of recognition is available.[1]

An example would be a case in which at the time of the decree of judicial separation the sole link between the parties and the state of origin was the habitual residence of the respondent. That decree would be recognised under the Convention.[2] If it is later 'converted into a divorce'[3] in the same state, the divorce will be recognised notwithstanding the fact that the respondent has lost his habitual residence in that state.

1   Convention, art 5.
2   Ibid, art 2, 1.
3   These words are used in ibid, art 5, to indicate the necessary relationship between the separation and the divorce.

Findings of fact

3.23   Article 6 of the Convention provides, in part, 'Where the respondent has appeared in the proceedings, the authorities of the State in which recognition of a divorce or legal separation is sought shall be bound by the findings of fact on which jurisdiction was assumed'.[1]

The object of this provision was to limit the scope for the case to be re-opened in the state in which recognition was sought; but it is far from clear that it is effective. A major reason for this is the exclusion of divorces granted by default—over 90% of British divorces—by a decision taken at the Eleventh Session.[2]

But even in the context of contested cases, the provision may be very limited in effect. Although the matter seems to have had little or no discussion, successive explanatory documents take a very restricted view of 'findings of fact', holding that nationality and domicile are essentially questions of law and that even habitual residence involves legal interpretation of facts.[3] The practical operation of the provision must therefore be in real doubt.

1   Convention, art 6, first paragraph.
2   See Procès-verbal No 6 (12 October 1968), *Actes et documents de la Onzième Session* Tome II, pp 123–126.
3   Eg the Explanatory Report of P. Bellet and B. Goldman, para 38; ibid, p 217.

Reservations and qualifications

3.24 The Convention contains some fairly complicated provisions which restrict the operation of the basic recognition rules. Some require the making of a formal Reservation at the time of ratification or accession; but others do not. Their number increased as the text reached finality, in an attempt to meet the special objections of particular delegations.

Without making any formal Reservation, any contracting state may refuse to recognise a divorce if, at the time it was obtained (as opposed to the date of the institution of proceedings, the more usual relevant date), both the parties were nationals of a state which did not provide for divorce, and of no other state.[1] In place of this power of refusing recognition, a contracting state may make a Reservation under art 19, 2. This would provide that the state in question would not recognise a divorce if, at the time it was obtained, both parties were *habitually resident* in a state which did not permit divorce. Having made such a Reservation, the state cannot rely on the nationality point.[2]

The above rules only apply where *both* spouses are nationals of, or habitually resident in, the state which does not provide for divorce. A rather different form of Reservation may be made by a contracting state which itself does not provide for divorce. This would exclude recognition of a divorce *one* party to which is a national of a state whose law did not, at the date the divorce was obtained, provide for divorce.[3] No 'habitual residence' counterpart is available.

As a general rule recognition of a divorce may not be refused on the ground that the internal law of the state addressed would not allow divorce on the same facts, nor because a law was applied other than that applicable under the rules of private international law of that state.[4] However a Reservation may be made reserving the right to refuse to recognise a divorce where both parties were, at the time of the divorce, nationals of the state addressed (and of no other state) and a law other than that indicated by the rules of private international law of that state was applied, unless the result reached was the same as would have been reached by the law indicated by those rules.[5] Given the common law tradition of applying the lex fori and of refusing to examine the factual grounds relied on by the foreign court, these points will not be important in most Commonwealth contexts but are of considerable interest within the civil law tradition.

1 Convention, art 7.
2 Ibid, art 19, 2. The power to make this Reservation was inserted at the request of the Irish delegation.
3 Convention, art 20. If the state making the Reservation later introduces provision for divorce into its own law, the Reservation ceases to have effect: ibid, art 20, second paragraph. See art 21 for a similar Reservation available to states lacking provision for legal separation.
4 Convention art 6, second paragraph.
5 Ibid, art 19, 1.

Grounds for refusing recognition

3.25 The Convention indicates a number of circumstances in which individual divorces, of a type which would generally be entitled to recognition, may be refused recognition.

The first set of grounds relate to the requirements of natural justice. A divorce may be refused recognition if, in the light of all the circumstances, adequate steps were not taken to give notice of the proceedings for a divorce to the respondent; or if, in all the circumstances, he was not afforded a sufficient opportunity to present his case.[1] It is for the judge in the state addressed to be satisfied that these procedural requirements have been complied with; it is not necessarily sufficient to demonstrate that the formalities prescribed by the law of the state of origin have been complied with if the judge in the state addressed finds that those formalities were inadequate. Accordingly, the provision is *not* limited to default judgments, for in some legal systems a judgment may be pronounced in what are regarded as defended proceedings despite inadequate notice having been given to the defendant.[2]

The second set of grounds relate to conflicting, or potentially conflicting, decisions. If the matrimonial status of the parties has already been determined, either in the state addressed or elsewhere in circumstances entitling the decision to be recognised in that state,[3] a later divorce incompatible with the earlier decision may be refused recognition.[4] The provision is carefully limited: only divorces (and not negative decisions or ancillary orders) *later than* the contrary decision are within its terms. If proceedings are in train in two or more contracting states at the same time, the problem of *litispendence*, the Convention merely enables proceedings in one state to be suspended;[5] the law of the individual state will govern the exercise of that power.

Finally, in the traditional language of the Hague Conference, recognition may be refused 'if such recognition is manifestly incompatible with ... public policy (ordre public)' in the state addressed.[6] This phrase is more fully discussed elsewhere.[7]

1   Convention, art 8.
2   See *Actes et Documents de la Onzième Session* Tome II, p 66 (Report of the Special Commission of June 1967, citing French and Egyptian procedure in particular).
3   Semble, not necessarily in accordance with the recognition rules laid down by the Convention itself.
4   Convention, art 9.
5   Ibid, art 12.
6   Ibid, art 10.
7   See para 4.12 below.

Federal and composite states

3.26   The Convention contains detailed provisions for its application in respect of states having two or more legal systems applying either in different territorial units or (as is sometimes the case in family law) to different categories of persons (eg adherents of a particular religion).

Where territorial factors are found, any reference to the law of the state of origin is to be construed as referring to the law of the territory in which the divorce was obtained;[1] any reference to domicile or residence in that state, to domicile or residence in that territory;[2] and any reference to the law of the state in which recognition is sought, to the law of the forum.[3]

Where personal characteristics are the basis of the differential application of law, any reference to the law of a contracting state is to be construed as a reference to the legal system specified by the law of that state.[4] The same rule is applied where a reference is made to the law of a third state having two or more systems of law.[5]

The Convention allows a state to declare that the Convention provisions apply in respect of only one or more of its several systems of law.[6] This applies to 'personal' as well as 'territorial' distinctions; for example, the Convention could be applied to the Canadian provinces but not the territories, or to Jews living in Israel but not Moslems.

The interpretative provisions dealing with these 'federal' issues should, it is submitted, be given a wide interpretation. For example, 'any reference to the law of the state of origin' need not be read as limited to provisions in which the words 'the law of the state of origin' apply; art 13 is not the sort of interpretation section found in statutes in most Commonwealth jurisdictions. Accordingly, art 13 is relevant in interpreting, for example, art 1, which speaks of a divorce legally effective in another contracting state where it was obtained; it seems impossible to deny that this contains a reference to the law of the state of origin.[7]

1   Convention, art 13, 1.
2   Ibid, art 13, 3.
3   Ibid, art 13, 2.
4   Ibid, art 15.
5   Ibid, art 16.
6   Ibid, art 23; the declaration may be modified from time to time.
7   Cf Dicey and Morris *The Conflict of Laws* (10th edn, 1980) p 350, where the opposite view is taken.

Retrospectivity

3.27   Although the matter was controversial, the authors of the Convention decided that it should in principle apply regardless of the date on which the divorce or legal separation was obtained.[1] Accordingly it applies to divorces obtained before the state of origin became a contracting party, and to divorces obtained before the Convention was signed. However, a Reservation is permitted, to be made not later than ratification or accession, by which a state reserves the right not to apply the Convention to divorces obtained before the date upon which the Convention comes into force in respect of that state.[2] It is, of course, possible for a state to enter such a Reservation but to be prepared to recognise some divorces obtained before the relevant date, or to recognise all such divorces subject to certain special conditions.[3]

1   Convention, art 24, first paragraph.
2   Ibid, art 24, second paragraph; once the Convention came into force, states ratifying or acceding are bound from the sixtieth day after the deposit of the relevant instrument: ibid, arts 27, second paragraph and 28, third paragraph.
3   This course was followed by the United Kingdom. See para 3.37 below.

Non-exclusivity of the Convention

3.28   The contracting states to The Hague Convention are not prevented from applying other and more favourable rules to the recognition of foreign divorces.[1] Nor are they disabled from relying upon existing conventions or from entering into further conventions on the same subject-matter, but (in an unusual provision) are 'to refrain' from entering into such conventions which are incompatible with The Hague Convention 'unless for special reasons based on regional or other ties'.[2] The Commonwealth does not operate its cooperative legal arrangements through the device of conventions, but the Commonwealth association would undoubtedly be a 'tie' that could be relied upon if the need arose.

1   Convention, art 17.
2   Ibid, art 18.

C. UNITED KINGDOM LEGISLATION

The Hague Convention and United Kingdom law

3.29   In November 1970 the English and Scottish Law Commissions published a joint report[1] on the legal implications for the United Kingdom of ratifying The Hague Convention, the Government having previously announced its decision in principle to proceed to ratification. The Commissions duly advised upon the legislation necessary to give effect to the Convention, but went a good deal further, recommending a more thorough reform of the law of both England and Scotland. They recommended a new set of rules, based on the Convention provisions and providing for the recognition of all divorces caught by those provisions but both wider and less complex, which would apply to divorces obtained in any country, whether or not a contracting state; and they also recommended the retention of some, but not all, of the existing common law bases of recognition. The resulting Recognition of Divorces and Legal Separations Act 1971 is a complex statute because of the combination of Convention and common law bases; its text, as amended to date, is set out in Appendix B.

In considering the Convention provisions, the Commissions lament their complexity, due in large part to the addition of further requirements ('reinforcing factors') to the basic elements of habitual residence and nationality. These factors were designed to discourage forum-shopping, but the Commissions argued, in effect, that forum-shopping is best discouraged by jurisdictional rather than recognition rules.[2] The Convention rules were in some respects stricter than those already found acceptable in the United Kingdom, and the Commissions disliked the distinction drawn in the nationality area between the nationality of the petitioner and that of the respondent; the respondent's nationality is not a basis for recognition under the Convention's rules though might well be relevant under *Indyka v Indyka*[3] and, in principle, both spouses 'should realise that the national law of the other may be relevant in relation to their status'.[4] By widening the rules, a simpler set of tests could be framed, suitable for use by registrars of marriages, who in practice are the officers most likely to be faced with a question as to the validity of an earlier divorce.[5]

The Commissions recommended that their new rules should apply to all foreign divorces. A limitation to contracting states of The Hague Convention would be a complicating factor, requiring the use of subordinate legislation to declare which states were contracting parties from time to time, and would produce apparent injustice, United Kingdom courts recognising a decree from State A but having to refuse a decree granted, in virtually identical circumstances, in (a non-contracting) State B.[6]

So far as existing common law bases of recognition were concerned, the Commissions urged the retention of the domicile basis and its 'rider', the rule in *Armitage v A-G*;[7] these rules were 'widely known and operate smoothly'.[8] But the other common law bases should not be retained: the rule in *Travers v Holley*[9] because most deserving cases to which it applied would fall within the Convention provisions; *Indyka v Indyka*[10] because it 'is inherently vague and the source of much uncertainty where certainty is desirable'.[11]

All the Commissions' recommendations were accepted and are reflected in the Recognition of Divorces and Legal Separations Act 1971 which is considered in the paragraphs which follow.

1   Law Com No 34; Scot Law Com No 16.
2   Ibid, para 29(a).
3   [1969] 1 AC 33, [1967] 2 All ER 689, HL.
4   Report, para 29(c).
5   Ibid, para 29(b).
6   Ibid, para 19.
7   [1906] P 135; see para 2.05 above.
8   Report, para 20(c).
9   [1953] P 246, [1953] 2 All ER 794, CA; see para 2.06 above.
10 [1969 1 AC 33, [1967] 2 All ER 689, HL; see para 2.09 above. See Report, paras 22–25.
11 Ibid, para 25.

The Recognition of Divorces and Legal Separations Act 1971 (UK)

3.30   'So far from simplifying the former rules, the effect of this Act and the later Domicile and Matrimonial Proceedings Act 1973 has been to create a series of new legal conundrums which are extremely difficult to resolve'.[1]

Although not formally divided into Parts, the sections of the Act do fall into four main groups. Section 1 deals with divorces granted in the British Isles, and is considered later.[2] Sections 2 to 5 contain the rules for the recognition of what are termed 'overseas divorces', based upon but (as the Law Commissions recommended) wider than the rules of The Hague Convention. Section 6 continues the effect of some of the common law bases of recognition in relation to 'divorces obtained outside the British Isles'. Sections 7, 8 and 10 contain provisions, applying generally but based in part on the rules of The Hague Convention as to refusal of recognition, retrospectivity and other matters.

1   Per Ormrod LJ in *Quazi v Quazi* [1980] AC 744 at 786, CA.
2   Para 3.40 below.

'Overseas divorces'

3.31   The category of 'overseas divorces' to which the Convention-based rules in s 3 to 5 apply is defined in effect by s 2, which refers to divorces obtained 'by means of judicial or other[1] proceedings in any country outside the British Isles'[2] and which 'are effective under the law of that country'.[3]

The text of the Act departs in drafting from the corresponding art 1 of The Hague Convention, but it was not intended to bear a different meaning. It has already been argued[4] that the reference in the Convention to a divorce being legally effective under the law of the country of origin is to be construed, in the case of federal or composite states, as being to effectiveness under the law of the relevant territorial unit, and it is clear that 'it is a legitimate aid to the construction of any provisions of the Act that are ambiguous or vague to have recourse to the terms of the treaty in order to see what was the obligation in international law that Parliament intended that this country should be enabled to assume'.[5] Unfortunately, in the Act there is a specific provision to the effect that 'country' may be so interpreted, but this provision[6] is limited to the interpretation of s 3 of the Act, and the argument from 'ambiguity' is a difficult one.

The practical significance of this controversy is that it is commonly argued[7] that if 'country' refers to a federation, a divorce will only be recognised if the other units of the federation would all give 'full faith and credit' to the decree, this being the test of federal effectiveness. This argument may, however, be too strongly influenced by the United States examples usually deployed. It is possible to have a federal or composite state in which there is no constitutional 'full faith and credit' doctrine; indeed, the United Kingdom itself is an example. Certainly in those cases, and arguably more generally, 'federal effectiveness' would seem to be satisfied by a demonstration that divorce is within the competence of the courts of the units as opposed to those of the federation itself.

This particular conundrum awaits judicial resolution. In a non-federal context 'effective' is relatively unproblematic. In *Quazi v Quazi*,[8] which involved a series of extra-judicial divorces, the question was whether a purported divorce was given legal effect, was recognised by, the legal system. A divorce granted by an incompetent court, in the sense of one lacking divorce jurisdiction, or by a judge appointed by an unconstitutional or rebel regime,[9] will lack this effectiveness. But there are some difficulties in the more general proposition advanced by Dr North[10] that if in the circumstances a foreign court would rescind its own decree, that decree might be regarded as lacking 'effectiveness'. An illustration might be one in which the divorce was obtained by the fraud of both parties as to facts establishing the jurisdiction of the foreign court.[11] In these circumstances a United Kingdom court would be bound by the findings of jurisdictional fact made by the foreign court;[12] could not rely solely on 'fraud', which is not a ground for refusing recognition under the Act; and would in any event find it difficult to deny that, at least until rescinded, the decree *was* legally effective in the state of origin.

1 For the effect of the Act in relation to extra-judicial divorces, see para 3.38 below.
2 Recognition of Divorces and Legal Separations Act 1971 (UK), s 2(a). 'British Isles' is defined (s 10(2)) as meaning the United Kingdom, the Channel Islands and the Isle of Man.
3 Ibid, s 2(b).
4 Para 3.26 above.
5 *Quazi v Quazi* [1980] AC 744 at 808, HL, per Lord Diplock.
6 Recognition of Divorces and Legal Separations Act 1971 (UK), s 3(3).
7 Dicey and Morris *The Conflict of Laws* (10th edn, 1980) pp 350–351; P. M. North *The Private International Law of Matrimonial Causes in the British Isles and the Republic of Ireland* p 174.
8 [1980] AC 744, [1979] 3 All ER 897, HL.
9 Cf *Adams v Adams* [1971] P 188 (decree pronounced by judge appointed by unconstitutional regime in what was then Southern Rhodesia refused recognition in England; although argued a few days after the signature of The Hague Convention, the case was before the 1971 Act).
10 Op cit, p 176.
11 North cites the facts of *Gaffney v Gaffney* [1975] IR 133 (Sup Ct of Ireland).
12 Recognition of Divorces and Legal Separations Act 1971 (UK), s 5(1)(a); see para 3.33 below.

Bases of recognition of 'overseas divorces'

3.32 Section 3 of the Act sets out the bases of recognition of 'overseas divorces'. As in The Hague Convention, they entail the factors of habitual residence, domicile and nationality,[1] but the rules in the Act are much simpler and more inclusive.

A decree will be recognised if at the date of the commencement of the proceedings in the state of origin:

(1) either spouse was habitually resident there;[2]
(2) in cases where the law of the state of origin uses the concept of domicile as a ground of jurisdiction in matters of divorce or legal separation,[3] either spouse was domiciled there within the meaning of that law;[4]
(3) either spouse was a national of that country.[5]

In federal or composite states comprising territories in which different systems of law are in force in matters of divorce, the question is whether either spouse was habitually resident or domiciled (in the above sense) in the relevant territory; but nationality relates to the country of which the territory is a part.[6]

It will be noted that each basis is available if either spouse, husband or wife, petitioner or respondent, has the prescribed link with the state of origin; and the link need be shown to exist only at the relevant date, there being no requirement that it should have continued for a stated period.

Subject to the other conditions laid down by the Act being satisfied, a divorce decree will be recognised if the foreign court took jurisdiction on the ground of domicile even if the notion of domicile is radically different from that obtaining in the United Kingdom, even if it causes 'English eyebrows to rise a little'; the phrase was used by Ormrod J in *Messina v Smith*[7] commenting on the effect of the Act, then a Bill before Parliament, on a divorce granted in Nevada on the basis of domicile established by six weeks' residence. The Act does not follow The Hague Convention in excluding the dependent domicile of a wife; given that by definition the husband would also be domiciled in the state of origin and the Act allows the domicile of either spouse to be relied upon, the Convention rule would be meaningless.[8]

Nationality is, in this as in other contexts, a matter for the state whose nationality is in issue. Naturalisation in the United Kingdom (or elsewhere) may not in the law of the state of origin terminate the propositus's citizenship of that state. This was the position in *Torok v Torok*;[9] had proceedings in train in the country of origin (Hungary, which the parties had left 17 years earlier) resulted in a divorce decree, it would have been recognised under the Act.

The Act follows the provisions of the Convention in respect of cross-petitions[10] and of decrees by 'conversion' after a legal separation.[11]

1   Cf paras 3.18–3.21 above.
2   Recognition of Divorces and Legal Separations Act 1971 (UK), s 3(1)(a).
3   For the meaning of this phrase, see para 3.20 above.
4   Recognition of Divorces and Legal Separations Act 1971 (UK), s 3(2).
5   Ibid, s 3(1)(b).
6   Ibid, s 3(3).
7   [1971] P 322, [1971] 2 All ER 1046.
8   See Law Com No 34, para 21; cf Convention, art 3, second paragraph.
9   [1973] 3 All ER 101, [1973] 1 WLR 1066.
10 Recognition of Divorces and Legal Separations Act 1971 (UK), s 4(1). (The reference to s 3(1)(a) or (b) is not intended to exclude the domicile basis, for s 3(2), which gives effect to that basis, does so by an extended interpretation of s 3(1)(a) which is equally relevant in this context).
11 Ibid, s 4(2). See para 3.22 above.

Findings of fact

3.33   Article 6 of The Hague Convention provides that where the respondent has appeared in the proceedings, the authorities of the state in which recognition of a divorce is sought are bound by the findings of fact on which jurisdiction was assumed in the state of origin;[1] it has already been noted[2] that in the context of the Convention this provision appears to have very limited effects. The English and Scottish Law Commissions recommended that a more extensive provision should be included in United Kingdom legislation based on the Convention,[3] and this is reflected in s 5 of the Recognition of Divorces and Legal Separations Act 1971.

The Act extends the original provision in a number of ways. It makes it clear that findings of fact made by implication are included.[4] It declares that 'finding of fact' includes a finding that either spouse was habitually resident[5] or domiciled in, or a national[6] of the state of origin.[7] It provides not only that findings of fact are conclusive when both spouses took part in the proceedings,[8] and appearance amounts to taking part,[9] but also that they are sufficient proof in other cases unless the contrary is shown.[10]

1   Convention, art 6, first paragraph.
2   Para 3.23 above.
3   Law Com No 34, paras 31–34.
4   Recognition of Divorces and Legal Separations Act 1971 (UK), s 5(1).
5   See *Cruse v Chittum* [1974] 2 All ER 940 at 943 (finding in Mississippi of 'actual and bona fide residence of a year and upwards', semble, treated as equivalent to a finding of habitual residence, or possibly of domicile; the case was undefended and the judgment is not clear on this point).
6   See *Torok v Torok* [1973] 1 WLR 1066 at 1069 (national of Hungary; obiter, as no decree had actually been pronounced there).
7   Recognition of Divorces and Legal Separations Act 1971 (UK), s 5(2).
8   Ibid, s 5(1)(a).
9   Ibid, s 5(2).
10   Ibid, s 5(1)(b).

Preservation of certain common law bases of recognition

3.34   Section 6 of the Recognition of Divorces and Legal Separations Act 1971 (UK) as originally enacted was in the following form:

'6.—This Act is without prejudice to the recognition of the validity of overseas divorces and legal separations—

(a)   by virtue of any rule of law relating to divorces or legal separations obtained in the country of the spouses' domicile or obtained elsewhere and recognised as valid in that country;
(b)   by virtue of any enactment other than this Act;

but, save as aforesaid, no such divorce or legal separation shall be recognised as valid except as provided in this Act.'

This preserved the common law domicile basis of recognition[1] and the rule in *Armitage v A-G*,[2] and the effect of the Indian and Colonial Divorce Jurisdiction Act 1926 as amended and certain other statutes,[3] but abolished all other common law bases of recognition and precluded the development of any new common law bases.

A much more elaborate text was substituted by the Domicile and Matrimonial Proceedings Act 1973 and is included in the version printed in Appendix B. The change was necessitated by the abolition of the dependent domicile of a married woman; the parties might now be domiciled in different countries. Under the amended text it is *not* sufficient that the divorce should be obtained in, or recognised in, the country of the domicile of one spouse. It must be shown that the divorce is recognised under the law of the domicile of each spouse,[4] or, having been granted in the domicile of one spouse, is recognised as valid under the law of the domicile of the other spouse.[5]

1   Ie, domicile in the sense of the law of the state addressed. See para 2.02 above.
2   [1906] P 135; see para 2.05 above.
3   Apart from the Colonial and Other Territories (Divorce Jurisdiction) Acts 1926–1950 (UK), these include the Indian Divorces (Validity) Act 1921 (UK), the Kenya Divorces (Validity) Act 1922 (UK) and the Matrimonial Causes (War Marriages) Act 1944 (UK). In *Vervaeke v Smith* [1981] Fam 77, CA, Sir John Arnold P expressed the opinion that nullity decrees (and, presumably, divorces) were capable of recognition under the Foreign Judgments (Reciprocal Enforcement) Act 1933. This point had been agreed between the parties, but was not fully endorsed in argument before the Court of Appeal. Cumming-Bruce and Eveleigh LJJ expressly

doubted the applicability of the 1933 Act. Certainly the 1933 Act was not taken into account by the English and Scottish Law Commissions in their 1970 Report (Law Com No 34). The point was not touched on in the House of Lords. ([1982] 2 All ER 144, HL).
4 Recognition of Divorces and Legal Separations Act 1971 (UK), s 6(3) as substituted in 1973.
5 Ibid, s 6(2) as substituted in 1973.

Remarriage

3.35 Where a divorce is recognised in the United Kingdom under the Recognition of Divorces and Legal Separations Act 1971, including the common law rules preserved by the Act, neither spouse is precluded from remarrying in the United Kingdom[1] on the ground that the validity of the divorce would not be recognised in any other country.[2] This gives effect to art 11 of The Hague Convention, and overrules in English law the decision in *R v Brentwood Superintendent Registrar of Marriages, ex p Arias*.[3]

1 The phrase 'in the United Kingdom' was not in the draft Bill prepared by the Law Commissions, but the limitation was probably implied. If the marriage takes place outside the United Kingdom, the law of the domicile will be relevant in testing the capacity of the parties, even, it would seem, if the marriage takes place in another contracting state to The Hague Convention.
2 Recognition of Divorces and Legal Separations Act 1971 (UK), s 7.
3 [1968] 2 QB 956, [1968] 3 All ER 279. See para 3.15 above.

Grounds for refusing recognition

3.36 A divorce obtained outside the British Isles and otherwise entitled to recognition under the Recognition of Divorces and Legal Separations Act 1971 *must* be refused recognition if by the law of the part of the United Kingdom in which recognition is sought (including its rules of the conflict of laws) there was no subsisting marriage between the parties.[1]

Such a divorce *may* be refused recognition if, and only if,

(1) it was obtained by a spouse without such steps having been taken for giving notice of the proceedings to the other spouse as, having regard to the nature of the proceedings and all the circumstances, should reasonably have been taken;[2]
(2) it was obtained by a spouse without the other spouse having been given (for any reason other than lack of notice) such opportunity to take part in the proceedings as, having regard to those same factors, he should reasonably have been given;[3] or
(3) recognition would manifestly be contrary to public policy.[4]

There appear to be no reported cases in which the ground of want of notice has been relied on. The common law cases arising on similar facts have already been considered;[5] as the statutory ground is discretionary—the decree *may* be refused recognition—the distinctions drawn in those cases may well be relied upon under the Act.

A number of cases have attracted the ground of want of opportunity to take part. In *Hack v Hack*,[6] a divorce was obtained in Missouri where the husband was habitually resident. The wife, who lived in England, argued that she was prevented by lack of money and shortage of time from attending the Missouri proceedings, from being represented there or from filing an answer or other defence. She failed on the facts, as she had some 35 days in which to send the necessary instructions; the financial aspects do not seem to have been fully explored.

Those aspects were much more important in *Joyce v Joyce and O'Hare*.[7] Again the wife was resident in England and on 17 April 1975 she was served with a divorce petition relating to proceedings in Quebec. A decree nisi was pronounced in Quebec on 4 July 1975. In the interval the wife's English solicitors corresponded energetically with the Quebec Bar and the Province's Legal Services Commission and the Registrar of the relevant court; despite their efforts, no Quebec legal representation or legal aid was obtained and although the letter to the Court Registrar was said to have been added to the dossier it later emerged that it was deemed ineligible to be shown to the judge. Lane J refused to recognise the Quebec divorce. Her Ladyship listed some of the factors to be examined:[8]

(a)   Had the complaining party been given the right to be heard?
(b)   Had she been given the facility to take not just a formal but an effective part in the proceedings?
(c)   The availability of financial aid.
(d)   The steps taken by the party to put forward her case.
(e)   The availability of remedies in the foreign jurisdiction, including the enforceability of any financial orders.

In addition, because the court had a discretion, it was proper to consider the wider aspects of the case, the implications for any children or new partners (and any children of a new union), the presence of property in England, and the public interest in preventing the party and any children becoming a charge on the social security system.

That the list of relevant factors given by Lane J in *Joyce v Joyce* is not exhaustive is clear from the 'disastrous' case of *Newmarch v Newmarch*[9] which has some factual similarities. In that case the wife was served in England on 14 October 1974 with a divorce petition presented by her husband in the Supreme Court of New South Wales. The husband alleged desertion by the wife, an allegation she was at all times anxious to contest (and in the view of the English court would have been able successfully to contest). She faced the usual difficulty over the legal costs of defending an action in Australia, but Australian solicitors were instructed to file a defence. Those instructions were received in October 1974, and the Australian solicitors indicated on a number of occasions their intention of acting upon them; but despite repeated letters and a cable failed so to act. The divorce proceedings were heard as an undefended suit in October 1975 and the decree absolute was expedited to take effect 14 days later. As in *Joyce v Joyce* a letter had been sent by the English solicitors to the New South Wales court, but was not seen by the judge.

On these facts, Rees J recognised the divorce decree. The approach he adopted is clear from this passage in the judgment:

'The terms of the section [ie s 8 of the Recognition of Divorces and Legal Separations Act 1971] make it clear that the court has a discretion whether or not to refuse recognition of a foreign decree, even in cases where one spouse has not been given a reasonable opportunity to take part in the proceedings, and even where its recognition would manifestly be contrary to public policy. The words of the section clearly import that even in those circumstances recognition "may be refused" not "shall be refused". In exercising its discretion, in my judgment, this court should have regard to all the surrounding circumstances which would include a full investigation of the facts relied upon to support a refusal of recognition; the likely circumstances if the petitioning spouse[10] had been given the opportunity to take part in the proceedings; an assessment of what the legitimate objectives of the petitioning spouse are, and to what extent those objectives can be achieved if the foreign decree remains valid, and what the likely consequences to the spouses and any children of the family would be if recognition were refused.'[11]

His Lordship's reasoning was essentially that even if the Australian solicitors had acted upon their instructions, a divorce would have been obtained by the husband. Although his petition alleged desertion, he could have amended it to rely on the 'no fault' separation ground in the law of New South Wales, or, by waiting a few more months, rely upon the ground of one year's separation available under the Family Law Act 1975 of Australia. The wife's main concern was to obtain maintenance and in all the circumstances she could obtain that maintenance despite the foreign divorce; the New South Wales courts had made a provisional order on the husband's application discharging a mainten- ance order made in England and sent to Australia for enforcement. Rees J, however, refused to confirm this order, so that the maintenance order in the wife's favour remained in force and could be varied so as to increase the amount.

The striking feature of *Newmarch v Newmarch* is the way in which the principles governing the recognition of divorce decrees are interpreted to take account of the real objectives of the parties and of the existence and workings of the Commonwealth maintenance orders enforcement procedures considered in the next Chapter. Where the foreign divorce decree originates from outside the Commonwealth, the financial implications, in the absence of any effective arrangements for the enforcement of financial provision orders, may be very different.

The ground for refusing recognition as 'manifestly ... contrary to public policy' was relied on, as an alternative ground for decision, in *Joyce v Joyce*.[12] Lane J stated her conclusion in a single sentence, and this should not, it is submitted, be interpreted as accepting the arguments of counsel, who appeared to base his public policy argument on the fact that the husband was evading his responsibilities so that the wife had to turn to social security benefits.[13] These facts alone would seem quite insufficient to support the application of the public policy doctrine.

A clear case for the application of the doctrine arose in *Kendall v Kendall*.[14] The parties married in Akrotiri in 1964, and, after a period in England, lived together in Bolivia in 1973–4. In 1974 the wife wished to return to Cyprus for reasons connected with the education of the children of the marriage, and signed at her husband's request documents in Spanish which she believed to be emigration papers. They were in fact papers authorising divorce proceedings to be commenced in her name, and without her knowledge a divorce was later obtained in Bolivia on evidence which was at least in part perjured. So, it was said that there were no children, and no jointly-owned property, and that the wife was in employment; all this was untrue. It was 'manifestly' wrong to recognise the decree, which would in all probability be set aside by any Bolivian court made aware of the facts.

---

1   Recognition of Divorces and Legal Separations Act 1971 (UK), s 8(1). Cf art 9 of The Hague Convention which contains a related provision.
2   1971 Act, s 8(2)(a)(i); cf Convention, art 8.
3   1971 Act, s 8(2)(a)(ii); cf Convention, art 8 which speaks of the 'opportunity to present his case'.
4   1971 Act, s 8(2)(b); cf Convention, art 10.
5   See para 2.13 above.

6   (1976) 6 Fam Law 177; see also the details of the case given in *Joyce v Joyce and O'Hare* [1979] Fam 93 at 107–108.
7   [1979] Fam 93, [1979] 2 All ER 156.
8   At 111–113.
9   [1978] Fam 79, [1978] 1 All ER 1. The adjective is Rees J's: at 85.
10 Ie the spouse seeking a denial of recognition.
11 [1978] Fam 79 at 95; this passage was cited with approval in *Sharif v Sharif* (1980) Fam Law 216 per Wood J, where an Iraqi talak was refused recognition under Recognition of Divorces and Legal Separations Act 1971, s 8(2)(a)(ii) where the wife was unable to travel to Iraq or instruct lawyers there, despite the fact that no effective defence would have been available to her.
12 [1979] Fam 93 at 114.
13 At 96.
14 [1977] Fam 208, [1977] 3 All ER 471.

Rectrospectivity

3.37   The Hague Convention applies to all decrees, including those granted before the Convention was signed or entered into force in any particular state; but there is power by Reservation to curtail this element of rectrospectivity.[1] The English and Scottish Law Commissions discussed the question in their Report on the Convention.[2] They took the view that while in theory a retrospective change in the law could cause injustice, particularly in its effect on financial and property matters where the parties may have arranged their affairs on a particular set of legal expectations, in practice such cases were likely to be very few in number. This was because the Convention rules were not radically different in their effect from those which had developed at common law (so that changes in the legal position would not be numerous) and, at the same time, the common law position, especially since *Indyka v Indyka*,[3] had been so uncertain that the parties' legal and financial advisers had necessarily given cautious advice, designed to cater for most contingencies.

The resulting recommendation of the Commissions was that the principle of rectrospective application should be accepted with certain saving provisos. One would protect those who had acquired property rights on the basis of the validity or invalidity of a foreign decree, on succession, under a marriage contract, a trust, or in respect of pensions or annuities. A second would leave unaffected any decision of a United Kingdom court taken before the legislation came into effect. Section 10(4) of the Recognition of Divorces and Legal Separations Act 1971 gives full effect to these recommendations.

1   See para 3.27 above.
2   Law Com No 34, paras 45–50.
3   [1969] 1 AC 33, [1967] 2 All ER 689, HL.

Extra-judicial divorces

3.38   There is no doubt that the authors of The Hague Convention intended that it should apply to extra-judicial divorces, but it is also clear that the full complexity of the issues was not appreciated in the debates at The Hague.[1] It is therefore not surprising that there are some difficulties in applying the provisions of the Recognition of Divorces and Legal Separations Act 1971 (UK) to extra-judicial divorces.

Sections 2 to 5 of that Act giving effect to the Convention apply to divorces which 'have been obtained by means of judicial or other proceedings in any country outside the British Isles' and 'are effective under the law of that country'.[2] It was thought at one time that 'other proceedings' covered only a limited class of extra-judicial divorces. The word 'proceedings' was held by the Court of Appeal in *Quazi v Quazi* to imply that 'the state or some official organisation recognised by the state must play some part in the divorce process at least to the extent that, in proper cases, it can prevent the wishes of the parties or one of them, as the case may be, from dissolving the marriage tie as of right'.[3] In the House of Lords, however, this limitation was not supported, though varying opinions were held by members of the House as to the precise scope of the term.

Lord Diplock was content to hold that a talaq obtained in Pakistan, where notification to a public officer is required, with conciliation procedures being made available, was covered by the Act, despite the inability of the state to prevent the talaq taking effect.[4] Lord Salmon would construe s 2 as applying 'amongst other things, to overseas divorces obtained by proceedings other than judicial proceedings if such divorces are effective under the law of the country in which they are obtained',[5] a statement which, with respect, does nothing to explain the language of the Act and which, in its use of the phrase 'amongst other things' adds a strange element of uncertainty. Lord Fraser would include non-forensic or non-judicial proceedings, so long as there was 'some regular definite form'; subject to that, any divorce would be within s 2 if it were legally effective in the country of origin.[6] Lord Scarman would construe s 2 as applying 'to any divorce which has been obtained by means of any proceeding, ie any act or acts, officially recognised as leading to divorce in the country where the divorce was obtained, and which itself is recognised by the law of the country as an effective divorce'.[7]

Effectiveness under the law of the state of origin is therefore the most important limiting factor in s 2. In appropriate cases it is clear that this will involve a reference to the conflict of laws rules of that state, and even to its rules as to renvoi.[8] For example, the law of the state of origin may refer to that of some other country so as to give effectiveness to a decree which would not satisfy the ordinary domestic rules of the state of origin.[9] Or, conversely, there may be a reference to the law of a foreign country by way of imposing an extra requirement, failure to meet which would prejudice the effectiveness of a divorce satisfying the ordinary domestic rules of the country of origin.[10]

If an extra-judicial divorce is entitled to recognition in accordance with the provisions of s 3 to 5 of the Act, it may still be challenged under s 8, ie the section setting out grounds upon which recognition may be refused. Section 8 speaks of 'notice of the proceedings' and of the 'opportunity to take part in the proceedings'; if there are no proceedings, there will accordingly be the possibility of the refusal of recognition.[11] In *Sharif v Sharif*[12] it was held that a 'bare' talak, ie one involving no such reference to an official body as is required in Pakistan, would fall into this category but it is submitted that the better view is that advanced by the editors of Dicey and Morris,[13] that s 8(2), which is discretionary, should not be strictly interpreted in the case of talaks 'because no amount of notice would enable the wife successfully to contest the husband's unilateral divorce, and therefore it would be pointless to insist on an empty formality'.

Extra-judicial divorces may also be recognised under the common law rules preserved and extended by s 6 of the Act.[14] The provisions of s 8(2) will apply in such cases, but the debates about 'proceedings' and 'effectiveness' under s 2 are irrelevant.[15]

---

1   See para 3.17 above.

2   Recognition of Divorces and Legal Separations Act 1971 (UK), s 2.
3   [1980] AC 744 at 789, CA.
4   [1980] AC 744 at 809, HL.
5   Ibid, at 811.
6   Ibid, at 814.
7   Ibid, at 824. Viscount Dilhorne agreed with the speeches of Lords Diplock and Scarman.
8   See ibid, at 804 per Lord Diplock.
9   Eg, a reference to the law of the domicile of the parties as in *Qureshi v Qureshi* [1972] Fam 173, [1971] 1 All ER 325. See the example given by Dr North in his *Private International Law of Matrimonial Causes in the British Isles and the Republic of Ireland* at p 231.
10   Eg, the reference by Thai law to the law of the nationality of the parties in respect of a divorce by consent (khula) meeting the general requirements of the Civil Code of Thailand: see *Quazi v Quazi* [1980] AC 744, esp at 824.
11   Cf *Viswalingham v Viswalingham* (1979) 1 FLR 15 at 19, CA.
12   (1980) 10 Fam Law 216, per Wood J.
13   10th edn, 1980, p 363.
14   See para 3.34 above.
15   For extra-judicial divorces granted in the British Isles, see para 3.39 below.

Extra-judicial divorces: the Domicile and Matrimonial Proceedings Act 1973 (UK)

3.39   In 1973, the United Kingdom made further provision as to the recognition of extra-judicial divorces. Section 16(1) of the Domicile and Matrimonial Proceedings Act 1973 (UK) provides that

'No proceeding[1] in the United Kingdom, the Channel Islands or the Isle of Man shall be regarded as validly dissolving a marriage unless instituted in the courts of law of one of those countries.'

This applies to any divorce obtained on or after 1 January 1974,[2] and will cover all forms of extra-judicial divorce. Extra-judicial divorces obtained in the British Isles before 1 January 1974 are recognised in England (or in any other British Isles jurisdiction) under the common law rules; the Recognition of Divorces and Legal Separations Act 1971 does not apply to such divorces because they were not 'granted under the law of any part of the British Isles'.[3]

Section 16(2) contains a more elaborate provision:

'Notwithstanding anything in section 6 of the Recognition of Divorces and Legal Separations Act 1971 (as substituted by section 2 of this Act), a divorce which—

(a)   has been obtained elsewhere than in the United Kingdom, the Channel Islands and the Isle of Man; and

(b)   has been so obtained by means of a proceeding other than a proceeding in a court of law; and

(c)   is not required to be recognised by any of the provisions of sections 2 to 5 of that Act to be recognised as valid,

shall not be regarded as validly dissolving a marriage if both parties to the marriage have throughout the period of one year immediately preceding the institution of the proceeding been habitually resident in the United Kingdom.'[4]

This provision is designed to prevent evasion of s 16(1) by the simple device of a short trip by ferry or hovercraft to an adjacent jurisdiction. Its complexity derives from the need to continue to honour the United Kingdom's treaty obligations under The Hague Convention; section 16(2)(c) is designed with this in mind. An extra-judicial divorce in, say, Calais, must be recognised under the Convention if one party is a French national and the other provisions of the Convention as given effect in the Recognition of Divorces and Legal Separations Act 1971 are complied with.

1 This has the same meaning as 'proceedings' in s 2 of the Recognition of Divorces and Legal Separations Act 1971: *Quazi v Quazi* [1980] AC 744, [1979] 3 All ER 897, HL. This leaves uncertain the position of 'bare talaks', which were surely within the mischief aimed at by s 16(1) of the 1973 Act but which *might* not be 'proceedings' under s 2 of the 1971 Act.
2 Domicile and Matrimonial Proceedings Act 1973 (UK), s 16(3).
3 Recognition of Divorces and Legal Separations Act 1971 (UK), s 1.
4 This provision is also with effect from 1 January 1974: Domicile and Matrimonial Proceedings Act 1973 (UK), s 16(3).

British Isles divorces

3.40 The Recognition of Divorces and Legal Separations Act 1971 (UK) makes provision in respect of decrees granted in the British Isles, which includes England and Wales, Scotland, Northern Ireland, Guernsey, Jersey and the Isle of Man.[1] A decree granted after 1 January 1972,[2] if it was granted under the law of any part of the British Isles,[3] is recognised throughout the United Kingdom,[4] subject only to s 8 which contains the grounds upon which recognition must or may be refused.[5] The recognition of divorces granted before 1 January 1972 is governed by the common law rules; there is no restrospectivity in the case of British Isles divorces.

1 Recognition of Divorces and Legal Separations Act 1971 (UK), s 10(2).
2 Ibid, ss 1, 10(5).
3 Ie, excluding extra-judicial divorces: see para 3.39 above.
4 Recognition of Divorces and Legal Separations Act 1971 (UK), s 1.
5 See para 3.36 above.

D. COMMONWEALTH LEGISLATION INFLUENCED BY THE HAGUE CONVENTION

Commonwealth legislation on the United Kingdom model

3.41 A number of Commonwealth jurisdictions have enacted legislation based closely upon the model of the Recognition of Divorces and Legal Separations Act 1971 of the United Kingdom. They include the Falkland Islands[1] together with the Falkland Islands' Dependencies[2] and the British Antarctic Territory,[3] Gibraltar,[4] Guernsey,[5] Hong Kong,[6] Jersey,[7] the Isle of Man,[8] and Trinidad and Tobago.[9] In the case of Guernsey, Hong Kong and Jersey the model used is strictly that of the 1971 Act of the United Kingdom, and does not reflect the amendments made to that Act by the Domicile and Matrimonial Proceedings Act 1973 (UK). The United Kingdom Act of 1971 is in force in Saint Helena[10] and may well be treated as applicable in other jurisdictions whose courts are directed to apply 'English practice' in matrimonial cases.

1 Matrimonial Causes Ordinance 1979, No 14, Part V (ss 48–55).
2 Application of Colony Law Ordinance 1980, DSI of 1980, applying the Falklands Islands ordinance.
3 Falklands Islands Laws (Application) Regulation 1980, Reg. 1/80, applying the Falklands Islands ordinance.
4 Domicile, Matrimonial Proceedings and Recognition of Divorces and Legal Separations Ordinance 1974, No 23, ss 7–14.
5 Recognition of Divorces and Legal Separations (Bailiwick of Guernsey) Law 1972.
6 Matrimonial Causes Ordinance, cap 179, RL, Part IX (ss 55–62).
7 Recognition of Divorces and Legal Separations (Jersey) Law 1973.
8 Recognition of Divorces and Legal Separations (Isle of Man) Act 1972, cap 12.
9 Matrimonial Proceedings and Property (Amendment) Act 1982, No 20, s 8 (inserting new s 62A–62H in the Matrimonial Proceedings and Property Act, cap 45:51 RL).

10   Recognition of Divorces and Legal Separations (Application) Order 1976 (St Helena), LN
      13 of 1976. For Ascension, see Application of English Law (Ascension) Ordinance 1973, No
      1 of 1973; for Tristan da Cunha see Interpretation and General Law Ordinance, cap 54 (St
      Helena) and Tristan da Cunha Ordinances (Application) Ordinance, cap 118 (St Helena),
      Sch 1.

Australia and Barbados

3.42   Provisions on the recognition of overseas decrees, including decrees of
nullity of marriage, were made in s 104 of the Family Law Act 1975[1] of
Australia. They have been adopted unchanged in Barbados, as Part X of the
Family Law Act 1981.[2] The Australian text is about to be amended by the
Family Law Amendment Bill currently before the Australian Parliament;[3] the
proposed changes are designed principally to include legal separations and to
deal with cases in which the petition is presented by the spouses jointly.

The current text of the legislation as in force in Australia is reproduced in
Appendix B.

It is clear that the Family Law Act provisions are modelled closely on the
rules of The Hague Convention, but there are a number of differences. Section
104(3) can be compared with art 2 of the Convention:

(1)   Where the Convention uses the term 'habitual residence', the Act prefers
       to speak of a person being 'ordinarily resident'; it is doubtful whether this
       would produce any significant differences in practice.
(2)   Similarly the Act[4] prefers the phrase 'the last place of cohabitation' to
       'last habitually resided there together',[5] but the effect should be the same.
(3)   More significantly, s 104(3)(c) of the Act enables a decree to be recognised
       on the basis of the domicile (semble, in accordance with Australian
       notions of domicile) of either spouse in the state of origin of the decree.
       But there is no provision corresponding to art 3 of the Convention which
       refers to the availability in certain cases of the test of domicile as the term
       is used in the state of origin.[6]

In a number of other respects the Act does not correspond to the provisions
of the Convention. The grounds for refusing recognition are stated in s 104(4)
of the Act in terms derived in part from the earlier Matrimonial Causes Act
1959 of Australia,[7] though with the addition of references to fraud and to cases
where recognition would manifestly be contrary to public policy; they are
mandatory grounds for refusing recognition, not discretionary, for a decree
'shall not be recognised as valid' under s 104(3)[8] if the circumstances are
established. The Hague Convention has discretionary rules at the corresponding point.[9]

The rules as to the binding effect of findings of jurisdictional facts by the
foreign court are stated in s 104(7) in words taken from the earlier Matrimonial
Causes Act 1959 of Australia. The interpretation of that earlier provision,
currently in force in Fiji, Nigeria and Papua New Guinea, has already been
examined,[10] and its effect was seen to be limited. The Family Law Amendment
Bill before the Australian Parliament in 1983 will, if enacted, substitute a new
s 104(7) in terms influenced by the corresponding provisions in the United
Kingdom Act.[11] The revised text proposed is as follows:

'For the purposes of this section, a court in Australia is considering the validity of a
dissolution or annulment of a marriage, or a legal separation of the parties to a marriage,
effected under a law of an overseas country—

(a) where the respondent appeared in the proceedings for the dissolution, annulment or separation—
  (i) is bound by the findings of fact on the basis of which a court of the overseas country assumed jurisdiction to grant the dissolution, annulment or separation; and
  (ii) may treat as proved any other facts found by a court of the overseas country or otherwise established for the purposes of the law of the overseas country; or
(b) where the respondent did not appear in the proceedings for the dissolution, annulment or separation—may treat as proved any facts found by a court of the overseas country or otherwise established for the purposes of the law of the overseas country.'[12]

The Family Law Act 1975, like its predecessor the Matrimonial Causes Act 1959 of Australia, preserves the common law rules of recognition. The interpretation of the text, taken directly from the 1959 Act, has already been considered.[13] Section 104(8) which was new in 1975 seems at first sight to preserve the rule in *Armitage v A-G*,[14] but it actually has a much wider effect. Its effect is that if a decree of Country A would be entitled to recognition in Australia, either under the new bases of recognition introduced by the Act or under the common law rules preserved by it, Australian courts will also recognise any decree which would be recognised as valid by the courts of Country A, wherever obtained. So, for example, a decree obtained in Nevada, with which state neither party had any real connection, will be recognised as valid in Australia (subject to the rules as to natural justice and public policy) if it would have been recognised on the date it was granted in the courts of the country of the respondent's nationality.[15]

Extra-judicial divorces are clearly covered by the Act.[16] However in *El Oueik v El Oueik*,[17] one reason for refusing recognition to a divorce granted in what was described as a 'Moslem court' in Lebanon, was that the husband 'in spite of being domiciled in Australia and an Australian citizen, resorted to the Moslem court ... purely for procuring a divorce and avoiding his responsibilities towards' his wife.[18] This was held to make recognition 'manifestly contrary to public policy', giving a very wide interpretation to that concept. It is submitted that the decision should not be followed on this point; the decree was in any event not entitled to recognition under the rules of s 104(3) of the Act, and had been obtained in circumstances which were contrary to natural justice.

1 Act No 53, 1975.
2 No 29 of 1981. Part X comprises ss 79–85.
3 See clause 42 of the Bill as introduced.
4 Family Law Act 1975 (Australia), s 104(3)(b)(ii), 104(3)(f).
5 The Hague Convention, art 2, (2)(b), art 2, (5)(b).
6 See para 3.20 above.
7 Cf s 92(6) of the current Fijian legislation reproduced in para 3.04 above.
8 But not if the decree is recognised under the common law rules preserved by Family Law Act 1975, s 104(5).
9 The Hague Convention, arts 8 and 10. The Family Law Act has no provision corresponding to arts 9 (conflicting decisions) and 12 (lis alibi pendens).
10 See para 3.06 above.
11 Recognition of Divorces and Legal Separations Act 1971 (UK), s 5; see para 3.33 above.
12 Family Law Amendment Bill, cl 42(g), as first introduced.
13 See para 3.05 above, in reference to the text as enacted as s 92(4) of the Matrimonial Causes Act of Fiji.
14 [1906] P 135. See para 2.05 above.
15 Family Law Act 1975 (Australia), s 104(3)(d) read with s 104(8).

16   See ibid, s 104(10); cf the corresponding provision of the earlier Matrimonial Causes Act 1959 (Australia) reproduced (as s 92(7) of the Matrimonial Causes Act of Fiji) in para 3.04 above.

17   (1977) FLC 76,173 (NSW Sup Ct).

18   At 76,177.

Bermuda

3.43   The Recognition of Divorces and Legal Separations Act 1977 of Bermuda,[1] though strongly influenced by the United Kingdom model, departs from it in significant respects. In particular it is much closer in its detailed rules to the terms of The Hague Convention; and it abrogates the common law rules rather than retaining and extending them.

Section 3 of the Act provides as follows:

'(1) The validity of an overseas divorce or legal separation shall be recognized in Bermuda if—

(a)   at the date of the institution of proceedings in the country in which it was obtained either spouse was habitually resident in that country; or

(b)   at that date both spouses were nationals of that country; or

(c)   at that date the petitioner was a national of that country and one of the following further conditions was fulfilled, that is to say—

    (i)   the petitioner was habitually resident there;

    (ii)   he had habitually resided there continuously for a period of one year, being a period falling wholly or partly within the period of two years immediately preceding the institution of the said proceedings.

(2) The validity of an overseas divorce shall also be recognized in Bermuda if, at the date of the institution of proceedings in the country in which it was obtained, the petitioner was a national of that country and both the following further conditions were fulfilled, that is to say—

(a)   he was present in that country at that date;

(b)   he and the respondent last habitually resided in a country whose law, at that date, did not provide for divorce.

(3) In relation to a country the law of which uses the concept of domicile as a ground of jurisdiction in matters of divorce or legal separation, the references in subsections (1) and (2) to habitual residence include a reference to domicile within the meaning of that law.

(4) In this section, as respects proceedings other than judicial proceedings the expressions "petitioner" and "respondent" respectively refer to the spouse initiating the proceedings and the other spouse.[2]

(5) In relation to a country comprising territories in which different systems of law are in force in matters of divorce or legal separation, the provisions of subsections (1) to (4) (except those relating to nationality) shall have effect as if each territory were a separate country.'

It will be seen that this corresponds closely to arts 2 and 3 of The Hague Convention,[3] but with one difference. Article 2,1 of the Convention refers to the habitual residence of *the respondent*, but s 3(1)(a) of the Bermuda Act to the habitual residence of *either spouse*. In this respect the lead of the United Kingdom, on the advice of the English and Scottish Law Commissions, was followed, but the implications were not fully worked out. This is clear from s 3(1)(c)(i) of the Bermuda Act which follows the Convention in using the habitual residence of the petitioner as a 'reinforcing factor' relevant when found in combination with the petitioner's nationality. In fact, given the form of s 3(1)(a), the petitioner's habitual residence would stand alone as a basis for recognition regardless of his nationality, so that s 3(1)(c)(i) is unnecessary.

The other distinctive feature of the Bermuda Act is to be found in s 6, which provides that

'No overseas divorce or legal separation shall be recognised as valid in Bermuda except as provided in this Act.'

Although there are traces in the Act of the distinction drawn in the United Kingdom legislation between 'overseas divorces' and other divorces 'obtained outside [Bermuda]',[4] it is clear that s 6 abrogates the common law bases for recognition; the marginal note reads 'Other grounds no longer recognised'. Accordingly the domicile basis, and the rule in *Armitage v A-G*[5] are swept away.

The Bermuda legislation pays particular attention to the position of dependent territories. Section 1 declares that 'country' includes a colony or dependent territory of any country and that 'a person shall be deemed to be a national of a colony or dependent territory if the law of such colony or dependent territory recognizes him as a national of the country on which the colony or dependent territory is dependent'. This is a rather strange provision. It is related in part to art 22 of The Hague Convention which allows contracting states to exclude certain categories of their nationals for the purposes of the Convention, but it operates much more obliquely. Suppose that a divorce granted in Montserrat, a colony of the United Kingdom, were being considered in Bermuda. Montserrat would clearly be 'a country'. If the recognition of the divorce depended upon the nationality of both spouses, or of the petitioner with a 'reinforcing factor', the Bermuda court would have to decide whether *by the law of Montserrat* the spouses or the petitioner had either a local Montserrat nationality or United Kingdom nationality. In practice the latter would be the crucial question; presumably the law of Montserrat would, by its conflict of laws rules, refer the question to the law of the United Kingdom, so that the British Nationality Act 1981 would govern; but the drafting is difficult.

1 No 20 of 1977.
2 Cross-petitions are dealt with in s 4(1).
3 See paras 3.18–3.21 above.
4 Compare the heading to ss 2 to 5 of the Bermuda Act ('Overseas Divorces and Legal Separations') with the use in s 8(1) of the phrase 'a divorce or legal separation obtained outside Bermuda'.
5 [1906] P 135.

Cayman Islands

3.44 The Matrimonial Causes Law 1976 of the Cayman Islands[1] contains, in section 7, a version of the United Kingdom Recognition of Divorces and Legal Separations Act 1971. The text is much shortened and the effect is rather different at a number of points. The provision reads as follows:

'7. (1) The Court will recognise the decree or order of a foreign court or other legally effective proceeding with reference to the marital status of the parties to a marriage where, irrespective of whether the grounds for the making of such decree or order would, in the Islands, be grounds for making a similar decree or order, the Court is satisfied that with respect to the country within which the foreign court has jurisdiction either spouse was at the date of the petition giving rise to the proceedings (whether in the first instance for legal separation or divorce) and culminating in such decree or order—

(a)   habitually resident in that country; or
(b)   a national of that country; or
(c)   domiciled in that country under the law relating to domicil there appertaining;
      and

the Court is satisfied that the foreign court, tribunal or authority was competent in that country to make the decree or order or other legally effective pronouncement:

Provided that the validity of such decree or order of a foreign court granting a divorce or judicial separation shall not be recognized in the Islands if it was granted at a time when, according to the law of the Islands, there was no subsisting marriage between the parties; and

Provided further that recognition by virtue of this section may be refused if such decree or order was obtained by one spouse—

(a)   without such steps having been taken for giving notice of the proceedings to the other spouse as, having regard to the nature of the proceedings and all the circumstances, should reasonably have been taken; or

(b)   without the other spouse having been given such opportunity to take part in the proceedings as, having regard to the matters aforesaid, should reasonably have been given;

or recognition would manifestly be contrary to public policy.

(2) Where the validity of a decree of divorce pronounced by a foreign court is entitled to recognition by virtue of subsection (1) neither spouse shall be precluded from re-marriage in the Islands on the grounds that the validity of the divorce would not be recognised in some other country.

(3) Nothing in this section shall be construed as requiring the recognition of any finding of fact made in the proceedings of the foreign court other than findings of fact upon which the jurisdiction was assumed, which latter findings shall be binding upon the Court.'

It would seem, though the matter is not made clear, that this set of rules replaces the common law rules which are impliedly abrogated.

The differences between the Cayman Islands and the United Kingdom legislation include the following:

(1)   The reference to the irrelevance of the grounds for divorce relied upon[2] is a novelty, though it restates long-established practice at common law.[3]

(2)   The use of the concept of nationality is not accompanied by any provision dealing with the federal state problems such as are presented by United States divorces;[4] this would seem a serious defect in the Law.

(3)   The domicile of either spouse in the state of origin and in accordance with the law of that state is relevant whether or not that law uses domicile as a jurisdictional basis in cases of divorce or legal separation.[5]

(4)   No provision is made for decrees obtained on a cross-petition.[6]

(5)   The provisions as to the binding nature of findings of fact as to the jurisdiction of the foreign court are different; the findings are binding in all cases, even in cases in which one party did not appear.[7]

1   No 9 of 1976.
2   Matrimonial Causes Law 1976 (Cayman Is), s 7(1).
3   See para 2.04 above.
4   See para 3.31 above.
5   Matrimonial Causes Law 1976 (Cayman Is), s 7(1)(c). Cf Recognition of Divorces and Legal Separations Act 1971 (UK), s 3(2).
6   Cf Recognition of Divorces and Legal Separations Act 1971 (UK), s 4(1).
7   Matrimonial Causes Law 1976 (Cayman Is), s 7(3). Cf Recognition of Divorces and Legal Separations Act 1971 (UK), s 5.

Nauru

3.45 The heroic nature of the legislation of Nauru has already been noted in connection with the reform of the law of domicile. It is evident once again in relation to the recognition of foreign decrees, as is clear at once from the title of the Recognition of Foreign Divorces, Legal Separations and Nullity of Marriages Act 1973.[1] The inclusion of nullity decrees is a striking innovation; indeed even extra-judicial nullity decrees are contemplated.

The Act follows the United Kingdom model very closely, save for the insertion of references to nullity decrees. So s 3 declares that the principal provisions have effect 'as respects the recognition in Nauru of the validity of foreign divorces, legal separations, annulments of marriage and declarations of invalidity of marriage, that is to say, divorces, legal separations, annulments of marriage and declarations of invalidity of marriage which (a) have been obtained by means of judicial or other proceedings in any country other than Nauru; and (b) are effective under the law of that country'.[2]

Three other points of difference can be noted between the Nauru and the United Kingdom legislation. The first is the preservation in effect of the rule in *Travers v Holley*[3] by s 4(1)(c) which provides for the recognition of a foreign decree if the proceedings by means of which it was obtained were held in the exercise in the country of origin of a jurisdiction similar to any jurisdiction conferred on the Family Court of Nauru by s 44 of the Matrimonial Causes Act 1973 of Nauru. It is not entirely clear whether, as under the rule in *Travers v Holley*, it is sufficient that the foreign court exercised jurisdiction in circumstances which, mutatis mutandis, would give the Nauru court jurisdiction; or whether it must expressly or impliedly claim jurisdiction on a ground corresponding to one relied upon in Nauru.[4]

A second point of difference is that all other common law bases for recognition are excluded.[5]

Finally it is provided that

'nothing in this Act shall affect the validity of any marriage celebrated before the commencement of this Act where the capacity of either party thereto to marry was dependent upon the validity of a foreign divorce or annulment of marriage or upon the invalidity of a previous marriage, if at the time when the marriage was celebrated the foreign divorce or annulment of marriage or the invalidity of the previous foreign marriage would have been recognised in Nauru.'[6]

This has no direct counterpart in the United Kingdom.

1 No 12 of 1973.
2 Recognition of Foreign Divorces etc Act 1973 (Nauru), s 3. Cf Recognition of Divorces and Legal Separations Act 1971 (UK), s 2.
3 [1953] P 246, [1953] 2 All ER 794, CA. See paras 2.06–2.07 above.
4 See para 2.07 above.
5 Recognition of Foreign Divorces etc Act 1973 (Nauru), s 7.
6 Ibid, proviso (a). The commencement date was 1 November 1973.

CHAPTER 4

Financial Provision
The Enforcement of Maintenance

A. INTRODUCTORY

Financial provision for spouses and children

4.01 Many jurisdictions now possess comprehensive and sophisticated codes regulating the financial and property aspects of family relationships, including those involving illegitimate children. It was of course not always so; outside the divorce courts, resorted to by relatively few, the emphasis was often on enforcing the right of an innocent wife or child to such maintenance by the husband or father as would prevent the claimant becoming a 'destitute person',[1] depending upon public assistance. Courts now engage in much more elaborate assessments of the immediate and longer-term needs of all concerned parties, seeking to allocate the capital assets and income of the parties so that those changing needs are properly met.

It is beyond the scope of this book to trace the history of this development or to essay a comparative study of the powers of courts in the different Commonwealth jurisdictions. The important point is the very great variety of orders which can be made in at least some jurisdictions and which may therefore require recognition or enforcement elsewhere. This can be illustrated by reference to one piece of legislation, the Family Law Act 1975 of Australia. So far as parties to a marriage and their children are concerned this gives the courts power, inter alia,

 (i) to make any order altering the property interests of the parties, including an order requiring the making of a settlement or a transfer of property;

 (ii) to order payment of a lump sum, in one amount or by instalments;

 (iii) to order periodical payments;

 (iv) to order that payments ordered to be paid be secured in such manner as the court may direct;

 (v) to order payments in respect of a child to be made to a specified individual or public authority;

 (vi) to appoint or remove trustees;

 (vii) to make orders of a temporary or permanent nature, including orders pending the disposal of proceedings, and consent orders;

 (viii) to approve, register and enforce certain maintenance agreements; and

 (ix) to set aside or restrain the making of transactions designed to defeat the court's powers.[2]

Although affiliation orders are not directly governed by the Act, it does govern the inter-state enforcement of such orders, including not only orders for the maintenance of the 'ex-nuptial' child, but also for the maintenance of the mother of the child before and after her confinement, the payment of medical, surgical, hospital and nursing expenses of the confinement, and of funeral expenses in relation to the child or its mother.[3]

In many countries, orders may be made either in superior courts (especially in divorce cases) or in summary courts; some courts have power to make orders ancillary to foreign divorce decrees recognised under their law.[4]

1 Until quite recent times the phrase featured in the short titles of Acts dealing with maintenance in the Australian states and in New Zealand.
2 Family Law Act 1975, Pt VIII, especially ss 79, 80, 86–89.
3 Ibid, s 109.
4 Eg New Zealand: Family Proceedings Act 1980, s 70(5). A similar power is under discussion in England: Law Commission Working Paper No 77, 1980, on Financial Relief after Foreign Divorce.

Scope of the present examination

4.02 It is proposed to examine here the recognition and enforcement of those orders which can be described as 'financial', maintenance in its widest sense including the various forms of lump sum orders, but not those orders which can be described as 'property' orders, such as orders for the transfer of property or the variation of settlements. So far as property orders concern immovable property the general principles of the conflict of laws refer most questions to the lex situs and those questions seldom arise in a context of enforcement overseas. The variation of trusts and of settlements may well give rise to practical difficulties, for the English courts have asserted their power, in the divorce jurisdiction, to vary a settlement of foreign property even if the trustees are also foreign.[1] The courts have however exercised considerable restraint, refusing to contemplate the making of an order which would be ineffective in the relevant foreign jurisdiction.[2] The principles governing the variation of trusts in the conflict of laws are uncertain and ill-developed.[3]

1 *Nunneley v Nunneley and Marrian* (1890) 15 PD 186; *Forsyth v Forsyth* [1891] P 363.
2 *Goff v Goff* [1934] P 107; *Wyler v Lyons* [1963] P 274, [1963] 1 All ER 821.
3 The subject is currently under examination by the Hague Conference on Private International Law.

Aspects of the problem

4.03 If the person claiming maintenance, typically but by no means necessarily a wife, and the person from whom maintenance is claimed are at all times resident in the same jurisdiction, no recognition problem arises. The claim and any variation or enforcement procedures following the making of the original order will be wholly within the competence of a single legal system and governed by its law. Hereafter the terms 'creditor' and 'debtor' will be used so far as convenient to describe the parties; at various times and in various pieces of legislation the creditor may be described as a claimant, an applicant, a petitioner, a payee or a beneficiary, with a corresponding range of words applying to the debtor, but some uniformity may well assist the reader.

Problems begin to appear whenever creditor and debtor live, at any stage in the process, in different jurisdictions. One major group of cases involves the making of a maintenance order in Country A, where both parties were then living, and the subsequent removal of the debtor to Country B. It is plainly in the interests of justice that the creditor should be able to enforce the order he has already obtained in a competent court and should not be required to begin fresh proceedings. Accordingly procedures have developed for the *enforcement of maintenance orders* in countries other than their country of origin.

It will be appreciated that there are many factual variations within this class of case. The creditor as well as the debtor may have left Country A; they may both be living in Country B or in separate countries. The debtor may now live in Country B but may have so arranged his affairs that his assets are substantially in Country C. The links between the parties and the various relevant countries may be more or less strong; eg the country in which the maintenance order was originally obtained may have been the domicile of origin of both parties, or merely the country of residence of the debtor.

Most maintenance orders involve periodical payments, and one of their characteristics is that as the circumstances of the parties change (as children grow up, or as new partners are found) there will be pressure from either creditor or debtor for variation in the amounts to be paid, or in some cases for revocation of the order. If an order made in Country A is being enforced in Country B, each party being resident in one of those countries, difficult questions arise as to the proper forum for applications for variation or revocation, and as to the law to be applied.

A second major group of cases sees the parties living in different countries before litigation can be commenced. Typically, a wife is deserted by a husband who travels abroad before she can take any steps to obtain a maintenance order. She wishes to assert her claim to maintenance, but quite apart from the legal issues (which court or courts have jurisdiction in the circumstances and which law should govern?) a deserted wife with perhaps no sources of income faces very real practical difficulties in obtaining any effective court order. This problem, the *enforcement of maintenance claims* is more complex than that of the enforcement of an existing order; though, of course, if a claim is successfully pursued, so that an order is obtained, the issues which arise when variation or revocation is sought are common to the two types of case.

Something must be said by way of introduction as to the problems encountered in each type of case, that is in relation to the enforcement of maintenance orders and to the enforcement of maintenance claims.

Enforcement of maintenance orders

4.04   Rules for the enforcement of foreign judgments are to be found in almost all legal systems, but are primarily designed with money-judgments in mind. As Gutteridge observed in 1948

'One need not be surprised that methods designed to enforce payment of large sums of money in respect of commercial transactions have proved to be wholly unsuited to the recovery of small sums due periodically from persons resident abroad. The enforcement of maintenance orders calls for a procedure which is simple, inexpensive and rapid in its operation. The courts entrusted with the duty of enforcing foreign maintenance orders are, as a general rule, courts of inferior jurisdiction, with laymen as judges,[1] who should not be required to deal with difficult questions of private international law or to unravel the network of technicalities in which the law relating to the enforcement of foreign judgments has become entangled.'[2]

Countries both in the civil law and the common law traditions have developed rules which make it difficult to apply the usual enforcement procedures to foreign maintenance orders. In some civil law countries a judgment-creditor under a foreign judgment must apply for exequatur, an order that the judgment be made enforceable, and this procedure is not necessarily either swift or sure.[3]

As Pelichet observes, exequatur 'will not only require considerable time (an enquiry by a lawyer who deals with the exequatur proceedings in a foreign country, a possible request for legal aid, overburdening of courts, etc) but also requires courage and a certain amount of optimism on the part of the petitioner' who may well be 'not only materially destitute but ... also ... lacking in intellectual and moral resources'.[4]

A particular cause of difficulty and uncertainty is the civil law concept of ordre public. Recognition or enforcement of a foreign judgment may be denied if it offends against the ordre public of the receiving state, as is most likely to be the case where local citizens are involved. The application of the concept can be seen from a decision of the French Cour de Cassation in 1976.[5] A German court had ordered a Frenchman to make regular maintenance payments in respect of an illegitimate child of which he was held to be the father. Enforcement of this order was sought in France under the Hague Convention on the Recognition and Enforcement of Maintenance Obligations in respect of Children 1958, which allows enforcement to be refused if the order is 'manifestly' contrary to the ordre public of the receiving state. It was held that enforcement of an order based on the uncorroborated statements of the mother would be manifestly contrary to French ordre public.

In common law countries (and in some civil law jurisdictions such as Quebec[6]) the primary obstacle to the enforcement of maintenance orders under the general foreign judgments rules is the condition developed under these rules that the judgment must be 'final and conclusive'. A foreign judgment which does not finally determine the respective rights of the parties will not be enforced.[7] Although it has been argued[8] that this rule should not have been applied to maintenance orders, there is abundant authority from many jurisdictions for the proposition that where the foreign court has power to vary the amount of periodical payments under a maintenance order that order will be regarded as not being 'final and conclusive' and will not be enforced; it is only in cases where accrued arrears cannot be the subject of variation that limited enforcement of the order, in respect of those arrears, will be possible.[9] Legislation in common law jurisdictions on the enforcement of foreign judgments in general is seldom of assistance in respect of maintenance orders. In many cases maintenance orders are expressly excluded;[10] other legislation reproduces the 'final and conclusive' requirement,[11] or is limited to judgments of superior courts[12] or to judgments pronounced within the preceding 12 months.[13]

It is clear from this brief review that specific legislation is needed if the enforcement of maintenance orders is to be satisfactorily secured. Commonwealth countries enacted such legislation at an early stage, and have since developed and refined the basic legislative model.[14] Civil law countries have found it harder to reach a common mind, but much effort has secured a number of international conventions which form the basis for a comprehensive system of enforcement.[15]

---

1   Gutteridge overstates his case at this point; the lay element in the administration of justice is not as great in most other jurisdictions as in England, and he clearly had the English experience in mind.

2   H. C. Gutteridge 'The International Enforcement of Maintenance Orders' (1948) 2 ILQ 155 at 157.

3   See J. K. Grodecki 'Enforcement of Foreign Maintenance Orders: French and English Practice' (1959) 8 ICLQ 18; P. Contini 'International Enforcement of Maintenance Obligations' (1953) 41 California LR 106 at 108–109.

4   M. Pelichet 'Report on Maintenance Obligations in Respect of Adults in the Field of Private

International Law' *Actes et Documents de la 12e Session*, Hague Conference, Tome IV, p 13 at pp 48–49.

5   Cour de cassation, 18 May 1976. See Clunet 1977, 485 (noted by A. Huet). See the collection of cases in TMC Asser Instituut, *Les Nouvelles Conventions de la Haye*, vol 2, pp 90–96.

6   J.-G. Castel *Droit International Privé Québécois* pp 264–266.

7   *Nouvion v Freeman* (1889) 15 App Cas 1; see Dicey and Morris *The Conflict of Laws* (10th edn, 1980) pp 1092–1094.

8   J. K. Grodecki 'Enforcement of Foreign Maintenance Orders: French and English Practice' (1959) 8 ICLQ 18 at 34–36.

9   See para 4.11 below.

10   Eg the legislation of most, but not all, the Canadian jurisdictions based on the uniform Reciprocal Enforcement of Judgments Act.

11   Eg the Foreign Judgments (Reciprocal Enforcement) Act 1933 (UK), s 1(2) and corresponding legislation in many Commonwealth jurisdictions.

12   This is true of both the Administration of Justice Act 1920 (UK) and the Foreign Judgments (Reciprocal Enforcement) Act 1933 (UK), though not of all legislation modelled upon these Acts (eg the Canadian uniform Acts and the Foreign Judgments Act 1971, no 72, of South Australia). The 1933 Act was amended in the United Kingdom by the Civil Jurisdiction and Judgments Act 1982, Sch 9, to include judgments of specified subordinate courts.

13   So the Administration of Justice Act 1920 (UK), where the period may be extended by the receiving court; in a number of jurisdictions, again including South Australia and the Canadian jurisdictions, a period of six years has been substituted.

14   See Chapters 5 and 6.

15   See Chapter 7.

Enforcement of claims for maintenance

4.05   The position of a maintenance creditor who has been unable to obtain a maintenance order before the debtor travels abroad is full of difficulties. On the face of it, the creditor can choose whether to apply for an order in his own country or in that in which the debtor is now living; in practice both may prove virtually impossible.

Taking proceedings in the debtor's country has certain advantages. There is likely to be little difficulty in persuading the courts of that country that they have jurisdiction; and once an order is obtained—and so long as the debtor does not change his country of residence again—the difficulties in enforcing the order will be no greater than those experienced in any maintenance case. But the creditor's legal advisers will soon point to the disadvantages. It would almost certainly be necessary to employ lawyers in the debtor's country to act as agents for the creditor's own solicitors; only such agents will know the procedure to be followed and be able to advise on the law applied in their courts. It is by no means certain that legal aid will be available, either from the authorities in the creditor's country or from those in the debtor's, to finance such international litigation. If the factual basis of the creditor's claim is disputed, as it might well be in an affiliation context for example, there are further difficulties in obtaining evidence in a form acceptable to the foreign courts; the difficulties are not insurmountable but further expenditure may have to be incurred. All in all the obstacles are more than sufficient to deter a creditor who is, almost by definition, impecunious.

It is much more attractive to commence proceedings in the courts of the creditor's own country. The difficulty here is the legal one of jurisdiction; it is quite probable that the courts will not have jurisdiction over the absent debtor. So, for example, the English courts may in certain cases have jurisdiction in divorce against a respondent not resident in England provided always that the petition is duly served upon him,[1] and will be able to make financial provision orders in the divorce proceedings; but the creditor may not wish to invoke the divorce jurisdiction, and it is not always certain that the resulting order would be recognised abroad. The English magistrates' courts, the forum in which an application for maintenance would normally be made, have no jurisdiction where the debtor is abroad, so that avenue is closed.

Once again special legal machinery is needed to overcome these problems, *either* by providing machinery for the transmission of claims for maintenance to the debtor's country and for their prosecution there by an official agency at public expense, *or* by enabling the courts of the creditor's country to take jurisdiction in a way which will afford some protection to the debtor's interests and also some guarantee that any order made will be recognised abroad. Commonwealth legislation pursues the latter approach;[2] a more recent international convention the former.[3]

1 Matrimonial Causes Rules 1977, r 117(1).
2 See paras 5.12 et seq.
3 See paras 7.17 et seq.

The size of the problem

4.06 Statistical information about the number of cases in which a maintenance order or a claim for maintenance needs to be enforced in a foreign jurisdiction is not readily available. What data can be gleaned are concerned with the use made of certain existing enforcement schemes; those schemes are evidently well used and this gives some impression of the size of the problem as a whole, some cases falling, for one reason or another, outside the scope of existing procedures.

So, in the ten-year period 1967–1976, 2,395 maintenance orders made in England and Wales or Northern Ireland (including provisional orders) were sent to overseas jurisdictions; 1,418 were received for confirmation or registration having originated overseas.[1] No fewer than 66 different jurisdictions were involved, and the list[2] covers Commonwealth jurisdictions in all parts of the world, underlining the need for comprehensive coverage. Nor is this merely a reflection of the special position of the United Kingdom in terms of Commonwealth activity. In the three-year period 1971–1973, the Province of British Columbia received 1,602 orders and sent 1,102; although the great majority were from other Canadian jurisdictions or from the United States, Australia, Austria, England, Fiji, Germany, Hong Kong, Northern Ireland, New Zealand and South Africa were also represented.

1 Home Office statistics supplied to the author.
2 Antigua and Barbuda, Australia (all states and both mainland territories; this was before the Family Law Act 1975 superseded state legislation), Bahamas, Barbados, Belize, Bermuda, Botswana, Canada (all jurisdictions except Prince Edward Island, Quebec and the Yukon Territory), Cayman Islands, Cyprus, Falkland Islands, Fiji, Gambia, Ghana, Gibraltar, Gilbert and Ellice Islands (now Kiribati and Tuvalu), Guernsey, Guyana, Hong Kong, India, Jamaica, Jersey, Kenya, Lesotho, Malawi, Malaysia, Malta, Isle of Man, Mauritius, Montserrat, New Zealand, Nigeria, Papua New Guinea, St Christopher and Nevis, St Lucia, St Vincent and the Grenadines, Seychelles, Sierra Leone, Singapore, Sri Lanka, Swaziland, Tanzania, Trinidad and Tobago, Uganda, the Virgin Islands, Zambia, Zimbabwe, and also three jurisdictions now outside the Commonwealth, Aden, Pakistan and South Africa.

Order of treatment

4.07 It is not possible to deal separately with the enforcement of maintenance orders and of maintenance claims. They are interwoven in practice and in the legislative treatment they have received in the Commonwealth.

It is proposed to examine first the extent to which maintenance orders can be recognised and enforced at common law or under legislation applying generally to foreign judgments. There will then follow a full examination of the Commonwealth schemes designed specifically to deal with maintenance orders, including maintenance claims.[1] A shorter account will be given of the United States' position, as Commonwealth countries are developing reciprocal enforcement arrangements with individual states of the United States, and of the international conventions dealing with maintenance orders or maintenance claims to which Commonwealth countries are parties.[2] Finally an attempt will be made to state the geographical scope of maintenance orders legislation in the Commonwealth by means of a country by country survey.[3]

1   See Chapters 5 and 6.
2   See Chapter 7.
3   See Chapter 8.

B. ENFORCEMENT AT COMMON LAW

Enforcement of foreign maintenance orders at common law

4.08   The traditional common law procedure for enforcing a foreign judgment is an action on the judgment-debt. The plaintiff relies on the judgment and does not have to address himself once again to the original cause of action. It is, however, not every foreign judgment which will be enforced in this way; a number of conditions have to be satisfied.[1]

The first is that the foreign court should be regarded under the rules of the conflict of laws of the receiving state as having had jurisdiction. The second is that it should be 'final and conclusive'. The third is a negative condition, that the judgment should not be impeachable as being based on fraud or as being contrary to natural justice or the public policy of the receiving court.

The application of these rules in the context of maintenance orders is examined in the paragraphs which follow.

1   See generally Dicey and Morris *The Conflict of Laws* (10th edn, 1980) pp 1043–1092; Castel *Canadian Conflict of Laws* pp 419–511; Nygh *Conflict of Laws in Australia* (3rd edn, 1976) Chapter 6.

The jurisdiction requirement

4.09   An action at common law on a foreign maintenance order cannot be maintained unless the foreign court is regarded as having had jurisdiction to make it. This topic is made more complicated by the range of circumstances in which a maintenance order can be made; the order can be the subject of separate proceedings in which the creditor seeks an order for maintenance and no other relief, or it can be ancillary to other proceedings, most commonly for divorce but sometimes for nullity of marriage or a finding of paternity.[1]

The jurisdiction of a foreign court to make a maintenance order in separate proceedings is governed by the rules applying generally to jurisdiction in personam. The traditional, but increasingly misleading, starting-point for an examination of these rules is the judgment of Buckley LJ in *Emanuel v Symon*[2] where five cases are identified:

'(1) Where the defendant is a subject of the foreign country in which the judgment has been obtained.' The nationality of the defendant is not in fact a ground upon which Commonwealth courts themselves claim jurisdiction at common law, and commentators are agreed that it is very doubtful whether it can be relied upon as a basis for recognising the jurisdiction of a foreign court.[3] The case is a difficult one to apply in federal states or in other contexts in which citizenship does not identify a particular jurisdiction, as was the case under earlier Commonwealth understandings of a common 'British' nationality.[4] Early cases, containing almost always no more than dicta, favour this basis for recognition,[5] but more recent indications are to the contrary.[6]

'(2) Where [the defendant] was resident in the foreign country when the action began.' This can be regarded as the standard, uncontroversial case. The only area of uncertainty concerns its possible extension to include cases in which though not 'resident' the defendant was physically present in the foreign country. There is some authority for this extension, provided that the defendant was duly served with process.[7]

'(3) Where the defendant in the character of plaintiff has selected the forum in which he is afterwards sued.' This is again uncontroversial. An example in a maintenance context is *Burpee v Burpee*[8] where after a husband had secured a divorce by an unopposed petition in the State of Washington he was ordered to pay maintenance to his former wife; the order was held enforceable in British Columbia.

'(4) Where [the defendant] has voluntarily appeared.' The existence of this principle is undisputed, but its application in cases in which the defendant enters some form of limited or conditional appearance to contest the jurisdiction of the foreign court or to urge the foreign court to exercise its discretion not to take jurisdiction is highly controversial. The cases indicate that anything going beyond the barest protest is likely to be interpreted as amounting to a voluntary appearance.[9]

'(5) Where [the defendant] has contracted to submit himself to the forum in which the judgment was obtained.' Commercial contracts commonly contain choice-of-court clauses. There is no reason why a maintenance agreement should not do so, but that would be unusual; the parties to such an agreement are usually very anxious to avoid litigation and will specify some other form of arbitration if any provision on the point is included in the agreement.

No other basis for the recognition of jurisdiction in personam at common law has been established, though the fact of the defendant having been domiciled in the foreign country at the commencement of the action has some support in Canadian cases.[10] It is clear that the fact of process having been served out of the jurisdiction will not be a sufficient basis for the recognition of the judgment.[11]

1   See next para.
2   [1908] 1 KB 302 at 309.
3   Eg Dicey and Morris *The Conflict of Laws* (10th edn, 1980) p 1056 ('cannot ... safely be relied upon today'); Castel *Canadian Conflict of Laws* p 427 ('not yet settled ... no clear-cut decision'); Nygh *Conflict of Laws in Australia* (3rd edn, 1976) p 79 ('validity of this recognition rule is in doubt').
4   See *Warner v Fischer* [1875] 13 SCR (NSW) 346; *Dakota Lumber Co v Rinderknecht* (1905) 6 Terr LR 210; *Gavin Gibson & Co Ltd v Gibson* [1913] 3 KB 379; *Marshall v Houghton* (1922) 68 DLR 308 at 311.
5   *Douglas v Forrest* (1828) 4 Bing 686 (but see Dicey and Morris, op cit, p 1056); *Schibsby v Westenholz* (1870) LR 6 QB 155 at 161; *Fowler v Vail* (1879) 4 OAR 267 at 272; *Rousillon v Rousillon* (1880) 14 Ch D 351 at 371; *Bugbee v Clergue* (1900) 27 OAR 96 at 108 (affd 31 SCR 66); *Gavin Gibson & Co Ltd v Gibson* [1913] 3 KB 379 at 388; *Harris v Taylor* [1915] 2 KB 580 at 591; *Marshall v Houghton* (1923) 33 Man R 166; *Forsyth v Forsyth* [1948] P 125 at 132.

6   *Rainford v Newell-Roberts* [1962] IR 95; *Blohn v Desser* [1962] 2 QB 116 at 123; *Rossano v
     Manufacturers Life Insurance Co Ltd* [1963] 2 QB 352 at 382; *A-G of British Columbia v Buschkewitz*
     [1971] 3 WWR 17 at 21; *Vogel v R & A Kohnstamm Ltd* [1973] QB 133, [1971] 2 All ER 1428;
     Patterson v D'Agostino (1975) 58 DLR (3d) 63.
7   *Carrick v Hancock* (1895) 12 TLR 59; *Forbes v Simmons* (1914) 20 DLR 100.
8   [1929] 3 DLR 18.
9   *Harris v Taylor* [1915] 2 KB 580; *Kennedy v Trites* (1916) 10 WWR 412; *Henry v Geoprosco
     International* [1976] QB 726, [1975] 2 All ER 702. See Dicey and Morris, op cit, pp 1047–
     1049; Castel, op cit, pp 433–438.
10   See Castel, op cit, p 431, n 90 citing dicta in ten cases; but Castel himself appears not to
     support such a basis of recognition.
11   *Re Kenny* [1951] 2 DLR 98; *Coatham v Vetter* [1973] 1 WWR 238 (both maintenance order
     cases).

The jurisdiction requirement: ancillary orders

4.10   Maintenance orders are frequently made in the course of divorce proceedings. The question arises, given that the rules for the recognition of foreign
divorces (and of other matrimonial decrees such as those of nullity of marriage)
differ from the rules for the recognition of foreign judgments in personam,
which set of rules should apply.

The first type of case which can present itself is one in which the foreign court
is regarded as having jurisdiction in the principal matter (eg to dissolve the
marriage) but in which the in personam rules are not satisfied. For example
the divorce is pronounced on the basis of the petitioner's present or past
domicile in the forum, but the defendant has no subsisting links with that
country. The authorities are unsatisfactory. In *Phillips v Batho*,[1] Scrutton J
allowed the plaintiff to enforce by an action in England an award of damages
for adultery given against a co-respondent in divorce proceedings in India. It
was clear that the Indian court did not have jurisdiction under the usual in
personam rules, but Scrutton J said, 'The English Courts will recognize and
enforce the judgments as to status of the Indian Courts in matters within their
jurisdiction, and I think they will also recognize and enforce the ancillary
orders as to damages, such as they themselves make in similar cases.'[2] *Phillips
v Batho* is almost certainly incorrect in treating damages for adultery as ancillary
to the divorce decree,[3] but that does not necessarily invalidate the wider
proposition that an ancillary order can be recognised on the jurisdictional
grounds proper to the principal matter. The point arose in a maintenance
context in *Summers v Summers*,[4] where the decision accords with the principle of
Phillips v Batho though that case was not cited. The judgment in *Summers v
Summers* is marred, however, by a failure to distinguish clearly between two
questions, whether the English courts had jurisdiction under their own law to
entertain divorce proceedings (which they clearly had) and whether the divorce would be recognised under the Ontario conflict of laws rules (a question
the judge did not address).

Although these decisions are open to considerable criticism, and despite the
strong objections formulated by Read,[5] it is submitted that the principle of
recognising orders ancillary to a decree which is itself entitled to recognition is
a desirable one, under the general principle that recognition rules should reflect
jurisdictional practice. But the principle is not clearly established and the
Recognition of Divorces and Legal Separations Act 1971 (UK) expressly
declares that it does not require the recognition of maintenance, custody or
other ancillary orders made by the foreign court.[6]

The converse case arises when a maintenance order is made as an ancillary order in foreign divorce proceedings and the divorce (or other principal decree) is not entitled to recognition; can the ancillary order be upheld if the rules as to recognition of judgments in personam are satisfied? The point arose in *Simons v Simons*.[7] An English court refused to recognise a decree of divorce pronounced in Massachusetts at a time when the parties were resident but not domiciled in that state. It was argued that the maintenance order made in the Massachusetts proceedings was a valid judgment in personam. Goddard LJ (sitting at first instance) held that 'where a Court has assumed a jurisdiction to decree a divorce, which neither according to its own law nor according to the law of this country it had in fact jurisdiction to do, ... an order which it makes consequent on that assumption of jurisdiction, even if it is an order in personam, must suffer the same fate as the rest of the decree'.[8]

Simons v Simons has been described by Morris as 'a highly unsatisfactory decision'.[9] The criticism is that Goddard LJ assumed that the Massachusetts court ordered maintenance only because it had ordered divorce, that is it could only make a maintenance order as an ancillary order; it may have been, however, that the Massachusetts court could have ordered maintenance in separate proceedings. Morris's argument does however ignore the fact that the maintenance order was in fact made as an ancillary order; it is by no means clear that weight should be given to the possibility that a separate jurisdiction existed in Massachusetts when that jurisdiction was not invoked in the instant case. Another aspect of the reasoning in *Simons v Simons* is suspect; Goddard LJ relied upon *Papadopoulos v Papadopoulos*[10] where Hill J, speaking of a Cypriot court, said, 'Having no power to declare [a] marriage null and void, it had no power to make an order for maintenance consequential upon a decree of nullity.'[11] This dictum is clearly obiter, for in *Papadopoulos v Papadopoulos* there was no attempt to bring an action in England on a Cypriot maintenance order, for the good reason that the Cypriot court had made no such order and had instead given damages for breach of promise of marriage.

The principle applied in *Simons v Simons*, the soundness of which it is submitted survives these criticisms, that an ancillary order falls with the principal decree has been applied in two Canadian cases;[12] in neither of those cases was it argued that the order could be upheld as a valid judgment in personam.

There remains the question which orders are to be classed as ancillary orders. As has already been noted,[13] the balance of authority favours the exclusion from the category of ancillary orders of awards of damages for adultery against co-respondents. A Canadian court has taken the same view of an award of maintenance pending suit made in English divorce proceedings, holding that that phase of proceedings constituted an action in personam not ancillary to any action in rem involving status.[14]

1   [1913] 3 KB 25.
2   Ibid, at 32.
3   See *Redhead v Redhead and Crothers* [1926] NZLR 131 and *Patterson v D'Agostino* (1975) 58 DLR (3d) 63, which are inconsistent with *Phillips v Batho*; and *Jacobs v Jacobs and Ceen* [1950] P 146, where it is criticised.
4   (1958) 13 DLR (2d) 454.
5   Read *Recognition and Enforcement of Foreign Judgments* pp 262–268.
6   S 8(3).
7   [1939] 1 KB 490, [1938] 4 All ER 436.
8   Ibid, at 496.
9   (1952) 29 BYIL 283 at 307.
10   [1930] P 55.
11   Ibid, at 69.
12   *Re Ducharme v Ducharme* (1963) 39 DLR (2d) 1; *Re Needham v Needham* (1964) 43 DLR (2d)

405. 'If decree or primary stock was not viable then the shoot grafted to it would die with it': *Gwyn v Mellen* (1978) 90 DLR (3d) 195 at 202 per McKenzie J (see n 14 below).
13   Para 2.16 above.
14   *Gwyn v Mellen* (1978) 90 DLR (3d) 195 (affd, on grounds not affecting this point (1979) 101 DLR (3d) 608).

The 'final and conclusive' requirement

4.11   No action at common law on a foreign judgment will succeed unless the court is satisfied that the judgment is 'final and conclusive' in respect of the sums claimed. As Dicey and Morris observes,[1] the expression is repetitive; only a single test is imposed.

The leading case applying this test to maintenance orders is *Harrop v Harrop*.[2] A wife sought to enforce in England, by an action on a judgment of the Judicial Commissioner of Perak, arrears due in respect of five monthly payments of maintenance. She failed, Sankey J holding that the Perak judgment, being capable of variation in subsequent proceedings in the Perak court, was not final and conclusive. He based himself on *Nouvion v Freeman*,[3] which was not a maintenance case but one involving a Spanish 'remate' judgment in civil proceedings, where Lord Watson had said that English courts would not give effect to a foreign judgment 'which is liable to be abrogated or varied by the same Court which issued it'.[4] Sankey J held that an order could not be said to be final and conclusive if '(1) an order has to be obtained for its enforcement,[5] and (2) on application for such an order the original judgment is liable to be abrogated or varied'.[6]

A learned commentator[7] has argued with some justification that the opinions in *Nouvion v Freeman* were being quoted out of context, but that scarcely justifies his conclusion that *Harrop v Harrop*[8] is 'of dubious authority'. The case has been cited without criticism in a score of cases, and Sankey J does advance a sound reason of policy for applying the principle in a maintenance orders context: 'to give effect to the order in this country would enable the plaintiff to obtain in this country a greater benefit from it than she could obtain from it in Perak, for here the defendant is not entitled to take the point that there is a change of circumstances which is open to him [under the Perak Enactment]'.[9] The importance of this point is clear from the way in which the law has developed in some United States jurisdictions, where the matter is much affected by the 'full faith and credit' principle. Those American courts which have held it possible at common law to enforce 'retroactively modifiable decrees for alimony and support' from another jurisdiction have insisted that the defendant must be allowed to advance, in the state in which enforcement is sought, any mitigating defences which would be available to him under the law of the original forum.[10] Such a development would not be open to courts in most Commonwealth jurisdictions, where it would be seen as reopening the merits in an unacceptable way.

Within a matter of months *Harrop v Harrop* was followed in England[11] and (without being aware of the English cases) the Appellate Division of the Supreme Court of Alberta had reached the same conclusion in *Maguire v Maguire*.[12] In that case an action in Alberta for arrears under a Minnesota judgment for alimony failed as the amount of payments, past as well as future, was variable by further order of the Minnesota court, and despite a vigorous dissent from Meredith CJCP who relied on the fact that all the circumstances of the parties, who were both now resident in Alberta, made it virtually certain that no variation would be ordered.[13]

A formidable number of subsequent decisions have accepted the principle in *Harrop v Harrop* that a maintenance order variable retrospectively by further order of the original court is not final and conclusive.[14] Limits to the principle were set by the English Court of Appeal in *Beatty v Beatty*.[15] An action was brought on a New York alimony order. Under the law of New York, the court could vary the amounts of future payments but could not interfere with accrued instalments. It was argued by counsel for the defendants that to be final and conclusive a judgment had to be invariable in all respects, but this argument was firmly rejected; the existence of the rule that the possibility or actual pendency of an appeal does not render a judgment other than final and conclusive demonstrated that such an extensive argument was untenable. Accordingly the New York order was enforceable in the sense that an action in respect of payments which had already fallen due could be maintained.

This conclusion accorded with a number of earlier Australian and Canadian decisions, none of which were actually cited in *Beatty v Beatty*, in which arrears of alimony due under a foreign order had been held enforceable, in cases where it appeared that the arrears could not be affected by subsequent variation.[16] The same principle has been widely applied in all types of maintenance cases,[17] included cases in which a lump sum judgment has consolidated arrears[18] and in which the making of the original order by consent has been regarded (the principle being stretched to its limits) as giving the order a finality it might otherwise lack.[19]

In those Commonwealth jurisdictions which allow retrospective variation of their own orders, the plaintiff who wishes to establish that a foreign maintenance order is final and conclusive will have the burden of proving that the foreign law on the point is different from that of the forum.[20] In jurisdictions which do not themselves have retrospective variation the judgment will probably be assumed to be final and conclusive, at least on this point, unless the defendant raises the issue;[21] the plaintiff would then still have the burden of proving that the judgment met all the conditions for enforceability.

1 Dicey and Morris *The Conflict of Laws* (10th edn, 1980) p 1094. See generally pp 1094–1096.
2 [1920] 3 KB 386.
3 (1889) 15 App Cas 1.
4 Ibid, at 13.
5 The status of this first element in Sankey J's rule is unclear. The point has seldom arisen in subsequent cases, but see *Martin (otherwise Ellington) v Trofimuk (Martin Estate)* (1960) 32 WWR 520 where the fact that a Californian support order could not be enforced there without an application to the court by the creditor was held to bar enforcement in Alberta.
6 [1920] 3 KB 386 at 399. He also relied on *De Brimont v Penniman* (1873) 10 Blatch 436, a case roundly criticised in Grodecki 'Enforcement of Foreign Maintenance Orders: English and French Practice' (1959) 8 ICLQ 18 at 31.
7 Grodecki, op cit, at 35–36.
8 And also *Re Macartney, Macfarlane v Macartney* [1921] 1 Ch 522.
9 [1920] 3 KB 386 at 401. Note that this point depends upon the international nature of the case. Many authorities sometimes cited in this connection deal with the wholly different question whether an order for alimony or maintenance creates a debt enforceable by an action at law in the *same* jurisdiction: eg *Bailey v Bailey* (1884) 13 QBD 855; *Keys v Keys* [1919] 2 IR 160; *Jachowicz v Bate* (1958) 14 DLR (2d) 99; *Kergan v Kergan* (1964) 49 DLR (2d) 280.
10 See *Worthley v Worthley* 283 P 19 (Cal 1955) and the authorities and literature there cited.
11 *Re Macartney, Macfarlane v Macartney* [1921] 1 Ch 522 (posthumous affiliation order in Malta, variable from time to time according to circumstances of child).
12 (1921) 64 DLR 180.
13 'It is not enough to say that, though substantially impossible, [variation] is in a technical sense legally possible; one might as well, out of the law courts, base an argument in favour of substantial worldly advantage on the ground that the moon may be made of green cheese': (1921) 64 DLR 180 at 187.

14   *M'Donnell v M'Donnell* [1921] 2 IR 148; *Davis v Davis* (1922) SR (NSW) 185; *Smith v Smith*
     [1923] 2 DLR 896; *McIntosh v McIntosh* [1942] 4 DLR 70; *Estate H v Estate H* 1952 (4) SA 168;
     Re The Maintenance Orders Enforcement Ordinance, Re Antrobus (a debtor) (1954) 27 KLR 94; *Ashley
     v Gladden* [1954] 4 DLR 848; *Smith v Smith* [1955] 1 DLR 229; *Re Hunter (a debtor)* (1955) 28
     KLR 120; *Beddell v Hartmann* [1956] BR 157; *Re Paslowski v Paslowski* (1957) 11 DLR (2d)
     180; *Webb v Murray, ex p Murray* (1962) ALR (Malawi) 205; *Hirschowitz v Hirschowitz* 1965 (3)
     SA 407; *Ruck v Ruck* (1980) 11 Alta LR (2d) 397.
15   [1924] 1 KB 807.
16   *Splatt v Splatt* (1889) 10 LR (NSW) 227; *Swaizie v Swaizie* (1899) 31 OR 324; *Robertson v
     Robertson* (1908) 16 OLR 170; *Wood v Wood* (1916) 28 DLR 367.
17   *Meyers v Meyers* [1935] OWN 547; *Ellenberger v Robins* (1940) 78 CS 1; *Patton v Reed* (1972) 30
     DLR (3d) 494; *Lear v Lear* (1974) 51 DLR (3d) 56; *McLean v McLean* [1979] 1 NSWLR 620;
     Stark v Stark (1978) 94 DLR (3d) 556.
18   *Burpee v Burpee* [1929] 3 DLR 18 (semble, the facts being ill-reported).
19   *Hadden v Hadden* (1898) 6 BCR 340 (see *Maguire v Maguire* (1921) 64 DLR 180).
20   See *Lear v Lear* (1974) 51 DLR (3d) 56; *Smith v Smith* [1955] 1 DLR 229; *Ruck v Ruck* (1980) 11
     Alta LR (2d) 397.
21   Cf *Smith v Smith* [1923] 2 DLR 896.

Impeachment of foreign orders: public policy

4.12   An action at common law on a foreign judgment will fail if the judgment
is 'impeachable' on certain grounds. Two of those grounds, that the judgment
was obtained by fraud or in proceedings which were contrary to natural justice,
depend on principles of importance in respect of foreign judgments generally
and full treatment is beyond the scope of the present work.[1] The third ground,
that enforcement would be contrary to the public policy of the country in
which it is sought, has been discussed in a family judgments context and is
therefore examined here. It constitutes the common law equivalent of the ordre
public principle,[2] but has a much narrower effect.

A broad, and it is submitted unacceptably broad, formulation appeared in
early editions of Dicey's textbook: 'An action (semble) cannot be maintained
on a valid foreign judgment if the cause of action in respect of which the
judgment was obtained was of such a character that it would not have supported an action in England.'[3] This rule was cited and approved by Astbury J
in *Re Macartney, Macfarlane v Macartney*.[4] However as the judgment makes clear,
the point did not really arise in view of Astbury J's decision on other points in
the case,[5] and the point is discussed only by citation from an early New York
case, *De Brimont v Penniman*,[6] in which an action on a French judgment ordering
support of a husband by his wife's parents was dismissed. Although the New
York court noted that the French judgment was 'not in conformity with our
laws' it seems to be clear that the objections to it were on more general grounds
of public policy, and a wish to protect American citizens from incurring, by
imprudent marriages, burdens under French laws which were seen as properly
having domestic and not extra-territorial effect.

The same broad principle was adopted in the Supreme Court of the Irish
Republic in *Mayo-Perrott v Mayo-Perrott*.[7] The court held that an order for costs
in an English divorce decree could not be enforced by an action in Ireland.
Irish public policy as expressed in article 41 of the Constitution disapproved of
divorce; to enforce the order for costs, which could not be treated as severable
from the divorce decree, would be to assist in carrying out something wholly
rejected by the public policy of the state. Maguire CJ quoted the former Dicey
rule (without attribution),[8] and other members of the court noted that comparable proceedings could not be instituted in Ireland.

This broad principle has been criticised (obiter) in a subsequent English case. In *Phrantzes v Argenti*[9] Lord Parker CJ cited with approval from the New York decision *Loucks v Standard Oil Co of New York*:[10] 'Our own scheme of legislation may be different. We may even have no legislation on the subject. That is not enough to show that public policy forbids us to enforce the foreign right.' It was rejected in a maintenance context in the Ontario case of *Burchell v Burchell*.[11] A court in Ohio having granted a divorce awarded the husband alimony; he sought to enforce this order in Ontario and was successful despite an argument that no such order could have been made in the Ontario courts.

All the cases cited in this paragraph can be regarded as authority for the existence of a narrower public policy principle. If a foreign judgment substantially offends the public policy of the receiving state, enforcement may be refused. In *Re Macartney*[4] the right to maintenance of an illegitimate child, even beyond the age of majority, out of the estate of the putative father was held to be contrary to the established policy of England. In *De Brimont v Penniman*[6] an obligation to support a son-in-law was similarly treated as contrary to the public policy of New York. The constitutional guarantees for marriage were the basis of the decision in *Mayo-Perrott v Mayo-Perrott*.[7] *Burchell v Burchell*[11] contains no denial of the existence of a public policy rule, which was also recognised (though held inapplicable on the facts) in the New Zealand case of *Connor v Connor*.[12] In that case an order for costs made in a Victorian divorce case was held registrable under New Zealand money-judgments recognition legislation despite the fact that the creditor was in receipt of legal aid in Victoria.

It is clear therefore that foreign maintenance orders may be impeached on public policy grounds. Unfortunately the scope of public policy is notoriously unclear, and it may be that it decreases as courts come to have greater understanding of the principles underlying foreign legal decisions.

1   See Dicey and Morris *The Conflict of Laws* (10th edn, 1980) pp 1081–1086, 1088–1092.
2   See para 4.04 above.
3   Dicey (2nd edn) p 414.
4   [1921] 1 Ch 522.
5   Ibid, at 528.
6   (1873) 10 Blatch 436.
7   [1958] IR 336.
8   Ibid, at 342.
9   [1960] 2 QB 19 at 31–34.
10 224 NY 99 (1918) per Cardozo J.
11 [1926] 2 DLR 595.
12 [1974] 1 NZLR 632.

C. ENFORCEMENT AS A MONEY-JUDGMENT

Enforcement of foreign maintenance orders under foreign judgments legislation: 1920 model

4.13   Almost all Commonwealth jurisdictions have legislation for the reciprocal enforcement of foreign judgments. This legislation supplements, and in some cases replaces,[1] the common law action on the foreign judgment-debt. It was designed to deal primarily with the enforcement of money-judgments in civil and commercial matters rather than with maintenance orders, but in

some circumstances may be (and in practice sometimes is) used as an alternative means of enforcing a foreign maintenance order. A full examination of the
legislation is beyond the scope of this volume;[2] it is proposed here to draw
attention only to those features of the various legislative models found in the
Commonwealth which are particularly relevant to their possible use in a
maintenance context.

One legislative model is based upon the Administration of Justice Act 1920[3]
of the United Kingdom. It has been adopted in a large number of jurisdictions
and its influence can also be seen in the legislation in force in South Australia[4]
and in the several successive versions of a uniform Act prepared by the
Conference of Commissioners on Uniformity of Legislation in Canada and
adopted with some modifications in the common law jurisdictions of Canada.[5]

The original 1920 model, but not the South Australian and Canadian
derivatives, is limited to judgments obtained in 'superior' courts.[6] This does of
course immediately preclude its use in respect of maintenance or other orders
made in inferior or summary courts. The provisions as to the jurisdiction of the
foreign court substantially reflect the common law rules, except that there is a
reference to the debtor being 'ordinarily resident' and not merely resident in
the country of origin;[7] as no minimum period of residence is prescribed, this
distinction is not likely to be of practical significance.

The 1920 model does not, however, contain any provision corresponding to
the 'final and conclusive' requirement found at common law. It does prohibit
registration of a foreign judgment where the debtor satisfies the registering
court either than an appeal is pending or that he is entitled and intends to
appeal;[8] but an application for variation is not the same as an appeal. The
Canadian Uniform Act contains a provision barring registration where 'the
judgment debtor would have a good defence if an action were brought on the
original judgment', and this clearly applies the 'final and conclusive' requirement[9] so as to render variable maintenance orders unregistrable.[10]

The public policy principle is expressly adopted in the 1920 model legislation
in a broadly drafted provision: 'No judgment shall be ordered to be registered
if ... the judgment was in respect of a cause of action which for reasons of
public policy or for some other similar reason could not have been entertained
by the registering court.'[11] An unsuccessful attempt to rely on this provision in
a maintenance context is reported in *Re Reciprocal Enforcement of Judgments Act,
Mackowey v Mackowey*,[12] on the identical provision in the British Columbia
legislation. It was argued that a judgment granted in Alberta in respect of
arrears due under a maintenance agreement should not be enforced in British
Columbia in view of the express provision in the agreement against the bringing
of claims against the husband. As such a judgment could have been obtained
in British Columbia itself there was no ground for refusing registration to the
Alberta judgment.

The current text of the Canadian Uniform Reciprocal Enforcement of
Judgments Act expressly excludes orders for alimony or maintenance and
affiliation orders. This particular exclusion is, however, omitted in the Act as
in force in the Provinces of New Brunswick, Ontario and Saskatchewan.

The 1920 model legislation only applies to judgments granted in the courts
of countries designated as reciprocating countries for the purpose.[13]

---

1   See Foreign Judgments (Reciprocal Enforcement) Act 1933 (UK), s6 (foreign judgments
     which can be registered under the Act not to be enforceable otherwise) and corresponding
     provisions in jurisdictions using the 1933 model.

2 See a later volume in this series by Professor K. W. Patchett.
3 10 & 11 Geo 5, c 81, Part II.
4 Foreign Judgments Act 1971, No 72 (South Australia).
5 See Castel *Canadian Conflict of Laws* pp 535–557; K. Nadelmann 'Enforcement of Foreign Judgments in Canada' (1960) 38 CBR 68. The provinces of New Brunswick and Saskatchewan have also adopted a Foreign Judgments Act prepared by the Commissioners in 1933 which in effect codifies the conditions upon which an action can be brought upon a foreign judgment.
6 Administration of Justice Act 1920 (UK), s 9(1).
7 Ibid, s 9(2)(b).
8 Ibid, s 9(2)(e).
9 *Re Guildhall Insurance Co and Jackson* (1968) 69 DLR (2d) 137.
10 Note the citation of *Smith v Smith* [1955] 1 DLR 229 (action at common law) in *Re Reciprocal Enforcement of Judgments Act, Mackowey v Mackowey* (1954) 14 WWR 190 at 191.
11 Administration of Justice Act 1920 (UK), s 9(2)(f).
12 (1954) 14 WWR 190.
13 Administration of Justice Act 1920 (UK), s 14.

Enforcement of foreign maintenance orders under foreign judgments legislation: 1933 model

4.14 The other principal model for legislation providing for the reciprocal enforcement of judgments in the Commonwealth is that based upon the Foreign Judgments (Reciprocal Enforcement) Act 1933[1] of the United Kingdom, which is capable of application to judgments granted in non-Commonwealth as well as Commonwealth countries.[2]

In its original form the 1933 Act, like its 1920 forerunner, was applicable only to judgments of 'superior courts'.[3] In the United Kingdom, legislation has recently removed this limitation,[4] but where it survives it clearly limits the potential use of the Act in a maintenance context quite drastically. A further limitation arises from the requirement that orders made under the Act must specify not only the country concerned but also the particular courts of that country whose judgments are within the Act's scope. So, for example, the United Kingdom in 1955 applied the legislation to the Australian Capital Territory and specified the Supreme Court of the Territory.[5] That court then exercised a jurisdiction in matrimonial causes which it has now lost; the jurisdiction is now exercised by the Family Court of Australia to which the United Kingdom Act does not apply even if it is sitting in the Capital Territory.

As in the 1920 model, the provisions as to the jurisdiction of the foreign court closely follow the common law rules.[6] The public policy principle is more narrowly stated, however: registration will only be set aside if the registering court is satisfied 'that the enforcement of the judgment would be contrary to public policy in the country' of that court.[7]

The 1933 model, unlike its predecessor, expressly requires that to be registrable an order must be 'final and conclusive as between the parties',[8] and as at common law this excludes all those maintenance orders capable of full variation by the court of origin. Accordingly, the model in its original form can only apply, in the present context, to a maintenance order made by a superior court (normally in a divorce jurisdiction) which cannot be varied and was made in circumstances which would give the court jurisdiction in personam over the defendant. Should these conditions be satisfied, which is most unlikely, so that registration under the Act is possible, no other form of enforcement proceedings can be taken.[9]

1   23 & 24 Geo 5, c 13.
2   S 1(1): 'any foreign country'.
3   Ibid.
4   Civil Jurisdiction and Judgment Act, Sch 9.
5   Reciprocal Enforcement of Judgments (Australian Capital Territory) Order 1955, SI 1955/559.
6   Foreign Judgments (Reciprocal Enforcement) Act 1933 (UK), s 4(2).
7   Ibid, s 4(1)(a)(v).
8   Ibid, s 1(2)(a).
9   Ibid, s 6.

CHAPTER 5

The Commonwealth Maintenance Orders Scheme

Early initiatives

5.01 The problem of enforcing maintenance orders or rights to maintenance against absent defendants is most likely to emerge in federal or composite states or other areas within which there is considerable movement of population. So in the United Kingdom the Summary Jurisdiction (Process) Act 1881[1] went some way towards a solution by providing for the service and execution in Scotland of process issued out of courts of summary jurisdiction in England and vice versa. In South Africa, provisions were enacted in the four colonies existing before the creation of the Union of South Africa dealing specifically with the enforcement of maintenance orders; in Cape Colony and Natal the legislation conferred powers to enforce orders from other South African colonies only, but that in Transvaal and the Orange Free State enabled the Government to proclaim reciprocal regulations extending to 'any part of Her Majesty's Dominions' which had corresponding legislation; no use was made of this power.[2]

The most significant initiative came, however, from New Zealand which negotiated reciprocal arrangements with the Australian states in 1910.[3] The scheme applied to maintenance orders including affiliation orders; it provided for the enforcement of orders made abroad (the New Zealand Act referring to orders 'made in any part of the Commonwealth of Australia, or elsewhere out of New Zealand'[4]), and for the making of orders in the local forum ex parte against absent defendants.

1 44 & 45 Vict, c 24.
2 See the intervention of Mr Malan at the Imperial Conference of 1911 (*Minutes*, Cd 5745, pp 208–209).
3 For a full account see Diane C. Dzwiekowski 'The Reciprocal Enforcement of Affiliation Orders', 22 RFL 29, pp 41 et seq. The resulting legislation was the Destitute Persons Act 1910, No 38 (New Zealand); the Interstate Destitute Persons Relief Act 1910, No 1008 (Tasmania); the Interstate Destitute Persons Relief Act 1912, No 2401 (Victoria); the Interstate Destitute Persons Relief Act 1912, No 30 (Western Australia); the Interstate Destitute Persons Relief Act 1914, No 9 (Queensland); and the Interstate Destitute Persons Relief Act 1919, No 33 (New South Wales).
4 Destitute Persons Act 1910 (NZ), s 80(1).

The Imperial Conference 1911

5.02 Having taken legislative action itself, New Zealand placed the matter on the agenda of the Imperial Conference 1911, proposing 'that in order to relieve both wives and children and the poor relief burdens of the United Kingdom and her dependencies, reciprocal provisions should be made throughout the constituent parts of the Empire with respect to destitute and deserted persons'. In accordance with the procedures of the Conference, papers were produced by the interested departments of the 'Home Government'. Their tone was unenthusiastic.

The fullest paper was a memorandum by the Local Government Board, England. It contained the germ of the idea which was later to be the basis of the Commonwealth scheme:

'It would be necessary to adopt and to obtain legislative sanction for a principle, hitherto unrecognised here, of allowing orders to be made against a defendant, not merely in his absence, but without proof that the proceedings had been brought to his notice. If an order were thus obtained, it would probably be considered that it should be regarded as provisional, and that if and when the whereabouts of the fugitive was ascertained, it might be transmitted thither for enforcement upon giving the defendant notice of the order, whereupon he would have an opportunity of appealing to a court of the country where he was resident.'[1]

Although recognising the equitable justification for such a procedure, the Board was hostile: a defendant might 'be placed at a considerable disadvantage in presenting what might be a complete defence'; 'grave hardship might be inflicted if the suggested procedure were extended so as to embrace proceedings in bastardy matters', an extension which was 'on many grounds' undesirable; and it was questionable on administrative grounds whether 'the advantage to be gained would be at all commensurate with the cost'.[2] The Local Government Board, Ireland, expressly agreed with these conclusions,[3] and the Home Office in a memorandum of a single paragraph doubted the practical utility of the proposals and commented on the serious risk of injustice and of disproportionate expenditure.[4]

The Local Government Board, Scotland, took a quite different view. They had consulted their Inspectors of Poor who reported that the problem was real, and of increasing size, and unanimously supported the idea of a change in the law, especially believing that it would have a deterrent effect. The Board would include bastardy cases, at least where paternity had been established or admitted before the father travelled abroad. The procedural ideas of the Board were equally independent; they discussed a 'quasi-criminal procedure', the colonial authorities in effect enforcing payments under threat of deportation or extradition.[5]

It is surprising in view of the history of the matter in his own country that in the first sentence of his speech at the Conference, Dr Findlay for New Zealand disclaimed any suggestion that affiliation orders should be included. If this was a tactical manoeuvre, it was successful, for there was general support for the proposal, Mr Malan of South Africa suggesting a circular to the different dominions to elicit responses to outlined legislation. The United Kingdom's spokesman, Mr Burns, summarised the hostile views in the memoranda but, perhaps sensing the mood of the meeting, suggested that the matter be remitted to the law officers of the various governments with a view to proceeding as Mr Malan had proposed. He advanced the view that desertion would have to be made a deportable offence, but did not press this view in the face of Dr Findlay's renewed explanation of the Australasian procedure.

With some verbal adjustment the proposal was adopted, the Chairman saying that 'it is quite clear that we ought to have further inquiry into this matter'.[6]

1   *Imperial Conference 1911: Papers Laid Before the Conference* (Cd 5746-1) p 224.
2   Ibid, p 225.
3   Ibid, p 226.
4   Ibid, p 228.
5   Ibid, pp 227-228.
6   For the debate see *Imperial Conference 1911: Minutes* (Cd 5745) pp 206-211.

Draft legislation

5.03 The 'further inquiry' took the form of an Interdepartmental Conference held at the Colonial Office on 20 March 1912 under the chairmanship of Sir Hartmann Just.[1] It appeared to be accepted on all sides that a positive response had to be made to the Imperial Conference resolution;[2] the representative of the Local Government Board for Scotland[3] indicated the size of the problem by reporting that in the previous year there were 122 cases in Glasgow in which it was known that husbands had gone to the dominions and had deserted their wives and families, leaving them to become chargeable to the Poor Law authorities.

The Conference examined first those cases in which a final order had been made in the United Kingdom before the defendant left the jurisdiction. It was agreed that there was no objection to making these enforceable in other jurisdictions by analogy with the Judgments Extension Act 1868, provided 'of course' that there was reciprocity, the reciprocating countries being designated by Order-in-Council.

On the second class of case, where the defendant left before an order could be obtained against him, Mr H. C. Biron, a police magistrate, took up and developed the suggestion made to the Imperial Conference:

'It might be possible to adopt the plan of making in the Courts of this country provisional orders for maintenance on the application of a deserted wife, which orders should become effective on being confirmed by the Courts in the Colonies. The procedure would, roughly speaking, be that the wife should apply to the Court for an order and should be granted that order if she made out a prima facie case; the whole record would then be submitted to the Court in the Dominion within whose jurisdiction the defendant was resident, and that Court should then confirm the order if it thought fit to do so or hear the defences which might be alleged by the husband.'[4]

With the added possibility of a remission of the case for the taking of further evidence,[5] the suggestion was adopted.

The first draft Bill included affiliation orders[6] and in other respects gave effect to the decisions of the Interdepartmental Conference. It went through a number of drafts and favourable comments were received from all the overseas governments concerned, except for some of the Canadian provinces.[7]

The 1914-1918 War both delayed legislation and made the problem more acute. In 1919 there was concerted pressure upon the Colonial Office from Boards of Guardians (ie, the bodies responsible for administering the Poor Law) in England, 30 of which petitioned 'that a court should be established in this country and in each of the British Colonies to consider matrimonial causes in which one of the parties is resident in another part of the Empire and that the authority of such courts should be enforceable in all parts of the Empire'.[8] It was in response to this pressure that a new version of the draft Bill, omitting affiliation orders, was enacted in the United Kingdom as the Maintenance Orders (Facilities for Enforcement) Act 1920[9] and circulated to other jurisdictions with a request that corresponding legislation be enacted locally.[10]

1   The record of this conference is the first item in a collection of 'Correspondence relating to the draft Maintenance Orders (Facilities for Enforcement) Bill', Public Record Office, London, class CO 886 7 (Dominions 57). The departments represented were the Home and Colonial Offices and the Local Government Boards for England and Scotland.

2   'It was ... agreed by all the members of the Conference that the procedure proposed was open to considerable objection, but that if the object of the Imperial Conference was to be carried out, it was, in their opinion, the least objectionable that could be devised.'

3   Mr E. F. Macpherson.

4   Page 5 of the collected Correspondence.
5   On the analogy of s 5 of the Extradition Act 1873 (36 & 37 Vict, c 60).
6   Circulated to interested departments 28 April 1913; no 8 in the collected Correspondence.
    The affiliation orders question was not discussed at the Interdepartmental Conference.
7   Probably Ontario and Quebec, but this is not clear from the published records. Cf Diane C.
    Dzwiekowski 'Reciprocal Enforcement of Affiliation Orders' 22 RFL 29 at 65 (n 28).
8   See 39 HL Official Report (5th series) cols 513–514.
9   10 & 11 Geo 5, c 33 (16 August 1920), reproduced in Appendix C.
10 General Circular CO 47330/20 dated 8 October 1920.

The 1920 model and its development

5.04   Legislation based on the model of the Maintenance Orders (Facilities for Enforcement) Act 1920 of the United Kingdom was rapidly enacted in almost all overseas jurisdictions to which it was circulated. That legislation remains in force in a large number of jurisdictions, often with only very minor amendments reflecting constitutional changes, developments in the judicial or administrative structure, or the process of preparing successive editions of Revised Laws.

In a few jurisdictions, experience in operating the legislation prompted steps to develop and refine the original text. This was the case in Australian jurisdictions (including Papua New Guinea, then a territory of Australia) which in 1964 and the immediately following years introduced substantially uniform Acts incorporating a number of refinements and an improved system of enforcement via an official known as 'the Collector of Maintenance'.[1] This Australian experience was drawn on by the United Kingdom draftsman in preparing the Act which is the basis of 'the 1972 model', the Maintenance Orders (Reciprocal Enforcement) Act 1972, which is considered in detail below.[2] The Australian state Acts have all now been superseded by the Family Law Act 1975, a federal Act, which incorporates many of their features. It departs so substantially (perhaps more in drafting and presentation than in its practical effect) from the other Commonwealth models that it too is separately examined below.[3]

A rather similar pattern of development occurred in New Zealand. The original 1921 statute was replaced by a new version with substantial improvements in 1963;[4] further changes were made in 1968[5] and the current statute dates only from 1980.[6] It also requires separate treatment.[7]

The most interesting, and in some ways surprising, developments occurred in Canada. None of the Canadian jurisdictions (including Newfoundland, then separate) took action to adopt the 1920 model. Although the matter was briefly mentioned at a number of conferences of the Commissioners on the Uniformity of Legislation in Canada,[8] it was only after the 1939–45 War that British Columbia, Manitoba and Saskatchewan each enacted legislation closely following the 1920 model; their text was adopted by the Commissioners at their 1946 Conference.[9]

Since 1946 great interest has been taken in Canada in the maintenance orders legislation. The original model has been repeatedly adjusted by the Commissioners, who adopted amendments to their recommended texts in 1956, 1958, 1963, 1970, 1973 and 1979.[10] There has been a remarkable volume of case law, which has in turn stimulated the production of commentaries in the legal literature.[11] Because the Uniform Act remains identifiably a development of the 1920 model, much of the case law is directly relevant in those jurisdictions retaining the original text; for this reason Canadian developments are taken into account in the main examination of the 1920 model which follows.

1   For an account of the special features of this State legislation, see J. D. McClean and K. W. Patchett *Preliminary Report on the Reciprocal Enforcement of Judgments within the Commonwealth* (1975), para 109–115.
2   See paras 6.18–6.26 below.
3   See paras 6.09–6.17 below.
4   Destitute Persons Amendment Act 1963, No 63 (NZ).
5   Domestic Proceedings Act 1968, No 62 (NZ), Part VIII.
6   Family Proceedings Act 1980, No 94 (NZ), Part VIII.
7   See paras 6.01–6.08 below.
8   See the Commissioners' *Proceedings* for 1921, p 18; for 1924, p 15; for 1928, p 17; for 1929, p 12; for 1945, p 24; and Diane C. Dzwiekowski 'The Reciprocal Enforcement of Affiliation Orders', 22 RFL 29 at pp 48–49.
9   For the text see the Commissioners' *Proceedings* for 1946, p 69.
10 The texts are in the *Proceedings* as follows: 1956, p 89; 1958, p 97; 1963, p 127; 1970, p 340; 1973, p 347; 1979, p 216; the last, current, text, also appearing in the collected edition of current Uniform Acts, is reproduced in Appendix C.
11 Notably D. Mendes da Costa 'Enforcement of Judgments and Orders across Canada', Canadian Bar Association Continuing Education Seminars, 1974, which also examines the difficult question of the relationship between the (federal) Divorce Act and the (provincial) maintenance orders statutes.

Scope of the 1920 model: 'maintenance orders'

5.05   The legislation prepared in 1920 is drafted with the emphasis on the procedures which were to be made available. Some major policy decisions, as to the scope of the new procedures in terms of the types of order to which they might apply and as to choice-of-law questions, are reflected in the interpretation section. In its original form this includes the following provisions:

'the expression "maintenance order" means an order other than an order of affiliation for the periodical payment of sums of money towards the maintenance of the wife or other dependants[1] of the person against whom the order is made, and the expression "dependants" means such persons as that person is, according to the law in force in the part of His Majesty's dominions in which the maintenance order was made, liable to maintain.'[2]

Some reference has already been made to the exclusion of affiliation orders from consideration at the Imperial Conference;[3] it requires further treatment when the various Commonwealth legislative models have been examined.[4]

A central feature of the definition is its limitation to cases where periodical payments of sums of money are ordered. Lump sum orders, settlements of property and other types of financial provision are excluded.[5] Orders in respect of hospital and funeral expenses, even if payable by instalments and so capable of being treated as 'periodical payments', will be excluded as not being 'towards the maintenance' of the creditor, unless some hospital bills could be treated as at least in part in respect of maintenance expenses.

The category of eligible 'dependants' is defined by reference to the law in force where the maintenance order was made.[6] This is an important rule. It operates as a choice-of-law rule, making it clearly irrelevant whether the jurisdiction in which enforcement is sought would include the creditor in its own category of 'dependants'. So, for example, an order in favour of grandparents, or step-children, or foster-children, or a mother-in-law would all be included so long as a duty of support existed in the country where the order was first obtained. The Act does not say in so many words that the decision of the court as to the existence of this duty under its own law is conclusive. So, to the extent that it is possible to challenge a maintenance order presented for registration and enforcement,[7] a court could perhaps review the question whether the creditor really was qualified under the relevant law. Such an argument was advanced and considered (and rejected on the merits) in *Harris v Harris*,[8] but the context there was the confirmation of an overseas provisional order.

It could be argued that, unlike 'dependants', the term 'wife' is undefined, so that the question whether the creditor was entitled to be treated as a 'wife' might be determined in accordance with the conflict of laws rules of the forum, which might lead to the application of a law other than that of the country making the original order. This argument can be met in a number of ways:

(i) At a practical level, it is difficult to imagine cases where anything would turn on the point. It is, for example, arguable that 'wife' does not include 'ex-wife', so that orders made after a divorce, or at least after a decree absolute, are not covered. This argument was advanced in the Nigerian case of *Foley v Foley*,[9] but rejected on the ground that the order made in favour of an ex-wife existed because she *was* a wife at an earlier date. The Law of Marriage Act 1971 of Tanzania meets this argument by referring to 'the wife or former wife or husband or former husband',[10] and a Canadian definition considered below speaks of a 'former wife or reputed wife' (the scope of the required 'repute' being sadly unclear). However, nothing turns on any of this; if the creditor is not a 'wife', she will certainly qualify as a 'dependant'. The only way the point could arise would be if a court in State A made a maintenance order in favour of, say, the second wife of a polygamous husband. When the order was registered and enforcement sought in State B, the argument was advanced that the court in State A misunderstood its own law, and that there was no duty of support under that law in such a case. It might then be argued for the creditor that here was an order made in favour of someone who was a 'wife' *under the law of State B*, and that no further enquiry into the correctness of the view taken of the law of State A was in order. It is not at all surprising that no such cases have even been reported!

(ii) As a matter of interpretation, it seems clear that the wife is *included* in the wider class of 'dependants': the Act uses the phrase 'wife *or other* dependants'. That being so, the decisive question in every case is whether a duty of support existed, whether qua 'wife' or in some other role, under the law of the country in which the orders were first made.

The original 1920 definition has gone through a series of modifications in successive recommended texts of the Canadian Commissioners. Their 1946 text defined 'maintenance order' in the same words as the original 1920 Act;[11] the 1956 text made insubstantial verbal changes.[12] In 1958 the definition was redrafted:

'an order for the periodical payment of money as alimony or as maintenance for a wife or former wife or reputed wife or a child or any other dependant of the person against whom the order was made.'[13]

For the reasons already given the spelling out of additional categories of dependants made no real difference; the reference to alimony met a suggestion that 'maintenance' should be read restrictively in contexts in which it was distinguished from 'alimony'. The crucial change was the omission of the words 'other than an order of affiliation', so bringing affiliation orders within the scope of the Act.[14]

Another definition was recommended in 1963; it was designed to help settle difficulties that had arisen as to the severance of provisions of an order dealing with other matters[15] but also met some quibbles about the title of the order:

'an order, judgment, decree or other adjudication of a court that orders or directs, or contains provisions that order or direct, the periodical payment of money as alimony, or maintenance, or support for a dependant of the person against whom the order, judgment, decree or adjudication was made.'[16]

This definition was incorporated unchanged in the revised Uniform Act adopted in 1973.[17] The final stage to date was the adoption of a further revised Uniform Act in 1979, with a more fragmented style. 'Order' is defined as

'an order or determination of a court providing for the payment of money as mainten-ance by the respondent named in the order for the benefit of the claimant named in the order, and includes the maintenance provisions of an affiliation order,'[18]

and there are related definitions of 'claimant', 'court', 'maintenance' and 'respondent'.[19]

Of the Canadian provinces, Prince Edward Island retains the 1946 defini-tion,[20] Manitoba the 1958 form[21] (and British Columbia save for the addition of a reference to 'parent'[22]); New Brunswick,[23] Newfoundland,[24] Nova Scotia[25] and Saskatchewan[26] have adopted the 1963 definition; and Alberta[27] and Ontario[28] have legislated for the 1979 revision. There is little to be said in favour of such variety, especially as the differences are trivial except in respect of affiliation orders.

One further variant remains to be noted. The Indian Act, taking local procedures into account, expressly provides that orders made by a court in the exercise of either civil or criminal jurisdiction are included.[29]

1 There is an interesting study to be made of the spelling of this word, 'dependents' being preferred in a number of jurisdictions which in other respects slavishly followed the original.
2 Maintenance Orders (Facilities for Enforcement) Act 1920 (UK), s 10. See also s 11(c) including (for the purposes of the application of the Act to Ireland) certain orders made under the Poor Relief (Ireland) Acts 1839-1914; out of an abundance, almost certainly a super-abundance, of caution, some overseas draftsmen incorporated this provision in their local legislation.
3 See para 5.02 above.
4 See paras 6.31-6.33 below.
5 See *Swirhun v Swirhun* (1979) 9 RFL (2d) 353 (order for payment of arrears due under separation agreement held *not* to be a maintenance order).
6 For this point in the context of provisional orders, see para 5.15 below.
7 See para 5.09 below.
8 [1949] 2 All ER 318, DC.
9 [1959] LLR 82 (High Ct of Lagos).
10 Law of Marriage Act 1971, No 5, s 141(2).
11 1946 Uniform Act, s 2 (but note the spelling of 'dependents').
12 1956 Uniform Act, s 2(d): 'payment of money' (not 'of sums of' money) and '*any* other dependant'. Note however s 2(c) which, unnecessarily, spells out that the governing law as to dependants is that in which the maintenance order is 'sought'.
13 1958 Uniform Act, s 2(d).
14 See *Re Reciprocal Enforcement of Maintenance Orders Act, Re Todesco v Zabkar* (1965) 53 WWR 589 (BC) on the definition as adopted in British Columbia.
15 See s 6A recommended for insertion in the existing (1958) Uniform Act, and see para 5.08 below.
16 Section 2(d) of the (1958) Uniform Act amended as recommended in 1963.
17 Uniform Reciprocal Enforcement of Maintenance Orders Act 1973, s 1(d).
18 Uniform Reciprocal Enforcement of Maintenance Orders Act 1979, s 1(h).
19 Ibid, s 1(c)(e)(g)(m). 'Maintenance' is defined as including support or alimony.
20 Reciprocal Enforcement of Maintenance Orders Act, c R8 (PEI), s 1(d).
21 Reciprocal Enforcement of Maintenance Orders Act, c M20 (Man), s 2(1)(d).

22 Family Relations Act, s 70 (BC) as amended in 1981–2.
23 Reciprocal Enforcement of Maintenance Orders Act, c R–4 (NB), s 1 (as amended in 1977).
24 Maintenance Orders (Enforcement) Act, c 224 (Newf), s 2(c) (as amended in 1979).
25 Maintenance Orders Enforcement Act, M–1 RL (NS), s 1(d).
26 Reciprocal Enforcement of Maintenance Orders Act, c R4 (Sask), s 2(1)(d).
27 Reciprocal Enforcement of Maintenance Orders Act 1980 (Alb), s 1(i).
28 Reciprocal Enforcement of Maintenance Orders Act 1982 (Ont), s 1(h).
29 Maintenance Orders Enforcement Act 1921, No 18 (India), s 2.

Transmission of maintenance orders

5.06   Any system for the enforcement of foreign judgments has to provide for
the text of the judgment in question to be made available in some reliable form
to the court in which enforcement is sought. Perhaps the most common method
is for the judgment-creditor to obtain a certified copy of the judgment from the
original court and lay it before the court with his request for enforcement. That
type of procedure is not the most suitable in the maintenance context, because
it requires procedural steps to be taken by the creditor in two jurisdictions; and
although a lawyer would see the procedural steps as being very simple, a
harassed and impecunious deserted wife would see them in a very different
light. What is required is the simplest procedure involving a single application
which, if successful, will set in train all the necessary procedures for the
transmission of the order to the new jurisdiction, its registration there and its
due enforcement against the debtor.

Accordingly, the 1920 model legislation provides for action by the court in
the enacting jurisdiction which made the original maintenance order, involving
the sending by the court to the Secretary of State of a certified copy of the
order.[1] The Act envisages, without actually formally requiring, onward transmission of the copy;[2] action by the authorities in the receiving jurisdiction,
including its transmission to and registration in an appropriate court and the
taking of steps leading to the enforcement of the order, is provided for in the
corresponding legislation in that jurisdiction.[3]

It must be proved to the relevant court that the person against whom the
order was made is resident in a jurisdiction to which the Act extends. It is
presumably for the creditor to provide the necessary evidence. In England, the
Rules of the Supreme Court deal with the case where the maintenance order
is a High Court order: a certified copy of the order is lodged in the court
registry together with an affidavit stating the applicant's reasons for believing
that the debtor is resident in a jurisdiction to which the 1920 Act extends
together with full particulars, so far as known to the applicant, of the debtor's
address and occupation and any other information which may be required by
the law of his new country of residence for the purpose of the enforcement of
the order.[4] The decision that the evidence is sufficient is taken by the registrar.[5]
There are no corresponding rules in other English courts, but justices' clerks
received guidance as to the transmission of documents in an advisory Home
Office Circular in 1925.[6]

A few variant forms of these provisions exist. The Canadian Uniform Act
adopted in 1946 specifically requires the transmission by the court to be 'on
the request of the person in whose favour the order was made', a formula
retained in successive versions of the Act until the 1979 revision. The 1979
Uniform Act makes no reference to an application to a court by the creditor,
but it does require the Attorney General receiving a document for transmission

under the Act to send it to the proper officer of the reciprocating state concerned.[7] It is not clear that this covers certified copies of final orders, and the 1979 Uniform Act in dealing with the registration of final orders made elsewhere does not require that they be received via the authorities of the country of origin of the order.[8] Legislation to adopt the 1979 text has been passed in Alberta[9] and Ontario;[10] all other Canadian provinces use the formula recommended in 1946.

A number of Canadian jurisdictions impose a further requirement, that the original order should have been made on the application of a dependant resident, semble at that time and not necessarily at any later time, in the jurisdiction.[11] This requirement was included in the 1973 Uniform Act but the reasons for the change are not clear.

The Ghana legislation requires the application for transmission to be made by 'the applicant for the order'.[12] This may well have been intended to have the same effect as the 1946 Canadian formula, but is in fact more restrictive. If a wife applies for an order which is made in favour of herself and her children, the children, although 'dependants' and 'persons in whose favour the order was made', cannot apply for transmission of the order; this appears to be the case even if the wife has died.

1   Maintenance Orders (Facilities for Enforcement) Act 1920 (UK), s 2; 'certified copy' is defined (ibid, s 10) as a copy certified by the proper officer of the court to be a true copy.
2   Ibid, s 2: the copy is sent 'for transmission'.
3   Cf ibid, ss 1(1), 6(1) and para 5.07 below.
4   RSC Ord 105, r 2(2)(4)(6).
5   RSC Ord 105, r 2(3)(4).
6   Home Office Circular 469, 726/4, dated 15 June 1925.
7   1979 Uniform Act, s 11(2).
8   Ibid, s 2(1).
9   Reciprocal Enforcement of Maintenance Orders Act 1980, c 44 (Alb).
10   Reciprocal Enforcement of Maintenance Orders Act 1982 (Ont).
11   British Columbia (Family Relations Act, Cap 121, RL 1979, s 70.2), Manitoba (Reciprocal Enforcement of Maintenance Orders Act, c M20, s 4), and Saskatchewan (Reciprocal Enforcement of Maintenance Orders Act, c R-4, s 5).
12   Courts Act 1971, Act 372 (Ghana), s 87.

Registration of final orders

5.07   The provisions as to the enforcement of final maintenance orders in the legislation on the 1920 model are in principle very simple. An order made in a reciprocating country is registered in a court in the receiving country and is then enforceable in the same way as any order originally made by that court.

The procedure was based upon that provided in the Judgments Extension Act 1868 and it is an unfortunate feature of the 1920 maintenance orders legislation that the statutory language used at this point, although somewhat simplified, does reflect all too clearly the prolixity of the 1868 model.[1]

A maintenance order received under the Act 'shall be registered'.[2] It is clear that this is an administrative and not a judicial act,[3] and that there is no room for the exercise of any discretion by the registering officer, whether he be the clerk or the magistrate.[4] Accordingly an application to the court for registration will be misconceived.[5] The safeguard lies in the channel by which orders are transmitted, the official channel from Minister to Minister (or in the original legislation, from Governor to the Secretary of State for the Colonies), and because the use of that official channel is a protection against fraud its use is mandatory, and an order received by any other means cannot be registered.[6]

The legislation applies to maintenance orders made 'whether before or after the passing of this Act'. In a few statutes[7] these words are omitted, but it is not thought that this omission has any significance, especially in the context of a revised edition of the Laws.

1   Compare s 1(1) of the Maintenance Orders (Facilities for Enforcement) Act 1920 (UK) with s 1 of the Judgments Extension Act 1868; and for a judicial comment on the resulting tautologies, see para 5.11 below.
2   S 1(1) of the 1920 Act (UK).
3   *Pilcher v Pilcher* [1955] P 318 at 331, per Lord Merriman P.
4   *Severin v Severin* 1951 (1) SA 225 at 228 (T), per Roper J. See also *Ex p Worth* 1951 (4) SA 230 (SR) (registration 'automatic'); *Smart v Smart* [1954] SR 12 ('very much a formality'); *McGregor v McGregor* [1957] NZLR 686.
5   *Re Reciprocal Enforcement of Maintenance Orders Act; Re Todesco v Zabkar* (1965) 53 WWR 589 (BC).
6   This is most clearly expressed in the Kenyan case, *Re The Maintenance Orders Enforcement Ordinance, Re Antrobus (a debtor)* (1954) 27 KLR 94, expressly followed in Ontario: *Re Villeneuve and Villeneuve* (1977) 15 OR (2d) 341.
7   Eg Prince Edward Island: Reciprocal Enforcement of Maintenance Orders Act, R-8 RL 1974, s 2(1).

Registration of final orders: severance of maintenance provisions

5.08   The 1920 model legislation, and indeed all the various legislative models, use the concept of a maintenance order. This can mean no more than an order made by a court about maintenance; there is nothing in the phrase which requires that the order made should have been the only order made by the court, or that the question of maintenance should have been the primary issue before the court. Accordingly, it is submitted that the Kenya Supreme Court was quite correct in rejecting, in *Re the Maintenance Orders Enforcement Ordinance, Re Antrobus (a debtor)*,[1] the argument that a provision as to maintenance included in a divorce decree was not a maintenance order.

Unfortunately a different view was taken in Manitoba in *Re Fleming and Fleming*.[2] Williams CJQB held that a maintenance award in an Alberta divorce could not be registered under the Maintenance Orders (Facilities for Enforcement) Act of Manitoba. He held that the definition of 'maintenance order' excluded orders which gave other relief and that the Act gave him no power to register part of an order (or, as the learned judge preferred to characterise this award) part of a judgment. The decision was followed in Saskatchewan.[3]

This interpretation provoked a legislative response in Manitoba, and the text of the Uniform Act recommended by the Canadian Commissioners was amended in 1970 to include a provision in these terms:

'Where it appears to the court that an order received for registration contains matter, or forms part of a judgment, that deals with matter, other than an order for maintenance, the order may be registered in respect of those matters only which constitute a maintenance order.'[4]

This, or a similar, provision can be found in the current legislation in British Columbia, Manitoba, New Brunswick and the Northwest Territories.[5] The legislation in Nova Scotia and Saskatchewan follows the 1973 Uniform Act in defining an order as including one which 'contains provisions' as to maintenance, and the 1979 Uniform Act adopted in Alberta and Ontario is to the same effect. It is submitted that as the view taken in *Antrobus* is to be preferred, the legal position is the same even in jurisdictions which have made no legislative provision on the point.

A not dissimilar point has been taken in those jurisdictions where the definition of 'maintenance orders' excludes affiliation orders. It was argued in New South Wales[6] that this exclusion did not apply to an order concerned wholly with the periodical payment of sums for maintenance, even if that order was consequent upon a finding of paternity made at an earlier date.[7] The argument failed, as did a similar argument in the Northwest Territories of Canada under the provision quoted above.[8]

1 (1954) 27 KLR 94.
2 (1959) 19 DLR (2d) 417, 28 WWR 241.
3 *Wilson v Wilson* (1966) 58 DLR (2d) 191.
4 1958 Uniform Act as amended in 1970, s 3(1.1).
5 See *Re Rhinhart v Rhinhart* (1973) 35 DLR (3d) 555 (Terr Ct).
6 *Re Cook, ex p Pezzuto* [1965] NSWR 895, under s 2 of the Maintenance Orders (Facilities for Enforcement) Act 1923 (NSW) (repealed).
7 Cf the distinction carefully drawn in the New Zealand model between orders 'in' and 'consequent upon' affiliation orders: see para 6.02 below.
8 *Miller v Shaw* [1974] 1 WWR 72 (Mag Ct).

Challenging the registration of final orders

5.09 Because registration is a wholly administrative act, there can be no appeal from it,[1] and the better view, adopted after some hesitation in the South African courts, would seem to be that proceedings to set aside the registration are equally inappropriate,[2] but the court will take notice of any challenges by the debtor when proceedings are taken to enforce the registered order. In Ontario, however, a different practice has become accepted, and there are a number of reported cases in which motions to expunge the registration of an order were entertained, and in some cases succeeded.[3]

It is clear that the registering court will not order enforcement of a registered order if it is satisfied that procedural irregularities mean that the order was not properly registrable, as in *Re Villeneuve and Villeneuve*[4] where a Quebec decree reached the Ontario court not through the official channels prescribed in the Ontario Act (and indeed in all 1920-model statutes) but via the ex-wife creditor and a court in Nova Scotia. It is equally clear, on the other hand, that the registering court cannot and will not look behind the order to re-open the merits of the case as argued, or as arguable, before the original court: a Kenyan court refused to examine whether the Zimbabwe court of origin had been correct in deciding that a child was a dependant under its own law.[5] More difficult are cases involving fraud or want of jurisdiction on the part of the original court.

It is possible that a registering court will consider allegations that the original order was obtained by fraud. The Supreme Court of British Columbia considered just such an argument in *Patton v Reed*,[6] but in that case the court was considering an action at common law to enforce an order made in Idaho, which (Idaho not being within the list of reciprocating countries) could not be registered under the maintenance orders legislation; the argument failed on the merits. Because of the danger of re-opening the merits, it is submitted that, in the absence of specific statutory provision, courts should be reluctant to hear argument based on fraud.

The legislation imposes no requirements as to the jurisdiction of the original court. The intention seems to have been that, as in cases under the Judgments Extension Act 1868, the fact that a court in a reciprocating country had made an order was a sufficient basis for registration and enforcement. So it has been held in Alberta that the registration provisions were designed to remove maintenance orders from such jurisdictional rules.[7] A different view has been taken in other Canadian jurisdictions, following the leading case of *Re Kenny*:[8]

A maintenance order was made in British Columbia by a stipendiary magistrate. Process had been served out of the province, in Ontario where the respondent was resident. When steps were taken to enforce the order in Ontario, enforcement was refused and registration set aside. The Ontario court held that it was not only able but was required to investigate questions as to the jurisdiction of the British Columbia court, and that the order was made without jurisdiction, both in terms of what the magistrate was competent to do in terms of British Columbia law and in the international sense, British Columbia having no jurisdiction in personam against a respondent resident elsewhere.

Re Kenny was referred to without disapproval by Locke J in the Supreme Court of Canada in *A-G for Ontario v Scott*[9] in which the constitutionality of other provisions in the maintenance orders legislation was in issue, and has subsequently been followed both in Ontario[10] and elsewhere.[11]

The volume of Canadian case law on challenges to the registration of registered final orders has led to statutory modifications of the earlier Uniform Acts. The text recommended by the Commissioners in 1963 allowed the debtor to apply to have the registration set aside, and requires the court to set aside the registration if the original court acted without jurisdiction under the conflict of laws rules of the registering country; or if the order was obtained by fraud.[12] In 1970, a right of appeal against registration was also allowed,[13] but since 1979 appeals have been restricted to 'rulings, decisions or orders of a court' which will not include registration. The 1979 recommended text contains more limited provisions for setting aside registration, the sole stated grounds being that 'the order was obtained by fraud or error or was not a final order'; the meaning of 'error' in this provision is unclear.[14]

---

1   *Severin v Severin* 1951 (1) SA 225 (T); *Marendaz v Marendaz* 1955 (2) SA 117 (C).
2   *S v Simpson* 1964 (1) SA 61 at 65 (N). Cf *Marendaz v Marendaz* 1955 (2) SA 117 at 127.
3   *Re Kenny* [1951] 2 DLR 98; *Re Needham v Needham* (1964) 43 DLR (2d) 405 (successful); *Summers v Summers* (1958) 13 DLR (2d) 454 (unsuccessful on the merits).
4   (1977) 15 OR (2d) 341.
5   *Re The Maintenance Orders Enforcement Ordinance, Re Antrobus (a debtor)* (1954) 27 KLR 94 at 99. See also *Foley v Foley* [1959] LLR 82 (similar case re status of ex-wife; Lagos court refused to examine question settled by original order).
6   (1972) 30 DLR (3d) 494.
7   *Coopey v Coopey* (1961) 36 WWR 332 (where however the authorities to the contrary cited below where not referred to).
8   [1951] 2 DLR 98 (Ontario CA).
9   (1956) 1 DLR (2d) 433 at 441.
10   *Re Ducharme v Ducharme* (1963) 39 DLR (2d) 1 (where the order was also ancillary to a divorce decree made without jurisdiction); *Re Needham v Needham* (1964) 43 DLR (2d) 405 (same points). Cf *Summers v Summers* (1958) 13 DLR (2d) 454, where *Re Kenny* distinguished on the facts.
11   *Coatham v Vetter* [1973] 1 WWR 238 (Sask) (where original court had competence under its own law but not jurisdiction in the international sense; case brought under Saskatchewan Act considered below). Cf *Gwyn v Mellen* (1978) 90 DLR (3d) 195 (BC) (*Re Kenny* distinguished).
12   Found now in New Brunswick (Reciprocal Enforcement of Maintenance Orders Act, s 2.2(3)) and Saskatchewan (Reciprocal Enforcement of Maintenance Orders Act, s 4(3)).
13   Found now in British Columbia (Family Relations Act, as amended in 1982, s 70.7).
14   The 1979 text is now found in Alberta (Reciprocal Enforcement of Maintenance Orders Act 1980, ss 2(6), 15) and Ontario (Reciprocal Enforcement of Maintenance Orders Act 1982, ss 2(6), 15). Manitoba has appeal provisions restricted in terms similar to the 1979 text, but enacted in 1968 (Reciprocal Enforcement of Maintenance Orders Act, s 8).

Enforcement of registered final orders: arrears

5.10 Registration enables the registering court to enforce the maintenance order. That is indeed the whole point of the exercise. The standard text of the legislation places a duty upon the court, and, perhaps more significantly, upon the officers of the court, to take 'all such steps for enforcing the order as may be prescribed'[1] by the appropriate rules.

When a court is considering the enforcement of its own maintenance orders, it will exercise a certain discretion in respect of arrears. If arrears have accumulated to a considerable extent, it may be quite unrealistic to order their payment; it may be wiser to remit some or all the arrears so as to give the debtor a realistic level of payments. The soundness of this strategy is not altered when the maintenance order is one originally made in another jurisdiction, but it could be argued that to remit arrears accrued under such an order would be to vary the order, a step beyond the competence of the registering court.[2]

The point was considered in *Pilcher v Pilcher (No 2)*.[3] The earlier proceedings in the same case had established that the registering court had no power to vary or revoke the order. The magistrate then declined to remit any arrears on the ground that this would be to take a power of variation 'by the back-stairs'.[4] In the Divisional Court, Lord Merriman P rejected this view: 'by remitting arrears one does not revoke an order. The two things are entirely distinct'.[5]

Accordingly, a registering court will adopt in respect of arrears under a registered order its usual approach to the exercise of discretion. In many jurisdictions this will attract what is sometimes known as 'the rule against hoarding', though it is better described as a practice or a guideline. This practice, as followed in the English courts,[6] was expressly referred to in *Pilcher v Pilcher (No 2)*, and has also been applied in a reciprocal enforcement context in Saskatchewan.[7] The position in British Columbia is less clear. The Court of Appeal of that province in *Meek v Enright*[8] held that there was no discretion enabling the registering court 'to decline to enforce the order or any part thereof'. The question formulated in the stated case is regrettably unclear, and both judgments are open to criticism: Bull JA asserted, quite incorrectly, that *Pilcher v Pilcher (No 2)* could be distinguished as 'the statute in that case contained a specific power to "remit"';[9] McFarlane JA based himself on a passage from *Dicey and Morris* dealing with early attitudes to the enforcement of foreign money-judgments at common law. In the later case of *Harris v Harris*,[10] the judge avowedly followed *Meek v Enright* in dismissing a debtor's application for the cancellation of arrears, which formed part of a misconceived application for the variation of the Californian order, but went on to give full consideration to the possibility of remitting arrears, declining to do so only in the exercise of his discretion on the merits. In New South Wales, the one-year rule has been held applicable, though in the instant case[11] it was waived on the merits, the period being just over one year and the case having run into procedural delays prior to registration.

When a final order is registered then 'from the date of such registration' it is of the same force and effect as an order made by the registering court.[12] This phrase influenced a South African court[13] to hold in 1955 that there could be no enforcement of arrears accruing before the date of registration. However the legislation does *not* say that the order has the force and effect of an order made *on the date of registration* by the registering court; unlike the position considered below in respect of provisional orders, there is one order, that of the original court, which is made enforceable in its own terms.[14] Accordingly, the better view is that arrears due before the date of registration may be recovered, and there is New Zealand authority to this effect.[15] The latest text of the Canadian Uniform Act provides for such enforcement,[16] and the British Columbia legislation secures the same result in a different way.[17]

1   Maintenance Orders (Facilities for Enforcement) Act 1920 (UK), s 6(1).
2   See para 5.11 below.
3   [1956] 1 All ER 463, [1956] 1 WLR 298.
4   Ibid, at 300.
5   Ibid, at 301.
6   For the English practice see *Luscombe v Luscombe* [1962] 1 All ER 668, [1962] 1 WLR 313, CA; *Freeman-Thomas v Freeman-Thomas* [1963] P 157, [1963] 1 All ER 17; *Ross v Pearson* [1976] 1 All ER 790; Matrimonial Causes Act 1973, s 32.
7   *Olsen v Olsen* (1973) 12 RFL 326, following *McMillan v McMillan* [1949] 2 DLR 762 (Sask CA). For the Ontario practice see *Coffey v Coffey* (1968) 70 DLR (2d) 459; *Snyder v Snyder* (1973) 12 RFL 335; *Patry v Patry* (1974) 16 RFL 332; *Re Gurney* (1975) 22 RFL 172. See also *Winters v Winters* (1977) 3 RFL (2d) 389.
8   (1977) 81 DLR (3d) 108.
9   Ibid, at 113.
10 (1980) 110 DLR (3d) 483. Compare *Patton v Reed* (1972) 30 DLR (3d) 494 (BC Sup Ct) (one-year rule not applied; but order not registered under reciprocal enforcement statute); *Stark v Stark* (1978) 94 DLR (3d) 556 (similar case in Alberta); *Re Sheppard* (1969) 5 DLR (3d) 458 (similar case in Northwest Territories; one-year rule applied).
11 *Nelson v Nelson* [1964–5] NSWR 447 (Sup Ct).
12 Maintenance Orders (Facilities for Enforcement) Act 1920 (UK), s 1(1).
13 *Marendaz v Marendaz* 1955 (2) SA 117 (C).
14 Cf *Re Pasowysty and Foreman* (1969) 5 DLR (3d) 427 at 430, per Rae J.
15 *Wedge v Wedge* [1960] NZLR 373 at 375 (a decision under the 1921 Act).
16 Recommended text of 1979, s 9(3). See Reciprocal Enforcement of Maintenance Orders Act 1980 (Alberta), s 9(3); Reciprocal Enforcement of Maintenance Orders Act 1982 (Ontario), s 9(3).
17 Family Relations Act (British Columbia) as amended in 1982, s 70.1(3) ad finem.

Variation or revocation of registered final orders

5.11   A question which has attracted a great deal of litigation and controversy is whether, once a final order has been registered, the registering court has power to vary or to revoke it. Almost all the authorities support the view that it has no such power.

The statutory language which has been repeatedly examined by the courts provides that once it is registered, the order shall 'be of the same force and effect, and, subject to the provisions of this Act, all proceedings may be taken on such order as if it had been an order originally obtained in the court in which it is so registered, and that court shall have power to enforce the order accordingly'.[1] One court, taking the view that these words gave power to vary, modify or discharge the order, declared that they 'are unambiguous and need no aid in interpretation';[2] another, taking the opposite view, lamented the tautology of the language,[3] which hinders its clear interpretation.

The existence of a power to vary or revoke a registered final order was declared in the Manitoba case of *Re Fleming and Fleming*[4] in 1959. It is clear that this was obiter, for the order in question was held not to be registrable in the first place; and no attention was paid to the considerable body of authority to the contrary.[5] The only other decision supporting a power to vary is from Alberta. In *Re Short v Short*,[6] a registered final order had been varied, and an attempt to quash that variation by certiorari failed. Counsel for the applicant cited no directly relevant authorities against *Re Fleming and Fleming* which was followed.

The contrary view, that a registering court cannot vary or revoke a registered final order, was taken in South Australia in 1947[7] and was the subject of full consideration by the English Divisional Court in *Pilcher v Pilcher*[8] in 1955. An order originally made in Gibraltar was registered in England. It was subsequently varied by an English magistrates' court, but the chairman of the bench tried unsuccessfully to cancel that order for variation when he reflected upon the fact that there had been no proper service of process upon the creditor, who was resident in Spain. (There existed no power to serve process out of the jurisdiction, which is one reason why the 'shuttlecock' procedure is required by the provisions enabling a registering court to vary or revoke a provisional order which it has confirmed.)[9] Lord Merriman criticised the drafting of section 1(2) of the Act:

'[I]t is not obvious why, having enacted that the order is of the same force and effect as if it had originally been made in [the registering court], it was necessary to enact that all proceedings may be taken upon such order as if it had originally been obtained [in that court], nor, having enacted that *all* proceedings may be taken upon it, to enact further that the court shall have power to enforce the order accordingly.'[10]

Lord Merriman was persuaded by the contrast between the provisions dealing with confirmed provisional orders, where variation and revocation are clearly possible, and for which detailed procedures are prescribed, and the much sparser words relevant to registered final orders, that some limit had to be placed upon the apparent generality of the words 'all proceedings may be taken on such an order'. He held that enforcement only was possible, and not variation or revocation or discharge. This conclusion might be inconvenient, not least in cases where the creditor had died but the order remained technically registered and enforceable, but was required by the statutory language.

Pilcher v Pilcher has been expressly followed in a large number of jurisdictions. They include New Zealand,[11] Singapore,[12] and Zimbabwe,[13] and (in similar cases before the same peripatetic judge) Kenya[14] and Malawi.[15] In Canada, courts in British Columbia,[16] Ontario,[17] the Northwest Territories[18] and Saskatchewan[19] have all preferred *Pilcher v Pilcher* to *Re Fleming and Fleming*.

The 1972 model legislation (and the 1979 version of the Canadian Uniform Act) contain provisions enabling registered final orders to be varied or revoked.[20] Certain earlier Canadian provisions can be briefly mentioned. In Ontario, the Reciprocal Enforcement of Maintenance Orders Amendment Act 1967 added a new section 6 to the principal Act; this provided for the severance of maintenance provisions in the order from 'any other question determined by the order or judgment' and enabled the Ontario court to 'deem the provision for maintenance to be a provisional order for maintenance'.[21] The precise meaning of this section (now repealed) was never made clear, but in *Hearn v Hearn*[22] it was held that it did not enable the court to divide a simple maintenance order, treating the finding of facts on which the order was based as an 'other question' and the actual order as to maintenance as a provisional order which could be modified prior to its confirmation.

New Brunswick adopted in 1974 a provision suggested by the Uniform Law Commissioners in the previous year that, subject to certain cases caught by the Divorce Act of Canada, 'an order registered under section 2 [of the New Brunswick Act, ie a registered final order] shall, for the purpose of subsequent enforcement, variation or rescission be deemed to have been made provisionally in the State where the dependent resides and confirmed in New Brunswick'.[23] No other province took similar action, which is not now recommended by the Uniform Law Commissioners.

Finally a little-known Alberta statute, the Alimony Orders Enforcement Act provides an alternative method of registering certain orders made in other jurisdictions for alimony or maintenance; and such orders are expressly declared to be variable in Alberta.[24]

1   Maintenance Orders (Facilities for Enforcement) Act 1920, s 1(1) (UK).
2   *Re Fleming and Fleming* (1959) 19 DLR (2d) 417 at 428, per Williams CJQB (Manitoba).
3   *Pilcher v Pilcher* [1955] P 318 at 329, per Lord Merriman P.
4   (1959) 19 DLR (2d) 417.
5   The only case cited to this effect was *Lupton v Lupton* [1946] 2 DLR 286, which was a decision under the Ontario Reciprocal Enforcement of Judgments Act, not the maintenance orders legislation.
6   (1962) 40 WWR 592 (Supreme Ct of Alberta, Kirby J).
7   *Jarvis v Jarvis* [1947] SASR 12 under the now superseded South Australian state legislation. The same position obtained in both Australia and New Zealand in respect of maintenance orders made by Supreme Courts in the divorce jurisdiction and registered in a court of summary jurisdiction for enforcement: Finlay and Bissett-Johnson *Family Law in Australia* p 477; *Wilson v Morris* [1929] NZLR 901.
8   [1955] P 318, [1955] 2 All ER 644.
9   See para 5.19 below.
10 At 329; emphasis in original. The reason is historical; see para 5.07 above.
11 *McGregor v McGregor* [1957] NZLR 686. The New Zealand legislation was amended in 1963 to give power to vary: Destitute Persons Amendment Act 1963, s 9.
12 *Humphrey v Humphrey* (1956) 22 MLJ 201 (Singapore: District Court Appeal).
13 *Smart v Smart* [1954] SR 12. See also *Ex p Charlesworth* 1951 SR 146 (obiter); also reported sub nom *Ex p Worth* 1951 (4) SA 230.
14 *Re Hunter (a debtor), ex p Hunter* (1955) 28 KLR 120.
15 *Webb v Murray, ex p Murray* (1962) 2 ALR (Malawi) 205.
16 *Re Pasowysty and Foreman* (1969) 5 DLR (3d) 427; *Falkner v Falkner* [1974] 3 WWR 446; *Meek v Enright* (1977) 81 DLR (3d) 108.
17 *Knowles v Knowles* (1974) 17 RFL 123; *Hearn v Hearn* (1975) 25 RFL 314 (see Comment by Diane C. Dzwiekowski (1976) 54 CBR 795). See also *Lowe (Allum) v Lowe* (1974) 26 RFL 327 at 328.
18 *Re Rhinhart v Rhinhart* (1973) 35 DLR (3d) 555.
19 *Olsen v Olsen* (1973) 12 RFL 326; *Winters v Winters* (1977) 3 RFL (2d) 389 (obiter).
20 See paras 5.19 and 6.25.
21 S 6(b).
22 (1975) 25 RFL 314. See also *Lowe (Allum) v Allum* (1974) 26 RFL 327 and *Knowles v Knowles* (1974) 17 RFL 123; and Cornelia Schuh 'Variation of Final Orders under Maintenance Reciprocity Legislation' (1977) 25 Chitty's LJ 159.
23 Reciprocal Enforcement of Maintenance Orders Act, R-4 RL 1973, s 2.1(4), inserted by 1974, c 45 (Supp), s 4.
24 Alimony Orders Enforcement Act, cap A-40, RL 1980, s 18. The only reported case under the Act seems to be *Martin v Martin* (1960) 31 WWR 643, which casts little light upon its origins or function.

Provisional orders

5.12   Reference has already been made to the original proposal that the problem of the deserted wife seeking maintenance from a husband who had already left the jurisdiction could be met by the device of making a 'provisional order' in the courts of her country of residence, an order which would only become effective on being confirmed by a court in the country to which the husband had gone.[1] This proposal was duly incorporated in the 1920 model legislation, and is indeed its most distinctive and characteristic feature.[2]

Accordingly the legislation confers power upon courts in the enacting jurisdiction to make provisional orders of maintenance against the debtor,[3] despite his absence from the jurisdiction and the lack of any service of process upon him. The power can only be exercised if it is proved that the debtor is resident in a country within the geographical scope of the reciprocal enforcement scheme; there is no merit in a provisional order which cannot in fact be confirmed.

The court may only make a provisional order 'if after hearing the evidence it is satisfied of[4] the justice of the application'.[5] This is rather an odd provision; a court is not to be expected to act in a way which it recognises as being contrary to justice, and perhaps for that reason the phrase is omitted in the latest recommended text of the Canadian Commissioners.[6] However, the point would seem to be that the court does not merely act as a post-box for the applicant; it will not make an order unless satisfied that such action is appropriate, and as the order has to be an order for a specific level of payments the court's enquiry must be a fairly detailed one. Because of the absence of the respondent, the enquiry is necessarily restricted, and this led the Chief Justice of Canada in *Bailey v Bailey*[7] to describe the events in the court as 'in the nature of an ex parte proceeding to establish a prima facie case'; but it has to be noted that the Act does not use the expression 'prima facie case' and arguably more is required.

So, an Australian magistrate, writing as one who had had experience of having to decide whether or not to confirm an overseas provisional order, urged a careful testing of the case before a provisional order was made:

'What we have here is cooperative action of two courts and each must be regarded as playing a constructive part in the ultimate decision. Otherwise there would be no point in giving the originating court power to make a *provisional order*; it would have been sufficient to have a system for taking the dependant's evidence on commission, leaving it entirely to the confirming court to make all necessary orders. The provisional order must be regarded as expressing some opinion on the merits of the case; indeed, it is to be hoped that originating courts will not be content merely to record what the dependant and her witnesses care to depose, but will probe the evidence to some extent, at least exploring any self-evident contradictions or weaknesses and asking whether there is any relevant correspondence which might be put in. It must be remembered that the hearing in the original court is necessarily ex parte, and it is a pity that the legislation was not drafted in the first place in terms inviting the court of origin to play a more active part in testing the evidence than courts in the English tradition are accustomed to do.'[8]

The only procedural guidance in the legislation is the direction that the evidence of any witness must be put in writing in the form of a deposition.[9] Until 1979, the recommended Uniform Act in Canada provided for shorthand transcripts as an alternative to depositions; the current text speaks of 'a sworn statement setting out or summarizing the evidence given in the proceeding'.[10] The supply of this information to the confirming court is clearly essential to the reciprocal enforcement scheme, but its limitations must be conceded. A Prince Edward Island judge observed in one case: 'As is not unusual in these cases, the transcript of evidence ... leaves something to be desired. Much of it is the result of leading questions, and since neither it nor, for that matter, the evidence here [ie, in the confirming court] is subject to cross-examination there is virtually no way to test credibility.'[11]

The court making a provisional order may make any order open to it if a summons had been duly served on the respondent and he had failed to appear at the hearing.[12] Clearly, therefore, it is the law of the jurisdiction in which the court is sitting which is alone relevant. But the order is of 'no effect unless and until confirmed by a competent court' abroad.[13] For this reason, there is no appeal against a provisional order; there is no *effective* order against which to appeal; there is, however, a right of appeal against a refusal to make a provisional order.[14] Strictly it would seem that a provisional order should not be taken as finally determining any issue between the parties. There is a provision in the current recommended text of the Canadian Commissioners' Uniform Act allowing fresh decisions to be made by the original court if the first provisional order is not confirmed,[15] and in an earlier text the marginal note to this provision read 'Doctrine of res judicata restricted';[16] it is submitted that that doctrine was not in fact applicable.

1   See para 5.02 above.
2   See Maintenance Orders (Facilities for Enforcement) Act 1920 (UK), ss 3 (making of provisional orders) and 4 (confirmation of such orders). Note that the current Tanzanian legislation omits in toto provision for the making and confirmation of provisional orders, being restricted to the registration and enforcement of final orders. The reason for this omission is not known; in the earlier separate legislation for Tanganyika and Zanzibar the full 1920 scheme was provided for.
3   Ibid, s 3(1).
4   In Mauritius, the text reads '... satisfied with the justice of the application': Maintenance Orders (Facilities for Enforcement) Ordinance, cap 191, RL, s 5(1).
5   Maintenance Orders (Facilities for Enforcement) Act 1920 (UK), s 3(1). See *Collister v Collister* [1972] 1 All ER 334, [1972] 1 WLR 54, DC.
6   1979 Uniform Act, s 3(1).
7   (1968) 68 DLR (2d) 537 at 544 per Cartwright CJC.
8   Professor G. Sawyer 'Confirmation of Provisional Maintenance Orders: The British Commonwealth System' (1960) 34 Australian LJ 233 at 234.
9   Maintenance Orders (Facilities for Enforcement) Act 1920 (UK), s 3(2).
10 1979 Uniform Act, s 3(3)(b).
11 *Wells v Wells* (1978) 7 RFL (2d) 271 per CR McQuaid J at 272. See para 5.14 below.
12 Maintenance Orders (Facilities for Enforcement) Act 1920 (UK), s 3(1).
13 Ibid.
14 Maintenance Orders (Facilities for Enforcement) Act 1920 (UK), s 3(6). The Indian Act (The Maintenance Orders Enforcement Act 1921 (India), No 18) contains no corresponding provision; an appeal may, however, be available under some more general rule.
15 1979 Uniform Act, s 3(6).
16 1973 Uniform Act, s 6(9).

Jurisdiction to make a provisional order

5.13   Apart from providing, in effect, that process is to be deemed to have been duly served upon the respondent, the 1920 model legislation contains no special jurisdictional rules for the making of a provisional order. Where the point has been discussed it has usually been assumed that this is a matter for the internal law of the country of the court before which the application is made. This means that attention must be paid to any rules in that law as to the connection between the *applicant*, and possibly the *subject-matter*, and the court, for by definition the respondent is resident abroad. So, for example, a magistrates' court in England has jurisdiction in maintenance cases 'if at the date of the making of the application either the applicant or the respondent ordinarily resides within the commission area for which the court is appointed'.[1]

The question was considered by a Divisional Court in *Collister v Collister*.[2] The respondent husband had lived all his life in the Isle of Man, where the parties married, lived together and eventually separated; thereafter the wife went to England, became ordinarily resident in Manchester and applied to the Manchester City magistrates for a provisional order. The court expressed some initial surprise at the 'proposition that a lady can come to Manchester (or elsewhere in England and Wales) from any of the many territories to which the Act of 1920 extends and obtain from the justices a provisional order against her husband, with whom she has always hitherto lived in that territory, and who has always been and still remains there' and noted that 'she may have arrived from Christmas Island, or the Falkland Islands, or the Niger delta, not from the Isle of Man.'[3] The court was, however, satisfied that provided the applicant satisfied the normal jurisdictional requirements for maintenance cases, in the instant case by her ordinary residence in Manchester,[4] there was no obstacle to the court's jurisdiction; in particular it was quite irrelevant that the cause of complaint (eg cruelty or constructive desertion) arose elsewhere.

In *Collister v Collister* the issue as to jurisdiction was raised in the country where the provisional order had been made. The point might also be taken before the court asked to confirm the order. This occurred in *Re Wheat*[5] where a provisional order made in South Africa was sent to England for confirmation. The facts were remarkably similar to those in *Collister v Collister*, the wife having obtained the provisional order in the town in which she had become resident having been deserted by her husband in Saint Helena. The English Divisional Court satisfied itself that, under the South African legislation as to the jurisdiction of magistrates' courts,[6] the wife's residence within the court's area was a sufficient basis upon which the order could be made. The matter was treated as governed wholly by South African law, and no attempt was made to invoke any rule of English law which might deny recognition to the claimed jurisdiction.

The issue has received repeated, and sometimes confused, attention in the Canadian jurisdictions. The confusion can be illustrated by reference to the Ontario case of *Meyers v Meyers*.[7] A husband had deserted his wife in Ontario, where both had been living; she went to Manitoba and there obtained a provisional maintenance order, which was transmitted to Ontario for confirmation. The Ontario court refused to confirm the order because on the proper construction *of the relevant Manitoba legislation* the Manitoba court had no jurisdiction. Thus far, the approach is entirely consistent with that adopted in *Re Wheat*; but unfortunately the judge continues by referring to the purpose of the *Ontario* Act, suggesting thereby that he was applying a rule of Ontario law to determine the propriety of the assumption of jurisdiction in Manitoba.

Similarly, in *Douglas v Douglas*[8] a Saskatchewan judge, asked to confirm a provisional order made in British Columbia, correctly referred to the British Columbia statute but then, in effect, declined to apply it, believing it to be 'inconceivable' that a wife could select a jurisdiction not linked to the cause of complaint.

Even the Supreme Court of Canada could not quite escape some muddling of ideas. In *Bailey v Bailey*,[9] on appeal from Manitoba, the Supreme Court considered the question whether an Ontario provisional order should have been confirmed in Manitoba despite the fact that the matrimonial disputes arose in Manitoba alone. Cartwright CJC held, quite correctly, that the question was whether, *under the Ontario statute*, the Ontario court had jurisdiction; a question he answered in the affirmative. But he then concluded his judgment with a summary of the position under the reciprocal enforcement legislation as a whole, saying that it was incorrect to limit provisional orders to cases in which a court would have jurisdiction to make a final and binding order of maintenance.

As a result, there is a tendency amongst Canadian judges and commentators to state the issue in terms of whether a provisional order will be confirmed if the husband has *never* resided in the country of origin, and the ground of complaint did not arise there. The answer now generally given to this question is 'yes', in the supposed light of *Bailey v Bailey*,[10] but there are isolated decisions in which a different view is taken. An illustration is *MacEachern v Pfaff*:[11] a provisional order was made in Nova Scotia for the support of a woman and her illegitimate child. An Ontario court was invited to confirm the order. The judge recognised that Nova Scotia law was applicable, but this, he thought, could not be the case when the debtor was neither domiciled nor resident there and cohabitation had not taken place there. In the result the order was confirmed only in respect of the child and that by reference to the policies of Ontario law.

1   Domestic Proceedings and Magistrates' Courts Act 1978 (UK), s 30(1), as amended by the Magistrates' Courts Act 1980 (UK), Sch 7.
2   [1972] 1 All ER 334, [1972] 1 WLR 54, DC.
3   Ibid, at 58.
4   Under the then-applicable Matrimonial Proceedings (Magistrates' Courts) Act 1960 (UK), s 1(2).
5   [1932] 2 KB 716, DC.
6   Deserted Wives and Children Protection Act 1895 (Cape of Good Hope), No 7, s 2.
7   [1953] 2 DLR 255 (Ont).
8   (1966) 58 WWR 42 (Sask).
9   (1968) 68 DLR (2d) 537 (Sup Ct Can).
10 See *Burak v Burak* [1949] 1 WWR 300 (Sask); *Andrie v Andrie* (1967) 60 WWR 53 (Sask) (not following *Douglas v Douglas*, above; cited with approval in *Bailey v Bailey*); *Woods v Woods* (1972) 9 RFL 220 (Sask). Cf *Re Maintenance Orders (Facilities for Enforcement) Act, Hawryluk v Hawryluk* (1965) 54 WWR 661 (Sask), applying the legislation of the court making the provisional order, and finding no jurisdiction.
11 (1974) 19 RFL 123 (Ont).

Confirmation of provisional orders

5.14   Once a provisional order is made, it is transmitted through official channels (in the original legislation the Governor of the appropriate colonies and the Secretary of State for the Colonies in London; many jurisdictions have substituted references to their own Attorney-General and a phrase such as 'the appropriate authorities' in other jurisdictions) to the country in which the debtor is resident. A certified copy of the order is provided, together with the depositions, 'a statement of the grounds on which the making of the order might have been opposed if the person against whom the order is made had been duly served with a summons and had appeared at the hearing',[1] and the available information for identifying the debtor and ascertaining his whereabouts.[2]

When the order is received, and it appears to the appropriate officer of the government concerned that the debtor is indeed resident in his jurisdiction, the papers are sent to the appropriate court,[3] usually the court for the area within which the debtor is said to be living. A summons is issued calling upon the respondent to show cause why the order should not be confirmed.[4]

If the respondent duly appears his case is heard. The proceedings are virtually ex parte, for the creditor under the provisional order is neither present nor represented. Under the Kenyan legislation, a legally qualified member of the staff of the Attorney-General's department may appear[5] but elsewhere the court clerk or registrar will take the necessary procedural steps and, while not exactly cross-examining, ask questions to clarify the respondent's case.[6]

The court in deciding whether to confirm the order may well be faced with conflicting evidence, neither party's evidence having been tested by cross-examination. A Prince Edward Island judge has suggested that 'where there is, as there usually is, conflict in evidence, the court must assume the truth lies somewhere in between'.[7] However, the legislation clearly places the burden upon the debtor to satisfy the court that the order ought not to be confirmed,[8] and Sawyer has argued that 'if the confirming court on reading the depositions and considering the evidence of the husband is left undecided as to the relevant facts, so that if acting otherwise than under this legislation it would dismiss the [creditor's] case, it should under this legislation confirm the provisional order',[9] and it is difficult to resist this view.

In some cases the difficulty can be eased by the use of the 'shuttlecock' or remission procedure which is another characteristic feature of the 1920 model legislation. The Act provides that if the respondent appears and satisfies the confirming court 'that for the purpose of any defence it is necessary to remit the case to the court which made the provisional order for the taking of any further evidence' the court may take this step.[10] An Indian court has given a wide interpretation to this provision, saying that in a case where the evidence before the confirming court cannot be tested by cross-examination (as will almost inevitably be the case) and introduces matter not mentioned in evidence as recorded in the documents accompanying the provisional order, a referral for further evidence is desirable.[11]

The power to remit to the original court is, however, limited by the words 'for the purpose of any defence'. It is not at all clear what this means. The situation is one in which the respondent has appeared and has at least persuaded the court not to confirm the order immediately. He may have done this by raising some defence, in the narrow sense, for example he may have produced evidence to the effect that the claimant has done something which ends her entitlement to maintenance, such as, in some legal systems, remarrying. Or he may have produced evidence casting some real doubts on the veracity of the evidence before the original court as to, for example, the alleged desertion. Or he may produce evidence of the financial commitments of himself or the applicant which suggest that the level of maintenance proposed is excessive. Professor Sawyer has argued for a limited meaning of the phrase 'for the purpose of any defence', suggesting that if the evidence before the confirming court is such that the respondent is discharging his burden of proof there should be no reference back: 'It would be an intolerable nuisance if these cases could be transmitted backwards and forwards for reply, rebutter, surrebutter and so forth. Dependants should be encouraged when obtaining a provisional order to tell the whole story, with the utmost candour, anticipating as far as possible the kinds of defence which these stories usually suggest.'[12] This view seems very hard on the applicant; the 'encouragement' Sawyer describes may well be very desirable, but who is to provide it? If a wife appears unrepresented to apply ex parte for a provisional order, is the court to administer a whole series of questions along the lines, 'If your husband comes up with this, that or the other story, what would your answer be?'

It seems, despite the possible delays that may result, desirable that the 'shuttlecock' procedure should be used liberally. Critics of the 1920 scheme usually seize upon the fact that there is no one court which is in a position to hear both sides of the case at first hand; the 'shuttlecock' device is designed to mitigate this as far as possible. The 1979 recommended text of the Canadian Commissioners takes this view, requiring any court, before making a confirmation order in a reduced amount[13] or before denying maintenance, to decide whether to remit the matter back for further evidence.[14]

The legislation does not spell out in detail what happens when a reference back is decided upon, in particular what documents are sent to the court which made the provisional order. In practice some sort of reasoned statement of the points in issue is essential, and could conveniently be accompanied by a set of depositions or a transcript of the evidence taken in the confirmation proceedings. The legislation does contemplate the possibility that the court which made the provisional order, having taken further evidence (which in practice will often, but not necessarily, be further evidence by the applicant), will decide to rescind the provisional order on the ground that it should not have been made.[15] This surely implies consideration by that court of the whole of the evidence in the case, including that taken in the confirming court; but it must be admitted that the Act does not expressly say so.

Professor Sawyer has raised one further point arising out of a case he decided in the Australian Capital Territory.[16] If the rules as to the admissibility of evidence applicable in the confirming court (and under the general principles of the conflict of laws, evidence is a matter for the lex fori) exclude evidence which is relevant and which would be admissible in the court which made the provisional order, can it be received by the confirming court and then sent on remission of the case to the court which made the provisional order in the expectation that the order will there be rescinded? The answer would seem to be 'no'; if the law of evidence excludes material there really is no way in which it can be 'received' in this fashion.

1   For this 'statement of grounds' see below, para 5.16.
2   Maintenance Orders (Facilities for Enforcement) Act 1920 (UK), s 3(3).
3   Ibid, s 4(1).
4   Ibid.
5   Maintenance Orders Enforcement Act, cap 154 RL (Kenya), s 6(8).
6   G. Sawyer 'Confirmation of Provisional Maintenance Orders: The British Commonwealth System' (1960) 34 Australian LJ 233.
7   McQuaid J in *Wells v Wells* (1978) 7 RFL (2d) 271 at 272; see also the passage cited in para 5.12 above.
8   Maintenance Orders (Facilities for Enforcement) Act 1920 (UK), s 4(4).
9   Sawyer, op cit, at p. 234.
10   Maintenance Orders (Facilities for Enforcement) Act 1920 (UK), s 4(5).
11   AIR 1928 Bom 117 at 121.
12   Sawyer, op cit, at p 236.
13   For this power, see para 5.17 below.
14   1979 Uniform Act, s 5(6); for the power to make interim orders in such cases, see ibid, s 5(7).
15   Maintenance Orders (Facilities for Enforcement) Act 1920 (UK), s 3(4).
16   Sawyer, op cit, at p 235.

Confirmation of provisional orders: choice of law

5.15   The device of a provisional order which is of no effect unless and until it is confirmed by a court in another jurisdiction is a legal novelty. It is not surprising that it has been explained in a number of different ways; in particular, some judges have seen the resulting order as essentially an order made by the confirming court, the role of the original court being essentially that of a prompter; others have seen it as an order emanating from the original court but subject to a requirement of approval by another tribunal.

So a Saskatchewan judge has described the proceedings in the original court as 'merely an initiating proceeding looking to the effective judicial action in [the country of the confirming court] for the purposes of which it is a means of adducing a foundation in evidence'.[1] In another Saskatchewan case[2] it was said that confirmation proceedings, despite their title, were for an original order. This approach was adopted by the Supreme Court of Canada in *A-G for Ontario v Scott*.[3] The issue in that case was the constitutionality of the reciprocal enforcement legislation as enacted in Ontario, and it was desirable, in order to uphold the legislation, to reject any suggestion that the Ontario courts acting as confirming courts were being made subordinate to foreign tribunals. So the court repeatedly emphasised that the provisional order was merely a 'preliminary step',[4] 'the order made must derive its legal force and effect entirely from the applicable Ontario statute'.[5]

At the other extreme is the view of the Supreme Court of Cyprus that confirmation proceedings 'are mainly designed to give additional opportunity of defending proceedings instituted in a foreign court'.[6] A less extreme version is to be found in an Ontario judgment delivered 20 years after the *Scott* case; the legislation was described as 'a procedural mechanism acting somewhat as an interstate extension cord for maintenance orders already made and those yet to be made'.[7] Commentators generally dissent from the extreme position taken in *Scott*.[8]

Lying behind these varying formulations is an important choice of law issue. If the creditor initiates proceedings in State A, which produce a provisional order, an order of no effect unless and until confirmed in State B, which law applies to determine the substantive issues between the parties? The answer is: the law of State A; and, it may be added, it is entirely proper to give this answer and yet also accept the statement in the *Scott* case that the eventual order derives its legal effect from the legislation in force in the confirming state, for there is no reason why that legislation should not require certain issues to be governed by the law of another country.

That the law of the country of origin governs is clear from the 1920 Act. The court making a provisional order is required to transmit with the order itself 'a statement of the grounds on which the making of the order might have been opposed',[9] and these are clearly grounds under the law of that court. When proceedings are taken for the confirmation of an order, the respondent may 'raise any defence which he might have raised in the original proceedings had he been a party thereto, but no other defence'.[10] The effect is to allow defences existing under the law of the country in which the provisional order was made, but to exclude those applicable to maintenance claims brought in the ordinary way in the confirming court.

Some case law exists supporting a different view. In *Re Morrissey and Morrissey*[11] a court in Saskatchewan refused to confirm an order made in British Columbia in favour of a child over the age of 16, that age being the maximum age for a support obligation under Saskatchewan law. The court's reasoning requires close examination. It turned, not on any general proposition as to choice of law, but on the definition of 'dependant'. In s 2(1)(c) of the Saskatchewan Act,[12] this word was defined as

'a person that a person against whom a maintenance order is sought or has been made is liable to maintain according to the law in force in the state where the maintenance order is sought or was made',

and the court held that the references to an order being 'sought' were apt in the case of confirmation proceedings. This seems an unlikely interpretation, in view of the inclusion in the same Act of the 'statement of grounds' procedure not examined in *Morrissey*. In any event, it is not an interpretation available in jurisdictions retaining the standard 1920 text, in which no reference is made to the law of the state where the order is 'sought'.[13]

Insofar as *Morrissey* seems to be authority for any wider proposition, the balance of case-law is heavily against it. It has been expressly disapproved in a number of cases, for example *Re Ross and Polak*[14] where the Alberta courts confirmed a Saskatchewan provisional order in favour of an illegitimate child despite the absence of a formal finding of paternity, as required in Alberta law. A similar result was obtained in the Ontario case of *MacEachern v Pfaff*.[15] In circumstances similar to those in the *Morrissey* case itself, courts have applied the law of the country in which the provisional order was made.[16]

An important application of the choice-of-law rule concerns the level of payments set in the order. In *Peagram v Peagram*[17] the English court was asked to confirm a New South Wales order for periodical payments considerably in excess of the maximum amount then permitted in English law. The Divisional Court held that the English limit was irrelevant as New South Wales law governed. The precise point had in fact been anticipated in India, where the Indian court's power to confirm a provisional order is expressed to be 'notwithstanding any pecuniary limit imposed on [the court's] power by any law for the time being in force in India'.[18]

The application of the law of the court making the provisional order can now be regarded as firmly established,[19] despite judicial comment that it can in some cases lead to injustice. Considering a situation in which an Alberta wife, deserted by her husband, had taken her children to Saskatchewan and there obtained a provisional order, Allen JA pointed out that this could be unfair if the law of Saskatchewan were more generous to the wife than that of Alberta.[20] The point, in traditional conflict of laws language, is that the application of the lex fori (in the sense of the *original* forum) could encourage 'forum-shopping'. However, the number of cases in which a claimant changes residence for this purpose must be tiny and there is every reason to keep jurisdictional and choice-of-law rules as simple as possible in this context.

The 1979 revision of the Canadian Commissioners' Uniform Act retains the choice-of-law rule but modifies the procedure. This aspect is considered below.

1   *Re Morrissey and Morrissey* (1969) 7 DLR (3d) 174 at 179, per Fresen DCJ.
2   *Skakun v Skakun* (1976) 29 RFL 185.
3   (1956) 1 DLR (2d) 433.
4   Per Abbott J at 447; cf per Rand J at 438: 'the preliminary ground and condition of which is a step taken elsewhere'.
5   Per Locke J at 442. See R. N. Komar 'Some Problems in The Reciprocal Enforcement of Maintenance Orders' (1978) 1 Family Law Review 82.
6   *Christou v Christou* [1964] Cyprus LR 336.
7   *Works v Holt* (1976) 22 RFL 1 at 9 per Beaulieu PCJ.
8   See Komar, op cit; A. Thompson 'Commentary on the Maintenance Orders (Facilities for Enforcement) Act' (1964) 4 Rhodesia LJ 133, 149.
9   Maintenance Orders (Facilities for Enforcement) Act 1920 (UK), s 3(3).
10 Ibid, s 4(3).
11 (1969) 7 DLR (3d) 174. See also *Cooper v Cooper* (1973) 13 RFL 20 (Ont).
12 Reciprocal Enforcement of Maintenance Orders Act 1968, following the 1956 Uniform Act of the Canadian Commissioners.
13 Cf Maintenance Orders (Facilities for Enforcement) Act 1920 (UK), s 10.
14 (1971) 18 DLR (3d) 436 (App Div).
15 (1974) 19 RFL 123 (Ont).
16 *Woods v Woods* (1972) 9 RFL 220 (Sask); *Pittam v Bolton* (1972) 13 RFL 383 (Ont). See also *Works v Holt* (1976) 22 RFL 1 (Ont) (affiliation).
17 [1926] 2 KB 165, DC; followed in *Harris v Harris* [1949] 2 All ER 318, DC.
18 Maintenance Orders Enforcement Act 1921, No 18 (India), s 7(4). The same provision, dealing with the power to confirm with modifications (see para 5.17 below), provides that the maximum sum to be awarded shall be that prescribed in the provisional order.
19 Relevant cases in addition to those already cited include *Wensing v Wensing* (1974) 17 RFL

102 (Ont); *Dickson v Dickson* (1976) 30 RFL 253 (Ont); *Hennessey v Hennessey* (1976) 3 RFL (2d) 140; *Carson v Carson* (1979) 9 RFL (2d) 209 (PEI); *Swirhun v Swirhun* (1979) 9 RFL (2d) 353.
20   *Re Ross and Polak* (1971) 18 DLR (2d) 436 at 459–60.

Confirmation of provisional orders: the statement of grounds of defence

5.16 Subordinate courts, such as those commonly involved in the reciprocal enforcement of maintenance orders, are seldom required to apply the law of another country. It was for this reason that the 1920 model legislation includes provision for the supply of a 'statement of grounds on which the order might have been opposed'.[1] The statement is 'conclusive evidence that those grounds are grounds on which objection may be taken'[2] but as Lord Merriman pointed out in *Harris v Harris*[3] 'it is not exclusive of the possibility that other grounds of objection were open'. It is open to the defendant to raise any defence which he might have raised in the proceedings which led to the making of the provisional order had he been a party to them; the decision to include a provision to this effect in the 1920 legislation was a considered one, the original 1913 draft having included as a possible alternative a rule that the statement should be 'conclusive evidence of the grounds on which objection may be taken'.

Judges and commentators have criticised the 'statement of grounds' system, without perhaps making due allowance for the difficulties facing subordinate courts in some jurisdictions. In *Re Ross and Polak*[4] an appellate judge complained that a form had been supplied listing a number of possible defences many of which were clearly not applicable to the facts of the case, no attempt having been made by deletions or additions to make the statement more suitable. An Australian magistrate[5] has complained of the brevity and formality of the statement, suggesting that the court making a provisional order could at least provide a copy of its own statute governing maintenance orders. In fact brevity and formality is enjoined in some jurisdictions, which include a list of grounds in the procedural rules made under their Act.[6]

An extreme illustration of brevity, which cannot be explained by reference to any such prescribed list, is reported in the Hong Kong case of *Leong Fatt Chee v Lee Miew Long*.[7] Here a wife had obtained a provisional order in the courts of Singapore, and this was transmitted to Hong Kong with a 'statement of grounds' listing only (1) the defence that the respondent was not in fact the applicant's husband; and (2) that the amount of maintenance fixed in the provisional order was disproportionate to his means. The respondent husband sought to rely on the wife's desertion and infidelity. It was held, on appeal, that he could so do, provided that he established that the defences would have been available in Singapore. Creedon J suggested that a court receiving a 'statement of grounds' which it believes to be inaccurate should address an enquiry to the court of origin rather than struggling on with poor information.[8]

Difficulties are likely to be most acute when a Commonwealth jurisdiction applies its reciprocal enforcement legislation to non-Commonwealth jurisdictions where the 'statement of grounds' technique is unknown. Canadian experience suggests that United States' courts are in difficulties here, sometimes supplying unhelpful or misleading lists[9] or simply a copy of their maintenance legislation.[10] An American commentator, in graphic language which deserves repetition, asserted that

'the good judges, the imaginative judges and the "hell benders" will make a long and careful list, broad enough to include just about everything under the sun. The tired judges, the stolid judges and those who want "to get" the "dirty rascal" who refuses to support his family will make a short list. Every judge will have a serious problem. He does not know the defendant or what his side of the story may be. So it is like asking a tailor to make a suit of clothes "to fit everybody".'[11]

The 1979 text of the Canadian Commissioners Uniform Act abandons the statement of grounds of defence. Instead a court making a provisional order is required to transmit 'a copy of the enactments under which the respondent is alleged to have an obligation to maintain the claimant',[12] that is the legislation on maintenance obligations in general, *not* the legislation on reciprocal enforcement under which the provisional order is made. Under the 1979 Uniform Act there are unusual provisions about choice of law. The relevant provision requires the application of the law of the reciprocating state, ie that in which the provisional order was made, 'where [that law] is pleaded to establish the obligation of the respondent to maintain a claimant resident in that state'.[13] It is not clear what is meant in this context by 'pleaded', nor what is intended in a case where the court making the provisional order had jurisdiction under its own law to make an order in respect of a claimant not resident in that state. If the relevant law is not pleaded, an interim order may be made but the substantive proceedings are adjourned for up to 90 days during which the Attorney-General is to notify the appropriate officer of the reciprocating state of 'the requirement to plead and prove' the relevant law.[14] If this requirement is not complied with (and it is not clear *who* is expected to act) the confirming court is to apply its own law.[15] These provisions appear likely to present a number of practical difficulties and cannot be regarded as satisfactory.

1   Maintenance Orders (Facilities for Enforcement) Act 1920 (UK), s 4(1). See para 5.14 above.
2   Ibid, s 4(3).
3   [1949] 2 All ER 318 at 321 DC. See, to the same effect, *Bailey v Bailey* (1968) 68 DLR (2d) 537 at 544 (Sup Ct Can).
4   (1971) 18 DLR (3d) 436 at 459 per Allen JA.
5   Professor G. Sawyer 'Confirmation of Provisional Maintenance Orders: The British Commonwealth System' (1960) 34 Australian LJ 233 at 235.
6   Eg Nigeria, Appendix to Rules of Court made under the Maintenance Orders Act, cap 114, RL 1958. The form in general use in England and some other jurisdictions is similar, but appears to lack any statutory basis.
7   [1963] HKLR 760.
8   At 768.
9   *Goodman v Goodman* (1974) 14 RFL 243 (Ont). See D. Mendes da Costa 'Enforcement of Judgments and Orders across Canada' *CBA Continuing Education Seminars No 2 (1974)* p 118.
10   *Gaon v Gaon* (1976) (Ont; unreported), cited in R N Komar 'Some Problems in the Reciprocal Enforcement of Maintenance Orders' (1978) 1 Family Law Rev 85; cf *Goodman v Goodman* above.
11   W. J. Brockelbank of Idaho, cited B. C. Barker (1975) 33 Univ Toronto Faculty LR 253 at 260.
12   1979 Uniform Act, s 3(3).
13   Ibid, s 6(1).
14   Ibid, s 6(3); proof may be by production of a copy of the relevant enactment: s 6(2).
15   Ibid, s 6(4). Section 6(5) refers to a statement of grounds, but this is a statement of the grounds upon which the making of the *confirmation* order might have been opposed, a complete novelty.

Confirmation of provisional orders: the court's discretion

5.17   Unlike the registration of an overseas final order, the confirmation of a provisional order is clearly a judicial and not merely an administrative act.[1] If the debtor fails to appear in the proceedings for the confirmation of the order, or fails to satisfy the court that the order ought not to be confirmed, the court may confirm the order 'either without modification or with such modifications as to the court after hearing the evidence may appear just'.[2]

Permitted modifications include a variation in the amount of the prescribed payments[3] in the light of the defendant's evidence as to his financial resources and commitments, but it is not clear what else is included. Sawyer records[4] his own action as a magistrate in refusing to confirm an order insofar as it dealt with children, having decided on the facts not to confirm it for the wife's own benefit, on the ground that to do so would be to inflict such a drastic change upon the provisional order as could not be described as a 'modification'. This seems an over-cautious view, for similar surgery has been carried out in Ontario[5] and is clearly contemplated in Canadian legislation based on the 1973 recommended Uniform Act of the Canadian Commissioners which speaks of an order which 'has not been confirmed in respect of one or more dependants'.[6]

So far as the financial aspects are concerned, it has been expressly held in South Australia that the power to modify covers quantum and the method and times of payment, and also the conversion of currency so that sums are payable in a currency convenient to the debtor;[7] the Uniform Acts recommended by the Canadian Commissioners have since 1956 made specific provision for the conversion of currencies.[8]

There is a paucity of reported cases on the operation of this aspect of the reciprocal enforcement scheme. It seems appropriate to refer at this point to *Re McK*[9] decided under the Maintenance Orders (Reciprocal Enforcement) Act 1972 (UK); that legislation is considered more fully below, and the case arose in rather different circumstances from those now under consideration, but the practical aspects of the problem are the same. A final maintenance order was made in the High Court in England in favour of a wife and six children and against a successful consultant radiologist living in Australia. Acting in the belief that the husband earned the equivalent of £12,000 per annum after tax, that his living expenses in Australia were comparable to those in England, and that maintenance payments would be tax-deductible in Australia (as they would have been in England), the order was for a payment of £3,000 a year in favour of the wife, and just over £2,000 a year divided between the six children. The order was registered in Sydney, where a magistrate later made a provisional order reducing the amount payable to the wife to £275 a year. He found that the husband had only £11,000 a year after tax, and that maintenance payments did not qualify for tax deduction; he also believed, as a result of evidence known to the husband to be false, that the wife could earn a substantial income.[10]

Re McK illustrates the difficulty these cases present. Latey J commented on these difficulties and suggested that it would have been reasonable and practicable for the wife to have been given notice of the husband's application for the provisional order of variation with a short statement of the grounds relied upon; she could have filed an affidavit in response. The difficulty of course is that these procedures would complicate, and increase the cost of, the reciprocal enforcement system; as between wealthy, or relatively wealthy, parties they may be acceptable, but many orders are for quite small sums and both parties may have limited means.[11]

The 1920 legislation is unclear as to the date from which payments begin when a provisional order is confirmed, but a natural reading of the provision that the order has no effect unless and until confirmed suggests that the obligation to pay commences only on confirmation. Since 1973 the recommended text of the Canadian Uniform Act has allowed the confirming court to fix an earlier date, but not a date before that of the original provisional order.[12]

1   See AIR 1928 Bom 117 at 119.
2   Maintenance Orders (Facilities for Enforcement) Act 1920 (UK), s 4(4).
3   Subject in India to a prohibition on any increase of the sum payable: Maintenance Orders Enforcement Act 1920 (India) No 18, s 7(4).
4   G. Sawyer 'Confirmation of Provisional Maintenance Orders: The British Commonwealth System' (1960) 34 Australian LJ 233 at p 236.
5   *MacEachern v Pfaff* (1974) 19 RFL 123. Cf *Killen v Killen* 1981 SLT 77 (Sh Ct) (a case under 1972 model legislation).
6   1973 Uniform Act, s 5(9).
7   *Jarvis v Jarvis* [1947] SASR 12 at 20 per Abbott J.
8   1956 Uniform Act, s 6(8). See 1979 Uniform Act, s 7(9) for the latest version.
9   (1976) Times, 14 July (High Court).
10   Under the procedures of the Maintenance Orders (Reciprocal Enforcement) Act 1972 (UK), further proceedings ensued in England and the payment to the wife was raised to £2,250.
11   Similar evidential problems were discussed in one aspect of the complex case of *Newmarch v Newmarch* [1978] Fam 79 [1978] 1 All ER 1, where again the husband had a substantial income.
12   1973 Uniform Act, s 7(10); 1979 Uniform Act, s 5(5).

Appeals

5.18   The standard 1920 model legislation gives the debtor, in cases where a provisional order has been confirmed, 'the same right of appeal, if any, against the confirmation of the order as he would have had against the making of the order had the order been an order made by the court confirming the order'.[1] This is not the most smoothly drafted provision, but the test seems to be what right of appeal would exist against an ordinary maintenance order made in the confirming court. The rule seems to be one which is both convenient to the debtor and his advisers and one which does no injustice to the creditor. It is however reversed in the Nigerian Act, which makes the existence of a right of appeal dependent on the existence of a corresponding right in the reciprocating territory,[2] a rule which must create difficulties in practice.[3]

There is no appeal against a refusal to confirm a provisional order, but in some jurisdictions such a refusal may be open to challenge in other ways, for example by seeking mandamus or certiorari on a point of law. The point is discussed rather obscurely in *Peagram v Peagram*,[4] but the discussion was clearly obiter as what was there involved was an appeal by way of case stated by a creditor against a modification (to reduce the sums payable) made by a court which *did* confirm the order.

Since 1963, the Uniform Act recommended by the Canadian Commissioners has included provision for a right of appeal against a refusal to confirm an order,[5] and the 1979 text gives a similar right to the Attorney-General.[6] Newfoundland, Nova Scotia and Prince Edward Island are the only provinces without some such provision.

1   Maintenance Orders (Facilities for Enforcement) Act 1920 (UK), s 4(7).
2   Maintenance Orders Act (Nigeria), cap 114, RL 1958, s 6(7).
3   There is no provision as to appeals in the Indian Maintenance Orders Enforcement Act 1921; but there may be a corresponding power under general legislation.
4   [1926] 2 KB 165, DC.
5   1958 Uniform Act, s 6(6a), as amended in 1963.
6   1979 Uniform Act, s 14; similar provisions had been enacted in Saskatchewan (Reciprocal Enforcement of Maintenance Orders, cap R-4, s 7(7)).

Variation and revocation of provisional orders

5.19   In contrast with the position in respect of registered final orders,[1] the 1920 model legislation does contain provisions concerning the variation and revocation of orders made as provisional orders. However, the legislation is not entirely satisfactory, probably because the issues had not been fully thought through in 1920. It is necessary to distinguish a number of different fact-situations.

The first is one in which a provisional order was made in State A, and has been duly confirmed in State B. An application is then made to the original court in State A, most probably by the creditor for an increase in the level of payments. The legislation declares that the confirmation of a provisional order 'shall not affect any power of a court of summary jurisdiction to vary or rescind that order'.[2] If the order is rescinded, the rescission takes effect immediately, but if it is varied the variation is by what is in effect a provisional order (though it is not formally so described) and does not have any effect unless and until confirmed; the thinking behind this set of rules is that rescission is to the advantage of the debtor and no reference to a court in his country of residence is necessary to safeguard his interests. The original 1920 text just quoted refers to 'a court of summary jurisdiction' without specifying that it will be the court which made the original order; the Canadian jurisdictions have always specified that court.[3]

A second situation arises if a similar application is made to the court in State A, for the variation, or conceivably the revocation, of its provisional order *before* that order has been confirmed elsewhere. The 1920 legislation does not deal expressly with this point, but it appears a reasonable inference from the provision already cited that, the court retaining its powers even after confirmation, it enjoys them a fortiori in the period before confirmation. The Canadian Commissioners' 1973 Uniform Act expressly refers to this type of case and provides that the court in State A may, within 12 months of the date of the original provisional order, proceed by way of re-opening the case rather than by insisting on a fresh application; the outcome, however, is not strictly a variation of the original order but a new provisional order made in the re-opened proceedings.[4] The period is reduced to 6 months in the comparable provision in the 1979 recommended text.[5]

A third case is that in which confirmation proceedings have begun in State B but the court there has referred the case back to the original State A court for the taking of further evidence, using the full opportunities of the 'shuttlecock' procedure. The court in State A is given express power in such cases to rescind the provisional order where it appears 'that the order ought not to have been made';[6] it appears that variation is impossible for the court is directed in any other case to proceed by sending the new evidence back to the confirming court.[7] The 1979 Canadian Uniform Act denies the court in State A the power to rescind; where further evidence is taken it must be provided to the court in State B, but the court in State A may make such 'recommendations' as it thinks fit.[8]

An application for variation or rescission may be addressed, usually by the debtor, to the confirming court. The 1920 legislation provides that once a provisional order has been confirmed, it may be varied or rescinded as if it had originally been made by the confirming court.[9] It is not at all clear what procedure is envisaged. It was pointed out, obiter, in *Pilcher v Pilcher*[10] that variation proceedings normally require service of a summons on the respondent, which will usually be impossible if he is out of the jurisdiction, and no express power is given to proceed in the absence of such service. Lord Merriman expressed the view that Parliament must have intended the use of the 'shuttle-cock' procedure, in effect variation by a provisional order needing confirmation in the other court. The difficulty with this view is that the relevant provision in the Act[11] expressly refers to the power to remit a case for the purpose of taking any necessary further evidence, and that seems to indicate that in most cases such a remission is unnecessary.

The 1920 text is silent on the law to be applied by the confirming court in exercising its power to vary or rescind the order. It has already been noted that the law of the state in which the provisional order was made governs the substantive issues which arise in the confirmation proceedings,[12] and in the discussions on the early drafts of the 1920 legislation it was suggested that the grounds for variation and rescission should similarly be those available in the law of the country from which the provisional order originated. It was eventually decided not to include such a rule; it was thought that the rule would be difficult to operate in practice and that it was not necessary in the interests of justice.[13] In practice applications are most commonly in respect of the level of payments and the disputes are about the respective needs and resources of the parties; it was evidently thought that in this type of case nothing very much turned on choice-of-law questions. Other types of case can arise, however, for example those concerning the effect of a divorce[14] and later legislative models have had to tackle the choice-of-law issues.[15]

The 1979 Uniform Act recommended by the Canadian Commissioners contains a new set of rules governing the variation and revocation both of registered final orders and confirmed provisional orders. Unless both parties accept the jurisdiction of the court,[16] the exercise of this power depends upon the remission of the case to a court in a reciprocating state for the taking of evidence from the creditor, or (where the creditor is not ordinarily resident in a reciprocating state) the giving of notice to the creditor (in effect involving service ex iuris), or (in the case of an application by a creditor for variation or rescission of a final order) the use of the provisional order procedure.[17]

1   See para 5.11 above.
2   Maintenance Orders (Facilities for Enforcement) Act 1920 (UK), s 3(5).
3   See 1946 Uniform Act, s 5(9). For the recast provisions in the 1979 text, see below.
4   Uniform Reciprocal Enforcement of Maintenance Orders Act 1973, s 6(9).
5   Uniform Reciprocal Enforcement of Maintenance Orders Act 1979, s 3(6).
6   Maintenance Orders (Facilities for Enforcement) Act 1920 (UK), s 3(4).
7   Ibid.
8   1979 Uniform Act, s 3(5).
9   Maintenance Orders (Facilities for Enforcement) Act 1920 (UK), s 4(6).
10   [1955] P 318 at 330–1 per Lord Merriman.
11   Ie, s 4(6) of the UK Act of 1920.
12   See para 5.15 above.
13   See clause 4(5) of the draft prepared in 1913, the Colonial Office letter of 28 April 1913 and Home Office response of 15 July 1913.
14   See para 5.21 below.
15   See the conflicting answers in the Australian legislation and the 1972 United Kingdom Act, paras 6.16 and 6.25 below.
16   1979 Uniform Act, s 7(4).
17   Ibid, s 7(6)(7)(8). Cf. the legislative models referred to in n 15 above.

Payments under registered or confirmed orders

5.20   A number of points are worthy of note in connection with the actual making of payments under a registered final order or a confirmed provisional order.

As with any international payment, there may be exchange control or fiscal barriers to be overcome. An example of the latter received judicial attention in *Re Coffeen and Schlosser*.[1] This concerned 'withholding tax', a tax commonly levied on payments to non-residents. The wife obtained an order for maintenance as part of divorce proceedings in New York; the payments to her would be tax-free in New York, being paid out of the taxed income of the husband. The order was registered in Ontario, where the husband was resident, and the wife took proceedings in that province to enforce the registered order. The Ontario court held that by taking those proceedings the wife submitted to Canadian tax law, and could not enforce payment of more than 85% of the sums due, Canadian withholding tax being due as to 15%. The judge mentioned, without indicating a view, that the balance, the 15%, might still be owing to the wife and so enforceable as against the husband (even if he had paid the sum to the tax authorities) should he travel to a jurisdiction outside Canada. This clearly raises important policy questions, notably whether maintenance payments should in fact be within the scope of such taxation.

The conversion of currency can create problems. In the case of a provisional order, it is possible to modify the sum payable as part of the confirmation proceedings so that the debtor pays a fixed sum expressed in his local currency (normally the currency in which he will himself be paid wages); the disadvantage of this step is that the creditor's income is subject to the fluctuations of exchange rates. There is no power to modify a final order on registration, so the debtor's obligation will remain expressed in the creditor's local currency; in this case he may have to pay a variable sum.

Since 1956 the recommended text of the Canadian Uniform Act has provided for final orders to be registered and for provisional orders to be confirmed in terms expressed in Canadian currency, the exchange rate being that current at the date of the original order. In the 1979 text, the relevant date is expressed as that on which 'the order was made or last varied'.[2]

The transmission of sums of money can also entail expense. The legislation in most jurisdictions is silent on the point, but in practice official channels are used and the costs are apparently absorbed in the court service budget. A different assumption moved the Select Committee of the Indian Legislature to insert into the text of the Indian Act, in justice to applicants, a provision requiring a court registering or confirming an overseas order to direct that charges for the transmission of maintenance payments should be payable by the debtor in addition to the sums for maintenance.[3]

1 (1975) 62 DLR (2d) 615 (Ont).
2 1956 Uniform Act, ss 3(3), 6(8); 1979 Uniform Act s 13(1). Prince Edward Island has no such provision, and Nova Scotia only in relation to registered final orders, the 'modification' power being presumably applied in the case of provisional orders.
3 Maintenance Orders Enforcement Act 1921, No 18 (India), s 9. Whether such orders are made in current practice is not known.

The effect of a divorce

5.21   In the absence of local matrimonial causes legislation to the contrary effect, the general position in Commonwealth jurisdictions appears to be that a maintenance order is not automatically discharged on the dissolution of the parties' marriage, whether order and divorce originate in the same country[1] or in different countries.[2] In the case of a maintenance order registered under the reciprocal enforcement scheme it follows that a divorce between the parties is no more than material which could be relied upon in an application for the variation or revocation of the order.

In the case of a final order registered under the 1920 legislation there is, as has already been noted, no power to vary or revoke the order by way of an application to the registering court.[3] In practice, therefore, a divorce cannot lead to any positive action by that court, and this has been recognised both in Zimbabwe[4] and (obiter) in England.[5] It has however been suggested in South Africa that in such circumstances the registering court will refuse to allow any process of execution to proceed.[6]

There is power to vary or revoke a confirmed provisional order[7] and the exercise of the power after a foreign divorce was considered in Ontario in *Wensing v Wensing*.[8] The Ontario judge was unwilling to revoke the order himself, taking the view that the effect of the divorce was a matter for the law of New Zealand, in which both the original provisional order and the divorce had been obtained. It is by no means clear that this choice-of-law rule is correct in principle,[9] but on the assumption that it is the procedural consequence, the remission of the case to New Zealand under the power dealing with the 'taking of further evidence',[10] involved some stretching of the legislation.

1   *Bragg v Bragg* [1925] P 20, DC. See Dicey and Morris *The Conflict of Laws* (10th edn, 1980) pp 406–9.
2   *Wood v Wood* [1957] P 254, [1956] 3 All ER 645, CA; *Qureshi v Qureshi* [1972] Fam 173, [1971] 1 All ER 325; *Newmarch v Newmarch* [1978] Fam 79, [1978] 1 All ER 1.
3   See para 5.11 above.
4   *Smart v Smart* [1954] SR 12 (which concerned a final order despite its mistaken registration as if it had been a provisional order).
5   *Pilcher v Pilcher* [1955] P 318 at 332, DC, per Lord Merriman P.
6   *S v Simpson* 1964 (1) SA 61 at 65 (N).
7   See para 5.19 above.
8   (1974) 17 RFL 102 (Ont Prov Ct).
9   For choice of law see para 5.19 above.
10 Under the Ontario equivalent of s 4(6) of the Maintenance Orders (Facilities for Enforcement) Act 1920 (UK).

CHAPTER 6

Variant Commonwealth Maintenance Orders Legislation

A. THE NEW ZEALAND MODEL

Development of the New Zealand legislation

6.01 Having done much to stimulate the creation of the 1920 model legislation, New Zealand duly enacted a Maintenance Orders (Facilities for Enforcement) Act in 1921. This was thoroughly revised in 1963 by the Destitute Persons Amendment Act[1] which introduced a number of features novel to Commonwealth practice. The new model was adopted in Western Samoa in 1967[2] and many of its features are reflected in the Regulations (of much earlier date) still in force in the Cook Islands and Niue.[3] The New Zealand provisions were further modified and re-enacted in the Domestic Proceedings Act 1968[4] and the process was repeated to produce the current text, Part VIII of the Family Proceedings Act 1980.[5]

A distinctive characteristic of the New Zealand model is that it abandons the principle of reciprocity. It applies automatically in respect of all Commonwealth countries, defined to include the Republic of Ireland and any territory for whose international relations the government of a country that is a member of the Commonwealth is responsible.[6] There is no requirement of reciprocity of any sort in these cases, and, while many countries have designated New Zealand in the extension orders made under their own Acts, there are many which have no reciprocal provision: this is more markedly the case for Western Samoa, the Cook Islands and Niue. Nor is reciprocity required before the Act, with any specified modifications, is applied to 'designated countries'; any country can be so designated, though in practice reciprocity will no doubt be taken into account before the Minister issues the required Gazette notice.[7]

1 No 63 of 1963.
2 Maintenance and Affiliation Act, No 7 of 1967 (W Samoa). This Act is uncertain in its treatment of affiliation orders which are not referred to in the definition of 'maintenance order' in s 2; but it appears from s 62 that some maintenance orders made in an affiliation context are included, and they are expressly *excluded* in s 73(1) (provisional orders for confirmation overseas).
3 Cook Islands Maintenance Enforcement Regulations 1948/134 of New Zealand.
4 No 62 of 1968.
5 No 94 of 1980.
6 Family Proceedings Act 1980 (NZ), s 2 (which also includes the Cook Islands, Niue and Tokelai). See also the Commonwealth Countries Act 1977, No 31 (NZ).
7 Family Proceedings Act 1980 (NZ), s 135 governs designation of countries. The Republic of South Africa is the only example, having been named in an Order in Council under the predecessor provision, Destitute Persons Amendment Act 1963, s 12.

'Maintenance orders'

6.02 The New Zealand legislation applies to a large class of maintenance orders. 'Maintenance order' is defined for the purposes of Part VIII of the Act as including a subsisting order (including an order 'in or consequent on' an affiliation order[1]) for the payment by any person of a periodical sum of money towards the maintenance of a person whom the first-mentioned person is, according to the law in force in the place where the order is made, liable to maintain;[2] a subsisting order for the payment of a sum in respect of the funeral expenses of a child in respect of whom a paternity order has been made;[3] a subsisting order for the payment to the mother of a child in respect of whom a paternity order has been made of a sum in respect of expenses reasonably incurred by her by reason of the pregnancy and the birth of the child and towards her support during the pregnancy and for such period thereafter (not exceeding one month) as the court specifies;[4] and any such order as subsequently varied.[5]

The distinction carefully drawn between orders 'in' affiliation orders and those 'consequent on' such an order is a distinctive feature of the New Zealand legislation but the practical significance of the distinction is much reduced in the latest (1980) Act; in earlier texts a more generous attitude was shown to the latter type of order.

So far as orders in respect of funeral and pregnancy expenses are concerned, the Act speaks of orders 'of the kind described' in sections which relate to orders made by courts in New Zealand.[6] The intention seems to be to include similar orders made in other jurisdictions but this is not made as clear as might be desired.

1   'Affiliation order' is further defined as an order declaring a person to be a parent of a child; it need not contain maintenance provisions: Family Proceedings Act 1980 (NZ), s 2.
2   Ibid.
3   Ibid, s 78(1)(b).
4   Ibid, s 78(2).
5   Ibid, s 2.
6   Section 2 refers to s 78 which empowers the New Zealand Family Court to make certain types of order, and which uses the expression 'paternity order' defined (in s 2) as one made under s 51 (again dealing with powers of New Zealand courts).

Transmission of maintenance orders

6.03   The New Zealand Act omits to provide for the transmission through official channels of final orders made by courts in New Zealand. This may well have been thought to be necessary given the abandonment of the principle of reciprocity; it could make for difficulties if New Zealand were to legislate in a way which assumed the co-operation of the authorities of other countries including those with whom no discussions (such as necessarily precede the making of reciprocal extension orders) had taken place. It is, however, quite clear from the Act that New Zealand orders are expected to be registered abroad in appropriate circumstances, for there are provisions dealing with situations which may then arise.

So the Act[1] deals with the variation or extension by a court in New Zealand of a New Zealand maintenance order registered in a country outside New Zealand. If the court finds that it has grounds to make an order varying or extending the original maintenance order, and that the respondent (in the usual case, the debtor) is not resident in New Zealand, it is given power to proceed by way of a provisional order requiring confirmation overseas. This provision was a novelty in Commonwealth practice when first introduced, though a similar result could be achieved by a liberal interpretation of the power to make provisional orders in the 1920 model legislation.[2]

A further novelty is the power given to a court in New Zealand to confirm a provisional order made elsewhere cancelling, varying or suspending a final order originally made in New Zealand but registered abroad.[3] (The 1920 texts do not allow for the variation or revocation of final orders in the registering court,[4] but the New Zealand Act has comprehensive provisions applying equally to registered final orders and to confirmed provisional orders.[5]) The power to confirm is limited by the requirement that the New Zealand court must be satisfied that an order similar to the order as confirmed could have been made there under the Family Proceedings Act.[6]

1 Family Proceedings Act 1980 (NZ), s 147(2). See ibid, s 147(3) for applicable limitations on the court's power; cf para 6.07 below.
2 Ie by treating s 3 of the Maintenance Orders (Facilities for Enforcement) Act 1920 (UK),· which speaks of 'an application ... for a maintenance order' as including applications for variation.
3 Family Proceedings Act 1980 (NZ), s 139.
4 See para 5.11 above.
5 See para 6.07 below.
6 Family Proceedings Act 1980 (NZ), s 139(6).

Registration of final orders

6.04 Provision is made for the registration in New Zealand, by filing a certified copy in the office of a district court, of a maintenance order made by any court in a Commonwealth or designated country or of an order made as a provisional order by any such court and confirmed in another Commonwealth or designated country.[1] As in the case of the 'export' of final orders for transmission elsewhere, nothing is said about the use of official channels, nor is there any express requirement that the debtor should be resident in New Zealand. There is however a provision, new in 1980, that, where an order is registered in New Zealand and it appears to the Secretary for Justice that the debtor is not resident in New Zealand, the Secretary must send a certified copy of the order and other relevant documents[2] to the responsible authority[3] either in the Commonwealth or designated country where the order was first made or to the responsible authority in any other Commonwealth or designated country.[4] The latter course would be appropriate where the debtor is believed to have moved on to a third country; in this case the responsible authority in the original country must be notified of the action that has been taken.[5]

An unusual provision declares that an order that has been registered in New Zealand remains an order of the court of the country in which the order was made.[6] This is presumably intended to ensure that orders of variation or discharge made in the original court will be entitled to recognition. The order is however enforceable as if made in New Zealand[7] and can be discharged or varied there.[8]

The debtor may apply for the setting aside of the registration of the order. The Act provides that the registration *must* be set aside on proof that the order is not one to which the registration power applies, and that the registration *may* be set aside in the case of an order made in or consequent upon an affiliation order where the debtor did not appear in the original proceedings and those proceedings were not duly brought to his notice.[9]

1 Family Proceedings Act 1980 (NZ), s 135. The earlier text (Domestic Proceedings Act 1968, s 71) excluded provisional orders made in, but not those consequent upon, an affiliation order.
2 Listed in Family Proceedings Act 1980 (NZ), s 143(2).
3 Defined as 'the appropriate authority in that country for the discharge of the functions

contemplated by Part VIII of this Act in relation to that authority': ibid, s 2. Semble the
second 'authority' is a mistake for 'country'.
4   Ibid, s 143(1).
5   Ibid, s 143(3).
6   Ibid, s 141(1).
7   Ibid, s 141(2).
8   Ibid, s 142; see para 6.07 below.
9   Ibid, s 137.

Provisional orders

6.05   New Zealand district courts are given power to make provisional orders
against a person who is proved either to be resident in a country outside New
Zealand or to have left New Zealand with the intention of so residing.[1] This
form of words avoids the difficulty which may be experienced by the newly-
deserted wife in establishing that the husband has acquired a residence in a
particular country, and also enables prompt action to be taken even during
the husband's journey to his new place of residence. The court may make an
order 'where after hearing the evidence it is satisfied of the truth of the matters
stated in the application'.[2] In view of the ex parte nature of the proceedings,
this is a more appropriate criterion than the reference in the 1920 text to 'the
justice of the application'.[3]

Because of the absence of necessary reciprocity in the New Zealand Act, the
possibility exists that a court will be asked to make a provisional order against
a debtor who has become resident in some country which has no legislation
compatible with the Commonwealth system. Such an order would plainly be
worthless, so it is provided in the Act that no provisional order shall be made
unless it appears that the order is one which may be confirmed under the law
of the country in which the respondent resides or intends to reside.[4] This is in
addition to the usual requirement that the order must be one which could have
been made, as a final order, had the respondent been served with process but
had failed to appear at the hearing.[5]

There are novel provisions concerning the relationship between provisional
orders and maintenance agreements registered under the Act. If it appears to
the New Zealand court that the agreement could, under the law of the country
in which the respondent resides, be enforced as an order, no provisional order
may be made; that is, enforcement of the existing agreement is preferred. If
such a facility does not exist and a provisional order is made, its confirmation
has the effect of cancelling the registration of the agreement in New Zealand.[6]

If a court overseas considering the confirmation of a New Zealand provisional order refers the matter back for the taking of further evidence, the New
Zealand court may discharge the order, absolutely or in order to make a fresh
provisional order.[7] The rights of appeal conferred by the Act include a right of
appeal not only against a refusal to make a provisional order but also against
the discharge of a provisional order under this power.[8]

Once a New Zealand order has been confirmed in an overseas court it
becomes for all the purposes of New Zealand law an order of the district court
that made the provisional order.[9] This entails the right to vary or revoke the
order, and the Act speaks of orders varying, discharging or suspending such an
order. If the order is discharged or suspended or is varied only so as to remit
arrears (all cases likely to be welcomed by the debtor), the New Zealand court
makes the decision, which is merely notified through official channels to the
confirming court.[10] If any other variation is to be made then, unless the

respondent is residing in New Zealand at the time of the variation, it must be by provisional order requiring confirmation overseas.[11]

1   Family Proceedings Act 1980 (NZ), s 147(1).
2   Ibid, s 147(2).
3   Maintenance Orders (Facilities for Enforcement) Act 1920 (UK), s 3(1).
4   Family Proceedings Act 1980 (NZ), s 147(3)(a).
5   Ibid, s 147(3)(b).
6   Ibid, s 147(4).
7   Ibid, s 147(8)(a).
8   Ibid, s 147(9) applying s 174.
9   Ibid, s 148(1).
10 Ibid, s 148(3)(b), (5).
11 Ibid, s 148(2), 3(a).

Confirmation of provisional orders

6.06   The provisions as to the confirmation of provisional orders made over-seas[1] follow the 1920 model with minor variations. For example there is no express reference to the respondent's residence in New Zealand, but the requirement of the issue of a summons or warrant implies that.[2]

The principal departure from the traditional pattern concerns affiliation orders. Until 1980, New Zealand law did not allow the confirmation of provisional orders 'in' (as opposed to 'consequent on') an affiliation order, and even in the case of consequential orders gave a special defence in the confirmation proceedings that the respondent had been given no notice of the proceedings.[3] The 1980 Act includes all types of affiliation order but allows the defendant to raise the defence that he is not the father of the child and had no notice of the original proceedings.[4] It may be that this provision is in a sense cosmetic, in that the defence would surely be available in the original proceedings and so capable of being relied on in the confirmation proceedings;[5] but it may conceivably be intended to allow reliance on this defence as a New Zealand rather than a foreign defence, so that, for example, New Zealand rules as to admissible evidence would apply in full.

If any provisional order is confirmed in New Zealand, the court has power to order the payment of a sum on account of maintenance between the date of the making of the provisional order and its confirmation.[6] A right of appeal exists against the confirmation or a refusal to confirm an order.[7]

1   Family Proceedings Act 1980 (NZ), s 138.
2   Ibid, s 138(3).
3   Domestic Proceedings Act 1968 (NZ), s 64(4).
4   Family Proceedings Act 1980 (NZ), s 138(5)(a).
5   Ie, under ibid, s 138(4).
6   Ibid, s 138(9).
7   Ibid, s 140, applying ss 173 and 174 (rehearings and appeals).

Variation and discharge of registered or confirmed orders

6.07   The original 1920 model legislation makes provision for the variation and rescission of an overseas provisional order which has been confirmed but is silent in respect of registered final orders.[1] The New Zealand Act has provisions applying in both contexts. They can be summarised as follows:

(i)   If both the creditor and the debtor become resident in New Zealand, the court may substitute a new order for the registered or confirmed order;[2]

(ii)   In any case, the court may, for the purposes of New Zealand law, discharge, vary or suspend the operation of the registered or confirmed order or remit arrears wholly or in part;[3]

(iii)   Where an order of the type described in the last paragraph could, if made as a provisional order, be confirmed under the law of the country in which the maintenance order was made, the New Zealand court may (but is not required to) exercise its powers by provisional order.[4]

1   See paras 5.11 and 5.19 above.
2   Family Proceedings Act 1980 (NZ), s 142(5).
3   Ibid, s 142(1).
4   Ibid, s 142(2).

Other features of the New Zealand model

6.08   A number of the features which have been found useful in Canadian jurisdictions have been incorporated in the New Zealand Act. For example, there are provisions as to the conversion of currency; but where the latest recommended text of the Canadian Uniform Act refers to the rate of exchange applicable on the day the order was made or last varied, the Family Proceedings Act 1980 selects the date of registration or confirmation.[1] It also provides for Registrar's certificates as to sums paid under an order being evidence of the facts stated.[2]

The Family Proceedings Act 1980, in new provisions not brought into force with the bulk of the Act, enables New Zealand to ratify the United Nations Convention for the Recovery of Maintenance Abroad. This convention is discussed below.[3]

1   Family Proceedings Act 1980 (NZ), s 153. Cf 1979 Canadian Uniform Act, s 13(1).
2   Family Proceedings Act 1980 (NZ), s 154.
3   Paras 7.17–7.23 below. For the New Zealand provisions, see Family Proceedings Act 1980, ss 144–146 and 149. The title used in the text differs slightly from the actual title, which speaks of the Recovery Abroad of Maintenance.

B. THE AUSTRALIAN MODEL

Development of the Australian legislation

6.09   The Australian legislation dealing with the reciprocal enforcement of maintenance orders acquired many of its characteristic features at the same period, the mid-1960s, as did that in New Zealand. Substantially uniform legislation was enacted in the various states and territories of Australia in 1964 and following years; it contained two sets of provisions, one dealing with inter-state enforcement and the other with overseas enforcement. The overseas enforcement provisions were plainly influenced by the much-used inter-state scheme.

The Commonwealth of Australia, ie the federal authority, has concurrent legislative competence in this field with the states, and it exercised its powers to enact the Family Law Act 1975[1] which superseded the state and territorial legislation. By creating the Family Court of Australia and unifying Australian law on the subject it rendered much of the former inter-state enforcement legislation unnecessary; corresponding provisions were enacted only in relation to affiliation and similar orders which remain state matters.[2] The Act also made use of a different legislative technique, under which most of the substantive provisions relevant to the present topic were relegated to Regulations made under it.[3] Many of the principles of the earlier legislation do, however, survive.

The earlier Australian model is still in force in Papua New Guinea.[4]

1   Act No 53, 1975. A number of amending Acts have been passed and a major Family Law Amendment Bill was introduced in 1981 and, in the same form, in 1982.
2   Family Law Act 1975, s 67; Family Law Regulations 1975, reg 139.
3   SR 1975/210. The Australian Government Publishing Service produces a *Family Law Handbook* which contains an up-to-date text of the Act and Regulations. In the paragraphs which follow 'Act' and 'Regulations' refer respectively to the Family Law Act and the Family Law Regulations.
4   Maintenance Orders Enforcement Acts 1970, Nos 23 and 51 of 1970 (PNG); see para 8.69 below.

'Maintenance orders'

6.10   For the purposes of the Act and the Regulations, 'maintenance order' is defined[1] as meaning 'an order with respect to the maintenance of a party to a marriage[2] or of a child of a marriage[3] who has not attained the age of 18 years or, to the extent provided by the regulations, an order of the kind referred to in section 109'.

Section 109 deals with affiliation orders and sets out eight types of order in a most comprehensive definition:

'(a)   the expenses of maintaining, for a period immediately before her confinement or expected confinement, a woman who has been, or is expected to be, confined for the purposes of childbirth;

(b)   medical, surgical, hospital or nursing expenses in respect of the confinement of such a woman;

(c)   the expenses of maintaining such a woman for a period immediately following her confinement;

(d)   the expenses of maintaining a woman who is expecting a child, where the order was made by reason that she was expecting the child;

(e)   an amount in respect of the maintenance of an ex-nuptial child who has not attained the age of 18 years where the order was made on the basis that the person against whom the order was made is a parent of the child;

(f)   funeral expenses in respect of an ex-nuptial child, where the order was made on the basis that the person against whom the order was made is a parent of the child;

(g)   funeral expenses in respect of the mother of an ex-nuptial child, where the order was made on the basis that the person against whom the order was made is the father of the child; or

(h)   medical, surgical, hospital or nursing expenses in respect of a person, where the order was made by reason that an order for the payment of expenses referred to in a preceding paragraph has been made in relation to that person.'

1   Act, s 110(1), applied for the purposes of the relevant Regulations by reg 139C.
2   Defined, Act s 4(1).
3   Defined, Act s 5(1).

Reciprocity and restricted reciprocity

6.11   The Australian legislation draws a distinction between a 'reciprocating country' and a 'country with restricted reciprocity'.[1] This is a most important distinction, giving the legislative scheme a different effect in relation to different countries and different types of order. But it is also a difficult distinction; the terminology was taken over from the earlier state legislation, where it was never entirely appropriate, and it is even less so in the context of the 1975 Act.

Under the earlier legislation, a country whose courts had jurisdiction to make orders all of which were of the same kinds as those which could be made in the Australian state in question was eligible to become a reciprocating country.[2] This was so even if it would not actually enforce the whole range of the Australian state's orders. So *actual* reciprocity was not required. Any country the courts of which could make orders of a kind unknown to the Australian state, for example an order for a lump sum payment to a government agency taking over the care of an illegitimate child on a permanent basis, could only be a country with restricted reciprocity. In such a case only those orders made in the overseas country which were known to the Australian State would be enforced there.

The effective position is similar under the Family Law Act. An official summary of the Act states that 'orders from countries with restricted reciprocity may only be registered [in Australia] if they are similar to orders that can be made or enforced under the Act'.[3]

However, the Act nowhere states the criteria for the classification of a country as reciprocating or as having restricted reciprocity. The definitions in the Act merely refer to the countries listed in the appropriate regulations as falling into one or other category.[4] Nor are the regulations entirely clear. So, reg 144(3) limits the duty of the Secretary of the Attorney-General's Department to send for registration orders from countries with restricted reciprocity to 'those of a kind referred to in section 74 of the Act [which deals with the maintenance of a party to a marriage or a child of a marriage] or sub-regulation (2)'. The latter sub-regulation refers to a number of types of order, both a wider class, orders of a kind referred to in s 109[5] or consequent upon such an order, and a narrower class, such orders made in proceedings to which the defendant was not a party.

These rather obscure definitions have caused some confusion. One aspect of this will be evident from the attempt, below, to describe the present geographical scope of the Australian Act. Another concerns the use of the same concepts in the Papua New Guinea Act. Although 'countries with restricted reciprocity' is defined there as comprising countries whose courts have jurisdiction to make maintenance orders not of the same kind as those in Papua New Guinea,[6] the relevant regulations list only two countries with 'restrictions', the United Kingdom and Jersey, and indicate as the nature of the restriction that orders from those countries are 'enforceable in Papua only'.[7] This is a relic of the position under the earlier separate Ordinances for Papua and New Guinea,[8] but it seems doubtful whether it is intra vires the current Act.

1　Act, s 110(1).
2　Eg, Maintenance Act 1964 (New South Wales), s 96(2).
3　The official *Family Law Handbook* (1980 edn) p 23, para 27.7, referring to Regulations, reg 144(3).
4　Act, s 110(1). The Regulations are regs 142 and 143.
5　Reproduced in para 6.10 above.
6　Maintenance Orders Enforcement Act 1970, No 23 (PNG), s 59(2).
7　Maintenance Orders Enforcement Regulations, No 54 of 1971 (PNG), 2nd Schedule.
8　See further para 8.69 below.

Transmission of maintenance orders

6.12　Under the Australian provisions, the procedure for the transmission of a final order for registration overseas may be initiated by the registrar of the court by which it was made or in which it is registered of his own motion, as well as at the request of the creditor.[1] It can operate whenever it appears that the debtor is 'resident in or is proceeding to' a reciprocating country or a country with restricted reciprocity.[2] Like the phrase used in the New Zealand Act[3] this minimises any gap in enforcement while the debtor is in transit; it is more liberal than the New Zealand phrase, for the debtor need not be shown actually to have left Australia. So, for example, a Victorian wife could seek to have the procedure set in motion in respect of her husband who was proceeding to Singapore, even if he was still in Western Australia awaiting the arrival of a ship on which he had booked a passage.

The procedure is not available in the case of Australian affiliation orders[4] unless the debtor appeared in the proceedings in which the order was made, or was duly served with a summons to appear, or consented to the making of the order.[5]

There is no express provision in the Act or Regulations preserving the power of the Australian court to vary or rescind an order despite its transmission overseas. It is thought that this power does nonetheless exist, and there is a related provision enabling the court to take steps to have the registration of the order overseas cancelled if it appears that the debtor is not resident in or proceeding to the registering country or if 'there is some other good reason why the order should no longer be enforceable in that country'.[6]

If an overseas court varies, discharges, suspends or revives an Australian order registered there by means of a provisional order, the Australian court has jurisdiction to confirm that order.[7]

1 Regulations, reg 145(1).
2 Ibid.
3 Family Proceedings Act 1980 (NZ), s 147(1) (applicable to provisional orders only).
4 Ie, orders within Act, s 109, set out in para 6.10 above.
5 Regulations, reg 145(2).
6 Ibid, reg 149(1).
7 Ibid, reg 154.

Registration of final orders

6.13 Before an overseas order is registered in Australia, the Secretary of the Attorney-General's Department must receive the relevant documents, including certificates that the order is enforceable (ie in a legal, but not a practical sense) in the overseas country, and of arrears, and there must appear to be reasonable grounds for believing that the debtor is resident in or proceeding to Australia.[1] Overseas affiliation orders[2] will not be registered if the documents suggest that the defendant was not served with process and did not appear or consent to the order.[3] The restrictions on the types of orders registrable when the country of origin is one 'with restricted reciprocity' have already been noted.[4] It is expressly provided that arrears payable under the order, ie, before the date of registration, are enforceable in Australia.[5] When an order is registered a notice to that effect, with a certified copy of the order and details of any arrears due, is served on the debtor.[6]

The Australian Act goes rather further than its Canadian and New Zealand counterparts in respect of the setting aside of the registration of an overseas final order. The case provided for is one in which a maintenance order (other than an affiliation order) has been made overseas and the defendant was not served with a summons, did not appear, and did not consent to the making of the order. In such a case the debtor may apply within six months of service of notice upon him that the order has been registered in Australia for the discharge (or variation or suspension) of the order and may raise any matter which he could have raised under the Family Law Act 1975 had the original proceedings taken place in Australia.[7] In effect, the Australian legislators have permitted these, inherently suspect, orders to be registered in Australia but in return have given unusually generous safeguards to the debtor.

While an order is registered in Australia, proceedings to enforce it may be taken by the creditor, the registrar of a court having jurisdiction under the Act (presumably, in practice, that in which the order is registered), or by an official appointed as Collector or Deputy Collector of Maintenance under the law of any state or territory.[8]

If an overseas court varies, discharges, suspends or revives one of its orders which has been registered in Australia, and does so by means of a provisional order, the Australian court has power to confirm that order.[9]

1   Regulations, reg 144(1).
2   Ie of a kind referred to in Act, s 109 (see para 6.10 above) or consequent upon such an order.
3   Regulations, reg 144(2).
4   See para 6.11 above.
5   Regulations, reg 144(5).
6   Ibid, reg 144(6) as substituted in 1977. An Australian court will not look behind the certificate of arrears: *Koss and Koss* (1982) FLC 77,498.
7   Ibid, reg 152.
8   Ibid, regs 148 and 132(7), both as amended in 1977.
9   Ibid, reg 154.

Provisional orders

6.14   The power to make provisional orders (including provisional affiliation orders which were not possible under the earlier state Acts[1]) is in fairly standard form. There are three features of note:

(i)   The procedure is available when the defendant is 'proceeding to' an overseas country within the scheme;[2]

(ii)   It is expressly provided that on a reference back from the confirming court, under the 'shuttlecock' procedure, the Australian court can make a fresh provisional order, and is expressly permitted to have regard for this purpose to the evidence given in the other court;[3] and

(iii) Confirmation by an overseas court raises a rebuttable presumption, capable of being relied upon in subsequent Australian proceedings, that the defendant was resident in that country at the time of the confirmation.[4]

There is no express provision as to powers of the Australian courts to vary or discharge a provisional order made by them.[5]

1   Eg Maintenance Act 1964 (New South Wales), s 81.
2   Regulations, reg 147(1).
3   Ibid, reg 147(5)(6).
4   Ibid, reg 147(8).
5   The provisions of ibid, reg 149, enabling the Australian court to secure the cancellation of the registration of an Australian maintenance order in an overseas court are semble inapplicable.

Confirmation of provisional orders

6.15   Here also the Australian scheme follows the general pattern with a few modifications. One is the provision in respect of defendants 'proceeding to'

Australia[1] which has been encountered in other contexts. Much more interesting is regulation 146(5):

'On the hearing of the application [to confirm the order] it shall be open to the respondent to raise any ground of opposition that he could have raised in the original proceedings *or any ground of opposition that he could have raised had the proceedings in which the provisional overseas order was made been heard in Australia* and the statement [of grounds of opposition supplied by the court of origin] shall be conclusive evidence that the grounds referred to in that statement are *the* grounds of opposition that could have been raised in the original proceedings.'[2]

This is remarkable in, semble, preventing the defendant from raising any defence open to him under the law of the country which made the provisional order but which was omitted from the statement supplied with the order; and even more remarkable in that it allows defences under Australian law to be relied upon.

At the hearing of the confirmation proceedings, the creditor is entitled to appear in person or be represented by a legal practitioner, but provision is also made for him to be represented by a registrar, an officer of the Attorney-General's Department or a Collector (or Deputy Collector or Assistant Collector) of Maintenance under the law of a state or territory.[3]

The power to remit the provisional order to the original court for the taking of further evidence is in general terms, ie it is not limited to a remission 'for the purpose of any defence',[4] a limitation which would be inappropriate in view of the choice of law rule allowing Australian defences to be relied upon. When a provisional order is remitted under this power, the Australian court may make an interim order for periodical payments.[5]

1 Regulations, reg 146(1)(d)(i).
2 Italics added.
3 Regulations, reg 146(4A) added in 1977.
4 Ibid, reg 146(6)(c); cf para 5.14 above.
5 Ibid, reg 146(8).

Variation and discharge of registered or confirmed orders

6.16 There are detailed provisions in the Act, applying equally to registered final orders and confirmed provisional orders, as to the variation or discharge of orders or the cancellation of their registration. An Australian court in which an order is registered or confirmed must direct the cancellation of the registration on receipt of a written request from the court that made the order or from some other competent authority in the country of that court.[1] The debtor or creditor may apply for an order discharging, suspending, reviving or varying the overseas order; in this case it is expressly provided that the law to be applied is the law currently in force in Australia under the Family Law Act.[2] An order made on such an application must be made as a provisional order if any court of the overseas country in which the original order was made would have jurisdiction to confirm it.[3]

1 Regulations, reg 150.
2 Ibid, reg 151.
3 Ibid, reg 153(1).

Other features of the Australian model

6.17 The Act contains provisions as to the conversion of currency, selecting as the applicable rate of exchange the telegraphic rate prevailing on the date on which the order becomes an enforceable order in Australia, ie the date of its registration or confirmation.[1] It also deals with the translation of documents not in English, including provision as to the costs of the translation which may be ordered to be borne by a party or the Australian Legal Aid Office.[2]

The Act provides for the making of regulations to give effect to the United Nations Convention on the Recovery Abroad of Maintenance 1956,[3] and in the Amendment Bill before Parliament in 1982 a similar power was added in respect of the Hague Convention on the Recognition and Enforcement of Decisions Relating to Maintenance Obligations 1973;[4] neither power has been exercised.

1   Regulations, reg 171.
2   Ibid, reg 172.
3   Act, s 111.
4   Ibid, s 111A added under cl 46 of the Bill as introduced.

C. THE 1972 UNITED KINGDOM MODEL

Introductory

6.18   In 1972, the United Kingdom Parliament enacted the Maintenance Orders (Reciprocal Enforcement) Act,[1] which contains a thoroughly revised version of the 1920 model, obviously drawing on experience in Canada, New Zealand and in the Australian states and territories. Legislation based on the 1972 Act is to be found in Bermuda, the Falkland Islands (and its Dependencies, and in the British Antarctic Territory), Fiji, Gibraltar, Hong Kong, Malta, the Isle of Man, Nauru, Saint Helena (and Ascension) and Singapore, though for various reasons set out in the relevant paragraphs of Chapter 8 not all this legislation is fully operational. At the 1973 Meeting of Commonwealth Law Ministers the Act was discussed, and a developed version of it, produced after a series of regional meetings of government legal officers, was received at the corresponding meeting in 1980 and is reproduced below.[2]

The Act contains three distinct sets of provisions. Part I, comprising sections 1–24, is the revised version of the 1920 Act. Part II, comprising s 25–39, gives effect in United Kingdom law to the United Nations Convention on the Recovery Abroad of Maintenance, examined below.[3] Section 40 (in Part III) enables variant schemes to be devised and applied to meet particular needs. It has been used to apply a modified form of Part I in relation to the Republic of Ireland; to give effect to the Hague Convention on the Recognition and Enforcement of Decisions relating to Maintenance Obligations, examined below,[4] by means of a more radical revision of Part I; and to apply a version of Part II in relation to various states of the United States of America.[5]

1   Cap 18.
2   See Appendix C. See also para 6.29, below
3   Paras 7.17–7.23.
4   Paras 7.03–7.16.
5   For details and citations see para 8.87 below.

United Kingdom law and the Brussels Convention

6.19   In the United Kingdom itself, the operation of the 1972 Act will be affected, once the Civil Jurisdiction and Judgments Act 1982 is brought fully into force, by the Brussels Convention of 1968 on jurisdiction and the enforcement of judgments in civil and commercial matters. This is a product of the European Community, which does of course contain no other Commonwealth member countries, but its effects cannot be ignored.

As maintenance orders are within the scope of the Convention, its effect is to exclude certain bases on which the English courts would otherwise have jurisdiction in such cases. If the defendant is domiciled (in the special sense in which that term is used in the Civil Jurisdiction and Judgments Act 1982) in another contracting state to the Convention, or in another part of the United Kingdom itself, the English courts will only have jurisdiction to make a maintenance order (a) if it is made as an ancillary order in divorce or similar proceedings;[1] (b) if the court is a court for the place where the creditor is domiciled (in that sense) or is habitually resident;[2] (c) if the defendant is resident in a Convention country within Part II of the 1972 Act, ie a country within the United Nations Convention;[3] (d) if the defendant is resident in a country to which a version of the 1972 Act has been applied by Order in Council under s 40 thereof, and the jurisdictional provisions applying derive from an international convention;[4] or (e) the defendant enters an appearance other than solely to contest the jurisdiction.[5] The same jurisdictional tests apply to applications for variation or revocation.

The Brussels Convention also contains provisions as to the enforcement of orders; the provisions as to maintenance orders to be enforced in the United Kingdom were made as similar as possible to those under the 1972 Act.[6] However, an order will not be recognised under the Convention if the court in which it was made decided a preliminary question as to the status of some person in a way which conflicts with a rule of English private international law.[7]

Affiliation orders are within the scope of maintenance proceedings for the purposes of the Brussels Convention, but it seems that contribution orders obtained from putative fathers by government agencies will be within the Convention as ordinary money-judgments.[8]

1 Civil Jurisdiction and Judgments Act 1982, Sch 1, art 1, para 2(1), and art 5(2), and Sch 4, art 5(2).
2 Ibid, Sch 1, art 5(2) and Sch 4, art 5(2).
3 Ibid, Sch 1, art 57.
4 Ibid. The Order in Council made in respect of the Hague Convention does not qualify, for although the Order contains jurisdictional provisions they are not based on anything in the Convention itself.
5 Ibid, Sch 1, art 18 and Sch 4, art 18.
6 Ibid, Sch 1, arts 31–45.
7 Ibid, Sch 1, art 27(4).
8 Professor Schlosser's official Report, *Official Journal* 1979 C59/77 at para 97(e).

'Maintenance orders'

6.20 The definition of 'maintenance order' in the 1972 legislation is much fuller, and much wider in scope, than in the earlier United Kingdom Act. It is

'an order (however described) of any of the following descriptions, that is to say:
(a)   an order (including an affiliation order or order consequent upon an affiliation order) which provides for the periodical payment of sums of money towards the maintenance of any person, being a person whom the person liable to make payments under the order is, according to the law applied in the place where the order was made, liable to maintain; and

(b)   an affiliation order or order consequent upon an affiliation order, being an order
which provides for the payment by a person adjudged, found or declared to be a
child's father of expenses incidental to the child's birth or, where the child has
died, of his funeral expenses.'[1]

When s 37(1) and Schedule 11 to the Civil Jurisdiction and Judgments Act
1982 (UK) are brought into force, the definition will be further widened: in
place of the reference to 'periodical payment of sums of money' there will
appear 'payment of a lump sum or the making of periodical payments'; this
reflects the increasing use of lump sum orders in the matrimonial jurisdiction
and the desirability of their being brought within the maintenance orders
scheme (for the same order may deal both with a lump sum and with continuing
periodical payments) rather than being left to the legislation on the enforcement of foreign judgments in general.

The words 'however described', together with the wide definition of 'court'[2]
as including 'any tribunal or person having power to make, confirm, enforce,
vary or revoke a maintenance order', are designed to exclude technical arguments based on the particular nature of the order. This reflects Canadian
developments[3] and also the coming together in some jurisdictions of government agencies dealing respectively with the actual enforcement of maintenance
orders and with the social security system.[4]

Any assessment of this definition of 'maintenance order' must take into
account the flexibility of the reciprocity provisions in the Act. A territory can
be designated as a reciprocating country either as regards maintenance orders
generally, ie all those which fall within the definition, or as regards one or more
specified classes only.[5] This flexibility has been much used in practice, and in
the majority of cases a country has been designated subject to some exclusion;
the details are analysed below.[6]

In favour of this approach is the argument that flexibility is desirable to take
account not only of legal provisions (and changes) in the reciprocating country
but also of actual experience in particular cases. The law of a particular country
may provide for the enforcement of certain classes of order, or for the confirmation of provisional orders, but the attitude of the local courts or other circumstances may mean that in practice great difficulty is experienced in obtaining
the desired result. It is possible for a country in which such circumstances arose
to be declared a reciprocating country for a more restricted class of orders,
those in relation to which there is a reasonable prospect of successful proceedings. On the other hand, the approach adopted in the Act produces
considerable complexity, both in the orders made under it and in the
negotiations which must take place with the other country before designations
can be made. It is not clear that it has any advantages over the simpler
system used in Australia,[7] nor that reciprocity of any sort is essential.
The New Zealand experience of a system in which all reliance on reciprocity is
abandoned and with it the whole business of extension orders designating
particular countries suggests that that is entirely satisfactory, and very much
simpler.[8]

The scope of the Act is not limited to Commonwealth countries, but is open
to any country which will confer reciprocal benefits. Because of the special
features of the Commonwealth 'shuttlecock' procedure which is the basis of
Part I of the Act, it is likely that non-Commonwealth countries will be the
subject of Orders under s 40 (application of the Act with adaptations and
modifications).

1 Maintenance Orders (Reciprocal Enforcement) Act 1972 (UK), hereafter referred to as 'Act', s 21(1).
2 Ibid.
3 See the 1979 text of the Canadian Commissioners' Uniform Act, s 1(b)(d).
4 New Zealand was cited in the discussions leading up to the Act; there enforcement was vested in the Department of Social Security.
5 Act, s 1(2).
6 See para 8.87 below.
7 See para 6.11 above.
8 See further para 8.07 below.

Transmission of maintenance orders

6.21 The transmission procedure is commenced by the creditor making application to a prescribed officer of the court; the court itself is not involved.[1] The debtor must be resident in a reciprocating country and the prescribed officer must be 'satisfied' on this score;[2] there is no provision for the 'in transit' cases falling within the Australian and New Zealand Acts.

The provisions as to the documentation required were based on the corresponding provisions in the former legislation of the Australian states and territories. Extensive documentation is required, including a photograph of the debtor if one is available, and the Secretary of State, acting as the transmitting authority, is only to act if he is satisfied that the statement relating to the whereabouts of the payer gives sufficient information to justify the sending of the order.[3]

In January 1976, arrangements were announced in the United Kingdom, after consultations with the Australian, Canadian, New Zealand and South African authorities, to improve the quality of available information and so make it more likely that the debtor would be traced.[4] The arrangements applied to the transmission of a final order under the 1972 Act, but also to provisional orders, corresponding cases under the 1920 Act and even cases where the United Kingdom court had as yet insufficient information even to justify the making of an order. The principal feature of the arrangements was an agreed Enquiry Form, seeking full details about the person concerned, eg his occupation, description, details of his journey to the reciprocating country (such as the airline concerned), names and addresses of possible contacts in that country with whom he might have been in touch, and a specimen signature and photograph.

When s 37(1) of and Part II of Schedule 11 to the Civil Jurisdiction and Judgments Act 1982 are brought into force, the 1972 Act will be amended so as to provide for reciprocal enforcement founded on the presence of assets. So an order will be transmitted to a country in which the debtor is *not* resident but in which he has assets, the prescribed officer being required to satisfy himself as to the nature and location of those assets.[5]

1 Act, s 2(1)(3).
2 Ibid, s 2(4).
3 Ibid.
4 Home Office Circular 8/1976, dated 23 January 1976.
5 Act, s 2(1)(4) as amended by Civil Jurisdiction and Judgments Act 1982, Sch 11, para 9.

Registration of final orders

6.22 The provisions as to the registration in the United Kingdom of overseas orders extend, as do the corresponding New Zealand provisions,[1] to orders made as provisional orders in one reciprocating country and confirmed in another.[2] Although the process remains an administrative one, without any procedure for setting aside registration, both the Secretary of State and the officers of the court concerned are required to consider the residence and whereabouts of the debtor. A court officer satisfied that the debtor is not in fact residing within the jurisdiction of the court returns the order to the Secretary of State with such information as is available as to the debtor's whereabouts;[3] if the Secretary of State finds that the debtor is not resident in the United Kingdom, he sends the order and other relevant documents either back to the responsible authority in the country in which the order was made or on to the responsible authority in another reciprocating country.[4]

Following Australian and New Zealand precedents, the Act provides for the registration of overseas orders in magistrates' courts in England, even if the orders originated in a superior court in the reciprocating country. Under the 1920 Act, orders of the latter class had to be registered in the High Court which made enforcement and variation a more complex matter.[5] High Court enforcement machinery remains available in certain cases in respect of any order originally registered in a magistrates' court.[6]

When s 37(1) of and Part III of Schedule 11 to the Civil Jurisdiction and Judgments Act 1982 are brought into force, reciprocal enforcement will be available on the basis of the presence of assets as well as residence. Accordingly, s 6 of the 1972 Act will be amended to refer to the fact of the debtor having assets in England as an alternative to being resident there.[7]

1   Family Proceedings Act 1980 (NZ), s 136(b).
2   Act, s 6(1).
3   Ibid, s 6(4).
4   Ibid, s 11.
5   Ibid, s 6; cf Maintenance Orders (Facilities for Enforcement) Act 1920 (UK), s 1(2).
6   Maintenance Orders Act 1958, s 1(4) as amended by Act, Sch.
7   Act, s 6(2)(4) as amended by Civil Jurisdiction and Judgments Act 1982, Sch 11, para 10.

Provisional orders

6.23   Three features of the provisions as to provisional orders, which are otherwise in standard form, are worthy of note. A difficulty which can arise where a court can only order maintenance if it also makes an order providing for the legal custody of the child is removed in this context: the applicant is deemed for the purpose to have custody under a court order.[1] Where a United Kingdom provisional order has been confirmed overseas, and, the marriage having been dissolved or annulled, the creditor remarries, the order ceases to have effect.[2] Finally, a United Kingdom order which has been confirmed overseas can be enforced in the United Kingdom if the debtor returns to that country; it was not at all clear that this was the case under the 1920 Act.[3]

1   Act, s 3(3).
2   Ibid, s 42 as amended by Domestic Proceedings and Magistrates' Courts Act 1978, Sch 2, para 37. Cf Matrimonial Proceedings and Property Act 1970, s 30(2) as amended by Domestic Proceedings and Magistrates' Courts Act 1978, Sch 2, para 48, applying a similar rule to cases under the 1920 Act; and cf also, for the effect of divorce on maintenance orders, para 5.21, above.
3   Act, s 3(6): 'for all purposes'.

Confirmation of provisional orders

6.24   The provisions as to the confirmation of overseas provisional orders contain only two novelties. One, inspired by similar provisions in other Commonwealth models, allows the confirming court to order that sums be payable under the order from a date earlier than the date of confirmation, but not earlier than that on which the original provisional order was made.[1] The other is the abandonment of the traditional term 'modification', the Act allowing a confirming court to make 'such alterations as it thinks reasonable.'[2] It is doubtful whether any change of substance was intended, but certainly 'alteration' is as general a term as could have been chosen.

1 Act, s 8(8).
2 Ibid, s 7(2)(ii).

Variation and revocation of orders

6.25 The Act contains comprehensive provisions as to variation and revocation of orders in different circumstances.

In the case of a United Kingdom final order registered abroad, it is expressly declared that courts in the United Kingdom retain jurisdiction to enforce, vary or revoke the order.[1] Similarly, it is declared that an order made in the United Kingdom as a provisional order and confirmed overseas may be enforced, varied or revoked in the United Kingdom.[2] In the latter case this is 'subject to section 5'; in fact *both* types of case are effected by s 5, which provides that the variation of either type of order may be by way of provisional order and must be by such an order if the effect of the variation is to increase the rate of payments, unless both the creditor and the debtor appear in the proceedings or the applicant appears and process was duly served upon the respondent.[3] The Act recognises the power of the court of registration to vary or revoke the order,[4] and also empowers the United Kingdom court which made the original order to confirm a provisional order made overseas varying or revoking it.[5]

So far as overseas orders registered in the United Kingdom are concerned, the terminology of the Act does not correspond to that used in other Commonwealth models. By section 7(5), when an overseas provisional order is confirmed in the United Kingdom, it must be registered in the confirming court, and the term 'registered order' therefore includes both registered final orders and confirmed provisional orders.[6]

Variation of a registered order may be by provisional order and must be by such an order unless both the creditor and the debtor are residing in the United Kingdom; or the application is made by the creditor; or the variation is a reduction in the rate of payments and is made solely on account of a change in the financial circumstances of the debtor and the courts in the country in which the original order was made would not have power under their own law to confirm a provisional order.[7]

Revocation may equally be by way of a provisional order. In this case, a provisional order must be used unless both the creditor and the debtor are residing in the United Kingdom.[8]

The choice-of-law rules are unusual. In considering variation, the United Kingdom court will always apply its own law. Revocation being a more drastic step, the court is required to apply the law of the country in which the registered order was made. If there is some doubt as to whether the ground upon which the applicant relies really does amount to a sufficient ground for revocation under that law, then the United Kingdom court, if it finds there are reasonable grounds for believing such a ground to exist, may make a provisional order requiring confirmation in the reciprocating country.[9]

The registration of an order must be cancelled if the order is revoked, or if the prescribed officer of the registering court is of opinion that the debtor has ceased to reside within the jurisdiction of the court. In this case the order is returned to the Secretary of State unless the debtor is believed to be residing within the jurisdiction of another United Kingdom court in which case it is sent to the prescribed officer of that court.[10]

The Act proceeds on the basis that if a judgment is registered in England, this gives jurisdiction to vary or revoke, subject to the requirements already noted as to the use of provisional orders. To comply with the Brussels Convention 1968, the Civil Jurisdiction and Judgments Act 1982 will, when brought fully into force, provide that a registered order may not be varied or revoked if neither the creditor nor the debtor is resident in the United Kingdom.[11] This new rule will have general effect and is not limited to cases with a European Community aspect.

1   Act, s 2(5).
2   Ibid, s 3(6).
3   Ibid, s 5(1)(2)(3).
4   Ibid, s 5(7)(8).
5   Ibid, s 5(5).
6   See ibid, s 21(1).
7   Ibid, s 9(1)(2).
8   Ibid, s 9(1)(3).
9   Ibid, s 9(4).
10   Ibid, s 10(1)(2)(3). These provisions will be amended when the Civil Jurisdiction and Judgments Act 1982, Sch 11, para 13, is brought into force, so as to refer to the 'presence of assets' as well as the 'residence' criterion.
11   Ibid, s 9(1B) inserted by Civil Jurisdiction and Judgments Act 1982, Sch 11, para 12.

Other features of the model

6.26   The Act contains provisions as to conversion of currency, affecting both registered orders and statements of arrears. The relevant date for both purposes is the date on which the order first became a registered order or (if it is earlier) that on which it was confirmed in the United Kingdom, except that where an order is varied the date is the date upon which the variation order was registered or (if it is earlier) the date upon which it was confirmed there.[1]

There are generally-worded powers both as to the taking of evidence in the United Kingdom in response to a request from a court in a reciprocating country and as to requests to courts in such a country for the purpose of any proceedings in the United Kingdom under Part I of the Act.[2]

1   Act, s 16.
2   Ibid, s 14; see s 13 for admissibility of evidence. See *Killen v Killen* 1981 SLT 77 (Sh Ct) for the practical aspects, in a Scottish context.

D. OTHER COMMONWEALTH MODELS

Barbados

6.27   The Maintenance Orders (Reciprocal Enforcement) Act 1974 of Barbados,[1] which has been reproduced mutatis mutandis in the current legislation of Anguilla,[2] is an attempt to combine the models enacted in the United Kingdom in 1920 and 1972. Each model had been adopted in Barbados, as the Maintenance Orders (Facilities for Enforcement) Act 1922[3] and the Foreign

Maintenance (Reciprocal Enforcement) Act 1972,[4] and there must have seemed merit in the idea of conflating the two texts.

Unfortunately the result is unsatisfactory; as a result of a series of drafting mistakes the legislation is probably wholly unworkable. Three matters require particular comment:

(i) Part X of the Act deals with applications by persons in Barbados for recovery of maintenance in a reciprocating state and vice versa. It is closely based upon the relevant provisions in Part II of the Maintenance Orders (Reciprocal Enforcement) Act 1972 of the United Kingdom, which were designed to give effect to the United Nations Convention on the Recovery Abroad of Maintenance 1956.[5] In the Barbados Act, however, there is no reference to the Convention or to a separate class of 'convention countries'[6]; instead reference is made to 'reciprocating states', and under s 34 a country can only be designated as a reciprocating state for all the purposes of the Act. The result is that only a country which has legislation compatible with the traditional Commonwealth scheme and which is also a party to, or at least has legislation based upon, the United Nations Convention can become a reciprocating state. This greatly reduces the potential usefulness of the Barbados legislation.

(ii) Part VI of the Act contains provisions as to the variation and revocation of maintenance orders made abroad and confirmed or registered in Barbados. The provisions are based upon s 9 of the United Kingdom Act of 1972. Unfortunately, apart from in the heading to Part VI, the marginal note to s 16, and the opening reference to a court in Barbados in which an order is 'confirmed or registered', the term 'confirmed' is not used. The substantive provisions follow the United Kingdom drafting in speaking solely of a 'registered order'; the draftsman failed to note that in the United Kingdom, but not in Barbados, a provisional order which has been confirmed is thereupon registered, so that a 'registered order' in the United Kingdom text comprises both registered final orders and confirmed provisional orders. A careless omission of words in s 16(10) when compared with the United Kingdom text, s 9(8), does nothing to add to one's confidence in the workability of this Act.

(iii) Finally, the definition of 'affiliation order' in s 2 of the Barbados Act is limited to orders made under s 6 of the Affiliation Proceedings Act 1963 (Barbados), and contains no words apt to describe orders of the same general type originating abroad.

1 Act 1974–50.
2 Maintenance Orders (Reciprocal Enforcement) Ordinance 1978, No 8 of 1978 (Anguilla).
3 Act 1922–4.
4 Act 1972–28.
5 See paras 7.17–7.23 below.
6 Cf Maintenance Orders (Reciprocal Enforcement) Act 1972 (UK), s 25.

Quebec

6.28 Although this book is primarily concerned with the common law jurisdictions of the Commonwealth, Quebec's position as a civil-law province within a federation generally in the common law tradition makes its law of particular interest.[1] Since 1952 Quebec has had a Reciprocal Enforcement of Maintenance Orders Act, in French *loi d'execution reciproque d'ordonnances alimentaires*.[2] Although expressed in a form which respects 'both the stylistic concision characteristic of the civil law and the general principles of Quebec's private international law',[3] the Quebec Act follows, as to all the substantive issues as to the meaning of maintenance and the handling of final and provisional orders, the recommendations of the Canadian Commissioners on the Uniformity of Legislation. It is slightly old-fashioned, not having been amended since its introduction, despite the recommendations of the Civil Code Revision Office in 1972. It can only be applied, for example, to other provinces of Canada.

One special feature of the current Act is its use of ordre public.[4] Section 4 reads (in the English translation):

'To have the benefit of the provisions of this Act, the judgment rendered in another Province of Canada must be in conformity with the laws and rules of public order in force in the Province of Quebec, especially those relating to marriage.'

The abortive 1972 Draft Bill similarly provided for the setting aside of the registration of an order which was 'manifestly contrary to Quebec public order'.[5] So long as the scope of Quebec recognition provisions is substantially limited to the orders of other Canadian provinces, it may be that ordre public will have limited effect; other Canadian jurisdictions are unlikely to make orders so offensive to the eyes of Quebec's judges.[6]

Special arrangements exist between Quebec and France. By the Act to Secure the Carrying Out of the Entente between France and Quebec Respecting Mutual Aid in Judicial Matters,[7] decisions as to support obligations handed down in France have pleno iure the authority of res judicata in Quebec subject to certain conditions.[8]

In the Final Report of the Civil Code Revision Office on the reform of the Civil Code of Lower Canada, Book IX contained new proposed rules on the recognition and enforcement of support obligations. Articles 79 and 80 of the proposed text in its English form read as follows:

'79   The courts of Quebec recognize and enforce decisions rendered outside Quebec with regard to support when:

1. at the time of the action, one of the parties was domiciled within the jurisdiction of the authority seized:
2. at the time of the action, one of the parties was a national of the State of the authority seized; or
3. the defendant has contested on the merits without challenging the jurisdiction of the authority seized.

80   A decision rendered outside Quebec which orders periodic payment of support may be recognized and declared enforceable as regards payments accrued and accruing.'

Certain other provisions of the proposed Code are also applicable.[9] So a decision would not be enforceable in Quebec if the defendant proved that it was not enforceable in its state of origin[10] or was obtained by 'fraud in the procedure'.[11] Default judgments are only recognised if the defendant was duly served with process in accordance with the law of the state of origin, and even then may be refused recognition if the defendant did not have sufficient time to present his defence.[12] Unless a default judgment is involved, findings of fact on which the court of origin based its jurisdiction bind the Quebec courts.[13] 'Settlements' are enforceable in the same way as decisions.[14]

Although regarded as an important working document, these proposals have not been implemented and the matter remains under review.

1   See generally J.-G. Castel *Droit International Privé Québécois.*
2   Now cap E-19, RL. Reforming legislation was under consideration during 1982.

3　Report of the Committee on Private International Law, Civil Code Revision Office (1973), p 8.
4　For this concept see para 4.12 above.
5　Draft Bill, art 6, 1.
6　See Ethel Groffier 'La loi québécoise d'execution reciproque d'ordonnances alimentaires' (1973) 51 CBR 419.
7　Cap A-20.1, RL.
8　Title VII.
9　Art 81.
10　Art 60, 3.
11　Art 60, 5.
12　Art 61.
13　Art 64.
14　Art 70. Cf para 7.05 below; the Hague Conference work is an important influence on the Quebec proposals.

The Commonwealth Secretariat's Draft Model Bill

6.29　After considering the question of the reciprocal enforcement of maintenance orders at their 1973, 1975 and 1977 meetings, the Commonwealth Law
Ministers encouraged detailed consideration of the matter at a series of regional
meetings. These meetings of government legal officers were organised by the
Commonwealth Secretariat, and separate reports are published of the
meetings in Basseterre (St Kitts), Apia (Western Samoa) and Nairobi (Kenya).
In the course of these regional meetings a draft Model Bill was elaborated,
based upon the United Kingdom's Maintenance Orders (Reciprocal Enforcement) Act 1972 but departing from that model in a number of respects. A
definitive version of the Bill, reproduced below,[1] was published in 1981.

　The model Bill, like the 1972 United Kingdom Act, contains provisions[2]
designed to give effect in the enacting jurisdiction to the United Nations
Convention on the Recovery Abroad of Maintenance 1956. Unlike the 1972
Act it also contains provisions[3] dealing with the Hague Convention on the
Recognition and Enforcement of Decisions relating to Maintenance Obliga-
tions.

　In Part I of the Act, which contains the revised version of the traditional
Commonwealth scheme, a wide definition of 'maintenance orders' is used,
reflecting some features of the Australian definition.[4] A novelty in the Bill is its
use of prescribed forms for use in connection with the transmission of orders
and related documents between countries, a system used with much success
under the Hague Convention on the Service Abroad of Judicial and Extra-
Judicial Documents in Civil and Commercial Matters. The various forms are
not set out in the Bill but in draft subordinate legislation also published by the
Commonwealth Secretariat.

　In other respects the draft selects the most appropriate solution from those
available in existing Commonwealth legislation.[5]

1　See Appendix C.
2　Draft Bill, cl 23–30.
3　Ibid, cl 31–41.
4　Ibid, cl 2(1).
5　Detailed Notes on Clauses and the relevant draft Rules are contained in the Commonwealth Secretariat publication *International Conventions concerning Applications for and Awards of Maintenance* (1981).

E. SPECIAL CASES—MAINTENANCE AGREEMENTS AND AFFILIATION ORDERS

Maintenance agreements

6.30 It is of course quite a common practice for the payment of maintenance to be the subject of a private agreement between the parties. This can involve the support of illegitimate children, but is much more common on the separation of a married couple. The agreement is enforceable as any other contract. However, in a number of jurisdictions the courts may also become involved. The courts may be given power to vary or revoke the provisions of a maintenance agreement, usually to take account of the changed financial circumstances of the parties.[1] Or, it may be thought desirable to improve the enforceability of maintenance agreements by providing a facility for their registration in a court, with the consequence that they can be enforced—and usually varied or revoked—as if they had been made as court orders.[2]

This sort of development raises the question whether, at least in the latter type of case, provision should be made within the reciprocal enforcement scheme for the enforcement of overseas maintenance orders. The 1979 text of the Canadian Commissioners' Uniform Act defines 'final order' as including 'the maintenance provisions in a written agreement between a claimant and a respondent where those provisions are enforceable in the state in which the agreement was made as if contained in an order of a court of that state'.[3] A maintenance agreement registered in a New Zealand court is also within the general definition of 'maintenance order' in the Family Proceedings Act 1980,[4] but this is not clearly stated as applicable to Part VIII dealing with the enforcement of overseas orders.[5]

The fullest provision is made in the Family Law Act 1975 of Australia, and the Family Law Regulations made thereunder.[6] The provisions only apply in respect of prescribed overseas countries, currently New Zealand and Papua New Guinea.[7] The Regulations contain provisions, comparable to those for the registration of an overseas final maintenance order, for the registration of overseas maintenance agreement, which becomes enforceable as if it were an agreement entered into in Australia and registered under the Family Law Act.[8] Registration must be cancelled at the request in writing of the parties or the overseas court or other relevant overseas authority.[9] Similarly, a maintenance agreement registered in an Australian court under the Family Law Act will be sent to the appropriate court or authority in any country which would enforce it, at the request in writing of a person having rights under the agreement.[10]

1 See, eg, Matrimonial Causes Act 1973 (UK), ss 34–36.
2 See, eg, Family Law Act 1975 (Australia), ss 86–88.
3 1979 Uniform Act, s 1(f)(i).
4 Family Proceedings Act 1980 (NZ), s 2.
5 Compare sub-para (a)(i) of the definition with sub-paras (a)(ii) and (a)(iii); but the effect would appear to be that (a)(i) applies generally.
6 Family Law Act 1975 (Australia), s 89; Family Law Regulations, regs 155–156.
7 Family Law Act 1975, s 4(1); Family Law Regulations, reg 170.
8 Family Law Regulations, reg 155.
9 Ibid, reg 155A added in 1977.
10 Ibid, reg 156.

Treatment of affiliation orders

6.31 As has already been noted, the original New Zealand legislation and the Australian states' Acts based upon it included affiliation orders along with other types of maintenance orders.[1] At the Imperial Conference the New Zealand delegate expressly excluded affiliation orders, and this appeared to be the mind of the Conference. Strangely, the first 1913 draft of what eventually became the 1920 model legislation nonetheless included affiliation orders. They were later again excluded, and it is clear that a conscious decision was taken to exclude all types of affiliation order from the Commonwealth scheme.[2]

Affiliation orders remained within the Australian inter-state enforcement scheme, and in Western Australia the same policy was applied in the local version of the 1920 legislation,[3] a decision which should have had the result of making it impossible to find reciprocating states. In more recent years the inclusion of affiliation orders has become much more general. The Canadian Commissioners' Uniform Act has since 1958 applied to affiliation orders, and all jurisdictions except Prince Edward Island have amended their legislation in this direction. At the international level, the various Hague Conventions[4] and (less clearly) the United Nations Convention[5] apply to affiliation orders. New Zealand, the pioneering jurisdiction within the Commonwealth, moved some way in its Domestic Proceedings Act 1968 where a carefully qualified recognition was extended to affiliation orders, and adopted a more liberal position in the Family Proceedings Act 1980. Australia, in the Family Law Act 1975, and the Canadian Commissioners in their 1979 Uniform Act include affiliation orders, but with some special provisions. The legislation based on the Maintenance Orders (Reciprocal Enforcement) Act 1972 of the United Kingdom equates affiliation orders with other maintenance orders for all purposes. Some of these variants are examined in more detail below.[6]

In a number of countries there exist what are sometimes styled 'contribution orders', in effect affiliation orders made against the putative father but on the application not of the mother but of the government agency which has taken over the care of the illegitimate child. As yet there is only a limited willingness to enforce such orders (and this is evidenced by the frequency with which they are excluded from the scope of extension orders made under the 1972 United Kingdom Act[7]), but whether this is a result of unfamiliarity or of a reluctance to come to the aid of an official agency, whose claims may be less attractive than those of a deserted mother, is not clear.

1   Destitute Persons Act 1910, No 38 (NZ), s 2. See, for the whole topic, Diane C. Dzwiekowski 'The Reciprocal Enforcement of Affiliation Orders' 22 RFL 29.
2   See Colonial Office letter to the Home Office, 5 August 1914, on the subject of provisional affiliation orders.
3   Reciprocal Enforcement of Maintenance Orders Act 1921, No 27 (Western Australia), s 2.
4   Paras 7.02–7.16 below.
5   Para 7.18 below.
6   Para 6.33 below.
7   See the details given in para 8.87 below.

The arguments

6.32   When the 1920 legislation was first introduced into the British House of Commons, the Under Secretary of State for the Colonies explained that 'the nature of the evidence in cases of affiliation, and the possibility, at any rate, of unwarranted charges being brought makes it much more difficult to try such cases at a distance of many thousands of miles.'[1] He foresaw difficulties in securing reciprocal arrangements if any other policy was adopted. Very similar arguments were repeated at the Commonwealth Law Ministers' Meeting in 1973, when the United Kingdom reported that it had in fact changed its policy.

There are two types of answer to these objections. An affiliation order will in practice almost always contain both a declaration that the defendant has been adjudged to be the father of the child and an order that he should make periodical payments on account of the maintenance of the child. The precise nature of the former declaration is not entirely clear—whether or not it is a judgment as to status, one in rem,[2]—but it was strongly urged by Lord Hailsham of St Marylebone LC at the 1973 Law Ministers' Meeting that, at least for the purposes of enforcement in private international law, the maintenance obligation was separable from questions of status. Although criticised, notably by Professor R. H. Graveson who was a British delegate at the Hague Conference in 1956, this same distinction was the basis of the Hague Conventions of 1956 and 1958 and was re-asserted on their revision in 1972–3. As M. Verwilghen comments:

'The great majority of Delegates [at The Hague] felt that the recognition and enforcement of that part of a foreign decision which relates to maintenance should, in principle, be independent of the effectiveness, in the State addressed, of that part of the said decision which concerns the status of persons or any other matter.'[3]

The second type of answer is at a more practical level. It is not at all clear why proof of paternity should be regarded as altogether more difficult than proof of adultery or any other factual basis for the making of a maintenance order. Grave doubts were expressed when the 1920 scheme was being prepared as to the wisdom of the procedure of provisional orders, with the two parties appearing before different courts, so that no one tribunal could judge the strength of each side's case at first hand. Practical experience has largely quieted these doubts, and it may well be that the same will be true in the affiliation context. In United Kingdom experience the defendant in affiliation proceedings admits paternity in some 75% of cases; difficult questions of proof will therefore arise only in a minority of cases.

Even if proof of paternity is regarded as being in a category of its own, it is important to realise that this is only an argument against a procedure for the confirmation of provisional affiliation orders. It is no argument against the registration and enforcement of an overseas final affiliation order made after the normal process of adjudication. This is perhaps especially the case in a Commonwealth context, for it may be assumed that safeguards such as the requirement of corroboration are common to all jurisdictions.

1   132 HC Official Report (5th series) col 2160.
2   See on this point the discussion by Diane C. Dzwiekowski, 22 RFL 29 at pp 30–40.
3   *Actes et Documents de la Douzième Session* vol 4, Report on the Enforcement Convention, para 38. See also his paras 129–132 concerning the corresponding art 2 of the Applicable Law Convention.

Special provisions applicable to affiliation

6.33   Some of the current legislative texts contain special provisions applying to affiliation cases. So the 1979 text of the Canadian Commissioners' Uniform Act makes it clear that the affiliation issue may be determined as part of proceedings under the reciprocal enforcement legislation, if it has not previously been determined by a court of competent jurisdiction; and in proceedings to confirm a provisional order, even if the provisional order makes no reference to affiliation.[1] These provisions make clear the Commissioners' determination to incorporate affiliation cases fully within the scheme of their legislation, but the Uniform Act also makes it clear that if affiliation is determined in the course of reciprocal enforcement proceedings the effect of the determination is limited to those proceedings.[2]

In Australia, overseas final affiliation orders[3] will not be registered under the Family Law Act 1975 if it appears that the defendant was not duly served with a summons to appear in the original proceedings and did not appear or consent to the making of an order.[4] Overseas provisional affiliation orders may be confirmed in Australia, but (as with all provisional orders) any defence available under the Family Law Act may be raised by the debtor,[5] which gives full protection to his interests. There is no restriction on the making of provisional affiliation orders in Australia,[6] but there are restrictions on the transmission abroad of final orders[7] which correspond to those on the registration in Australia of overseas final orders.[8]

The New Zealand Family Proceedings Act 1980 integrates affiliation orders more fully than did the earlier Domestic Proceedings Act 1968 (which forbade the confirmation of provisional affiliation orders).[9] The current Act allows the registration of overseas affiliation orders, providing however that the registration of such an order (including orders made both 'in' and 'consequent on' an affiliation order) may be set aside if the defendant did not appear in the original proceedings and those proceedings were not duly brought to his notice.[10] In proceedings for the confirmation of provisional affiliation orders from overseas, the defendant may raise the defence that he is not the father of the child and had had no notice of the original proceedings.[11]

1   1979 Uniform Act, s 4(1)(2).
2   Ibid, s 4(3).
3   For this purpose 'affiliation order' includes any order within Family Law Act 1975, s 109 (reproduced in para 6.10 above).
4   Family Law Regulations 1975 (Australia), reg 144(2).
5   Ibid, reg 146(5).
6   Ibid, reg 147.
7   Ibid, reg 145(2).
8   Text and note 5, above.
9   This is still the position in Western Samoa.
10   Family Proceedings Act 1980 (NZ), s 137(b).
11   Ibid, s 138(5).

CHAPTER 7

Financial Provision
International Developments

Introduction

7.01 The Commonwealth system for the recognition and enforcement of maintenance orders remains one of the most satisfactory, and in its developed forms one of the most sophisticated, of the international instruments dealing with the problem. A great deal of other work has been carried out, and is directly relevant to the Commonwealth jurisdictions, either because they can usefully become party to international arrangements which can supplement their existing legislation, or, in the case of legislation in the United States, because there is a model sufficiently similar to the Commonwealth scheme for it to be treated as giving reciprocal benefits and so opening the way to bilateral designations between jurisdictions in the United States and Commonwealth countries.

At the end of the 1920s, more than a decade after the Imperial Conference had initiated the preparation of the Commonwealth scheme, a number of international bodies began to study the enforcement of maintenance obligations. The Nordic countries were able to agree the Convention of Oslo 1931, which dealt with maintenance orders originating from courts or other agencies, and included affiliation orders.[1] In 1929 the League of Nations invited the Rome Institute for the Unification of Private Law to work in the area and it produced a preliminary draft convention in 1938, which was revised and re-issued in 1949.[2]

The work was taken over by the United Nations, the Economic and Social Council agreeing in 1951 to the preparation of one or more international instruments.[3] A Committee of Experts met in Geneva in 1952 and prepared two drafts;[4] the Economic and Social Council took the view that progress should only be made with the second, which was designed to facilitate the making of claims for maintenance in the country of the debtor's residence.[5] This work led in due course to the United Nations Convention on the Recovery Abroad of Maintenance 1956, the details of which are considered below.[6]

Meanwhile, the Hague Conference on Private International Law had resumed its work after the interruption during the war years. Work was set in hand towards the preparation of a Convention on the Law Applicable to Maintenance Obligations in Respect of Children, a choice-of-law convention which was agreed in 1956. In view of the limitations the United Nations had imposed upon its own work, the Hague Conference also tackled the question of the enforcement of maintenance orders. The United Nations view was that this could best be dealt with by bilateral treaties; the Hague Conference preferred a multilateral approach, with a remarkable dissent from the United Kingdom whose delegation argued that a multilateral approach was inappropriate—an extraordinary position given the development of the Commonwealth scheme.[7] In the result a second Hague Convention, this dealing with the Recognition and Enforcement of Decisions Relating to Maintenance Obligations towards Children, was drafted in 1956 and signed in 1958.

Both of these Hague conventions were limited to cases involving children. It was clearly desirable to make similar provision in respect of adults and at the 12th Session of the Conference in 1972 and at a session of a Special Commission in 1973 two new conventions were drafted dealing with a wider range of maintenance obligations; they are examined below.[8]

1 For details of this and other early work, see Gutteridge 'The International Enforcement of Maintenance Orders' (1948) 2 ILQ 155; and *L'Execution à L'Etranger des Obligations Alimentaires* Rome Institute (Unidroit), Doc 13(1) (1938) with Appendix (1949).
2 For texts see *Unification of Law* (1948) p 212; (1954) p 199.
3 See P. Contini (Legal Adviser to the Committee of Experts charged with the work), 'International Enforcement of Maintenance Obligations' 41 California LR 106 (1953).
4 Doc E/AC 39/1 of 18 September 1952. The first of these drafts, on the enforcement of orders, is reproduced in *Actes et Documents de la Huitième Session* (of the Hague Conference), vol 2, pp 173–178.
5 Resolution No 527 (XVII) of 26 April 1954.
6 Paras 7.18–7.23 below.
7 *Actes et Documents de la Huitième Session* vol 2, p 156.
8 Paras 7.02–7.17 below.

A. HAGUE CONVENTIONS

The Hague Applicable Law Convention

7.02 In Commonwealth practice, a court invited to make a maintenance order will apply to its own law. As the leading treatise remarks, 'It has never been doubted that the court ... always applies its own law, irrespective of the domicile of the parties.'[1] Not only is this established practice, but there is little evidence of dissatisfaction with it. Given that many maintenance orders are made in subordinate courts, there are strong arguments for excluding reference to foreign legal principles; and it can be argued that the elements of discretion involved, and the importance of the social context within which that discretion is used, make the correct application of foreign legal principles peculiarly difficult.

However, within the Commonwealth reciprocal enforcement schemes, there are circumstances in which courts, including subordinate courts, are required to apply the law of some other jurisdiction. So, taking examples under United Kingdom legislation, the question 'who is a dependant?' is answered by reference to the law of the country in which the original order (or provisional order) was made.[2] Defences available under the law of the country in which a provisional order was made are relevant in confirmation proceedings in other jurisdictions.[3] In certain cases, revocation of an order must be based on a consideration of the law under which the order was originally made.[4] It can, however, be said that the relevant law is always the lex fori; the peculiarity of the Commonwealth scheme is that a case may have more than one forum, and rules once applicable as the then lex fori may remain applicable despite the transfer of some aspects of the case to a second (or third) forum.

Civil law tradition is averse to the application of the lex fori in this way, and this is reflected in the Hague Applicable Law Convention of 1973 which, like its predecessor of 1956, favours the law of the habitual residence of the creditor. The justifications advanced for this approach are both theoretical and practical:

'Firstly . . ., the aim of the maintenance obligation is to protect the creditor. As he is the focal point of the institution, he must be considered in the reality of his daily life and not in the purely legal attributes of his person, as he will use his maintenance to enable him to live. Indeed in this field it is wise to appreciate the concrete problem arising in connection with a concrete society: that in which the [creditor] lives and will live. Secondly, this system facilitates a degree of harmonization within each State: all maintenance creditors living in that State will be put on the same footing. In practice also, the system undoubtedly has its advantages in the case of plurality of debtors. Finally, it is well-known that this connecting factor represents a meeting point of States traditionally favouring nationality and States using domicile as the preferred connecting factor.'[5]

Although there are no common law states amongst the signatories to the Convention,[6] it was designed to provide a set of model rules which were thought likely to commend themselves to countries with diverse legal traditions. Accordingly, and because of some parallels with the Enforcement Convention considered below, a brief account of those rules is presented here.

Under the Convention, a court in a contracting state applies

(i)   the internal law of the habitual residence of the maintenance creditor;
(ii) if under the above law, the creditor is unable to obtain maintenance from the debtor, the law of the common nationality of the maintenance creditor and the maintenance debtor; and
(iii) if the parties have no common nationality, or the creditor is unable to obtain maintenance from the debtor under the law of their common nationality, then the law of the authority seised of the case, ie the lex fori.[7]

The applicable law so identified governs, inter alia, to what extent and from whom the creditor may claim maintenance; who is entitled to bring proceedings and the time limits for their institution; and, in the case of a claim for reimbursement by a public body, the extent of the debtor's obligation to pay.[8]

These general rules are set aside in a number of special cases identified in the convention. Where maintenance issues arise in the context of proceedings for divorce, separation, or nullity of marriage, the law applied to the matrimonial question will govern maintenance obligations between the spouses, including future variations, and this rule applies both in the contracting state whose courts granted the divorce or other remedy and in a contracting state in which the decree is entitled to recognition.[9] It is to be noted that this provision is limited to obligations between spouses and does not apply to the maintenance of children of the marriage; the division of the issues in this way could prove very difficult in practice.

A second special case is that of claims to contribution or reimbursement of benefits provided for a maintenance creditor by a public body. The law to which the public body is subject governs such claims.[10]

A third special case concerns obligations between persons related collaterally or by affinity. Such claims may be excluded altogether from the effective scope of the Convention by Reservation; in other cases, the debtor escapes liability if no obligation exists under

(i)   if the parties have a common nationality, the law of that nationality; and
(ii) in other cases, the internal law of the debtor's habitual residence.[11]

A contracting state may refuse to apply the law designated as applicable under the Convention if, and only if, it is manifestly incompatible with its public policy (ordre public).[12] In all cases, and even if the applicable law provides otherwise, the needs of the creditor and the resources of the debtor must be taken into account in determining the amount of maintenance.[13]

1 Dicey and Morris *The Conflict of Laws* (10th edn, 1980) p 404, citing *Sealey v Callan* [1953] P 135, [1953] 1 All ER 942; *Cammell v Cammell* [1965] P 467, [1964] 3 All ER 255; and *Schmidt v Schmidt* (1963) 43 DLR (2d) 61.
2 Maintenance Orders (Facilities for Enforcement) Act 1920 (UK), s 10; Maintenance Orders (Reciprocal Enforcement) Act 1972 (UK), s 21(1).
3 1920 Act, s 4(3); 1972 Act, s 7(2).
4 1972 Act, s 9(4).
5 M. Verwilghen, Report of the Special Commission, para 58 in *Actes et Documents de la Douzième Session* Tome IV, p 117.
6 Belgium, France, Italy, Luxembourg, Netherlands, Portugal, Switzerland and Turkey. Belgium and Turkey have not yet ratified the Convention.
7 Applicable Law Convention, arts 4–6.
8 Ibid, art 10.
9 Ibid, art 8. See ibid, art 14(3) for the power by reservation to include cases of divorces, etc, granted by default in a country other than that in which the respondent had his habitual residence.
10 Ibid, art 9.
11 Ibid, arts 7, 14(1)(2) (reservations).
12 Ibid, art 11, first paragraph.
13 Ibid, art 11, second paragraph.

The Hague Enforcement Convention

7.03 The Convention on the Recognition and Enforcement of Decisions Relating to Maintenance Obligations was signed at The Hague on 2 October 1973. Ten states have ratified the Convention (Czechoslovakia, France, Italy, Luxembourg, Netherlands, Norway, Portugal, Sweden, Switzerland and the United Kingdom). Belgium, Finland, the German Federal Republic and Turkey are signatories which have yet to ratify. Australian legislation to enable that country to accede to the Convention was introduced in 1982.[1] It is understood that Denmark, Japan and Spain are taking steps towards accession, and a number of Commonwealth jurisdictions are also giving consideration to the matter.

The Convention is limited to what would, in terms of the Commonwealth reciprocal enforcement schemes, be described as 'final' orders. Article 4 refers to 'provisionally enforceable decisions', but this refers to decisions which are subject to further review in the country of origin yet are enforceable as an interim measure; a 'provisional order' within the Commonwealth schemes would clearly not be a 'provisionally enforceable decision' for the purposes of the Convention for it wholly lacks effect until it is confirmed.

The scope and principles of the Convention are examined in the following paragraphs.[2]

1 See para 6.09 above.
2 There is a large literature, though only a small amount is in English. See D. F. Cavers (1973) 21 Am Jo Comp L 154, 593 and (1981) 81 Columbia LR 994; H. Battifol (1973) Rev crit de d i p, 261; A. E. van Overbeck (1973) 29 Annuaire suisse de droit international 135.

Scope of the Convention

7.04 The Convention applies in respect of a broad category of maintenance obligations, those 'arising from a family relationship, parentage, marriage or affinity, including a maintenance obligation towards an infant who is not legitimate, between (1) a maintenance creditor and a maintenance debtor; or (2) a maintenance debtor and a public body which claims reimbursement of benefits given to a maintenance creditor.'[1] The Convention follows the example of Commonwealth legislation in avoiding any direct definition of maintenance, in terms of the content of the concept. The Convention does not even refer to the payment of money as an essential feature, but this is plainly envisaged and art 22 contains a reference to the 'transfer of funds payable as maintenance'.

The range of family relationships included is a large one. Illegitimate children are increasingly within Commonwealth legislation as the opposition to the enforcement of overseas affiliation orders gradually disappears. However the Convention also applies to maintenance obligations in favour of grandparents, collaterals and even relatives by marriage, and such obligations do exist in some legal systems. By art 26(2)(a)(b), a contracting state may however make a Reservation, reserving the right *not* to recognise or enforce a decision or settlement in respect of maintenance obligations between persons related collaterally or between persons related by affinity.[2] The United Kingdom made a qualified Reservation, something not expressly allowed in the Convention, in the following terms:

'The United Kingdom . . . reserves the right provided for in article 26(2) not to recognise or enforce a decision or settlement in respect of maintenance obligations between persons related collaterally and between persons related by affinity *unless that decision or settlement requires the maintenance debtor to make payments to a person who is a child of the family (for the purposes of the law of England and Wales and Northern Ireland) or who is a child of the maintenance creditor who has been accepted as child of the family by the maintenance debtor (for the purposes of the law of Scotland).'*

The italicised words ensure that United Kingdom courts will enforce orders made abroad in cases where its own courts would be prepared to make orders even though the child in question might fall into the specified categories (collaterals and relatives by affinity) and would not be entitled by virtue of being in one of those categories to maintenance in United Kingdom law. It is presumably also hoped that, despite the existence of a Reservation, other contracting states will recognise United Kingdom orders falling within the italicised words. It has to be said that this hope may not be realised; and that the implementation of the Reservation in United Kingdom law is handled in a most obscure way, the relevant definition of 'maintenance order' being qualified by a proviso referring to the possibility of a Reservation without indicating its actual existence or its terms.

Further powers to enter reservations are conferred by art 26. The more drastic allows a contracting state to exclude, in effect, maintenance obligations in respect of adults, those maintenance creditors who have attained the age of 21 or married, from the scope of the Convention. The point of this provision is that it enables a state to accept the improvements contained in the 1973 Convention (as compared with the earlier 1956 Convention which was limited to cases involving children) without extending the scope of enforcement to adult cases. Its content has, however, been described by the official *rapporteur* as 'mysterious' and 'not very elegant'.[4] The other possible Reservation, made by the United Kingdom, is to exclude cases where the relevant order does not provide for the periodical payment of maintenance, but only for example for the payment of a lump sum to an ex-wife or in respect of the funeral expenses of an illegitimate child.[5]

1   Convention, art 1, first paragraph.

2 The making of such a Reservation also has the effect of preventing such a state from seeking the recognition and enforcement of any orders it may make which fall within the prescribed classes: ibid, art 26, second paragraph.
3 Reciprocal Enforcement of Maintenance Orders (Hague Convention Countries) Order 1979, SI 1979/1317, Sch 2, para 21.
4 *Actes et Documents de la Douzième Session*, Tome IV, p 429 (M. Verwilghen).
5 Convention, art 26, first paragraph (3).

'Decisions' and 'settlements'

7.05 The Convention is primarily concerned with 'decisions' relating to maintenance obligations, as its title indicates. These decisions may be given either by a judicial or an administrative authority in a contracting state,[1] however that decision is described,[2] ie as a judgment, order, arrêt, or ruling. Other provisions of the Convention, notably art 6, make it clear that the proceedings giving rise to the decision must comply with the principles of natural justice and to that extent must be at least quasi-judicial.

The Convention also applies to certain 'settlements'. The Convention text betrays the awkwardness of this concept in terms of the traditional common law categories, the English text actually quoting the equivalent in the French text, *transaction*, as a gloss. The settlement must be made 'by or before' a competent judicial or administrative authority; the French text speaks of *transactions passes dans cette matière devant ces autorités*, '*devant*' being given an extended meaning in the English text. What is meant is an agreement between the parties settling the dispute between them and in some way approved or noted or registered in or before a court or other authority so that it becomes enforceable in the country in which it was made.[3] Some common law jurisdictions have the practice of making certain types of maintenance agreement, especially those made at the time of a divorce, 'rules of court'; this seems to be an example of a 'settlement' in the Convention usage, as are the institutions known in civil law countries as *Vollstreckbarer-Prozessvergleich, dading*, or *schikking*.

Decisions and settlements modifying previous decisions or settlements are within the scope of the Convention;[4] this is so even if the original was from a non-contracting state. If a decision or settlement does not relate solely to a maintenance obligation, the effect of the Convention is limited to the parts of the decision or settlement which do concern maintenance obligations.[5]

This 'severability' concept was also found in the 1958 Convention and gave rise to considerable controversy, especially in cases in which a finding of paternity was accompanied by an order as to the payment of maintenance, but the principle that maintenance orders could be enforced even if the decision as to personal status was incapable of recognition has been well accepted in the courts and was firmly re-iterated at The Hague when the 1973 Convention was under consideration.[6]

1 Convention, art 1, second paragraph.
2 Ibid, art 2, first paragraph.
3 See M. Verwilghen *Actes et Documents de la Douzième Session* Tome IV, pp 395-396.
4 Convention, art 2, second paragraph.
5 Ibid, art 3. See also art 10.
6 See decisions of the French Cour de Cassation, 9 July 1975 (D. 1975. IR. 208); of the Oberlandesgericht Koln, 10 April 1979 (Fam RZ 1979, 718) and the Italian Corte di Cassazione, 29 November 1976; the other cases collected in the TMC Asser Instituut's collection *Les Nouvelles Conventions de la Haye* (vol 1, pp 194-198; vol 2, pp 66-72); and M. Verwhilghen, op cit, at pp 399-400.

Reciprocity

7.06   As the Convention's preamble makes clear, it is based on reciprocity, and so only extends to decisions and settlements originating in other contracting states.[1] If however a decision (or settlement) is given in a non-contracting state but is subsequently varied in a contracting state, *the decision (or settlement) effecting the variation* will be entitled to recognition and enforcement under the Convention.[2] Strictly that is all the Convention requires, but the United Kingdom legislation giving effect to the Convention provides that when a maintenance order, from whatever country, is varied by a competent court in a Hague Convention country, *the order as varied* is enforceable, so giving effect to what was almost certainly the intention of the authors of the Convention.[3]

1   Convention, art 1, first paragraph.
2   Ibid, art 2, second paragraph.
3   Reciprocal Enforcement of Maintenance Orders (Hague Convention Countries) Order 1979, SI 1979/1317, Sch 2, para 21.

Conditions for recognition and enforcement

7.07   Chapter II of the Convention, which consists of arts 4 to 12 inclusive, sets out the rules for the recognition and enforcement of 'decisions'. Article 21, the sole article in Chapter V, deals with 'settlements' and provides that a settlement enforceable in its state of origin is to be recognised and enforced subject to the same conditions as a decision 'so far as such conditions are applicable to it'. This is in effect a drafting device, which avoids the need for constant repetition of the phrase 'decisions or, so far as the context allows, settlements'; the same device will be used here, so that what is said about 'decisions' in the following discussion applies mutatis mutandis to 'settlements'.

The basic rule is that a decision rendered in another contracting state will be recognised or enforced if two conditions are satisfied.[1] One is that it is no longer subject to 'ordinary forms of review' in the state of origin;[2] the other is that the authority rendering the decision is treated as having jurisdiction under the principles set out in the Convention.[3]

1   Convention, art 4, first paragraph.
2   See para 7.08 below.
3   See para 7.09 below.

'Ordinary forms of review'

7.08   The foreign decision must no longer be subject to ordinary forms of review in the state of origin.[1]

This rule corresponds to certain aspects of the familiar Commonwealth requirement in respect of the enforcement of money-judgments that the order be 'final and conclusive'.[2] However, it does not operate, as that formula does, to prevent the enforcement of an order merely because it may be subject to variation in later proceedings; the question is rather whether the current proceedings have reached a sufficient degree of finality or 'maturity'.

The 1958 Hague Convention used in the same context the requirement that *la decision est passée en force de chose jugée* in the state of origin.[3] This phrase lacks an English equivalent, and common lawyers are driven to use Latin, for the issue is one of 'res judicata'. However, in the mid-1960s, and in particular at the Extraordinary Session of 1966 dealing with the enforcement of foreign money-judgments, the Hague Conference decided to substitute a reference to a judgment being no longer subject to the ordinary forms of review. Professor Fragistas, commenting on the 1966 decision, wrote:

'In reality, this variation was merely a change of terminology. In The Hague Conventions, the expression *"force de chose jugée"* has always been equivalent to "no longer subject to ordinary forms of review". All that has happened is that the problem is shifted to one of defining "ordinary forms of review". Just as the notion of res judicata is not the same in all countries, so also with that of ordinary forms of review. In two countries sharing the same basic principles of judicial organisation and civil procedure, appeals serving more or less the same function may be considered "ordinary" in one of those countries but "extraordinary" in the other. To give one example, resort to "cassation" or "review", basically similar institutions, are considered extraordinary forms in France and Greece but as ordinary forms in Italy, Germany and Austria.'[4]

This difficulty is more theoretical than practical. It may mean that the reciprocity which is the basis of the Convention is less than perfect, but in a particular case no practical issue should arise. This is because a party seeking recognition or enforcement of a decision must furnish any document necessary to prove that the decision is no longer subject to the ordinary forms of review in the state of origin,[5] so that the view of that country's legal system would appear to be conclusive.

No express provision on this point is included in the United Kingdom legislation giving effect to the Hague Convention, nor in the Model Bill produced for the Commonwealth Secretariat. It is unlikely that any decision not complying with the requirement would be transmitted for enforcement.

1 Convention, art 4, first paragraph.
2 See para 4.11 above.
3 1958 Convention, art 2(3).
4 *Actes et Documents de la Dixième Session, Execution des jugements* p 372 (Author's translation from French original).
5 1973 Convention, art 17, first paragraph (2).

Jurisdiction

7.09 Four bases of jurisdiction are established by the Convention. The first is that *either* the maintenance debtor *or* the maintenance creditor had his habitual residence in the state of origin at the time when the proceedings were instituted.[1] So far as this provision deals with cases in which only the maintenance creditor was habitually resident in the state of origin, it was a controversial novelty to the delegates from some of the civil law countries represented at The Hague, but it presents no difficulties to countries in the common law tradition. By art 28, dealing with federal or composite states, the reference to habitual residence is to be interpreted as being to habitual residence in the territorial unit in which the decision was rendered.[2]

The second basis is that *both* parties were nationals of the state of origin at the time when the proceedings were instituted.[3] The Convention does not attempt to resolve the various questions of dual nationality which might arise; it would seem to be sufficient to show that each party did possess the relevant nationality in accordance with the law of that state, other possible nationalities being irrelevant.

The third basis is that the defendant had submitted to the jurisdiction of the authority, either expressly or by defending on the merits of the case without objecting to the jurisdiction.[4] This basis is defined by reference to 'the defendant', which in some cases, for example applications for variation, may mean the maintenance creditor.

The fourth basis is more complex. It arises 'if the maintenance is due by reason of a divorce or a legal separation, or a declaration that a marriage is void or annulled [which will include decrees of nullity] obtained from an authority of [the state of origin] recognised as having jurisdiction in that matter, according to the law of the state addressed'.[5] So if a maintenance order is made in divorce proceedings in State A, in which state neither party was habitually resident nor had nationality, but in which both were domiciled in the sense of domicile used in State B, prima facie the order is not entitled to recognition in State B under any of the earlier bases. If however State B applies the common law rule that divorce decrees of the common domicile of the parties are entitled to recognition, the maintenance order as well as the decree itself will be recognised under this fourth rule. It is not essential that the maintenance decision be taken in the divorce, separation or nullity proceedings; it is enough if the maintenance is 'due by reason of' the divorce, etc. The United Kingdom legislation giving effect to The Hague Convention does not follow the Convention text very closely at this point. It provides that an authority will be regarded as having jurisdiction if, 'in the case of an order made by reason of a divorce ..., the court is recognised by the law of the part of the United Kingdom in which enforcement is sought as having jurisdiction *to make the order*'.[6] The result may well be the same, but the refusal to use the Convention language is odd.

1   Convention, art 7(1).
2   Ibid, art 28, first paragraph (4). The United Kingdom legislation giving effect to The Hague Convention contains no provision corresponding to the Convention provision on this point.
3   Convention, art 7(2).
4   Ibid, art 7(3).
5   Ibid, art 8.
6   Reciprocal Enforcement of Maintenance Orders (Hague Convention Countries) 1979, SI 1979/1317, Sch 2, para 6.

Findings as to jurisdiction

7.10   The authority in the state in which recognition or enforcement is sought is bound by the findings of fact on which the authority of the state of origin based its jurisdiction.[1] This provision is almost identical with that in the Divorce Convention of 1970,[2] but is not wholly clear. What is intended is that a decision in the state of origin that a party was habitually resident there or was a national of that state or had submitted to the jurisdiction may not be re-opened, except in cases of fraud in a matter of procedure,[3] in the state addressed. It is not entirely clear whether the 'finding' has to be mentioned in the decision, or made express in some other way; and the word 'fact' is presumably to be given an interpretation which will not exclude rulings on nationality, for example, which might well involve points of law.

1   Convention, art 9.
2   Divorce Convention, art 6, first paragraph: see para 3.23 above.
3   1973 Convention, art 5(2); although art 9 is not expressly subject to the fraud provision this must surely have been intended.

Provisionally enforceable decisions and provisional measures

7.11   Some states, especially perhaps those in which delays in litigation are a major problem, make use of decisions which are 'provisionally enforceable'.

Such decisions are by definition interim in nature and further proceedings, which may include the ordinary forms of review, are contemplated; but the decision so far reached can be enforced. This type of decision is to be distinguished from orders for alimony pendente lite, which are final orders although limited in duration, and from 'provisional orders' as used in the Commonwealth maintenance orders schemes which are not themselves enforceable. Few Commonwealth jurisdictions appear to have any exact counterpart of the provisional decisions spoken of in the Convention, which are essentially features of civil law systems.

This last fact is important for the Convention in providing that such decisions and related 'provisional measures' shall be recognised and enforced in another contracting state, despite the availability of ordinary forms of review, limits this rule to cases in which the state addressed itself uses the device of provisionally enforceable decisions and provisional measures.[1]

1 Convention, art 4, last paragraph.

Review and variation

7.12 As in all international conventions on the recognition and enforcement of foreign judgments, a cardinal principle is that there may be no review of the merits. This principle is applied in the present Convention in art 12, 'unless this Convention otherwise provides'. This seems not to be a real exception, for what is intended is merely that the receiving court must be satisfied as to the applicability of the Convention, and as to the adequacy of documentation, and may examine certain grounds on which recognition may be refused which are considered below.

The Convention's *rapporteur*, M. Verwilghen, commented in this connection:

'It is most important to remember that the authority addressed *qualitate qua* can, in no case, *modify* the contents of the foreign decision. For example, it is not for it to reduce the amount of the maintenance allowance, to change periodicity of payments or to allow days of grace. Its role is restricted to the granting or refusal of the recognition or enforcement of a maintenance decision and nothing more.'[1]

That being so, it is surprising to find that the United Kingdom legislation giving effect to the Convention makes provision for the variation in the United Kingdom of orders registered there under the Convention.[2] The United Kingdom Government took the view that the Convention was silent on the question of variation and therefore did not forbid it; that is, variation in subsequent proceedings is permissible, even if the initial decision must be to recognise and enforce the order in the form in which it is presented. It is not at all clear how service of process can be effected if variation proceedings are allowed under such legislation; the silence of the Convention has practical consequences in this area, and it is believed that the United Kingdom interpretation is unjustified, having been influenced by a desire to make the applicable rules as closely similar as possible to those applying under the Commonwealth scheme.

1 *Actes et documents de la douzième session* Tome IV, p 417.
2 Reciprocal Enforcement of Maintenance Orders (Hague Convention Countries) Order 1979, SI 1979/1317, Sch 2, para 9.

Grounds for refusing recognition

7.13   The Convention sets out five grounds upon which the recognition or enforcement of a decision may be refused.

The first and broadest ground is the traditional one of public policy, that recognition or enforcement is 'manifestly' incompatible with the public policy (ordre public; the French phrase is used in the English text) of the state addressed.[1] Courts will not lightly invoke this power. An example is the English decision of a Divisional Court in *Armitage v Nanchen*[2] where the mother of an illegitimate child sought to register in England a Swiss affiliation order made some nine years previously. The putative father argued that registration would be contrary to English public policy, relying on three features of the Swiss proceedings, the fact that the court did not hear certain witnesses who had been examined earlier by the judge who prepared the dossier in the case, the court's error in referring to a probability of 96.25% instead of 91.25% in the serological evidence (which was only one type of evidence relied upon), and its selective use of a medical report as to the effect of haemorrhoids on sexual desire and ability. The Divisional Court referred to the cases on public policy in divorce and nullity contexts[3] before holding that the Swiss court had examined the defendant's case with a degree of practicality and conscientiousness which rendered the public policy point 'virtually unarguable'. *Armitage v Nanchen* may be contrasted with a decision of the Cour d'Appel of Amiens[4] under the corresponding provisions of the 1958 Convention; a German order made against a French putative father in default of his appearance and on the sole evidence of the Youth Office was held to be manifestly incompatible with the French conception of international public policy on the essential question of proof.

The second is that the decision was obtained by fraud 'in connection with a matter of procedure'.[5] This does not raise the merits of the case, but if, for example, the pleadings or other documents had been forged, then 'fraud unravels all'.

The third ground for refusing recognition or enforcement is that proceedings between the same parties and having the same purpose are pending before an authority of the state addressed and those proceedings were the first to be instituted.[6] This is the case of lis alibi pendens, and although the Convention's *rapporteur*, M. Verwhilgen, has suggested[7] that one element of the classic case, the requirement that the actions should be based on the same 'cause of action', is missing, nothing seems to turn on the point. If maintenance claims are in issue in two states in pending proceedings, the authority before which the first claim was made *may* (not must) refuse to recognise or enforce any order made in the second state.

The fourth ground deals with a related problem. If there are in existence two incompatible decisions, both entitled to recognition and enforcement, the state addressed must be able to choose between them. The Convention so provides, covering both cases in which one decision was made in the state addressed and those in which both decisions originate in other contracting states and are entitled to recognition and enforcement in the state addressed.[8]

The fifth ground concerns default judgments. They gave rise to some difficulty under the earlier 1958 Convention; there such judgments were to be refused recognition and enforcement if the defaulting party, through no fault of his own, had no knowledge of the proceedings or could not make a deface.[9] In a number of cases concerning Danish orders (*bidragsresolution*) where the debtor had appeared in the paternity phase of the proceedings but not in respect of the later administrative decision as to the amount of maintenance, it was held that the decision was to be recognised and enforced;[10] the power to refuse recognition was given a restricted interpretation. It seems likely that a different result would be reached under the 1973 Convention: a default decision may be recognised or enforced only if notice of the institution of the proceedings, including notice of the substance of the claim, had been served on the defaulting party in accordance with the law of the state of origin and if, having regard to all the circumstances, that party had sufficient time to enable him to defend the proceedings.[11] 'The substance of the claim' must relate to the claim for maintenance itself.

1 Convention, art 5(1).
2 27 April 1982; see (1983) 13 Family Law 14.
3 *Von Lorang v Administrator of Austrian Property* [1927] AC 641, HL; *Gray (orse Formosa) v Formosa* [1963] P 259, [1962] 3 All ER 419; *Lepre v Lepre* [1965] P 52, [1963] 2 All ER 49; *Middleton v Middleton* [1967] P 62, [1966] 1 All ER 168.
4 2 April 1978, (1979) Rev crit d i p, 641.
5 Convention, art 5(2).
6 Ibid, art 5(3).
7 *Actes et Documents de la Douzième Session* p 413.
8 Convention, art 5(4).
9 1958 Convention, art 2(2), proviso.
10 Landesgericht Hamburg, 16 August 1974, 17 T 6/73, and other decisions collected in the TMC Asser Instituut's *Les Nouvelles Conventions de la Haye* vol 2, pp 82 et seq.
11 1973 Convention, art 6.

The time factor

7.14 In principle, the Convention applies to all decisions rendered in contracting states irrespective of their date.[1] In the case of a decision providing for the periodical payment of maintenance, enforcement relates to arrears, ie in respect of payments already due, as well as to future payments.[2] However, where a decision has been rendered before the date upon which the Convention entered into force as between the state of origin and the state addressed, it is to be enforced in the latter state only in respect of payments falling due after that date.[3]

1 Convention, art 24, first paragraph.
2 Ibid, art 11.
3 Ibid, art 24, second paragraph.

Procedure

7.15 Chapter III of the Convention, consisting of arts 13 to 17 inclusive, deals with the procedure for obtaining the recognition or enforcement of decisions. The general rule is that the lex fori governs, meaning in this context the law of the state addressed, that in which recognition or enforcement is sought,[1] and this accords with the general principles of private international law on procedural questions.

The Convention does however contain some specific rules which override any general rules in the lex fori. So, art 17 contains a list of the documentation which an applicant must produce (including translations in certain cases into the language of the state addressed); if the documentation is incomplete or insufficient for the purpose of establishing that the decision does come within the terms of the Convention, the authority addressed must allow a specified period of time for the production of the necessary documents,[2] a rule designed to prevent a creditor with limited resources being wholly non-suited on technical grounds without being given an adjournment in which to correct procedural errors.

As in other recent Hague Conventions there are provisions about legal aid, security for costs, and legalisation. Where a maintenance creditor receives legal aid in the state of origin, and legal aid for this purpose includes 'complete or partial legal aid or exemption from costs or expenses', he is entitled in the state addressed 'to benefit from the most favourable legal aid or the most extensive exemption from costs or expenses provided for by the law of the state addressed.'[3] This means that once the creditor has the status of a legally-aided person he need no longer comply with any means tests or other requirements under the law of the state addressed; he is entitled without more ado to the maximum level of benefit provided. Security for costs may not be required,[4] and no form of legalisation of the foreign documents involved can be insisted upon.[5]

An unusual provision, which may operate to override the usual rules of the lex fori, is that partial recognition or enforcement of a decision can always be applied for.[6] This is not the same thing as the severance of one part of a decision from another to exclude, for example, a finding as to personal status not within the scope of a 'decision relating to maintenance obligations.'[7] The purpose is rather to enable a creditor to 'tone down' his application, perhaps to minimise the risk of the application of the public policy provision.[8]

1   Convention, art 13.
2   Ibid, art 17, second paragraph.
3   Ibid, art 15.
4   Ibid, art 16.
5   Ibid, art 17, last paragraph. See also art 22 re transfer of funds.
6   Ibid, art 14.
7   Cf ibid, arts 3 and 10.
8   See *Actes et Documents de la Douzième Session* p 131; cf EEC Judgments Convention 1968, art 42(2).

Claims by public bodies

7.16   Chapter IV of the Convention, arts 18 to 20 inclusive, contains some additional provisions relating to claims by 'public bodies'. The expression 'public body' is not further defined, but what is clearly intended is an agency, such as a Youth Service or a Social Security Office, providing benefits to those in need. Two different situations are covered: one is where the original decision in the state of origin was in favour of a public body (eg a contribution order in favour of an English local authority which had received a child into care and sought to recover a contribution towards the maintenance of the child from the putative father); the other is that in which a public body seeks to obtain recognition or enforcement for its own benefit of an order originally made in favour of an individual maintenance creditor.

In the first case the public body may obtain recognition and enforcement of a decision awarding reimbursement of maintenance expenses if (a) reimbursement can be obtained by the public body under the law to which it is subject, *and* (b) the existence of a maintenance obligation between the creditor and debtor is provided for by the internal law applicable under the rules of private international law of the state addressed.[1] In the great majority of cases, the public body obtaining an order in the state of origin will be an agency created under the law of that state, so that requirement (a) will be satisfied and established by the very existence of the original decision. However, the Convention allows the state addressed to apply its own conflict of laws rules to identify the law to which the public body is subject, and to examine the position under that law if it is not that of the state of origin. Similarly, in this context the state addressed is enabled to apply its own conflicts rules to determine the existence of the primary obligation between maintenance debtor and maintenance creditor, to which obligation that asserted by the public body is in a sense secondary.

Rather different considerations apply where the parties to the original decision were the individual maintenance creditor and maintenance debtor themselves. In accordance with the basic principles on which the Convention is founded, that decision cannot be re-examined on its merits. But if a public body now seeks to have that decision recognised or enforced, the question of its entitlement so to act can be examined. The public body will succeed only if it is entitled to seek recognition or claim enforcement '*ipso jure*, under the law to which it is subject',[2] a law identified in accordance with the conflict of laws rules of the state addressed.

1 Convention, art 18.
2 Ibid, art 19.

Relationship with other Conventions

7.17 The Convention is designed to replace the earlier 1958 Convention, and art 29 gives it that effect as between contracting states who were also parties to that earlier Convention. Of much greater importance from a Commonwealth point of view is art 23 which declares that the Convention does not restrict the application of other rules of law, derived from an international instrument or not, as to the recognition and enforcement of maintenance orders. A Commonwealth country can, therefore, accede to the Convention without prejudice to the existing Commonwealth scheme which is not technically based on any 'international instrument' but rather, as has been seen, on shared tradition and experience.

B. UNITED NATIONS DEVELOPMENTS

The United Nations Convention

7.18 Some reference has already been made[1] to the preliminary work which led to the preparation of the United Nations Convention on the Recovery Abroad of Maintenance in June 1956. The Convention has attracted a large number of states as parties, including Barbados, Sri Lanka and the United Kingdom. Australia, Fiji and New Zealand have enabling legislation but have not yet acceded. The full list of parties is as follows: Algeria, Argentina, Austria, Barbados, Belgium, Brazil, Central African Republic, Chile, Czechoslovakia, Denmark, Ecuador, Finland, France,[2] Germany (Federal Republic), Greece, Guatemala, Haiti, the Holy See, Hungary, Israel, Italy, Luxembourg, Monaco, Morocco, Netherlands,[3] Niger, Norway, Pakistan, Philippines, Poland, Portugal, Spain, Sri Lanka, Suriname, Sweden, Switzerland, Tunisia, Turkey, United Kingdom, Upper Volta and Yugoslavia. In addition Bolivia, Columbia, Cuba, Dominican Republic, El Salvador, Kampuchea, and Mexico have signed but not ratified the Convention; the Chinese Nationalist regime had ratified the Convention. It came into effect on 25 May 1957.

1   See para 7.01 above.
2   Including the overseas departments (Guadeloupe, Guiana, Martinique and Reunion) and French Polynesia, Mayotte, New Caledonia and St Pierre and Miquelon.
3   Including the Netherlands Antilles.

Scope of the Convention

7.19   The United Nations Convention is notably terse in its drafting, in market contrast with the Hague texts. Its object is declared to be the facilitation of the recovery of 'maintenance to which a person . . . who is in the territory of one of the Contracting Parties, claims to be entitled from another person, . . . who is subject to the jurisdiction of another Contracting Party'.[1] It deals with *claims* for maintenance, and not therefore with those cases in which a maintenance order already exists; the enforcement of such orders is of course the subject of the Hague Enforcement Convention. Within the Commonwealth schemes, the solution preferred is that of the provisional order confirmed in the debtor's country, but this presumes a basic similarity of procedure and approach which cannot be found on a world-wide basis; the United Nations Convention provides an alternative device, essentially machinery by which a claim can be transmitted by official channels for consideration in the courts of the defendant's country.

There is no definition of 'maintenance' and no limitation to cases in which periodical payments rather than lump sums are claimed. It is suggested that 'maintenance' is wide enough to include the support of any dependant, including spouses, ex-spouses, and children (legitimate or not) and presumably any other person regarded as a dependant in the law of the state addressed, but would almost certainly not cover cases of, for example, funeral or medical expenses which can be ordered to be paid under some maintenance statutes.

Equally no definition is given of 'subject to the jurisdiction of' a contracting party. It is for each state to apply its own law, including its rules of the conflict of laws, to determine the scope of the Convention, for the Convention is about the making of claims which are to be tested in all respects by the law of the state addressed. In the United Kingdom legislation giving effect to the Convention the phrase 'subject to the jurisdiction of' in relation to the United Kingdom is rendered as 'residing in',[2] and by specifying the local procedural rules to be applied claims by ex-spouses are excluded;[3] no such restrictions apply in relation to claims being sent from the United Kingdom to another Convention country.[4]

Article 8 declares that the Convention applies also to applications for the variation of maintenance orders. 'Variation' would appear to include revocation. Where the creditor seeks variation, for example an increase in the level of periodical payments, the effect of this provision is clear; the same machinery as was made available for the original claim will be put into use in respect of the application for variation. However, the position is less clear when the debtor seeks variation. No international machinery is needed, for he will in the usual case be applying directly to the courts of the country in which he is resident; questions of the service of process on the creditor are left to the lex fori. It seems possible however that in such cases ancillary provisions of the Convention, notably those of art 7 which enable evidence to be obtained from the courts of other contracting states in relation to 'an action for maintenance' will apply.

1   Convention, art 1(1).
2   Maintenance Orders (Reciprocal Enforcement) Act 1972 (UK), s 27(1).
3   Ibid, ss 27-30.

4   Ibid, s 26.

Reciprocity

7.20   The Convention is firmly based on reciprocity. It only applies as between contracting states, and one state party may only rely on the Convention as against another to the extent that it is itself bound by the Convention.[1]

1   Convention, art 18.

Transmitting and receiving agencies

7.21   The main feature of the convention system is the establishment of Transmitting and Receiving Agencies in each contracting state. The function of the Transmitting Agency is to receive applications from claimants in its country and to send them in due form to the Receiving Agency in the defendant's country for action to be taken on the claimant's behalf. Each contracting state must designate 'one or more judicial or administrative agencies' to act as Transmitting Agencies.[1] This formula gives considerable freedom to set up an appropriate structure, so that a federal country can have a number of Agencies and any country remains free to specify local agencies within its own system through which a claimant must approach the national Transmitting Agency. This latter device is used in the United Kingdom, where the application to the Secretary of State (the Transmitting Agency) must be made through the clerk of the magistrates' court for the district in which the claimant resides or, in Scotland, the sheriff clerk or sheriff clerk depute for the jurisdiction within which he resides;[2] the local officer's function is to advise and assist the claimant,[3] and the procedure is not intended to place further obstacles in the claimant's path.

The raison d'etre of the Transmitting Agencies is that they have a duty to take all reasonable steps to ensure that the requirements of the law of the state addressed are complied with.[4] Each contracting state is bound to supply the Secretary-General of the United Nations with information as to its law and procedure in respect of maintenance claims which the Secretary-General can make available to the various Transmitting Agencies. In particular the information is 'as to the evidence normally required . . . for the proof of maintenance claims, of the manner in which such evidence should be submitted and of other requirements to be complied with' under the relevant law.[5]

Each contracting state is required to designate 'a public or private body' to act as a Receiving Agency.[6] The terms 'public' and 'private' are not defined, and the range of choice seems to be very wide: a judicial or government office, a social security agency, or even a private charitable foundation could be designated. Only a single body may be designated; even federal states are so restricted.

1   Convention art 2(1).
2   Maintenance Orders (Reciprocal Enforcement) Act 1972 (UK), s 26(3)(5)(6).
3   Ibid, s 26(3).
4   Convention, art 3(4).
5   Ibid, art 3(2).
6   Ibid, art 2(2).

Forwarding the claim

7.22   Once the claimant's application is received by the Transmitting Agency, the Agency is under an obligation to transmit the documents detailing and supporting the claim 'unless satisfied that the application is not made in good faith'.[1] The Transmitting Agency must, before transmitting the documents, satisfy itself that they are regular in form so far as its own law is concerned,[2] and must also take all reasonable steps to ensure that the law of the state addressed is also complied with.[3] The Agency may also, but is not obliged to, indicate a view on two matters. It may express to the Receiving Agency an opinion as to the merits of the case and may recommend that free legal aid and exemption from costs be given to the claimant.[4] The Convention provides no criteria by reference to which these powers are to be exercised. An Agency will presumably have no difficulty in recommending free legal aid in almost all cases, knowing that the recommendation will only be acted upon if the law of the receiving state so allows. The opinion on the merits is much more difficult, and indeed surprising; there is no hearing or other opportunity to test the claimant's case so that it is far from clear how an Agency can formulate an opinion and what weight a Receiving Agency should attach to it.

The Receiving Agency must take all appropriate steps for the recovery of maintenance including 'the settlement of the claim and, where necessary, the institution and prosecution of an action for maintenance and the execution of any order or other judicial act for the payment of maintenance'.[5] The institution of court proceedings is neither the inevitable nor the preferred mode of response; the Receiving Agency is intended to act as a wise solicitor would advise, pursuing the claim in the most effective and economical manner available.

If one is needed under the law of the receiving state, the claimant will have furnished the Receiving Agency with a power of attorney.[6] Whether or not this is done, it is made clear that the acts of the Receiving Agency are 'subject always to the authority given by the claimant',[7] an authority which may be limited.

Whatever actions or proceedings are commenced by the Receiving Agency in the courts or tribunals will be governed by the lex fori.[8]

1   Convention, art 4(1). The documents and data to be supplied are detailed in ibid, art 3(3)(4).
2   Ibid, art 4(2).
3   Ibid, art 3(4).
4   Ibid, art 4(3).
5   Ibid, art 6(1).
6   Ibid, art 3(3).
7   Ibid, art 6(1).
8   Ibid, art 6(3).

Procedure

7.23   Article 5 of the Convention contains provisions for the transmission via the machinery established under the Convention of 'any order, final or provisional, and any other judicial act, obtained by the claimant for the payment of maintenance in a competent tribunal of any of the Contracting Parties'. This is *not* a provision leading to the recognition and enforcement of orders as under the Commonwealth schemes or the Hague Enforcement Convention. It provides a channel for the transmission of the relevant documents but creates no new obligation upon the receiving state to register or enforce any order evidenced by the documents. A Receiving Agency may take exequatur or registration proceedings in accordance with the law of the receiving state,[1] but that will be subject to the existence and applicability of such procedures under the existing law. 'Provisional' in this context has the same meaning as in the Hague Enforcement Convention, referring to an interim order and not to the 'provisional orders' found in the Commonwealth schemes.[2]

The Convention contains provisions for obtaining evidence by Letters of Request.[3] This enables the court or other tribunal in the state of the Receiving Agency to address requests for further evidence to the authorities of the other state involved. It is limited to cases in which Letters of Request are known to the laws of the two contracting states involved, and is presumably not intended to exclude reliance on any other Convention or other arrangements designed to serve the same purpose.

Neither the Transmitting nor the Receiving Agency may charge fees in respect of services rendered under the Convention.[4] No security for costs may be required of a claimant on account of his alien or non-resident status,[5] and in proceedings under the Convention claimants are to receive equal treatment and the same exemptions in the payment of costs and charges as are given to nationals or residents of the forum state.[6]

1   Convention, art 5(3).
2   See para 5.12 above.
3   Convention, art 7.
4   Ibid, art 9(3).
5   Ibid, art 9(2).
6   Ibid, art 9(1).

C. THE UNITED STATES UNIFORM ACT

The Uniform Reciprocal Enforcement of Support Act

7.24   The United States National Conference of Commissioners on Uniform State Laws has adopted a series of Uniform Reciprocal Enforcement of Support Acts. A brief account is given here of the currently recommended text; although neither a Commonwealth nor an international instrument, the Act is important as being the basis of a growing number of bilateral arrangements between individual states of the United States and Commonwealth jurisdictions. It contains features broadly comparable to the Commonwealth schemes, though there are also significant similarities between the Act and the United Nations Convention.

The first Uniform Act was adopted in 1950 with amendments in 1952 and 1958. By 1957 it had been adopted in all the states, and it remains the basis of the current law in 21 states,[1] the District of Columbia, Guam, Puerto Rico and the (American) Virgin Islands. The 1968 Revised Act is the basis of the law in the remaining 29 states.[2]

All references in the paragraphs which follow are to the 1968 Revised Act.

1   Alabama, Alaska, Connecticut, Delaware, Georgia, Hawaii, Indiana, Iowa, Maryland, Massachusetts, Michigan, Minnesota, Mississippi, Missouri, New York, Oregon, South Carolina, Tennessee, Texas, Utah and Washington.
2   Arizona, Arkansas, California, Colorado, Florida, Idaho, Illinois, Kansas, Kentucky, Louisiana, Maine, Montana, Nebraska, Nevada, New Hampshire, New Jersey, New Mexico, North Carolina, North Dakota, Ohio, Oklahoma, Pennsylvania, Rhode Island, South Dakota, Vermont, Virginia, West Virginia, Wisconsin and Wyoming.

Registration of foreign support orders

7.25   Part IV of the Act contains provisions for the registration of foreign support orders. The provisions were first incorporated in the recommended

Uniform Act in 1958, and some jurisdictions have not given effect to the recommendations.[1]

'Support order' in the Act means any judgment, decree or order of support in favour of an 'obligee' whether temporary or final, or subject to modification, revocation or remission, regardless of the kind of action or proceeding in which it was entered.[2] An obligee may register such an order made in a foreign jurisdiction in a court in the enacting state,[3] and on registration it is treated in the same manner as a support order issued by a court in that state.[4] The registration is confirmed if no petition to vacate it is received by the court within a prescribed period.[5] As in a few of the Commonwealth statutes, a local official (usually a prosecuting attorney) is appointed to represent the creditor, and has the duty of taking enforcement proceedings.[6] In enforcement proceedings the debtor (the 'obligor') may present only matters that would be available to him as defences in an action to enforce a foreign money judgment, a provision which effectively precludes any re-examination of the merits of the case.[7]

1   Alaska, Connecticut, Hawaii, Michigan, Mississippi, Oregon, Puerto Rico, the (American) Virgin Islands and (despite its adoption of the bulk of the 1968 Act) Kentucky.
2   Act, s 2(n).
3   Act, s 36. For procedure see s 39. Registration, as in the corresponding case under most Commonwealth Acts is a purely ministerial action: *Pinner v Pinner* 234 SE 2d 633 (NC, 1977).
4   Act, s 40(a).
5   Act, s 40(b).
6   Act, ss 38, 39(b).
7   Act, s 40(c). See *O'Halloran v O'Halloran* 580 SW 2d 870 (Tex Civ App, 1979).

Initiating and responding courts

7.26 Where a claimant for maintenance is in one state but the debtor in another, the claimant petitions the appropriate court in his own state which is described in the Act as 'the initiating State'. An official, usually the prosecuting attorney, is appointed to represent him,[1] and the petition is considered by the court to determine whether it 'sets forth facts from which it may be determined that the obligor owes a duty of support and that a court of the responding state may obtain jurisdiction of the obligor or his property'.[2] The law of the state in which the obligor is present determines the existence of a duty of support during the period of his presence.[3] The resulting certificate of the initiating court is not unlike a 'provisional order' in the Commonwealth scheme; it is not an enforceable judgment, but does involve an assessment of the strength of the claimant's case.

The relevant documents are transmitted to the appropriate court in the 'responding state' where a prosecuting attorney is required to take appropriate action to press the claim.[4] If at the hearing the obligor denies the existence of a duty of support or raises a defence, the court may adjourn the proceedings to allow further evidence to be taken, including evidence by deposition which may be ordered to be taken before a judge of the initiating court.[5] This last device mirrors the 'shuttlecock' procedure of the Commonwealth schemes and was first introduced in 1968. The Act is silent on the question of the variation or revocation of an order eventually made in the responding court, and in this respect the Act is less developed than its Commonwealth counterparts.

These provisions are available in respect not only of other states of the

Union, but also any foreign jurisdiction in which a substantially similar reciprocal law is in force.[6]

1 Act, s 12.
2 Act, s 14.
3 Act, s 7.
4 Act, s 18.
5 Act, s 20.
6 Act, s 2(m).

CHAPTER 8

Financial Provision
The Commonwealth Position
Surveyed

A. GENERAL CONSIDERATIONS

Introduction

8.01 Almost every Commonwealth jurisdiction has in its statute book legislation based directly or indirectly on the ideas first embodied in the Maintenance Orders (Facilities for Enforcement) Act 1920 of the United Kingdom. In
the great majority of jurisdictions, the legislation closely follows the original
model with only such amendments as have been dictated by constitutional
developments or changes in the structure of the courts. In this sense the
geographical spread of the legislation is very great; in this sense, Dzwiekowski
was justified in exclaiming that 'certainly by 1927, at the very latest, almost
the entire British Empire was linked into the network of reciprocity'.[1]

The effective geographical scope of the Commonwealth maintenance orders
scheme cannot, however, be judged on this criterion alone. It is necessary to
examine the actual 'extent' of the legislation in a second sense. The primary
sense of that word, at least in legislative usage within the United Kingdom,
refers to an Act extending to a country *as part of its law*; in this sense we say that
the Maintenance Orders (Reciprocal Enforcement) Act 1972 extends to the
whole of the United Kingdom, including Scotland, but its predecessor, the
1920 Act, extended only to England and Ireland (later, Northern Ireland).
The secondary sense is used in provisions corresponding to s 12 of the 1920 Act.

Section 12(1) provides, under a marginal heading 'Extent of Act':

'Where His Majesty is satisfied that reciprocal provisions have been made by the
legislature of any part of His Majesty's dominions outside the United Kingdom for the
enforcement within that part of maintenance orders made by courts within England
and Ireland, His Majesty may by Order in Council extend this Act to that part, and
thereupon that part shall become a part of His Majesty's dominions to which this Act
extends.'

It is plain from the words of this provision that legislation will have been passed
by the overseas legislature; that legislation will be part of the law of that
jurisdiction, and will satisfy the pre-condition imposed by s 12 for the application of the United Kingdom Act in respect of that jurisdiction, of orders made
by the courts there or to be registered in those courts.

Later paragraphs in this chapter will state for each Commonwealth jurisdiction the legislation in force as part of its law, and will set out the 'extent' of
that legislation in this secondary sense, examining the reciprocating countries
designated by extension orders made under the local Act. It will be seen from
this survey that 'the network of reciprocity' is far from being comprehensive,
which has prompted suggestions that the present requirement of designating
reciprocating countries should be removed.[2] There are, however, a number of

commonly occurring difficulties which require examination by way of introduction to that survey.

1 Diane C. Dzwiekowski 'The Reciprocal Enforcement of Affiliation Orders' 22 RFL 29 at p 48.
2 See para 8.07 below.

Permissible extensions

8.02 In its original form, the Commonwealth maintenance orders scheme was seen very much as an 'Imperial' scheme, with reciprocal arrangements limited to the British Empire. Section 12(1) of the 1920 Act, already quoted,[1] enabled the Act to be extended to 'any part of His Majesty's dominions outside the United Kingdom', and s 12(2) included 'any British protectorate'. One of the difficulties experienced in the early years of the scheme was caused by unsatisfactory adaptations of this section in legislation corresponding to it. The Colonial Office circulated a draft provision and a number of jurisdictions duly amended their Acts to adopt the suggested formula, which spoke of 'any British possession or any territory under His Majesty's protection'.[2]

This formula with its reference to 'British possession' is still to be found in some fifteen Commonwealth jurisdictions, principally in the Caribbean and Pacific Ocean areas.[3] In 1920 the phrase was perhaps appropriate to describe even those countries which came to be known as dominions, and in nationality law the terms 'British subject' and 'Commonwealth citizen' were largely equivalent in United Kingdom law until the passage of the British Nationality Act 1981. Constitutional developments within the Commonwealth, as colonial territories proceed to independence, make the phrase increasingly inappropriate (not to say, embarrassing). A literal interpretation, it might be argued, would restrict the phrase to the remaining dependent territories of the United Kingdom; but practice is undoubtedly to give a much more generous interpretation. Even the most liberal interpretation would be strained were it desired to treat as 'British possessions' those few Commonwealth countries which were never subject to United Kingdom sovereignty, eg Western Samoa; Scotland would certainly not be a British possession.

It must be emphasised that this problem, and the related issues shortly to be examined, do not strictly raise the question of 'state succession' familiar, especially in relation to treaty obligations, in public international law. The issue concerns the effect of constitutional changes on legislative provisions in other countries, and can arise both on independence and on the adoption (then or at a later date) of republican forms of government.

The latter change is particularly relevant where the phrase 'Her Majesty's dominions' is used. In the maintenance orders context, this phrase, either alone or in combination with other phrases, is used in a number of jurisdictions,[4] including at least one (Sri Lanka) which has itself become a republic.

It is the practice in the United Kingdom and in certain other Commonwealth countries[5] to legislate so as to ensure the continued operation of existing law despite independence and the change to republican status. A recent example is in the Kiribati Act 1979, passed when the Gilbert Islands became the Republic of Kiribati. Section 3(1) provides in part that 'all existing law to which this section applies, whether being a rule of law or a provision of an Act of Parliament or of any other enactment or instrument whatsoever ... shall, unless and until provision to the contrary is made by Parliament or some other authority having power in that behalf, have the same operation in respect of Kiribati and persons and things belonging to or connected with Kiribati, as it would have had apart from this subsection if there had been no change in the status of Kiribati'.[6] Such legislation, coupled with the provisions in the constitutional documents of the former colony, will ensure the operation of existing law in both the United Kingdom and the ex-colony. What has never been fully tested is whether legislation in a third country can be re-interpreted in the light of these developments, and without explicit local provision.

Partly with these questions in mind, many jurisdictions have revised their legislation, by substituting,[7] or in some cases by adding as an alternative,[8] a reference to 'any Commonwealth country'. Various formulae are to be found, with some references to 'Commonwealth states' and others to 'Commonwealth states and territories'. There are unfortunately difficulties even with these formulae. A unitary member of the Commonwealth, such as Jamaica or Singapore, presents no problem. But is a province of Canada a 'Commonwealth country'? Are dependent territories of the United Kingdom, which are indisputably 'British possessions', within the term 'Commonwealth country'? Similar difficulties may arise in connection with the various island territories associated with Australia and New Zealand,[9] as well as with special cases such as Brunei.

In some jurisdictions the constitution or an Interpretation Act contains a definition of 'Commonwealth' which obviates these difficulties. Another very satisfactory technique is that first adopted in New Zealand (and recently copied in Barbados): the Commonwealth Countries Act specifies the member countries of the Commonwealth in a Schedule (capable of amendment by Order); makes it clear that any territory for the international relations of which a Commonwealth country is responsible is within the term 'Commonwealth', and provides for the continued operation of existing law in respect of those Commonwealth countries of which Her Majesty is not Head of State.[10]

A growing number of jurisdictions impose no limit on the class of countries to which their legislation may be extended. Some make separate provision for Commonwealth and other countries,[11] a practice which does reflect the fact that very few foreign, ie non-Commonwealth, countries have a system corresponding to the 'shuttlecock' procedure required for full reciprocity; but most[12] simply say that any country may be designated a reciprocating state.

1   See para 8.01 above.
2   General Circular 61319/29 dated 12 June 1929.
3   Antigua and Barbuda, Brunei, Cyprus (and Akrotiri and Dhekelia), Dominica, Grenada, Kiribati, Montserrat, Nigeria, St Christopher and Nevis, St Lucia, St Vincent and the Grenadines, Solomon Islands, Turks and Caicos Islands, and the Virgin Islands. For citations see the country-by-country survey commencing at para 8.09 below.
4   Belize, Christmas Island, Cocos (Keeling) Islands, Guernsey, Jersey, Mauritius (where the reference is expressly to the Queen of the United Kingdom), and Sri Lanka.
5   Eg New Zealand; see n 10 below, for the more recent practice there.
6   See also the Zimbabwe Act 1979, Sch 2, para 3: in that case a specific reference was made to the continued application of the Order in Council extending to Southern Rhodesia the Maintenance Orders (Facilities for Enforcement) Act 1920.
7   Bahamas, Fiji (1920 Act), Gambia, Guyana, Jamaica, Kenya, Lesotho, Isle of Man, Mauritius, Sierra Leone, Swaziland, Trinidad and Tobago, Tuvalu, Uganda, Zambia and Zimbabwe.
8   Cayman Islands, Seychelles and Sri Lanka.
9   Ie Christmas Island, Cocos (Keeling) Islands, Cook Islands and Niue.
10 Commonwealth Countries Act 1977, No 31 (New Zealand); Commonwealth Countries Act 1980, No 52 (Barbados).
11 Cook Islands, New Zealand, Niue, Western Samoa; all are jurisdictions which extend their provisions to all Commonwealth countries automatically, without specific extension orders: see para 8.07 below.

12   Including all those with legislation on the 1972 model (Ascension, Bermuda, British Antarctic
     Territory, Falkland Islands, Fiji (1974 Act), Gibraltar, Hong Kong, Malta (1974 Act),
     Nauru, St Helena, Singapore and the United Kingdom) and Anguilla, Australia (including
     Christmas Island and the Cocos (Keeling) Islands), Bangladesh, Barbados, Botswana,
     Canada (all jurisdictions except Quebec), Ghana, India, Malawi, Malaysia and Tanzania.

Obsolete extensions

8.03   Legislation on the 1920 model contains no provision corresponding to
that in the 1972 model[1] that extension orders may be varied or revoked by a
subsequent order; contraction of the system was evidently not contemplated.
In some jurisdictions such a power will be conferred under some more general
provision or may be regarded as implied, but it is at least possible that the lack
of any express provision reinforces administrative inertia. This results in the
survival of extension orders designating Aden, British Burma, and Her Majesty's Court at Zanzibar, all of which are plainly obsolete.

Of potentially greater importance are questions, related to those discussed
in the last paragraph, of a state succession nature.[2] There seems to be no
difficulty in 'translating' designations where changes of nomenclature require
this, for example Ghana for the Gold Coast, and Guyana for British Guiana.
Similarly, it is assumed that the division or fragmentation of a designated state,
such as the division of the Gilbert and Ellice Islands by the separation of
Tuvalu from Kiribati or the dissolution of the Leeward Islands into separate
units formed from its 'presidencies', generally leads to the successor units all
receiving the status of reciprocating country. This cannot be applied universally; the violent origins of Bangladesh and that country's refusal to treat itself
as a successor to Pakistan have to be weighed, and the separation of a unit
which was formerly partially self-governing (eg the Turks and Caicos Islands
from Jamaica) gives rise to special problems noted in the country-by-country
survey which follows. The succession of Singapore to the position of 'the Straits
Settlements' in the maintenance orders scheme appears to be uncontroversial
in Singapore, despite the difference in the geographical limits of the units;
similarly Malaysia is generally treated as having succeeded to the earlier
Malaya, whether or not the East Malaysian states of Sabah and Sarawak had
been brought within the scheme.

The existence of these and similar questions is unfortunate in that the
potential user of the maintenance order procedures may be discouraged if he,
or in practice his legal advisers, cannot find a reference to the overseas jurisdiction under its present title.

1   See s 45(1) of the Maintenance Orders (Reciprocal Enforcement) Act 1972 (UK).
2   Though, as was pointed out in the last paragraph, the issue is *not* strictly one of state succession
    to treaty obligations. On that issue see Lester 'State Succession to Treaties in the Common-
    wealth' (1963) 12 ICLQ 475. As the maintenance orders scheme, with the obsolete exception
    of Zanzibar, does not involve the designation of *courts*, the point taken in a money-judgments
    context in *Re Lowenthal and Air France* [1967] EA 75 (High Ct of Kenya) that superior courts of
    Zambia were not the same as the 'Superior Courts of Northern Rhodesia' specified in Kenyan
    legislation does not arise.

'England and Ireland'

8.04   The Maintenance Orders (Facilities for Enforcement) Act 1920 of the
United Kingdom was designed to secure reciprocity between England and
Ireland on the one hand and 'other parts of His Majesty's Dominions and
Protectorates' on the other. When the Act was sent to overseas jurisdictions

with a request that corresponding legislation be enacted locally,[1] no specific guidance was given as to the appropriate adaptations. With very few exceptions[2] the overseas draftsman adjusted the text so that the local legislation applied automatically to 'England and Ireland' but could be extended to other jurisdictions by order.

In 1929 further advice was offered by the Colonial Office.[3] This pointed out some unsatisfactory features of colonial legislation which had followed the imperial model too slavishly. In some cases orders had to be transmitted via the Secretary of State in London even if destined for a neighbouring colony; in others provisional orders were only possible if the respondent was in England or Ireland; in others depositions were only admissible in evidence if they originated from England or Ireland. A new formula was suggested which ensured that jurisdictions designated by extension orders, and their Governors, were substituted as appropriate for the references to 'England or Ireland' and the Secretary of State.

What is remarkable about the 1929 Circular is its omission of any reference to constitutional developments in Ireland. Although the 1920 Act uses the term 'Ireland' this had, since the establishment of the Irish Free State in December 1922, to be adapted to read as a reference to Northern Ireland only so far as the law of the United Kingdom was concerned[4] and all extension orders made in the United Kingdom after 1922 expressly excluded orders made in or intended for registration in the Irish Free State.

However the 1920 Act continued in force as part of the law of the new Irish state with corresponding adaptations.[5] No extension orders have ever been made under it in Ireland, and when in 1974 Ireland first made provision for the reciprocal enforcement of maintenance orders with the United Kingdom a fresh Act[6] was passed for the purpose rather than an amendment of the 1920 Act. Technically the 1920 Act remains part of the law of Ireland and extends to those territories named in extension orders made in the United Kingdom prior to the separation of the Irish Free State.[7] A large number of jurisdictions retain the expression 'England and Ireland'[8] and some have added an express reference to 'Eire'[9] or 'the Republic of Ireland';[10] but there is little correlation between the list of such jurisdictions and those in respect of which the 1920 Act is technically in force in Ireland. In practice, however, no reciprocal arrangements involving the Irish Republic are in use except those between Ireland and the United Kingdom jurisdictions.[11]

---

1   Colonial Office General Circular CO 47330/20 dated 8 October 1920.
2   A notable exception was India: the Maintenance Orders Enforcement Act 1921, s 3 applies the Act to reciprocating territories without making any special mention of 'England and Ireland', which were the subject of the first extension order (F.120, 6 March 1922).
3   General Circular CO 61319/29 dated 12 June 1929.
4   Irish Free State (Consequential Adaptation of Enactments) Order 1923, SR & O 1923/405 (UK).
5   See Adaptation of Enactments Act 1922, s 3; Constitution (Consequential Provisions) Act 1937, s 2.
6   Maintenance Orders Act 1974, No 16.
7   These are (no attempt having been made to express the list in modern terms): Basutoland, Bechuanaland, Bermuda, British Solomon Islands Protectorate, Cyprus, the Falkland Islands, the Gambia, Gibraltar, the Gilbert and Ellice Islands, Gold Coast (including Ashanti and the Northern Territories), Grenada, Hong Kong, the Leeward Islands, Malta, the Isle of Man, Mauritius, New Zealand, Nigeria, Northern Rhodesia, Nyasaland, Queensland, St Lucia, St Vincent, Seychelles, Somaliland Protectorate, Southern Rhodesia, the Straits Settlements, Swaziland, Tasmania, Trinidad and Tobago, Western Australia, and Zanzibar.
8   Botswana, Cayman Islands, Cyprus, Fiji (1967 Act), Guyana, Kiribati, Lesotho, Malawi,

Mauritius, Nigeria, St Lucia, St Vincent and the Grenadines, Sierra Leone, the Solomon Islands, and Zambia.

9 Kenya.

10 Bahamas, Fiji (1920 Act amended in 1966 and interpreting 'Ireland'), Gambia, Swaziland and Uganda.

11 I am grateful to Mr Roger Hayes, member of the Irish Law Reform Commission, for his help in tracing the position in Irish law.

'Unilateral reciprocity'

8.05   As the country-by-country survey will demonstrate, there are a number of cases in which country A has legislation declaring country B to be a reciprocating country (and declaring that country B has or is about to confer reciprocal benefits) but no effective reciprocal legislation can be traced in country B. This phenomenon of 'unilateral reciprocity' has a number of possible explanations, one of which is simply administrative error or misunderstanding. Rather more respectable reasons are related to the enactment of fresh legislation. When an improved version of the relevant legislation is enacted it does not always provide for the continued validity of extension orders made under the corresponding Act now repealed. Barbados provides a clear illustration of this, a considerable number of reciprocal arrangements being 'lost' as a result. The enactment of the Family Law Act 1975 by the Commonwealth of Australia, an assertion of federal legislative competence in an area previously the subject of state legislation, produced a complex pattern of unilateral reciprocity which is described more fully below.[1] Other instances are fully noted in the country-by-country survey.

Where unilateral reciprocity is found, the legislation is not wholly inoperative. A final maintenance order made in country B will be registered and enforced in country A; this procedure requires no action in country B so that the gap in that country's legislation is irrelevant. But the 'shuttlecock' procedure involving the confirmation of one country's provisional order by the courts of the other, or co-operation between courts in matters of variation or of evidence, will be impossible—though it may on occasion actually take place if the defect in the legal machinery is overlooked.

1   Para 8.14 below.

The resulting pattern

8.06   Potentially, the Commonwealth maintenance orders scheme is of universal application throughout Commonwealth jurisdictions. It is indeed the case that a maintenance order made in Lesotho could be enforced against a defaulting husband in the Bailiwick of Guernsey, and the Prince Edward Islander who took refuge in Papua New Guinea would not be beyond the reach of enforcement procedures. But there are other, more likely, cases which are not covered: there are no reciprocal arrangements between the Gambia and Ghana, between Ontario and any of the Commonwealth Caribbean countries, or between India and Hong Kong.

There are certainly some jurisdictions which have sought to achieve as fully comprehensive coverage as possible. Guernsey and Jersey are the outstanding examples, each building up an enormous list of reciprocating countries in a very short time. The original motion at the Imperial Conference of 1911 asked that 'reciprocal provisions should be made throughout the constituent parts of the Empire'. The actual legislation guaranteed reciprocity only as between the enacting jurisdiction and 'England and Ireland', and the Colonial Office did not encourage any attempt at universal coverage. In 1924, the Colonial Secretary, noting that 50 territories had enacted legislation, but that few had made direct arrangements between themselves, observed, 'I do not, however, consider it necessary that each Colony or Protectorate should extend reciprocal arrangements to all others in which the necessary measures have been adopted, and I am content to leave to the local authority in each case the selection of the Dominions, Colonies or Protectorates with which it is desired to reciprocate'.[1] Although this policy was no doubt realistic at a time when travel was much more difficult, and much less common, than it is today, the result was incomplete coverage for many years even within some natural regional groupings such as the Caribbean.

The current position is still one of patchy coverage, most adequate within the federal states such as Canada, good in the Caribbean and in East and Central Africa, but more limited elsewhere; there is only a very small amount of reciprocity between countries in different regions. Where such links exist, they may reflect patterns of migration (eg from India to Malaysia and some of the Pacific jurisdictions), but may also be the result either of individual cases arising in practice in which the parties have persuaded the authorities to act or of actions by the peripatetic legal officers of former Colonial Office days creating links with a jurisdiction in which they had previously served.

1   General Circular dated 24 June 1924 (Public Record Office, London, reference CO 854 60).

Abolition of the requirement of reciprocity

8.07   New Zealand, one of the pioneers in the field of reciprocal enforcement legislation,[1] was also the first jurisdiction to abandon the requirement of reciprocity. Legislation in New Zealand, and its counterparts in the Cook Islands, Niue and Western Samoa, applies automatically to all Commonwealth jurisdictions without the necessity for the making of any extension orders. It is immaterial that the overseas jurisdiction may not have enacted corresponding legislation or may not have extended its legislation to New Zealand.

Reciprocity was an essential feature of the scheme first mooted in 1911 and enacted from 1920. At that stage it was almost certainly a political necessity; the notion of providing such enforcement facilities was novel, and most of the jurisdictions were dependencies. There was not the confidence that Commonwealth countries have come to feel in their shared judicial tradition.

There appears to be considerable support for the view that those considerations are no longer as persuasive. Given the almost universal adoption of the Commonwealth scheme in the statute books of Commonwealth jurisdictions, the negotiation of reciprocal arrangements is often a formality, at least where similar definitions of 'maintenance orders' are used. Yet experience has shown that the business of preparing extension orders and of keeping the list accurate and up-to-date is one of the greatest obstacles to an effective Commonwealth scheme. It must be very hard for a party in Country A seeking to enforce an order in Country B to be told that both countries have the relevant legislation, in identical terms it may be, but that, for want of Orders-in-Council it cannot help her. On the basis of discussions at regional meetings of law officers, the model legislation prepared for Commonwealth Law Ministers in 1980 follows the New Zealand lead in abolishing the requirement of reciprocity.[2]

1   See para 5.01 above.
2   See Appendix C.

B. THE COUNTRY-BY-COUNTRY SURVEY

The country-by-country survey

8.08　The paragraphs which follow examine the position in each Commonwealth jurisdiction. In each case the current statute is identified, indicating on which model it is based and any special peculiarities. The permissible extensions under the Act are stated, and the jurisdictions to which the Act has been extended are listed. So far as possible an indication is given of cases of unilateral reciprocity involving each country. Jurisdictions are examined in alphabetical order, the Australian, Canadian and United Kingdom jurisdictions grouped under those headings; an account of the position in the Republic of South Africa which remains for some purposes within the Commonwealth scheme completes the survey.

Akrotiri and Dhekelia

8.09　These 'Sovereign Base Areas' remained under British sovereignty after the establishment of the Republic of Cyprus. The Maintenance Orders (Facilities for Enforcement) Law[1] of Cyprus remains in force, with certain adaptations to reflect the constitutional position.[2] The extent of the Law would appear to be the same as that of the Cyprus Law;[3] no extension orders have been made expressly for Akrotiri and Dhekelia, and the relevant legislation in force in the United Kingdom refers only to 'Cyprus'.

1　Cap 16, RL 1959 (of Cyprus).
2　Laws (Adaptation and Interpretation) (Consolidation and Extension) Ordinance, No 5 of 1968.
3　See para 8.41 below.

Anguilla

8.10　Anguilla was formerly part of the State of St Christopher–Nevis–Anguilla; after a period of somewhat anomalous separation dating from 1969 its present status was declared in the Anguilla Act 1980 (UK). It is assumed that orders designating St Christopher–Nevis–Anguilla as a reciprocating territory continue to apply to both Anguilla and St Christopher and Nevis, and that earlier orders applying to 'the Leeward Islands' (of which St Christopher–Nevis–Anguilla was a presidency) also continue to apply to Anguilla.[1]

　　In the law of Anguilla, however, such issues do not arise. The Maintenance Orders (Reciprocal Enforcement) Ordinance 1978[2] follows the unsatisfactory model of the Barbados Act of 1974.[3] It has been extended only to the United Kingdom,[4] where reciprocal provisions are in force.

1　A difficult case is Bermuda's order, made in 1975 but referring to the Leeward Islands. See para 8.21 below.
2　No 8 of 1978.
3　See para 6.27 above.
4　SRO 4/1979.

Antigua and Barbuda

8.11　Antigua and Barbuda was, until 1957, a presidency of the Leeward Islands, and its Maintenance Orders (Facilities for Enforcement) Act,[1] which follows the 1920 model, was originally enacted by the legislature of the Leeward Islands. The Act extends to England and Northern Ireland[2] and is capable of further extension to any 'British possession or territory under Her Majesty's protection'.[3]

The Act has been extended to the Bahamas,[4] Belize,[5] Bermuda,[4] Dominica,[6] Grenada,[4] Guyana,[7] Jamaica,[8] the States of Jersey,[9] the Isle of Man,[10] Montserrat,[11] St Christopher and Nevis,[12] St Lucia,[4] St Vincent and the Grenadines,[4] Trinidad and Tobago,[4] and the Virgin Islands.[11] In all these cases, reciprocal arrangements are in force; in a number of cases the other territory has extended its legislation to 'the Leeward Islands' and it is assumed that this extension continues to apply to Antigua. The Act also extends to Anguilla,[12] Barbados,[4] and the Turks and Caicos Islands,[13] but no reciprocal arrangements are currently in force in these territories. The Antigua legislation has also been extended to the Australian Capital Territory[14] and New South Wales,[5] but Antigua is not a reciprocating territory for the purposes of the Family Law Act 1975 of Australia.[15]

1   Cap 50, RL 1962.
2   S 3 as amended by the General Revision Ordinance 1961; the original Leeward Islands legislation applied to 'England and Ireland'.
3   S 12. For a discussion of the effect of this expression, see para 8.02 above.
4   LI Gaz, 30 August 1923.
5   LI Sub Leg (1924).
6   SRO (LI) 14/1945.
7   LI Gaz, 9 August 1922.
8   LI Gaz, 14 May 1925.
9   SRO (LI) 44/1954.
10 SRO 5/1962.
11 SRO 12/1957.
12 SRO 12/1957, as part of St Christopher–Nevis–Anguilla.
13 LI Gaz, 14 May 1925, as part of Jamaica.
14 SRO (LI) 6/1929.
15 See para 8.14 below.

Ascension

8.12   A local Ordinance on the 1920 model was repealed by the Maintenance Orders (Facilities for Enforcement) (Repeal) Ordinance 1978. The general legal position in Ascension is that English law applies unless a 'specific law', which includes legislation passed in Saint Helena, makes other provision.[1] It would appear that the Saint Helena legislation, applying a modified version of the Maintenance Orders (Reciprocal Enforcement) Act 1972 (of the United Kingdom), is in force; but, for reasons set out below, has almost no actual legal effect.[2]

1   Application of English Law (Ascension) Ordinance, 1973 No 1.
2   See para 8.71 below.

Australia

8.13   The principal Australian legislation has already been fully examined.[1] It remains to examine the geographical application of the Australian legislation, and to examine the special position in two of the island territories of the Commonwealth of Australia.

1   See para 6.09–6.17 above.

(a) The mainland states and territories and Norfolk Island

8.14 The Family Law Act 1975[1] is in force throughout the mainland of Australia (that is, in the States of New South Wales, Queensland, South Australia, Tasmania, Victoria and Western Australia and the Australian Capital Territory and the Northern Territory) and also in the Territory of Norfolk Island.[2] So far as the law of Australia is concerned, there is therefore a single list of countries which are declared to be either reciprocating countries or countries with restricted reciprocity[3] for the purposes of the Act.

The position is, however, rather more complicated, and it is necessary to examine the historical background. Legislation on the 1920 model was enacted at an early date in the various Australian jurisdictions, the subject being handled through state rather than Commonwealth (ie, federal) legislation. A considerable number of reciprocal arrangements were entered into, especially by New South Wales and Victoria, with other countries during the 1920s, and a large number of reciprocal arrangements were made by the Australian Capital Territory in 1928 and 1929. This latter development was the result of action in 1928 which persuaded the Colonial Office to issue a circular despatch[4] urging reciprocal arrangements with what was then formally known as the Seat of Government of the Commonwealth of Australia. In a number of jurisdictions the relevant Order, or its short title, referred simply to 'Australia' or 'the Commonwealth of Australia' although only the territory was in mind.

The adoption of substantially uniform legislation by the Australian jurisdictions in 1964 and following years led to the making of further reciprocal arrangements with overseas jurisdictions, especially by those states which hitherto had only named a limited number of reciprocating countries. By the time the Family Law Act 1975 was enacted by the Australian Parliament, a considerable number of overseas jurisdictions had designated all the Australian states and mainland territories as reciprocating countries; those overseas jurisdictions were suitable for inclusion in the new federal list of reciprocating countries for the purposes of the Family Law Act 1975.

There are, however, a number of countries[5] which are declared to be reciprocating countries under the Family Law Act 1975 which had not made reciprocal arrangements with all the mainland Australian jurisdictions. Some of these seem to be cases where the use of the term 'Australia' or 'the Commonwealth of Australia' in an order intended to refer only to the Australian Capital Territory created a false impression of comprehensive reciprocity, but at least four cases cannot be explained on this basis, New Brunswick having designated only states and no territories, the Isle of Man having designated all jurisdictions except Queensland, and Nauru and Tanzania having designated no part of Australia under their current legislation.

A much larger group of countries declared to be reciprocating countries under the Family Law Act 1975 had taken no action in respect of the Territory of Norfolk Island. The Australian authorities in implementing the Family Law Act 1975 seem to have decided to overlook this on the de minimis principle. It remains the case that a maintenance order made in Norfolk Island will be directly enforceable in few overseas jurisdictions, for those jurisdictions for the most part continue to designate the various Australian states and territories separately for the purposes of their own legislation and have not responded to the enactment of the Family Law Act 1975 by substituting a general designation of 'Australia, including Norfolk Island'.

Of those countries *not* declared to be reciprocating countries under the

Family Law Act 1975, some had in fact designated all the Australian jurisdictions.[6] A much larger group[7] had designated some only of the Australian jurisdictions; the designations remain in force despite the fact that now no Australian court can register and enforce maintenance orders from those countries. Strictly all these countries should rescind their designations of Australian jurisdictions, as reciprocity no longer exists.

The list which follows is the position in Australian law. The extent to which the law of other countries assumes the existence of some reciprocity with the whole or with parts of Australia is stated in the paragraphs dealing with the law of each country.

Under the Family Law Regulations,[8] the following countries are declared[9] to be reciprocating countries: Fiji, the Isle of Man, Kenya, Malawi, Malaysia, Manitoba, Nauru, New Zealand, Ontario, Papua New Guinea, Saskatchewan, Sierra Leone, Singapore, Sri Lanka, Tanzania (excluding Zanzibar), Trinidad and Tobago, the United Kingdom, and Zambia. The following countries are declared[10] to be 'countries with restricted reciprocity':[3] Alberta, British Columbia, California,[11] Cook Islands, Cyprus, Guernsey, Alderney and Sark, Hong Kong,[11] India, Jersey, Malta, Newfoundland, New Brunswick, Niue, Nova Scotia, Prince Edward Island, South Africa (excluding Namibia), and Western Samoa.

1 Act No 53, 1975, which came into force on 5 January 1976.
2 S 7 (extension of Act to Norfolk Island).
3 For the meaning of this phrase, see para 6.11 above.
4 General Circular 51349/28 dated 7 November 1928.
5 Including Cyprus, India and Sierra Leona. Cf Grenada where the error was avoided.
6 Including Falkland Islands, Kiribati, Solomon Islands and Tuvalu.
7 Including Antigua and Barbuda, Bahamas, Belize, Botswana, Dominica, Gambia, Ghana, Guyana, Jamaica, Lesotho, Mauritius, Montserrat, Nigeria, Saint Christopher and Nevis, Saint Lucia, Saint Vincent and the Grenadines, Swaziland, Uganda, the Virgin Islands, and Zimbabwe.
8 SR 1975 No 210.
9 Reg 143.
10 Reg 144.
11 California and Hong Kong were inserted by SR 1977, No 172, reg 43, with effect from 1 November 1977.

(b) The Territory of Christmas Island

8.15 The Maintenance Orders (Facilities for Enforcement) Ordinance 1963[1] made under the Christmas Island Act 1958–1963 of the Commonwealth of Australia is on the 1920 model with some modifications, for example the inclusion of a provision[2] governing the conversion of payments into Australian currency. The Ordinance may be applied[3] to any 'part of the Queen's dominions', any 'territory under the Queen's protection', any 'territory administered by the Government of a part of the Queen's dominions under the trusteeship system of the United Nations' or to 'any other country or part of a country'. It has been extended only to Hong Kong,[4] which makes reciprocal provision, and to Singapore,[5] which appears not to.

Christmas Island was administered as part of Singapore until, after a brief period as a separate colony of the United Kingdom, it was accepted as a territory of Australia. Until 1963, the Singapore legislation on maintenance orders was in force; it is possible that in some jurisdictions a designation of Singapore as a reciprocating country made while Christmas Island was a part of the Colony of Singapore might be held to include Christmas Island.

1   Ordinance No 3 of 1963 (amended by Ordinance No 5 of 1968 in respect of the title of the Administrator).
2   S 10.
3   S 5.
4   Notice 20 January 1968 (Commonwealth of Australia Gazette, 7 February 1968).
5   Notice 21 August 1978 (Gaz, 5 September 1978).

(c)   The Territory of Cocos (Keeling) Islands

8.16   The Maintenance Orders (Facilities for Enforcement) Ordinance 1960[1] made under the Cocos (Keeling) Islands Act 1955–1958 of the Commonwealth of Australia is on the 1920 model with some modifications; it is substantially identical with the Christmas Island Ordinance. The power to declare reciprocating countries is in the same terms as in that Ordinance. The Ordinance has been extended[2] to Brunei, Cook Islands, Bailiwick of Guernsey, Hong Kong, India, Jersey, Malaysia, the Isle of Man, Papua New Guinea,[3] Saint Vincent and the Grenadines, South Africa, Sri Lanka, and Western Samoa; in all these cases reciprocal arrangements exist. It has also been extended to all the Australian states and territories (including Christmas Island)[4] except Victoria, but the Cocos (Keeling) Islands are not designated under either the Family Law Act 1975 or the Ordinance in force in Christmas Island.

The Islands were transferred from the then Colony of Singapore in 1955. It is possible that in some jurisdictions a designation of Singapore before that date as a reciprocating country might be held to include the Cocos (Keeling) Islands.

1   Ordinance No 1 of 1960 (amended by Ordinance No 3 of 1975 in respect of the title of the Administrator).
2   Unless otherwise indicated, by Notice 27 February 1961 (Commonwealth of Australia Gazette, 23 March 1961).
3   Notice 2 May 1961, Gaz 11 May 1961.
4   Norfolk Island and Christmas Island by Notice 10 July 1961 (Gaz 22 July 1961); New South Wales by Notice 20 September 1961 (Gaz 12 October 1961).

The Bahamas

8.17   The Maintenance Order Facilities for Enforcement Act[1] follows the 1920 model. It extends to England, Northern Ireland and the Republic of Ireland.[2] The reference to the Republic of Ireland is inoperative, as that republic has no legislation actually applicable in respect of the Bahamas, and is in any case difficult because the rest of the Act, including the definition of a 'dependant',[3] is written in terms of countries 'of the Commonwealth'. The Act is capable of extension to 'any country of the Commonwealth other than England or Northern Ireland'.[4]

The Act has been extended to Antigua and Barbuda,[5] Belize,[6] Dominica,[7] Grenada,[8] Guyana,[8] Jamaica,[9] Montserrat,[5] New Zealand,[10] St Christopher and Nevis,[5] St Lucia,[9] St Vincent and the Grenadines,[8] Trinidad and Tobago,[9] and the Virgin Islands.[5] In all these cases, reciprocal arrangements are in force. The Bahamas Act has also been extended to Anguilla,[5] Barbados,[8] Bermuda[8] and the Turks and Caicos Islands,[11] but no reciprocal arrangements are currently in force in these territories. It has also been extended to the Australian Capital Territory,[12] but the Bahamas is not a reciprocating territory for the purposes of the Family Law Act 1975 of Australia.[13] Guernsey, Jersey and the Isle of Man have extended their legislation to the Bahamas, but no corresponding extension of the Bahamas legislation has been traced.

1   Cap 45, RL 1965.
2   S 3, as amended by an amending Ordinance in 1957 (No 1) and by Existing Laws Amendment Order 1974, SI 41A of 1974.
3   S 2.
4   S 12; see Ordinance 43 of 1964.
5   Off Gaz 1924, p 277 as part of the Leeward Islands.
6   Off Gaz 1928, p 115.
7   Off Gaz 1924, p 277 as part of the Leeward Islands, of which Dominica was a part until 1940.
8   Off Gaz 1924, p 227.
9   Off Gaz 1925, p 269.
10 SI 45/69.
11 Off Gaz 1925, p 269, as part of Jamaica.
12 Off Gaz 1929, p 13; the reference is to 'Australia' but it is clear that this refers only to the 'seat of government', ie the Capital Territory.
13 See para 8.14 above.

Bangladesh

8.18   The legislation in force in Bangladesh is the Maintenance Orders Enforcement Act 1921 of India,[1] as amended by the Maintenance Orders Enforcement (Amendment) Ordinance 1962 of Pakistan.[2] Unlike almost all legislation on the 1920 model, the Indian Act did not apply automatically to any country, not even England; its extent is, therefore, defined entirely by extension orders. By virtue of the Pakistani amending Ordinance, the Act can be extended to 'any country'[3] whether or not within the Commonwealth.

However, the Government of Bangladesh takes the view that on independence it did not inherit bilateral arrangements made by India or Pakistan, and treats the extension orders made before independence as ineffective. As no orders have been made subsequently, it follows that the Act is wholly inoperative.

1   No 18 of 1921 (India).
2   No 69 of 1962 (Pakistan).
3   S 3.

Barbados

8.19   The Maintenance Orders (Reciprocal Enforcement) Act 1974[1] is an unsatisfactory conflation of earlier legislation which it repealed.[2] The repeal of the earlier legislation caused the numerous extension orders made under it to lapse in March 1975, and the new Act has been extended only to the Province of British Columbia[3] and the United Kingdom.[4] A large number of other countries designate Barbados as a reciprocating territory, the relevant orders having been made before the 1974 Act.

1   No 50 of 1974.
2   For a discussion of the Act, see para 6.27 above.
3   SI 1977/131.
4   SI 1976/69.

Belize

8.20   Provisions on the 1920 model are contained in the Summary Jurisdiction (Procedure) Ordinance.[1] They extend to England and Northern Ireland[2] and are capable of further extension to 'any part of Her Majesty's dominions outside the United Kingdom'[3] a phrase which would seem to exclude Scotland and those Commonwealth countries which do not recognise Her Majesty as Head of State.[4]

The provisions have been extended[5] to Antigua and Barbuda[6], the Bahamas, Dominica,[7] Grenada, the Bailiwick of Guernsey,[8] Guyana, Jamaica, Jersey, the Isle of Man, Montserrat,[6] St Christopher and Nevis,[6] St Vincent and the Grenadines, and the Virgin Islands.[6] In all these cases reciprocal provisions are in force. Extensions of the Belize legislation to Anguilla,[6] Barbados and the Turks and Caicos Islands[9] are not matched by current reciprocal provisions; the same is true of extensions to the Australian Capital Territory and New South Wales as Belize is not a reciprocating territory for the purposes of the Family Law Act 1975 of Australia.[10]

1 Cap 24, RL. See ss 82–92 (part IX).
2 S 83.
3 S 92(1); s 92(2) defines this to include territories under HM protection and mandated territories.
4 Eg Guyana in the list below.
5 Unless otherwise noted, in the consolidated Order printed in RL as subsidiary to cap 24.
6 As part of the Leeward Islands.
7 Semble, as part of the Leeward Islands of which Dominica was one until 1940.
8 SI 1966/5.
9 As part of Jamaica.
10 See para 8.14 above.

Bermuda

8.21 The Maintenance Orders (Reciprocal Enforcement) Act 1974[1] is on the 1972 model. It has been extended[2] to Antigua and Barbuda,[3] Dominica,[4] Guernsey, Hong Kong,[5] Jersey, the Isle of Man, Montserrat,[3] St Christopher and Nevis,[3] St Vincent and the Grenadines, the United Kingdom and the Virgin Islands;[3] in all these cases reciprocal arrangement are in force. No such arrangements exist in Anguilla,[3] Barbados and New South Wales[6] to which the Bermuda Act has also been extended.

The repeal of earlier legislation in 1974 and the limited extension of the new Act has led to a situation in which a number of countries (including the Bahamas, Grenada, Guyana and Jamaica) regard Bermuda as a reciprocating country when Bermuda in fact makes no corresponding provision.

1 No 119 of 1974.
2 SRO 1975/66, unless otherwise noted.
3 As part of the Leeward Islands.
4 Sed quaere. Dominica ceased to be part of the Leeward Islands in 1940 and the use of the term Leeward Islands in an instrument made in 1975 is anachronistic. Dominica does make reciprocal provision in favour of Bermuda.
5 BR 24/78.
6 Bermuda is not a reciprocating country for the purposes of the Family Law Act 1975 of Australia; see para 8.14 above.

Botswana

8.22 Part III of the Judgments (International Enforcement) Act 1981[1] contains provisions as to maintenance orders on the 1920 model. The provisions apply to 'England, Wales, Ireland and the Island of Jersey and to any other country in respect of which the President, having regard to reciprocal provisions under the law of that country, by statutory instrument so provides'.[2]

There is no provision saving orders made under the corresponding provisions repealed in 1981. Those provisions, contained in the former Maintenance Act,[3] had also been extended[4] to the Cook Islands, the Bailiwick of Guernsey, India, Kenya, Lesotho, Malawi, the Isle of Man, New Zealand, Swaziland, Uganda,

Zambia and Zimbabwe; in all these cases reciprocal arrangements exist. There were also extensions to Pakistan and the Republic of South Africa, the validity of which was in some doubt owing to the limitation of the extension power in the earlier Act to Commonwealth countries. Further extensions existed to the Australian Capital Territory, New South Wales, Queensland, South Australia, Tasmania, Victoria and Western Australia, but Botswana is not a reciprocating country for the purposes of the Family Law Act 1975 of Australia. An extension of the earlier Botswana Act to Zanzibar had become inoperative, although the relevant Zanzibar legislation had not been formally repealed by the Tanzanian authorities. It appears, however, that all the extensions referred to in this paragraph have lapsed and require review and appropriate restoration by a statutory instrument under the new Act.

1   No 16 of 1981.
2   S 14(1).
3   Cap 29:04, RL.
4   By a (consolidating) Reciprocal Enforcement of Maintenance Orders Notice (published as subsidiary to cap 29:04, RL).

British Antarctic Territory

8.23   The Falkland Islands legislation, the Maintenance Orders (Reciprocal Enforcement) Ordinance 1979[1], which is on the 1972 model, is applied with adaptations by the Falkland Islands Laws (Application) Regulation 1979.[2] The corresponding subordinate legislation is not expressly so applied, nor has any been made for the territory. The legislation may, therefore, be wholly inoperative.

1   No 1 of 1979 as amended by No 16 of 1979 (Falkland Islands).
2   No 3 of 1979. The amending Ordinance was applied by Regulation No 1 of 1980.

British Indian Ocean Territory

8.24   The law of Mauritius (in the Chagas Archipelago) and of the Seychelles (in the Aldabra Group) as at 8 April 1965 applies.[1] There has been no further relevant legislation.

1   British Indian Ocean Territory Order 1965 (SI 1965/1 BIOT), art 15.

Brunei[1]

8.25   The Maintenance Orders (Reciprocal Enforcement) Enactment,[2] on the 1920 model, applies to England and Northern Ireland.[3] It is capable of further extension to 'any British possession or territory under Her Majesty's protection'[4] and has been extended[5] to the Cocos (Keeling) Islands, Hong Kong, Malaysia and Singapore, and in all the above cases reciprocal arrangements are in force.[6] An extension to Sri Lanka appears not to be reciprocated.

1   It has proved impossible to trace any developments later than 1960 in respect of Brunei.
2   Cap 10, RL 1951; originally Enactment No 1 of 1936.
3   S 3.
4   S 11. For this phrase, see para 8.02 above.
5   By the Maintenance Orders (Reciprocal Enforcement) Enactment (Extension) Order, printed in RL.
6   In the case of Singapore, by virtue of an order made by the Straits Settlements (of which Singapore was a part) and regarded in Singapore as remaining in force.

Canada

8.26 The development of the 1920 model legislation in the various Canadian jurisdictions, especially through the work of the Commissioners for the Uniformity of Law in Canada, has been examined in the context of the account in Chapter 5 of the 1920 scheme. The paragraphs which follow examine the geographical scope of the current legislation in each jurisdiction.

(a) Alberta

8.27 The Reciprocal Enforcement of Maintenance Orders Act 1980[1] is not yet in force. When it is proclaimed it will continue in force regulations made under the earlier Reciprocal Enforcement of Maintenance Orders Act.[2] That Act extends[3] to all other Canadian jurisdictions,[4] and to England, Fiji,[5] Jersey, New Zealand, Northern Ireland, Papua New Guinea, Scotland,[6] and South Africa;[7] in all these countries reciprocal arrangements are in force. It has been extended to all the states and mainland territories of Australia,[8] and Alberta is a country with restricted reciprocity for the purpose of the Family Law Act 1975 of Australia. An extension to Barbados is not now reciprocated. Ghana, Singapore and Zimbabwe all treat Alberta as a reciprocating country, but no corresponding order has been made in Alberta. The Alberta Act has also been extended to California.

1 R–7.1, RL (Act 44 of 1980).
2 R–7, RL.
3 Reg 167/70, unless otherwise indicated.
4 Quebec by reg 68/71.
5 Reg 73/76.
6 Reg 342/75.
7 Reg 293/71.
8 All reg 167/70, except Tasmania by reg 215/71.

(b) British Columbia

8.28 The current legislation, ie the Family Relations Act[1] and the Regulations made thereunder, applies[2] in respect of all other Canadian jurisdictions,[3] and of Barbados, Cook Islands, Fiji, Gibraltar,[4] Guernsey,[5] Hong Kong, Jersey,[5] the Isle of Man, New Zealand,[5] Papua New Guinea, Singapore, the United Kingdom[6] and Zimbabwe;[5] in all these cases reciprocal arrangements are in force. It also extends to all the states and mainland territories of Australia,[7] but not to Norfolk Island; British Columbia is a reciprocating country for the purposes of the Family Law Act 1975 of Australia.[8] Ghana regards British Columbia as a reciprocating country but no regulation has been made applying the British Columbia Act to Ghana.

British Columbia has been very active in negotiating reciprocal arrangements with non-Commonwealth countries. Its legislation applies[2] in respect of Austria, the German Federal Republic and West Berlin, Norway,[9] and South Africa.[10] Most significant are the extensive reciprocal arrangement with parts of the United States, including currently[2] California, Colorado, Connecticut, Kansas, Maine, Michigan, Minnesota,[11] Nebraska,[12] Nevada, New Hampshire, New Mexico, New York, North Dakota, Ohio, Oregon, Pennsylvania,[13] Vermont, Virginia, Washington and Wisconsin.[14]

1 Cap 121, RL 1979.
2 Reg 332/73 unless otherwise indicated.
3 Reg 19/58 (all except Quebec); reg 143/62 (Quebec).

4   Reg 716/75.
5   Reg 19/58.
6   Reg 432/73.
7   Reg 19/58 (all except S. Australia); reg 63/70 (S. Australia).
8   See para 8.14 above.
9   Reg 391/78.
10 Reciprocal arrangements are in force in South Africa.
11 Reg 364/79, applying the British Columbia legislation in part only.
12 Reg 514/75.
13 Reg 33/74.
14 Reg 189/78.

(c) Manitoba

8.29   The Reciprocal Enforcement of Maintenance Orders Act[1] applies[2] to all other Canadian jurisdictions and to Australia, England, Fiji, Guernsey, Jersey, the Isle of Man, New Zealand, Northern Ireland, Papua New Guinea, Scotland and Zimbabwe; in all these cases reciprocal arrangements are in force. Extensions of the Manitoba Act to Barbados and Ghana appear not to be reciprocated.

Manitoba also has reciprocal arrangements with a large number of the United States: Arizona, Arkansas, California, Colorado, Connecticut, Delaware, Georgia, Idaho, Illinois, Indiana, Kentucky, Louisiana, Maine, Minnesota, Montana, Nebraska, Nevada, New Hampshire, New Mexico, New York, North Carolina, North Dakota, Oklahoma, Oregon, Pennsylvania, Rhode Island, South Dakota, Tennessee, Texas, Utah, Vermont, Virginia, Washington, Wisconsin and Wyoming; and with the German Federal Republic.

1   M20, RL. Proposals for a replacement Act were under consideration in April 1982.
2   Reg 254/80 proclaimed in force May 1981.

(d) New Brunswick

8.30   The Reciprocal Enforcement of Maintenance Orders Act[1] applies in respect of all other Canadian jurisdictions[2] and to Fiji[3], the Isle of Man,[2] New Zealand,[2] Singapore[2] and the United Kingdom;[4] in all these cases reciprocal arrangements are in force. It also applies to all the states, but none of the territories, of Australia;[5] New Brunswick is a reciprocating country for the purposes of the Family Law Act 1975 of Australia.[6]

The Act also applies in respect of the following United States: California,[7] Connecticut,[8] Delaware,[9] Maine,[10] Maryland,[11] Massachusetts,[12] Montana,[13] New York,[14] North Carolina[15] and Oregon.[16]

1   R-4, RL 1973, as amended.
2   Reg 74-95.
3   Reg 75-44. By a charming misunderstanding, Fiji is listed as a State of Australia; an earlier Regulation (139 of 1963) went further, noting the Isle of Man as part of Australia.
4   Reg 74-95 (England and Northern Ireland); reg 74-104 (Scotland).
5   Reg 74-95 except for Queensland; reg 74-127 (Queensland).
6   See para 8.14 above.
7   Reg 75-116.
8   Reg 78-14.
9   Reg 79-29.
10 Reg 76-164.
11 Reg 80-123.
12 Reg 80-93.
13 Reg 80-61.

14 Reg 80–198.
15 Reg 79–86.
16 Reg 80–46.

(e) *Newfoundland*

8.31 The Maintenance Orders (Enforcement) Act[1] applies to countries listed in Schedule C to the Act as amended from time to time, a technique used also in Malaysia.

The listed jurisdictions include all the other Canadian jurisdictions and England, Guernsey, Jersey, the Isle of Man, New Zealand, Papua New Guinea, Singapore, and Zimbabwe; in all these cases reciprocal arrangements exist. All states and mainland territories of Australia are also listed; Newfoundland is a country 'with restricted reciprocity' for the purposes of the Family Law Act 1975 of Australia. The listing of Malta does not appear to be reciprocated.[2] Ghana regards Newfoundland as a reciprocating country, but does not appear in the Schedule to the Newfoundland Act.

1 Cap 224, RL 1970.
2 See para 8.61 below.

(f) *Northwest Territories*

8.32 The Maintenance Orders (Facilities for Enforcement) Ordinance[1] extends to all other Canadian jurisdictions except Quebec[2] and to the Cook Islands,[3] the Bailiwick of Guernsey,[4] Jersey,[5] the Isle of Man,[6] New Zealand,[3] Singapore,[7] South Africa[8] and Zimbabwe;[9] in all these jurisdictions reciprocal arrangements are in force. The Ordinance also extends to England and Northern Ireland;[10] the Territories are designated as a reciprocating country by the United Kingdom as a whole. Extensions to Barbados[11] and Malta[12] seem not to be reciprocated. Ghana lists the Territories as a reciprocating country, but no corresponding order seems to have been made in the Territories. The Ordinance also extends to the States of New York[13] and of California.[14]

1 M-4, RL, 1974. Note the Amendment Ordinance, 2nd Session 1980 c 15.
2 By various regulations as follows: Alberta, Revised Regulations 1980, reg 131; British Columbia, reg 137; Manitoba, reg 129; New Brunswick, reg 140; Newfoundland, reg 135; Nova Scotia, reg 136; Ontario, reg 138; Prince Edward Island, reg 134; Saskatchewan, reg 133; Yukon Territory, reg 130.
3 Reg 142.
4 Reg 145.
5 Reg 141.
6 Reg 139.
7 Reg 149.
8 Reg 147.
9 Reg 144.
10 Reg 132.
11 Reg 148.
12 Reg 143; see para 8.61 below.
13 Reg 146.
14 Reg 150.

(g) *Nova Scotia*

8.33 The Maintenance Orders Enforcement Act[1] extends to all the other Canadian jurisdictions except Quebec (which does, however, treat Nova Scotia as a reciprocating country),[2] and to the Cook Islands,[3] Guernsey,[4] the Isle of Man,[5] New Zealand,[3] Papua New Guinea,[6] Singapore,[7] the United Kingdom[8] and Zimbabwe,[9] in all of which countries reciprocal arrangement exist. The Nova Scotia Act has also been extended to all states and mainland territories of Australia except Queensland;[10] Nova Scotia is a country with 'restricted reciprocity' for the purposes of the Family Law Act 1975 of Australia.[11] Ghana, Gibraltar and Jersey treat Nova Scotia as a reciprocating country, but no corresponding orders have been made under the Nova Scotia Act.

1 M-1, RL.
2 Ontario by Order-in-Council of 8 February 1950; Alberta, British Columbia, Manitoba and Saskatchewan by Order-in-Council of 26 June 1951; Newfoundland and Prince Edward Is by Order-in-Council of 6 November 1951; New Brunswick by Order-in-Council of 5 June 1953; and Yukon Territory by Order-in-Council of 24 October 1953.
3 Order-in-Council, 19 October 1951.
4 Order-in-Council, 18 December 1956.
5 Order-in-Council, 10 October 1952.
6 Order-in-Council, 20 September 1960.
7 Order-in-Council, 3 July 1973.
8 Order-in-Council, 6 November 1973.
9 Order-in-Council, 29 October 1957.
10 By individual Orders-in-Council as follows: New South Wales, 9 February 1953; Victoria, 5 June 1953; Tasmania, 28 June 1957; Australian Capital Territory, 27 October 1958; Northern Territory, 10 February 1959; W. Australia, 22 March 1972; S Australia, 21 December 1973.
11 See para 8.14 above.

(h) Ontario

8.34 The Reciprocal Enforcement of Maintenance Orders Act 1982[1] replaced the earlier Act[2] and contained no provision that the designation of reciprocating states under the earlier Act should be carried forward.

The former legislation applied[3] to all other Canadian jurisdictions, and to the Cook Islands, Fiji, Ghana, Gibraltar, Guernsey, Jersey, the Isle of Man, New Zealand, Papua New Guinea,[4] the United Kingdom and Zimbabwe;[5] in all these cases reciprocal arrangements exist. The former Ontario Act also applied to 'the Commonwealth of Australia' and all the states and mainland territories of Australia;[6] Ontario is a reciprocating country for the purposes of the Family Law Act 1975 of Australia.[7] It also applied to South Africa[6] (where reciprocal arrangements exist), and to numerous of the United States: Arkansas, Arizona, California, Colorado, Delaware, Georgia, Louisiana, Maryland, Massachusetts, Michigan, Minnesota, Montana, Nebraska, Nevada, New Mexico, New York, North Carolina, North Dakota, Ohio, Oregon, Pennsylvania, South Dakota, Texas, Virginia, Washington, and Wisconsin. The Ontario Act did apply to Malta, but it is uncertain whether reciprocal arrangements were in force in Malta.[8]

1 See (1983) 9 CLB 42.
2 Cap 403, RL 1970.
3 Reg 893, RRO 1980 unless otherwise stated.
4 Reg 212/81 correcting a former reference to Papua *and* New Guinea.
5 Reg 212/81 amending a former reference to Southern Rhodesia.
6 Reg 212/81.
7 See para 8.14 above.
8 See para 8.61 below.

(i) Prince Edward Island

8.35 The Reciprocal Enforcement of Maintenance Orders Act[1] extends to all other Canadian jurisdictions[2] and to England,[3] the Bailiwick of Guernsey,[4] Jersey,[5] the Isle of Man,[3] New Zealand,[6] Northern Ireland,[3] Papua New

Guinea[7] and Zimbabwe;[8] in all these cases reciprocal arrangements are in force. The Act has been extended to all the states and mainland territories of Australia,[9] and Prince Edward Island is a reciprocating country for the purposes of the Family Law Act 1975 of Australia.[10] An extension to Malta may no longer be reciprocated;[11] Ghana treats Prince Edward Island as a reciprocating country but no extension order referring to Ghana has been traced.[12]

1 R-8, RL, 1974.
2 By orders of various dates as follows: Alberta, British Columbia, Manitoba, Nova Scotia and Saskatchewan, 12 November 1951; New Brunswick, 8 March 1952; Newfoundland and Ontario, 31 October 1951; Northwest Territories, 2 April 1953; Quebec, 4 June 1953; Yukon Territory, Order 146/53.
3 Order dated 21 November 1951.
4 Order 527/57.
5 Order 295/53.
6 Order 167/55.
7 Order 465/54.
8 Order 470/56.
9 By various orders as follows: Australian Capital Territory and Northern Territory, 582/55; New South Wales, 435/54; Queensland and Tasmania, 379/54; South Australia, 257/54; Victoria, 106/53; Western Australia 466/54.
10 See para 8.14 above.
11 Order 628/56; see para 8.61 below.
12 The information as to the extension of the Act may not be completely up-to-date; no orders made since 1973 have been seen.

(j) Quebec

8.36 The *loi sur l'execution reciproque d'ordonnances alimentaires*,[1] with the alternative title, in former compilations of Quebec statutes, of the Reciprocal Enforcement of Maintenance Orders Act, can be extended only to other Canadian jurisdictions. It has been extended to all the provinces, but not to the territories;[2] the possibility of amending the Act to enable it to be extended to jurisdictions outside Canada was under consideration by the Quebec Government in 1982.

In respect of one European country, France, specific action was taken in the Act to Secure the Carrying Out of the Entente between France and Quebec Respecting Mutual Aid in Judicial Matters,[3] whch provides for mutual aid by the two governments 'in locating and hearing alimentary debtors staying in their territory and in obtaining the voluntary recovery of alimentary pensions'[4] and in enforcing decisions as to support obligations.[5]

1 E-19, RL.
2 Reg 1-667.
3 A-20.1, RL.
4 Title VI, 3.
5 See para 6.28 above.

(k) Saskatchewan

8.37 The Reciprocal Enforcement of Maintenance Orders Act[1] extends to all the other Canadian jurisdictions except Quebec[2] and to Fiji,[3] Guernsey,[4] Jersey,[5] the Isle of Man,[6] New Zealand,[7] Papua New Guinea,[8] the United Kingdom,[9] and Zimbabwe;[10] in all these cases reciprocal arrangements exist. The Act has also been extended to all the states and mainland territories of Australia;[11] Saskatchewan is a reciprocating country for the purposes of the Family Law Act 1975 of Australia. An extension order to Barbados[12] is not now reciprocated.

The Saskatchewan Act has also been extended to a number of the United

States, namely California,[13] Delaware,[14] Maryland,[15] Massachusetts,[16] Minnesota,[17] New York,[18] North Carolina,[19] and North Dakota.[20]

1   R-4, RL 1978, amended by an Amendment Act 1980–1 c 11.
2   By orders as follows: Alberta 14 February 1948, British Columbia 26 May 1947, Manitoba 26 May 1947, New Brunswick 13 June 1952, Newfoundland 18 July 1952, Northwest Territories 14 January 1955, Nova Scotia 3 August 1951, Ontario 4 June 1949, Prince Edward Island 1 December 1951 and Yukon Territory 25 September 1953.
3   Reg 282/78.
4   4 January 1957.
5   17 December 1954.
6   2 June 1950.
7   8 May 1948.
8   17 August 1962.
9   Reg 15/79.
10   Reg 58/81 amending a former extension to S Rhodesia.
11   Australian Capital Territory 20 June 1958, New South Wales 24 October 1953, Northern Territory 3 April 1958, Queensland 24 January 1953, South Australia Reg 285/69, Tasmania 16 October 1954, Victoria 9 October 1953 and Western Australia 5 November 1954.
12   Reg 7/71.
13   Reg 213/78.
14   Reg 159/80.
15   Reg 256/80.
16   Reg 196/80.
17   Reg 220/79.
18   Reg 197/80.
19   Reg 158/80.
20   Reg 214/78.

(l) Yukon Territory

8.38   The Reciprocal Enforcement of Maintenance Orders Ordinance[1] extends to all other Canadian jurisdictions except Quebec,[2] and to the Cook Islands,[3] England,[4] Jersey,[5] the Isle of Man,[6] Northern Ireland,[4] New Zealand,[3] Singapore[7] and Zimbabwe;[8] in all these cases reciprocal arrangements are in force. The Ordinance has also been extended to the State of New York.[9] Fiji treats the Yukon Territory as a reciprocating country, but no corresponding order in the Territory has been traced.[10]

1   1980 (1st session), cap 25.
2   By various Commissioner's Orders as follows: Alberta, British Columbia and Ontario, 1 September 1953; Manitoba, 9 August 1951; New Brunswick, 5 November 1953; Newfoundland, 15 October 1953; Northwest Territories, 5 March 1952; Prince Edward Island, 12 August 1953; and Saskatchewan, 1 October 1953.
3   CO 21 August 1951.
4   CO 29 January 1951.
5   CO 1964/91, semble duplicating a previous CO of 1 June 1954.
6   CO 18 December 1951.
7   CO 1973/297.
8   CO 1956/125.
9   CO 1969/74.
10   The information as to the extension of the Ordinance may not be completely up-to-date; no orders made since 1973 have been seen.

Cayman Islands

8.39   The Maintenance Orders (Enforcement) Law[1] is on the 1920 model. It is unusual in that it extends not only to 'England and Ireland'[2] but also to Jamaica,[3] to which the Islands were constitutionally linked until 1962. The Law can be extended to 'any British possession, Commonwealth country, or any territory under Her Majesty's protection'[4] and has been extended to Belize.[5]

1 RL, originally Law 3 of 1935.
2 S 3. For a discussion of the effect of this expression, see para 8.04 above.
3 S 11. It seems likely that the Law also extends to the Turks and Caicos Islands, which were also linked to Jamaica until they became a separate colony in 1959. Unlike the Cayman Islands, the Turks and Caicos Islands were actually part of Jamaica. No reciprocal arrangements are in force in the Turks and Caicos Islands.
4 S 12.
5 Gaz, 7 October 1977. No reciprocating order had been made in Belize by 1 January 1978.

Cook Islands

8.40   The Cook Islands are constitutionally linked to New Zealand, and the Cook Islands Act 1915 (of New Zealand) contains provisions[1] which enable New Zealand orders to be enforced in the Islands. Of much wider importance are the Cook Islands Maintenance Enforcement Regulations 1948[2] which provide for the enforcement in the Islands of maintenance orders made by a court in 'H.M.'s dominions (including New Zealand) or in any British protectorate, mandated territory or place where H.M. exercises judicial powers'.[3] No designation of reciprocating territories is required; in this respect the New Zealand model[4] is followed, and the Regulations may indeed reflect an earlier version of that model.

A Family Law Bill is in draft which will replace the Regulations but (as at May 1981) it had not been finalised for presentation to the Legislative Assembly.

1 S 173.
2 1948/134 (New Zealand).
3 Reg 3.
4 See paras 6.01–6.08 above.

Cyprus[1]

8.41   The Maintenance Orders (Facilities for Enforcement) Law[2] is on the 1920 model. It applies to 'England and Ireland'[3] and can be extended to any 'British possession or any territory under Her Majesty's protection'.[4] The Law has been extended to Grenada[5] and Jersey,[6] both of which have reciprocating arrangements. An extension to South Africa[7] must now be regarded as of doubtful validity in view of South Africa's withdrawal from the Commonwealth. No extension order in respect of Guernsey or the Isle of Man can be traced, although their legislation does extend to Cyprus.

Three extension orders have been made in respect of Australian jurisdictions, New South Wales,[8] South Australia[9] and 'the Commonwealth of Australia'.[10] It is clear from its date that the last-named was intended to apply to the 'seat of government', ie the Australian Capital Territory. Australia has, however, designated Cyprus as a 'country with restricted reciprocity' under the Family Law Act 1975, which applies throughout the Commonwealth of Australia; it would appear that the Cypriot extension order referring to 'the Commonwealth of Australia' has been given its literal rather than its intended meaning.

Cyprus is a party to the United Nations Convention on the Recovery Abroad of Maintenance 1956. The Convention was ratified by the Convention on the Recovery Abroad of Maintenance (Ratification) Law 1978.[11] Procedural implementing legislation did not appear until 1981 when the Maintenance Orders (Facilities for Recovery) Law 1981[12] was passed. This Law is mainly based on

the relevant provisions in Part II of the Maintenance Orders (Reciprocal
Enforcement) Act 1972 of the United Kingdom.

1   For Akrotiri and Dhekelia, see para 8.09 above.
2   Cap 16 RL 1959.
3   S 3. For a discussion of the effect of this expression, see para 8.04 above.
4   S 11. This section does not appear to have been amended, despite the constitutional develop-
     ments since its enactment. For a discussion of its effect, see para 8.02 above.
5   Gaz 1925, p 181.
6   Gaz 1954, vol 2, p 577.
7   Gaz 1953, vol 2, p 709.
8   Gaz 1924, p 365.
9   Gaz 1954, vol 2, p 432.
10   Gaz 1928, p 870.
11   Law 50 of 1978. An official English translation is published by the Cyprus Ministry of Justice.
12   Law 43 of 1981. Only the Greek text is published.

Dominica

8.42   Dominica was a presidency of the Leeward Islands until 1940; its legislation was originally enacted by the legislature of the Leeward Islands and
extension orders made before 1940 and extending legislation to the Leeward
Islands are assumed to continue to apply to Dominica.[1]

The Maintenance Orders (Facilities for Enforcement) Ordinance[2] is on the
1920 model. It applies to England and Northern Ireland,[3] and can be extended
to any 'British possession or territory under Her Majesty's protection'.[4] It has
been extended to Antigua and Barbuda,[5] the Bahamas,[6] Belize,[7] Bermuda,[6]
Grenada,[6] the Bailiwick of Guernsey,[8] Guyana,[9] Jamaica,[10] Jersey,[11] the Isle of
Man,[12] Montserrat,[5] St Christopher and Nevis,[13] St Lucia,[6] St Vincent and
the Grenadines,[6] Trinidad and Tobago,[6] and the Virgin Islands.[5] The Ordinance appears also to extend to Anguilla,[13] Barbados,[6] and to the Turks and
Caicos Islands,[14] but no reciprocal arrangements are currently in force in those
territories. An early extension order in respect of Mauritius is recorded,[15] but
does not appear in consolidated lists in the other former presidencies of the
Leeward Islands; there is no reciprocal extension in Mauritius. The Dominica
Ordinance has been extended to the Australian Capital Territory[16] and New
South Wales,[17] but Dominica is not a reciprocating territory for the purposes
of the Family Law Act 1975 of Australia.[18]

1   This can create difficulties in practice. Many revised editions of legislation produce a conso-
     lidated list of countries to which an Act has been extended, but omit the date of the original
     order; further research is needed to discover whether the extension to the Leeward Islands
     was in fact before 1940.
2   Cap 12, RL 1962.
3   S 3.
4   S 12. For a discussion of the effect of this expression, see para 8.02 above.
5   SRO 54/1945.
6   Gaz, 30 August 1923. The position as regards reciprocal arrangements in Bermuda is obscure;
     see para 8.21 above.
7   Gaz, 28 August 1924.
8   SRO 20/1965.
9   Gaz, 9 August 1922.
10   Gaz, 14 May 1925.
11   SRO 1/1955.
12   SRO 24/1961.
13   SRO 54/1945 as part of St Christopher–Nevis–Anguilla.
14   Gaz, 14 May 1925, as part of Jamaica.
15   Gaz, 4 August 1921.

16   SRO 6/1929; the reference is to 'Australia' but it is clear that only the 'seat of government',
     ie the Capital Territory, was meant.
17   Gaz, 3 July 1924.
18   See para 8.14 above.

Falkland Islands

8.43   The Maintenance Orders (Reciprocal Enforcement) Ordinance 1979[1]
is on the 1972 model. It has been extended[2] to the Bailiwick of Guernsey,
Jersey, the Isle of Man, and New Zealand; in all these cases reciprocal arrangements are in force. The Ordinance also extends to all the states and mainland
territories of Australia, and to the United Kingdom, but reciprocal arrangements are not in force there; the Falkland Islands is designated under the
Maintenance Orders (Facilities for Enforcement) Act 1920 of the United
Kingdom, which is in force in England and Northern Ireland but not in
Scotland. The designation of the Falkland Islands as a reciprocating territory
by Grenada is not reciprocated.

1   No 1 of 1979. For a minor correction see an Amending Ordinance, No 16 of 1979.
2   See Order 6 of 1979 (22 August 1979).

Falkland Islands Dependencies

8.44   The Maintenance Orders (Reciprocal Enforcement) Ordinance[1] of the
Falkland Islands has been applied to the Dependencies.[2] However, as the
subordinate legislation of the Falkland Islands has not been expressly applied
to the Dependencies, and as no local subordinate legislation exists, the legislation may be wholly inoperative.

1   No 1 of 1979 as amended by No 16 of 1979.
2   Application of Colony Laws Ordinance 1980, No DS1 of 1980 (which by a strange error
     applied only the Amending Ordinance, deleting five words from the principal Ordinance) and
     the Application of Colony Laws Ordinance 1981, No DS1 of 1981 (correcting the error and
     applying the Principal Ordinance).

Fiji

8.45   Fiji, like the United Kingdom, has two relevant statutes. The Maintenance Orders (Facilities for Enforcement) Ordinance[1] on the 1920 model is
prospectively repealed by the 1972-model Maintenance Orders (Reciprocal
Enforcement) Act 1974,[2] but remains in force at present.

The Ordinance delared that it applied to England and Ireland,[3] the latter
specifically (but mistakenly) defined in 1966 to include both Northern Ireland
and the Republic of Ireland.[4] It is capable of further extension to 'any country
or territory of the Commonwealth or any territory under Her Majesty's protection'.[5] Only three extensions remain in force. In one case, that of the
Solomon Islands,[6] reciprocal arrangements exist. The designation of the Republic of South Africa would appear to have lapsed on its departure from the
Commonwealth[7] and that of Tanzania[8] is not reciprocated by Tanzania.

Under the 1974 Act, orders have been made extending it in respect of
Australia,[9] certain Canadian provinces (Alberta,[10] British Columbia,[11] Manitoba,[12] New Brunswick,[11] Ontario,[12] Saskatchewan,[12] and the Yukon Territory[12]), India,[13] Kiribati,[14] Nauru,[14] New Zealand,[15] Tuvalu[16] and Western
Samoa;[17] in all these cases reciprocal arrangements are in force. The Act has
also been extended to 'the United Kingdom including (sic) the Isle of Man

and the Channel Islands';[18] no order has been found making reciprocal provision in Guernsey, but the other jurisdictions have done so.

1   Cap 45, RL 1967.
2   No 16 of 1974.
3   S 3.
4   S 2, as amended by Ord 37 of 1966.
5   S 11, as similarly amended.
6   See RL 1957, referring to a collection of pre-1962 proclamations.
7   RL cites a pre-1962 proclamation, presumably made by reference to the 'Union of' South Africa but cited in RL in terms of the Republic.
8   LN 59/1972.
9   LN 31/1977.
10 LN 50/1976 (reciprocating order by Alberta not seen).
11 LN 182/1979.
12 LN 36/1977 (reciprocating orders by Sashatchewan and Yukon not seen).
13 LN 112/1978.
14 LN 58/80. No reciprocating order by Nauru has been traced, but it is known that the Nauru Cabinet had approved its principle in 1979.
15 LN 153/1977.
16 LN 57/1977.
17 LN 145/1979.
18 LN 134/1977.

The Gambia

8.46   The Maintenance Orders (Facilities for Enforcement) Act[1] is on the 1920 model. Its current text extends the Act to the United Kingdom and the Republic of Ireland.[2] So far as the reference to the United Kingdom is concerned, there is in fact only partial reciprocity; from the point of view of United Kingdom law, the legislation which has been extended to The Gambia[3] is in force only in England and Northern Ireland. The Republic of Ireland has no relevant legislation extending in practice to The Gambia, and the reference to the republic in The Gambia's Act is unrealistic.

The Act can be extended to 'any part of the Commonwealth' and has been extended to the Bailiwick of Guernsey,[4] Jersey,[5] the Isle of Man,[6] Nigeria,[7] and Sierra Leone;[8] in all these cases reciprocal arrangements exist. Extension orders have also been made in respect of the Australian Capital Territory,[9] New South Wales,[10] the Northern Territory of Australia,[11] Queensland,[11] South Australia,[11] and Western Australia,[11] but The Gambia is not a reciprocating territory for the purposes of the Family Law Act 1975 of Australia.[12]

1   Cap 114, RL.
2   S 3.
3   Ie the Maintenance Orders (Facilities for Enforcement) Act 1920 (UK).
4   LN 48/1956.
5   Proc 18 November 1954.
6   LN 21/1961.
7   Proc 8 November 1924.
8   Proc 11 September 1924.
9   Proc 3 January 1929. The reference is to 'the Commonwealth of Australia' (see RL, vol V, p 114) but it is clear that only the 'seat of government', ie the ACT, was intended.
10 Proc 10 February 1925.
11 LN 37/1973.
12 See para 8.14 above.

Ghana

8.47   The relevant legislation in Ghana is contained in sub-part II of the

Courts Act 1971.¹ Sections 84 to 92 inclusive are closely based upon the 1920 model, though the drafting is not identical. The provisions do not apply, without more, to any territory, but can be extended by subsidiary legislation to 'any country', whether or not in the Commonwealth.

The extent of the Ghanaian provisions is very doubtful. According to the Maintenance Orders (Reciprocal Enforcement) Instrument 1974,² they extend to Switzerland, the United Kingdom, three Australian states (Queensland, Tasmania, and Western Australia) and seven Canadian jurisdictions (Alberta, British Columbia, Newfoundland, the Northwest Territories, Nova Scotia, Ontario, and Prince Edward Island). Reciprocal arrangements do exist in the United Kingdom and in Ontario, but none of the other Canadian jurisdictions has entended its legislation to Ghana. Ghana is not a reciprocating territory for the purposes of the Family Law Act 1975 of the Commonwealth of Australia, and did not appear in the extension orders made in Queensland, Tasmania, and Western Australia under their separate Acts, now superseded.

On the other hand, Guernsey, Jersey, Nigeria, Sierra Leone, and Zambia all regard their legislation as extending to Ghana, despite the apparent lack of reciprocal arrangements by Ghana.

1 Cap 372, RL.
2 LI 979 (1974).

Gibraltar

8.48 The Maintenance Orders (Reciprocal Enforcement) Ordinance 1973¹ is on the 1972 model. It has been extended to Australia,² three provinces of Canada³ (British Columbia, Nova Scotia, and Ontario), Malta⁴ and the United Kingdom.⁵ In all these cases reciprocal arrangements are in force. Certain countries, Guernsey, Jersey, the Isle of Man, and Sierra Leone, regard Gibraltar as a reciprocating country under their own legislation, but no reciprocal extension has been made by Gibraltar; so far as the Channel Islands and the Isle of Man are concerned, this may be because they were thought (incorrectly) to be technically part of the United Kingdom.

1 No 23 of 1973.
2 LN 27/1978, in respect of certain classes of order.
3 LN 45/1975.
4 LN 48/1976.
5 LN 86/1973.

Grenada

8.49 The Maintenance Ordinance¹ contains provisions which follow the 1920 model. It extends to England and Northern Ireland² and can be further extended to 'any British possession or territory under Her Majesty's protection'.³

It has been extended⁴ to Antigua and Barbuda, the Bahamas, Belize, Cyprus,⁵ Dominica, Guernsey, Guyana, Jamaica, Jersey, Mauritius, Montserrat, Nigeria, St Christopher and Nevis,⁶ St Lucia, St Vincent and the Grenadines, Sri Lanka, Trinidad and Tobago, and the Virgin Islands; in all these cases reciprocal arrangements exist. The Grenada Ordinance has also been extended to Anguilla,⁶ Barbados, Bermuda, the Falkland Islands, and the Turks and Caicos Islands,⁷ where no reciprocal arrangements are currently in force. The published list in the Revised Laws also records an extension to 'Australia', probably meaning the Australian Capital Territory only; but Grenada is not a reciprocating territory for the purposes of the Family Law Act 1975 which now applies throughout the Commonwealth of Australia.[8]

1   Cap 180, RL 1958.
2   S 21.
3   S 29.
4   See footnote to s 29, RL, citing Proclamations of 1941, SRO 76/1941, and of 1956, SRO 38/1956.
5   For Akrotiri and Dhekelia, see para 8.09 above.
6   As part of St Christopher–Nevis–Anguilla.
7   As part of Jamaica.
8   See para 8.14 above.

Guernsey

8.50   The Bailiwick of Guernsey includes not only the island of Guernsey itself but also Alderney and Sark, each of which has a measure of autonomy. Many jurisdictions in extending their legislation to Guernsey in the late 1950s used the phrase 'the Island of Guernsey' and had to correct this to 'the Bailiwick of Guernsey' in subsequent amending legislation.

The Maintenance Orders (Facilities for Enforcement) (Guernsey) Law 1955 is on the 1920 model.[1] It can be extended to 'any part of Her Majesty's dominions outside Guernsey' including British protectorates.[2] Many of the territories designated as reciprocating countries do not now regard Her Majesty as Head of State but remain in the list.

The Law has been extended to a large number of jurisdictions. The Law currently extends[3] to Australia,[4] the Bahamas, Belize, Bermuda, Botswana, a number of Canadian jurisdictions,[5] Cook Islands, Dominica, England and Wales, the Falkland Islands, the Gambia, Grenada, Guyana, Jamaica, Kenya, Kiribati, Lesotho, Malawi, the Isle of Man, Mauritius, New Zealand, Northern Ireland, St Vincent and the Grenadines, Seychelles,[6] Singapore, Solomon Islands, Sri Lanka, Swaziland, Trinidad and Tobago, Tuvalu, Uganda, Zambia, and Zimbabwe; in all these cases reciprocal arrangements exist. The Law has also been extended to 'the Federation of Malaya'[7] and 'North Borneo';[8] despite the failure to cover Sarawak, the Malaysian Act has been extended to Guernsey. The Guernsey Law has also been extended[3] to Barbados, Cayman Islands, the Falkland Islands Dependencies, Ghana, Gibraltar, and Malta but no reciprocal arrangements exist in those jurisdictions. An extension to Aden would appear to be spent, and the position of that to South Africa is of uncertain status.[9]

1   Ordres en Conseil, vol XVI, p 161.
2   Art 10.
3   Unless otherwise stated by the (consolidating) Ordinance No 31 of 1959.
4   All states except Tasmania and the Northern Territory are covered by Ord 31/1959; Norfolk Island was added by Ord 16/1962 and Tasmania by Ord 33/1974. The territories of Christmas Island and the Cocos (Keeling) Islands are also named in Ord 31/1959; reciprocal arrangements are in force only in the latter.
5   British Columbia, Manitoba, Newfoundland, Northwest Territories, Nova Scotia, Ontario, Prince Edward Island, and Saskatchewan.
6   Ord 14/1961.
7   Ord 31/1959.
8   Ord 23/1960.
9   Both are listed in Ord 31/1959.

Guyana

8.51 The Maintenance Orders (Facilities for Enforcement) Act[1] is on the 1920 model. It applies to 'England or Ireland'[2] but can be extended to 'any Commonwealth territory'.[3]

It has been extended to Antigua and Barbuda,[4] the Bahamas,[5] Belize,[6] Dominica,[7] Grenada,[8] the Bailiwick of Guernsey,[9] Jamaica,[10] Jersey,[11] the Isle of Man,[12] Montserrat,[4] Nigeria,[13] St Christopher and Nevis,[4] St Lucia,[14] St Vincent and the Grenadines,[15] and Trinidad and Tobago.[16] In all these cases reciprocal arrangements exist. The Act appears also to extend to Anguilla,[4] Barbados,[17] Bermuda,[15] and the Turks and Caicos Islands;[18] no reciprocal arrangements are currently in force in those territories. The Guyana Act has also been extended to the Australian Capital Territory,[19] New South Wales[20] and the Northern Territory of Australia[14] but Guyana is not a designated reciprocating territory under the Family Law Act 1975 of Australia.[21]

1 Cap 45: 05, RL.
2 S 3; for a discussion of the effect of this phrase, see para 8.04 above.
3 S 12.
4 Order-in-Council, 19 September 1922, as part of the Leeward Islands, which are defined to *exclude* the Virgin Islands.
5 Order-in-Council, 23 September 1924.
6 Order-in-Council, 22 May 1928.
7 Order-in-Council, 19 July 1922, as part of the Leeward Islands, of which Dominica was a part until 1940.
8 Order-in-Council, 15 May 1923.
9 Order-in-Council, 16 October 1957.
10 Order-in-Council, 7 March 1925.
11 Order-in-Council, 18 March 1954.
12 Order-in-Council, 7 November 1961.
13 Order-in-Council, 18 May 1926.
14 Order-in-Council, 19 July 1922.
15 Order-in-Council, 22 August 1922.
16 Order-in-Council, 20 July 1922.
17 Order-in-Council, 3 April 1923.
18 Order-in-Council, 7 March 1925, as part of Jamaica.
19 Order-in-Council, 28 January 1929.
20 Order-in-Council, 3 February 1925.
21 See para 8.14 above.

Hong Kong

8.52 The Maintenance Orders (Reciprocal Enforcement) Ordinance,[1] which came into force on 31 January 1979, is on the 1972 model, corresponding to Part I of the Maintenance Orders (Reciprocal Enforcement) Act 1972 of the United Kingdom. Some small amendments were made in 1980:[2] in ss 6 (variation and revocation of maintenance order made in Hong Kong), 9 (enforcement of maintenance order made in Hong Kong) and 10 (variation and revocation of maintenance order registered in Hong Kong) references to sums being or ceasing to be payable from the date 'on which the order was made' are amended to refer to the date on which they are required to be paid under the terms of the order or (depending on the context) the effective date of the variation or revocation.

The Ordinance applies,[3] as regards maintenance orders generally, to Bermuda and the United Kingdom; and, as regards maintenance orders other than affiliation orders, to the Commonwealth of Australia 'and its territories',[4] 'the State of' British Columbia, Brunei, Malaysia, New Zealand, Singapore,[5] the Solomon Islands and Sri Lanka; in all these cases reciprocal arrangements exist. The Ordinance also applies to the Republic of South Africa (except as to affiliation orders) and reciprocal arrangements exist there. Jersey and the Isle of Man were designated under the legislation superseded by the Ordinance[6] but are not now included, perhaps in error, it being commonly but erroneously supposed that the Islands are within the United Kingdom.

1   Cap 188, RL 1977. (Originally cap 13 of 1977).
2   By Ord 31 of 1980. Ord 61 of 1981 made amendments, more numerous but less important, adjusting the designation of courts in Hong Kong.
3   LN 101/79.
4   Hong Kong is a country with 'restricted reciprocity' for the purposes of the Family Law Act 1975 of Australia, which is in force in all states, the mainland territories and Norfolk Island, but not in the other island territories; Hong Kong is, however, also designated as a reciprocating country in each of the island territories (Cocos (Keeling) Islands and Christmas Island).
5   See *Leong Fatt Chee v Lee Miew Long* [1963] HKLR 760.
6   Ie Maintenance Orders (Facilities for Enforcement) Ordinance, cap 15, RL 1969.

India

8.53   The Maintenance Orders Enforcement Act 1921[1] is generally on the 1920 model but contains a number of variations, mostly dating from its original enactment, but some reflecting later constitutional changes. It is in force throughout India except for the States of Jammu and Kashmir.[2]

The definition of 'maintenance order' contains the phrase 'made by a Court in the exercise of civil or criminal jurisdiction', to remove a doubt expressed when the Bill was first considered.[3] So far as provisional orders are concerned, there is no provision in the Indian Act for an appeal against a refusal to make the order; this presumably reflected features of the courts system in 1921, which may also explain a more general feature of the Act. This is the avoidance of any reference to collaboration directly between the two courts involved in a 'shuttlecock' exercise; all communication is via the Central Government even in those cases where the standard model allows for the direct remission of a case to an overseas court.[4] In respect of the confirmation of provisional orders received from overseas, there are two special features. The Indian court's power to confirm an order is expressed to be 'notwithstanding any pecuniary limit imposed on its power [ie to make a maintenance order] by any law for the time being in force in India'.[5] The same power is the subject of a proviso: 'Provided that no sum shall be awarded as maintenance under this section, or shall be recoverable as such, at a rate exceeding that proposed in the provisional order'.[6]

A novel feature of the Indian Act is a provision[7] that the court in India registering or confirming an order for maintenance may require the payer to pay any charges incurred in transmitting the periodical payments and that those transmission charges shall be recoverable in the same manner as costs.

So far as the extent of its application is concerned, the Indian Act has never applied automatically to any overseas jurisdiction, not even to England, as would the standard model. It can be applied to 'any country or territory outside India'.[8] It has been extended to Botswana,[9] the Cocos (Keeling) Islands,[10] Fiji,[11] Kenya,[12] Lesotho,[9] Malawi,[13] Malaysia,[14] the Isle of Man,[15] Mauritius,[16] Seychelles,[17] Singapore,[18] Sri Lanka,[19] Swaziland,[9] Uganda,[20] Zambia[21] and Zimbabwe;[22] in all these cases reciprocal arrangements are in force. The Act was extended to 'England and Ireland';[23] reciprocal arrangements apply throughout the United Kingdom, perhaps as a result of the heading of the relevant Indian Notification which uses the expression 'United Kingdom' though the text does not.[24] A rather similar position exists in respect of Australia: India is a reciprocating country under the Family Law Act 1975 of Australia[25] but extension orders seem to have been made in India in respect only of the Australian Capital Territory,[26] the Northern Territory[27] and Western Australia.[28] The Indian Act has also been extended to South Africa,[29] where no reciprocal provision seems to have been made; and to Burma,[30] no information being available as to reciprocal provision there. An extension to the former Somaliland Protectorate[31] would appear to be inoperative, though unrepealed.

1   Act 18 of 1921.
2   Ss 1(2) and 2 (as amended).
3   S 2.
4   See eg, s 7(5).
5   S 7(4).
6   Ibid, proviso.
7   S 9.
8   S 3 as amended by the Maintenance Orders Enforcement (Amendment) Act 1952 (No 47 of 1952).
9   SRO 2725, 26 August 1957.
10   GSR 29, 13 February 1958.
11   GSR 1225, 9 July 1971.
12   SRO 818, Gaz 1954, part 2, p 492.
13   SRO 3523, 16 November 1955.
14   GSR 351, 18 February 1972.
15   GSR 1005, 4 July 1964.
16   SRO 3389, Gaz 1954, part 2, p 2165.
17   SRO 2, 21 December 1954.
18   GSR 1224 of 1971.
19   GSR 1008, 28 October 1958.
20   SRO 2411, Gaz 1954, part 2, p 1805.
21   SRO 6, 23 December 1954.
22   SRO 1073, 8 May 1956.
23   For this phrase, see para 8.04 above.
24   See No F 120 dated 6 March 1922, Gaz 1922, Part 1, p 228, as cited in letter to the Legal Division of the Commonwealth Secretariat.
25   See para 8.14 above.
26   GSR 27, 13 February 1958.
27   GSR 28, same date.
28   GSR 1193, 10 December 1958.
29   Notification No 24/9/37, 28 July 1938; Gaz 1939, Part 1, p 1306.
30   SRO 673, 16 March 1956.
31   SRO 3425, 20 November 1954.

Jamaica

8.54   The Maintenance Orders (Facilities for Enforcement) Act[1] is on the 1920 model. It applies to England and Northern Ireland[2] and can be extended to 'any Commonwealth country'.[3] An ususual provision enables an extension order to be given retrospective effect to a day not earlier than 11 June 1923 (the date on which the Act was originally enacted);[4] no advantage seems to have been taken of this power.

The Act has been extended to Antigua and Barbuda,[5] the Bahamas,[6] Belize,[7] the Cayman Islands,[8] Dominica,[9] Grenada,[10] the Bailiwick of Guernsey,[11] Guyana,[10] Jersey,[12] Montserrat,[5] St Christopher and Nevis,[5] St Lucia,[13] St Vincent and the Grenadines,[14] Trinidad and Tobago,[15] and the Virgin Islands.[5] In all these cases reciprocal arrangements are in force. It appears also to extend to Anguilla,[5] Barbados[15] and Bermuda;[15] no reciprocal arrangements are currently in force in those territories. The Jamaica Act has also been extended to the Australian Capital Territory[16] and New South Wales[17] but Jamaica has not been designated as a reciprocating territory for the purposes of the Family Law Act 1975 of Australia.[18] The designation of Jamaica by the Isle of Man is not reciprocated.

1   Cap 233, RL 1973.
2   S 3.
3   S 12.
4   S 12(2).
5   Gaz Notice 198/1925, as part of the Leeward Islands.
6   Gaz Notice 100/1926.
7   Gaz Notice 418/1928.
8   Gaz Notice 52/1953.
9   Gaz Notice 198/1925, as part of the Leeward Islands of which Dominica was a part until 1940.
10   Gaz Notice 347/1925.
11   LN 31/1956.
12   Gaz Notice 55/1955.
13   Gaz Notice 96/1926.
14   Gaz Notice 887/1925.
15   Gaz Notice 198/1925.
16   Gaz Notice 52/1929. The reference is to the 'Commonwealth of Australia', but it is clear that only 'the seat of government', ie the ACT, is intended.
17   Gaz Notice 667/1925.
18   See para 8.14 above.

Jersey

8.55   The Maintenance Orders (Facilities for Enforcement) (Jersey) Law 1953[1] is on the 1920 model. It extends to any designated 'reciprocating country'[2] which must be a part of Her Majesty's dominions[3] including British protectorates.[4] Many of the territories designated as reciprocating countries do not now regard Her Majesty as Head of State, but remain in the list.

The Law has been extended[5] to Antigua and Barbuda,[6] Australia, Belize, Bermuda, Botswana, various parts of Canada (Alberta, Manitoba, Newfoundland, Northwest Territories, Ontario, Prince Edward Island, Saskatchewan, Yukon Territory), Cocos (Keeling) Islands, Cook Islands, Cyprus,[7] Dominica, England and Wales, Falkland Islands, Fiji, The Gambia, Grenada, the Bailiwick of Guernsey, Guyana, Jamaica, Kenya, Kiribati,[8] Lesotho, Malawi, Malaysia, the Isle of Man, Mauritius, Montserrat,[6] New Zealand, Nigeria, Northern Ireland, Pakistan,[9] Papua,[10] St Christopher and Nevis,[6] St Helena, St Lucia, St Vincent and the Grenadines, Seychelles, Sierra Leone, Singapore, Solomon Islands, South Africa,[11] Swaziland, Tuvalu,[8] Uganda, Virgin Islands,[6] Zambia and Zimbabwe; reciprocal arrangements are in force in all these territories.

It is commonly, but incorrectly, thought that Jersey is a part of the United Kingdom. A number of jurisdictions designated as reciprocating countries in Jersey have extended their legislation to the United Kingdom, but not to Jersey. They include Anguilla,[6] Barbados, the Canadian Provinces of British Columbia and Nova Scotia, Ghana, Gibraltar, Hong Kong, and Malta. Other territories designated as reciprocating territories by Jersey but not in fact having reciprocal arrangements are the Bahamas, Cayman Islands, Christmas Island, Sri Lanka, and the Turks and Caicos Islands. The designations of Aden and Zanzibar would appear to have no continuing effect.

1 No 15 of 1973.
2 Art 2.
3 Art 10(1).
4 Art 10(2).
5 Maintenance Orders (Facilities for Enforcement) (Jersey) Act 1962, No. 4330; an Act is a subsidiary instrument in the Jersey system.
6 As part of the Leeward Islands.
7 For Akrotiri and Dhekelia, see para 8.09 above.
8 As part of the Gilbert and Ellice Islands.
9 See Maintenance Orders (Facilities for Enforcement) (Jersey) Act 1965, No 4618.
10 But *not* to New Guinea; quaere how an order of a court having jurisdiction throughout Papua New Guinea would be treated.
11 See South Africa (Jersey) Law 1962.

Kenya

8.56 The Maintenance Orders Enforcement Act[1] follows the 1920 model. There are, however, a number of distinctive features. The first is that the definition of 'maintenance order', as a result of the partial repeal of that part of the standard definition which referred to the Poor Relief (Ireland) Acts 1839 to 1914, contains the words 'and includes an order or decree for the recovery or repayment of the cost of relief or maintenance'.[2] This appears to include all cases in which some public authority seeks to be recompensed for support payments which it has made. It is even arguable that the words include affiliation orders, despite their express exclusion a few lines earlier, but the argument would be unlikely to succeed.

The second distinctive feature is the inclusion of a provision enabling legal representation to be given to the applicant in proceedings for the confirmation of a foreign provisional order:

'At the hearing of any summons issued by virtue of this section or of any appeal against the confirmation under this section of a provisional order, any Crown Counsel or any person duly qualified as a barrister or solicitor holding office in the Attorney-General's Department may appear on behalf of the person upon whose application the maintenance order was made.'[3]

In other jurisdictions, the applicant's interests have, in effect, to be safeguarded either by the court itself, or its registrar.

The Act extends to 'the United Kingdom and Eire'.[4] The Republic of Ireland has in fact no relevant legislation extending in practice to Kenya. Reciprocal arrangements do exist with all parts of the United Kingdom, and with the following countries to which the Kenyan Act has been extended: Australia,[5] Botswana,[6] Cook Islands,[7] Bailiwick of Guernsey,[8] India,[9] Jersey,[10] Lesotho,[11] Malawi,[12] the Isle of Man,[13] Mauritius,[14] New Zealand,[7] Niue,[7] Seychelles,[15] Swaziland,[16] Uganda,[17] Western Samoa,[7] Zambia,[18] and Zimbabwe.[19] The Act is capable of extension to any Commonwealth country;[20] the application to Guernsey, Jersey and the Isle of Man is presumably in order, treating these as dependencies of the United Kingdom, but the extensions to 'the Union of South Africa'[21] and to Somaliland[22] must be taken to have lapsed.

Further extensions to Tanganyika[23] and 'His Britannic Majesty's Court at Zanzibar',[24] are not matched by reciprocal arrangements, and the Zanzibar Order is almost certainly to be regarded as inoperative.

1 Cap 154, RL 1962.
2 S2.
3 S6(8).

4   S 3.
5   Extension orders were made in respect of individual states and territories: Australian Capital
    Territory (Proc 121/1929), New South Wales (Proc 32/1925), Northern Territory (LN 338/
    1968), Queensland (LN 341/1968), South Australia (Proc 22/1943), Tasmania (LN 339/
    1968), Victoria (Proc 19/1927), and Western Australia (LN 340/1968). Kenya is a recipro-
    cating territory under the Family Law Act 1975 which applies throughout the Common-
    wealth of Australia (including Norfolk Island); see para 8.14 above.
6   Proc 70/1925.
7   LN 400/1956.
8   LN 510/1956.
9   Proc 4/1953.
10 Proc 28/1954.
11 Proc 71/1925.
12 Proc 25/1926.
13 LN 554/1961.
14 Proc 52/1925.
15 Proc 57/1923.
16 Proc 69/1925.
17 Proc 109/1930.
18 Proc 33/1925.
19 Proc 34/1925.
20 See s 10 of the Act, referring to s 95 of the Constitution which contains a list of Commonwealth
    member states.
21 Proc 38/1927.
22 Proc 35/1925.
23 Proc 39/1950.
24 Proc 3/1931.

Kiribati

8.57   The Maintenance Orders (Facilities for Enforcement) Ordinance,[1]
which is on the 1920 model, was originally enacted by the Gilbert and Ellice
Islands of which Kiribati was formerly part. It extends to 'England and
Ireland',[2] but can be further extended to 'any British possession or territory
under Her Majesty's protection'.[3]

It has been extended to Fiji,[4] the Bailiwick of Guernsey,[5] Jersey,[6] Nauru,[7]
New Zealand,[4] Papua New Guinea,[8] Solomon Islands,[4] and Western Samoa;[9]
in all these cases reciprocal arrangements are in force. The Kiribati Ordinance
has also been extended to all the Australian jurisdictions (ie the Australian
Capital Territory,[10] New South Wales,[11] Norfolk Island,[4] the Northern Territory,[4] Queensland,[4] South Australia,[12] Tasmania,[13] Victoria,[14] and Western
Australia[4]) but Kiribati has not been designated as a reciprocating country for
the purposes of the Family Law Act 1975 of Australia.[15] The designation of the
former Gilbert and Ellice Islands by the Isle of Man is not reciprocated in
Kiribati.

1   Cap 4, RL (of Gilbert and Ellice Islands), 1973.
2   S 3. For the effect of this phrase, see para 8.04 above.
3   S 12. For the effect of this phrase, see para 8.02 above.
4   Proc 4/1924.
5   LN 25/1965.
6   GN 29/1954.
7   LN 17/1978.
8   LN 16/1966.
9   Proc 5/1930.
10 Proc 1/1929.
11 Proc 4/1924.
12 Proc 5/1927.
13 Proc 13/1927.

14   Proc 1/1927.
15   See para 8.14 above.

Lesotho

8.58   The Maintenance Orders Proclamation[1] is on the 1920 model, with an additional provision[2] extending and modifying such provisions of Roman–Dutch law in force in Lesotho as relate to maintenance orders so as to secure consistency with the Proclamation. It applies to 'England or Ireland'[3] and can be extended to 'any country or territory within the Commonwealth'.[4]

The Proclamation has been extended to Botswana,[5] the Cook Islands,[6] the Bailiwick of Guernsey,[7] India,[8] Kenya,[9] Jersey,[8] Malawi,[10] New Zealand,[11] Swaziland,[5] Uganda,[12] Zambia,[5] and Zimbabwe.[13] In all these cases reciprocal arrangements are in force. The Proclamation has also been extended to most of the Australian jurisdictions,[14] but Lesotho is not a reciprocating country for the purposes of the Australian Family Law Act 1975.[15] The Lesotho Proclamation also extends to Namibia,[16] Pakistan,[17] and South Africa.[16] An extension to Zanzibar[18] can be regarded as ineffective. A designation of Lesotho by the Isle of Man appears not to be reciprocated.

 1   Proc No 75 of 1921.
 2   Art 11.
 3   Art 3.
 4   Art 12 as amended by Proc No 82 of 1956. See also Proc No 1 of 1962 and n 15 below.
 5   Notice 41/1922.
 6   Notice 36/1949.
 7   Notice 122/1956.
 8   Notice 126/1955.
 9   Notice 54/1925.
10   Notice 21/1925.
11   Notice 51/1925.
12   Notice 60/1925.
13   Notice 60/1922.
14   To the Australian Capital Territory (Notice 10/1929), New South Wales (Notice 140/1924), South Australia (Notice 11/1926), Tasmania (Notice 73/1925), Victoria (Notice 121/1926), and Western Australia (Notice 60/1925).
15   See para 8.14 above.
16   Notice 78/1923, and Proc No 1 of 1962 amending the principal Proclamation to allow these countries to be treated as reciprocating countries.
17   Notice 35/1957; the current status of this extension is very doubtful.
18   Notice 18/1925.

Malawi

8.59   The Maintenance Orders (Enforcement) Act[1] follows the 1920 model. It applies to 'England and Ireland',[2] and can be further extended to 'any country'.[3] Although the marginal note to the relevant provision continues to refer to *Commonwealth* countries, this limitation was removed in 1971.[4]

The Act has been extended to Australia,[5] Botswana,[6] the Bailiwick of Guernsey,[7] India,[8] Jersey,[9] Lesotho,[6] the Isle of Man,[10] Seychelles,[11] Singapore,[12] South Africa,[13] Swaziland,[6] Tanzania,[14] Uganda,[15] Zambia,[16] and Zimbabwe;[17] reciprocal arrangements exist in every case.

The Act is supplemented by provisions in the Service of Process and Execution of Judgments Act, enabling affiliation orders made in Zimbabwe or Zambia to be registered and enforced in Malawi.[18] These provisions are a relic of the former Federation of Rhodesia and Nyasaland of which Malawi was part.

1   Cap 26:04, RL.
2   S 3. For this phrase, see para 8.04 above.
3   S 11.
4   By the Maintenance Orders (Enforcement) (Amendment) Act 1971, No 40 of 1971.
5   A number of orders extended the Malawi Act to the various states and mainland territories
    of Australia: GN 222/1924 (New South Wales), GN 317/1928 (Queensland, South Australia,
    Tasmania, Victoria and Western Australia), GN 23/1929 (ACT), and GN 1/1972 (Northern
    Territory). Malawi is now a reciprocating territory under the Family Law Act 1975 of
    Australia: see para 8.14 above.
6   GN 58/1925.
7   GN 96/1956.
8   GN 105/1955.
9   GN 53/1961.
10 GN 189/1961.
11 GN 133/1923.
12 GN 232/1970.
13 GN 74/1972.
14 GN 189/1972.
15 GN 226/1924.
16 GN 2/1925.
17 GN 251/1925.
18 Cap 4:04, RL, Part IV.

Malaysia

8.60   The Maintenance Orders (Facilities for Enforcement) Act 1949[1] is on
the 1920 model. Originally enacted in West Malaysia, it was brought into force
in East Malaysia (ie Sabah and Sarawak) in 1971.[2] The extension of the Act to
foreign jurisdictions uses an unusual technique. All reciprocating countries are
designated in the Schedule to the Act, and the Yang di-Pertuan Agong is given
power to amend the Schedule from time to time.[3]

The Act currently extends to Australia,[4] Brunei, England, Wales and Northern Ireland, Cocos (Keeling) Islands, Cook Islands, Hong Kong, India, Jersey,
the Isle of Man, New Zealand, Niue, Papua (but not New Guinea), and
Singapore; in all these cases reciprocal arrangements are in force. The Malaysian Act has also been extended to Pakistan; no information about reciprocal
arrangements is available. It also extends to South Africa which has not
designated Malaysia; to Sri Lanka which has designated the 'Federation of
Malaya' and not Sabah or Sarawak; to the Bailiwick of Guernsey which
appears to have made reciprocal provision in respect of West Malaysia and
Sabah, and not Sarawak; and to the Isle of Man which has designated only
Sabah and Sarawak. The designation in the Schedule to the Malaysian Act of
'North Island' is inexplicable; no such distinct jurisdiction exists.

1   Act 34, RL (as revised, 1971).
2   Maintenance Ordinance (Extension) Order 1970, PU(A) 460/70.
3   S 11.
4   All states and mainland territories, and Norfolk Island.

Malta

8.61   The Maintenance Orders (Reciprocal Enforcement) Act 1974[1] is on the
1972 model, containing provisions corresponding to those in Part I of the
Maintenance Orders (Reciprocal Enforcement) Act 1972 of the United Kingdom. It also contains a provision[2] corresponding to s 40 of the United Kingdom
Act enabling the Act to be applied to specified countries with exceptions,
adaptations and modifications; no use has been made of this power. Section

20(2) of the Act contains a very wide power enabling the President by Order to 'make such further provision as he may deem necessary or expedient for any purposes aforesaid or with a view to or in view of the accession by Malta to any international convention relating to maintenance'; no use has yet been made of this power.

The Act has been applied to Australia,[3] Gibraltar,[4] and the United Kingdom;[5] in all these cases reciprocal arrangements are in force.

It is possible that the earlier Maintenance Orders (Facilities for Enforcement) Ordinance[6] remains in force in respect of certain countries. The Maltese authorities are using the technique of bringing into force the 1974 Act, including its repeal of the earlier Ordinance, in respect of named countries. The Ordinance presumably remains in force in respect of any other countries which had been designated as reciprocating countries for its purposes. It has not been possible to trace any orders made under the Ordinance, but Alberta, Guernsey, Jersey, the Isle of Man, Newfoundland, the Northwest Territories and Prince Edward Island all regard Malta as a reciprocating country by virtue of Orders made in their own jurisdiction before 1974.

1 Act No XX of 1974.
2 S 20(1).
3 LN 154 of 1977 in respect of orders affecting the parties to or the children of a marriage only; Malta is similarly a country with 'restricted reciprocity' for the purposes of the Family Law Act 1975 of Australia.
4 LN 43 of 1978.
5 LN 49 of 1975.
6 Cap 76, RL.

Isle of Man

8.62 The Maintenance Orders (Facilities for Enforcement) Act 1921 is on the 1920 model. It can be extended to any Commonwealth country.[1] A striking feature of the position in relation to this Act is that, although it has been extended to a large number of Commonwealth jurisdictions, a very high proportion of those designated jurisdictions do not in fact have reciprocal arrangements. One can only speculate as to the reasons for this 'unilateral reciprocity'; it seems likely that the appropriate officers in a number of overseas jurisdictions, unfamiliar with the constitutional position of the Isle of Man, assumed that the extension of their own legislation to 'England' or 'the United Kingdom' would be sufficient. (In fact the Isle of Man is not part of either of those jurisdictions.) A possible source of confusion is the principal order made in the Isle of Man, the Maintenance Orders (Facilities for Enforcement) Order 1963[2] which reproduces in an Annex the corresponding United Kingdom Order of 1959; this can have no legal significance for Manx law.

The Manx Act has been extended[3] to Antigua and Barbuda, Australia (mainland jurisdictions and Norfolk Island),[4] Belize, Bermuda, Botswana,[5] Canada (all jurisdictions except Quebec), Cocos (Keeling) Islands, Dominica, England and Wales,[6] Falkland Islands, Fiji, Gambia, the Bailiwick of Guernsey, Guyana, India,[5] Jersey, Kenya, Malawi, Mauritius, New Zealand, Northern Ireland,[6] Papua,[7] St Christopher and Nevis,[8] Seychelles, Sri Lanka,[9] South Africa,[10] Swaziland,[5] Trinidad and Tobago,[9] Uganda, Zambia, and Zimbabwe; in all these cases reciprocal arrangements do exist. However, there is no actual reciprocity in the following jurisdictions to which the Manx Act has also been extended: Anguilla,[8] Bahamas, Barbados, Brunei,[11] Cayman Islands, Christmas Island,[12] Falkland Islands Dependencies,[13] Gibraltar, Grenada,

Hong Kong, Jamaica, Kiribati,[14] Lesotho, Malta,[15] Nigeria, St Helena, Sierra Leone, Singapore, Solomon Islands, Tanzania,[16] Turks and Caicos Islands, Tuvalu,[14] and the Virgin Islands. The Act has also been extended to Pakistan;[17] information is not available as to reciprocal arrangements. The extension to Aden would seem to have no continuing effect. The Isle of Man is treated as a reciprocating country by Malaysia despite the extension of the Manx Act only to Sabah and Sarawak and not to West Malaysia.

The Maintenance Orders (Reciprocal Enforcement) Act 1978[18] is on the 1972 model but is not yet in force, and no orders designating reciprocating countries have been made.

1   S 11, as amended by the Matrimonial Proceedings (Magistrates' Courts) Act 1962, s 25.
2   Government Circular 43/63. See also GC 31/64 bringing up-to-date the text of the United Kingdom Order it reproduces.
3   Unless otherwise indicated by GC 43/63.
4   For Queensland see GC 31/64.
5   GC 54/64.
6   See GC 31/61 correcting a designation of the whole United Kingdom in GC 43/63.
7   But not New Guinea.
8   As part of St Christopher-Nevis-Anguilla, now divided.
9   GC 59/64.
10 No longer part of the Commonwealth, so status of extension unclear.
11 See para 8.25 above.
12 See GC 31/61, correcting an earlier designation of 'Christmas Islands'.
13 See para 8.44 above.
14 As part of the Gilbert and Ellice Islands, now divided.
15 See para 8.61 above.
16 GC 2/66.
17 Not part of the Commonwealth; GC 7/66.
18 1978, c 2.

Mauritius

8.63   The Maintenance Orders (Facilities for Enforcement) Ordinance[1] is on the 1920 model. It applies to 'England or Ireland'[2] and can be further extended to 'any country within the Commonwealth'.[3] The generality of this last provision is perhaps qualified by the unusual provision in the interpretation section, defining 'dependants' by reference to 'the law in force in the part of Her Majesty the Queen of the United Kingdom's dominions' in which the maintenance order was made;[4] the phrase would appear to exclude all Commonwealth states which do not acknowledge the Queen as Head of State.[5]

Subject to that important questionmark, the Ordinance has been extended to the Bailiwick of Guernsey,[6] Grenada,[7] India,[8] Jersey,[9] Kenya,[10] the Isle of Man,[11] Seychelles,[12] Sri Lanka,[13] and Uganda.[14] Reciprocal arrangements exist in all these cases. Extension orders exist in respect of the Australian Capital Territory,[15] New South Wales,[16] and Victoria[17] but Mauritius is not a reciprocating state for the purposes of the Family Law Act 1975 of Australia.[18] The extension of the Mauritius Ordinance to South Africa is presumably inoperative as a result of South Africa's withdrawal from the Commonwealth. Dominica deems Mauritius to be a reciprocating territory, but no corresponding extension order has been made by Mauritius.

1   Cap 191, RL.
2   S 3. For this phrase, see para 8.04 above.
3   S 12.
4   S 2.

5 This would limit the effective extent of the Mauritius Ordinance to the British Isles jurisdictions and Grenada.
6 Proc 2/1957.
7 Proc 29/1925.
8 Proc 11/1954.
9 Proc 4/1963.
10 Proc 7/1925.
11 Proc 26/1961.
12 Proc 16/1924.
13 Proc 34/1924.
14 Proc 5/1925.
15 Proc 8/1930.
16 Proc 9/1930.
17 Proc 10/1930.
18 See para 8.14 above.

Montserrat

8.64 Montserrat was until 1957 a presidency of the Leeward Islands and its Maintenance Orders (Facilities for Enforcement) Act,[1] which follows the 1920 model, was originally enacted by the Legislature of the Leeward Islands. The Act extends to England and Northern Ireland[2] and is capable of extension to any 'British possession or territory under Her Majesty's protection'.[3]

The Act has been extended to Antigua and Barbuda,[4] the Bahamas,[5] Belize,[6] Bermuda,[5] Dominica,[7] Grenada,[5] Guyana,[8] Jamaica,[9] Jersey,[10] St Christopher and Nevis,[11] St Lucia,[5] St Vincent and the Grenadines,[5] Trinidad and Tobago,[5] and the Virgin Islands.[4] In all these cases, reciprocal arrangements are in force; in many cases the other territory has designated 'the Leeward Islands' and this is assumed to continue to apply to Montserrat. The Act also appears to extend to Anguilla,[11] Barbados,[5] and the Turks and Caicos Islands,[12] but no reciprocal arrangements are currently in force in those territories. The Montserrat legislation has also been extended to the Australian Capital Territory[13] and New South Wales,[7] but Montserrat is not a reciprocating territory for the purposes of the Family Law Act 1975 of Australia.[14] A designation of Montserrat by the Isle of Man is not reciprocated.

1 Cap 48, RL 1962.
2 S 3.
3 S 12.
4 SRO 8/1957.
5 LI Gaz, 30 August 1923.
6 LI Sub Leg (1924).
7 SRO (LI) 14/1945.
8 LI Gaz, 9 August 1922.
9 LI Gaz, 14 May 1925.
10 SRO (LI) 44/1954.
11 SRO 8/1957 as part of St Christopher–Nevis–Anguilla.
12 LI Gaz, 14 May 1925, as part of Jamaica.
13 SRO (LI) 6/1929.
14 See para 8.14 above.

Nauru

8.65 The Maintenance Orders (Reciprocal Enforcement) Act 1973[1] is on the 1972 model, that is it contains provisions substantially identical to those in Parts I, II and III of the corresponding United Kingdom Act. The power to ratify the United Nations Convention on the Recovery Abroad of Maintenance conferred by Part III of the Nauru Act[2] has not been exercised; nor has that[3] to apply modified versions of the Act in respect of particular countries. The Act has been applied only to Kiribati,[4] where reciprocal arrangements are in force. Australia and Fiji both regard Nauru as reciprocating countries despite the absence of appropriate provision in Nauru; in the case of Fiji, which acted in 1980, this may since have been attended to in Nauru. In January 1979 it was reported[5] that the Nauru Cabinet had given a preliminary indication that it would be prepared to make orders in respect of Australia, Fiji, Hong Kong, New Zealand, Papua New Guinea, Solomon Islands, Tonga, and Tuvalu, but no report has been received of further action.

1   No 19 of 1973.
2   Ie ss 21–25.
3   Given by s 26.
4   Cabinet Order, 13 January 1978; this is in respect of Part II of the Nauru Act.
5   By the Secretary for Justice, Nauru.

New Zealand

8.66   The New Zealand legislation is fully examined above,[1] and this paragraph is concerned solely with the extent of its application.

The Family Proceedings Act 1980[2] contains provisions as to the enforcement of overseas maintenance orders[3] which apply automatically and with no requirement of reciprocity to all Commonwealth countries including every territory for whose international relations the government of any Commonwealth member country is responsible, the Republic of Ireland, the Cook Islands, Niue and Tokelau.[4] The relevant provisions may also be applied with or without modification to any other designated country;[5] South Africa and South-West Africa (Namibia) were so designated under a predecessor of the present legislation.[6]

1   See paras 6.01–6.08 above.
2   No 94 of 1980.
3   Ss 136–143; and see ss 150–154. Ss 144–146 and 149, which make provision enabling New Zealand to ratify the United Nations Convention on the Recovery Abroad of Maintenance, are not yet in force.
4   S 2. See also Commonwealth Countries Act 1977, No 31 of 1977.
5   S 135.
6   Destitute Persons Amendment Act 1963, No 63 of 1963. South Africa appears to be treated as a designated country under the 1980 Act, semble without any fresh notification under s 135 of the 1980 Act.

Nigeria

8.67   The Maintenance Orders Act,[1] a federal statute, is on the 1920 model. It extends to 'England or Ireland'[2] and is capable of further extension to 'any British possession or territory under Her Majesty's protection'.[3]

It has been extended to the Cook Islands,[4] The Gambia,[5] Grenada,[6] the Bailiwick of Guernsey,[7] Guyana,[8] Jersey,[9] New Zealand,[4] St Vincent and the Grenadines,[10] Sierra Leone,[4] and Zambia.[11] In these cases reciprocal arrangements are in force. Although the Nigerian Act has been extended to Ghana,[4] Ghana appears to have made no reciprocal provision. The Act has also been extended to the Australian Capital Territory,[12] New South Wales,[13] Victoria,[14] and Western Australia[15] but Nigeria is not designated as a reciprocating country under the Family Law Act 1975 of Australia.[16] The extension of the Nigerian Act to South Africa[17] is presumably ineffective since that country's withdrawal from the Commonwealth. A designation of Nigeria by the Isle of Man is not reciprocated.

1 Cap 114, RL 1958. It is not certain that the information in this paragraph is wholly up-to-date; legislative action since 1974 is not available.
2 S 3. For this phrase, see para 8.04 above.
3 S 11. For this phrase, see para 8.02 above.
4 Proc 1 of 1951.
5 Gaz, 1 Jan 1925.
6 Gaz, 11 June 1925.
7 LN 93/1959.
8 Gaz, 29 October 1925.
9 LN 174/1954.
10 Gaz, 9 April 1925.
11 GN 1354 (1945).
12 Gaz, 3 January 1929.
13 Gaz, 12 March 1925.
14 Gaz, 25 November 1926.
15 GN 1525 (1946).
16 See para 8.14 above.
17 GN 1875 (1947).

Niue

8.68 Although now self-governing, by virtue of the Niue Constitution Act 1974 (of New Zealand), Niue was formerly administered with the Cook Islands. The legislation in force for the enforcement of overseas maintenance orders is the Cook Islands Maintenance Enforcement Regulations 1948 of New Zealand.[1]

1 1948/134. See the entry relating to the Cook Islands, para 8.40 ante.

Papua New Guinea

8.69 The Maintenance Orders Enforcement Act 1970[1] is based upon the substantially uniform legislation introduced during the late 1960s in the Australian states and territories. At that date Papua New Guinea was an external territory of Australia, and the Act contained provisions[2] applying in Papua New Guinea the 'internal' system of reciprocal enforcement then operated between the various Australian jurisdictions; these provisions were repealed after Independence by the Maintenance Orders Enforcement (Amendment) Act 1976.[3]

The Papua New Guinea legislation applies to Australia including Norfolk Island and the territory of the Cocos (Keeling) Islands[4] and also[5] to several Canadian Provinces,[6] Cook Islands, Kiribati, New Zealand, Niue, Solomon Islands, and Tuvalu; reciprocal arrangements are in force in all these countries. A number of other countries are reciprocating countries in respect of Papua only; this is a survival of the position existing before 1959 under which there was separate legislation in Papua and New Guinea, the latter being capable of extension only to Australian states and territories and New Zealand.[7] Certain reciprocal arrangements made with Papua before 1959 remain in force. They include arrangements with the Isle of Man,[8] Jersey,[9] and Zimbabwe,[10] in all of which reciprocity exists. They also include designations, in respect of Papua, of the Federation of Malaya,[10] and of Sarawak[10]; despite the omission of Sabah, there is a reciprocal designation by Malaysia as a whole. Conversely, there is a designation of 'the United Kingdom' in respect of Papua,[9] but Papua is a reciprocating country in England and Northern Ireland only.

1   No 23 of 1970.
2   Division III.2 (ss 33–42).
3   No 49 of 1976, s 4.
4   All the Australian states except New South Wales, together with the mainland territories, the Cocos (Keeling) Islands and Norfolk Island were designated (Gaz, 28 July 1960 except for the Australian Capital Territory and Norfolk Island (for which see Gaz, 28 December 1961) and the Cocos (Keeling) Islands (Gaz, 27 December 1962)) as reciprocating states for the purposes of the Maintenance Orders (Facilities for Enforcement) Ordinance 1959, and such reciprocating states were deemed to be reciprocating countries for the purposes of the 1970 legislation by s 4(2A) (inserted by the Maintenance Orders Enforcement (Amedment) Ordinance 1970, No 51 of 1970, s 3). New South Wales was similarly designated on the same day but in respect of Papua only, but by the Maintenance Orders Enforcement (New South Wales Temporary Provisions) Ordinance 1962 was deemed to have been designated for the whole of Papua New Guinea. Norfolk Island is also separately designated in Sch 2 to the Maintenance Orders Enforcement Regulations, No 54 of 1971.
5   See Maintenance Orders Enforcement Regulations, No 54 of 1971, reg 13 and Sch 2.
6   Alberta, British Columbia, Manitoba, Newfoundland, Nova Scotia, Ontario, Prince Edward Island, and Saskatchewan.
7   An exception was the Maintenance Orders (Canada) (Facilities for Enforcement) Ordinance 1953 which applied in both Papua and New Guinea.
8   Gaz, 29 September 1960, continued in force by s 4(2A) of the 1970 Act.
9   Maintenance Orders Enforcement Regulations, No 54 of 1971, reg 13 and Sch 2.
10   Gaz, 28 July 1960, continued in force by s 4(2A) of the 1970 Act.

St Christopher and Nevis

8.70   St Christopher–Nevis–Anguilla was until 1957 a presidency of the Leeward Islands. After it had attained associated statehood, it was divided by the separation of Anguilla.[1] The Maintenance Orders (Facilities for Enforcement) Act of St Christopher and Nevis,[2] which is on the 1920 model, was originally enacted by the Legislature of the Leeward Islands. It extends to England and Northern Ireland[3] and is capable of further extension to any 'British possession or territory under Her Majesty's protection'.[4]

The Act has been extended to Antigua and Barbuda,[5] the Bahamas,[6] Belize,[7] Bermuda,[6] Dominica,[8] Grenada,[6] Guyana,[9] Jamaica,[10] Jersey,[11] the Isle of Man,[12] Montserrat,[5] St Lucia,[6] St Vincent and the Grenadines,[6] Trinidad and Tobago,[6] and the Virgin Islands.[5] In all these cases, reciprocal arrangements are in force; the other territory in many cases designates 'the Leeward Islands' and it is assumed that these extensions continue to apply to St Christopher and Nevis. The Act also extends to Barbados,[6] and the Turks and Caicos Islands,[13] but no reciprocal arrangements are currently in force in those territories. The St Christopher and Nevis Act has also been extended to the Australian Capital Territory[14] and New South Wales,[7] but St Christopher and Nevis is not a reciprocating territory for the purposes of the Family Law Act 1975[15] of Australia.

1   See, for Anguilla, para 8.10 above.
2   Cap 48, RL 1962.
3   S 3.
4   S 12. For this phrase, see para 8.02 above.
5   SRO 11/1957.
6   LI Gaz, 30 August 1923.
7   LI Sub Leg (1924).
8   SRO (LI) 14/1945.
9   LI Gaz, 9 August 1922.
10   LI Gaz, 14 May 1925.
11   SRO (LI) 44/1954.
12   SRO 8/1964.

13 LI Gaz, 14 May 1925 as part of Jamaica.
14 SRO (LI) 6/1929.
15 See para 8.14 above.

Saint Helena

8.71 By virtue of the English Law (Application) Ordinance 1970, the Maintenance Orders (Reciprocal Enforcement) Act 1972 of the United Kingdom is in force in Saint Helena,[1] with certain modifications (principally the omission of those provisions applying in Scotland or Northern Ireland, but also those dealing with legal aid,[2] and some others, eg the provision that Orders in Council under the Act are subject to annulment in pursuance of a resolution of either House of Parliament).[3] Although the position is far from clear, it is thought that Orders in Council made in the United Kingdom and designating reciprocating countries, applying modified versions of the Act, or implementing the United Nations Convention on the Recovery Abroad of Maintenance,[4] will not apply in Saint Helena in the absence of some express provision. If that interpretation of the position is correct there are no countries to which the Act applies so far as the law of Saint Helena is concerned. It would also appear to be the case that the application of the United Kingdom Act in Saint Helena is an inappropriate means of ensuring reciprocal treatment of maintenance orders as between the United Kingdom and Saint Helena themselves, and so far as English law is concerned Saint Helena is a reciprocating country (in England and Northern Ireland only) under the Maintenance Orders (Facilities for Enforcement) Act 1920 and not under the 1972 Act.

The position is made more complicated by the existence of a Maintenance Orders (Facilities for Enforcement) Ordinance of Saint Helena,[5] which was repealed in 1978[6] but with a saving for orders made thereunder. The Ordinance itself applied to 'England and Ireland',[7] but that provision seems not to have been saved. The extensions under the former Ordinance were to 'Aden Colony and Protectorate',[8] now South Yemen; to 'the Union of South Africa',[9] an extension now inappropriate in view of South Africa's departure from the Commonwealth (though South Africa still regards Saint Helena as a reciprocating country); and to Jersey.[10] It is difficult to resist the conclusion that Jersey is in fact the only reciprocating country remaining.

1 See LN 3(a) of 1978.
2 S 43.
3 S 45(2).
4 Ie under ss 1, 25 and 40.
5 Cap 67, RL.
6 Maintenance Orders (Facilities for Enforcement) (Repeal) Ordinance 1978, No 5 of 1978, but see savings in s 2.
7 For the effect of this phrase, see para 8.04 above.
8 Proc 1 of 1941.
9 Proc, 20 November 1944.
10 Proc 5 of 1961.

St Lucia

8.72 The Maintenance Orders (Facilities for Enforcement) Ordinance[1] is on the 1920 model. It extends to 'England and Ireland'[2] and can be extended to 'any British possession or territory under Her Majesty's protection'.[3]

It has been extended[4] to Antigua and Barbuda,[5] the Bahamas, Dominica,[6] Grenada, Guyana, Jamaica, Jersey,[7] the Isle of Man,[8] Montserrat,[5] St Christopher and Nevis,[5] St Vincent and the Grenadines, Trinidad and Tobago, and the Virgin Islands;[5] in all these cases reciprocal arrangements are in force. The St Lucia Ordinance has also been extended[4] to Anguilla,[5] the Australian Capital Territory,[9] Barbados, New South Wales[9] and the Turks and Caicos Islands,[10] but reciprocal arrangements are not in force in those jurisdictions.

1   Cap 11, RL 1957.
2   S 3. For this phrase, see para 8.04 above.
3   S 12. For this phrase, see para 8.02 above.
4   Unless otherwise indicated by orders consolidated in RL, vol 7, p 196.
5   As part of the Leeward Islands.
6   As part of the Leeward Islands, of which Dominica was a presidency until 1940.
7   Proc 5/1961.
8   Proc 29/1961.
9   St Lucia is not a reciprocating country under the Australian Family Law Act 1975; see para 8.14 above.
10 As part of Jamaica.

St Vincent and the Grenadines

8.73   The Maintenance Act[1] contains provisions on the 1920 model. They extend to 'England and Ireland'[2] and are capable of extension to 'any British possession or territory under Her Majesty's protection'.[3]

The Act has been extended to Antigua and Barbuda,[4] the Bahamas,[5] Belize,[6] Cocos (Keeling) Islands,[7] Dominica,[8] Grenada,[9] Guernsey,[10] Guyana,[11] Jamaica,[5] Jersey,[12] the Isle of Man,[13] Montserrat,[4] Nigeria,[5] St Christopher and Nevis,[4] St Lucia,[8] Trinidad and Tobago[14] and the Virgin Islands;[4] in all these cases reciprocal arrangements are in force. The St Vincent Act was also extended to the Australian Capital Territory[15] and to New South Wales,[5] but St Vincent is not a reciprocating country for the purposes of the Australian Family Law Act 1975.[16] The St Vincent Act has also been extended to Anguilla,[4] Barbados[5] and the Turks and Caicos Islands[17] but no reciprocal arrangements exist in those territories. It is probable that reciprocal arrangements exist with Singapore; the St Vincent Act was extended to 'the Straits Settlements'[5] and a reciprocating extension by the Straits Settlements authorities appears to be in force in Singapore.[18]

1   Act 1 of 1949, ss 21–29. See Title 15, ch 5, RL 1966 (never brought into force).
2   S 21. For this phrase, see para 8.04 above.
3   S 29. For this phrase, see para 8.02 above.
4   G 79/1922, as part of the Leeward Islands.
5   RL 1926, vol 1, p 364.
6   Proc 5/1928.
7   Proc 18/1958.
8   G 77/1922.
9   G 49/1922.
10 Proc 42/1955.
11 G 105/1922.
12 Proc 12/1963.
13 Proc 21/1961.
14 G 59/1922.
15 Proc 12/1928.
16 See para 8.14 above.
17 RL 1926, vol 1, p 364, as part of Jamaica.
18 See para 8.76 below.

Seychelles

8.74   The Maintenance Orders (Reciprocal Enforcement) Ordinance[1] is based on the 1920 model. It contains one additional provision in respect of the confirmation of provisional orders made overseas. Section 4(6) provides:

'If the court of England or Northern Ireland which made the provisional order shall for any reason vary or rescind an order confirmed under this section, such order varying or rescinding the original order shall not have effect in the Seychelles unless and until confirmed in the same manner as the original order.'

This reinforces the effect of s 5(5) of the 1920 model Act.

The Seychelles Act applies to England and Northern Ireland and its further extension is governed by unusually complex provisions. The Act may be extended to 'any British possession or any territory under Her Majesty's protection',[2] and to 'any country within the Commonwealth' not falling within the former class.[3] However the definition of 'dependants' is in terms of the law in force in some 'part of Her Majesty's dominions',[4] a phrase which makes the extension of the Act to Commonwealth countries which do not recognise the Queen as Head of State of doubtful validity.

The Act has been extended to the Bailiwick of Guernsey,[5] India,[6] Jersey,[5] Kenya,[7] the Isle of Man,[5] Malawi,[8] Mauritius[9] and Uganda.[10] Reciprocal arrangements are in force in all these cases.

1 Cap 71, RL.
2 S 1(1). For this phrase, see para 8.02 above.
3 S 1(2).
4 S 2.
5 Proc 7/1961.
6 Proc 8/1954.
7 Proc 15/1923.
8 Proc 8/1923.
9 Proc 12/1924.
10 Proc 10/1923.

Sierra Leone

8.75   The Maintenance Orders (Facilities for Enforcement) Act[1] is on the 1920 model. It applies to 'England and Ireland'[2] and can be extended to 'any territory within the British Commonwealth of Nations'.[3]

The effective extent of the Sierra Leone Act is very limited. It has been extended to The Gambia,[4] Jersey[5] and Nigeria,[6] and reciprocal arrangements are in force in those territories. It has also been extended to Ghana[7] and Gibraltar,[8] but reciprocal arrangements are not there in force. An extension order designated the Australian Capital Territory[9] in 1929; there appears to have been no extension to any other part of Australia, but Sierra Leone is a reciprocating country for the purposes of the Australian Family Law Act 1975. This appears to be the result of a misunderstanding; 'the Seat of Government of the Commonwealth of Australia' tends to be shortened to 'Australia' even in published official lists, including that supplied by the Sierra Leone Government. A designation of Sierra Leone by the Isle of Man is not reciprocated.

The Judicial Convention between Guinea and Sierra Leone, scheduled to the Sierra Leone–Guinea Relations Act 1964 provides[10] for the enforcement of 'civil judgments ... including judgments relating to marriage, divorce and other matters concerning civil status'. It is not clear whether this applies to maintenance orders. In the absence of express language the common law rule as to the need for the relevant order to be 'final and conclusive' would appear to operate, which almost certainly prevents the effectiveness of the Convention in respect of maintenance orders.[11]

1   Cap 101, RL 1960.
2   S 3. For this phrase, see para 8.04 above.
3   S 12.
4   Proc, 1 September 1924.
5   PN 33/1961.
6   Proc, 3 January 1925.
7   Proc, 1 October 1924.
8   Proc, 1 June 1929.
9   Proc, 2 February 1929.
10   Art V.
11   See para 4.11 above.

Singapore

8.76   Singapore has two pieces of legislation, one on the 1920 and one on the 1972 model. The former is the Reciprocal Enforcement of Maintenance Orders Act[1] which originally applied to England and Northern Ireland[2] and could be extended to 'any part of the British Commonwealth outside the United Kingdom'.[3] It is prospectively repealed by the second Act, the Maintenance Orders (Reciprocal Enforcement) Act 1975,[4] but the repealing provision has not yet been brought into force and it appears to be intended to transfer arrangements from one Act to the other only as occasion presents itself, and not as a planned exercise. The Maintenance Orders (Reciprocal Enforcement) Act 1975 is on the 1972 model, that is it contains provisions corresponding to those in Part I of the corresponding United Kingdom Act of 1972, but does not contain provisions such as are to be found in Parts II and III of that Act enabling effect to be given to the United Nations Convention on the Recovery Abroad of Maintenance or enabling a modified version of the general rules in the Act to be applied in respect of particular countries.

Singapore was formerly part of the Straits Settlements, and orders made by the Straits Settlements authorities are treated as continuing in force in Singapore; it is assumed, similarly, that designations by other countries of 'the Straits Settlements' apply to Singapore.

The Reciprocal Enforcement of Maintenance Orders Act has been applied to Australia,[5] several Canadian jurisdictions,[6] Cook Islands,[7] Guernsey,[8] Hong Kong,[9] India,[9] Jersey,[10] Malawi,[9] Niue,[7] Saint Vincent and the Grenadines,[11] Sri Lanka,[11] and Western Samoa;[7] in all these countries reciprocal arrangements are in force. The same is also true of South Africa[11] but this designation may well have lapsed on South Africa's departure from the Commonwealth. Reciprocal arrangements exist with Malaysia, but on the Singapore side the position is confused; designations exist in favour of the former Federated Malay States, Johore, Kedah, Perlis, Kelantan and Trengannu,[12] Sarawak[13] and Sabah,[14] but the other former Straits Settlements (eg Penang) are not expressly mentioned. An extension to Zambia[9] appears not to be reciprocated. Designations of Singapore by Christmas Island (formerly administered by Singapore) and by the Isle of Man are not reciprocated.

The Maintenance Orders (Reciprocal Enforcement) Act 1975 has been extended[15] to New Zealand (except in respect of provisional affiliation orders and certain orders for the payment of birth and funeral expenses of a child) and to the United Kingdom; in both cases reciprocal arrangements are in force.

1   Cap 26, RL.
2   S 3; the Act no longer applies to England and Northern Ireland, which are now under the 1975 Act referred to below.

3 S 11.
4 No 23 of 1975, effective from 3 May 1976 (GN 93 of 1976); the repeal is effected by s 19(1).
5 GN 592 of 1973; Singapore is a reciprocating country for the purposes of the Family Law Act
   1975.
6 Alberta, British Columbia, New Brunswick, Newfoundland, Northwest Territories, Nova
   Scotia, Saskatchewan and Yukon Territory (all GN 592 of 1973); no reciprocating order has
   been traced in Alberta or Saskatchewan.
7 GN S83 of 1960.
8 GN 403 of 1957.
9 GN S92 of 1973.
10 GN 2951 of 1954.
11 GN No 337/1930 of the Straits Settlements.
12 GN No 2566/1938 of the Straits Settlements.
13 GN No 1722/1939 of the Straits Settlements.
14 GN 1841 of 1954.
15 GN No S94 of 1976.

Solomon Islands

8.77 The Maintenance Orders (Facilities for Enforcement) Ordinance[1] is on
the 1920 model. It extends to 'England and Ireland'[2] and can be extended to
'any British possession or territory under Her Majesty's protection'.[3]

It has been extended to Fiji,[4] Guernsey,[5] Hong Kong,[6] Jersey,[7] Kiribati,[8]
New Zealand,[9] Papua New Guinea,[10] Tuvalu,[8] and Western Samoa;[11] in all
these cases reciprocal arrangements are in force. It has also been extended to
all the Australian states and mainland territories and to Norfolk Island;[12] but
the Solomon Islands are not a reciprocating country for the purposes of the
Family Law Act 1975 of Australia.[13] A designation of the Solomon Islands by
the Isle of Man is not reciprocated.

1 Cap 10, RL 1969.
2 S 3. For this phrase, see para 8.04 above.
3 S 12. For this phrase, see para 8.02 above.
4 Proc 4/1925.
5 Proc 5/1965.
6 Citation not available.
7 Proc 1/1959.
8 Proc 4/1925 as part of the Gilbert and Ellice Islands.
9 Proc 9/1928.
10 Proc 2/1966.
11 Proc 4/1930.
12 New South Wales by Proc 5/1924; Queensland, Western Australia, Norfolk Is. and the
   Northern Territory by Proc 4/1925; Victoria by Proc 2/1927; S. Australia by Proc 6/1927;
   Tasmania by Proc 12/1927; and the Australian Capital Territory by Proc 2/1929.
13 See para 8.14 above.

Sri Lanka

8.78 The Maintenance Orders (Facilities for Enforcement) Act[1] is on the
1920 model. It applies to England and Northern Ireland[2] and may be extended
to 'any British possession or any territory under Her Majesty's protection or
any country which is a member of the Commonwealth'.[3]

The Act has been extended to all the Australian states and mainland territories and to the territories of Cocos (Keeling) Islands and Norfolk Island,[4] to
Grenada,[5] the Bailiwick of Guernsey,[6] Hong Kong,[7] India,[8] the Isle of Man,[9]
Mauritius,[10] New Zealand[11] and Uganda;[12] in all these cases reciprocal
arrangements are in force. The same would appear to be the case in respect of

Singapore, by virtue of a Sri Lanka extension to 'the Straits Settlements'[13] and a reciprocating order by the Straits Settlements authorities which is treated as in force in Singapore.[14] The Sri Lanka Act has been extended to the 'Federation of Malaya',[15] and Sri Lanka is treated as a reciprocating country by Malaysia, but it seems that the Sri Lanka Act has never been extended to the East Malaysian states. Brunei and Jersey treat Sri Lanka as a reciprocating country, despite the absence of any reciprocating order in Sri Lanka; but Papua New Guinea does not despite the existence of orders extending the Sri Lanka Act to both Papua[16] and New Guinea.[17]

1   Cap 92, RL 1956.
2   S 3.
3   S 12, as amended by an Amending Act, cap 42 of 1956. The phrase 'Her Majesty's' is odd in legislation of a republican state, but no amendment has been made since the adoption of a republican constitution.
4   Australian Capital Territory (Gaz, 8 March 1929), New South Wales (Gaz, 21 November 1924), Northern Territory (Gaz, 28 November 1972), Queensland, South Australia and Tasmania (Gaz, 8 February 1972), Victoria (Gaz, 12 November 1926), Western Australia (24 March 1950), Cocos (Keeling) Islands (Gaz, 9 June 1959) and Norfolk Island (Gaz, 8 February 1972). Sri Lanka is a reciprocating country for the purposes of the Family Law Act 1975 of Australia.
5   Gaz, 24 July 1925.
6   Gaz, 31 October 1957.
7   Gaz, 29 March 1923.
8   Gaz, 20 October 1958. Earlier orders applying, inter alia, to 'British Burma' are presumably inoperative.
9   Gaz, 30 April 1965.
10 Gaz, 30 January 1925.
11 Gaz, 15 August 1924.
12 Gaz, 1 December 1924.
13 Gaz, 12 January 1923.
14 See para 8.76 above.
15 Gaz, 1 June 1957.
16 Gaz, 8 February 1972.
17 Gaz, 28 November 1972.

Swaziland

8.79   The Maintenance Orders Act 1921[1] is on the 1920 model with an additional provision[2] extending and modifying such provisions of Roman–Dutch law in force in Swaziland as relate to maintenance orders so as to secure consistency with the Act. It extends to all parts of the United Kingdom,[3] though reciprocal arrangements only exist in England and Wales and Northern Ireland. It may be extended to any country within the Commonwealth, to the Republic of Ireland, the Republic of South Africa, Namibia, and to any part of those countries.[4]

It has been extended to Botswana,[5] Cook Islands,[6] Guernsey,[7] India,[8] Jersey,[9] Kenya,[10] Lesotho,[5] Malawi,[11] the Isle of Man,[12] New Zealand,[13] South Africa,[14] Uganda,[15] Zambia[5] and Zimbabwe;[16] in all these cases reciprocal provisions are in force. Extension orders also exist in relation to the Australian Capital Territory,[17] New South Wales,[18] Queensland,[19] South Australia,[20] Tasmania,[21] Victoria[22] and Western Australia,[23] but Swaziland is not a reciprocating country for the purposes of the Family Law Act 1975 of Australia.[24] The extensions to Pakistan[25] and Zanzibar[26] would appear to be inoperative.

1   Act 77 of 1921.
2   S 11.
3   S 3 which actually refers to 'the United Kingdom or Northern Ireland'.

4   S 12.
5   N 43/1922.
6   N 38/1949.
7   N 124/1956.
8   N 129/1955.
9   N 171/1954.
10 N 50/1925.
11 N 23/1925.
12 N 109/1964.
13 N 53/1925.
14 N 103/1962.
15 N 59/1925.
16 N 62/1922.
17 N 12/1929.
18 N 142/1924.
19 N 56/1925.
20 N 13/1926.
21 N 75/1925.
22 N 123/1926.
23 N 62/1925.
24 See para 8.14 above.
25 N 37/1957.
26 N 20/1925.

Tanzania

8.80   At one time both Tanganyika and Zanzibar, the component parts of Tanzania, had legislation on the 1920 model. The Zanzibar legislation[1] appears never to have been formally repealed, but is inoperative. The Tanganyika Ordinance[2] has been repealed and has been partially replaced by some provisions[3] of the Law of Marriage Act 1971.[4]

The 1971 Act, which refers in the relevant provisions expressly to Tanganyika rather than the whole of Tanzania, contains a modified version of that part of the 1920 model which deals with the registration of final orders. There is no re-enactment of the 'shuttlecock' provisions dealing with provisional orders and their confirmation; it is not known why the decision was taken to limit the new Act in this way.

The Act applies to orders for the maintenance 'of the wife or former wife or husband or former husband or infant child of the person against whom the order is made'.[5] Only two extension orders are known to have been made, so that the Act applies only to orders from Malawi[6] and the United Kingdom,[7] where reciprocal arrangements exist. Australia, Fiji and the Isle of Man also regard Tanzania as a reciprocating country despite the apparent absence of Tanzanian extension orders. A number of countries regard Zanzibar or 'His Britannic Majesty's Court at Zanzibar' as within the scope of their legislation,[8] and Zimbabwe regards Tanganyika (but not Zanzibar) as within its Act.

The Judgments Extension Ordinance[9] enables decrees for 'any debt' from courts in Kenya, Uganda, Malawi or Zanzibar to be transferred to and executed in Tanganyika. It is not clear whether this can be applied to maintenance or affiliation orders, bearing in mind the need at common law for orders to be 'final and conclusive' before being enforceable as judgment-debts.

1   Maintenance Orders (Enforcement) Decree, cap 11, RL 1961.
2   Maintenance Orders (Enforcement) Ordinance, cap 275, RL 1950.
3   Ss 141–144.
4   Act 5 of 1971.
5   S 141(2).
6   GN 4/1973.

7 GN 72/1976. The United Kingdom in designating Tanzania as a reciprocating country expressly excludes Zanzibar.
8 Botswana, Jersey, Kenya, Lesotho, Swaziland, and Uganda.
9 Cap 7, RL 1950.

Tonga

8.81   Tonga has no specific legislation on the enforcement of overseas main-tenance orders. The view of the Crown Solicitor's Office in Nuku'alofa is that the Maintenance Orders (Facilities for Enforcement) Act 1920 of the United Kingdom applies directly by virtue of the Civil Law Act of Tonga which authorises Tongan courts to apply statutes of general application which were in force in England on 18 October 1966.[1] The nature of the system of reciprocal extension orders does however make it difficult to accept this view; it would appear unlikely to carry weight in any other jurisdiction in the face of an Act applying to 'England' and not specifically extended to Tonga.

1   Letter from the Acting Crown Solicitor to the Legal Division of the Commonwealth Secretariat, 19 December 1978.

Trinidad and Tobago

8.82   The Maintenance Orders (Enforcement) Act[1] is on the 1920 model. It applies to England and Northern Ireland[2] and is capable of extension to 'any Commonwealth territory'.[3]

It has been extended[4] to Antigua and Barbuda,[5] Dominica,[6] Grenada, Guernsey,[7] Guyana, Jamaica, the Isle of Man,[8] Montserrat,[5] St Christopher and Nevis,[5] St Lucia, St Vincent and the Grenadines, and the Virgin Islands;[5] in all these cases reciprocal arrangements are in force. Separate extensions were made to all the states, but only one of the territories, of Australia;[9] despite this incomplete coverage, Trinidad and Tobago is a reciprocating country for the purposes of the Family Law Act 1975 of Australia.[10] The Trinidad and Tobago Act also extends to Anguilla,[5] Barbados and the Turks and Caicos Islands,[11] but no reciprocal arrangements are in force in those jurisdictions.

1   Cap 45:03, RL 1981.
2   S 2.
3   S 12.
4   The 1981 Edition of the Laws contains a Reciprocal Enforcement Maintenance Order (sic) which lists the relevant countries, without in most cases citing the proclamation by which the extension was effected. Where a citation is retained, it is noted below.
5   As part of the Leeward Islands.
6   Dominica was part of the Leeward Islands until 1940; as the extension of the Trinidad and Tobago Act to the Leeward Islands appears to date from 1923, it includes Dominica.
7   Proc 153/1956.
8   Proc 132/1964.
9   Covered are the Australian Capital Territory, New South Wales, Queensland, South Australia, Tasmania, Victoria and Western Australia (the last four by Proc 29/1974); the Northern Territory and Norfolk Island are not covered.
10   See para 8.14 above.
11   As part of Jamaica.

Tristan da Cunha

8.83   English law is generally applied in Tristan da Cunha,[1] and this includes relevant statute law. The need in the maintenance orders context for specific extension orders makes it difficult to determine what, if any, effect follows from the application of the statutory provisions themselves, Tristan da Cunha not being expressly mentioned in any extension orders made in England or else-where.

1 Interpretation and General Law Ordinance, cap 54 of Saint Helena as applied by the Tristan da Cunha Ordinances (Application) Ordinance, cap 118 (of Saint Helena), Sch 1.

Turks and Caicos Islands

8.84 The Maintenance Orders (Facilities for Enforcement) Ordinance[1] is on the 1920 model. It applies to the United Kingdom[2] and is capable of extension to 'any British possession or territory under Her Majesty's protection'.[3] No extension orders have been made, and although the Ordinance is derived from Jamaican legislation (the Islands forming part of Jamaica until 1959) it is believed that extension orders made in Jamaica are not in force under the Islands Ordinance.

Reciprocal arrangements are in force in the United Kingdom, and a large number of other countries[4] have legislation which is thought to extend to the Turks and Caicos Islands, having been made in respect of Jamaica before 1959. Jersey and the Isle of Man expressly extend their legislation to the Turks and Caicos Islands.

1 Cap 35, RL.
2 S 3, as amended by the Maintenance Orders (Facilities for Enforcement) (Amendment) Ordinance 1974, No 11 of 1974.
3 S 12.
4 Antigua and Barbuda, the Bahamas, Belize, Cayman Islands, Dominica, Grenada, Guernsey, Guyana, Montserrat, St Christopher and Nevis, St Lucia, St Vincent and the Grenadines, Trinidad and Tobago and the Virgin Islands.

Tuvalu

8.85 The Maintenance (Miscellaneous Provisions) Ordinance,[1] Part II of which contains provisions for the reciprocal enforcement of maintenance orders on the 1920 model, was originally enacted by the Gilbert and Ellice islands of which Tuvalu was formerly part. It extends to 'England and Ireland',[2] but can be further extended to 'any British possession or territory under Her Majesty's protection';[3] 'British possession' is defined[4] to mean 'any part of Her Majesty's dominions other than the United Kingdom'.

It has been extended to Fiji,[5] the Bailiwick of Guernsey,[6] Jersey,[7] New Zealand,[5] Papua New Guinea,[8] Solomon Islands,[5] and Western Samoa;[9] in all these cases reciprocal arrangements are in force. The Tuvalu Ordinance has also been extended to all the Australian jurisdictions (ie the Australian Capital Territory,[10] New South Wales,[11] Norfolk Island,[5] the Northern Territory,[5] Queensland,[5] South Australia,[12] Tasmania,[13] Victoria[14] and Western Australia[5]) but Tuvalu has not been designated as a reciprocating country for the purposes of the Family Law Act 1975 of Australia.[15] A designation of the former Gilbert and Ellice Islands by the Isle of Man is not reciprocated in Tuvalu.

1 Cap 4, RL 1978.
2 S 3. For the effect of this phrase, see para 8.04 above.
3 S 12.
4 In the Interpretation and General Clauses Ordinance.
5 Proc 4/1924.
6 LN 25/1965.
7 GN 29/1954.
8 LN 16/1966.

9   Proc 5/1930.
10   Proc 1/1929.
11   Proc 4/1924.
12   Proc 5/1927.
13   Proc 13/1927.
14   Proc 1/1927.
15   See para 8.14 above.

Uganda[1]

8.86   The Maintenance Orders Enforcement Act[2] is on the 1920 model. It applies to England, Northern Ireland and the Republic of Ireland; the application to the Republic of Ireland is, however, probably unrealistic, there being no legislation in the Republic effectively conferring reciprocal benefits on Uganda. The Uganda Act is capable of extension to any Commonwealth country.[3]

The Act has been extended[4] to Botswana, the Bailiwick of Guernsey, India, Jersey, Kenya, Lesotho, Malawi, the Isle of Man, Mauritius, New Zealand, Seychelles, Sri Lanka, Swaziland and Zambia; in all these cases reciprocal arrangements are in force. The Act has also been extended to the Australian Capital Territory, New South Wales, South Australia and Tasmania, but Uganda is not a reciprocating country for the purposes of the Family Law Act 1975 of Australia.[5] An extension to Zanzibar would appear to be inoperative.

1   The troubled political situation in Uganda in recent years makes it difficult to trace the development of the laws. No changes in relevant legislation subsequent to 1970 have been traced, but this information may not be complete.
2   Cap 49, RL.
3   S 9.
4   No citations are available.
5   See para 8.14 above.

United Kingdom

8.87   As some of the current legislation in the United Kingdom is in force as part of the law of England and Wales and of Northern Ireland, and not in Scotland, it is necessary to deal with this legislation separately.

(a) England and Wales, and Northern Ireland

The Maintenance Orders (Facilities for Enforcement) Act 1920[1] can be applied to 'any part of Her Majesty's dominions outside the United Kingdom'[2] and to 'any British protectorate'.[3] Although many countries to which the Act has been applied are now republics, or have their own monarchies, the Act remains applicable as a result of provisions in specific legislation passed in the United Kingdom whenever a change of status occurs.

The Act applies[4] to Anguilla,[5] Antigua and Barbuda,[5] Bahamas, Belize, Botswana, Brunei, certain Canadian jurisdictions (Newfoundland, Prince Edward Island and the Yukon Territory), Cayman Islands, Cyprus (including Akrotiri and Dhekelia), Dominica, the Falkland Islands, Gambia, Grenada, the Bailiwick of Guernsey, Guyana, Jamaica, Jersey, Kiribati,[6] Lesotho, Malawi, Malaysia,[7] the Isle of Man, Mauritius, Montserrat,[5] Nigeria, Papua,[8] St Christopher and Nevis, St Helena, St Lucia, St Vincent and the Grenadines, Seychelles, Sierra Leone, Solomon Islands, Sri Lanka, Swaziland, Trinidad and Tobago, Tuvalu,[6] Uganda, Virgin Islands,[5] Zambia and Zimbabwe. In all these cases reciprocal arrangements are in force; in a few countries[9] the

United Kingdom as a whole is designated as the reciprocating country despite the Act not being part of the law of Scotland. Extensions to the Falkland Islands Dependencies and to the Territories of Christmas Island and the Cocos (Keeling) Islands appear not to be reciprocated. Extensions to Aden, Somaliland Protectorate and Zanzibar appear to be inoperative.

(b) The whole United Kingdom

The Maintenance Orders (Reciprocal Enforcement) Act 1972[10] contains three different sets of provisions. Part I, a developed version of the 1920 Act, can be extended to 'any country or territory outside the United Kingdom',[11] and a country may be designated as a reciprocating country either generally or in respect of designated classes of order.

Part I has been extended in respect of all classes of maintenance order to Barbados,[12] Bermuda,[12] the Canadian Province of British Columbia,[13] Fiji,[14] Gibraltar,[13] Hong Kong,[14] Malta[12] and Singapore;[14] in all cases reciprocal arrangements are in force.

Limited designations under Part I exclude different classes of order in particular cases. The exclusions are noted here using the following symbols:

A = affiliation orders
B = provisional affiliation orders
C = maintenance orders of the description contained in paragraph (b) of the definition of 'maintenance order' in s 21(1) of the Act, ie 'an affiliation order or order consequent upon an affiliation order, being an order which provides for the payment by a person adjudged, found or declared to be a child's father of expenses incidental to the child's birth or, where the child has died, of his funeral expenses'
D = orders obtained by or in favour of a public authority.

Such designations refer to all the Australian states, mainland territories and Norfolk Island (all D),[15] the Canadian provinces of Alberta (BCD),[14] Manitoba (B),[13] New Brunswick (ACD),[12] Nova Scotia (CD),[13] Ontario (C),[13] and Saskatchewan (BC)[14] and the Northwest Territories (ACD),[12] Ghana (AC),[12] India (ACD),[12] Kenya (AC),[12] New Zealand (BC),[13] the Republic of South Africa (AC),[12] Tanzania excluding Zanzibar (ACD)[14] and the Turks and Caicos Islands (ACD).[14] Reciprocal designations of the United Kingdom exist in all except South Africa, which appears not to have amended its legislation to include Scotland; the Tanzanian designation of the United Kingdom does not in fact confer full reciprocal benefits owning to the limited nature of the Tanzanian provisions.[16]

Under s 40 of the Act, Part I of the Act may be applied with exceptions, adaptations and modifications prescribed by Order in Council in respect of certain countries. One version has been applied in respect of the Republic of Ireland[17] and a second, more radically modified, in respect of 'Hague Convention countries', that is[18] Czechoslovakia, France, Italy,[19] Luxembourg,[20] Netherlands (including the Netherlands Antilles),[21] Norway, Portugal, Sweden and Switzerland.

Part II of the Act, giving effect to the United Nations Convention on the Recovery Abroad of Maintenance 1956 applies to the following countries which have been designated as 'convention countries':[22] Algeria, Austria, Barbados, Belgium, Brazil, Central African Republic, Chile, Czechoslovakia, Denmark, Ecuador, Finland, France,[23] Germany (the Federal Republic and

West Berlin), Greece, Haiti, Holy See, Hungary, Israel, Italy, Luxembourg, Monaco, Morocco, Netherlands (including the Netherlands Antilles), Niger, Norway, Pakistan, Philippines, Poland, Portugal, Spain, Sri Lanka, Sweden, Switzerland,[24] Tunisia, Turkey, Upper Volta and Yugoslavia. A slightly modified version is applied[25] to specified states of the United States: Arizona, Arkansas, California, Colorado, Connecticut, Delaware,[26] Florida, Idaho, Illinois, Indiana, Kansas, Kentucky, Louisiana, Maine, Maryland,[26] Massachusetts,[26] Michigan, Minnesota, Missouri,[26] Montana, Nebraska, Nevada, New Hampshire, New Mexico, New York, North Carolina, North Dakota, Ohio, Oklahoma, Oregon, Pennsylvania, Rhode Island,[26] South Dakota,[26] Tennessee,[26] Texas, Utah,[26] Vermont, Virginia, Washington, Wisconsin and Wyoming.

1   10 & 11 Geo 5, c 33.
2   S 12(1).
3   S 12(2).
4   Maintenance Orders (Facilities for Enforcement) Order 1959, SI 1959/377 as amended by SI 1974/557, SI 1975/2188 and SI 1979/116 and by the Pakistan Act 1973, s 4(4).
5   As part of the Leeward Islands.
6   As part of the Gilbert and Ellice Islands.
7   The references are to 'the Federation of Malaya', 'North Borneo' (ie Sabah) and Sarawak.
8   But *not* New Guinea.
9   Anguilla, Falkland Islands, Gambia, Papua and Swaziland.
10   1972 cap 18.
11   S 1(1).
12   Reciprocal Enforcement of Maintenance Orders (Designation of Reciprocating Countries) Order 1975, SI 1975/2187.
13   Reciprocal Enforcement of Maintenance Orders (Designation of Reciprocating Countries) Order 1974, SI 1974/556.
14   Reciprocal Enforcement of Maintenance Orders (Designation of Reciprocating Countries) Order 1979, SI 1979/115.
15   Australian Capital Territory, New South Wales, Northern Territory, Queensland, South Australia, Tasmania and Victoria: SI 1974/556 as amended by SI 1979/115; Norfolk Island and Western Australia: SI 1979/115.
16   See para 8.80 above.
17   Reciprocal Enforcement of Maintenance Orders (Republic of Ireland) Order 1974, SI 1974/2140.
18   For the modifications see Reciprocal Enforcement of Maintenance Orders (Hague Convention Countries) Order 1979, SI 1979/1317. The countries are designated, subject to the following notes, in Sch 1.
19   Inserted by SI 1981/1674.
20   Inserted by SI 1981/1845.
21   Inserted by SI 1981/837.
22   S 25(1). The designation is by the Recovery Abroad of Maintenance (Convention Countries) Order 1975, SI 1975/423.
23   Including Guadeloupe, French Guiana, Martinique and Reunion (overseas departments of France); and the Comoro Archipelago (most of which is now independent), French Polynesia, the French Territory of the Afars and Issas (now independent), New Caledonia and its dependencies, and St Pierre and Miquelon.
24   Inserted by SI 1978/279.
25   Recovery of Maintenance (United States of America) Order 1979, SI 1979/1314.
26   Inserted by SI 1981/606.

Vanuatu

8.88   Vanuatu has no legislation on the reciprocal enforcement of maintenance orders; indeed, it has no matrimonial causes legislation of any sort, one result of the fragmentary nature of written law under the former Anglo-French Condominium administration (of the New Hebrides).

Virgin Islands

8.89 The (British) Virgin Islands were until 1957 a presidency of the Leeward Islands. The Maintenance Orders (Facilities for Enforcement) Act,[1] which is on the 1920 model, was originally enacted by the Legislature of the Leeward Islands. It extends to England and Northern Ireland[2] and is capable of extension to 'any British possession or territory under Her Majesty's protection'.[3]

The Act has been extended to Antigua and Barbuda,[4] the Bahamas,[5] Belize,[6] Bermuda,[5] Dominica,[7] Grenada,[5] Guyana,[8] Jamaica,[9] Jersey,[10] Montserrat,[4] St Christopher and Nevis,[4] St Lucia,[5] St Vincent and the Grenadines[5] and Trinidad and Tobago;[5] in all these cases reciprocal arrangements are in force. The Act also extends to Barbados[5] and the Turks and Caicos Islands,[11] but no reciprocal arrangements are currently in force in those territories. The Act has also been extended to all the states of Australia (New South Wales is the subject of two separate extension orders) and the Australian Capital Territory,[12] but the Virgin Islands are not a reciprocating country for the purposes of the Family Law Act 1975 of Australia.[13] A designation of the Virgin Islands by the Isle of Man is not reciprocated.

1   Cap 46, RL 1961.
2   S 3.
3   S 12. For this phrase, see para 8.02 above.
4   SRO 8/1957.
5   LI Gaz, 30 August 1923.
6   LI Sub Leg (1924).
7   SRO (LI) 14/1945.
8   LI Gaz, 9 August 1922.
9   LI Gaz, 14 May 1925.
10 SRO (LI) 44/1954.
11 LI Gaz, 14 May 1925 as part of Jamaica.
12 SRO 39/1972 for all except New South Wales (also LI Sub Leg (1924)) and the Australian Capital Territory (SRO (LI) 6/1929).
13 See para 8.14 above.

Western Samoa

8.90 Part IX of the Maintenance and Affiliation Act 1967[1] contains provisions corresponding to those in the Destitute Persons Amendment Act 1963 of New Zealand,[2] an earlier version of the current New Zealand legislation. Unlike the more recent versions of that legislation, the Western Samoan Act consistently excludes orders made in an affiliation order.[3]

The provisions apply automatically in respect of all Commonwealth countries, defined[4] to include not only members of the Commonwealth but also every territory for whose international relations the Government of any Commonwealth country is responsible and the Republic of Ireland. Section 71 enables the Head of State to apply ss 62–70 to other, non-Commonwealth, countries; s 72 contains limited provisions as to the registration of maintenance orders made in foreign, and specifically in non-Commonwealth, countries designated by the Head of State; neither of these powers has been exercised.

1   No 7 of 1967.
2   No 63 of 1963, repealed by the Domestic Proceedings Act 1968 (New Zealand).
3   See s 62 (registration of Commonwealth country orders), s 64 (confirmation of provisional Commonwealth country orders) and s 73 (provisional orders for confirmation overseas).
4   S 2(1).

Zambia

8.91 The Maintenance Orders (Enforcement) Act[1] is on the 1920 model. It applies to 'England and Ireland'[2] and can be extended to 'any country within the Commonwealth'.[3] It has been extended to Botswana,[4] the Cook Islands,[5] the Bailiwick of Guernsey,[6] India,[7] Jersey,[8] Kenya,[9] Lesotho,[4] Malawi,[10] the Isle of Man,[11] New Zealand,[5] Nigeria,[12] Niue[5] and Uganda;[13] in all these cases reciprocal arrangements are in force. The Zambian Act was also extended to 'Gold Coast Colony,'[14] but Zambia is not a reciprocating country under the Ghanaian legislation. The Zambian Act has also been extended to all the states and mainland territories of Australia,[15] and Zambia is a reciprocating country for the purposes of the Family Law Act 1975 of Australia.

South Africa regards Zambia as a reciprocating country but the Zambian Act does not extend to South Africa, and indeed cannot be so extended in view of its limitation to Commonwealth countries. Similarly, Zimbabwe treats Zambia as a reciprocating country despite the fact that Zambia has not applied its Act to Zimbabwe; there is provision for the reciprocal enforcement of affiliation orders as between Zambia, Zimbabwe and Malawi, a survival of their former federal relationship,[16] but other types of maintenance order are expressly excluded. Singapore regards Zambia as a reciprocating country, but again there appears to be no designation of Singapore by Zambia.

1 Cap 212, RL.
2 S 3. For a discussion of this term, see para 8.02 above.
3 S 11.
4 GN 64/1922.
5 GN 341/1963.
6 GN 162/1957.
7 GN 318/1954.
8 GN 307/1953.
9 GN 15/1925.
10 GN 169/1924.
11 GN 14/1952.
12 GN 62/1946.
13 GN 177/1924.
14 GN 218/1946.
15 New South Wales (GN 30/1925), Queensland, South Australia and Tasmania (SI 267/1970), Victoria (GN 49/1927), Western Australia (GN 24/1955), Australian Capital Territory (GN 58/1929), and the Northern Territory (SI 16/1972).
16 Service of Process and Execution of Judgments Act.

Zimbabwe

8.92 The Maintenance Orders (Facilities for Enforcement) Act[1] is on the 1920 model. It applies to England and Northern Ireland and can be extended to 'any territory within the Commonwealth, including Scotland'.[2] It has been extended to Botswana,[3] several Canadian jurisdictions,[4] Cook Islands,[5] the Bailiwick of Guernsey,[6] India,[7] Jersey,[8] Kenya,[9] Lesotho,[3] Malawi,[10] the Isle of Man,[11] New Zealand,[12] Papua (but not New Guinea)[13] and Swaziland;[3] in all these cases reciprocal arrangements exist. Extensions to 'Tanganyika'[14] and Zambia[15] appear not to be reciprocated. Similarly, extensions to several Australian jurisdictions exist,[16] but Zimbabwe is not a reciprocating country for the purposes of the Family Law Act 1975 of Australia. An extension to Aden[6] is now inoperative. Orders were made applying the Zimbabwe Act to South Africa[17] and South-West Africa (Namibia),[18] and Zimbabwe is treated as a reciprocating country by South Africa; but the position is unclear in view of the limitation of the Zimbabwe Act to other Commonwealth jurisdictions and the express suspension of the reciprocal arrangements with South Africa by the illegal régime in Southern Rhodesia during its tenure of power.

1   Cap 36, RL, 1974.
2   S 2.
3   GN 324/1922. Pre-1953 orders appear to have been consolidated in GN 197/1953, but it has not proved possible to obtain the text of that Notice.
4   GN 30/1957 lists Alberta, British Columbia, Manitoba, Newfoundland, Northwest Territories, Ontario, Prince Edward Island, Saskatchewan and Yukon Territory and GN 467/1956 designated Nova Scotia; reciprocal arrangements exist in all except the two first-named jurisdictions.
5   GN 260/1949.
6   GN 373/1957.
7   GN 394/1956.
8   GN 839/1953.
9   GN 38/1925.
10 GN 96/1926.
11 GN 819/1951.
12 GN 68/1925.
13 GN 108/1956.
14 GN 251/1959.
15 GN 572/1922.
16 New South Wales (GN 634/1924), Queensland (GN 654/1924), South Australia (GN 103/1926), Victoria (GN 626/1926), Western Australia (GN 39/1925) and the Australian Capital Territory (GN 148/1929).
17 GN 338/1923.
18 GN 25/1955.

Republic of South Africa

8.93   South Africa is of course no longer part of the Commonwealth and for that reason the continued designation of 'the Union of South Africa' or of the Republic by a number of Commonwealth jurisdictions for the purpose of their legislation on the reciprocal enforcement of maintenance orders is of doubtful validity. It might however be useful to set out the position in South African law.

The Reciprocal Enforcement of Maintenance Orders Act[1] is a revised version, still recognisably on the 1920 model, of legislation dating from 1923.[2] Countries to which the earlier legislation applied are deemed to be 'proclaimed countries' for the purposes of the current Act. Proclaimed countries include South-West Africa (Namibia)[3] and the 'homeland' states of Bophuthatswana[4] and Venda,[5] which are regarded by South Africa as independent; the states and mainland territories of Australia except Tasmania,[6] and also the Cocos (Keeling) Islands, Botswana, California,[7] certain Canadian jurisdictions,[8] Cyprus, England, Fiji, Guernsey, Hong Kong,[9] Jersey,[10] Kenya, Lesotho, Malawi, the Isle of Man, Mauritius, New Zealand, Nigeria, Northern Ireland, Saint Helena, Sarawak, Singapore, Swaziland, Zambia, and Zimbabwe. South Africa is a country with restricted reciprocity for the purposes of the Family Law Act 1975 of Australia. Subject to the doubts caused by South Africa's departure from the Commonwealth, reciprocal arrangements appear to exist in all the Commonwealth countries listed except Zambia and Zimbabwe. In addition, India, Malaysia and Saskatchewan regard South Africa as a reciprocating country despite the apparent lack of reciprocity except in so far as the South African Act applies to one state (Sarawak) of Malaysia.

1   No 80 of 1963.
2   The original Act was the Maintenance Orders Act 1923, No 15 of 1923.

3   Proc R 345, 30 September 1960 (a consolidating instrument). The 1963 Act is itself now in force as part of the law of South-West Africa (Namibia): s 10A, inserted by Reciprocal Enforcement of Maintenance Orders Amendment Act 1970 (No 40 of 1970), s 6.
4   Proc R 105, 5 May 1978.
5   Proc R 310, 28 December 1979.
6   Proc R 345, 30 September 1960 (a consolidating instrument), which lists all the following countries unless otherwise indicated.
7   Proc R 1, 8 January 1971.
8   Alberta (Proc R 175, 13 August 1971), British Columbia (Proc R 175, 3 August 1962), Ontario (Proc R 345, 30 September 1960) and the Northwest Territories (Proc R 160, 19 June 1970).
9   Proc R 274, 1963.
10   Proc R 131, 19 May 1961.

CHAPTER 9

Custody of Children

Introduction

9.01 It is the common experience of judges and practitioners in many jurisdictions that with changing social attitudes towards divorce and the growing
prevalence of 'no-fault' divorces, divorce litigation centres increasingly upon
questions of property and of the custody of children. The bitterness of disputes
over the children is readily understood. After the pain of marital breakdown,
the care of the children of the marriage offers consolation and a continuing
focus for affection, for hope for the future. A custody contest can see projected
all the tensions in the parents' relationship, each party justifying his or her case
by the belief that what is being done is for the child's sake, to prevent the
serious harm which would surely be the result of continued influence by the
other party on the child's future development.

The whole matter is much more difficult when the dispute crosses national
boundaries. The factor of distance is important in itself: what had hitherto
been an amicable separation with generous access for the non-custodial parent
may be transformed by the decision of the custodial parent to move to a
different country perhaps thousands of miles away. Access becomes a meaningless fiction, and the custody issue is decisive.

Legal factors also come into play. Different countries may adopt different
approaches to the custody issue: one may regard the father as having a natural
priority; another may favour the mother's claims, especially in the case of girls
or young children; apparent agreement that such presumptions are unsound
and should give way to a test of the 'welfare of the child' may conceal differences
in actual practice. It may be tempting for one party to a dispute to seek the
forum most likely to give a favourable ruling; and, faced with an unfavourable
ruling in one jurisdiction, to seek to re-open the matter in another, playing the
courts of one country off against those of the other.

This chapter is concerned with these international cases. It must be stressed
that the questions to be examined are not limited to the recognition in one
country of custody *orders* made in another, although that is the issue most
frequently relevant. The exercise of custody rights in a country for a period of
time, whether they are rights created by a court order, or by a separation
agreement, or simply through the exercise of parental responsibilities, creates
a situation, a settled environment within which a child is growing up. If the
continued existence of that situation is ended, the child being removed to a
second country (either by the (legal or de facto) custodian or by abduction by
another person), the courts of that second country must decide what weight to
give to the previous history; the existence of a court order is not decisive in
setting the limits of the problem.

In the conflict of laws rules of Commonwealth countries, questions of the
rights and duties of parents and guardians and disputes as to custody are seen
as being governed by the lex fori. This does not mean that the appointment of

a guardian by a foreign court will not be recognised. A guardian appointed by the courts of the country in which the child was to be found at the time, or of which he was a national, will be entitled to act in any jurisdiction, but the courts of that jurisdiction remain free to appoint a local guardian of their own choosing.[1] The general position appears to be the same in custody matters; a court is never obliged at common law to enforce a foreign custody order, which is simply part of the history of the case before it. It is the great variety of other circumstances contributing to that history which makes for the difficulty of the present topic.

The first part of the chapter attempts to review the position at common law. Attention is then given to a number of attempts in Commonwealth jurisdictions to regulate aspects of the matter by statutory provision, and to the Hague Convention on the Civil Aspects of International Child Abduction, 1980, which is already seen as likely to be influential in Commonwealth legislation and practice.

1   See *Johnstone v Beattie* (1843) 10 Cl & Fin 42; *Stuart v Bute* (1861) 9 HLC at 440; *Nugent v Vetzera* (1866) LR 2 Eq 704; *Re P(GE)* (*an infant*) [1965] Ch 568, [1964] 3 All ER 977, CA; and generally Dicey and Morris *The Conflict of Laws* (10th edn, 1980) pp 437-443.

A. THE COMMON LAW POSITION

Some illustrative cases

9.02   It may be helpful to the reader to present at this stage the outline facts of a number of cases to indicate the range of situations which present themselves.

1. Children were born in Alberta to a married couple domiciled in that province. The marriage broke down and in 1966 the divorce court awarded custody to the father, and later a possession order when the mother delayed delivery up of the children. The mother commenced proceedings in Alberta in 1968 in a fresh attempt to obtain custody, but they were adjourned. In 1969 the mother, with a man friend, arrived at the father's house and forcibly removed the children; the two men came to blows. The mother and her friend took the children to British Columbia, and the mother sought custody in the Supreme Court of British Columbia.[1]

2. A child was born in England in 1962. His parents' marriage was dissolved in 1965 on account of the husband's adultery with a New Zealand lady whom he subsequently married. The mother had custody but the father had access which continued during a period of residence in Cyprus. In 1972, the father and his second family emigrated to New Zealand. The child spent six weeks with them in December 1972–January 1973 and again in July–September 1973. At the end of the second period, the boy, now twelve years of age, indicated that he did not want to return to England. The father sought custody in the Supreme Court of New Zealand.[2]

3. Two children were born in California in 1966 and 1968 respectively. After an adulterous affair lasting some three years, the father left leaving the children with their mother. He petitioned for divorce, asking that the mother be given custody, but on finding that his wife had a drink problem he amended the

petition to seek custody. Some months later, after a court-appointed social worker had recommended that the mother be given custody, the father removed them to British Columbia, hoping to avoid a costly and possibly unsuccessful custody dispute in California. Fourteen months later, his application for custody was heard in the Supreme Court of British Columbia; there was evidence that the mother was now living in 'an untidily kept shack' in an area unserved by water. In the meantime, the California court, ignorant of the children's abduction, had given custody to the mother and prohibited their removal from that state.[3]

In all these cases there had at some stage been a determination of the custody issue by a competent foreign court; in some cases this was a recent decision, but in case 2 a number of years had elapsed. Cases 1 and 3 involve an abduction by one parent of the child, but in the latter case this was not in breach of any final court order, that being made only after the removal of the children. In none of the cases were the children born in the jurisdiction whose courts were now seised of the case; in cases 2 and 3 the de facto custodian had substantial links with that country.

In all cases the court now seised of the matter had jurisdiction, if only because of the presence of the child. The initial question is whether that jurisdiction should be exercised in such a way as to lead the court into a full examination of the merits de novo; or should the child be returned to the country from which he had come, either because the foreign decision should be given considerable persuasive weight or so that any re-examination of the case should be in a forum which could be regarded as a more appropriate one.

1   The facts are those of *Re Lyon and Lyon* (1969) 10 DLR(3d) 287.
2   The facts are those of *E v F* [1974] 2 NZLR 435.
3   The facts are those of *Walker v Walker* [1974] 3 WWR 48 (BC).

McKee v McKee

9.03   On this question, the Canadian case of *McKee v McKee*, which went on appeal to the Judicial Committee of the Privy Council, remains the leading Commonwealth authority. It is cited in the great majority of reported cases, though not always to the same effect. For this reason, and because of the illuminating divergence of judicial attitudes found in the case, it requires consideration at some length.

The child Terry McKee was born in 1940. In 1942 custody was given to his father in divorce proceedings in California, but in 1945 the Superior Court of California gave custody to the mother, finding that the child was being kept in unsuitable conditions, in a place subject to severe weather conditions and in the charge of aged hired servants. This decision was affirmed by a majority in the Court of Appeal[1] and the father's right to custody finally expired in January 1947.[2] Before then he had brought the child to Ontario. The mother brought habeas corpus proceedings in Ontario. Holding that the Californian order was not conclusive, especially as California was not, at the material times, the domicile of the child, Wells J decided that despite the 'obvious and flagrant breach of a solemn agreement' by the father, the issue of custody required a consideration of the child's welfare. On the merits, custody was restored to the father.[3]

Wells J's decision was affirmed by a majority in the Ontario Court of Appeal.[4] The majority, strongly influenced by the English decision of *Re B's*

Settlement,[5] held that the trial judge applied the right test and, on the merits, that the changes in circumstances between 1945 and 1947 justified his order. Robertson CJO dissented:

'It is my opinion that the Courts of this Province should leave the dispute regarding the custody of the infant to the Courts of the country to which these people belong. It is not a question of jurisdiction, but rather one of comity between friendly nations'.[6]

The Supreme Court of Canada, by a 4–3 majority, reversed the Ontario courts. The minority (Taschereau, Kellock and Fauteux JJ) rested upon the right of the child, whatever the merits or otherwise of his father's conduct, to the protection of the law of Ontario and its welfare principle.[7] The majority (Kerwin, Estey, Lock and Cartwright JJ) ordered the return of the child to his mother in the United States. Cartwright J recognised that foreign custody orders were not binding, and that the welfare principle was well-established. But he denied that the losing party to a custody dispute in one jurisdiction could, by the simple expedient of taking the child with him across the border, become entitled to have the whole question retried in the courts of the second jurisdiction and to have them reach a new and independent judgment as to what was best for the child.[8] Putting the point another way, comity and the sound administration of justice required courts to enforce the custody orders made after full enquiry by competent courts elsewhere.

The Privy Council reversed the judgment of the Supreme Court of Canada.[9] That fact has often been interpreted, not least in the Canadian courts, as meaning that Cartwright J's proposition was rejected, and therefore that the converse was true; that the courts of the country to which a child was abducted were required to make a full enquiry into the merits. In truth, the Judicial Committee decided no such thing. They held that Cartwright J had addressed himself to the wrong issue. What had actually happened was that the Ontario courts had chosen to re-examine the merits; the real issue was not whether that was *obligatory*, just because the child was there, but whether it was *permissible* at all, and the eventual decision was that it was indeed permissible. As Lord Simonds put it:

'Once it is conceded that the court of Ontario had jurisdiction to entertain the question of custody and that it need not blindly follow an order made by a foreign court, the consequence cannot be escaped that it must form an independent judgment on the question, though in doing so it will give proper weight to the foreign judgment. What is the proper weight will depend on the circumstances of each case. It may be that, if the matter comes before the court of Ontario within a very short time of the foreign judgment, and there is no new circumstance to be considered, the weight may be so great that such an order as the Supreme Court made [ie for the immediate return of the child to the custodian under the foreign order] ... could be justified. But if so, it would not be because the court of Ontario, having assumed jurisdiction, then abdicated it, but because in the exercise of its jurisdiction it determined what was for the benefit of the infant.'[10]

It is not always recognised that the Privy Council's decision in *McKee v McKee* did not require the court to re-examine all aspects of the case. It is true that Lord Simonds said in a much-quoted passage[11] that there was 'no via media between the abdication of jurisdiction ... and the consideration of the case on its merits', and many courts have been misled by that. It is, however, quite clear from the longer passage cited that in some cases at least evidence of the foreign court's order and of no change of circumstances will be sufficient to enable the court to order the child's return; in one sense the merits have been examined—and, incidentally, the duty of the court, mandatory in many jurisdictions, to give first consideration to the welfare of the child has been honoured—but the full circumstances on which the foreign court grounded its order are not reopened.

Understood in this sense, *McKee v McKee* leaves courts with a great deal of freedom; or, put another way, gives so little guidance that it is not surprising that courts while protesting loyalty to the principles of the case have adopted a range of different stances.

1   174 P 2d 18 (Cal, 1946).
2   Not 1946 as stated by Wells J, [1947] 4 DLR 579 at 583.
3   *Re McKee* [1947] 4 DLR 579 (Ont).
4   *Re McKee* [1948] 4 DLR 339 (Ont CA).
5   [1940] Ch 54.
6   [1948] 4 DLR 339 at 345.
7   *McKee v McKee* [1950] 3 DLR 577 at 596 (Sup Ct Can).
8   Ibid, at 582-3.
9   [1951] AC 352, [1951] 1 All ER 942, PC.
10 Ibid, at 364.
11 Ibid, at 365. See *Re H (infants)* [1966] 1 All ER 886 at 891, per Willmer LJ commenting on the 'inconsistency' of Lord Simond's remark with other passages in his opinion.

Review on the merits

9.04   In a number of countries, *McKee v McKee* has been interpreted as requiring a full review of the case on the merits. For example, in *Menasce v Menasce*,[1] a court in Zaire (then the Belgian Congo) had given custody to the mother. The father eventually kidnapped the child and took him to Prince Edward Island. In habeas corpus proceedings the trial judge ordered the immediate return of the child without reviewing any evidence as to the welfare of the child in the present circumstances; on appeal the Supreme Court ordered a trial on the merits, citing *McKee v McKee*. A similar case is *Re Stalder and Wood*.[2] The Court of Session in Scotland had given custody to the father, but the mother was allowed to take the child for a holiday in Canada, having given assurances as to its return. In the event, she remained in Manitoba. The Manitoba Court of Appeal, by a majority, and without citing any previous authority, reversed the trial judge's peremptory order for the return of the child to Scotland and ordered a trial on the merits in Manitoba.

The courts of New Zealand have adopted a similar stance. In *Re B (infants)*[3] the parents (he an Italian by origin, she a New Zealander) had lived in New South Wales until the wife, without warning the husband, returned to her parents in New Zealand taking the children with her. The husband obtained an interim order for custody in New South Wales and applied to the New Zealand court for an immediate order granting him leave to remove the children from the jurisdiction. He relied upon dicta in English cases disapproving of kidnapping and emphasising the importance of comity,[4] but Haslam J giving the judgment of the Court of Appeal said this:

'It would appear that, although in England the prevalence of "kidnapping" cases has reached the proportions of a local problem, the Courts of this country will prefer, in view of the terms of our Guardianship Act,[5] the opinion of the Privy Council delivered by Lord Simonds in *McKee v McKee*, where the Judicial Committee re-affirmed that the "infant's welfare is the paramount consideration" and that the Court in whose jurisdiction the child happens to be should "give affect to the foreign judgment without further enquiry" only when it is "in the best interests of that infant that it [ie the Court] should not look beyond the circumstances in which its [ie the foreign] jurisdiction was invoked".'[6]

Despite some hardship to the father, the Court of Appeal upheld an order directing an early trial on the merits of the mother's application for custody.

In *E v F*,[7] the facts of which have already been given,[8] the trial judge indicated that he would have ordered the return of the child to England in order to do justice to the mother's position, were it not for *Re B*; having been led into a review of the merits of the case, he found that he had to allow the child to remain in New Zealand.[9]

1   (1965) 40 DLR (2d) 114 (PEI).
2   (1975) 54 DLR (3d) 157 (Man CA).
3   [1971] NZLR 143, CA.
4   *Re T (infants)* [1968] Ch 704 at 714, CA, per Harman LJ; *Re E (D) (an infant)* [1967] Ch 287, [1967] 1 All ER 329, per Cross J (affd [1967] Ch 761, [1967] 2 All ER 881, CA); see para 9.06 below.
5   Ie Guardianship Act 1968 (NZ), s 23(1) (Welfare of the child the first and paramount consideration).
6   [1971] NZLR 143 at 145 CA.
7   [1974] 2 NZLR 435.
8   Para 9.02 above.
9   See also *Re Woodhams (infants)* [1952] GLR 313 (NZ) (*McKee v McKee* followed; return of child ordered after review on merits, some children having actually died while in care of abductor); *C v C* [1973] 1 NZLR 129 (*Re B* followed; child returned after review of merits).

No review on the merits; peremptory return

9.05   Canadian commentators detect a tendency towards an increasingly narrow interpretation of *McKee v McKee*. '*McKee v McKee* stresses that the paramount consideration in matters of custody is the welfare of the child. The courts today stress that the welfare of the child is generally better served if he is ordered to be returned to his place of ordinary residence and custody determined there'.[1] 'The application of judicial creativity together with the adoption of the viewpoint that *McKee v McKee* need not be followed leaves considerable flexibility for a court to refuse jurisdiction on custody matters where a foreign order is at issue except in the very exceptional or altered circumstances where the child is endangered in some way'.[2]

In part these comments are based on the judgment of a local judge of the British Columbia Supreme Court in *Re Lyon and Lyon*.[3] Kennedy Co CtJ held that in view of the abolition of appeals to the Judicial Committee of the Privy Council, Canadian courts were not 'absolutely committed' to follow Privy Council decisions reached before that abolition. He expressly preferred the majority view of the Supreme Court of Canada in *McKee v McKee*[4] and so 'refused jurisdiction'.

Other decisions, while not rejecting the authority of *McKee v McKee*, interpret it as allowing peremptory return without a consideration of the merits, even in cases where no final custody order had been made in the foreign country concerned,[5] or as indicating a need for a review of the merits only where the court was convinced that to return the child at once 'at the very least, would be gravely prejudicial' to the child.[6] Speaking of cases involving different provinces of Canada, Miller J of the Supreme Court of Alberta has observed:

'Since the *McKee* decision the ability of people to move from one jurisdiction to another has markedly increased and a tendency is evident, from recent decisions, for courts to decline to exercise jurisdiction, even if it is available, on the basis that the court of the

Province of ordinary residence is probably in a better position, because of the availability of witnesses, to determine the matter.'[7]

Such forum conveniens considerations are, of course, easier to reconcile with loyalty to a welfare principle than is a policy of returning children as a sanction against the growing practice of abduction or kidnapping.

1 Christine Davies 'Interprovincial Custody' (1978) 56 CBR 17 at p 23.
2 J-G Castel *Canadian Conflict of Laws* vol 2, p 230.
3 (1969) 10 DLR (3d) 287.
4 [1950] 3 DLR 577 (Sup Ct Can); revsd [1951] AC 352, [1951] 1 All ER 942, PC.
5 *Prosser-Jones v Prosser-Jones* (1972) 7 RFL 150 (Man) (child taken to Manitoba in breach of undertaking, divorce proceedings being pending in England, returned); *Furjan v Furjan* (1975) 23 RFL 321 (PEI) (child taken to PEI in breach of Ontario separation agreement; return ordered as unfair to let abductor profit).
6 *Dalshaug v Dalshaug* (1973) 41 DLR (3d) 475 (Alta S Ct, App Div) (children taken to Alberta in breach of Saskatchewan custody order; return ordered in the absence of evidence of prejudice). See also *Re Loughran and Loughran* (1972) 30 DLR (3d) 385 (Ont CA), and the Canadian cases cited in the next paragraph.
7 *Hilborn v Hilborn* (1977) 2 RFL (2d) 5 (Alta).

Return of the abducted child unless grave risk of harm

9.06 A related approach which has found favour at different times in many jurisdictions is to enforce what might be called 'foreign custody rights' as against a kidnapper or abductor by ordering the prompt return of the child in the absence of clear evidence that this would expose the child to the risk of serious harm.

In some jurisdictions this was the usual rule adopted in pre-*McKee* days. In South Africa and Zimbabwe, for example, a common formulation in early cases was that foreign custody orders would be enforced unless there was clear evidence that the person given custody under the foreign order was 'an improper person' to enjoy it.[1] This approach was rejected in Zimbabwe in 1954 in *Ferrers v Ferrers*[2] as inconsistent with the Privy Council's decision in *McKee v McKee*,[3] which required the court now seised of the case to form an independent judgment on the evidence before it, and *Ferrers v Ferrers* has been repeatedly applied in Southern African jurisdictions.[4]

The English Court of Appeal, however, adopted something akin to the earlier approach in *Re H (infants)*[5] where a mother had brought children to England in breach of an agreement which had been incorporated into a divorce decree granted in Mexico and also in a consent order in the State of New York, where the family had been resident. The Court of Appeal approved the observation of Cross J at first instance that 'the sudden and unauthorised removal of children from one country to another is far too frequent nowadays, and ... it is the duty of all courts in all countries to do all they can to ensure that the wrong-doer does not gain an advantage by his wrongdoing'[6] and approved equally of his order for the return of the children for a full trial of the merits in New York. This approval emphasised the judge's satisfaction that the children would come to no harm if their father took them to New York; it was also noted that this was the right course even if, after the hearing in New York, the ultimate decision was to return the children to England and largely to sever their links with their father. *McKee v McKee* though 'treated with the utmost respect'[7] was given little weight.

A similar approach was applied by the English Court of Appeal in *Re T (infants)*,[8] a case in which no court order existed in Alberta, the jurisdiction from which the child had been abducted. 'The removal of children from their home and their surroundings by one of their parents who happens to live in or have connections with another country is a thing against which the court should set its face. . . . Unless there is good reason to the contrary, it should not countenance proceedings of that kind'.[9]

The 'good reasons to the contrary' were not, it seems, limited to factors adverse to the person claiming the return of the child. In *Re E(D) (an infant)*,[10] the mother, although she had at one stage been deprived of the custody of the child by a New Mexico court on the ground of unfitness, was described as 'of charm and intelligence'; but, while the *Re H* principle was again reasserted, the Court of Appeal accepted that on the facts, the child's father having died and its only real relationship being with its English aunt, it would be 'disastrous' to terminate that relationship by ordering a return to the United States.

There are other cases which suggest that the loyalty of the English courts to the *Re H* doctrine was somewhat precarious. An example is *Re T A (infants)*[11] in which four children, three of whom (the youngest aged 11) had lived since birth in Malta and the fourth had lived there for 14 years, were abducted by their mother to England during an adjournment in Maltese proceedings concerning access, custody having been given to the father in a separation agreement. Rees J repeated the *Re H* principle, that where children ordinarily resident abroad had been removed to England by force, stealth or fraud the court would order their immediate return to the home country unless positively satisfied that to do so would cause real danger to the mental, physical or moral well-being of the children concerned. But the result of the case was that the children were to remain with their mother in England. Although much was made of the father's alleged adultery with his maidservants, the mother's adultery was not considered as affecting her fitness to keep the children. The key factors, to judge from the short report available, was that 'the children were now extremely hostile towards the father' and were 'settled happily in England'. No doubt the ages of the children made their views carry significant weight, but the supposedly governing principle seems to have been set aside quite lightly, for a hearing in Malta could have led to a similar result.

The English approach was reviewed in an important judgment of Buckley LJ in the Court of Appeal in *Re L (minors)*[12] in which the developing principles were tested against the decisions of the Privy Council in *McKee v McKee*[13] and of the House of Lords in *J v C*[14] where the primacy of the welfare principle in wardship and custody cases had been re-emphasised. In *Re L (minors)* the decision on the merits was to uphold an order returning children to Germany, whence their mother had removed them (but not in breach of any existing court order). The importance of the case lies in the passage in which Buckley LJ examines how the 'kidnapping' cases relate to the wider emphasis on the welfare principle, that the welfare of the child is *always* the first and paramount consideration. The passage deserves to be quoted at length:

'Where the court has embarked on a full-scale investigation of the facts, the applicable principles, in my view, do not differ from those which apply to any other wardship case. The action of one party in kidnapping the child is doubtless one of the circumstances to be taken into account, and may be a circumstance of great weight; the weight to be attributed to it must depend on the circumstances of the particular case. Where a court makes a summary order for the return of a child to a foreign country without investigating the merits, the same principles, in my judgment, apply, but the decision must be justified on somewhat different grounds.

To take a child from his native land, to remove him to another country where, maybe, his native tongue is not spoken, to divorce him from the social customs and contacts to which he has been accustomed, to interrupt his education in his native land and subject him to a foreign system of education, are all acts (offered here as examples and of course not as a complete catalogue of possible relevant factors) which are likely to be psychologically disturbing to the child, particularly at a time when his family life is also disrupted. If such a case is promptly brought to the attention of a court in this country, the judge may feel that it is in the best interests of the infant that these disturbing factors should be eliminated from his life as speedily as possible. A full investigation of the merits of the case in an English court may be incompatible with achieving this. The judge may well be persuaded that it would be better for the child that those merits should be investigated in a court in his native country than that he should spend in this country the period which must necessarily elapse before all the evidence can be assembled for adjudication here. Anyone who has had experience of the exercise of this delicate jurisdiction knows what complications can result from a child developing roots in new so'l, and what conflicts this can occasion in the child's own life. Such roots can grow rapidly. An order that the child should be returned forthwith to the country from which he has been removed in the expectation that any dispute about his custody will be satisfactorily resolved in the courts of that country may well be regarded as being in the best interests of the child. In my judgment, the decision of this court in *Re H (infants)* was based on considerations of this kind.

As citations which I have already made disclose, judges have more than once reprobated the acts of "kidnappers" in cases of this kind. I do not in any way dissent from those strictures, but it would, in my judgment, be wrong to suppose that in making orders in relation to children in this jurisdiction the court is in any way concerned with penalising any adult for his conduct. That conduct may well be a consideration to be taken into account, but, whether the court makes a summary order or an order after investigating the merits, the cardinal rule applies that the welfare of the infant must always be the paramount consideration.'[15]

This judgment has been described as the locus classicus on the matter,[16] and it is clear that it is no longer correct for an English judge to take the position that a kidnapped child should be returned in the absence of an obvious risk of harm. In *Re C (minors)*[17] the Court of Appeal expressed disapproval of a first instance judgment which had proceeded on that basis. In that case the children's mother had died and a dispute arose between their stepfather, maternal grandmother and aunt, all living in California, and their father who had abducted them to England. The trial judge felt unable to order the return of the children to California because of the cannabis-smoking habits of the stepfather which he saw as exposing the children to a risk of harm. The Court of Appeal reached the same result, that the children should remain in England, but based its judgment on the welfare principle. It seemed very likely that a Californian court, especially in the light of a court welfare officer's report available to the Court of Appeal, would give custody to the father; a journey to California leading eventually to a return to England was not in the best interests of the children.

If the approach under examination in this paragraph has been repudiated in England, there is evidence that it is taking a new lease of life in Canada. In *Re DJC and WC*,[18] influenced by English cases decided before *Re L (minors)* which was not cited, Wright J of the Ontario High Court spoke of the duty to return a kidnapped child (in this context, to another Canadian province) in the absence of a reasonable apprehension of serious harm to the child if it were returned. Similarly in *Burgess v Burgess*,[19] the Appeal Division of the Nova Scotia Supreme Court, considering a number of English cases decided during the 1960s, ordered the return to England of a boy abducted by his father. *McKee v McKee*[20] was interpreted as allowing the prompt return of a kidnapped child; there was no evidence that the child would be harmed if returned. Finally in *Re O and O*[21] the Ontario High Court, assuming that approach to be correct, examined the nature of the evidence required to establish a risk of harm. There, allegations of homosexual incest were made against the father seeking the return of his son, detained in Ontario at the end of an access visit. It was held that it was sufficient that the court was satisfied of the risk of harm on the preponderance of evidence;[22] this standard of proof was not reached on the facts.

Similarly, although a more recent Scottish case has asserted that the Scottish approach accords with that now adopted in England,[23] Scottish courts have also used words not unrelated to those used in *Re H*. In *Thomson Petitioner*,[24] Lord Stott held that 'unless there is something to indicate that the welfare of the child will be adversely affected or unless some change of circumstances has taken place which requires investigation by the Scottish court, the Scottish court will return the child to the court of pre-eminent jurisdiction'.[25] This latter court is that of the domicile of the child, so that different considerations would apply if a child were abducted in defiance of an order made by the court of some other country.

1   Eg *Leyland v Chetwynd* 18 SC 239 (Cape); *Berlyn v De Smidt* 1911 SR 117; *Fairfield v Fairfield* 1925 CPD 297.
2   1954 (1) SA 514 (SR).
3   [1951] AC 352, [1951] 1 All ER 942, PC.
4   *Righetti v Pinchen* 1955 (3) SA 338 (D); *Riddle v Riddle* 1956 (2) SA 739 (C); *Hubert v Hubert* 1960 (3) SA 181 (W); *Mashaoane v Mashaoane* 1962 (1) SA 628 (D) at 638–9; *Jagoe v Jagoe* 1969 (4) SA 59 (R).
5   [1966] 1 All ER 886, CA.
6   [1965] 3 All ER 906 at 912.
7   [1966] 1 All ER 886 at 890, CA.
8   [1968] Ch 704, CA.
9   Per Harman LJ at 715. Cf *Re A* (*infants*) [1970] Ch 665, [1970] 3 All ER 184, CA (application of *Re H* refused where case not regarded as a kidnapping one, children having travelled from Jersey to England by consent).
10 [1967] Ch 761, [1967] 2 All ER 881, CA.
11 (1972) 116 Sol Jo 78.
12 [1974] 1 All ER 913, [1974] 1 WLR 250, CA.
13 [1951] AC 352, [1951] 1 All ER 942, PC.
14 [1970] AC 668, [1969] 1 All ER 788, HL.
15 [1974] 1 All ER 913 at 925–926.
16 *Re C* (*minors*) [1978] Fam 105 at 112, CA, per Ormrod LJ.
17 [1978] Fam 105, [1978] 2 All ER 230, CA.
18 (1974) 51 DLR (3d) 351 (Ont). The point was not discussed on appeal: (1975) 57 DLR (3d) 694 (Ont CA).
19 (1977) 75 DLR (3d) 486.
20 [1951] AC 352, [1951] 1 All ER 942, PC.
21 (1980) 117 DLR (3d) 159 (Ont).
22 Not following *Nielsen v Nielsen* (1971) 16 DLR (3d) 33 at 37 where proof beyond reasonable doubt was required.
23 *Campins v Campins* 1979 SLT (Notes) 41 (First Division).
24 1980 SLT (Notes) 29 (decided in 1978).
25 See also *Sargeant v Sargeant* 1973 SLT (Notes) 27 (First Division); *Campbell v Campbell* 1977 SLT 125; *Lyndon v Lyndon* 1978 SLT (Notes) 7.

International co-operation

9.07   A decision of the Full Bench of the Kerala High Court in India deserves a paragraph on its own. In *Feldman v Chacko*[1] a father removed children to India in breach of a court order made in Germany. The court felt obliged to order the return of the children to Germany in the interests of international comity, but accepted a remarkable 'package' of safeguards. With the co-operation of the German consular representatives in Kerala, the Indian court was to be supplied every three months with a written report as to the children's welfare from the parish priest of the German township in which the children were to live, so that the priest was acting as an extra-territorial court welfare officer. The mother undertook to bring the children to India for at least one month every three years, and to submit the case for full review on the occasion of the first triennial visit.

A number of comments can be made about this case. It is obviously an unusual case, for not many parents would have the financial resources to undertake regular trips from Germany to India. It is also puzzling in that the 'safeguards' are precarious indeed. If the parish priest were to report, for example, that the children were in poor health, or had forgotten their father and did not want to visit India again, it is not at all clear what steps would be open to the father or the Indian court, the children being in Germany where the courts had unequivocally given custody to the mother. Finally, the case involved some sort of co-operation from the German consular authorities; such international co-operation may be very desirable, and The Hague Convention considered below[2] contains relevant provisions, but it cannot be secured in the absence of international agreement.

1 AIR 1970 Kerala 1.
2 See paras 9.25-9.33 below.

The weight attaching to the foreign order

9.08 It is evident that no consistent approach can be found in Commonwealth jurisdictions. Some guidance can be salvaged from a review of Commonwealth case law, even if it is limited to an indication of questions which courts commonly ask themselves. One such question concerns the weight to be given to the foreign custody order, assuming one exists, in the current circumstances of the case.

So in *McKee v McKee* itself, in a passage already quoted,[1] Lord Simonds emphasised that a very recent decision of the foreign court would carry great weight, and the same point was made in the English Court of Appeal in *Re H (infants)*.[2] In the New Zealand case of *C v C*,[3] three factors were examined in connection with the foreign order: the status of the court (so that an order made in a superior court would carry more weight than one made in a subordinate jurisdiction); the nature of the proceedings (so that a decision reached after a full hearing, both parties being represented by counsel, would carry more authority than, for example, an order made ex parte); and the legal principles applied (more weight being given to a judgment based upon principles, for example that of the paramountcy of the child's welfare, similar to those adopted by the court now seised of the case).

The weight attaching to a foreign order diminishes sharply if 'changed circumstances' are established. The illness of one claimant since the date of the original order is a clear illustration.[4] The formation of definite views by a teenage child may well have the same effect.[5] The danger is, of course, that 'change of circumstances' arguments will give an undue advantage to a kidnapping parent, who can rely on the fact that the child is now settled in a secure home (the kidnapping being some evidence that former arrangements were insecure!) and generally gain from the passage of time: 'roots grow rapidly'.[6]

1   [1951] AC 352 at 365, PC.
2   [1966] 1 All ER 886 at 890–1, CA, per Willmer LJ.
3   [1973] 1 NZLR 129. For Australian views, see para 9.16 below.
4   *Re Maloney and LeBlanc* (1973) 41 DLR (3d) 463 (Alta).
5   *E v F* [1974] 2 NZLR 435, where the original order was made nine years earlier. For this case see paras 9.02 and 9.04 above.
6   *Re L (minors)* [1974] 1 All ER 913 at 926, CA.

The welfare of the child

9.09   As the preceding review has shown, most courts now give primacy to the welfare of the child, either in accordance with legislation applying generally to custody disputes or by reference to common law principles. An Australian court, upholding the award of custody to a kidnapping father, commented, 'if it were a question of justice as between the parties, [the mother] would have a genuine grievance at being deprived of custody by the court. But the court's concern is with the child and its welfare, and to that principle the "justice" of the situation as between the parties must be subordinated.'[1]

In considering the child's welfare his physical well-being will of course be considered,[2] but in international disputes the child's cultural development is also prominent, for example the language in which he has been educated to date. *In the Marriage of Reihana and Reihana*[3] provides a strong illustration, the Family Court of Australia ordering the return from Queensland to New Zealand of the child of a Maori father and non-Maori mother, referring both to the child's cultural roots and to the greater experience of the New Zealand courts in cross-cultural matters.

As a Nova Scotia court has emphasised, welfare must be very generally interpreted. 'It means the material well-being of the children equally with their psychological and spiritual well-being; it means that their need for food and clothing and shelter is to be given consideration in conjunction with their real need for love and affection and parental care and training. It means the development of a young human being.'[4]

However, there is danger in applying the 'welfare' test in international cases. In his preliminary paper on abduction prepared for the Hague Conference, Adair Dyer observed, 'The legal standard "the best interests of the child" is at first view of such vagueness that it seems to resemble more closely a sociological paradigm than a concrete juridical standard. How can one put flesh on its bare bones without delving into assumptions concerning the *ultimate* interests of a child which are derived from the moral framework of a particular culture?'[5] Professor Elisa Pérez-Vera, in her Explanatory Report on the Hague Convention, develops the point: 'We cannot ignore the fact that recourse by internal authorities [ie, those of a particular country] to such a notion involves the risk of their expressing particular cultural, social etc attitudes which themselves derive from a given national community and thus basically imposing their own subjective value judgments upon the national community from which the child has recently been snatched'.[6] In other words the 'welfare principle' in international cases can be a mere front, no doubt one assumed from the best motives, for the particular viewpoint of the court most recently seised of the case.

1   *In the Marriage of Schenck and Schenck* (1981) FLC 76,234 (Full Ct of Family Ct of Australia).
2   Eg *Re Woodhams (infants)* [1952] GLR 313 (NZ) (ill-treatment by abductor); *Re O and O* (1980) 117 DLR (3d) 159.
3   (1980) FLC 75,282 (Australian Fam Ct).
4   *Re Winsor* (1963) 48 MPR 445 at 447, per Furlong CJ, applied in *Re Wright* (1964) 49 DLR (2d) 460 (NS).

5   *Actes et documents de la quatorzième session* Tome III, p 22 (italics in original).
6   Ibid, at p 413.

B. STATUTORY INTERVENTION IN THE COMMONWEALTH

The Canadian Uniform Act of 1974

9.10   The foregoing attempt to impose some systematic order on the 'wilderness of single instances' in international child custody disputes has not concealed the disarray which exists at the level of the basic approach to be adopted. Statutory reformulation could do much to reduce the uncertainty, and the Uniform Law Conference of Canada began to investigate the issue after its 1971 meeting; the initiative came largely from Manitoba on the prompting of the Manitoba section of the Canadian Bar Association. The 1974 Conference adopted a Uniform Act,[1] designed in the words of the Manitoba Commissioners to ensure that in enacting jurisdictions there would be 'no haven for "civil kidnappers" even if such havens existed elsewhere'.[2]

As its title suggests, the Extra-Provincial Custody Orders Enforcement Act is limited to cases in which a court order exists, either one limited to matters of custody and access or one dealing with other matters (eg dissolution of marriage) but including custody and access provisions.[3] In such cases the basic duty of the courts in enacting jurisdictions is to enforce the order, making such orders as it considers necessary to give effect to the order,[4] for example an order returning the child to its proper custodian. In other words, the main thrust of the Act is to eliminate fresh consideration of the merits in the jurisdiction to which a child has been removed, and so to secure obedience to the extra-provincial order with the minimum of delay.

Reported cases indicate that this objective is achieved,[5] though not always without some delay. In one of the earliest cases, a child was kept in Prince Edward Island after a period of access due to end on 31 July 1976, in breach of an Ontario order. Enforcement of the Ontario order was sought promptly but an appeal was not dismissed until September 1977.[6]

There are however a number of important qualifications upon the basic rule in the Uniform Act. An order need not be enforced if the child concerned did not, at the time the custody order was made, 'have a real and substantial connection with the province, state or country in which the custody order was made'. The test of 'real and substantial connection' was expressly derived from the divorce case of *Indyka v Indyka*[7] and has produced, as could have been predicted, a crop of reported cases.

So in *Gergely v Gergely*[8] an interim custody order was made in British Columbia two months after the child had been removed there from Saskatchewan. Enforcement of the order was refused. The court held that the test of 'real and substantial connection' was one of ordinary residence. The child's ordinary residence was still in Saskatchewan. A similar decision was reached in another Saskatchewan case, *Labrecque v Labrecque*,[9] where an order had been made in Alberta one month after mother and child had moved there.

However in *Godwalt v Godwalt*[10] enforcement was refused on the ground that the order in question had been made after the child had ceased to 'reside' in the relevant jurisdiction; but the judgment is devoid of argument. The decision is inconsistent with two more recent and more fully considered cases. In the first[11] the Manitoba court agreed to make a custody order despite the fact that the child had been taken from the province some five weeks earlier, and expressly considered the likelihood of its enforcement in Nova Scotia to which the child had gone. The child had been born in Manitoba and was still there when the application for custody was presented; the abduction occurred a few days before the hearing of the application.

The most recent case was fully argued in the Alberta Court of Appeal and leave to appeal to the Supreme Court of Canada was refused by the latter court. In *Read v Read*[12] an English custody order was made in 1976 and renewed in 1981. In 1979, the child's father removed the child to Alberta; when his whereabouts were traced, proceedings were taken to enforce the English order. The Court of Appeal held, for the purposes of recognising the 1976 order, that the child had a real and substantial connection with England at least until its removal; and, in connection with possible variation of the order,[13] that that connection remained despite the abduction. It rejected an argument that the passage of time before the father's whereabouts were discovered broke the connection; this would mean that 'the more successful the kidnapping, the greater the chance that the wrongdoer [would] succeed', an unacceptable principle.[14]

As in the divorce context, the 'real and substantial connection' test is little more than a formulation of the issue, giving little firm guidance to the courts seeking to apply it.

1 Uniform Law Conference 1974 Report, pp 114-15. The text of the Act (as enacted in Alberta) is reproduced in Appendix D, below.
2 1974 Report, p 111.
3 Uniform Act, s 1 (definition of 'custody order'). In *Read v Read* [1982] 2 WWR 25 (Alta CA) the court had to consider the effect of an English wardship; the English court had entrusted the care of the ward to its mother, and this was held to amount to a custody order in her favour for the purposes of the Extra-Provincial Enforcement of Custody Orders Act 1977 of Alberta, despite the argument that the ward was technically in the care of the court.
4 Uniform Act, s 2.
5 Eg *Re Carrier* (1979) 16 RFL (2d) 16 (NB). Cf *Durham v Windley* (1978) 8 RFL (2d) 79 (Sask) where enforcement not sought but fresh custody order refused because of existence of enforceable order.
6 *McLean v McLean* (1977) 13 N & PEIR 513 (PEI CA).
7 [1969] 1 AC 33, [1967] 2 All ER 689, HL (see para 2.09 above); Manitoba Commissioners' Report in 1974 Uniform Law Conference Report at p 111.
8 (1978) 5 RFL (2d) 365 (Sask).
9 [1981] 2 WWR 383 (Sask).
10 (1979) 9 RFL (2d) 67 (Sask).
11 *Re Brew and MacDiarmid* (1982) 131 DLR (3d) 744 (Man).
12 [1982] 2 WWR 25 (Alta CA).
13 See para 9.11 below.
14 [1982] 2 WWR 25 at 32.

Powers of variation

9.11 The Uniform Act gives the court asked to enforce an extra-provincial order two different powers of variation, which amount to further qualifications upon the basic duty of enforcement.

The first variation power exists only if the child has ceased to have a real and substantial connection[1] with the jurisdiction in which the custody order was made or was last enforced *and* either the child now has such a connection with the enforcing jurisdiction or all the parties are resident there.[2] Although the Act makes no express reference to periods of time, and despite what was said in *Read v Read*,[3] this is likely to mean that after a certain time has elapsed, and the child acquires roots in the jurisdiction to which he had been taken, the conclusiveness of the original order will be lost.[4] The reality of these fears is perhaps indicated by the decision in *Hayes v Hayes*.[5] A custody order in favour of grandparents had been made in British Columbia. They then took the child to Saskatchewan; in proceedings under the Uniform Act as enacted in that province, it was held that two months having elapsed, that being 'more than negligible' in the life of a young child, the mother could apply for the variation of the order on the 'real and substantial' connection basis. If this power of variation exists, the court in exercising it is directed to give first consideration to the welfare of the child regardless of the wishes or interests of the adult parties.[6]

The second power is described, in a marginal note, as an 'extraordinary power'. The court may vary the original order in any case, that is regardless of questions as to the jurisdiction with which the child was or is substantially connected, where it is satisfied that the child 'would suffer serious harm if the child remained in or was restored to the custody of the person named in the custody order'.[7] The word 'extraordinary' in the marginal note is presumably intended to signify that the power should be exercised only in clear cases, but the provision as a whole could be used to change the spirit of the Act. Peremptory return is clearly meant to be the general rule; 'return unless there is evidence of a risk of harm' is not quite the same thing.

1 For 'real and substantial connection' in this context, see para 9.10 above.
2 Uniform Act, s 3(1). 'Residence' will not be held to exist when the party is present solely for the purpose of the proceedings: ibid, s 3(2).
3 [1982] 2 WWR 25 (Alta CA); see para 9.10 above.
4 Cf Christine Davies 'Interprovincial Custody' (1978) 56 CBR 17 at p 36. See ibid at pp 33–5 for an examination of various possible permutations, involving third jurisdictions in some cases.
5 (1981) 23 RFL (2d) 214 (Sask).
6 Uniform Act, s 3(3).
7 Ibid, s 4.

Legislation based upon the Uniform Act of 1974

9.12 The 1974 Act has been adopted in Alberta,[1] British Columbia,[2] Manitoba,[3] New Brunswick,[4] Newfoundland,[5] Prince Edward Island[6] and Saskatchewan.[7] The position in Nova Scotia and Quebec is examined in the paragraphs which follow.

A new Uniform Act was recommended by the Uniform Law Conference in 1981; it is examined below, and is gradually replacing the 1974 model.

1 Extra-Provincial Enforcement of Custody Orders Act 1977, cap 20 (Alberta).
2 Originally in 1976. See now Family Relations Act, cap 121 RL (BC), ss 38–42.
3 Extra-Provincial Custody Orders Enforcement Act, cap C360, RL (Man) (originally 1975, cap 4).
4 Child and Family Services and Family Relations Act 1980, cap C-2.1 (NB), s 130 (originally 1977, cap E-15).
5 Extra-Provincial Custody Orders Enforcement Act 1976, No 24 (Newf).
6 Extra-Provincial Custody Orders Enforcement Act 1975, cap 68 (PEI).
7 Extra-Provincial Custody Orders Enforcement Act, cap E18, RL (Sask) (originally 1977-8 cap 14).

Nova Scotia

9.13 In 1976, Nova Scotia enacted the Reciprocal Enforcement of Custody Orders Act.[1] Although clearly based upon the model of the 1974 Uniform Act, the Nova Scotia legislation differs from it in important respects.

This Act gives much greater weight to the foreign order. Unlike the Uniform

Act, there is no general power to vary the foreign order when the child has acquired a real and substantial connection with Nova Scotia. The only power to vary, and therefore to refuse to enforce, the foreign order is in cases where the child would suffer serious harm if it remained with[2] or was restored to the person named in the order.[3] Again, enforcement of an order cannot be refused on the ground that, at the time it was made, the child had no real and substantial connection with the jurisdiction whose courts made the order.

However, the Nova Scotia Act only extends to reciprocating states, to territorial legal units in Canada or outside Canada making reciprocal provision and designated by order of the Governor in Council.[4] It is unfortunately not known whether any orders have been made under this power.

1   1976 cap 15 (NS).
2   The official print has 'remained *in*', which must be an error.
3   Reciprocal Enforcement of Custody Orders Act 1976 (NS), s 4(1). The welfare principle is applicable in deciding how to exercise this power: ibid, s 4(2).
4   Ibid, ss 2(d), 6(2).

Quebec

9.14   Apart from special arrangements between Quebec and France, given effect by the Act to Secure the Carrying Out of the Entente between France and Quebec Respecting Mutual Aid in Judicial Matters[1] (which, subject to certain conditions, gives French custody decisions the authority of res judicata in Quebec), Quebec has very limited statutory provision at present.

The Youth Protection Act[2] provides that where, by a judgment of a competent court having no jurisdiction in Quebec, the rights of the parents of a child have been established, specified, changed, annulled or contemplated in any manner whatsoever, the judgment must be considered executory in Quebec unless a decision or an order of the Quebec courts intervenes in the same matter. The final words indicate that the freedom of the Quebec courts is in no way limited, and this principle was very largely retained in the proposals of the Civil Code Revision Office on the Reform of the Civil Code of Lower Canada in 1977. Book IX of the Report contained the following draft provision:

'Article 78. The courts of Quebec recognize decisions rendered outside Quebec in matters of custody of children and parental authority when

1.   at the time of the action, the child was domiciled or was present within the jurisdiction of the authority seized; or
2.   at the time of the action, the child was a national of the State of the authority seized.

These decisions may nonetheless be reviewed by the courts of Quebec if such a review is in the interests of the child.'

The final sentence of this article would enable the merits to be fully re-examined in Quebec. In addition certain other proposed articles of the revised Code would enable recognition to be refused on other grounds, such as 'fraud in the procedure' practised in the foreign court.[3]

1   Cap A-20.1, RL (Quebec), Title VII.
2   Cap P-34.1, RL (Quebec), s 131.
3   Art 60, 5, applied by art 81.

Australia 1975

9.15   The Family Law Act 1975[1] of the Commonwealth of Australia contains provisions relating to the registration of 'overseas custody orders'. An overseas custody order is an order made by a court in a prescribed overseas country, which currently means in New Zealand[2] or Papua New Guinea[3] only, for custody of or access to a child below the age of 18 years, or an order varying or discharging any such order.[4]

When an overseas custody order is registered in a court in Australia under the Act it has the same force and effect as if it were an order made by that court.[5] Registration is effected by the Secretary to the Attorney-General's Department sending a certified copy of the order, together with a certificate from a court officer or other appropriate authority in the overseas country that the order is enforceable there, to the registrar of either the Family Court of Australia or a Supreme Court of a state or territory of Australia.[6] The Secretary takes this action only if he has reasonable grounds for believing that the child who is the subject of the order, a parent of that child, or a person having the right to custody of or access to that child, is present in or proceeding to Australia.[7] Once registered the order is enforceable throughout Australia until the registration (including any concurrent registration) is cancelled.[8]

A court in Australia which has become aware of an overseas order registered under these provisions is forbidden from exercising jurisdiction in custody or access matters unless either

(a) every person having rights of custody or access under the order consents to the exercise of jurisdiction by the court; or

(b) the court is satisfied that there are 'substantial grounds for believing that the welfare of the child will be adversely affected' if the court does not exercise jurisdiction.[9]

If the court decides to entertain the proceedings, it may only make an order as to custody or access if the applicant for such an order satisfies the court either

(a) that the welfare of the child is likely to be adversely affected if the order is not made; or

(b) that there has been such a change in the circumstances of the child[10] that the order ought to be made.[11]

When an Australian court, acting under these provisions, substantially varies an overseas order, the registrar of the court must notify the overseas court or some other appropriate authority in the overseas country, supplying three copies of the Australian court's order and the reasons for the order, a copy of the depositions, and such further material as the court may direct.[12]

Some aspects of these provisions were examined by the Full Court of the Family Court of Australia in 1982.[13] An interim custody order made in New Zealand was registered in Australia; a variation of the order by a judge of the Australian Family Court was set aside on appeal as the statutory criteria for the exercise of jurisdiction were not satisfied. However a new trial was ordered because of some legal issues raised by Strauss J who argued that interim orders were not within the scope of the Australian provisions. His Honour based this conclusion not on an analysis of those provisions but because the New Zealand legislation dealing with the transmission of orders for enforcement overseas expressly excludes interim orders.[14] It is, with respect, difficult to see the relevance of this to the Australian legislation. The Australian regulations expressly provide for the registration of overseas orders where the Australian court has received the relevant documents other than from the Secretary to the Attorney-General's Department,[15] but Strauss J said that this was probably intended to deal with emergencies; the regulations contain no express limitation of this sort.

The principles behind the provisions in the Family Law Act 1975 of Australia are broadly comparable with those in the Uniform Act recommended in the previous year by the Canadian Commissioners. In particular the circumstances in which an Australian court may exercise jurisdiction despite the existence of an overseas custody order[16] can be compared with the powers of variation of extra-provincial orders under the Canadian Uniform Act.[17] The Australian Act makes no use in this context of the 'real and substantial connection' test; the mere fact that links have come to exist with Australia is not a ground for intervention; but that fact may, of course, be relevant to welfare criteria. The welfare basis for intervention, ie that there are substantial grounds for believing that the child's welfare would be adversely affected if the court did not intervene, is more broadly drawn than the Canadian Uniform Act's 'extraordinary power' in cases of anticipated 'serious harm'. Clearly much depends on the spirit in which the two sets of provisions are applied.

1   Act 53 of 1975.
2   Family Law Act 1975 (Australia), s 4(1).
3   Ibid, and Family Law Regulations 1975, SR 1975 No 210, r 170 (as amended by SR 1977 No 172, r 52).
4   Family Law Act 1975, s 60.
5   Ibid, s 68(2).
6   Family Law Regulations 1975, r 140(1). See text to note 15 below.
7   Ibid.
8   Ibid, r 140(5).
9   Family Law Act 1975, s 68(3).
10 Semble, since the date of the original order or its most recent variation; this is left implicit in the text of the Act.
11 Family Law Act 1975, s 68(4).
12 Family Law Regulations 1975, r 140(7).
13 *In the Marriage of Mentor and Mentor* (1982) FLC 91-210.
14 Guardianship Act 1968, (NZ) s 22L(1) as inserted by the Guardianship Amendment Act 1979 (NZ), s 2.
15 Family Law Regulations 1975 (Australia), r 140(6).
16 Text to note 9 above.
17 Cf para 9.11 above.

Unregistered orders

9.16   The Family Law Act 1975 contains a number of provisions applicable to overseas orders, even if they have not been registered under the Act. Section 64 provides for the issue of warrants for the purpose of giving effect to orders, and these provisions are available in respect of orders made by a court of a prescribed overseas country (ie New Zealand or Papua New Guinea[1]); no reference is made to prior registration in Australia. The warrant may provide for the stopping and searching of any vehicle, vessel or aircraft, the entry and search of any named premises or place, the taking of possession of the child and the child's delivery to the person entitled to custody or access or some other named person or authority (including a person or authority in or from a prescribed overseas country).[2]

Of more general importance is the tendency for Australian courts to apply the principles of the legislation generally to custody orders made in overseas countries other than New Zealand and Papua New Guinea. The Full Court of the Family Court of Australia adopted this approach in *In the Marriage of Khamis*[3] in 1978. Evatt CJ and Ellis SJ expressed the matter as follows:

'Where the earlier custody order is made by an overseas court of appropriate jurisdiction and that court has recently considered the issues in full and has made a custody order applying the rule that the child's welfare or interests are the paramount consideration, the Australian court should be reluctant to act inconsistently with that order unless the exceptions set out in s 68(4) are met. In determining appropriate jurisdiction regard should be paid not only to the status of the court but also to the provisions of s 39(4) which define the custody jurisdiction of the Family Court.

A too great willingness of courts to assume custody jurisdiction de novo where a party has taken a child from a country in breach of an order of the local court could encourage such behaviour. It is not in the interests of children to be put at the risk of endless series of abductions. It remains true, however, that a custody order is never final, and an overseas order cannot have higher standing than a local order. Nothing that has been said derogates from the main principle that the welfare of the child is the paramount consideration. Nevertheless, the welfare of a child is not served by repeated litigation unless there is clearly a case for a further review of custody.'[4]

However, the Full Court, and especially Watson SJ, emphasised that not every foreign order was entitled to equal respect; an ex parte order in the foreign jurisdiction would carry little weight. (This was despite the fact that a foreign ex parte order would, if made in a 'prescribed overseas country' be entitled to registration in Australia.[5]) Watson SJ set out questions which could properly be asked when a foreign order was being weighed:

'First, what is the law of the foreign country? Does it apply the "best interests of the child" rule? If it does are there religious and cultural considerations in that country which so affect its application therein that the law applied is not in fact similar?

Secondly, what is the nature of the tribunal which made the order? Is it a court which specializes in family law matters? Are its judicial officers professional or lay? Was the order arrived at by a judicial process or by some other means, eg, a panel or a board either solely or partially comprised of non-lawyers? It is perhaps not so much the status of the foreign tribunal but its composition and methods which is the more relevant consideration.

Thirdly, what was the nature of the hearing which led to the making of the order? Were both parents present? Were the conflicting claims fully examined? Did the court have the assistance of family reports from trained observers such as psychologists or social workers, etc?'[6]

In a most interesting submission to The Hague Conference on Private International Law as part of the preparations for the 14th Session which drafted The Hague Convention on the Civil Aspects of International Child Abduction,[7] the Australian Government expressly considered whether the approach adopted in *In the Marriage of Khamis* was consistent with that of the Privy Council in *McKee v McKee*.[8] The government took the view that there was consistency, the Australian decisions (and by extension the Family Law Act provisions they reflect) merely 'fleshing out' the broad framework set in *McKee v McKee*.

1 See para 9.15 above, notes 2 and 3.
2 Family Law Act 1975 (Australia), s 64(9) (custody cases) and (10) (access cases), both as substituted by the Family Law Amendment Act 1976 (No 63), s 22.
3 (1978) 34 FLR 150.
4 At 158. See also *In the Marriage of P and B* (1978) 32 FLR 350; *In the Marriage of Reihana and Reihana* (1980) FLC 75 at 282; *In the Marriage of Schenck and Schenck* (1981) FLC 76 at 234.
5 But cf Guardianship Act 1968 (NZ), s 22L(1) as inserted by the Guardianship Amendment Act 1979 (NZ), s 2, excluding ex parte orders from the provisions as to the transmission overseas of New Zealand Orders, and, for the possible relevance of that exclusion in Australia, *In the Marriage of Mentor and Mentor* (1982) FLC 91, 210 (para 9.15 above).
6 (1978) 34 FLR 150 at 167.

7   *Actes et Documents de la Quatorzième Session* Tome III, pp 63–69 (and especially at p 68).
8   [1951] AC 352, [1951] 1 All ER 942, PC. See para 9.03 above.

Prospective amendments

9.17   The Family Law Amendment Bill, first introduced into the Australian Parliament in 1981 but still under consideration in 1983, contains a number of relevant provisions. It strengthens the provisions designed to prevent the removal from Australia of children subject to custody, guardianship or access orders,[1] but also amends the provisons as to overseas custody orders.

The first amendment clarifies the original text by making it clear that only changes in circumstances since the making of the overseas custody order can be regarded as relevant when the jurisdiction of an Australian court is invoked.[2]

The second deals with the situation in which there are conflicting orders, that is an Australian order as to custody or access *and* an order on the same subject but to a different effect made in the courts of a prescribed overseas country (ie New Zealand or Papua New Guinea[3]); it is immaterial whether the overseas order was made before or after the Australian order. The new provisions will require the Australian court, on the application of any person entitled to custody or access under the overseas order, to discharge the Australian order unless

(a)   every person having rights of custody or access under the overseas order[4] consents to the cancellation of the registration of that order; or

(b)   the court is satisfied that there are substantial grounds for believing that the welfare of the child will be adversely affected if the overseas order continues to operate; or

(c)   the court is satisfied that changes in the circumstances of the child since the making of the overseas order indicate that that order should not continue to operate.[5]

If one of these sets of circumstances is made out, the court must cancel the registration in Australia of the overseas order.[6]

1   Clause 25 of the Bill as introduced, adding new ss 70A and 70B to the principal Act.
2   Clause 23(a), amending s 68(4)(b) of the Act.
3   See para 9.15 above, notes 2 and 3.
4   Ie, including the applicant.
5   Clause 23(b), inserting a new s 68(5) into the Act.
6   Ibid, inserting a new s 68(6) into the Act.

New Zealand 1979

9.18   In 1979 the New Zealand Parliament enacted the Guardianship Amendment Act,[1] inserting sections 22A to 22L into the Guardianship Act 1968. The new sections contain provisions substantially corresponding to those in the Family Law Act 1975 of Australia,[2] together with various administrative and evidential provisions some of which are covered by regulations in Australia.

An interesting provision concerns the costs of returning abducted children, a matter of very real practical importance. Section 22G provides that where a New Zealand court has issued a warrant for the purpose of enforcing an overseas custody order which had been registered in New Zealand, it may 'if it thinks just' order any person who has knowingly abducted, or is deliberately holding, the child in contravention of the overseas order to pay the whole or part of the cost of returning the child to the person entitled to custody under that order, including the cost and travelling expenses of any necessary escort.

1 No 52 of 1979 (NZ).
2 An important difference is that 'overseas custody order' in the New Zealand Act is defined so as to exclude interim orders, orders made ex parte, and orders made in the prescribed overseas country varying, discharging or made in substitution for a New Zealand order enforceable in that overseas country: Guardianship Act 1968 (NZ), s 2(1) as substituted by the Guardianship Amendment Act 1979 (NZ), s 3(1) and Sch. Cf para 9.15 above.

Barbados 1981

9.19 The Family Law Act 1981 of Barbados[1] contains provisions corresponding to those in the Family Law Act 1975 of Australia as to the registration and effect of overseas custody orders. The provisions[2] apply in respect of orders made in a country declared by the Attorney-General to be a prescribed overseas country for the purposes of the Act;[3] so far as is known no such declarations have been made.

1 No 29 of 1981.
2 Family Law Act 1981 (Barbados), ss 39, 46, 47.
3 Ibid, s 2(1).

The United States model: the Uniform Child Custody Jurisdiction Act

9.20 Some account should be given of the Uniform Child Custody Jurisdiction Act adopted in 1968 by the National Conference of Commissioners on Uniform State Laws. Not only is it in force in the great majority of United States jurisdictions,[1] but it was an important influence on the form, if not the detailed content, of the Canadian Uniform Act of 1981.[2]

As its title indicates, the Uniform Act approaches the problem in large measure as a jurisdictional issue. In a section declaring the general purposes of the Act, two of the purposes listed are to:

'avoid jurisdictional competition and conflict with courts of other states in matters of child custody which have in the past resulted in the shifting of children from state to state with harmful effects on their well-being' and to
'assure that litigation concerning the custody of a child takes place ordinarily in the state with which the child and his family have the closest connection . . .'[3]

To further these purposes, the Uniform Act vests jurisdiction in custody matters as far as may be in the child's 'home state' to the exclusion of any other state in which the child may be physically present.[4] The 'home state' is that in which the child had lived with a parent or person acting as parent for at least six consecutive months.[5] That state retains jurisdiction for six months after a child has been removed or kept away from the state but a parent continues to live there.[6] Another state has jurisdiction only if

(a) it is in the child's best interests that the jurisdiction exists, the child and at least one adult party having a significant connection with the state, *and* 'substantial evidence' as to the child's present and future care is available there;[7] or
(b) the child is present in the state and has either been abandoned or requires emergency steps to protect it from harm;[8] or
(c) no other state appears to have jurisdiction and the best interests of the child require the exercise of jurisdiction by the forum state.[9]

These rules are reinforced by provisions prohibiting the exercise of jurisdiction when proceedings have already been commenced in a state 'exercising jurisdiction substantially in conformity with this Act'[10] and permitting disclaimer of jurisdiction on forum non conveniens grounds.[11] Further, under what is known as the 'clean hands doctrine' a court may decline to exercise jurisdiction if that is just and proper and the petitioner 'has wrongfully taken the child from another state or has engaged in similar reprehensible conduct'.[12]

Where a custody order has already been made in the courts of another state acting in accordance with the jurisdictional principles of the Act,[13] the order is to be recognised and enforced.[14] So long as the state in which the order was made retains jurisdiction under the Act's principles, the courts in no other state may vary the order.[15] Exactly when the original state loses this exclusive jurisdiction to vary the order is unclear: the Commissioners' notes make it plain that the mere fact that another state becomes the child's 'home state' is not sufficient, but jurisdiction will cease if no claimant to custody remains living in the state of origin.

The Act was drafted with the practices of United States jurisdictions in mind. Section 23, however, declares that 'the general policies of this Act extend to the international area'; it is presumably for the courts to work out how best to give practical effect to these 'general policies' in international cases.

1   Alabama, Arizona, Arkansas, California, Colorado, Connecticut, Delaware, Florida, Georgia, Hawaii, Idaho, Illinois, Indiana, Iowa, Kansas, Kentucky, Louisiana, Maine, Maryland, Michigan, Minnesota, Missouri, Montana, Nebraska, Nevada, New Hampshire, New Jersey, New York, North Carolina, North Dakota, Ohio, Oklahoma, Oregon, Pennsylvania, Rhode Island, South Dakota, Virginia, Washington, West Virginia, Wisconsin and Wyoming.
2   For a recent commentary see Brigitte M. Bodenheimer 'Interstate Custody: Initial Jurisdiction and Continuing Jurisdiction under the UCCJA' (1981) 14 Fam LQ 203. See also by the same author 'The International Kidnapping of Children: the United States Approach' (1977) 9 Fam LQ 83, and 'Progress under the Uniform Child Custody Act and Remaining Problems: Punitive Decrees, Joint Custody and Excessive Modification' (1977) 65 Cal LR 978.
3   Uniform Act, s 1(a)(1), (3).
4   Ibid, s 3.
5   Ibid, s 2(5).
6   Ibid, s 3(a)(1).
7   Ibid, s 3(a)(2).
8   Ibid, s 3(a)(3).
9   Ibid, s 3(a)(4).
10   Ibid, s 6.
11   Ibid, s 7.
12   Ibid, s 8(a), which relates to petitions for an initial custody order. Cf ibid, s 8(b) for 'modification decrees'.
13   Ie under provisions corresponding to those in the Act, or in factual circumstances meeting its jurisdictional standards.
14   Uniform Act, s 13.

British proposals

9.21   An important Working Paper was published in 1976 by the English and Scottish Law Commissions.[1] The scope of the paper was limited to jurisdiction and enforcement of custody orders within the United Kingdom and matters affecting overseas orders were postponed for later consideration.[2] Recognising the example of the United States Uniform Child Custody Jurisdiction Act 1968, the Commissions favoured legislation setting out clear rules of jurisdiction which would serve to discourage 'kidnapping'; welfare considerations would remain paramount once jurisdiction was found properly to exist.

The existing jurisdictional rules at common law are based on the physical presence of the child within the jurisdiction or the child's nationality.[3] The Law Commissions' view was that none of the existing rules was satisfactory, and they also rejected 'ordinary residence' as both too uncertain and as possibly likely to favour an abductor.[4] In the end the Commissions favoured habitual residence, with a clear definition:

'(1) The general rule should be that a court in a United Kingdom country should have jurisdiction to entertain wardship or independent[5] custody proceedings if, and only if, the child in question is habitually resident in that country at the date of the commencement of the proceedings.

(2) Unless it is established that the habitual residence of a child is in some other country, it should be presumed that his habitual residence is in the country where he has resided cumulatively for the longest period in the year immediately preceding the commencement of the proceedings.

(3) In cases where the child's residence has been changed without lawful authority during the year immediately preceding the commencement of the proceedings, no account should be taken of the period of that changed residence in reckoning the periods of the child's residence for the purposes of (2) above.'[6]

The Commissions expressed no decided view about the possibility of jurisdiction by consent of the parties as an alternative ground.

The effect of these proposals is not unlike that of the United States Uniform Act's provisions as to 'home state' jurisdiction.[7] The British proposals are more explicit than the Uniform Act in dealing with the continuing jurisdiction of a court which has made a custody order to vary or revoke it or substitute a fresh order; this would continue until a court in another United Kingdom country made a custody order in matrimonial proceedings, or in wardship or custody proceedings on the basis that the child was then habitually resident in that country.[8]

The crucial question in drafting legislation in this area concerns the exceptional powers of a court which does not have jurisdiction under the general rules to intervene. The United States Uniform Act is fairly liberal on this point,[9] but the Law Commissions would allow such jurisdiction only where the child was physically present and 'the immediate intervention of the court is necessary for the protection of the child'.[10] Even then such an 'emergency order' would be superseded by any order made in the country of the child's habitual residence or by a court in which matrimonial proceedings were continuing.[11]

The Law Commissions also examine the question of concurrent proceedings and the need for provisions as to the staying of one set of proceedings.[12] In matrimonial cases, where, as under the existing law, a court properly seised of matrimonial matters would retain the power to make custody orders, the power would not be exercised if a court in another United Kingdom country had made a custody order in matrimonial proceedings within the previous six months.[13]

The Law Commissions have not yet made a Final Report, nor have they indicated a view on the international aspects of the problem.

1   Law Com WP No 68; Scottish Law Com Memorandum No 23.
2   Ibid, para 1.3.
3   See paras 3.40 ff of the Law Commissions' paper, and Dicey and Morris *The Conflict of Laws* (10th edn, 1980) pp 424 ff. The nationality basis presents particular difficulties in federal states where custody tends to be a state matter but nationality is federal. For differing views in Australia, see *Kelly v Panayioutou* [1980] 1 NSWLR 15n: *McM v C (No 2)* [1980] 1 NSWLR 27; *Romeyko v Whackett (No 2)* (1980) 25 SASR 531; cf *McM v C (No 1)* [1980] 1 NSWLR 1. For Scottish use of domicile see Law Commissions' paper, paras 3.44–3.52.

4   Ibid, para 3.67.
5   Ie, independent of matrimonial proceedings.
6   Law Commissions' paper, para 3.78.
7   See para 9.20 above, text to notes 5 and 6.
8   Law Commissions' paper, para 3.91.
9   See para 9.20 above, text to notes 7-9. Cf for a rather different perception of the United States provisions, Law Commissions' paper, para 3.93.
10   Ibid, para 3.95.
11   Ibid.
12   Ibid, para 5.17.
13   Ibid, para 3.34.

The Canadian Uniform Act of 1981

9.22 In 1981 the Uniform Law Conference of Canada approved a new recommended Uniform Act, entitled the Uniform Custody Jurisdiction and Enforcement Act. The title indicates that a concern for the enforcement of orders, such as had been the basis of the earlier Uniform Act, was combined with an emphasis on jurisdictional matters; the latter was derived to some considerable extent from the United States approach considered above,[1] but elements of forum conveniens thinking were also to be found in Canadian case law.[2] So, the stated purposes of the Canadian Uniform Act include the avoidance of the exercise of concurrent jurisdiction by courts in more than one jurisdiction[3] as well as the more effective enforcement of custody and access orders.[4]

Like the United States model, the Canadian Uniform Act seeks to impose a restriction on the broad jurisdiction of courts in custody matters. Like the English and Scottish Law Commissions, the Canadian Commissioners favoured the habitual residence of the child,[5] but have a different approach to its definition. Generally, a child's habitual residence will be where he last resided with both parents, or with one parent under a court order or with the consent of the other parent, or with a foster-parent 'on a permanent basis'.[6] Abduction will only alter the habitual residence if 'there has been acquiescence or undue delay in commencing due process by the person from whom the child is removed or withheld'.[7]

There are, however, some exceptions to the habitual residence rule. The first involves the 'real and substantial connection' of the child with the jurisdiction in which proceedings are commenced. So the courts in that jurisdiction will have jurisdiction, despite the habitual residence of the child elsewhere, if a number of further conditions are satisfied:

(a)   the child must be physically present in the jurisdiction;
(b)   substantial evidence concerning the best interests of the child must be available there;
(c)   proceedings must not be pending in any court in the place[8] of habitual residence of the child;
(d)   there must be no extra-provincial custody order which has been recognised[9] by a court in the province now seised of the case; and
(e)   it must be appropriate, on the balance of convenience, for the court to exercise jurisdiction.[10]

In addition, if the child is physically present, the court may exercise jurisdiction to make or vary a custody or access order if it is satisfied, on the balance of probabilities, that the child would otherwise 'suffer serious harm'.[11]

Even if the court cannot exercise jurisdiction under any of these provisions, it may still make an interim order; it need not order the immediate return of the child but may, for example, maintain the status quo on the condition that proceedings are promptly commenced in the courts of another jurisdiction.[12]

1   Para 9.20 above.
2   Eg in *Hilborn v Hilborn* (1977) 2 RFL (2d) 5 (Alta), cited in para 9.05 above.
3   Uniform Act, s 2(b). The Act is reproduced in Appendix D.
4   Ibid, s 2(d).
5   Ibid, s 3(1)(a).
6   Ibid, s 3(2).
7   Ibid, s 3(3). For power to disclaim jurisdiction on forum non conveniens grounds, see ibid, s 5.
8   Semble, meaning 'country'; a more limited meaning would have unfortunate results.
9   *Not* 'would be entitled to recognition'.
10 Uniform Act, s 3(1)(b).
11 Ibid, s 4.
12 Ibid, s 6.

Enforcement of custody orders

9.23 The Canadian Uniform Act of 1981 also contains provisions on the enforcement of extra-provincial custody orders, the matter dealt with in the earlier 1974 recommended Act.

The duty to give effect to an extra-provincial order is much more heavily qualified than in the earlier Act. The only qualification in the 1974 Act concerned the case in which the order had been made by a court in a jurisdiction with which the child had no real and substantial connection. This is replaced by a provision entitling a court to refuse recognition to a custody order made by a court in circumstances which would not, mutatis mutandis, have given jurisdiction under the terms of the Uniform Act, s 3.[1] However, recognition may also be refused:

(a) if the respondent was not given reasonable notice of the extra-provincial proceedings;

(b) if the respondent was not given an opportunity to be heard by the extra-provincial tribunal;[2]

(c) if the law applied by that tribunal did not require it to have regard for the best interests of the child; or

(d) if the order is seen as contrary to the public policy of the province now seised of the matter.[3]

If two or more conflicting extra-provincial orders survive all these hurdles to recognition, the court resolves the conflict between them by favouring the order appearing to be most in accord with the best interests of the child.[4]

Power is given to supersede an extra-provincial order entitled to recognition under the Uniform Act where there has been a material change of circumstances which affects or is likely to affect the best interests of the child. This generous ground for intervention is subject to jurisdictional rules. Either the child must be habitually resident in the province now seised of the case, or, if that test is not satisfied, the child must be physically present in that province, have ceased to have a real and substantial connection with the place where the order was made, have acquired such a connection with the province concerned, and it must be shown that substantial evidence concerning the best interests of the child is available there and that it is appropriate, on the balance of convenience, for jurisdiction to be exercised.[5]

In addition, the power exists to supersede an extra-provincial order where the court is satisfied, on the balance of probability, that the child would otherwise suffer serious harm.[6]

The Uniform Act also contains detailed provisions as to the machinery by which orders are to be enforced.[7]

1　1981 Uniform Act, s 7(1)(e). Cf para 9.10 above.
2　Cases in which the respondent was entitled to be heard but had inadequate time to prepare the case would seem to be ones in which no 'reasonable notice' was given; where distance and lack of financial resources prevent the respondent from appearing the position is unclear: does 'opportunity' mean one realistic in all the circumstances?
3　1981 Uniform Act, s 7(1)(a)-(d).
4　Ibid, s 7(3).
5　Ibid, s 8(1). Cf s 3 of the 1974 Uniform Act: para 9.11 above.
6　1981 Uniform Act, s 9. Cf s 4 of the 1974 Uniform Act: para 9.11 above.
7　1981 Uniform Act, ss 10-16.

Assessment and adoption of the Uniform Act

9.24　The 1981 Uniform Act is much more elaborate than its predecessor of 1974, covering a greater number of issues and in much more detail. It probably remains true that, as under the earlier Act, the interpretation of 'real and substantial connection' is crucial. This is because, although the primary basis of jurisdiction is habitual residence, which will seldom be affected by an abduction, a combination of the physical presence of the child and its 'real and substantial connection' with the province concerned will often serve almost as well. It seems very likely that the central issues in contested cases under the Uniform Act as adopted in the provinces of Canada will concern the extent to which the passage of time and the putting down of new 'roots' creates the necessary connection; and an examination of that issue may well involve looking at all the circumstances of the case.

The text recommended by the Uniform Law Conference was based upon legislative proposals before the Ontario Legislative Assembly. The Children's Law Reform Amendment Act 1982 of Ontario[1] enacts the relevant provisions.[2] They are under active consideration in a number of other provinces, but priority seems to be being given to legislation based upon The Hague Convention considered below.

1　Cap 82 of 1982.
2　Children's Law Reform Act 1977 (cap 41) (Ont), ss 25, 29, 30, 32, and 48-53, all as added by the Children's Law Reform Amendment Act 1982 (Ont), s 1.

C. THE HAGUE CONVENTION OF 1980

Introduction

9.25　A Convention on the Civil Aspects of International Child Abduction was negotiated during the Fourteenth Session of The Hague Conference on Private International Law in October 1980, and at the close of the Session was signed by Canada, France, Greece and Switzerland. It has since been signed by Belgium, Portugal and the United States.

The Commonwealth had an unusually close association with the preparation of the Convention. The subject was first put upon the Agenda of The Hague Conference at the suggestion of Canada. The subject, and the then draft Convention, was discussed by Commonwealth Law Ministers at their Barbados Meeting in April-May 1980,[1] the final communiqué expressing the view that the proposals were an appropriate response to the problem and the hope that a large number of countries would accede to any resulting convention as a matter of priority. The Commission of The Hague Conference which drafted the Convention was presided over by the United Kingdom delegate,[2] and a Commonwealth Secretariat Observer delegation[3] was present and was also represented at a pre-Conference meeting between the Commonwealth member countries present at the Session.

The Convention was the subject of keen debate, and represented a concerted effort by representatives of countries with different initial positions.[4] Its principal provisions are examined in the paragraphs which follow.[5]

1   See also paper LMM(80) 16 and the annexed report 'The International Abduction of Children by a Parent or Guardian' by J. M. Eekelaar. The paper reviews, inter alia, the European Convention on the Recognition and Enforcement of Decisions Concerning Custody and on Restoration of Custody of Children adopted by the Council of Europe in November 1979 and signed (but not ratified) by Cyprus.
2   Professor A. E. Anton of the Scottish Law Commission.
3   The present author, Mr J. M. Eekelaar and Dr O. Aina.
4   The papers and debates are published in *Actes et Documents de la Quatorzième Session* Tome III. For commentaries on the Convention, see the official Explanatory Report by Professor Elisa Pérez-Vera (ibid, p 425); A. E. Anton 'The Hague Convention on International Child Abduction' (1981) 30 ICLQ 537; and J. M. Eekelaar *The Hague Convention on the Civil Aspects of International Child Abduction* (Commonwealth Secretariat 1981).
5   The text of the Convention, excluding its Final Clauses, is reproduced in Appendix D.

Aims and methods of the Convention

9.26   The philosophy of the Convention has been stated as being that 'the struggle against the great increase in international child abductions[1] must always be inspired by the desire to protect children and should be based upon an interpretation of their true interests'.[2] Yet the word 'abduction' appears nowhere in the text of the Convention, but only in its title; and the only reference to 'the interests of children' is in the preamble. It would be more accurate, perhaps, to describe the Convention as seeking to secure the enforcement of rights to custody and access.

Unlike the United States and Canadian Uniform Acts, the Convention does not seek to regulate jurisdiction in custody matters, a task which seemed unlikely to be fruitful in an international context. On the other hand it is not limited to the recognition and enforcement of custody orders for, as the experience of common law countries has shown clearly, disputes can arise and abductions take place before any court order or other written instrument comes into existence.

The Convention contains a mixture of types of provisions. Some contain rather general language, with more than a touch of exhortation about them; others impose precisely-worded obligations; others establish detailed administrative procedures, using the Central Authority device much favoured in recent Hague Conventions. So, art 1, in setting out the objects of the Convention, states that they are:

'(a)   to secure the prompt return of children wrongfully removed to or retained in any Contracting State; and

(b)   to ensure that rights of custody and of access under the law of one Contracting State are effectively respected in the other Contracting States.'

Paragraph (a) applies whether the child concerned has links with another contracting state or not. If a child is abducted *to* a contracting state from any place in the world, art 2, read with art 1(a), obliges the contracting state to 'take all appropriate measures', using 'the most expeditious procedures available' to deal with the situation; but no precise machinery or specific steps are prescribed in the Convention. Paragraph (b), however, operates as between contracting states, and other provisions of the Convention spell out the obligations entailed in some detail; the specific provisions of the Convention apply only where a child was habitually resident in a contracting state immediately before any breach of custody or access rights.[3]

1   For some statistics, see the Replies of Governments to a Hague Conference Questionnaire: *Actes et Documents de la Quatorzième Session* Tome III, pp 61 ff; and a paper by International Social Service, ibid, pp 130–143.
2   E. Pérez-Vera, Explanatory Report, para 24 (ibid, p 431).
3   Convention, art 4.

Central Authorities

9.27   Chapter II of the Convention, which comprises arts 6 and 7 only, requires a contracting state to designate a Central Authority[1] to discharge the duties imposed by the Convention on such authorities.

The term 'Central Authority' has been used in a number of Hague Conventions, especially those dealing with civil procedure. What is entailed is the nomination of some agency or office or officer, usually within the Government Service of the particular state, to carry out (almost invariably as part of a much wider remit) functions arising under the Convention. The Central Authorities are required to 'co-operate with each other',[2] and therefore constitute the point of reference in communications between states on this subject; but it is clear from the Convention that within a particular contracting state no structure is imposed. So, the various measures to be taken by a Central Authority may be taken 'directly or through an intermediary',[3] and may well be handled through appropriate child welfare agencies, or other official agencies (such as those concerned with legal aid) or the police service.

The specific functions listed in art 7, second paragraph, fall into a number of categories. One is investigatory, to discover the whereabouts of a child wrongfully removed or retained. Others are functions perhaps best described as social work functions: to take provisional measures to protect the child, to secure voluntary settlement or amicable resolution of the issues, and to exchange information as to the child's social background. Others again have a legal flavour: to initiate proceedings, to provide legal aid and the participation of counsel or legal advisers (or to facilitate these matters). Administrative functions include making arrangements for the safe return of a child or for access. Finally there is the exchange of information specifically about the operation of the Convention. Certainly in a large country, many of these functions will have to be discharged through the appropriate agency in the local district concerned.

1   Or in states with more than one system of law or 'autonomous territorial organizations' one or more Central Authorities: Convention, art 6, second paragraph.
2   Convention, art 7, first paragraph.

Wrongful removal or retention of a child

9.28   Article 3 of the Convention provides that the removal or retention of a child[1] is to be considered wrongful where:

(a)   it is in breach of rights of custody attributed to a person, an institution or any other body, either jointly or alone, under the law of the state[2] in which the child was habitually resident immediately before the removal or retention; and

(b) at the time of removal or retention those rights were actually exercised, either jointly or alone, or would have been so exercised but for the removal or retention.

The rights of custody may arise by operation of law or by reason of a judicial or administrative decision, or by reason of an agreement having legal effect under the law of that state;[3] the notion of 'rights of custody' is declared to include rights relating to the care of the person of the child and, in particular, the right to determine the child's place of residence.[4]

These provisions are very widely drawn. They will include a parent's rights as the natural guardian of his child (without any court order); the rights of an institution or social welfare agency to whom those rights have been transferred by a court order or by a decision of an administrative body (or in appropriate cases of the agency itself[5]); rights under a custody order made in divorce or guardianship proceedings; and rights under certain types of separation agreements.[6]

Custody rights must be those which 'were actually exercised ... or would have been exercised but for the removal or retention'. Professor Anton has suggested that 'too much must not be read into the words "actually exercised" '; he argues that they would apply to the rights of a mother who, being in hospital, had actually left the child in the care of its grandmother.[7] A similarly broad reading of 'would have been exercised' has been canvassed by Eekelaar, taking the case of a removal by the parent with the de facto care of the child immediately the other parent commences custody proceedings. He argues that the failure of the non-custodial parent to take charge of the child directly is on the understanding that the court will be allowed to decide the matter; knowing of the other parent's rejection of this understanding, he 'would have' acted but for the child's removal.[8] This takes the meaning of the phrase to its limits, especially as the arrangement or understanding allowing a parent de facto care of the child could well constitute a legally effective agreement giving custody, in the Convention sense, exclusively to that parent.

1   The child must be under 16 years of age: Convention, art 4.
2   In effect, the *contracting* state: see Convention, art 4, providing that the child must have been resident in a contracting state immediately before any breach of custody or access rights. The reference to the law of the state includes a reference to its rules of the conflict of laws; see E. Pérez-Vera, Explanatory Report, para 66.
3   Convention, art 3, second paragraph.
4   Ibid, art 5(a).
5   Eg an English local authority, which has power by resolution in certain circumstances to assume the parental rights of children placed in its care by the parents: Child Care Act 1980 (UK), s 3.
6   It appears that the phrase 'having legal effect' is to be interpreted widely; the intention was *not* to limit the scope of the provision to, eg, agreements incorporated in some court order or otherwise officially approved: E. Pérez-Vera, Explanatory Report, para 70.
7   (1981) 30 ICLQ 537 at 546, n 29.
8   *The Hague Convention on the Civil Aspects of International Child Abduction* (Commonwealth Secretariat, 1981) at pp 22–23.

Return of children: procedures

9.29 The Convention makes available procedures designed to secure the return of a child who has been wrongfully removed or retained; but nothing in the Convention limits any existing power of a judicial or administrative authority to order the return of the child at any time.[1]

A request for assistance in securing the return of the child may be addressed to the Central Authority of any contracting state.[2] The text of the Convention expressly mentions the possibility of applying to the Central Authority of the child's habitual residence, because the applicant for assistance is most likely to be there, but whichever Central Authority is approached must 'directly and without delay' transmit the application to the Central Authority of any contracting state in which it believes the child to be.[3] The Fourteenth Session of The Hague Conference which produced the Convention also, as part of the Final Act of the Session, approved a model Form of Request for return and recommended states to make use of it in cases falling within the Convention. The form contains all the material specified in the text of the Convention as having to be contained in an application for assistance,[4] together with further details (eg photographs, passport numbers, dates of the parents' marriage) which might prove relevant. The use of the form is not mandatory, and it is not part of the text of, nor an Annex to, the Convention; this latter point is to facilitate the amendment and improvement of the form in the light of experience with its use.

The Central Authority of the contracting state where the child is must take or cause to be taken all appropriate measures in order to obtain the voluntary return of the child.[5] This reflects the duty placed upon Central Authorities, and already noted, to seek voluntary settlement of the dispute by an 'amicable resolution of the issues' wherever possible;[6] such an outcome is clearly likely to be in the long-term interests of the child.

The Central Authority may also initiate or facilitate the institution of judicial or administrative proceedings to secure the return of the child.[7] Those authorities are required to act 'expeditiously'[8] and expedition is encouraged by an unusual provision: if a decision has not been reached within six weeks of the date of commencement of proceedings the applicant or the Central Authority is entitled to a statement as to the reasons for the delay.[9] The judicial or administrative authorities may take notice directly of the laws of the state of habitual residence of the child, and of any judicial or administrative decisions[10] taken there, without recourse to the specific procedures normally required for proof of foreign law or recognition of foreign decisions.[11] There is also provision for an authority to request the applicant to obtain from the authorities of the state of the child's habitual residence a decision or determination that the removal or retention of the child was wrongful within the meaning of art 3 of the Convention.[12] Professor Pérez-Vera, in her Explanatory Report,[13] stresses the voluntary nature of this procedure: the return of the child cannot be made conditional upon its use; it is a further means of facilitation and this is emphasised by the duty placed on Central Authorities so far as practicable to assist applicants to obtain the requested decision;[14] in some cases their duty 'to provide information of a general character as to the law of their State'[15] may prove sufficient, and more specific information may be available in a certificate or affidavit concerning the relevant law which may accompany or supplement the application.[16]

1　Convention, art 18.
2　Ibid, art 8, first paragraph.
3　Ibid, art 9.
4　Ie in ibid, art 8, second paragraph.
5　Ibid, art 10.

6   Ibid, art 7, second paragraph, (c).
7   Ibid, (f).
8   Ibid, art 11, first paragraph.
9   Ibid, art 11, second paragraph.
10   Including decisions not 'formally recognised' in that state.
11   Convention, art 14.
12   Ibid, art 15.
13   Explanatory Report, para 120.
14   Convention, art 15.
15   Ibid, art 7, second paragraph, (e).
16   Ibid, art 8, third paragraph, (f).

Return of children: substantive rules

9.30   The crucial articles in the Convention are arts 12 and 13, and a great deal of time was occupied in their elaboration at the Fourteenth Session of The Hague Conference.[1]

Article 12 sets forth a general rule:

'Where a child has been wrongfully removed or retained in terms of Article 3 and, at the date of the commencement of the proceedings before the judicial or administrative authority of the Contracting State where the child is, a period of less than one year has elapsed from the date of the wrongful removal or retention, the authority concerned shall order the return of the child forthwith.'

There are important qualifications upon this general rule, which are considered below. At this point, the nature of the general rule requires some examination.

Its main feature is the use of a time-limit, a year, rather than any inexact formula such as a test of real and substantial connection or even of habitual residence. One of the difficulties with a time-limit is the possibility of injustice where an abducting parent successfully conceals the whereabouts of the child for a long period; to meet this difficulty an earlier draft of the Convention provided for a time limit of six months, to run from the date of the breach of custody rights or, where the residence of the child was unknown, from the date of the discovery of the child; an overall time limit of twelve months was applicable in all cases.[2] The Conference decided however upon a single time limit, and selected a period of one year. Attempts to fix a shorter period were met by arguments, advanced forcefully by the United States delegation, that this would threaten the position of parents seeking the return of children, especially those without legal advice, and could also prejudice the chances of a voluntary settlement of the matter. As Professor Pérez-Vera observes, any time limit is arbitrary but one year was the 'least bad' answer.[3]

However, the minority who remained anxious that a time limit of one year was too short were met by the second paragraph of art 12:

'The judicial or administrative authority, even where the proceedings have been commenced after the expiration of the period of one year referred to in the preceding paragraph, shall also order the return of the child, unless it is demonstrated that the child is now settled in its new environment.'

The inclusion of this provision was agreed to by a narrow majority.[4] It effectively restores a two-stage approach: during the first year return will be mandatory (with qualifications still to be noted); thereafter it will still be mandatory (subject to those same qualifications) in the absence of proof that the child 'is now settled in its new environment'. A child who has been moved from place to place will not fall within the latter phrase.

Article 13 contains the qualifications, the cases in which the return of the child need *not* be ordered:

'Notwithstanding the provisions of the preceding Article, the judicial or administrative authority of the requested State is not bound to order the return of the child if the person, institution or other body which opposes its return establishes that—

(a)   the person, institution or other body having the care of the person of the child was not actually exercising the custody rights at the time of removal or retention, or had consented to or subsequently acquiesced in the removal or retention; or

(b)   there is a grave risk that his or her return would expose the child to physical or psychological harm or otherwise place the child in an intolerable situation.

The judicial or administrative authority may also refuse to order the return of the child if it finds that the child objects to being returned and has attained an age and degree of maturity at which it is appropriate to take account of its views.

In considering the circumstances referred to in this Article, the judicial and administrative authorities shall take into account the information relating to the social background of the child provided by the Central Authority or other competent authority of the child's habitual residence.'

The provisions as to the exercise of custody rights merely reinforce the earlier definition of wrongful removal or retention; and those as to the expressed wishes of the child reflect the reality of situations in which teenage children are involved. The crucial paragraph is that lettered (b). This does *not* permit 'an omnibus survey of the child's general condition'[5] which would examine all aspects of the problem in terms of the welfare of the child. 'Physical' and 'psychological' harm are intended to be strictly defined, and do not include broader economic or educational matters. The reference to the possible 'intolerable situation' will include special cases such as those of political refugees.

One further provision needs to be noted in this context. Article 20 provides that the return of the child may be refused 'if this would not be permitted by the fundamental principles of the requested State relating to the protection of human rights and fundamental freedoms'. This article was included after protracted negotiations to protect the position of certain countries, notably Ireland, where constitutional provisions giving certain guarantees to citizens in respect of the family made some 'public policy' escape-route essential. The article is, however, much more restrictively drafted than the customary provision in Hague Conventions with its reference to matters 'manifestly contrary to public policy'; the inclusion of that form of clause was expressly rejected.

It is *not* a sufficient ground for refusing to return the child that to do so would be contrary to a custody decision previously given in the requested state or entitled to recognition there.[6] The judicial or administrative authorities may however in exercising any discretion 'take account of the reasons for that decision'.[7]

Finally, the Convention stresses that a decision concerning the return of the child is not to be taken as a determination on the merits of any custody issue.[8]

1   See procès-verbaux 6–10, 15–16, 18 of the 3rd Commission, *Actes et Documents de la Quatorzième Session* Tome III, pp 288–319, 360–366, and 389.
2   See ibid, p 168 (art 11 of the Preliminary Draft).
3   Explanatory Report, para 107 (ibid, p 458).
4   14 votes to 10: ibid, p 316.
5   The phrase is Mr Eekelaar's: *The Hague Convention on the Civil Aspects of International Child Abduction* (1981) p 20.
6   Convention, art 17.
7   Ibid.
8   Ibid, art 19.

Access

9.31 One of the objects of The Hague Convention is to ensure that rights of access under the law of one contracting state are effectively respected in the other contracting states.[1] In international cases, especially those involving long distances, the financial and logistical difficulties in the way of the exercise of rights of access may be more significant than any reluctance on the part of the custodial parent to allow access. However, cases do of course arise in which a parent refuses to allow the actual exercise of clear rights of access, and the Convention makes an attempt to deal with these cases.

As with custody cases, Central Authorities have a major role. An application may be made to a Central Authority to make arrangements for organising or securing the effective exercise of rights of access. A Central Authority is under a duty 'to promote the peaceful enjoyment of access rights and the fulfilment of any conditions to which the exercise of those rights may be subject'.[2] This would presumably include, for example, the provision of an element of supervision if that was required under the terms of a court order or binding agreement. Central Authorities are to take steps to remove, as far as possible, all obstacles to the exercise of access rights;[3] this would obviously include tracing a child whose whereabouts are unknown, but it is doubtful if it would carry a duty to provide financial assistance.

If proceedings must be taken, the Central Authorities may take appropriate steps as in the custody context.[4]

1 Convention, art 1(b).
2 Ibid, art 21, which forms the sole article of Chapter IV on Rights of Access.
3 Ibid.
4 Ibid.

Ancillary provisions

9.32 Chapter V of the Convention contains a large number of general provisions ancillary to the major provisions already examined. Some are provisions commonly included in Conventions negotiated at The Hague such as prohibitions upon the requirement of security for costs (the cautio judicatum solvi)[1] or of legalisation.[2] Others are more specifically related to the subject-matter of the Convention.

So the Convention requires that applications and other documents sent to a Central Authority be accompanied by a translation into an official language of the requested state, or, if that is not feasible, into French or English; a contracting state may by Reservation object to the use of either French or English but not to both.[3] A Central Authority may also require that the application be accompanied by a written authorisation to act, a power of attorney or similar document; this is to meet the requirements of the law as to civil procedure in some signatory countries.[4] When it is 'manifest' that the Convention's requirements are not fulfilled or that the application is otherwise not well founded, a Central Authority may in effect reject the application in limine, notifying the applicant of its reasons.[5]

Article 26 contains some important provisions as to costs and expenses. The general rule is that Central Authorities and other public services of contracting states should carry all the costs of applications under the Convention on their normal budget, making no charge either to other Central Authorities or to the applicant. To this rule there are two exceptions. The first concerns the expenses 'incurred or to be incurred' in implementing the return of the child;[6] the payment of these expenses may be required, apparently from the applicant although the Convention is not entirely clear on the point.[7] The words quoted suggest that payment in advance may be required. The second exception concerns expenses resulting from lawyers' participation or court proceedings; by making a Reservation, a contracting state may declare that it will not accept the obligation to pay such expenses except insofar as they are covered by its system of legal aid and advice;[8] legal aid and advice is to be made available to nationals of contracting states and persons habitually resident in those states on matters relating to the Convention on the same terms as it is available to nationals and habitual residents of the requested state.[9]

The Convention contains provisions dealing with cases in which a state has different systems of law applicable to different territorial units or to different categories of persons, making it clear that it applies at the international level and not as between different units of one state.[10]

The Convention is not retrospective: it applies in respect of wrongful removals or retentions occurring after its entry into force.[11] This and other restrictions on the Convention's effectiveness in securing the return of children may be derogated from by two or more contracting states as between themselves.[12]

1   Convention, art 22.
2   Ibid, art 23.
3   Ibid, art 24.
4   Ibid, art 28.
5   Ibid, art 27.
6   Semble, this provision is inapplicable to cases involving only the exercise of access rights (where expenses may be incurred).
7   Convention, art 26, second paragraph.
8   Ibid, third paragraph.
9   Ibid, art 25.
10 Ibid, arts 31–33; on art 33, see E. Pérez-Vera, Explanatory Report, para 142 (*Actes et Documents de la Quatorzième Session* Tome III, p 470).
11 Convention, art 35.
12 Ibid, art 36.

Assessment and adoption of the Convention

9.33   There seems little doubt that The Hague Convention is the best available model for legislative action designed to deal with international child custody disputes.

Its merits include its comprehensive coverage of the various situations that can arise; it is not limited to the narrower area of the enforcement of existing custody orders, and deals with cases in which the care of the child has become vested in persons other than the parents or in institutions. The wisdom of the decision not to seek agreement on uniform jurisdictional rules is self-evident; on the international plane, the difficulties in this approach, whatever its virtues within the United States or Canada, are too great. Above all the Central Authorities device, which has proved so successful in civil procedure Conventions negotiated at The Hague, promises to afford realistic assistance to the parties and their advisers in what can be extremely difficult situations.

At a more technical level, one can accept the estimate of the President of the Commission which elaborated the text. It is:

'simple in application, in its general structure, and in the definition of the key concepts it utilises. It is simple also in the sense that it admits of no reservations in relation to its central rules and no counter-reservations of any kind. It includes various compromise solutions which ideally some States would have preferred not to make; but the fact that these compromises were admitted points to the feeling among delegates that as few States as possible should be precluded from ratifying the Convention. It was appreciated, that is to say, that the effectiveness of the Convention may depend less upon its precise terms than upon its adoption by a relatively large number of States.'[1]

Support for the Convention may well depend in turn on the views of governments as to the balance struck in the crucial arts 12 and 13.[2] The 'twelve-month rule' and the balancing provisions as to 'physical and psychological harm', operating in a context which is essentially one of jurisdiction, not of ultimate decision-making, would seem to be well within the spirit of Commonwealth practice and a great deal more precise and simple in formulation.

The Canadian Uniform Law Conference has already produced a simple Model Act designed to give effect to the Convention which is scheduled to it. A number of provinces have already introduced draft legislation; Acts passed include those in Alberta,[3] New Brunswick[4] and Ontario.[5] A further draft Model Bill, giving effect to the Convention provisions by a different technique, was prepared by Mr Eekelaar for the Commonwealth Secretariat.[6] It is submitted that action by many Commonwealth governments should follow.

1 Professor A. E. Anton (1981) 30 ICLQ at 556.
2 See para 9.30 above.
3 Family Relations Act 1982, c 8 (Alberta).
4 International Child Abduction Act 1982, c I-12.1 (New Brunswick).
5 Children's Law Reform Amendment Act 1982, c 20 (Ontario).
6 See *The Hague Convention on the Civil Aspects of International Child Abduction* (Commonwealth Secretariat, 1981).

Appendices

Domicile: Selected Texts

(1) DOMICILE ACT 1976

(New Zealand)

1. Short title and commencement.—(1) This Act may be cited as the Domicile Act 1976.

(2) This Act shall come into force on a date to be appointed by the Governor-General by Order in Council.

2. Interpretation.—In this Act, unless the context otherwise requires—
'Country' means a territory of a type in which, immediately before the com-
    mencement of this Act, a person could have been domiciled:
'Union' means a nation comprising 2 or more countries.

3. Domicile before commencement.—The domicile that a person had at a time before the commencement of this Act shall be determined as if this Act had not been passed.

4. Domicile after commencement.—The domicile that a person has at a time after the commencement of this Act shall be determined as if this Act had always been in force.

5. Wife's dependent domicile abolished.—(1) Every married person is capable of having an independent domicile; and the rule of law whereby upon marriage a woman acquires her husband's domicile and is thereafter during the subsistence of the marriage incapable of having any other domicile is hereby abolished.

(2) This section applies to the parties to every marriage, wherever and pursuant to whatever law solemnised, and whatever the domicile of the parties at the time of the marriage.

6. Children.—(1) This section shall have effect in place of all rules of law relating to the domicile of children.

(2) In this section 'child' means a person under the age of 16 years who has not married.

(3) A child whose parents are living together has the domicile for the time being of its father.

(4) If a child whose parents are not living together has its home with its father it has the domicile for the time being of its father; and after it ceases to have its home with him it continues to have that domicile (or, if he is dead, the domicile he had at his death) until it has its home with its mother.

(5) Subject to subsection (4) of this section, a child whose parents are not living together has the domicile for the time being of its mother (or, if she is dead, the domicile she had at her death).

(6) Until a foundling child has its home with one of its parents, both its parents shall, for the purposes of this section, be deemed to be alive and domiciled in the country in which the foundling child was found.

7. Attainment of independent domicile.—Subject to any rule of law relating to the domicile of insane persons, every person becomes capable of having an independent domicile upon attaining the age of 16 years or sooner marrying, and thereafter continues so to be capable.

8. Domicile to continue.—The domicile a person has immediately before becoming capable of having an independent domicile continues until he acquires a new domicile in accordance with section 9 of this Act, and then ceases.

9. Acquisition of new domicile.—A person acquires a new domicile in a country at a particular time if, immediately before that time—
(a)   He is not domiciled in that country; and
(b)   He is capable of having an independent domicile; and
(c)   He is in that country; and
(d)   He intends to live indefinitely in that country.

10. Deemed intention.—A person who ordinarily resides and intends to live indefinitely in a union but has not formed an intention to live indefinitely in any one country forming part of the union shall be deemed to intend to live indefinitely—
(a)   In that country forming part of the union in which he ordinarily resides; or
(b)   If he does not ordinarily reside in any such country, in whichever such country he is in; or
(c)   If he neither ordinarily resides nor is in any such country, in whichever such country he was last in.

11. Domicile of origin not to revive.—A new domicile acquired in accordance with section 9 of this Act continues until a further new domicile is acquired in accordance with that section; and the rule of law known as the revival of domicile of origin whereby a person's domicile of origin revives upon his abandoning a domicile of choice is hereby abolished.

12. Standard of proof.—The standard of proof which, immediately before the commencement of this Act, was sufficient to show the abandonment of a domicile of choice and in the acquisition of another domicile of choice shall be sufficient to show the acquisition of a new domicile in accordance with section 9 of this Act.

13. Domicile in unions.—A person domiciled in a country forming part of a union is also domiciled in that union.

14. Consequential amendments and repeals.—[not reproduced]

(2) UNIFORM AUSTRALIAN DOMICILE ACT
as enacted as DOMICILE ACT 1981

(Queensland)

1. Short title.—This Act may be cited as the *Domicile Act* 1981.

2. Commencement.—(1) Section 1 and this section shall commence on the day on which it is assented to for and on behalf of Her Majesty.

(2) Except as provided in subsection (1), this Act shall commence on a day to be appointed by Proclamation.

3. Interpretation.—In this Act, save where a contrary intention appears—
'Commonwealth of Australia' means the territory comprising the States and the Australian Capital Territory, the Jervis Bay Territory and the Northern Territory of Australia;
'country' includes any state, province or other territory—
(a) that is one of two or more territories that together form a country; and
(b) domicile in which can be material for any purpose of the laws of Queensland;
'union' means any country that is a union or federation or other aggregation of two or more countries and includes the Commonwealth of Australia.

4. Operation of Act.—(1) The domicile of a person at a time before the commencement of this section shall be determined as if this Act had not been enacted.

(2) The domicile of a person at a time after the commencement of this section shall be determined as if this Act had always been in force.

(3) Nothing in this Act affects the jurisdiction of any court in any proceedings commenced before the commencement of this section.

(4) This Act has effect to the exclusion of the application of the laws of any other country relating to any matter dealt with by this Act.

5. Abolition of rule of dependent domicile of married woman.—The rule of law whereby a married woman has at all times the domicile of her husband is abolished.

6. Abolition of rule of revival of domicile of origin.—The rule of law whereby the domicile of origin revives upon the abandonment of a domicile of choice without the acquisition of a new domicile of choice is abolished and the domicile a person has at any time continues until he acquires a different domicile.

7. Capacity to have independent domicile.—(1) A person is capable of having an independent domicile if—
(a) he has attained the age of 18 years; or
(b) he is, or has at any time been, married,
and not otherwise.

(2) Subsection (1) does not apply to a person who, under the rules of law relating to domicile, is incapable of acquiring a domicile by reason of mental incapacity.

8. Domicile of certain children.—(1) In this section—

(a) 'child' means a person under the age of 18 years who is not, and has not at any time been, married; and

(b) references to the parents of a child include references to parents who are not married to each other.

(2) Where, at any time, a child has his principal home with one of his parents but his parents are living separately and apart or the child does not have another living parent, the domicile of the child at that time is the domicile that that parent has at that time and thereafter the child has the domicile that that parent has from time to time or, if that parent has died, the domicile that that parent had at the time of death.

(3) Where a child is adopted, his domicile—

(a)   if, upon his adoption, he has two parents—is, at the time of the adoption and thereafter, the domicile he would have if he were a child born in wedlock to those parents; and

(b)   if, upon his adoption, he has one parent only—is, at the time of the adoption, the domicile of that parent and thereafter is the domicile that that parent has from time to time or, if that parent has died, the domicile that that parent had at the time of death.

(4) A child ceases to have, by virtue of subsection (2), the domicile or last domicile of one of his parents if—

(a)   he commences to have his principal home with his other parent; or

(b)   his parents resume or commence living together.

(5) Where a child has a domicile by virtue of subsection (2) or (3) immediately before he ceases to be a child, he retains that domicile until he acquires a domicile of choice.

(6) Where the adoption of a child is rescinded, the domicile of the child shall thereafter be determined in accordance with any provisions with respect to that domicile that are included in the order rescinding the adoption and, so far as no such provision is applicable, as if the adoption had not taken place.

9. Intention for domicile of choice.—The intention that a person must have in order to acquire a domicile of choice in a country is the intention to make his home indefinitely in that country.

10. Domicile in union.—A person who is, in accordance with the rules of the common law as modified by this Act, domiciled in a union but is not, apart from this section, domiciled in any particular one of the countries that together form the union is domiciled in that one of those countries with which he has for the time being the closest connection.

11. Evidence of acquisition of domicile of choice.—The acquisition of a domicile of choice in place of a domicile of origin may be established by evidence that would be sufficient to establish the domicile of choice if the previous domicile had also been a domicile of choice.

(3) PART I OF THE DOMICILE AND MATRIMONIAL PROCEEDINGS ACT 1973

(United Kingdom)

PART I

DOMICILE

1. (1) Subject to subsection (2) below, the domicile of a married woman as at any time after the coming into force of this section shall, instead of being the same as her husband's by virtue only of marriage, be ascertained by reference to the same factors as in the case of any other individual capable of having an independent domicile.

(2) Where immediately before this section came into force a woman was married and then had her husband's domicile by dependence, she is to be treated as retaining that domicile (as a domicile of choice, if it is not also her domicile of origin) unless and until it is changed by acquisition or revival of another domicile either on or after the coming into force of this section.

3. (1) The time at which a person first becomes capable of having an independent domicile shall be when he attains the age of sixteen or marries under that age; and in the case of a person who immediately before 1st January 1974 was incapable of having an independent domicile, but had then attained the age of sixteen or been married, it shall be that date.

4. (1) Subsection (2) of this section shall have effect with respect to the dependent domicile of a child as at any time after the coming into force of this section when his father and mother are alive but living apart.

(2) The child's domicile as at that time shall be that of his mother if—
(a)   he then has his home with her and has no home with his father; or
(b)   he has at any time had her domicile by virtue of paragraph (a) above and has not since had a home with his father.

(3) As at any time after the coming into force of this section, the domicile of a child whose mother is dead shall be that which she last had before she died if at her death he had her domicile by virtue of subsection (2) above and he has not since had a home with his father.

(4) Nothing in this section prejudices any existing rule of law as to the cases in which a child's domicile is regarded as being, by dependence, that of his mother.

(5) In this section, 'child' means a person incapable of having an independent domicile; and in its application to a child who has been adopted, references to his father and his mother shall be construed as references to his adoptive father and mother.

Divorce: Selected Texts

(1) HAGUE CONVENTION ON THE RECOGNITION OF DIVORCES AND LEGAL SEPARATIONS 1970

(omitting the Final Clauses in articles 26 to 31)

The States signatory to the present Convention.
Desiring to facilitate the recognition of divorces and legal separations obtained in their respective territories.
Have resolved to conclude a Convention to this effect, and have agreed on the following provisions:

ARTICLE 1
The present Convention shall apply to the recognition in one Contracting State of divorces and legal separations obtained in another Contracting State which follow judicial or other proceedings officially recognised in that State and which are legally effective there.

The Convention does not apply to findings of fault or to ancillary orders pronounced on the making of a decree of divorce or legal separation; in particular, it does not apply to orders relating to pecuniary obligations or to the custody of children.

ARTICLE 2
Such divorces and legal separations shall be recognised in all other Contracting States, subject to the remaining terms of this Convention, if, at the date of the institution of the proceedings in the State of the divorce or legal separation (hereinafter called 'the State of origin'):
(1)   the respondent had his habitual residence there; or
(2)   the petitioner had his habitual residence there and one of the following further conditions was fulfilled—
    (a)   such habitual residence had continued for not less than one year immediately prior to the institution of proceedings;
    (b)   the spouses last habitually resided there together; or
(3)   both spouses were nationals of that State; or
(4)   the petitioner was a national of that State and one of the following further conditions was fulfilled—
    (a)   the petitioner had his habitual residence there; or
    (b)   he had habitually resided there for a continuous period of one year falling, at least in part, within the two years preceding the institution of the proceedings; or
(5)   the petitioner for divorce was a national of that State and both the following further conditions were fulfilled—
    (a)   the petitioner was present in that State at the date of institution of the proceedings and

(b)   the spouses last habitually resided together in a State whose law, at the date of institution of the proceedings, did not provide for divorce.

ARTICLE 3

Where the State of origin uses the concept of domicile as a test of jurisdiction in matters of divorce or legal separation, the expression 'habitual residence' in Article 2 shall be deemed to include domicile as the term is used in that State.

Nevertheless, the preceding paragraph shall not apply to the domicile of dependence of a wife.

ARTICLE 4

Where there has been a cross-petition, a divorce or legal separation following upon the petition or cross-petition shall be recognised if either falls within the terms of Articles 2 or 3.

ARTICLE 5

Where a legal separation complying with the terms of this Convention has been converted into a divorce in the State of origin, the recognition of the divorce shall not be refused for the reason that the conditions stated in Articles 2 or 3 were no longer fulfilled at the time of the institution of the divorce proceedings.

ARTICLE 6

Where the respondent has appeared in the proceedings, the authorities of the State in which recognition of a divorce or legal separation is sought shall be bound by the findings of fact on which jurisdiction was assumed.

The recognition of a divorce or legal separation shall not be refused—

(a)   because the internal law of the State in which such recognition is sought would not allow divorce or, as the case may be, legal separation upon the same facts, or,

(b)   because a law was applied other than that applicable under the rules of private international law of that State.

Without prejudice to such review as may be necessary for the application of other provisions of this Convention, the authorities of the State in which recognition of a divorce or legal separation is sought shall not examine the merits of the decision.

ARTICLE 7

Contracting States may refuse to recognise a divorce when, at the time it was obtained, both the parties were nationals of States which did not provide for divorce and of no other State.

ARTICLE 8

If, in the light of all the circumstances, adequate steps were not taken to give notice of the proceedings for a divorce or legal separation to the respondent, or if he was not afforded a sufficient opportunity to present his case, the divorce or legal separation may be refused recognition.

ARTICLE 9

Contracting States may refuse to recognise a divorce or legal separation if it is incompatible with a previous decision determining the matrimonial status of the spouses and that decision either was rendered in the State in which recognition is sought, or is recognised, or fulfils the conditions required for recognition, in that State.

ARTICLE 10
Contracting States may refuse to recognise a divorce or legal separation is such recognition is manifestly incompatible with their public policy ('ordre public').

ARTICLE 11
A State which is obliged to recognise a divorce under this Convention may not preclude either spouse from remarrying on the ground that the law of another State does not recognise that divorce.

ARTICLE 12
Proceedings for divorce or legal separation in any Contracting State may be suspended when proceedings relating to the matrimonial status of either party to the marriage are pending in another Contracting State.

ARTICLE 13
In the application of this Convention to divorces or legal separations obtained or sought to be recognised in Contracting States having, in matters of divorce or legal separation, two or more legal systems applying in different territorial units—
(1)   any reference to the law of the State of origin shall be construed as referring to the law of the territory in which the divorce or separation was obtained;
(2)   any reference to the law of the State in which recognition is sought shall be construed as referring to the law of the forum; and
(3)   any reference to domicile or residence in the State of origin shall be construed as referring to domicile or residence in the territory in which the divorce or separation was obtained.

ARTICLE 14
For the purposes of Articles 2 and 3 where the State of origin has in matters of divorce or legal separation, two or more legal systems applying in different territorial units—
(1)   Article 2, sub-paragraph (3), shall apply where both spouses were nationals of the State of which the territorial unit where the divorce or legal separation was obtained forms a part, and that regardless of the habitual residence of the spouses;
(2)   Article 2, sub-paragraphs (4) and (5), shall apply where the petitioner was a national of the State of which the territorial unit where the divorce or legal separation was obtained forms a part.

ARTICLE 15
In relation to a Contracting State having, in matters of divorce or legal separation, two or more legal systems applicable to different categories of persons, any reference to the law of that State shall be construed as referring to the legal system specified by the law of that State.

ARTICLE 16
When, for the purposes of this Convention, it is necessary to refer to the law of a State, whether or not it is a Contracting State, other than the State of origin

or the State in which recognition is sought, and having in matters of divorce or legal separation two or more legal systems of territorial or personal application, reference shall be made to the system specified by the law of that State.

ARTICLE 17

This Convention shall not prevent the application in a Contracting State of rules of law more favourable to the recognition of foreign divorces and legal separations.

ARTICLE 18

This Convention shall not affect the operation of other conventions to which one or several Contracting States are or may in the future become Parties and which contain provisions relating to the subject-matter of this Convention.

Contracting States, however, should refrain from concluding other conventions on the same matters incompatible with the terms of this Convention, unless for special reasons based on regional or other ties; and, notwithstanding the terms of such conventions, they undertake to recognise in accordance with this Convention divorces and legal separations granted in Contracting States which are not Parties to such other conventions.

ARTICLE 19

Contracting States may, not later than the time of ratification or accession, reserve the right—

(1) to refuse to recognise a divorce or legal separation between two spouses who, at the time of the divorce or legal separation, were nationals of the State in which recognition is sought, and of no other State, and a law other than that indicated by the rules of private international law of the State of recognition was applied, unless the result reached is the same as that which would have been reached by applying the law indicated by those rules;

(2) to refuse to recognise a divorce when, at the time it was obtained, both parties habitually resided in States which did not provide for divorce. A State which utilises the reservation stated in this paragraph may not refuse recognition by the application of Article 7.

ARTICLE 20

Contracting States whose law does not provide for divorce may, not later than the time of ratification or accession, reserve the right not to recognise a divorce if, at the date it was obtained, one of the spouses was a national of a State whose law did not provide for divorce.

This reservation shall have effect only so long as the law of the State utilising it does not provide for divorce.

ARTICLE 21

Contracting States whose law does not provide for legal separation may, not later than the time of ratification or accession, reserve the right to refuse to recognise a legal separation when, at the time it was obtained, one of the spouses was a national of a Contracting State whose law did not provide for legal separation.

ARTICLE 22

Contracting States may, from time to time, declare that certain categories of persons having their nationality need not be considered their nationals for the purposes of this Convention.

ARTICLE 23

If a Contracting State has more than one legal system in matters of divorce or legal separation, it may, at the time of signature, ratification or accession, declare that this Convention shall extend to all its legal systems or only to one or more of them, and may modify its declaration by submitting another declaration at any time thereafter.

These declarations shall be notified to the Ministry of Foreign Affairs of the Netherlands, and shall state expressly the legal systems to which the Convention applies.

Contracting States may decline to recognise a divorce or legal separation if, at the date on which recognition is sought, the Convention is not applicable to the legal system under which the divorce or legal separation was obtained.

ARTICLE 24

This Convention applies regardless of the date on which the divorce or legal separation was obtained.

Nevertheless a Contracting State may, not later than the time of ratification or accession, reserve the right not to apply this Convention to a divorce or to a legal separation obtained before the date on which, in relation to that State, the Convention comes into force.

ARTICLE 25

Any State may, not later than the moment of its ratification or accession, make one or more of the reservations mentioned in Articles 19, 20, 21 and 24 of the present Convention. No other reservation shall be permitted.

Each Contracting State may also, when notifying an extension of the Convention in accordance with Article 29, make one or more of the said reservations, with its effect limited to all or some of the territories mentioned in the extension.

Each Contracting State may at any time withdraw a reservation it has made. Such a withdrawal shall be notified to the Ministry of Foreign Affairs of the Netherlands.

Such a reservation shall cease to have effect on the sixtieth day after the notification referred to in the preceding paragraph.

(2) RECOGNITION OF DIVORCES AND LEGAL SEPARATIONS ACT 1971

(United Kingdom)

(as amended by the Domicile and Matrimonial Proceedings Act 1973)

Whereas a Convention on the recognition of divorces and legal separations was opened for signature at The Hague on 1st June 1970 and was signed on behalf of the United Kingdom on that date:

And whereas with a view to the ratification by the United Kingdom of that Convention, and for other purposes, it is expedient to amend the law relating to the recognition of divorces and legal separations:

Be it therefore enacted, etc.

Decrees of divorce and judicial separation granted in British Isles

1.—Subject to section 8 of this Act, the validity of a decree of divorce or judicial separation granted after the commencement of this section shall if it was granted under the law of any part of the British Isles, be recognised throughout the United Kingdom.

Overseas divorces and legal separations

2.—Sections 3 to 5 of this Act shall have effect, subject to section 8 of this Act, as respects the recognition in the United Kingdom of the validity of overseas divorces and legal separations, that is to say, divorces and legal separations which—

(a) have been obtained by means of judicial or other proceedings in any country outside the British Isles; and

(b) are effective under the law of that country.

3.—(1) The validity of an overseas divorce or legal separation shall be recognised if, at the date of the institution of the proceedings in the country in which it was obtained—

(a) either spouse was habitually resident in that country; or

(b) either spouse was a national of that country.

(2) In relation to a country the law of which uses the concept of domicile as a ground of jurisdiction in matters of divorce or legal separation, subsection (1) (a) of this section shall have effect as if the reference to habitual residence included a reference to domicile within the meaning of that law.

(3) In relation to a country comprising territories in which different systems of law are in force in matters of divorce or legal separation, the foregoing provisions of this section (except those relating to nationality) shall have effect as if each territory were a separate country.

4.—(1) Where there have been cross-proceedings, the validity of an overseas divorce or legal separation obtained either in the original proceedings or in the cross-proceedings shall be recognised if the requirements of paragraph (a) or (b) of section 3(1) of this Act are satisfied in relation to the date of the institution either of the original proceedings or of the cross-proceedings.

(2) Where a legal separation the validity of which is entitled to recognition by virtue of the provisions of section 3 of this Act or of subsection (1) of this section is converted, in the country in which it was obtained, into a divorce, the validity of the divorce shall be recognised whether or not it would itself be entitled to recognition by virtue of those provisions.

5.—(1) For the purpose of deciding whether an overseas divorce or legal separation is entitled to recognition by virtue of the foregoing provisions of this Act, any finding of fact made (whether expressly or by implication) in the proceedings by means of which the divorce or legal separation was obtained and on the basis of which jurisdiction was assumed in those proceedings shall—

(a) if both spouses took part in the proceedings, be conclusive evidence of the fact found; and

(b) in any other case, be sufficient proof of that fact unless the contrary is shown.

(2) In this section 'finding of fact' includes a finding that either spouse was

habitually resident or domiciled in, or a national of, the country in which the divorce or legal separation was obtained; and for the purposes of subsection (1) (a) of this section, a spouse who has appeared in judicial proceedings shall be treated as having taken part in them.

General provisions

6.—(1) In this section 'the common law rules' means the rules of law relating to the recognition of divorces or legal separations obtained in the country of the spouses' domicile or obtained elsewhere and recognised as valid in that country.

(2) In any circumstances in which the validity of a divorce or legal separation obtained in a country outside the British Isles would be recognised by virtue only of the common law rules if either—

(a)   the spouses had at the material time both been domiciled in that country; or

(b)   the divorce or separation were recognised as valid under the law of the spouses' domicile,

its validity shall also be recognised if subsection (3) below is satisfied in relation to it.

(3) This subsection is satisfied in relation to a divorce or legal separation obtained in a country outside the British Isles if either—

(a)   one of the spouses was at the material time domiciled in that country and the divorce or separation was recognised as valid under the law of the domicile of the other spouse; or

(b)   neither of the spouses having been domiciled in that country at the material time, the divorce or separation was recognised as valid under the law of the domicile of each of the spouses respectively.

(4) For any purpose of subsection (2) or (3) above 'the material time', in relation to a divorce or legal separation, means the time of the institution of proceedings in the country in which it was obtained.

(5) Sections 2 to 5 of this Act are without prejudice to the recognition of the validity of divorces and legal separations obtained outside the British Isles by virtue of the common law rules (as extended by this section), or of any enactment other than this Act; but, subject to this section, no divorce or legal separation so obtained shall be recognised as valid in the United Kingdom except as provided by those sections.

7. Where the validity of a divorce obtained in any country is entitled to recognition by virtue of sections 1 to 5 or section 6(2) of this Act or by virtue of any rule or enactment preserved by section 6(5) of this Act, neither spouse shall be precluded from re-marrying in the United Kingdom on the ground that the validity of the divorce would not be recognised in any other country.

8.—(1) The validity of—

(a)   a decree of divorce or judicial separation granted under the law of any part of the British Isles; or

(b)   a divorce or legal separation obtained outside the British Isles

shall not be recognised in any part of the United Kingdom if it was granted or obtained at a time when, according to the law of that part of the United Kingdom (including its rules of private international law and the provisions of this Act), there was no subsisting marriage between the parties.

(2) Subject to subsection (1) of this section, recognition by virtue of sections

2 to 5 or section 6(2) of this Act or of any rule preserved by section 6(5) thereof of the validity of a divorce or legal separation obtained outside the British Isles may be refused if, and only if—

(a)   it was obtained by one spouse—

    (i)   without such steps having been taken for giving notice of the proceedings to the other spouse as, having regard to the nature of the proceedings and all the circumstances, should reasonably have been taken; or

    (ii)   without the other spouse having been given (for any reason other than lack of notice) such opportunity to take part in the proceedings as, having regard to the matters aforesaid, he should reasonably have been given; or

(b)   its recognition would manifestly be contrary to public policy.

(3)   Nothing in this Act shall be construed as requiring the recognition of any findings of fault made in any proceedings for divorce or separation or of any maintenance, custody or other ancillary order made in any such proceedings.

9.   [Repealed]

10.—(1)   This Act may be cited as the Recognition of Divorces and Legal Separations Act 1971.

(2)   In this Act 'the British Isles' means the United Kingdom, the Channel Islands and the Isle of Man.

(3)   In this Act 'country' includes a colony or other dependent territory of the United Kingdom but for the purposes of this Act a person shall be treated as a national of such a territory only if it has a law of citizenship or nationality separate from that of the United Kingdom and he is a citizen or national of that territory under that law.

(4)   The provisions of this Act relating to overseas divorces and legal separations and other divorces and legal separations obtained outside the British Isles apply to a divorce or legal separation obtained before the date of the commencement of those provisions as well as to one obtained on or after that date and, in the case of a divorce or legal separation obtained before that date—

(a)   require, or, as the case may be, preclude, the recognition of its validity in relation to any time before that date as well as in relation to any subsequent time; but

(b)   do not affect any property rights to which any person became entitled before that date or apply where the question of the validity of the divorce or legal separation has been decided by any competent court in the British Isles before that date.

(5)   Section 9 of this Act shall come into operation on the passing of this Act and the remainder on 1st January 1972.

(3) FAMILY LAW ACT 1975

(Commonwealth of Australia)

104.   (1)   In this section—

'applicant', in relation to the dissolution or annulment of a marriage, means the party at whose instance the dissolution or annulment was effected;

'marriage' includes a purported marriage that is void;

'overseas country' means a country, or part of a country, outside Australia;

'relevant date', in relation to a dissolution or annulment of a marriage, means the date of the institution of the proceedings that resulted in the dissolution or annulment;

'respondent', in relation to the dissolution or annulment of a marriage, means a party to the marriage not being the party at whose instance the dissolution or annulment was effected.

(2) For the purposes of this section, a person who is a national of a country of which an overseas country forms part shall be deemed to be a national of that overseas country.

(3) A dissolution or annulment of a marriage effected in accordance with the law of an overseas country shall be recognised as valid in Australia where—

(a)   the respondent was ordinarily resident in the overseas country at the relevant date;

(b)   the applicant was ordinarily resident in the overseas country at the relevant date and either—

    (i)   the ordinary residence of the applicant had continued for not less than 1 year immediately before the relevant date; or

    (ii)   the last place of cohabitation of the parties to the marriage was in that country;

(c)   the applicant or the respondent was domiciled in the overseas country at the relevant date;

(d)   the respondent was a national of the overseas country at the relevant date;

(e)   the applicant was a national of the overseas country at the relevant date and either—

    (i)   the applicant was ordinarily resident in that country at that date; or

    (ii)   the applicant had been ordinarily resident in that country for a continuous period of 1 year falling, at least in part, within the 2 years immediately before the relevant date; or

(f)   the applicant was a national of, and present in, the overseas country at the relevant date and the last place of cohabitation of the parties to the marriage was in an overseas country the law of which, at the relevant date, did not provide for dissolution of marriage or annulment of marriage, as the case may be.

(4) A dissolution or annulment of a marriage shall not be recognized as valid by virtue of sub-section (3) where—

(a)   under the common law rules of private international law, recognition of its validity would be refused on the ground that a party to the marriage had been denied natural justice or that the dissolution or annulment was obtained by fraud; or

(b)   recognition would manifestly be contrary to public policy.

(5) Any dissolution or annulment of a marriage that would be recognized as valid under the common law rules of private international law but to which none of the preceding provisions of this section applies shall be recognized as valid in Australia, and the operation of this sub-section shall not be limited by any implication from those provisions.

(6) Notwithstanding anything contained in this section, the annulment in accordance with the law of an overseas country of a marriage solemnized under Part V of the *Marriage Act* 1961 or of that Act as amended, being an annulment

on the ground only of non-compliance with the formalities prescribed by the law of the country in which the marriage was solemnized, shall not be recognized as valid in Australia.

(7) For the purposes of this section, a court in Australia, in considering the validity of a dissolution or annulment effected under the law of an overseas country, may treat as proved any facts found by a court of the overseas country or otherwise established for the purposes of the law of the overseas country.

(8) For the purposes of the preceding provisions of this section but without limiting the operation of those provisions, a dissolution or annulment of a marriage shall be deemed to have been effected in accordance with the law of an overseas country if it was effected in another overseas country in circumstances in which, at the relevant date, it would have been recognized as valid by the law of the first-mentioned overseas country.

(9) Where a dissolution or annulment of a marriage is to be recognized as valid in accordance with this section, the capacity of a party to that marriage to re-marry in accordance with the law of Australia is not affected by the fact that the validity of the dissolution or annulment is not recognized under the law of some other country.

(10) The preceding provisions of this section apply in relation to dissolutions and annulments effected whether by decree, legislation or otherwise, whether before or after the commencement of this Act, and, for the purposes of this section, any decree, legislation or other process by which it is established that a purported marriage was or is to become void shall be deemed to be an annulment of the marriage.

Financial Provision: Selected Texts

(1) THE MAINTENANCE ORDERS (FACILITIES FOR ENFORCEMENT) ACT 1920, CAP. 33

enacted in the United Kingdom on 16 August 1920 and circulated with a view to the enactment of corresponding local legislation in Colonial Office General Circular 47330/20 of 8 October 1920.

An Act to facilitate the enforcement in England and Ireland of Maintenance Orders made in other parts of His Majesty's Dominions and Protectorates and vice versa.

BE IT ENACTED, etc.

1. Enforcement in England and Ireland of maintenance orders made in His Majesty's dominions outside the United Kingdom.—(1) Where a maintenance order has, whether before or after the passing of this Act, been made against any person by any court in any part of His Majesty's dominions outside the United Kingdom to which this Act extends, and a certified copy of the order has been transmitted by the governor of that part of His Majesty's dominions to the Secretary of State, the Secretary of State shall send a copy of the order to the prescribed officer of a court in England or Ireland for registration; and on receipt thereof the order shall be registered in the prescribed manner, and shall, from the date of such registration, be of the same force and effect, and subject to the provisions of this Act, all proceedings may be taken on such order as if it had been an order originally obtained in the court in which it is so registered, and that court shall have power to enforce the order accordingly.

(2) The court in which an order is to be so registered as aforesaid shall, if the court by which the order was made was a court of superior jurisdiction, be the Probate, Divorce and Admiralty Division of the High Court, or in Ireland the King's Bench Division (Matrimonial) of the High Court of Justice in Ireland, and, if the court was not a court of superior jurisdiction, be a court of summary jurisdiction.

2. Transmission of maintenance orders made in England or Ireland.—Where a court in England or Ireland has, whether before or after the commencement of this Act, made a maintenance order against any person, and it is proved to that court that the person against whom the order was made is resident in some part of His Majesty's dominions outside the United Kingdom to which this Act extends, the court shall send to the Secretary of State for transmission to the governor of that part of His Majesty's dominions a certified copy of the order.

3. Power to make provisional orders of maintenance against persons resident in His Majesty's dominions outside the United Kingdom.— (1) Where an application is made to a court of summary jurisdiction in England or Ireland for a maintenance order against any person, and it is proved that that person is resident in a part of His Majesty's dominions outside the United Kingdom to which this Act extends, the court may, in the absence of that person, if after hearing the evidence it is satisfied of the justice of the application, make any such order as it might have made if a summons had been duly served on that person and he had failed to appear at the hearing, but in such case the order shall be provisional only, and shall have no effect unless and until confirmed by a competent court in such part of His Majesty's dominions as aforesaid.

(2) The evidence of any witness who is examined on any such application shall be put into writing, and such deposition shall be read over to and signed by him.

(3) Where such an order is made, the court shall send to the Secretary of State for transmission to the governor of the part of His Majesty's dominions in which the person against whom the order is made is alleged to reside the depositions so taken and a certified copy of the order, together with a statement of the grounds on which the making of the order might have been opposed if the person against whom the order is made had been duly served with a summons and had appeared at the hearing, and such information as the court possesses for facilitating the identification of that person, and ascertaining his whereabouts.

(4) Where any such provisional order has come before a court in a part of His Majesty's dominions outside the United Kingdom to which this Act extends for confirmation, and the order has by that court been remitted to the court of summary jurisdiction which made the order for the purpose of taking further evidence, that court or any other court of summary jurisdiction sitting and acting for the same place shall, after giving the prescribed notice, proceed to take the evidence in like manner and subject to the like conditions as the evidence in support of the original application.

If upon the hearing of such evidence it appears to the court that the order ought not to have been made, the court may rescind the order, but in any other case the depositions shall be sent to the Secretary of State and dealt with in like manner as the original depositions.

(5) The confirmation of an order made under this section shall not affect any power of a court of summary jurisdiction to vary or rescind that order: Provided that on the making of a varying or rescinding order the court shall send a certified copy thereof to the Secretary of State for transmission to the governor of the part of His Majesty's dominions in which the original order was confirmed, and that in the case of an order varying the original order the order shall not have any effect unless and until confirmed in like manner as the original order.

(6) The applicant shall have the same right of appeal, if any, against a refusal to make a provisional order as he would have had against a refusal to make the order had a summons been duly served on the person against whom the order is sought to be made.

4. Power of court of summary jurisdiction to confirm maintenance order made out of the United Kingdom.—(1) Where a maintenance order has been made by a court in a part of His Majesty's dominions outside the

United Kingdom to which this Act extends, and the order is provisional only and has no effect unless and until confirmed by a court of summary jurisdiction in England or Ireland, and a certified copy of the order, together with the depositions of witnesses and a statement of the grounds on which the order might have been opposed has been transmitted to the Secretary of State, and it appears to the Secretary of State that the person against whom the order was made is resident in England or Ireland, the Secretary of State may send the said documents to the prescribed officer of a court of summary jurisdiction, with a requisition that a summons be issued calling upon the person to show cause why that order should not be confirmed, and upon receipt of such documents and requisition the court shall issue such a summons and cause it to be served upon such person.

(2) A summons so issued may be served in England or Ireland in the same manner as if it had been originally issued or subsequently endorsed by a court of summary jurisdiction having jurisdiction in the place where the person happens to be.

(3) At the hearing it shall be open to the person on whom the summons was served to raise any defence which he might have raised in the original proceedings had he been a party thereto, but no other defence, and the certificate from the court which made the provisional order stating the grounds on which the making of the order might have been opposed if the person against whom the order was made had been a party to the proceedings shall be conclusive evidence that those grounds are grounds on which objection may be taken.

(4) If at the hearing the person served with the summons does not appear or, on appearing, fails to satisfy the court that the order ought not to be confirmed, the court may confirm the order either without modification or with such modifications as to the court after hearing the evidence may seem just.

(5) If the person against whom the summons was issued appears at the hearing and satisfies the court that for the purpose of any defence it is necessary to remit the case to the court which made the provisional order for the taking of any further evidence, the court may so remit the case and adjourn the proceedings for the purpose.

(6) Where a provisional order has been confirmed under this section, it may be varied or rescinded in like manner as if it had originally been made by the confirming court, and where on an application for rescission or variation the court is satisfied that it is necessary to remit the case to the court which made the order for the purpose of taking any further evidence, the court may so remit the case and adjourn the proceedings for the purpose.

(7) Where an order has been so confirmed, the person bound thereby shall have the same right of appeal, if any, against the confirmation of the order as he would have had against the making of the order had the order been an order made by the court confirming the order.

5. Power of Secretary of State to make regulations for facilitating communications between courts.—The Secretary of State may make regulations as to the manner in which a case can be remitted by a court authorised to confirm a provisional order to the court which made the provisional order, and generally for facilitating communications between such courts.

6. Mode of enforcing orders.—(1) A court of summary jurisdiction in which an order has been registered under this Act or by which an order has been confirmed under this Act, and the officers of such court, shall take all such steps for enforcing the order as may be prescribed.

(2) Every such order shall be enforceable in like manner as if the order were for the payment of a civil debt recoverable summarily:

Provided that, if the order is of such a nature that if made by the court in which it is so registered, or by which it is so confirmed, it would be enforceable in like manner as an order of affiliation, the order shall be so enforceable.

(3) A warrant of distress or commitment issued by a court of summary jurisdiction for the purpose of enforcing any order so registered or confirmed may be executed in any part of the United Kingdom in the same manner as if the warrant had been originally issued or subsequently endorsed by a court of summary jurisdiction having jurisdiction in the place where the warrant is executed.

7. Application of Summary Jurisdiction Acts 42 & 43 Vict c 49.—The Summary Jurisdiction Acts shall apply to proceedings before courts of summary jurisdiction under this Act in like manner as they apply to proceedings under those Acts, and the power of the Lord Chancellor to make rules under section twenty-nine of the Summary Jurisdiction Act, 1879, shall include power to make rules regulating the procedure of courts of summary jurisdiction under this Act.

8. Proof of documents signed by officers of court.—Any document purporting to be signed by a judge or officer of a court outside the United Kingdom shall, until the contrary is proved, be deemed to have been so signed without proof of the signature or judicial or official character of the person appearing to have signed it, and the officer of a court by whom a document is signed shall, until the contrary is proved, be deemed to have been the proper officer of the court to sign the document.

9. Depositions to be evidence.—Depositions taken in a court in a part of His Majesty's dominions outside the United Kingdom to which this Act extends for the purposes of this Act, may be received in evidence in proceedings before courts of summary jurisdiction under this Act.

10. Interpretation.—For the purposes of this Act, the expression 'maintenance order' means an order other than an order of affiliation for the periodical payment of sums of money towards the maintenance of the wife or other dependants of the person against whom the order is made, and the expression 'dependants' means such persons as that person is, according to the law in force in the part of His Majesty's dominions in which the maintenance order was made, liable to maintain; the expression 'certified copy' in relation to an order of a court means a copy of the order certified by the proper officer of the court to be a true copy, and the expression 'prescribed' means prescribed by rules of court.

11. Application to Ireland.—In the application of this Act to Ireland the following modifications shall be made:—

(a) The Lord Chancellor of Ireland may make rules regulating the procedure of courts of summary jurisdiction under this Act, and other matters incidental thereto:

(b)   Orders intended to be registered or confirmed in Ireland shall be transmitted by the Secretary of State to the prescribed officer of a court in
Ireland through the Lord Chancellor of Ireland:

(c)   The expression 'maintenance order' includes an order or decree for the
recovery or repayment of the cost of relief or maintenance made by virtue
of the provisions of the Poor Relief (Ireland) Acts, 1839 to 1914.

12. Extent of Act.—(1) Where His Majesty is satisfied that reciprocal provisions have been made by the legislature of any part of His Majesty's dominions outside the United Kingdom for the enforcement within that part of
maintenance orders made by courts within England and Ireland, His Majesty
may by Order in Council extend this Act to that part, and thereupon that part
shall become a part of His Majesty's dominions to which this Act extends.

(2) His Majesty may by Order in Council extend this Act to any British
protectorate, and where so extended this Act shall apply as if any such protectorate was a part of His Majesty's dominions to which this Act extends.

13. Short title.—This Act may be cited as the Maintenance Orders (Facilities
for Enforcement) Act, 1920.

(2) THE CANADIAN UNIFORM RECIPROCAL ENFORCEMENT OF MAINTENANCE ORDERS ACT

As adopted by the Conference of Uniform Law Commissioners 1979

1. Interpretation.—In this Act

(a)   'Attorney General' includes a person authorized in writing by the Attorney General to act for him in the performance of a power or duty under
this Act;

(b)   'certified copy' means, in relation to a document of a court, the original
or a copy of the document certified by the original or facsimile signature
of a proper officer of the court to be a true copy;

(c)   'claimant' means a person who has or is alleged to have a right to
maintenance;

(d)   'confirmation order' means a confirmation order made under this Act or
under the corresponding enactment of a reciprocating state;

(e)   'court' means an authority having jurisdiction to make an order;

(f)   'final order' means an order made in a proceeding of which the claimant
and respondent had proper notice and in which they had an opportunity
to be present or represented and includes
  (i)   the maintenance provisions in a written agreement between a claimant and a respondent where those provisions are enforceable in
the state in which the agreement was made as if contained in an
order of a court of that state, and
  (ii)   a confirmation order made in a reciprocating state;

(g)   'maintenance' includes support or alimony;

(h)   'order' means an order or determination of a court providing for the
payment of money as maintenance by the respondent named in the order
for the benefit of the claimant named in the order, and includes the
maintenance provisions of an affiliation order;

(i) 'provisional order' means an order of a court in (*the Province*) that has no force or effect in (*the Province*) until confirmed by a court in a reciprocating state or a corresponding order made in a reciprocating state for confirmation in (*the Province*);

(j) 'reciprocating state' means a state declared under section 18(2) or under an enactment repealed by this Act to be a reciprocating state and includes a province;

(k) 'registered order' means
   (i) a final order made in a reciprocating state and filed under this Act or under an enactment repealed by this Act with a court in (*the Province*),
   (ii) a final order deemed under section 2(3) to be a registered order, or
   (iii) a confirmation order that is filed under section 5(8);

(l) 'registration court' means the court in (*the Province*)
   (i) in which the registered order is filed under this Act, or
   (ii) that deemed a final order to be a registered order under this Act or under an enactment repealed by this Act;

(m) 'respondent' means a person in (*the Province*) or in a reciprocating state who has or is alleged to have an obligation to pay maintenance for the benefit of a claimant, or against whom a proceeding under this Act, or a corresponding enactment of a reciprocating state, is commenced;

(n) 'state' includes a political subdivision of a state and an official agency of a state.

2. Final orders of reciprocating state.—(1) Where the Attorney General receives a certified copy of a final order made in a reciprocating state before, on or after the day on which this Act comes into force with information that the respondent is in (*the Province*), the Attorney General shall designate a court in (*the Province*) for the purposes of the registration and enforcement and forward the order and supporting material to that court.

Filing for registration.—(2) On receipt of a final order transmitted to a court under subsection (1) or under a provision in a reciprocating state corresponding to section 5(8) (a), the proper officer of the court shall file the order with the court and give notice of the registration of the order to the respondent.

Claimant leaving province after final order made in province.—(3) Where a final order is made in (*the Province*) before, on or after the day on which this Act comes into force and the claimant subsequently leaves (*the Province*) and is apparently resident in a reciprocating state, the court that made the order shall, on the written request of the claimant, the respondent or the Attorney General, deem the order to be a registered order.

Variation of registered order.—(4) A registered order varied in a manner consistent with this Act, continues to be a registered order.

Setting aside a registered order.—(5) A respondent may, within one month after receiving notice of the registration of a registered order, apply to the registration court to set the registration aside.

Grounds.—(6) On application under subsection (5) the registration court shall set aside the registration if it determines that the order was obtained by fraud or error or was not a final order.

Disposition.—(7) An order determined not to be a final order and set aside under subsection (6) may be dealt with by the registration court under section 5 as a provisional order.

3. Making of provisional orders.—(1) On application by a claimant before, on or after the day on which this Act comes into force, a court may, without notice to and in the absence of a respondent, make a provisional order against the respondent.

Maintenance provisions in provisional orders.—(2) An order under subsection (1) may only include the maintenance provisions the court could have included in a final order in a proceeding of which the respondent had notice in (*the Province*) but in which he failed to appear.

Transmission of provisional orders.—(3) Where a provisional order is made, a proper officer of the court shall send to the Attorney General for transmission to a reciprocating state

(a)   three certified copies of the provisional order;

(b)   a sworn document setting out or summarizing the evidence given in the proceeding;

(c)   a copy of the enactments under which the respondent is alleged to have an obligation to maintain the claimant; and

(d)   a statement giving available information respecting identification, location, income and assets of the respondent.

Further evidence.—(4) Where, during a proceeding for a confirmation order, a court in a reciprocating state remits the matter back for further evidence to the court in (*the Province*) that made the provisional order, the court in (*the Province*) shall after giving notice to the claimant, receive further evidence.

Evidence and recommendations.—(5) Where evidence is received under subsection (4), a proper officer of the court shall forward to the court in the reciprocating state a sworn document setting out or summarizing the evidence with such recommendations as the court in (*the Province*) considers appropriate.

New provisional orders.—(6) Where a provisional order made under this section comes before a court in a reciprocating state and confirmation is denied in respect of one or more claimants, the court in (*the Province*) that made the provisional order may, on application within six months from the denial of confirmation, reopen the matter and receive further evidence and make a new provisional order for a claimant in respect of whom confirmation was denied.

4. Affiliation.—(1) Where the affiliation of a child is in issue and has not previously been determined by a court of competent jurisdiction, the affiliation may be determined as part of a maintenance proceeding under this Act.

Relation in proceeding respecting provisional order.—(2) If the respondent disputes affiliation in the course of a proceeding to confirm a provisional order for maintenance, the matter of affiliation may be determined even though the provisional order makes no reference to affiliation.

Limited effect of determination.—(3) A determination of affiliation under this section has effect only for the purpose of maintenance proceedings under this Act.

5. Making of confirmation orders.—(1) Where the Attorney General receives from a reciprocating state documents corresponding to those described in section 3(3) with information that the respondent is in (*the Province*), the Attorney General shall designate a court in (*the Province*) for the purpose of proceedings under this section and forward the documents to that court.

Procedure.—(2) On receipt of the documents referred to in subsection (1), the court shall, whether the provisional order was made before, on or after the day on which this Act came into force, (*issue process against*) the respondent in the same manner as it would in a proceeding under (*Provincial enactment*) for the same relief and shall proceed, taking into consideration the sworn document setting out or summarizing the evidence given in the proceeding in the reciprocating state.

Report to Attorney General.— (3) Where the respondent apparently is outside the territorial jurisdiction of the court and will not return, a proper officer of the court, on receipt of documents under subsection (1), shall return the documents to the Attorney General with available information respecting the whereabouts and circumstances of the respondent.

Orders of confirmation or refusal.— (4) At the conclusion of a proceeding under this section, the court may make a confirmation order in the amount it considers appropriate or make an order refusing maintenance to any claimant.

Commencement of payments.— (5) Where the court makes a confirmation order for periodic maintenance payments, the court may direct that the payments begin from a date not earlier than the date of the provisional order.

Further evidence.— (6) The court, before making a confirmation order in a reduced amount or before denying maintenance, shall decide whether to remit the matter back for further evidence to the court that made the provisional order.

Interim order.— (7) Where a court remits a matter under subsection (6), it may make an interim order for maintenance against the respondent.

Report and filing.— (8) At the conclusion of a proceeding under this section, the court, or a proper officer of the court, shall

(a) forward a certified copy of the order to the court that made the provisional order and to the Attorney General;

(b) file the confirmation order, where one is made; and

(c) where an order is made refusing or reducing maintenance give written reasons to the court that made the provisional order and to the Attorney General.

6. Choice of law.— (1) Where the law of the reciprocating state is pleaded to establish the obligation of the respondent to maintain a claimant resident in that state, the court in (*the Province*) shall take judicial notice of that law and apply it.

Proof of foreign enactment.— (2) An enactment of a reciprocating state may be pleaded and proved for the purposes of this section by producing a copy of the enactment received from the reciprocating state.

Adjournment.— (3) Where the law of the reciprocating state is not pleaded under subsection (1), the court (*in the Province*) shall

(a) make an interim order for maintenance against the respondent where appropriate;

(b) adjourn the proceeding for a period not exceeding 90 days; and

(c) request the Attorney General to notify the appropriate officer of the reciprocating state of the requirement to plead and prove the applicable law of that state if that law is to be applied.

Application of local law.— (4) Where the law of the reciprocating state is not pleaded after an adjournment under subsection (3), the court shall apply the law of (*the Province*).

Statement of local law.— (5) Where the law of a reciprocating state requires the court in (*the Province*) to provide the court in the reciprocating state with a statement of the grounds on which the making of the confirmation order might have been opposed if the respondent were served with (*process*) and had appeared at the hearing of the court in (*the Province*), the Attorney General shall be deemed to be the proper officer of the court for the purpose of making and providing the statement of the grounds.

7. Variation or rescission of registered orders.—(1) The provisions of this Act respecting the procedure for making provisional orders and confirmation orders apply with the necessary changes to proceedings, except under subsection (5), for the variation or rescission of registered orders.

Restricted jurisdiction.—(2) This section does not

(a)   authorize a provincially appointed judge to vary or rescind a registered order made in Canada by a Federally appointed judge; or

(b)   allow a registered order originally made under a Federal enactment to be varied or rescinded except as authorized by Federal enactment.

Powers of provincially appointed judge.—(3) Notwithstanding subsection (2), a provincially appointed judge may make a provisional order to vary or rescind a registered order made in Canada under a provincial enactment by a Federally appointed judge.

Acceptance of jurisdiction.—(4) Subject to subsections (2) and (3) a registration court has jurisdiction to vary or rescind a registered order where both claimant and respondent accept its jurisdiction.

Variation and rescission where respondent resides in the Province.—(5) Where the respondent is ordinarily resident in (*the Province*) a registration court may, on application by the claimant, vary or rescind a registered order.

Confirmation of provisional orders of variation and rescission.—(6) A registration court may make a confirmation order for the variation or rescission of a registered order where

(a)   the respondent is ordinarily resident in (*the Province*);

(b)   the claimant is ordinarily resident in a reciprocating state;

(c)   a certified copy of a provisional order of variation or rescission made by a court in a reciprocating state is received by the registration court through the Attorney General; and

(d)   the respondent is given notice of the proceeding and an opportunity to appear.

Application by respondent residing in the Province.—(7) A registration court may, on application by the respondent, vary or rescind a registered order where

(a)   the respondent is ordinarily resident in (*the Province*);

(b)   the claimant is ordinarily resident in a reciprocating state; and

(c)   the registration court, in the course of the proceeding, remits the matter to the court nearest to the place where the claimant lives or works for the purpose of obtaining evidence on behalf of the claimant,

or where

(d)   the respondent is ordinarily resident in (*the Province*);

(e)   the claimant is not ordinarily resident in a reciprocating state; and

(f)   the claimant is given notice of the proceeding.

Application by claimant resident in the Province.—(8) Where a claimant ordinarily resident in (*the Province*), applies for a variation or rescission of a final order and the respondent is apparently ordinarily resident in a reciprocating state, the court may make a provisional* order of variation or rescission and section 3 applies with the necessary changes to the proceeding.

8. Effect of variation or rescission of orders of (*the Province*) by courts in reciprocating states.—Where an order originally made in (*the Province*) is varied or rescinded in a reciprocating state under the law in that state corresponding to section 7, the order shall be deemed to be so varied or rescinded in (*the Province*).

9. Enforcement.—(1) The registration court has jurisdiction to enforce a registered order notwithstanding that the order
(a)   was made in a proceeding in respect of which the registration court would have had no jurisdiction; or
(b)   is of a kind that the registration court has no jurisdiction to make.
   (2) The provisions of (*the deserted spouses' and children's maintenance enactment of the Province*) for the enforcement of maintenance orders apply with the necessary changes to registered orders and interim orders made under this Act.
   Effect of registered order.—(3) A registered order, has, from the date it is filed or deemed to be registered, the same effect as if it had been a final order originally made by the registration court and may, both with respect to arrears accrued before registration, and with respect to obligations accruing after registration, be enforced, varied or rescinded as provided in this Act whether the order is made before, on or after the day on which this Act comes into force.
   Status of order.—(4) Where a registered order is registered with (*Supreme Court of Province*), it may be enforced as if it were an order of that court.
   Service not necessary.—(5) Where a proceeding is brought to enforce a registered order, it is not necessary to prove that the respondent was served with the order.
   Recording variations.—(6) Where a registered order is being enforced and the registration court finds that the order has been varied by a court subsequent to the date of registration, the registration court shall record the fact of the variation and enforce the order as varied.

10. Remedies of a state.—Where (*the Province*), a province, a state or a political subdivision or official agency of (*the Province*), a province or a state is providing or has provided support to a claimant, it has, for the purpose of obtaining reimbursement or to obtain continuing maintenance for the claimant, the same right to bring proceedings under this Act as the claimant.

11. Duties of the Attorney General.—(1) The Attorney General shall, on request in writing by a claimant or an officer or court of a reciprocating state, take all reasonable measures to enforce an order made or registered under this Act.
   Transmission of documents.—(2) On receipt of a document for transmission under this Act to a reciprocating state, the Attorney General shall transmit the document to the proper officer of the reciprocating state.
   Delegation.—(3) The Attorney General may, in writing, authorize a person to perform or exercise a power or duty given to the Attorney General under this Act.

* 'provincial' appears in the text printed in the Commissioners' 1979 *Proceedings*.

12. Documents from reciprocating states.—(1) Where a document signed by a presiding officer of the court in a reciprocating state or a certified copy of the document is received by a court in (*the Province*) through the Attorney General, the court in (*the Province*) may deem the document to be a provisional order or a final order, according to the tenor of the document, and proceed accordingly.

Terminology.—(2) Where in a proceeding under this Act a document from a court in the reciprocating state contains terminology different from the terminology of this Act or customarily in use in the court in (*the Province*), the court in (*the Province*) shall give a broad and liberal interpretation to the terminology so as to give effect to the document.

13.   Conversion to Canadian currency.—(1) Where confirmation of a provisional order or registration of a final order is sought and the documents received by a court refer to amounts of maintenance or arrears not expressed in Canadian currency, a proper officer of the court shall first obtain from a bank a quotation for the equivalent amounts in Canadian currency at a rate of exchange applicable on the day the order was made or last varied.

Certification.—(2) The amounts in Canadian currency certified on the order by the proper officer of the court under sub-section (1) shall be deemed to be the amounts of the order.

Translation.—(3) Where an order or other document received by a court is not in (*English or French*), the order or other document shall have attached to it from the other jurisdiction a translation in (*English or French*) approved by the court and the order or other document shall be deemed to be in (*English or French*) for the purposes of this Act.

14. Appeals.—(1) Subject to subsections (2) and (3), a claimant, respondent or the Attorney General may appeal any ruling, decision or order of a court in the (*the Province*) under this Act and (*the deserted spouses' and children's maintenance enactment of the Province*) applies with the necessary changes to the appeal.

Time for appeal by appellant.—(2) A person resident in the reciprocating state and entitled to appear in the court in the reciprocating state in the proceeding being appealed from, or the Attorney General on that person's behalf, may appeal within seventy-five days after the making of the ruling, decision or order of the court in (*the Province*) appealed from.

Time for appeal by person responding to appeal.—(3) A person responding to an appeal under subsection (2) may appeal a ruling, decision or order in the same proceeding within fifteen days after receipt of notice of the appeal.

Order in force pending appeal.—(4) An order under appeal remains in force pending the determination of the appeal, unless the court appealed to otherwise orders.

15. Evidentiary matters.—(1) In a proceeding under this Act, spouses are competent and compellable witnesses against each other.

Proof of documents.—(2) In a proceeding under this Act, a document purporting to be signed by a judge, officer of a court or public officer in a reciprocating state shall, unless the contrary is proved, be proof of the appointment, signature and authority of the person who signed it.

Sworn documents and transcripts.—(3) Statements in writing sworn by the maker, depositions or transcripts of evidence taken in a reciprocating state may be received in evidence by a court in (*the Province*) under this Act.

Proof of default.—(4) For the purposes of proving default or arrears under this Act, a court may receive in evidence a sworn document made by any person, deposing to have knowledge of, or information and belief concerning, the fact.

16. Statement of payments.—A registration court or a proper officer of it shall, on reasonable request of a claimant, respondent, the Attorney General, a proper officer of a reciprocating state or a court of the state, furnish a sworn itemized statement showing with respect to maintenance under an order

(a)   all amounts that became due and owing by the respondent during the twenty-four months preceding the date of the statement; and

(b)   all payments made through the court by or on behalf of the respondent during that period.

17. Transmission of documents by court where respondent leaves (*the Province*).—Where a proper officer of a court in (*the Province*) believes that a respondent under a registered order has ceased to reside in (*the Province*) and is resident in or proceeding to another province or state, the officer shall inform the Attorney General and the court that made the order of any information he has respecting the whereabouts and circumstances of the respondent and, on request by the Attorney General, a proper officer of the court that made the order or the claimant, shall send to the court or person indicated in the request

(a)   three certified copies of the order as filed with the court in (*the Province*); and

(b)   a sworn certificate of arrears.

18. Regulations.—(1) The Lieutenant Governor in Council may make such regulations as are ancillary to this Act and not inconsistent with it.

(2) The Lieutenant Governor in Council may, where satisfied that laws are or will be in effect in a state for the reciprocal enforcement of orders made in (*the Province*) on a basis substantially similar to this Act, by order, declare that state to be a reciprocating state.

19. Saving.—This Act does not impair any other remedy available to a claimant or another person, (*the Province*), a province, a state or a political subdivision of official agency of (*the Province*), a province or a state.

20. Transitional.—Any order made under an enactment repealed by this Act continues, insofar as it is not inconsistent with this Act, valid and enforceable, and may be rescinded, varied, enforced or otherwise dealt with under this Act.

21. Repeal.—The (*reciprocal enforcement of maintenance orders enactment presently in force in the Province*) is repealed.

(3) THE COMMONWEALTH SECRETARIAT'S DRAFT MODEL BILL

This draft legislation was published in 1981. Its origins and main features are described in paragraph 6.29, above.

An Act to make new provision to facilitate the enforcement of maintenance orders; to make provision with a view to the accession by [   ] to the United Nations Convention on the Recovery Abroad of Maintenance done at New York on 20th June 1956 and to the Convention on the Recognition and Enforcement of Decisions Relating to Maintenance Obligations done at The Hague on 2nd October 1973; and for connected purposes.

1. Short title.—This Act may be cited as the Maintenance Orders (Facilities for Enforcement) Act 198—.

2. Interpretation.—(1) In this Act—
'affiliation order' means an order (however described) adjudging, finding or declaring a person to be the father of a child, whether or not it also provides for the maintenance of the child;
'certificate of arrears', in relation to a maintenance order, means a certificate certifying that the sum specified in the certificate is to the best of the information or belief of the officer giving the certificate the amount of the arrears due under the order at the date of the certificate or, as the case may be, that to the best of his information or belief there are no arrears due thereunder at that date;
'certified copy', in relation to an order of a court, means a copy of the order certified by the registrar or other proper officer of the court to be a true copy;
'Commonwealth country' means any country outside [   ] which is an independent sovereign member of the Commonwealth or any territory for whose international relations any such country is responsible;
'competent court in a Hague Convention country' means any court in a Hague Convention country which has jurisdiction on one of the grounds specified in section 34(4);
'convention country' means a country designated by [Order] made under section 23;
'court' includes any tribunal or person having power to make, confirm, enforce, vary or revoke a maintenance order;
'court in a Hague Convention country' means any judicial or administrative authority in a Hague Convention country;
'Hague Convention' means the Convention referred to in section 31, and 'Hague Convention country' means a country designated by [Order] under that section.
'maintenance order' means an order (however described), including a settlement made by or before a competent court in a Hague Convention country, of any of the following descriptions, and in the case of an order which is not limited to the following descriptions, the part of the order which is so limited, that is to say:—

(a) an order (including an affiliation order or order consequent upon an affiliation order) which provides for the periodical payment of sums of money towards the maintenance of any person, being a person whom the person liable to make payments under the order is, according to the law applied in the place where the order was made, liable to maintain;

(b)   an affiliation order or order consequent upon an affiliation order, being an order which provides for the payment by a person adjudged, found or declared to be a child's father of expenses incidental to the child's birth, or, where the child has died, of his funeral expenses, or, where the mother of the child has died, of her funeral expenses; and

(c)   an order within the foregoing provisions of this definition made against a payer on the application of a public body which claims reimbursement of sums of money payable under the order with respect to the payee if reimbursement can be obtained by the public body under the law to which it is subject,

and, in the case of a maintenance order which has been varied (including a maintenance order which has been varied either by a court in [   ] or by a competent court in a Hague Convention country whether or not the original order was made by such a court) means that order as varied

Provided that the expression 'maintenance order' shall not include an order made in a Hague Convention country of a description which that country or [   ] has reserved the right under article 26 of The Hague Convention not to recognise or enforce;

'payee', in relation to a maintenance order, means the person entitled to payments for which the order provides;

'payer', in relation to a maintenance order, means the person liable to make payments under the order;

'prescribed' means prescribed by rules of court;

'provisional order' means (according to the context)—

(a)   an order made by a court in [   ] which is provisional only and has no effect unless and until confirmed, with or without alteration, by a competent court in a Commonwealth country; or

(b)   an order made by a court in a Commonwealth country which is provisional only and has no effect unless and until confirmed, with or without alteration, by a court in [   ] having power under Part I of this Act to confirm it;

'registered order' means an order which is for the time being registered in a court in [   ] under Part III;

'registering court', in relation to a registered order, means the court in which that order is for the time being registered;

'related documents' means—

(a)   the application on which the order was made;

(b)   a certificate of arrears signed by the registrar of the registering court;

(c)   a statement giving such information as he possesses as to the whereabouts of the payer; and

(d)   any relevant documents in his possession relating to the case.

'the responsible authority', in relation to a Commonwealth country, means any person who in that country has functions similar to those of the [Minister for Foreign Affairs] under Part I, and in relation to a Hague Convention country means the appropriate authority in that country.

(2)   Any reference in this Act to the payment of money for the maintenance of a child shall be construed as including a reference to the payment of money for the child's education.

PART I

ENFORCEMENT OF MAINTENANCE ORDERS MADE IN [   ] AND IN
COMMONWEALTH COUNTRIES

ORDERS MADE BY COURTS IN [   ]

3. Transmission of a maintenance order made in [   ] for registration in a Commonwealth country.—(1) This section applies to any maintenance order, not being a provisional order or an order made by virtue of a provision of Part III made, whether before or after the commencement of this Part, by a court in [   ].

(2) Where it appears that the payer under a maintenance order to which this section applies is residing in or is proceeding to a Commonwealth country, the registrar of the court by which the order was made [or in which it is registered] may, of his own motion or on the application of a payee under the order, send to the [Minister for Foreign Affairs] a Request for Registration in the prescribed form.

(3) The [Minister for Foreign Affairs] shall transmit the Request for Registration to the responsible authority in the Commonwealth country if he is satisfied that the statement relating to the whereabouts of the payer gives sufficient information to justify that being done.

(4) Nothing in this section shall be taken as affecting any jurisdiction of a court in [   ] with respect to a maintenance order to which this section applies, and subject to section 7 any such order may be enforced, varied or revoked accordingly.

4. Provisional orders for confirmation in a Commonwealth country.—(1) Where an application is made to a court in [   ] for a maintenance order against any person who is proved to be residing in or to be proceeding to a Commonwealth country, and the application is one on which the court would have jurisdiction to make a maintenance order if that person were resident in [   ] and a summons to appear before the court to answer the application had been duly served upon him, the court shall have jurisdiction to hear the application and may make a provisional order.

(2) Where a court makes a provisional order by virtue of this section, the registrar of the court shall send to the [Minister for Foreign Affairs] a Request for Confirmation in the prescribed form.

5. Effect of confirmation.—A provisional order made by virtue of section 4 which has been confirmed by a competent court in a Commonwealth country shall be treated for all purposes as if the court in [   ] which made the order had made it in the form in which it was confirmed and as if the order had never been a provisional order, and subject to section 7 any such order may be enforced varied, or revoked accordingly.

6. Further proceedings in respect of a provisional order.—(1) Where before a provisional order made by virtue of section 4 is confirmed, either—

(i)   a document, duly authenticated, setting out or summarising evidence taken in a Commonwealth country for the purpose of proceedings relating to the confirmation of the order is received by the court in [   ] which made the order; or

(ii)   that court, in compliance with a request made to it by a court in a

Commonwealth country, takes the evidence of a person residing in [   ] for the purpose of such proceedings,
the court in [   ] which made the order shall consider that evidence.

(2) If it appears to the court, having considered such evidence, that the provisional order ought not to have been made, or ought not to have been made in the form in which it was made—

(a) it shall, in such manner as may be prescribed, give to the person on whose application the order was made an opportunity to consider that evidence, to make representations with respect to it, and to adduce further evidence; and

(b) after considering all the evidence and any representations made by that person, it may revoke the provisional order, and may make a fresh provisional order.

(3) Where a court makes a fresh provisional order by virtue of the preceding sub-section, the registrar of the court shall send in the prescribed manner to the court in the Commonwealth country a Request for Confirmation in the prescribed form.

7. Variation and revocation in [   ] of orders.—(1) This section applies to a maintenance order which has been transmitted to a Commonwealth country in pursuance of section 3 and to a provisional order made by virtue of section 4 which has been confirmed by a competent court in a Commonwealth country.

(2) A court in [   ] which, having considered an application for the variation of an order to which this section applies, proposes to vary the order—

(a) may do so by a provisional order; and

(b) shall do so by a provisional order where it proposes to increase the rate of payments under the order unless either—

    (i) both the payer and the payee under the order appear in the proceedings; or

    (ii) the applicant appears and the appropriate process has been duly served on the other party.

(3) Where a court in [   ] makes a provisional order by virtue of this section, the registrar of the court shall send in the prescribed manner to the court in a Commonwealth country having power to confirm the provisional order a Request for Confirmation in the prescribed form.

8. Confirmation of provisional orders affecting orders made in [   ].—(1) This section applies to a maintenance order which has been transmitted to a Commonwealth country in pursuance of section 3 and to a provisional order made by virtue of secton 4 which has been confirmed by a competent court in a Commonwealth country.

(2) Where a certified copy of a provisional order made by a court in a Commonwealth country, being an order varying or revoking an order to which this section applies, together with a document duly authenticated, setting out or summarising the evidence given in the proceedings in which the provisional order was made, is received by the court in [   ] which made the order, that court may confirm or refuse to confirm the provisional order and if that order is an order varying the order, confirm it either without alteration or with such alterations as it thinks reasonable.

(3) For the purpose of determining whether a provisional order should be confirmed under this section, the court shall proceed as if an application for

the variation or revocation, as the case may be, of the order in question had been made to it.

9. Registration in [   ] court of maintenance order made in a Commonwealth country.—(1) This section applies to a maintenance order made before or after the commencement of this Part against any person by a court in a Commonwealth country, including a provisional order made by such a court which has been confirmed by a court in another Commonwealth country.

(2) Subject to the following provisions of this section, the registrar of a court in [   ] who receives from the [Minister for Foreign Affairs] a certified copy of an order to which this section applies shall register the order in the prescribed manner in the court.

(3) Before registering an order under this section, the registrar shall take such steps as he thinks fit for the purpose of ascertaining whether the payer is residing within the jurisdiction of the court, and if after taking those steps he is satisfied that the payer is not so residing he shall return the certified copy of the order to the [Minister of Foreign Affairs] with a statement giving such information as he possesses as to the whereabouts of the payer.

10. Setting aside registration.—The registration of an order under section 9 shall be set aside if the court in which the order has been registered is satisfied on an application by the payer that the order is not an order to which that section applies.

11. Confirmation and registration in [   ] of a provisional order made in a Commonwealth country.—(1) This section applies to a provisional order made before or after the commencement of this Part against any person by a court in a Commonwealth country.

(2) Where the registrar of a court in [   ] receives from the [Minister for Foreign Affairs] a certified copy of an order to which this section applies together with—

(a) a document, duly authenticated, setting out or summarising the evidence given in the proceedings in which the order was made; and

(b) a statement of the grounds on which the making of the order might have been opposed by the payer under the order,

the registrar shall cause proceedings to be commenced in the court for the confirmation of the order.

(3) If a summons to appear in the proceedings for the confirmation of the order cannot be duly served on the payer, the registrar shall return the certified copy of the order and documents which accompanied it to the [Minister for Foreign Affairs] with a statement giving such information as he possesses as to the whereabouts of the payer.

(4) Subject to the provisions of section 19, proceedings for the confirmation of the order shall be conducted as if an application for a maintenance order against the payer had been made to the court.

(5) At the hearing it shall be open for the payer to raise any defence which he might have raised in the original proceedings had he been present, but no other defence, and the statement received from the court which made the order of the grounds on which the making of the order might have been opposed

shall be conclusive evidence that the payer might have raised a defence on any of those grounds.

(6) If the payer establishes any such defence as he might have raised in the original proceedings, the court shall refuse to confirm the order, and the registrar shall return the certified copy of the order and the documents which accompanied it to the [Minister for Foreign Affairs].

(7) In any other case, the court shall confirm the order either without alteration or with such alteration as it thinks reasonable, and the registrar shall register the order in the prescribed manner.

12. Enforcement in [   ] of orders registered under Part I.—
(1) An order registered in a court in [   ] by virtue of section 9(2) or 11(7) may be enforced in [   ] as if it had been made by the court in which it is registered and as if that court had had jurisdiction to make it; and proceedings for or with respect to the enforcement of any such order may be taken accordingly.

(2) The registrar of the court by which an order is enforceable by virtue of this section shall take all such steps for enforcing the order as may be prescribed.

(3) In any proceedings for or with respect to the enforcement of an order which is for the time being registered in any court under this Part a certificate of arrears sent to the court or to the registrar thereof shall be evidence of the facts stated therein.

(4) Subject to subsection (5) sums of money payable under an order registered under this Part shall be payable in accordance with the order as from the date on which the order was made.

(5) A court confirming an order under section 11(7) may direct that the sums of money payable under it shall be deemed to have been payable in accordance with the order as from such date, being a date later than the date on which the order was made, as it may specify; and subject to any such direction an order so confirmed shall be treated as if it had been made in the form in which it was confirmed and as if it had never been a provisional order.

13. Variation and revocation of orders registered under Part I.—
(1) This section applies to orders registered in [   ] by virtue of section 9(2) or 11(7).

(2) The court in which an order to which this section applies is registered shall have the like power, on an application made by the payer or the payee, to vary or revoke the order as if the court had made the order and had had jurisdiction to make it.

(3) Where the court in which an order to which this section applies is registered varies the order it may do so by means of a provisional order and shall do so unless—
(a) both the payer and the payee are for the time being residing in [   ]; or
(b) the application is made by the payee; or
(c) the variation consists of a reduction in the rate of payments under the order and is made solely on the ground that there has been a change in the financial circumstances of the payer since the order was made or, in the case of an order registered by virtue of section 11(7), since the order was confirmed, and the courts in the Commonwealth country in which the order was made do not have power, according to the law in force in that country, to confirm provisional orders varying maintenance orders.

(4) When the court in which an order to which this section applies is registered revokes the order it may do so by means of a provisional order and shall do so unless both the payer and the payee are for the time being resident in [   ].

(5) On an application for the revocation of an order to which this section applies, the court shall, if both the payer and the payee are for the time being residing in [   ], apply the law of [   ], but shall in any other case apply the law of the Commonwealth country in which the order was made; but where the court is required by virtue of this sub-section to apply the law of a Commonwealth country it may make a provisional order if it has reason to believe that the ground on which the application is made is a ground on which the order could be revoked according to that law, notwithstanding that it has not been established that it is such a ground.

(6) Where a court makes a provisional order under this section, the registrar shall send in the prescribed manner to the court in the Commonwealth country which made the order a Request for Confirmation in the prescribed form.

14. Confirmation of provisional orders affecting orders registered under Part I.—(1) This section applies to orders registered in [   ] by virtue of section 9(2) or 11(7).

(2) Where a certified copy of a provisional order made by a court in a Commonwealth country, being an order varying or revoking an order to which this section applies, together with a document duly authenticated, setting out or summarising the evidence given in the proceedings in which the provisional order was made, is received by a court in [   ] in which an order to which this section applies is registered, that court may confirm or refuse to confirm the provisional order and if that order is an order varying the order, confirm it either without alteration or with such alterations as it thinks reasonable.

(3) For the purpose of determining whether a provisional order should be confirmed under this section, the court shall proceed as if an application for the variation or revocation, as the case may be, of the order in question had been made to it.

(4) The registrar of the court in which any order to which this section applies is registered shall register in the prescribed manner any order varying such an order.

15. Cancellation of registration and transfer of order.—(1) This section applies to orders registered in [   ] by virtue of section 9(2) or 11(7).

(2) Where an order to which this section applies is revoked
(a)   by an order made by the court in which it is registered; or
(b)   by a provisional order made by that court which has been confirmed by a court in a Commonwealth country and notice of the confirmation is received by the court in [   ]; or
(c)   by an order made by a court in a Commonwealth country and notice of the revocation is received by the court in [   ].
the registrar of that court shall cancel the registration; but any arrears due under the order at the date when its registration is cancelled shall continue to be recoverable as if the registration had not been cancelled.

(3) Where the registrar of a court in which an order to which this section applies is registered is of opinion that the payer has ceased to reside within the jurisdiction of that court, he shall cancel the registration of the order and

subject to sub-section (4) shall send the certified copy of the orders to the [Minister for Foreign Affairs].

(4) Where the registrar of a court in which an order to which this section applies is registered is of opinion that the payer is residing within the jurisdiction of another court in [   ], he shall transfer the order to that court by sending the certified copy of the order to the registrar of that other court, and that registrar shall subject to subsection (6) register the order in the prescribed manner in that court.

(5) Where the certified copy of an order is received by the [Minister for Foreign Affairs] under this section and it appears to him that the payer is still residing in [   ], he shall send the certified copy of the order to the registrar of the court within the jurisdiction of which it appears that the payer is residing, and the registrar of that court shall subject to sub-section (6) register the order in the prescribed manner in that court.

(6) Before registering an order under sub-section (4) or (5), the registrar shall take such steps as he thinks fit for the purpose of ascertaining whether the payer is residing within the jurisdiction of the court, and if after taking those steps he is satisfied that the payer is not so residing he shall return the certified copy of the order to the [Minister for Foreign Affairs] with a statement giving such information as he possesses as to the whereabouts of the payer.

(7) A registrar required by the provisions of this section to send to the [Minister for Foreign Affairs] or to the registrar of another court the certified copy of an order shall send with that copy—
(a)   a certificate of arrears signed by him;
(b)   a statement giving such information as he possesses as to the whereabouts of the payer; and
(c)   any relevant documents in his possession relating to the case.

16. Transmission of certain orders by [Minister for Foreign Affairs].

—(1) This section applies to maintenance orders received by the [Minister for Foreign Affairs] from the responsible authority in a Commonwealth country and to orders which have been registered in a court in [   ] by virtue of section 9(2) or 11(7).

(2) If it appears to the [Minister for Foreign Affairs] that the payer under an order to which this section applies is not residing or has ceased to reside in [   ], he shall send to the responsible authority of the Commonwealth country which in all the circumstances is appropriate—
(a)   the certified copy of the order in question and a certified copy of any order varying that order;
(b)   if the order has at any time been registered in a court in [   ], a certificate of arrears signed by the registrar of the court in which it was last registered;
(c)   a statement giving such information as the [Minister for Foreign Affairs] possesses as to the whereabouts of the payer; and
(d)   any other relevant documents in his possession relating to the case.

(3) Where the documents mentioned in sub-section (2) are sent to the responsible authority in a Commonwealth country other than that in which the order in question was made, the [Minister for Foreign Affairs] shall inform the responsible authority in the Commonwealth country in which the order was made of what he has done.

SUPPLEMENTAL

17. Appeals.—(1) No appeals shall lie from a provisional order made under any provision of this Part of this Act by a court in [   ].

(2) Where any court in [   ] refuses to make a provisional order in pursuance of section 4 or revokes a provisional order in pursuance of section 6, the applicant shall have the like right of appeal (if any) from the refusal to make, or the revocation of, the provisional order as he would have if that order were not a provisional order.

(3) Where in pursuance of any provision of this Part, any court in [   ] confirms or refuses to confirm a provisional order made by a court in a Commonwealth country (including a provisional order varying or revoking a maintenance order), the payer or payee under the order shall have the like right of appeal (if any) from the confirmation of, or refusal to confirm, the provisional order as he would have if that order were not a provisional order and the court which confirmed or refused to confirm it had made or, as the case may be, refused to make it.

(4) Where in pursuance of any provision in this Part, any court in [   ] makes, or refuses to make, an order varying or revoking a mainten-ance order made by a court in a Commonwealth country then, subject to sub-section (1), the payer or payee shall have the like right of appeal (if any) from that order or from the refusal to make it as he would have if the mainten-ance order had been made by the court in [   ].

(5) Nothing in this section (except sub-section (1)) shall be construed as affecting any right of appeal conferred by any other enactment.

18. Obtaining of evidence for the purposes of proceedings in a Com-monwealth country.—(1) Where for the purpose of any proceedings in a court in a Commonwealth country relating to a maintenance order to which this Part applies a request is made by or on behalf of that court for the taking in [   ] of the evidence of a person residing therein relating to matters specified in the request a court in [   ] shall have power to take that evidence, and, after giving notice of the time and place at which the evidence is to be taken to such persons and in such manner as it thinks fit, shall take the evidence in such manner as may be prescribed.

(2) Evidence taken by virtue of this section shall be sent in the prescribed manner by the registrar of the court to the court in the Commonwealth country by or on behalf of which the request was made.

19. Remission of case to a court in a Commonwealth country; interim orders.—(1) A court in [   ] may for the purpose of any proceedings in that court under this Part relating to an order to which this Part applies request a court in a Commonwealth country to take or provide evidence relating to such matters as may be specified in the request and may remit the case to that court for that purpose.

(2) A court in [   ] considering the confirmation of an order under section 11 and remitting the case in accordance with this section may make such interim order for periodical payments by the payer as it thinks fit.

20. Conversion of currency.—(1) Where the sums of money required to be paid under an order registered in a court in [   ] under this Part or specified in any statement of arrears due under a maintenance order made by a court in a Commonwealth country are expressed in a currency other than the currency of [   ], then, as from the relevant date, the sums shall be treated as such sums in the currency of [   ] as are equivalent thereto on the basis of the rate of exchange prevailing at that date.

(2) For the purposes of this section a written certificate purporting to be signed by an officer of any bank in [   ] certifying that a specified rate of exchange prevailed between currencies at a specified date and that at such rate a specified sum in the currency of [   ] is equivalent to a specified sum in another specified currency shall be evidence of the rate of exchange so prevailing on that date and of the equivalent sums in terms of the respective currencies.

(3) In this section 'the relevant date' means—

(a)   in relation to an order which is registered in a court in [   ] or to a statement of arrears due under a maintenance order made by a court in a Commonwealth country, the date on which the order is first registered under this Act;

(b)   in relation to an order which has been varied, the date on which the last order varying that order is registered under this Act.

21. Orders in foreign language.—Where a maintenance order sought to be registered or confirmed in [   ] under this Part is in a language other than English, the certified copy of the order shall have attached thereto, for all purposes of this Part, a translation in the English language approved by the registrar of the court, and upon such approval being given the order shall be deemed to be in the English language.

PART II

EXTENSION OF PART I TO NON-COMMONWEALTH COUNTRIES

22. Extension of Part 1 to non-Commonwealth countries.—The [Head of State] may by [Order] declare that the provisions of Part I, with such exceptions, adaptations and modifications as may be specified in the [Order] shall apply as if any country designated in the [Order] were a Commonwealth country.

PART III

RECIPROCAL ENFORCEMENT OF CLAIMS FOR THE RECOVERY OF MAINTENANCE

CONVENTION COUNTRIES

23. Convention countries.—The [Head of State] may by [Order] declare that any country or territory specified in the [Order], being a country or territory outside [   ] and not being a Commonwealth country or a country designated in an [Order] under section 22, to which the United Nations Convention on the Recovery Abroad of Maintenance done at New York on 20th June 1956 extends, is a convention country for the purposes of this Act.

APPLICATION BY PERSON IN [   ] FOR RECOVERY ETC OF MAINTENANCE IN A CONVENTION COUNTRY

24. Application by person in [   ].—(1) Where a person in [   ] ('the applicant') claims to be entitled to recover in a convention country maintenance from another person, and that other person is for the time being subject to the jurisdiction of that country, the applicant may apply to the [Minister for Foreign Affairs], in accordance with the provisions of this section, to have his claim for the recovery of maintenance from that other person transmitted to that country.

(2) Where the applicant seeks to vary any provision made in a convention country for the payment by any other person of maintenace to the applicant, and that other person is for the time being subject to the jurisdiction of that country, the applicant may apply to the [Minister for Foreign Affairs], in accordance with the provisions of this section, to have his application for the variation of that provision transmitted to that country.

(3) An application to the [Minister for Foreign Affairs] under this section shall be made through the registrar of the prescribed court who shall assist the applicant in completing an application which will comply with the requirements of the law of the convention country and shall send the application to the [Minister for Foreign Affairs], together with such other documents, if any, as are required by that law.

(4) On receiving an application from the registrar, the [Minister for Foreign Affairs] shall transmit it, together with any accompanying documents, to the appropriate authority in the convention country, unless he is satisfied that the application is not in good faith or that it does not comply with the requirements of the law of that country.

(5) The [Minister for Foreign Affairs] may request the registrar to obtain from the court of which he is registrar such information relating to the application as may be specified in the request, and it shall be the duty of the court to furnish the [Minister for Foreign Affairs] with the information he requires.

APPLICATION BY PERSON IN CONVENTION COUNTRY FOR RECOVERY OF
MAINTENANCE IN [   ]

25. Application by person in convention country.—(1) Where the [Minister for Foreign Affairs] receives from the appropriate authority in a convention country an application by a person in that country for the recovery of maintenance from another person ('the defendant') who is for the time being residing in [   ], he shall send the application, together with any accompanying documents, to the registrar of the prescribed court.

(2) On receiving the application in accordance with sub-section (1), the registrar shall cause proceedings to be commenced in the court for the consideration of the application.

(3) If a summons to appear in the proceedings cannot be duly served on the defendant, the registrar shall subject to sub-section (4) return the application, together with any accompanying documents, to the [Minister for Foreign Affairs] with a statement giving such information as he possesses as to the whereabouts of the defendant.

(4) If a registrar who receives an application in accordance with sub-section (1) is satisfied that the defendant is residing within the jurisdiction of another court in [   ], he shall send the application, together with any accompanying documents, to the registrar of that other court and shall inform the [Minister for Foreign Affairs] that he has done so.

(5) A registrar receiving an application under sub-section (4) shall proceed as if he had received it under sub-section (1).

(6) In any case not falling under sub-section (3) or (4), the court shall proceed as if the applicant were before the court.

(7) If the court makes an order on the application the registrar shall register the order in the prescribed manner in the court.

FURTHER PROVISIONS AS TO REGISTERED ORDERS

26. Transfer or return of orders.—(1) Where the registrar of the registering court is of opinion that the payer under a registered order has ceased to reside within the jurisdiction of the court he shall cancel the registration and, subject to sub-section (2), send a certified copy of the order and the related documents to the [Minister for Foreign Affairs].

(2) Where the registrar of the registering court is of opinion that the payer under a registered order is residing within the jurisdiction of another court in [   ], he shall transfer the order to that other court by sending a certified copy of the order and the related documents to the registrar of that court and, subject to sub-section (4), that registrar shall register the order in the prescribed manner in that court.

(3) Where a certified copy of an order is received by the [Minister for Foreign Affairs] under sub-section (1) and it appears to him that the payer under the order is still residing in [   ] he shall transfer the order to the court within the jurisdiction of which the payer is residing by sending the copy of the order and the related documents to the registrar of that court, and subject to sub-section (4), that registrar shall register the order in the prescribed manner in that court.

(4) Before registering an order in pursuance of sub-section (2) or (3), a registrar of a court shall take such steps as he thinks fit for the purpose of ascertaining whether the payer under the order is residing within the jurisdiction of the court, and if after taking those steps he is satisfied that the payer is not so residing he shall return the certified copy of the order and the related documents to the registrar or the [Minister for Foreign Affairs], as the case may be, from whom he received them, together with a statement giving such information as he possesses as to the whereabouts of the payer.

27. Enforcement of orders.—(1) The registrar of the court in which an order is registered under this Part shall take all such steps for enforcing the order as may be prescribed.

(2) A registered order which is registered in a court other than the court by which the order was made may be enforced as if it had been made by the registering court and as if that court had had jurisdiction to make it.

(3) In any proceedings for or with respect to the enforcement of a registered order, a certificate of arrears sent under section 26 to the registrar of the court shall be evidence of the facts stated therein.

28. Variation and revocation of orders.—(1) The registering court shall have jurisdiction to hear any application by the payer or the payee for the variation or revocation of a registered order where the defendant to the application is residing in [   ] or in a convention country.

(2) Where the [Minister for Foreign Affairs] receives from the appropriate authority in a convention country an application by a person in that country for the variation or revocation of a registered order, he shall send the application, together with any accompanying documents, to the registrar of the registering court.

(3) On receiving the application in accordance with sub-section (1), the

registrar shall cause proceedings to be commenced in the court for the consideration of the application.

(4) The court shall not proceed to the hearing of an application for the variation or revocation of a registered order unless

(a)   in the case of a defendant to the application residing in [   ], a summons to appear in the proceedings has been duly served on him; and

(b)   in the case of a defendant residing in a convention country, such notice of the proceedings as may be prescribed has been given to the defendant in the prescribed manner.

29. Obtaining of evidence for purpose of proceedings in [   ].—

(1) A court in [   ] may for the purpose of any proceedings in that court under this Part arising out of an application received by the [Minister for Foreign Affairs] from a convention country request the [Minister for Foreign Affairs] to make to the appropriate authority or court in the convention country a request for the taking in that country of the evidence of a person residing therein relating to matters connected with the application.

(2) A request made by a court under this section shall—

(a)   give details of the application in question;

(b)   state the name and address of the person whose evidence is to be taken; and

(c)   specify the matters relating to which the evidence of that person is required.

(3) If the [Minister for Foreign Affairs] is satisfied that a request made to him under this section contains sufficient information to enable the evidence of the person named in the request relating to the matters specified therein to be taken by a court or person in the convention country, he shall transmit the request to the appropriate authority or court in that country.

30. Taking of evidence at request of court in a convention country.

—(1) Where a request is made to the [Minister for Foreign Affairs] by or on behalf of a court in a convention country to obtain the evidence of a person residing in [   ] relating to matters connected with an application to which section 24 applies, the [Minister for Foreign Affairs] shall request such court, or such registrar or other officer of a court, as he may determine to take the evidence of that person relating to such matters connected with that application as may be specified in the request.

(2) The court by which or registrar or other officer by whom a request under sub-section (1) is received from the [Minister for Foreign Affairs] shall have power to take the evidence and, after giving notice of the time and place at which the evidence is to be taken to such persons and in such manner as it or he thinks fit, shall take the evidence of the person named in the request relating to the matters specified therein in such manner as may be prescribed; and the evidence so taken shall be sent in the prescribed manner by the registrar to the court in the convention country by or on behalf of which the request referred to in sub-section (1) was made.

PART IV

ENFORCEMENT UNDER THE HAGUE CONVENTION

HAGUE CONVENTION COUNTRIES

31. Hague Convention countries.—(1) The [Head of State] may by [Order] declare that any country or territory specified in the [Order], being a country or territory outside [   ] and not being a Commonwealth country or a country designated in an [Order] under section 22, in which the Convention on the Recognition and Enforcement of Decisions Relating to Maintenance Obligations concluded at The Hague on 2nd October 1973 is in force, is a Hague Convention country for the purposes of this Part.

(2) In relation to a Hague Convention country comprising territories in which different systems of law are in force in relation to the recognition and enforcement of maintenance orders, any reference to

(a) the law or procedure of a Hague Convention country; or

(b) a court in a Hague Convention country; or

(c) habitual residence in a Hague Convention country

shall have effect as if each territory were a separate Hague Convention country.

ORDERS MADE BY COURTS IN [   ]

32. Transmission of a maintenance order made in [   ] for registration in a Hague Convention country.—(1) This section applies to any maintenance order, not being a provisional order or an order made by virtue of a provision of Part III, made, whether before or after the commencement of this Part, by a court in [   ] if—

(a) either the payer or the payee had his habitual residence in [   ] at the time when the application for the maintenance order was made; or

(b) the payer and the payee were citizens of [   ] at that time; or

(c) the payer appeared in the proceedings in which the maintenance order was made and defended on the merits without objecting to the jurisdiction of the court.

(2) Where it appears that the payer under a maintenance order to which this section applies is residing in or is proceeding to a Hague Convention country, the registrar of the court by which the order was made [or in which it is registered] may, of his own motion or on the application of a payee under the order, send to the [Minister for Foreign Affairs] a Request for Enforcement in the prescribed form.

(3) The [Minister for Foreign Affairs] shall transmit the Request for Enforcement to the responsible authority in the Hague Convention country if he is satisfied that the statement relating to the whereabouts of the payer gives sufficient information to justify that being done.

(4) Nothing in this section shall be taken as affecting any jurisdiction of a court in [   ] with respect to a maintenance order to which this section applies, and, subject to section 33, any such order may be enforced, varied or revoked accordingly.

33. Variation and revocation in [   ] of orders.—(1) This section applies to a maintenance order which has been transmitted to a Hague Convention country by virtue of section 32.

(2) Where an application is made to a court in [   ] by the payee for the variation or revocation of an order to which this section applies, and the

payer is residing in a Hague Convention country, the registrar of the court shall send to the [Minister for Foreign Affairs] a notice of the application in the prescribed form, and the court may not vary or revoke the maintenance order unless—

(a)   it is satisfied that the notice of the application has been served on the payer in accordance with the law of the Hague Convention country in which he is residing not less than six weeks before the date of the hearing of the application; and

(b)   it has taken into account any representations made and any evidence adduced by or on behalf of the payer.

(3) Where a court in [   ] varies or revokes an order to which this section applies, the registrar of the court shall send to the [Minister for Foreign Affairs] a Notice of Variation or Revocation in the prescribed form.

ORDERS MADE BY COURTS IN HAGUE CONVENTION COUNTRIES

34. Registration in [   ] of maintenance order made in Hague Convention country.—(1) This section applies to a maintenance order made before or after the commencement of this Part against any person by a court in a Hague Convention country.

(2) Subject to the following provisions of this section, the registrar of a court in [   ] who receives from the [Minister for Foreign Affairs] a certified copy of an order to which this section applies shall register the order in the prescribed manner in the court.

(3) Before registering an order under this section, the registrar shall take such steps as he thinks fit for the purpose of ascertaining whether the payer is residing within the jurisdiction of the court, and if after taking those steps he is satisfied that the payer is not so residing he shall return the certified copy of the order to the [Minister for Foreign Affairs] with a statement giving such information as he possesses as to the whereabouts of the payer.

(4) (a)   The registrar may refuse to register the order if the court in the Hague Convention country by or before which the order was made did not have jurisdiction to make the order; and for these purposes a court in a Hague Convention country shall be considered to have jurisdiction if—

(i)   either the payer or the payee had his habitual residence in the Hague Convention country at the time when the proceedings in which the maintenance order was made were instituted; or

(ii)   the payer and the payee were nationals of that country at that time; or

(iii)   the defendant in those proceedings had submitted to the jurisdiction of the court, either expressly or by defending on the merits of the case without objecting to the jurisdiction; or

(iv)   in the case of a maintenance order made by reason of a divorce or a legal separation or a declaration that a marriage is void or annulled, the court is recognised by the law of [   ] as having jurisdiction in that matter.

(b)   In deciding whether a court in a Hague Convention country had jurisdiction to make a maintenance order the registrar shall be bound by any finding of fact on which the court based its jurisdiction.

(5) The registrar may refuse to register the order.

(a) if such registration is manifestly contrary to public policy;

(b) if the order was obtained by fraud in connection with a matter of procedure;

(c) if proceedings between the same parties and having the same purpose are pending before a court in [   ] and those proceedings were the first to be instituted; or

(d) if the order is incompatible with an order made in proceedings between the same parties and having the same purpose, either in [   ] or in another country provided that in the latter case the order fulfils the conditions necessary for its recognition and enforcement in [   ] under this Act.

(6) Without prejudice to sub-section (5), if the payer did not appear in the proceedings in the Hague Convention country in which the order was made, the registrar shall refuse to register the order unless

(a) notice of the institution of the proceedings, including notice of the substance of the claim, was served on the payer in accordance with the law of that Hague Convention country; and

(b) having regard to the circumstances, the payer had sufficient time to enable him to defend the proceedings.

35. Setting aside registration.—(1) The payer may apply to the court in which an order is registered under section 34 for the registration to be set aside.

(2) The court shall set aside the registration if it is satisfied that the order is not an order to which section 34 applies or that the registrar should have refused to register the order under subsection (6) of that section.

(3) The court may set aside the registration on any ground upon which the registrar might have refused to register the order under section 34.

36. Appeals against refusal to register.—The payee may appeal to the court against any refusal by the registrar to register an order to which section 34 applies.

37. Enforcement in [   ] of orders registered under section 34.—(1) An order registered in a court in [   ] by virtue of section 34 may be enforced in [   ] as if it had been made by the court in which it is registered and as if that court had jurisdiction to make it, and proceedings for or with respect to the enforcement of any such order may be taken accordingly.

(2) The registrar of the court by which an order is enforceable by virtue of this section shall take all such steps for enforcing the order as may be prescribed.

(3) In any proceedings for or with respect to the enforcement of an order which is for the time being registered in any court under section 42, a certificate of arrears sent to the court or the registrar thereof shall be evidence of the facts stated therein.

(4) Subject to subsection (5), sums of money payable under an order registered under section 42 shall be payable in accordance with the order as from the date on which the order was made.

(5) Where an order was made by a court in a Hague Convention country prior to the date of the entry into force of the Hague Convention between [   ] and that country, no sums of money falling due before that date shall be payable in accordance with the order.

38. Cancellation transfer and transmission of orders registered under section 34.—(1) This section applies to a maintenance order registered in a court in [   ] by virtue of section 34.

(2) Subject to the following subsections, section 15 and 16 shall apply in relation to orders to which this section applies as if the Hague Convention country in which the maintenance order was made was a Commonwealth country.

(3) In its application to the orders to which this section applies, section 15 shall be amended by the omission of subsection (2)(b).

(4) In its application to the orders to which this section applies, section 16 shall be amended by the omission in subsection (2) of the words 'which in all the circumstances is appropriate' and of subsection (3).

SUPPLEMENTAL

39. Obtaining of evidence for purpose of proceedings in [   ].— A court in [   ] may for the purpose of any proceedings in that court under this Part relating to a maintenance order to which this Part applies request the [Minister for Foreign Affairs] to make to the responsible authority in a Hague Convention country a request for the taking or provision of evidence relating to such matters as may be specified in the request.

40. Obtaining of evidence for the purpose of proceedings in a Hague Convention country.—(1) Where for the purpose of any proceedings in a court in a Hague Convention country relating to a maintenance order to which this Part applies a request is made by or on behalf of that court for the taking in [   ] of the evidence of a person residing therein relating to matters specified in the request, a court in [   ] shall have power to take that evidence and, after giving notice of the time and place at which the evidence is to be taken to such persons and in such manner as it thinks fit, shall take the evidence in such manner as may be prescribed.

(2) Evidence taken by virtue of this section shall be sent by the registrar of the court to the [Minister for Foreign Affairs] for transmission to the responsible authority in the Hague Convention country.

41. Conversion of currency.—Section 20 shall apply in relation to orders made by a court in a Hague Convention country as if that country were a Commonwealth country.

PART V

SUPPLEMENTAL

42. Provisional order to cease to have effect on remarriage.— (1) Where a court has, by virtue of section 4, made a provisional order consisting of or including a provision for periodical payments by a husband or wife and the order has been confirmed by a competent court in a Commonwealth country, then, if after the making of that order the marriage of the parties to the proceedings in which the order was made is dissolved or annulled but the order continues in force, that order or, as the case may be, that provision thereof shall cease to have effect on the remarriage of the payee except in relation to any arrears due under it on the date of such remarriage and shall not be capable of being revived.

(2) For the avoidance of doubt it is hereby declared that reference in this section to remarriage include references to a marriage which is by law void or voidable.

43. Admissibility of evidence given abroad.—(1) A statement contained in—

(a) a document, duly authenticated, which purports to set out or summarise evidence given in proceedings in a court in a Commonwealth country, a convention country, a Hague Convention country or a country designated in an [Order] under section 22; or

(b) a document, duly authenticated, which purports to set out or summarise evidence taken in such a country for the purpose of proceedings in a court in [   ] under this Act, whether in response to a request made on behalf of such a court or otherwise; or

(c) a document, duly authenticated, which purports to have been received in evidence in proceedings in a court in such a country, or to be a copy of a document so received,

shall in any proceedings in a court in [   ] under this Act (including any proceedings on appeal from any such proceedings) be admissible as evidence of any fact stated therein to the same extent as oral evidence of that fact is admissible in these proceedings.

(2) A document purporting to set out or summarise evidence given as mentioned in subsection (1)(a), or taken as mentioned in sub-section (1)(b), shall be deemed to be duly authenticated for the purposes of that sub-section if the document purports to be certified by the judge, magistrate, or other person before whom the evidence was given or, as the case may be, by whom it was taken, to be the original document containing or recording or, as the case may be, summarising, that evidence or a true copy of that document.

(3) A document purporting to have been received in evidence as mentioned in sub-section (1)(c), or to be a copy of a document so received, shall be deemed to be duly authenticated for the purposes of that sub-section if the document purports to be certified by a judge, magistrate or officer of the court in question to have been, or to be a true copy of a document which has been, so received.

(4) It shall not be necessary in any such proceedings to prove the signature or official position of the person appearing to have given such a certificate.

(5) Nothing in this section shall prejudice the admission in evidence of any document which is admissible in evidence apart from this section.

44. Order, etc., made abroad need not be proved.—For the purposes of this Act, unless the contrary is shown—

(a) any order made by a court in a Commonwealth country, a Hague Convention country or a country designated in an [Order] under section 22 purporting to bear the seal of that court or to be signed by any person in his capacity as a judge, magistrate or officer of the court, shall be deemed without further proof to have been duly sealed or, as the case may be, to have been signed by that person;

(b) the person by whom the order was signed shall be deemed without further proof to have been a judge, magistrate or officer, as the case may be, of that court when he signed it and, in the case of an officer, to have been authorised to sign it; and

(c) a document purporting to be a certified copy of an order made by a court in such a country shall be deemed without further proof to be such a copy.

45. Rules of court.—Without prejudice to the generality of the powers conferred under [the relevant legislation] [the appropriate authority] may make rules of court prescribing the practice and procedure under this Act.

46. Repeals.—The [Maintenance Orders (Facilities for Enforcement) Act 192-] is hereby repealed.

47. Transitional provisions.—(1) Where immediately before the commencement of Part I, a country was one to which the [Act repealed by s. 46] extended, the provisions of that Part shall apply to any order made under that Act by a court in [   ] against a person residing in that country and to any order made by a court in that country against a person residing in [   ] and transmitted to [   ] for the purpose of proceedings under that Act.

(2) Any proceedings brought under or by virtue of any provision of the [Act repealed by s. 46] in a court in [   ] which are pending immediately before the commencement of Part I shall be continued as if they had been brought under or by virtue of the corresponding provision of this Act.

48. Commencement.—This Act shall come into force on such day as the [Head of State] may by [Order] appoint and different days may be so appointed for different provisions or for different purposes.

(4) THE HAGUE CONVENTION ON THE RECOGNITION AND ENFORCEMENT OF DECISIONS RELATING TO MAINTENANCE OBLIGATIONS 1973

The States signatory to this Convention,

Desiring to establish common provisions to govern the reciprocal recognition and enforcement of decisions relating to maintenance obligations in respect of adults,

Desiring to coordinate these provisions and those of the Convention of the 15th of April 1958 on the Recognition and Enforcement of Decisions Relating to Maintenance Obligations in Respect of Children,

Have resolved to conclude a Convention for this purpose and have agreed upon the following provisions:

CHAPTER I—SCOPE OF THE CONVENTION

Article 1
This Convention shall apply to a decision rendered by a judicial or administrative authority in a Contracting State in respect of a maintenance obligation arising from a family relationship, parentage, marriage or affinity, including a maintenance obligation towards an infant who is not legitimate, between—
(1) a maintenance creditor and a maintenance debtor; or
(2) a maintenance debtor and a public body which claims reimbursement of benefits given to a maintenance creditor.
It shall also apply to a settlement made by or before such an authority

('transaction') in respect of the said obligations and between the same parties (hereafter referred to as a 'settlement').

Article 2

This Convention shall apply to a decision or settlement however described.

It shall also apply to a decision or settlement modifying a previous decision or settlement, even in the case where this originates from a non-Contracting State.

It shall apply irrespective of the international or internal character of the maintenance claim and whatever may be the nationality or habitual residence of the parties.

Article 3

If a decision or settlement does not relate solely to a maintenance obligation, the effect of the Convention is limited to the parts of the decision or settlement which concern maintenance obligations.

CHAPTER II—CONDITIONS FOR RECOGNITION AND ENFORCEMENT OF DECISIONS

Article 4

A decision rendered in a Contracting State shall be recognised or enforced in another Contracting State—

(1) if it was rendered by an authority considered to have jurisdiction under Article 7 or 8; and
(2) if it is no longer subject to ordinary forms of review in the State of origin.

Provisionally enforceable decisions and provisional measures shall, although subject to ordinary forms of review, be recognised or enforced in the State addressed if similar decisions may be rendered and enforced in that State.

Article 5

Recognition or enforcement of a decision may, however, be refused—

(1) if recognition or enforcement of the decision is manifestly incompatible with the public policy ('ordre public') of the State addressed; or
(2) if the decision was obtained by fraud in connection with a matter of procedure; or
(3) if proceedings between the same parties and having the same purpose are pending before an authority of the State addressed and those proceedings were the first to be instituted; or
(4) if the decision is incompatible with a decision rendered between the same parties and having the same purpose, either in the State addressed or in another State, provided that this latter decision fulfils the conditions necessary for its recognition and enforcement in the State addressed.

Article 6

Without prejudice to the provisions of Article 5, a decision rendered by default shall be recognised or enforced only if notice of the institution of the proceedings, including notice of the substance of the claim, has been served on the defaulting party in accordance with the law of the State of origin and if, having regard to the circumstances, that party has had sufficient time to enable him to defend the proceedings.

Article 7

An authority in the State of origin shall be considered to have jurisdiction for the purposes of this Convention—

(1) if either the maintenance debtor or the maintenance creditor had his habitual residence in the State of origin at the time when the proceedings were instituted; or

(2) if the maintenance debtor and the maintenance creditor were nationals of the State of origin at the time when the proceedings were instituted; or

(3) if the defendant had submitted to the jurisdiction of the authority, either expressly or by defending on the merits of the case without objecting to the jurisdiction.

Article 8

Without prejudice to the provisions of Article 7, the authority of a Contracting State which has given judgment on a maintenance claim shall be considered to have jurisdiction for the purposes of this Convention if the maintenance is due by reason of a divorce or a legal separation, or a declaration that a marriage is void or annulled, obtained from an authority of that State recognised as having jurisdiction in that matter, according to the law of the State addressed.

Article 9

The authority of the State addressed shall be bound by the findings of fact on which the authority of the State of origin based its jurisdiction.

Article 10

If a decision deals with several issues in an application for maintenance and if recognition or enforcement cannot be granted for the whole of the decision, the authority of the State addressed shall apply this Convention to that part of the decision which can be recognised or enforced.

Article 11

If a decision provided for the periodical payment of maintenance, enforcement shall be granted in respect of payments already due and in respect of future payments.

Article 12

There shall be no review by the authority of the State addressed of the merits of a decision, unless this Convention otherwise provides.

CHAPTER III—PROCEDURE FOR RECOGNITION AND ENFORCEMENT OF DECISIONS

Article 13

The procedure for the recognition or enforcement of a decision shall be governed by the law of the State addressed, unless this Convention otherwise provides.

Article 14

Partial recognition or enforcement of a decision can always be applied for.

Article 15

A maintenance creditor, who, in the State of origin, has benefited from complete or partial legal aid or exemption from costs or expenses, shall be entitled, in any proceedings for recognition or enforcement, to benefit from the most favourable legal aid or the most extensive exemption from costs or expenses provided for by the law of the State addressed.

Article 16
No security, bond or deposit, however described, shall be required to guarantee the payment of costs and expenses in the proceedings to which the Convention refers.

Article 17
The party seeking recognition or applying for enforcement of a decision shall furnish—

(1)   a complete and true copy of the decision;
(2)   any document necessary to prove that the decision is no longer subject to the ordinary forms of review in the State of origin and, where necessary, that it is enforceable;
(3)   if the decision was rendered by default, the original or a certified true copy of any document required to prove that the notice of the institution of proceedings, including notice of the substance of claim, has been properly served on the defaulting party according to the law of the State of origin;
(4)   where appropriate, any document necessary to prove that he obtained legal aid or exemption from costs or expenses in the State of origin;
(5)   a translation, certified as true, of the above-mentioned documents unless the authority of the State addressed dispenses with such translation.

If there is a failure to produce the documents mentioned above or if the contents of the decision do not permit the authority of the State addressed to verify whether the conditions of this Convention have been fulfilled, the authority shall allow a specified period of time for the production of the necessary documents.

No legalisation or other like formality may be required.

CHAPTER IV—ADDITIONAL PROVISIONS RELATING TO PUBLIC BODIES

Article 18
A decision rendered against a maintenance debtor on the application of a public body which claims reimbursement of benefits provided for a maintenance creditor shall be recognised and enforced in accordance with this Convention—

(1)   if reimbursement can be obtained by the public body under the law to which it is subject; and
(2)   if the existence of a maintenance obligation between the creditor and the debtor is provided for by the internal law applicable under the rules of private international law of the State addressed.

Article 19
A public body may seek recognition or claim enforcement of a decision rendered between a maintenance creditor and maintenance debtor to the extent of the benefits provided for the creditor if it is entitled *ipso jure*, under the law to which it is subject, to seek recognition or claim enforcement of the decision in place of the creditor.

Article 20
Without prejudice to the provisions of Article 17, the public body seeking recognition or claiming enforcement of a decision shall furnish any document necessary to prove that it fulfils the conditions of sub-paragraph 1, of Article 18 or Article 19, and that benefits have been provided for the maintenance creditor.

CHAPTER V—SETTLEMENTS

Article 21
A settlement which is enforceable in the State of origin shall be recognised and enforced subject to the same conditions as a decision so far as such conditions are applicable to it.

CHAPTER VI—MISCELLANEOUS PROVISIONS

Article 22
A Contracting State, under whose law the transfer of funds is restricted, shall accord the highest priority to the transfer of funds payable as maintenance or to cover costs and expenses in respect of any claim under this Convention.

Article 23
This Convention shall not restrict the application of an international instrument in force between the State of origin and the State addressed or other law of the State addressed for the purposes of obtaining recognition or enforcement of a decision or settlement.

Article 24
This Convention shall apply irrespective of the date on which a decision was rendered.

Where a decision has been rendered prior to the entry into force of the Convention between the State of origin and the State addressed, it shall be enforced in the latter State only for payments falling due after such entry into force.

Article 25
Any Contracting State may, at any time, declare that the provisions of this Convention will be extended, in relation to other States making a declaration under this Article, to an official deed ('acte authentique') drawn up by or before an authority or public official and directly enforceable in the State of origin insofar as these provisions can be applied to such deeds.

Article 26
Any Contracting State may, in accordance with Article 34, reserve the right not to recognise or enforce—

(1)   a decision or settlement insofar as it relates to a period of time after a maintenance creditor attains the age of twenty-one years or marries, except when the creditor is or was the spouse of the maintenance debtor;
(2)   a decision or settlement in respect of maintenance obligations
    a)   between persons related collaterally;
    b)   between persons related by affinity;

(3)   a decision or settlement unless it provides for the periodical payment of maintenance.

A Contracting State which has made a reservation shall not be entitled to claim the application of this Convention to such decisions or settlements as are excluded by its reservation.

Article 27
If a Contracting State has, in matters of maintenance obligations, two or more legal systems applicable to different categories of persons, any reference to the law of that State shall be construed as referring to the legal system which its law designates as applicable to a particular category of persons.

Article 28
If a Contracting State has two or more territorial units in which different systems of law apply in relation to the recognition and enforcement of maintenance decisions—

(1)   any reference to the law or procedure or authority of the State of origin shall be construed as referring to the law or procedure or authority of the territorial unit in which the decision was rendered;
(2)   any reference to the law or procedure or authority of the State addressed shall be construed as referring to the law or procedure or authority of the territorial unit in which recognition or enforcement is sought;
(3)   any reference made in the application of sub-paragraph 1 or 2 to the law or procedure of the State of origin or to the law or procedure of the State addressed shall be construed as including any relevant legal rules and principles of the Contracting State which apply to the territorial units comprising it;
(4)   any reference to the habitual residence of the maintenance creditor or the maintenance debtor in the State of origin shall be construed as referring to his habitual residence in the territorial unit in which the decision was rendered.

Any Contracting State may, at any time, declare that it will not apply any one or more of the foregoing rules to one or more of the provisions of this Convention.

Article 29
This Convention shall replace, as regards the States who are Parties to it, the Convention on the Recognition and Enforcement of Decisions Relating to Maintenance Obligations in Respect of Children, concluded at The Hague on the 15th of April 1958.

CHAPTER VII—FINAL CLAUSES
[not reproduced]

(5) THE UNITED NATIONS CONVENTION ON THE RECOVERY ABROAD OF MAINTENANCE

(omitting certain of the final clauses re signature, etc.)

PREAMBLE

Considering the urgency of solving the humanitarian problem resulting from the situation of persons in need dependent for their maintenance on persons abroad,

Considering that the prosecution or enforcement abroad of claims for maintenance gives rise to serious legal and practical difficulties, and

Determined to provide a means to solve such problems and to overcome such difficulties,

The Contracting Parties have agreed as follows:

Article 1
SCOPE OF THE CONVENTION

1.   The purpose of this Convention is to facilitate the recovery of maintenance to which a person, hereinafter referred to as claimant, who is in the territory of one of the Contracting Parties, claims to be entitled from another person, hereinafter referred to as respondent, who is subject to the jurisdiction of another Contracting Party. This purpose shall be effected through the offices of agencies which will hereinafter be referred to as Transmitting and Receiving Agencies.

2.   The remedies provided for in this Convention are in addition to, and not in substitution for, any remedies available under municipal or international law.

Article 2
DESIGNATION OF AGENCIES

1.   Each Contracting Party shall, at the time when the instrument of ratification or accession is deposited, designate one or more judicial or administrative authorities which shall act in its territory as Transmitting Agencies.

2.   Each Contracting Party shall, at the time when the instrument of ratification or accession is deposited, designate a public or private body which shall act in its territory as Receiving Agency.

3.   Each Contracting Party shall promptly communicate to the Secretary-General of the United Nations the designations made under paragraphs 1 and 2 and any changes made in respect thereof.

4.   Transmitting and Receiving Agencies may communicate directly with Transmitting and Receiving Agencies of other Contracting Parties.

Article 3
APPLICATION TO TRANSMITTING AGENCY

1.   Where a claimant is in the territory of one Contracting Party, hereinafter referred to as the State of the claimant, and the respondent is subject to the jurisdiction of another Contracting Party, hereinafter referred to as the State of the respondent, the claimant may make application to a Transmitting Agency in the State of the claimant for the recovery of maintenance from the respondent.

2.   Each Contracting Party shall inform the Secretary-General as to the evidence normally required under the law of the State of the Receiving Agency for the proof of maintenance claims, of the manner in which such evidence should be submitted, and of other requirements to be complied with under such law.

3.   The application shall be accompanied by all relevant documents, including, where necessary, a power of attorney authorizing the Receiving

Agency to act, or to appoint some other person to act, on behalf of the claimant. It shall also be accompanied by a photograph of the claimant and, where available, a photograph of the respondent.

4. The Transmitting Agency shall take all reasonable steps to ensure that the requirements of the law of the State of the Receiving Agency are complied with; and, subject to the requirements of such law, the application shall include:

(a) the full name, address, date of birth, nationality, and occupation of the claimant, and the name and address of any legal representative of the claimant;

(b) the full name of the respondent, and, so far as known to the claimant, his addresses during the preceding five years, date of birth, nationality, and occupation;

(c) particulars of the grounds upon which the claim is based and of the relief sought, and any other relevant information such as the financial and family circumstances of the claimant and the respondent.

Article 4
TRANSMISSION OF DOCUMENTS

1. The Transmitting Agency shall transmit the documents to the Receiving Agency of the State of the respondent, unless satisfied that the application is not made in good faith.

2. Before transmitting such documents, the Transmitting Agency shall satisfy itself that they are regular as to form, in accordance with the law of the State of the claimant.

3. The Transmitting Agency may express to the Receiving Agency an opinion as to the merits of the case and may recommend that free legal aid and exemption from costs be given to the claimant.

Article 5
TRANSMISSION OF JUDGMENTS AND OTHER JUDICIAL ACTS

1. The Transmitting Agency shall, at the request of the claimant, transmit, under the provisions or article 4, any order, final or provisional, and any other judicial act, obtained by the claimant for the payment of maintenance in a competent tribunal of any of the Contracting Parties, and, where necessary and possible, the record of the proceedings in which such order was made.

2. The orders and judicial acts referred to in the preceding paragraph may be transmitted in substitution for or in addition to the documents mentioned in article 3.

3. Proceedings under article 6 may include, in accordance with the law of the State of the respondent, exequatur or registration proceedings or an action based upon the act transmitted under paragraph 1.

Article 6
FUNCTIONS OF THE RECEIVING AGENCY

1. The Receiving Agency shall, subject always to the authority given by the claimant, take, on behalf of the claimant, all appropriate steps for the recovery of maintenance, including the settlement of the claim and, where necessary, the institution and prosecution of an action for maintenance and the execution of any order or other judicial act for the payment of maintenance.

2. The Receiving Agency shall keep the Transmitting Agency currently informed. If it is unable to act, it shall inform the Transmitting Agency of its reasons and return the documents.

3. Notwithstanding anything in this Convention, the law applicable in the determination of all questions arising in any such action or proceedings shall be the law of the State of the respondent, including its private international law.

Article 7
LETTERS OF REQUEST

If provision is made for letters of request in the laws of the two Contracting Parties concerned, the following rules shall apply:

(a) A tribunal hearing an action for maintenance may address letters of request for further evidence, documentary or otherwise, either to the competent tribunal of the other Contracting Party or to any other authority or institution designated by the other Contracting Party in whose territory the request is to be executed.

(b) In order that the parties may attend or be represented, the requested authority shall give notice of the date on which and the place at which the proceedings requested are to take place to the Receiving Agency and the Transmitting Agency concerned, and to the respondent.

(c) Letters of request shall be executed with all convenient speed; in the event of such letters of request not being executed within four months from the receipt of the letters by the requested authority, the reasons for such non-execution or for such delay shall be communicated to the requesting authority.

(d) The execution of letters of request shall not give rise to reimbursement of fees or costs of any kind whatsoever.

(e) Execution of letters of request may only be refused:
  (1) If the authenticity of the letters is not established;
  (2) If the Contracting Party in whose territory the letters are to be executed deems that its sovereignty or safety would be compromised thereby.

Article 8
VARIATION OF ORDERS

The provisions of this Convention apply also to applications for the variation of maintenance orders.

Article 9
EXEMPTIONS AND FACILITIES

1. In proceedings under this Convention, claimants shall be accorded equal treatment and the same exemptions in the payment of costs and charges as are given to residents or nationals of the State where the proceedings are pending.

2. Claimants shall not be required, because of their status as aliens or non-residents, to furnish any bond or make any payment or deposit as security for costs or otherwise.

3. Transmitting and Receiving Agencies shall not charge any fees in respect of services rendered under this Convention.

Article 10
TRANSFER OF FUNDS

A Contracting Party, under whose law the transfer of funds abroad is restricted, shall accord the highest priority to the transfer of funds payable as maintenance or to cover expenses in respect of proceedings under this Convention.

Article 11

FEDERAL STATE CLAUSE

In the case of a Federal or non-unitary State, the following provisions shall apply:

(a) With respect to those articles of this Convention that come within the legislative jurisdiction of the federal legislative authority, the obligations of the Federal Government shall to this extent be the same as those of Parties which are not Federal States;

(b) With respect to those articles of this Convention that come within the legislative jurisdiction of constituent States, provinces or cantons which are not, under the constitutional system of the Federation, bound to take legislative action, the Federal Government shall bring such articles with a favourable recommendation to the notice of the appropriate authorities of States, provinces or cantons at the earliest possible moment;

(c) A Federal State Party to this Convention shall, at the request of any other Contracting Party transmitted through the Secretary-General, supply a statement of the law and practice of the Federation and its constituent units in regard to any particular provision of the Convention, showing the extent to which effect has been given to that provision by legislative or other action.

Article 12

TERRITORIAL APPLICATION

The provisions of this Convention shall extend or be applicable equally to all non-self-governing, trust or other territories for the international relations of which a Contracting Party is responsible, unless the latter, on ratifying or acceding to this Convention, has given notice that the Convention shall not apply to any one or more of such territories. Any Contracting Party making such a declaration may, at any time thereafter, by notification to the Secretary-General, extend the application of the Convention to any or all of such territories.

Articles 13–16

[not reproduced]

Article 17

RESERVATIONS

1. In the event that any State submits a reservation to any of the articles of this Convention at the time of ratification or accession, the Secretary-General shall communicate the text of the reservation to all States which are Parties to this Convention, and to the other States referred to in article 13. Any Contracting Party which objects to the reservation may, within a period of ninety days from the date of the communication, notify the Secretary-General that it does not accept it, and the Convention shall not then enter into force as between the objecting State and the State making the reservation. Any State thereafter acceding may make such notification at the time of its accession.

2. A Contracting Party may at any time withdraw a reservation previously made and shall notify the Secretary-General of such withdrawal.

Article 18

RECIPROCITY

A Contracting Party shall not be entitled to avail itself of this Convention against other Contracting Parties except to the extent that it is itself bound by the Convention.

Articles 19–21
[not reproduced]

Custody of Children: Selected Texts

(1) UNIFORM EXTRA-PROVINCIAL CUSTODY ORDERS ACT (1974 VERSION) OF THE UNIFORM LAW COMMISSIONERS OF CANADA

[**The text reproduced is** that of the Extra-Provincial Enforcement of Custody Orders Act 1977 (cap 20) of Alberta.]

HER MAJESTY, by and with the advice and consent of the Legislative Assembly of Alberta, enacts as follows:

1. Definitions.—In this Act
(a) 'child' means a person who has not attained the age of 18 years:
(b) 'court' means a court in Alberta having jurisdiction to grant custody of a child;
(c) 'custody order' means an order, or that part of an order, of an extra-provincial tribunal that grants custody of a child to any person and includes provisions, if any, granting another person a right of access or visitation to the child;
(d) 'extra-provincial tribunal' means a court or tribunal outside Alberta with jurisdiction to grant custody of a child.

2. Enforcement.—(1) A court, on application by originating notice, shall enforce, and may make such orders as it considers necessary to give effect to, a custody order as if the custody order had been made by the court unless it is satisfied on evidence adduced that the child affected by that custody order did not, at the time the custody order was made, have a real and substantial connection with the province, state or country in which the custody order was made.

(2) The court, upon application ex parte, may make an interim order under subsection (1) and may direct that the interim order be served upon any persons, and in any manner, as the court may specify in the interim order.

3. Variation of custody orders.—(1) A court may at any time by order vary a custody order as if the custody order had been made by the court if it is satisfied
(a) that the child affected by the custody order does not, at the time the application for variation is made, have a real and substantial connection with the province, state or country in which the custody order was made or was last enforced, and
(b) that the child has a real and substantial connection with Alberta or all the parties affected by the custody order are resident in Alberta.
(2) A person is not resident in Alberta for the purposes of subsection (1),

clause (b) when that person is within Alberta solely for the purpose of making or opposing an application under this Act.

(3) In varying a custody order under this section, the court shall

(a)   give first consideration to the welfare of the child regardless of the wishes or interests of any person seeking or opposing the variation, and

(b)   treat the question of custody as of paramount importance and the question of access or visitation as of secondary importance.

4. Extraordinary power of court.—Notwithstanding any other provision of this Act, where a court is satisfied that a child would suffer serious harm if the child remained in or was restored to the custody of the person named in a custody order, the court may at any time vary the custody order or make such other order for the custody of the child as it considers necessary.

5. Copies of custody orders.—An application under this Act shall be accompanied by a copy of the custody order to which the application relates, certified as a true-copy by a judge, other presiding officer or registrar of the extra-provincial tribunal or by the person charged with keeping the orders of the extra-provincial tribunal and no proof is required of the signature or appointment of a judge, presiding officer, registrar or other person in respect of any certificate produced as evidence under this section.

6. Coming into force.—This Act comes into force on the day upon which it is assented to.

(2) UNIFORM CUSTODY JURISDICTION AND ENFORCEMENT ACT (1981 VERSION) OF THE UNIFORM LAW COMMISSIONERS OF CANADA

1. Interpretation.—(1) In this Act,

(a)   'court' means a (*provincial family court of enacting jurisdiction*), a county or district court or (*Superior Court of enacting jurisdiction*);

(b)   'extra-provincial order' means an order, or that part of an order of an extra-provincial tribunal that grants to a person custody of or access to a child;

(c)   'extra-provincial tribunal' means a court or tribunal outside (*enacting jurisdiction*) that has jurisdiction to grant to a person custody of or access to a child.

Child.—(2) A reference in this Act to a child is a reference to the child while a minor.

2. Purposes.—The purposes of this Act are,

(a)   to ensure that application to the courts in respect of custody of, incidents of custody of, access to and guardianship for children will be determined on the basis of the best interests of the children;

(b)   to recognise that the concurrent exercise of jurisdiction by judicial tribunals of more than one province, territory or state in respect of the custody of the same child ought to be avoided, and to make provision so that the courts of (*enacting jurisdiction*) will, unless there are exceptional circumstances, refrain from exercising or decline jurisdiction in cases where it is more appropriate for the matter to be determined by a tribunal having jurisdiction in another place with which the child has a closer connection;

(c)   to discourage the abduction of children as an alternative to the determination of custody rights by due process; and

(d)   to provide for the more effective enforcement of custody and access orders and for the recognition and enforcement of custody and access orders made outside *(enacting jurisdiction)*.

3. Jurisdiction.—(1) A court shall only exercise its jurisdiction to make an order for custody of or access to a child where,

(a)   the child is habitually resident in *(enacting jurisdiction)* at the commencement of the application for the order;

(b)   although the child is not habitually resident in *(enacting jurisdiction)*, the court is satisfied,

   (i)   that the child is physically present in *(enacting jurisdiction)* at the commencement of the application for the order.

   (ii)   that substantial evidence concerning the best interests of the child is available in *(enacting jurisdiction)*.

  (iii)   that no application for custody of or access to the child is pending before an extra-provincial tribunal in another place where the child is habitually resident.

  (iv)   that no extra-provincial order in respect of custody of or access to that child has been recognized by a court in *(enacting jurisdiction)*.

   (v)   that the child has a real and substantial connection with *(enacting jurisdiction)*, and

  (vi)   that, on the balance of convenience, it is appropriate for jurisdiction to be exercised in *(enacting jurisdiction)*.

Habitual residence.—(2) A child is habitually resident in the place where he resided,

(a)   with both parents;

(b)   where the parents are living separate and apart, with one parent under a separation agreement or with the implied consent of the other or under a court order; or

(c)   with a person other than a parent on a permanent basis for a significant period of time,

whichever last occurred.

Abduction.—(3) The removal or withholding of a child without the consent of the person having custody of the child does not alter the habitual residence of the child unless there has been acquiescence or undue delay in commencing due process by the person from whom the child is removed or withheld.

4. Serious harm to child.—Notwithstanding sections 3 and 7, a court may exercise its jurisdiction to make or to vary an order in respect of the custody of or access to a child where,

(a)   the child is physically present in *(enacting jurisdiction)*; and

(b)   the court is satisfied that the child would, on the balance of probabilities, suffer serious harm if,

   (i)   the child remains in the custody of the person legally entitled to custody of the child,

    (ii)   the child is returned to the custody of the person legally entitled to custody of the child, or

    (iii)   the child is removed from (*enacting jurisdiction*).

5. Declining jurisdiction.—A court having jurisdiction in respect of custody or access may decline to exercise its jurisdiction where it is of the opinion that it is more appropriate for jurisdiction to be exercised outside (*enacting jurisdiction*).

6. Interim powers of court.—Upon application, a court

(a)   that is satisfied that a child has been wrongfully removed to or is being wrongfully retained in (*enacting jurisdiction*); or

(b)   that may not exercise jurisdiction under section 3 or that has declined jurisdiction under section 5 or 8,

may do any one or more of the following:

1.   Make such interim order in respect of the custody or access as the court considers is in the best interests of the child.

2.   Stay the application subject to,
    i. the condition that a party to the application promptly commence a similar proceeding before an extra-provincial tribunal, or
    ii. such other conditions as the court considers appropriate.

3.   Order a party to return the child to such place as the court considers appropriate and, in the discretion of the court, order payment of the cost of the reasonable travel and other expenses of the child and any parties to or witnesses at the hearing of the application.

7. Enforcement of foreign orders.—(1) Upon application by any person in whose favour an order for the custody of or access to a child has been made by an extra-provincial tribunal, a court shall recognize the order unless the court is satisfied,

(a)   that the respondent was not given reasonable notice of the commencement of the proceeding in which the order was made;

(b)   that the respondent was not given an opportunity to be heard by the extra-provincial tribunal before the order was made;

(c)   that the law of the place in which the order was made did not require the extra-provincial tribunal to have regard for the best interests of the child;

(d)   that the order of the extra-provincial tribunal is contrary to public policy in (*enacting jurisdiction*); or

(e)   that, in accordance with section 3, the extra-provincial tribunal would not have jurisdiction if it were a court in (*enacting jurisdiction*).

    Effect of recognition of order.—(2) An order made by an extra-provincial tribunal that is recognized by a court shall be deemed to be an order of the court and enforceable as such.

    Conflicting orders.—(3) A court presented with conflicting orders made by extra-provincial tribunals for the custody of or access to a child that, but for the conflict, would be recognized and enforced by the court under subsection (1) shall recognize and enforce the order that appears to the court to be most in accord with the best interests of the child.

    Further orders.—(4) A court that has recognized an extra-provincial order may make such further orders under (*Act governing custody and access*) as the court considers necessary to give effect to the order.

8. Superseding order, material change in circumstances.—(1) Upon application, a court by order may supersede an extra-provincial order in respect of custody of or access to a child where the court is satisfied that there has been a material change in circumstances that affects or is likely to affect the best interests of the child and,

(a)   the child is habitually resident in (*enacting jurisdiction*) at the commencement of the application for the order; or

(b)   although the child is not habitually resident in (*enacting jurisdiction*), the court is satisfied,

   (i)   that the child is physically present in (*enacting jurisdiction*) at the commencement of the application for the order,

  (ii)   that the child no longer has a real and substantial connection with the place where the extra-provincial order was made,

 (iii)   that substantial evidence concerning the best interests of the child is available in (*enacting jurisdiction*),

 (iv)   that the child has a real and substantial connection with (*enacting jurisdiction*), and

  (v)   that on the balance of convenience, it is appropriate for jurisdiction to be exercised in (*enacting jurisdiction*).

   Declining jurisdiction.—(2) A court may decline to exercise its jurisdiction under this section where it is of the opinion that it is more appropriate for jurisdiction to be exercised outside (*enacting jurisdiction*).

9. Superseding order, serious harm.—Upon application, a court by order may supersede an extra-provincial order in respect of custody of or access to a child if the court is satisfied that the child would, on the balance of probability, suffer serious harm if,

(a)   the child remains in the custody of the person legally entitled to custody of the child;

(b)   the child is returned to the custody of the person entitled to custody of the child; or

(c)   the child is removed from (*enacting jurisdiction*).

10. Order restraining harassment.—Upon application, a court may make an order restraining any person from molesting, annoying or harassing the applicant or a child in the lawful custody of the applicant and may require the respondent to enter into such recognizance, with or without sureties, or to post a bond as the court considers appropriate.

11. Order where child unlawfully withheld.—(1) Where a court is satisfied upon application by a person in whose favour an order has been made for custody of or access to a child that there are reasonable and probable grounds for believing that any person is unlawfully withholding the child from the applicant, the court by order may authorize the applicant or someone on his behalf to apprehend the child for the purpose of giving effect to the rights of the applicant to custody or access, as the case may be.

   Order to locate and take child.—(2) Where a court is satisfied upon application that there are reasonable and probable grounds for believing,

(a)   that any person is unlawfully withholding a child from a person entitled to custody of or access to the child;

(b)   that a person who is prohibited by court order or separation agreement from removing a child from (*enacting jurisdiction*) proposes to remove the child or have the child removed from (*enacting jurisdiction*); or

(c)　that a person who is entitled to access to a child proposes to remove the child or to have the child removed from (*enacting jurisdiction*) and that the child is not likely to return,

the court by order may direct the sheriff or a police force, or both, having jurisdiction in any area where it appears to the court that the child may be, to locate, apprehend and deliver the child to the person named in the order.

Application without notice.—(3) An order may be made under subsection (2) upon an application without notice where the court is satisfied that it is necessary that action be taken without delay.

Duty to act.—(4) The sheriff or police force directed to act by an order under subsection (2) shall do all things reasonably able to be done to locate, apprehend and deliver the child in accordance with the order.

Entry and search.—(5) For the purpose of locating and apprehending a child in accordance with an order under subsection (2), a sheriff or a member of a police force may enter and search any place where he has reasonable and probable grounds for believing that the child may be with such assistance and such force as are reasonable in the circumstances.

Time.—(6) An entry or a search referred to in subsection (5) shall be made only between sunrise and sunset unless the court, in the order, authorizes entry and search at another time.

Expiration of order.—(7) An order made under sub-section (2) expires six months after the day on which it was made, unless the order specifically provides otherwise.

When application may be made.—(8) An application under subsection (1) or (2) may be made in an application for custody or access or at any other time.

12. Application to prevent unlawful removal of child.—(1) Where a court, upon application, is satisfied upon reasonable and probable grounds that a person prohibited by court order or separation agreement from removing a child from (*enacting jurisdiction*) proposes to remove the child from (*enacting jurisdiction*), the court in order to prevent the removal of the child from (*enacting jurisdiction*) may make an order under subsection (3).

Application to ensure return of child.—(2) Where a court, upon application, is satisfied upon reasonable and probable grounds that a person entitled to access to a child proposes to remove the child from (*enacting jurisdiction*) and is not likely to return the child to (*enacting jurisdiction*), the court in order to secure the prompt, safe return of the child to (*enacting jurisdiction*) may make an order under subsection (3).

Order by court.—(3) An order mentioned in subsection (1) or (2) may require a person to do any one or more of the following:

1.　Transfer specific property to a named trustee to be held subject to the terms and conditions specified in the order.

2.　Where payments have been ordered for the support of the child, make the payments to a specified trustee subject to the terms and conditions specified in the order.

3.　Post a bond, with or without sureties, payable to the applicant in such amount as the court considers appropriate.

4.　Deliver the person's passport, the child's passport and any other travel documents of either of them that the court may specify to the court or to an individual or body specified by the court.

Idem. provincial court.—(4) A (*provincial court*) shall not make an order under paragraph 1 of subsection (3).

Terms and conditions.—(5) In an order under paragraph 1 of subsection (3), the court may specify terms and conditions for the return or the disposition of the property as the court considers appropriate.

Safekeeping.—(6) A court or an individual or body specified by the court in an order under paragraph 4 of subsection (3) shall hold a passport or travel document delivered in accordance with the order in safekeeping in accordance with any directions set out in the order.

Directions.—(7) In an order under subsection (3), a court may give such directions in respect of the safekeeping of the property, payments, passports or travel documents as the court considers appropriate.

13. Further evidence.—(1) Where a court is of the opinion that it is necessary to receive further evidence from a place outside (*enacting jurisdiction*) before making a decision, the court may send to the Attorney General, Minister of Justice or similar officer of the place outside (*enacting jurisdiction*) such supporting material as may be necessary together with a request,

(a)   that the Attorney General, Minister of Justice or similar officer take such action as may be necessary in order to require a named person to attend before the proper tribunal in that place and produce or give evidence in respect of the subject-matter of the application; and

(b)   that the Attorney General, Minister of Justice or similar officer or the tribunal send to the court a certified copy of the evidence produced or given before the tribunal.

Cost of obtaining evidence.—(2) A court that acts under subsection (1) may assess the cost of so acting against one or more of the parties to the application or may deal with such cost as costs in the cause.

14. Referral to court.—(1) Where the Attorney General receives from an extra-provincial tribunal a request similar to that referred to in section 13 and such supporting material as may be necessary, it is the duty of the Attorney General to refer the request and the material to the proper court.

Obtaining evidence.—(2) A court to which a request is referred by the Attorney General under subsection (1) shall require the person named in the request to attend before the court and produce or give evidence in accordance with the request.

15. Information as to address.—(1) Where, upon application to a court, it appears to the court that,

(a)   for the purpose of bringing an application in respect of custody or access; or

(b)   for the purpose of the enforcement of an order for custody or access,

the proposed applicant or person in whose favour the order is made has need to learn or confirm the whereabouts of the proposed respondent or person against whom the order referred to in clause (*b*) is made, the court may order any person or public body to provide the court with such particulars of the address of the proposed respondent or person against whom the order referred to in clause (*b*) is made as are contained in the records in the custody of the person or body, and the person or body shall give the court such particulars as are contained in the records and the court may then give the particulars to such person or persons as the court considers appropriate.

Exception.—(2) A court shall not make an order on an application under subsection (1) where it appears to the court that the purpose of the application is to enable the applicant to identify or to obtain particulars as to the identity of a person who has custody of a child, rather than to learn or confirm the whereabouts of the proposed respondent or the enforcement of an order for custody or access.

Compliance with order.—(3) The giving of information in accordance with an order under subsection (1) shall be deemed for all purposes not to be a contravention of any Act or regulation or any common law rule of confidentiality.

Section binds Crown.—(4) This section binds the Crown to right of (*enacting jurisdiction*).

16. Contempt of orders of provincial court.—(1) In addition to its powers in respect of contempt, every (*provincial court*) may punish by fine or imprisonment, or both, any wilful contempt of or resistance to its process or orders in respect of custody of or access to a child, but the fine shall not in any case exceed $1,000 nor shall the imprisonment exceed ninety days.

Conditions of imprisonment.—(2) An order for imprisonment under subsection (1) may be made conditional upon default in the performance of a condition set out in the order and may provide for the imprisonment to be served intermittently.

17. True copy of extra-provincial order.—A copy of an extra-provincial order certified as a true copy by a judge, other presiding officer or registrar of the tribunal that made the order or by a person charged with keeping the orders of the tribunal is *prima facie* evidence of the making of the order, the content of the order and the appointment and signature of the judge, presiding officer, registrar or other person.

18. Court may take notice of foreign law.—For the purposes of an application under this Act, a court may take notice, without requiring formal proof, of the law of a jurisdiction outside (*enacting jurisdiction*) and of a decision of an extra-provincial tribunal.

(3) HAGUE CONVENTION ON THE CIVIL ASPECTS OF CHILD ABDUCTION 1981

[Excluding the Final Clauses in Chapter VI (arts 37-45)]

The States signatory to the present Convention,
Firmly convinced that the interests of children are of paramount importance in matters relating to their custody,
Desiring to protect children internationally from the harmful effects of their wrongful removal or retention and to establish procedures to ensure their prompt return to the State of their habitual residence, as well as to secure protection for rights of access,

Have resolved to conclude a Convention to this effect, and have agreed upon the following provisions—

CHAPTER I—SCOPE OF THE CONVENTION
Article 1
The objects of the present Convention are—
(a) to secure the prompt return of children wrongfully removed to or retained in any Contracting State; and
(b) to ensure that rights of custody and of access under the law of one Contracting State are effectively respected in the other Contracting States.

Article 2
Contracting States shall take all appropriate measures to secure within their territories the implementation of the objects of the Convention. For this purpose they shall use the most expeditious procedures available.

Article 3
The removal or the retention of a child is to be considered wrongful where—
(a) it is in breach of rights of custody attributed to a person, an institution or any other body, either jointly or alone, under the law of the State in which the child was habitually resident immediately before the removal or retention; and
(b) at the time of removal or retention those rights were actually exercised, either jointly or alone, or would have been so exercised but for the removal or retention.
The rights of custody mentioned in sub-paragraph (a) above, may arise in particular by operation of law or by reason of a judicial or administrative decision, or by reason of an agreement having legal effect under the law of that State.

Article 4
The Convention shall apply to any child who was habitually resident in a Contracting State immediately before any breach of custody or access rights. The Convention shall cease to apply when the child attains the age of 16 years.

Article 5
For the purposes of this Convention—
(a) 'rights of custody' shall include rights relating to the care of the person of the child and, in particular, the right to determine the child's place of residence;
(b) 'rights of access' shall include the right to take a child for a limited period of time to a place other than the child's habitual residence.

CHAPTER II—CENTRAL AUTHORITIES
Article 6
A Contracting State shall designate a Central Authority to discharge the duties which are imposed by the Convention upon such authorities.
    Federal States, States with more than one system of law or States having autonomous territorial organisations shall be free to appoint more than one Central Authority and to specify the territorial extent of their powers. Where a State has appointed more than one Central Authority, it shall designate the

Central Authority to which applications may be addressed for transmission to the appropriate Central Authority within that State.

Article 7
Central Authorities shall co-operate with each other and promote co-operation amongst the competent authorities in their respective States to secure the prompt return of children and to achieve the other objects of this Convention.

In particular, either directly or through any intermediary, they shall take all appropriate measures—

(a)   to discover the whereabouts of a child who has been wrongfully removed or retained;

(b)   to prevent further harm to the child or prejudice to interested parties by taking or causing to be taken provisional measures;

(c)   to secure the voluntary return of the child or to bring about an amicable resolution of the issues;

(d)   to exchange, where desirable, information relating to the social background of the child;

(e)   to provide information of a general character as to the law of their State in connection with the application of the Convention;

(f)   to initiate or facilitate the institution of judicial or administrative proceedings with a view to obtaining the return of the child and, in a proper case, to make arrangements for organising or securing the effective exercise of rights of access;

(g)   where the circumstances so require, to provide or facilitate the provision of legal aid and advice, including the participation of legal counsel and advisers;

(h)   to provide such administrative arrangements as may be necessary and appropriate to secure the safe return of the child;

(i)   to keep each other informed with respect to the operation of this Convention and, as far as possible, to eliminate any obstacles to its application.

CHAPTER III—RETURN OF CHILDREN
Article 8
Any person, institution or other body claiming that a child has been removed or retained in breach of custody rights may apply either to the Central Authority of the child's habitual residence or to the Central Authority of any other Contracting State for assistance in securing the return of the child.
The application shall contain—

(a)   information concerning the identity of the applicant, of the child and of the person alleged to have removed or retained the child;

(b)   where available, the date of birth of the child;

(c)   the grounds on which the applicant's claim for return of the child is based;

(d)   all available information relating to the whereabouts of the child and the identity of the person with whom the child is presumed to be.

The application may be accompanied or supplemented by—

(e)   an authenticated copy of any relevant decision or agreement;

(f)   a certificate or an affidavit emanating from a Central Authority, or other competent authority of the State of the child's habitual residence, or from a qualified person, concerning the relevant law of that State;

(g)   any other relevant document.

Article 9
If the Central Authority which receives an application referred to in Article 8 has reason to believe that the child is in another Contracting State, it shall directly and without delay transmit the application to the Central Authority of that Contracting State and inform the requesting Central Authority, or the applicant, as the case may be.

Article 10
The Central Authority of the State where the child is shall take or cause to be taken all appropriate measures in order to obtain the voluntary return of the child.

Article 11
The judicial or administrative authorities of Contracting States shall act expeditiously in proceedings for the return of children.

If the judicial or administrative authority concerned has not reached a decision within six weeks from the date of commencement of the proceedings, the applicant or the Central Authority of the requested State, on its own initiative or if asked by the Central Authority of the requesting State, shall have the right to request a statement of the reasons for the delay. If a reply is received by the Central Authority of the requested State, that Authority shall transmit the reply to the Central Authority of the requesting State, or to the applicant, as the case may be.

Article 12
Where a child has been wrongfully removed or retained in terms of Article 3 and, at the date of the commencement of the proceedings before the judicial or administrative authority of the Contracting State where the child is, a period of less than one year has elapsed from the date of the wrongful removal or retention, the authority concerned shall order the return of the child forthwith.

The judicial or administrative authority, even where the proceedings have been commenced after the expiration of the period of one year referred to in the preceding paragraph, shall also order the return of the child, unless it is demonstrated that the child is now settled in its new environment.

Where the judicial or administrative authority in the requested State has reason to believe that the child has been taken to another State, it may stay the proceedings or dismiss the application for the return of the child.

Article 13
Notwithstanding the provisions of the preceding Article, the judicial or administrative authority of the requested State is not bound to order the return of the child if the person, institution or other body which opposes its return establishes that—
(a)   the person, institution or other body having the care of the person of the child was not actually exercising the custody rights at the time of removal or retention, or had consented to or subsequently acquiesced in the removal or retention; or
(b)   there is a grave risk that his or her return would expose the child to physical or psychological harm or otherwise place the child in an intolerable situation.

The judicial or administrative authority may also refuse to order the return of the child if it finds that the child objects to being returned and has attained an age and degree of maturity at which it is appropriate to take account of its views.

In considering the circumstances referred to in this Article, the judicial and administrative authorities shall take into account the information relating to the social background of the child provided by the Central Authority or other competent authority of the child's habitual residence.

Article 14

In ascertaining whether there has been a wrongful removal or retention within the meaning of Article 3, the judicial or administrative authorities of the requested State may take notice directly of the law of, and of judicial or administrative decisions, formally recognised or not in the State of the habitual residence of the child, without recourse to the specific procedures for the proof of that law or for the recognition of foreign decisions which would otherwise be applicable.

Article 15

The judicial or administrative authorities of a Contracting State may, prior to the making of an order for the return of the child, request that the applicant obtain from the authorities of the State of the habitual residence of the child a decision or other determination that the removal or retention was wrongful within the meaning of Article 3 of the Convention, where such a decision or determination may be obtained in that State. The Central Authorities of the Contracting States shall so far as practicable assist applicants to obtain such a decision or determination.

Article 16

After receiving notice of a wrongful removal or retention of a child in the sense of Article 3, the judicial or administrative authorities of the Contracting State to which the child has been removed or in which it has been retained shall not decide on the merits of rights of custody until it has been determined that the child is not to be returned under this Convention or unless an application under this Convention is not lodged within a reasonable time following receipt of the notice.

Article 17

The sole fact that a decision relating to custody has been given in or is entitled to recognition in the requested State shall not be a ground for refusing to return a child under this Convention, but the judicial or administrative authorities of the requested State may take account of the reasons for that decision in applying this Convention.

Article 18

The provisions of this Chapter do not limit the power of a judicial or administrative authority to order the return of the child at any time.

Article 19

A decision under this Convention concerning the return of the child shall not be taken to be a determination on the merits of any custody issue.

Article 20

The return of the child under the provisions of Article 12 may be refused if this would not be permitted by the fundamental principles of the requested State relating to the protection of human rights and fundamental freedoms.

CHAPTER IV — RIGHTS OF ACCESS

Article 21

An application to make arrangements for organizing or securing the effective exercise of rights of access may be presented to the Central Authorities of the Contracting States in the same way as an application for the return of a child.

The Central Authorities are bound by the obligations of co-operation which are set forth in Article 7 to promote the peaceful enjoyment of access rights and the fulfilment of any conditions to which the exercise of those rights may be subject. The Central Authorities shall take steps to remove, as far as possible, all obstacles to the exercise of such rights.

The Central Authorities, either directly or through intermediaries, may initiate or assist in the institution of proceedings with a view to organizing or protecting these rights and securing respect for the conditions to which the exercise of these rights may be subject.

CHAPTER V — GENERAL PROVISIONS

Article 22

No security, bond or deposit however described, shall be required to guarantee the payment of costs and expenses in the judicial or administrative proceedings falling within the scope of this Convention.

Article 23

No legalization or similar formality may be required in the context of this Convention.

Article 24

Any application, communication or other document sent to the Central Authority of the requested State shall be in the original language, and shall be accompanied by a translation into the official language or one of the official languages of the requested State or, where that is not feasible, a translation into French or English.

However, a Contracting State may, by making a reservation in accordance with Article 42, object to the use of either French or English, but not both, in any application, communication or other document sent to its Central Authority.

Article 25

Nationals of the Contracting States and persons who are habitually resident within those States shall be entitled in matters concerned with the application of this Convention to legal aid and advice in any other Contracting State on the same conditions as if they themselves were nationals of and habitually resident in that State.

Article 26

Each Central Authority shall bear its own costs in applying this Convention.

Central Authorities and other public services of Contracting States shall not impose any charges in relation to applications submitted under this Convention. In particular, they may not require any payment from the applicant towards the costs and expenses of the proceedings or, where applicable, those arising from the participation of legal counsel or advisers. However, they may require the payment of the expenses incurred or to be incurred in implementing the return of the child.

However, a Contracting State may, by making a reservation in accordance with Article 42, declare that it shall not be bound to assume any costs referred to in the preceding paragraph resulting from the participation of legal counsel or advisers or from court proceedings, except insofar as those costs may be covered by its system of legal aid and advice.

Upon ordering the return of a child or issuing an order concerning rights of access under this Convention, the judicial or administrative authorities may, where appropriate, direct the person who removed or retained the child, or who prevented the exercise of rights of access, to pay necessary expenses incurred by or on behalf of the applicant, including travel expenses, any costs incurred or payments made for locating the child, the costs of legal representation of the applicant, and those of returning the child.

Article 27

When it is manifest that the requirements of this Convention are not fulfilled or that the application is otherwise not well founded, a Central Authority is not bound to accept the application. In that case, the Central Authority shall forthwith inform the applicant or the Central Authority through which the application was submitted, as the case may be, of its reasons.

Article 28

A Central Authority may require that the application be accompanied by a written authorisation empowering it to act on behalf of the applicant, or to designate a representative so to act.

Article 29

This Convention shall not preclude any person, institution or body who claims that there has been a breach of custody or access rights within the meaning of Article 3 or 21 from applying directly to the judicial or administrative authorities of a Contracting State, whether or not under the provisions of this Convention.

Article 30

Any application submitted to the Central Authorities or directly to the judicial or administrative authorities of a Contracting State in accordance with the terms of this Convention, together with documents and any other information appended thereto or provided by a Central Authority, shall be admissible in the courts or administrative authorities of the Contracting States.

Article 31

In relation to a State which in matters of custody of children has two or more systems of law applicable in different territorial units—
(a) any reference to habitual residence in that State shall be construed as referring to habitual residence in a territorial unit of that State;
(b) any reference to the law of the State of habitual residence shall be construed as referring to the law of the territorial unit in that State where the child habitually resides.

Article 32

In relation to a State which in matters of custody of children has two or more systems of law applicable to different categories of persons, any reference to the law of that State shall be construed as referring to the legal system specified by the law of that State.

Article 33

A State within which different territorial units have their own rules of law in respect of custody of children shall not be bound to apply this Convention where a State with a unified system of law would not be bound to do so.

Article 34

This Convention shall take priority in matters within its scope over the *Convention of October 5, 1961 concerning the powers of authorities and the law applicable in respect of the protection of minors*, as between Parties to both Conventions. Otherwise the present Convention shall not restrict the application of an international instrument in force between the State of origin and the State addressed or other law of the State addressed for the purposes of obtaining the return of a child who has been wrongfully removed or retained or of organizing access rights.

Article 35

This Convention shall apply as between Contracting States only to wrongful removals or retentions occuring after its entry into force in those States.

Where a declaration has been made under Article 39 or 40, the reference in the preceding paragraph to a Contracting State shall be taken to refer to the territorial unit or units in relation to which this Convention applies.

Article 36

Nothing in this Convention shall prevent two or more Contracting States, in order to limit the restrictions to which the return of the child may be subject, from agreeing among themselves to derogate from any provisions of this Convention which may imply such a restriction.

Index